Recovering the U. S. Hispanic Literary Heritage

Volume III

Edited, with an Introduction, by

María Herrera-Sobek and Virginia Sánchez Korrol

Recovering the U.S. Hispanic Literary Heritage

Arte Público Press
Houston, Texas
2000

This volume is made possible through grants from the Rockefeller Foundation, the National Endowment for the Arts (a federal agency), the Andrew W. Mellon Foundation, and the Lila Wallace-Reader's Digest Fund.

Recovering the past, creating the future

Arte Público Press
University of Houston
Houston, Texas 77204-2174

Jacket design by Ken Bullock

The Library of Congress has catalogued Volume I of
Recovering the U.S. Hispanic Literary Heritage as follows:

Recovering the U.S. Hispanic literary heritage / edited by Ramón Gutiérrez and Genaro Padilla.
    p.   cm.
    ISBN 1-55885-063-5 : $34.95. ISBN 1-55885-058-9 (trade pbk.)
: $17.95

    1. American literature — Hispanic American authors — History and criticism. 2. Hispanic American literature (Spanish) — History and criticism. 3. Hispanic Americans — Intellectual life. 4. Hispanic Americans in literature. I. Gutiérrez, Ramón A., 1951– . II. Padilla, Genaro M., 1949– .
PS153.H56R43   1993

                      92-45114
                      CIP

ISBN 1-55885-139-9 (Volume II)
ISBN 1-55885-251-4 (Volume III)

♾ The paper used in this publication meets the requirements of the American National Standard for Information Sciences—Permanence of Paper for Printed Library Materials, ANSI Z39.48-1984.

0 1 2 3 4 5 6 7 8 9   10 9 8 7 6 5 4 3 2 1

Contents

Part III
Chroniclers, Ethnographers, and Historians

Part IV
Identity and Affirmation: Contextualizing U. S. Hispanic Literature

Part V
Using Historical, Archival, and Oral Sources

Introduction

María Herrera-Sobek and
Virginia Sánchez Korrol

The past two decades bear witness to a re-evaluation of the origins and recursors of the Hispanic literary heritage of the United States. This phenomenon now plays a decisive role in rethinking the very nature of American literature, formulating new canonical parameters, and in determining the content of university classes taught on the subject. Scholars throughout Latin America, the Hispanic Caribbean and in European countries where specialties exist on U. S. Hispanics/Latino (as) have also begun to incorporate the new knowledge in professional assemblies and university settings. Periodization of the literature has borne similar scrutiny. As critics, researchers and academics recovered lost manuscripts, novels, poetry, historical narratives and examples of other literary genres, the antecedents of Hispanic American contributions are older than previously imagined. Timeframes have also been revised. As significant, the institutionalization of an Hispanic literary heritage has had transformative effects beyond academic and geo-political borders, changing the ways Hispanics think about themselves and each other.

As the literature on U. S. Hispanics continues to grow, all indicators point to a heightened sense of awareness and receptivity among Hispanic/Latinos (as), regardless of national origins, with respect to a collective agency and historical role in the formation of the United States. The validation of memory, identity, cultural affirmation and creative expression, tempered by considerations of gender, race and class, spans centuries as persons of Hispanic heritage have always figured in the making of the United States of America. As Spanish settlements: presidios or villas, pueblos and missions multiplied throughout the Americas, pre-dating Jamestown by at least one hundred years, the seeds of a comprehensive Latino/Hispanic experience are evident well before the massive migrations and immigrations of contemporary times. This buried past is the subject of prevailing historical investigation and literary criticism. The third volume of *Recovering the U. S. Hispanic Literary Heritage* offers a persuasive contribution in this direction.

Chronicles, travel narratives, diaries and testimonials; administrative, civil, military and ecclesiastical records; musical and theatrical compositions; prose, poetry and other rich primary sources constitute the earliest extant

1

Spanish American literature in what is today the United States. A wealth of information culled from the plastic and creative arts, architecture and folk traditions chronicle multi-faceted life in colonial settlements in the present-day regions of Florida, Louisiana, South Carolina, Georgia, Alabama, Missouri, Mississippi, Kansas, Arkansas, Nebraska, Texas, New Mexico, Arizona, Colorado and California. Moreover, such sources indicate as well, effective connections with Cuba, Puerto Rico and Santo Domingo. A common political, economic and socio-cultural web connected the Caribbean, South and Central America with U. S. Hispanic communities undeniably aiding and abetting the earliest population movements from one point to the other. Furthermore, such interactions engendered familiarity with Anglo-American and European merchants, bringing about modifications in lifestyles, diverse attitudes and world views. The founding of major administrative and commercial centers included cities such as Los Angeles, Santa Fe, Tucson, San Antonio, San Agustín, Santo Domingo, Havana and San Juan. Their early histories testify to the vitality of a period that set in motion enduring socio-cultural institutions and political-economic practices and that, while engendering syncretic *mestizaje*, also wove the earliest strands linking Spanish Americans.

To illustrate, between 1824 and 1830 trading ships from Mexico and newly constituted Latin American republics regularly traversed Pacific waters destined for Californian ports-of-call. Exchanges of goods and commodities between St. Louis and Santa Fe assumed broad international proportions as the trade route extended southward into Chihuahua, Aguas Calientes and Mexico City. Along the eastern seaboard, New England and Middle Atlantic commercial houses enjoyed a brisk trade based on the exchange of Puerto Rican and Cuban sugar, rum and molasses for manufactured goods. Although prohibited by Crown legalities in the colonial *Antillas*, barter ultimately paved the way for the movement of merchants, workers, students, political exiles and others forced to abandon home countries for unknown horizons, or for settlements inhabited by others of common heritage.

The mid- to late nineteenth century in particular bears witness to a flourishing production of mainland and émigré literature. Theatre emerged as a highly cultivated genre and *zarzuelas, entremeses* and other theatrical productions were presented to audiences in Hispanic communities throughout the Southwest, Southeast and the Northeast. *Testimonios*, exile political treatises, novels, plays and hundreds of small and large community presses bonded peripheral U. S. Hispanic communities with Latin American and Caribbean hubs, but also with mainland counterparts. Following the war with Mexico in 1848, newspapers especially afforded intimate glimpses into the ethos of large congregations of new "Americans" who happened to speak and write in Spanish. These reported every conceivable occurrence affecting the welfare of Latinos (as) in U. S. communities and their counterparts in derivative nations. The interests of Hispanic presses and the local communities they served were often one and the same. They increased awareness about perceived advantages accruing to the citizens of an affluent nation, but more importantly, rebuked the United States for failing to live up to treaty accords and Constitutional guarantees. The presses organized communities in socio-political action, disseminating the writings of leading figures of the period. Cultural affirmation of an Hispanic heritage increasingly interwoven into the historical fabric of the dominant Anglo nation shared center stage with critical issues of identity, and contested subjugation and discrimination.

In response to massive dispossession of Mexican Americans and the increased immigration across the border, Southwestern presses and journals imaged the chaotic clash of Anglo and Mexican American political and economic values, a bitter legacy of greed, corruption and outright larceny. Often bastions of cultural resistance to a pervasive American imperialism, community presses played important leadership roles, supported by writers, intellectuals, entrepreneurs and populations eager to define their own identity and defend themselves against assimilationist forces. The challenge, as Meyers illuminates in this volume, was how to become Americans on Hispanic terms.

In contrast, community presses in New York, Tampa-Ybor City, Key West and other regions of the eastern seaboard during the late nineteenth and early twentieth century, promoted revolution, supporting the struggle for Antillean independence. Such organs as *El Porvenir* and *La Patria,* opposed the oppressive colonial regime, spearheading the battle from diasporic shores. The written word sowed the seeds for liberation, radical labor organizing, working class culture and concepts of *hispanidad* or *latinismo* on U. S. soil, even as writers lived in one community while never fully severing ties with the homeland. Writer-activists such as the Cuban Cirilo Villaverde operated in two world contexts alongside a cadre of expatriot leaders, many of whom recorded their experiences for posterity. (Lazo, this volume). Among these were José Martí, Francisco González (Pachín) Marín and Sotero Figueroa, who formulated foundations for the Cuban and Puerto Rican revolutionary movement supported by sympathetic groups in New York, Tampa, New Orleans, Philadelphia and other revolutionary centers spanning the Americas. Their convictions were well known outside and within exile communities generally comprised of racially diverse, enlightened, working-class men and women, cigar and other skilled workers, intellectuals, professionals and former landowners.

In the first decades following the Cuban-Spanish-American War, attention shifts from independence to internal community concerns and issues, fostering status negotiations, inter-group relations, the organization of workers, unions and supportive socio-cultural structures. Essayists—such as the Cuban playwright Alberto O'Farrill, editor of the weekly *Gráfico*; Puerto Rican Jesús Colón; and Dominican Pedro Henríquez Ureña, who wrote in the widely read *Novedades*—emphasized cultural and linguistic conservation. They challenged acculturation and assimilation, defending their communities against American foreign and domestic imperialism. In so doing, they followed an honored tradition established by leading Antillean precursors, who had also lived and written in the United States.

Clearly, an affirmation of culture and self informed the core of literary works written in the newly acquired territories of the Southwest and among Hispanics in the North and Southeast. The buried past, however, brings a new set of ideological concerns to present generations. Painful questions regarding the Hispanic literary legacy must be acknowledged as this *herencia* is tainted by its inscription in a discourse that can only be characterized as a treatise of domination and of servitude. It is the discourse of an expanding Spain bent on conquering the Americas and its inhabitants and stamping its imperial seal on the face of the new continent. Chicano literature, as an important case in point, cannot deny its Mexican/Spanish origins, the writings of those who came to colonize the Southwestern states in the sixteenth through nineteenth centuries. Much of that writing is an imperialistic literature related to the conquest and colonization of the Southwest. It is a literature that describes the subjugation and near destruction of a native population, while at the same time, glorifying the deeds of conquest.

Such dramas as *Los Comanches* and *Los Moros y Cristianos* exemplify the *teatro de la conquista*, or theatre of conquest. Written approximately between 1778 and 1780, *Los Comanches* detailed a bloody encounter between New Mexicans and a band of Comanches that historically never took place. The play encapsulates the friction between Spanish and Indian settlements instituted by the Spanish *conquistador* Captain Juan de Oñate and subsequent settlers during the period of colonization. For the past two centuries, the drama continues to play annually for New Mexican audiences in commemoration of the Spanish victory and the displacement of indigenous peoples. However, as Anglo-Americans dispossessed Spanish/Mexicans of their lands and heritage, the drama assumed new relevancy as a legitimization of their former dominant status. Its longevity can be understood in terms of a ritual that functions as a semiotic sign whose meaning has changed dramatically with the passage of time. The drama has, therefore, served to communicate varying political systems and functions over time.

This literature, nonetheless, belongs to a Chicano literary patrimony, and indeed, informs the broader Hispanic literary birthright. When read from the perspective of recovering a collective Hispanic literary heritage, however, it sheds new light on darkened subjects. As Shields' analysis of colonial Franciscan documents elucidates in this volume, such reports become informative ethnographic treasures. Viewed from another perspective, the significance of the literature is, in the words of the scholar Genaro Padilla, in "the formative lines of literary practice that constitutes our cultural epistomology the topology of which has been broken by the dominant American hegemony, and often dismissed as Hispanophilic . . . the topological tree must be reillumined if we expect to situate ourselves within a discursive tradition that is socially empowering." Furthermore, Padilla posits proliferation of this material, understanding that it will ultimately result in multi-voiced and multi-ideological literary production. It is in the expanded discourse that these writings will receive the intertextual significance they deserve.

What then, does it mean to be Hispanic or Latino (a) in American society at the crossroads of the millennium? How have we persevered and created community in two world contexts? How indeed have we shaped the Americas? Like bridges to the past, the recovered heritage prepares the groundwork for understanding the complexity and totality of a U. S. Hispanic heritage. In the search process, scholars need to consider the confluences of the broader Latin American/Caribbean context, as well as that of the non-Hispanic United States. While historical investigation and literary criticism has, of necessity, prioritized much needed reconstruction of single group experiences, frequently imbued with a North American slant, current trends pinpoint the need for a compilation of a comprehensive Hispanic experience. Such an enterprise must recognize and preserve the integrity of individual national groups. Indeed, the abundance of recovered materials guide and compel us to do no less. But, at the same time, we must acknowledge that the literature and history of U. S. Hispanics legitimately belongs to the Americas; that the concept of Borderlands transcends imaginary geo-political or academic limitation and that Hispanic or Latino (a) heritage forms an indivisible chapter subject to its universality and specificity. The writings included in this volume are important contributions towards recovering a past that will, undoubtedly, inform a more unified future.

In *Part I: Rewriting the Present: Nineteenth Century Historical Novels,* we have grouped four contributors whose scholarly work deal with nineteenth-century novels. Three of these contributors focus on María Amparo Ruiz de Burton and one centers her optic on the New Mexican author, Manuel C. de Baca. All four authors are concerned with discursive strategies and their relationship to the historical context.

Amelia M. de la Luz Montes's article on the writings of María Amparo Ruiz de Burton explores the connection between letter writing and novel construction in the California author. Montes has made a major contribution to Chicano/a literature, to Women's Studies and American literary studies since she located more than eighty personal letters written by Ruiz de Burton in the latter half of the nineteenth century. These letters were in the archives of the Huntington Library in San Merino, California, and in the archives of the Santa Barbara Mission, also in California. Her study finds a direct link between these two processes insofar as the letters reflect the life experiences and problematics of Ruiz de Burton as lived in the California *ranchos*. Through a comparison of the two texts, i.e. the letters and the novels, we find that the California author's life experiences are very similar to those of the characters in both of her books *The Squatter and the Don* (1882) and *Who Would Have Thought It?* (1872).

Furthermore, Montes's article demonstrates how Ruiz de Burton's letters demolish the stereotypes commonly found in California, the West and in other parts of the United States regarding Mexican women. Through Ruiz de Burton's letters, we encounter an upper-class woman, politically savy, socially concerned about Californios and not a passive, air-headed *señorita,* as Mexican-California women of that era were frequently portrayed. Ruiz de Burton's personal correspondence certainly yields important information regarding the political and social life of Californios after the conquest, and Montes has done a sterling job of both discovering the Burton correspondence and highlighting its importance to literary studies.

Taking a different tangent but also focusing on one of the above novels by Ruiz de Burton, Jesse Alemán writes "Novelizing National Discourses: History, Romance, and Law in *The Squatter and the Don.*" His article focuses on the discourses of history and romance and how Ruiz de Burton cleverly subverts the structure of the latter in her novel *The Squatter and the Don* (1882). According to Alemán, the Californiana's subversion of the romance genre is done in order to underscore the oppression of her people. Alemán demonstrates how romantic notions of the settling of the West by Anglo American writers created a myth of "heroic" proportions and often erased the violent episodes of the Anglo American conquest. Alemán's agile mind deconstructs the structure of American romance novels and skillfully utilizes post colonial theories posited by Homi Bhabha, Benedict Anderson, Doris Sommers, Carl Gutiérrez Jones and Bahktin, as well as other scholars to interpret and examine Ruiz de Burton's narrative strategies.

The third critic focusing on Ruiz de Burton's work, José F. de Aranda, Jr., problematizes various issues appearing in the novel *Who Would Have Thought It?* (1872) as they relate to class, race, and gender and the Spanish and Anglo colonization projects in his essay "Breaking All the Rules: María Amparo Ruiz de Burton Writes a Civil War Novel." Aranda rightly underscores Burton's aristocratic background and questions her place as a "subaltern." In fact, Burton perceived herself as "white" of European descent and had her own racial prejudices toward Afro-Americans and Native Americans. Aranda perceptively amplifies on the issues of colonization in the nineteenth century and points out how Ruiz de Burton's novel was already grappling with this important political aspect.

Nineteenth-century Hispanic literature was not confined to California but in fact much of it was written in New Mexico. Erlinda Gonzales-Berry, in her article "*Como dios manda*: Political Messianism in Manuel C. de Baca's *Noches tenebrosas en el condado de San Miguel,*" examines a New Mexican author and proves once again that ideological concerns play a major role in the structuring of narrative fiction. Gonzales-Berry carefully teases out how C. de Baca wrote his novel *Noches tenebrosas en el condado de San Miguel* (1892) as a political ploy to convince the general Mexican American population of the righteousness of law and order. Since C. de Baca belonged to the ruling class, his narrative discourse was designed to condemn the radical Gorras Blancas, who were fighting against the inexorable encroachment on New Mexican lands by the recently arrived Anglo Texans. C. de Baca, therefore, is one of the few examples of Mexican American fiction writers who sided with conservative forces. Gonzales-Berry's contribution lies in demonstrating how class interest once again overrode ethnic solidarity, as Marxist scholars have frequently posited.

In *Part II: Women's Voices: The Construction of Ethnic and Gender Identities,* we included five essays. The first essay in this section is by Martha Eva Rocha Islas, who posits that most Mexican women who valiantly fought in the Mexican Revolution of 1910–1917, have been frequently relegated to the margins of history. She perceptively explores how one woman *soldadera* was wholeheartedly involved in the revolutionary project and sought to insert herself in history through her narrative texts. Such a woman was Leonor Villegas de Magnón. Rocha Islas's article, "Los textos narrativos y su importancia historeográfica: *Las Memorias* de Leonor Villegas de Magnón," focuses on the life of Villegas de Magnón and her memoir, *The Rebel,* and demonstrates how her writings demolished stereotypes regarding representations of passive Mexican women. Villegas de Magnón was an educated, middle-class woman possessing a liberal, democratic ideology. Her work, *The Rebel,* according to Rocha Islas, records from a woman's perspective an important moment in Mexican history. Magnón's text, therefore, deserves careful scrutiny, for it presents history in a different voice; a voice that is often marginalized or silenced but which needs to be heard loud and clear.

Amy Doherty undertakes a sensitive analysis of the short stories published by María Cristina Mena in *Century Magazine* during the 1913–1916 period. In her study entitled "Representing Mexico: María Cristina Mena's Short Fiction in *Century Magazine,* 1913–1916," Doherty underscores the historical context in which Mena was writing in the United States, which was mainly during the Mexican Revolution (1910–1917), and the difficulties in asserting her voice in the presentation of non-stereotypical, more rounded characters of Mexican descent to American audiences. American audiences desired the exotic images of the Other, i.e. the tantalizing seductive (yet subservient) Mexican woman. Doherty underlines Mena's struggle to escape the constraints placed on her creative production and demonstrates how the Mexican writer did not capitulate to the pressures visited upon her by the editors of *Century Magazine.* Of special interest are Mena's images of la Malinche, Coatlicue and the Virgen of Guadalupe in the three short stories analyzed by Doherty: "John of God, the Water-Carrier," "The Birth of the God of War," and "The Vine-Leaf." Doherty makes an excellent contribution by exploring author-publisher relations and the strategies used by one writer to subvert publication policies and make her voice heard on her own terms.

Louis Mendoza assertively challenges generational periodization paradigms as well as racialist and sexist paradigms posited by some revisionist
historians in his article "Confronting *la Frontera*: Identity and Gender: Poetry
and Politics in *La Crónica* and *El Demócrata Fronterizo*." In contrast to the
shortcomings Mendoza perceives in generational periodization and other revisionist historians' views, he posits the works of Sara Estela Ramírez, a
transborder poet, journalist and feminist activist living in the Laredo, Texas,
border area at the turn of the century (1897-1910). Ramírez's work consisted
mainly in writing for the newspaper *La Crónica* and *El Demócrata Fronterizo*,
in being the editor of the literary newspaper *La Corregidora*, in founding the
literary journal *Aurora,* and in writing for *Vésper: Justicia y Libertad* (a four
page weekly).

Mendoza underscores Ramírez's voice as a political activist in the Partido
Liberal Mexicano (PLM) as well as her creative production. The article's
importance lies in the connections the author makes between this early writer
and late twentieth century Chicanas. Ramírez is perceived as a precursor to contemporary Chicana political activists and writers.

Andrea Tinnemeyer, acutely aware of the innumerable problematics
invloved in translating texts, brilliantly examines Leonor Villegas de Magnón's
narrative strategies used in translating the novel *La Rebelde* into its English version *The Rebel* (1872) in her article "Mediating the Desire of the Reader in
Villegas de Magnón's *The Rebel*." Zeroing in on the political and ideological
vectors involved in the processes of a linguistic transfer, she explores the dialogic interaction between two axiological belief systems on both sides of the
border. Tinnemeyer's work teases out the relationship between an Anglo
American reading public and a Mexican American author and how the latter
was able to navigate through this treacherous terrain in order to meet Anglo
readers' expectations and desires without betraying her own voice and her
country. The translation of *La Rebelde,* therefore, was in reality a new text conceived and constructed with an Anglo American readership in mind.
Tinnemeyer's excellent application of Bahktinian theories and Reader
Reception theories aids her in pinpointing the different voices found in Villegas
de Magnón's novel.

Adhering to the topic of the importance of women's voices in constructing
gender identities, Virginia M. Bouvier carefully dissects the struggle for authoritative voice between interviewer and interviewees in her article "Framing the
Female Voice: The Bancroft Narratives of Apolinaria Lorenzana, Angustias de
la Guerra Ord, and Eulalia Pérez." Bouvier's analysis is centered on the Hubert
Howe Bancroft interviews undertaken in the 1870s and which consisted of
interviewing 160 elderly residents of California in order to write the history of
that state. Of the 160 interviews, half of the interviewees were Hispanic, and
Bouvier examines the oral histories recorded for Apolinaria Lorenzana,
Angustias de la Guerra Ord, and Eulalia Pérez. Her findings explicitly demon-

strate the struggle for narrative authority between the male Anglo interviewer and the Hispanic women. She found that the women constantly had to assert their discursive authority, since their voices were constantly deformed, erased, and challenged at every important turn of the interview. Nevertheless, the women found various discursive strategies in order to impose their voice over and above the male interviewer. For example, when Eulalia Pérez did not want to answer a question or discuss a topic, she feigned deafness! Bouvier makes an outstanding contribution toward the understanding of how orality challenges the written text and how women challenge gender constructions of the female subject.

Part III, titled *Chroniclers, Ethnographers, and Historians,* features María Herrera-Sobek, Barbara De Marco, Enrique Lamadrid, Charles A. Weeks, Marcela Salas, Shannon Moore, José Fernández, and E. Thomson Shields, Jr. The first article in this Section is by Herrera-Sobek and is titled "New Approaches to Old Chroniclers: Contemporary Critical Theories and the Pérez de Villagrá Epic." Her work applies contemporary post colonial theories as well as Reader Response theories in examining Villagrá's epic *Historia de la Nueva México, 1610.* In particular, Herrera-Sobek centers her attention on the various versions of the Aztlán myth extant in Mexico and the southwestern United States and compares them to the one found in Villagrá's epic poem of the conquest and settlement of New Mexico in the late sixteenth and early seventeenth centuries. Villagrá's poem is one of the earliest instances in which the Aztlán myth appears in a literary narrative. Its interest lies not only in the poet-soldier citing this myth in an early chronicle, but in the poem's deviation from standard versions found in Meso-American chronicles and in those variants cited by subsequent Mexican scholars. One salient difference is the incorporation of a female deity (possibly Coatlicue) in Villagrá's variant and the fact that there were two brothers who divided the lands into two kingdoms: north and south. One brother and his followers migrated south (the Aztecs) and another stayed and continued settling the Southwest.

Herrera-Sobek points out how Villagrá, a university-trained scholar, utilized classical Greek and Roman mythology to mediate between his European readership and the Native American experience. Her contribution lies in pointing out how contemporary literary theories, such as reader response and mythic analysis, can be fruitfully used in identifying the strategies conquest writers used in making the American experience comprehensible to a European audience.

Barbara De Marco also examines the strategies used in the construction of seventeenth century chronicles in her article "'Cantaron la Victoria': Historical Accounts of the 1680 Pueblo Revolt" and highlights the parallels between chronicles of the Spanish colonial era and hagiographic literature of the medieval period such as the *Cantigas de Santa María* (miracle tales) of Alfonso El Sabio. These *cantigas* or miracle narratives of medieval saints were popular during the thirteenth century in the Spanish peninsula. In particular, De Marco analyzes Fray Francisco de Ayeta's *Memorial* of the 1680 Pueblo Revolt and examines the similarities this document has with the *Cantigas*.

De Marco's article is important in pinpointing the origins and literary influences of the literature of the Southwest. She demonstrates how literature is not produced in a vacuum but is a product of long established literary traditions. In this sense, she underscores the importance of the Recovery Project since one of its goals is the recovery of colonial documents in order to understand and fully appreciate our contemporary literary experience.

In the article *"Los Comanches:* Text, Performance, and Transculturation in an Eighteenth Century New Mexican Folk Drama," Enrique Lamadrid explores the process of transculturation as exemplified in the performative aspects of the colonial period play, *Los Comanches,* still performed to New Mexican audiences today. Lamadrid points out how this colonial period play has been studied mostly from a historical or literary perspective and not from a performance angle. He cites the various strands of scholarship related to *Los Comanches* with respect to origins, date, and literary interpretation of the play. Some of these early folklore scholars include Arthur L. Campa, Aurelio M. Espinosa, and John E. Englekirk.

Aside from the important literary history on *Los Comanches* provided by Lamadrid, his contribution lies in perceptively noting how two arch enemies, the Spaniards and the Native Americans, who fiercely fought during the colonial period, have come together in relatively peaceful coexistence. He points out how the process of time and subsequent Anglo conquests have brought the two enemies together. The Hispanos and Native Americans have come together through *mestizaje* and friendship and, most likely, because they now find themselves "conquered" and marginalized by Anglo American society.

Marcela W. Salas analyzes the works of Félix Varela (*Jicoténcal,* 1826) and Francisco Sellén (*Hatuey,* 1891). She focuses on the manner in which the figure of the Indian was idealized and presented as a "noble savage" by Cuban rebel groups seeks independence in the nineteenth century. She further points out how the Indian was used in the construction of Cuban identity and how this ethnic group reinforced a national consciousness separate from the Spanish who controlled Cuba at the time. Salas underscores how the Black Legend was used by revolutionaries seeking to overturn Spanish control in Cuba. However, the Black Legend eventually served to construct a negative stereotype in the twentieth century. Salas's study is a lucid analysis of how nineteenth-century literature sheds light on contemporary behavior.

In "Negating Cultures, Saving Cultures: Franciscan Ethnographic Writings in Seventeenth Century *La Florida*," Tom Shields explores ethnographic content in Franciscan writings in *La Florida*. He finds a complex interplay of conversion, assimilation and acculturation that occurred in the daily execution of missionary duties. Intimate views of the very cultural practices that missionaries sought to eradicate are encoded in doctrinaire and journalistic reports. The written word, as Shields discovers in the Franciscan documents, played a major role in the evangelizing process and accounts, and maintained very effective records of indigenous lifestyle.

The practices of Spanish *conquistadores* in the conquest of seventeenth-century Florida contrast sharply with the work of Franciscan ethnographers, according to the Moore-Ross and Fernández. Exploring the complex nature and motivations of the Spanish conquerors, the authors turn to the chronicles of the Inca Garcilaso de la Vega, *La Florida del Inca* (1605), *Los Commentarios reales* (1609), and *La historia general del Perú* (1617). Intent on exalting Spanish courage and also Native American resistance in the conquest of that province, Garcilaso de la Vega offers important perspectives. Juxtaposing de la Vega's perspective with observations of other chroniclers allows the authors to reach certain conclusions and offers the reader some views on frontier negotiations useful for comparison with other volume essays.

Spanish successes in frontier negotiations with Native American nations in the Mississippi Valley rested, in good measure, on knowledge of Indian languages, culture, politics and economic realities according to Charles A. Weeks' "The Nogales Dispute of 1791–1792: Texts and Context." Documentation of the Nogales dispute provides rare insights into life in the lower valley at the twilight of the eighteenth century. Revealed as well is a complexity of cultures, defined by diversity and *mestizaje*, that enable understanding of ritual, symbols, political interests, and language.

The articles included in Section IV emphasize identity and cultural affirmation in recovered texts of the nineteenth and early twentieth century, and incorporate seldom acknowledged works of Dominican and Nicaraguan writers in the United States. Silvio Torres-Saillant's "Before the Diaspora: Early Dominican Literature in the United States" offers a general historical overview of Dominican writing. Torres-Saillant traces a U. S. Dominican presence from the earliest commercial and political interactions between the Dominican Republic and the United States. The late nineteenth and early twentieth centuries are particularly salient as they place leading Dominican figures in concert and alliance with Puerto Ricans, Cubans and other Latin American or Caribbean émigrés at a critical historical juncture. Outstanding among the Dominican writer/activists is Pedro Henríquez Ureña, well known for his journalistic endeavors and contributions to the development of an early Hispanic intellectual community. However, as Torres-Saillant makes clear, he was one among other Dominicans who left their literary mark in the United States.

In the same time period, Silvio Sirias' "The Recovery of Salomón de la Selva's *Tropical Town:* Challenges and Outcomes" centers on the work of the Nicaraguan writer during his extended sojourn in the United States. De la Selva's arrival in the United States mirrors Henríquez Ureña's as both came as students, became expatriots involved in the external politics of their respective countries and subsequently joined the academic ranks in American universities. However, de la Selva's work also rightfully belongs to the U. S. Hispanic literary tradition, as Sirias points out. His contributions, considered idiosyncratic among Nicaraguan *literati*, reflect the duality that characterizes contemporary Hispanic American literature.

In a similar vein, the man of action put forth by Rodrigo Lazo in "A Man of Action: Cirilo Villaverde as Trans-American Revolutionary Writer" is the political journalist Cirilo Villaverde. Lazo presents a gratifying perspective into the life of the Cuban activist who lived in the United States for almost half a century until his death in 1894. Villaverde deliberately chose a journalistic path in his political efforts to eliminate the Spanish colonial regime in Cuba. He wrote for the New York newspaper *El Espejo*. Lazo's article emphasizes the intellectual processes by which Villaverde moved away from the writing of fiction to prioritize political activism and journalism. These, he believed, were more effective in the struggle for Cuban independence. Villaverde's legacy poses a challenge to literary historians, for he engages the reader to consider and contextualize the highly politicized productivity of Cuban-Americans who published in newspapers in cities key to Antillean liberation such as New York, New Orleans and Philadelphia.

Antillean independence, anti-assimilationist sentiments and the processes of forging syncretic identity through the genre of theatre, particularly the integrative *teatro bufo,* is the subject of Kenya C. Dworkin y Méndez' article, "From Factory to Footlights: Original Spanish-language Cigar Workers' Theatre in Ybor City and West Tampa, Florida." With the implantation of the cigar industry in Florida in the 1870s, workers brought Cuban theatre and culture to Florida. The theatre and the public meeting house became the first structures to appear after the initial cigar factories. A highly political and sociocultural institution, monies raised by the workers' theatre paid for Cuban revolutionary activity, supported the Spanish Republic, built hospitals and clinics. Theatrical productions alleviated the tensions associated with "post colonial circumstances," such as transculturation and the creation of new identity, negotiating issues of class and ethnicity and developing communities that balanced *lo cubano* and the emerging American reality. Dworkin y Méndez draws important interconnections between political activism, particularly in the practice of *la lectura,* and the theatre arts for actors often honed their craft as readers in the cigar factories. The article analyzes the interactions of Spanish, Italian and Cuban immigrants in resisting assimilation while creating the space for a flourishing of cultural affirmation through theatre.

The last two articles in this section focus on the life and times of the Puerto Rican writer/activist Jesús Colón from two very different perspectives. Tim Libretti's "Looking Backward, Looking Forward: Jesús Colón's Left Literary Legacy and the Adumbration of a Third World Writing" highlights Colón's place and literary contributions as a worker, a Puerto Rican, a black man and committed supporter of the political left to both the Hispanic and the U. S. literary traditions. Colón's use of history and memory recovers a forgotten past that ultimately points to an idealistic and socially just future. An important legacy gleaned from Colón's writings, as Libretti elucidates, was the urgent need to create alternative literary institutions that would confront the marginalization of the working class, often found within minority communities, and challenge hegemonic distortions regarding Third World peoples and culture. The dominant themes of colonialism, racial oppression and discrimination eloquently expressed in Colón's writings about Puerto Rico reflect the conditions in which all Puerto Ricans found themselves.

The focus of Edwin Padilla's "Jesús Colón: Relación entre crónica periodista, lenguaje y público" reveals a little-known aspect of the writer's works as Padilla analyzes Colón's Spanish-language contributions to the newspaper, *Gráfico*, 1927–1929. Here Colón's essays, precursors to the edited volumes cited by Libretti, are written under the pseudonyms of Pericles Espada and Miquis Tiquis. In both voices, topics comprise a running commentary on New York Puerto Rican life, yet each assumes a different persona and political objective. Miquis Tiquis, an affected, superior individual, produces scathing satire, intended to caricature New York Latinos in their social exaggerations and shortcomings, perhaps with the hopes of effecting change. Pericles Espada, as the name implies, is both the orator, teacher and combatant who in his allegorical letters to his lover/native country hopes to prepare the latter for the ultimate encounter with the new political order, the United States.

Part V examines the different ways that researchers utilize historical, archival and oral sources. In "Social Identity on the Hispanic Texas Frontier," Gerald E. Poyo investigates the formation of social identity focusing on the relevance of the pre-1848 period, particularly for contemporary Chicano and Latino history. He describes the processes by which identity shifted from Mexican to Spanish American in the Texas of mid to late nineteenth century. Poyo documents the dynamics of shifting identity in primary sources pertaining to both San Antonio and Nacogdoches and concludes that in the early decades of the twentieth century, Tejanos reinvented the social definitions of their historical past. He makes a strong case for understanding the regional historical context in which socio-cultural concepts of identity operate.

The biographical writing and the newspapers of the day also serve to provide important insight into what Hispanics held as their particular cultural values. Newspapers in New Mexico flourished despite a limited literate population according to Doris Meyers' "Reading Early Neomexicano Newspapers: Yesterday and Today." The article centers on the delicate balance of transition from territory to statehood, a particularly intense socio-political interval in New Mexican history, when Spanish Mexican culture and identity supposedly evolved into Mexican American. The impact of the local press at that historical moment, the context in which it operated and its role in intellectual and social matters cannot be underestimated.

Life narratives or symbolic biographies composed of eulogies and funeral oratories often originated in the obituary columns of the day. As Gabriel Meléndez posits, this biographical form was an important means of self-representation that incorporated ethnic and gender identifiers and, by extension, contributed to the collective narrative of a people. In "Recovering Neo-Mexicano Biographical Narrative: *Cuarenta años de legislador,* The Biography of Casimiro Barela," Meléndez studies the life and times of a leading New Mexican political figure. What is particularly revealing in the Barela saga rests on the varying interpretations of his life and achievements. How the narrative changes in the retelling is a noteworthy contribution to our utilization of primary sources.

Luis Leal offers similar observations in his article "En torno a Joaquín Murrieta: Historia y literatura." The author laments the separation of history and literature pointing to literary criticism as the vehicle for resolving doubts regarding literary textual ambiguity. The case of Joaquín Murrieta traces historical antecedents of the legendary figure who emerges as a Mexican and not of Chilean origins. In search of the "real" Joaquín, Leal hones in on the earliest writings about Murrieta from the *California Gazette* to works written in France, Spain and Chile. For the author's purposes the historical method proves indispensable because it serves to separate myth from reality in the study of literary criticism.

Rodolfo Cortina, however, utilizes the historical novel as the window to the past that, in turn, reflects the present as he explores the nature of Cuban civil society. In his article "Varela's *Jicotencal* and the Historical Novel," Cortina posits that *Jicotencal,* one of the earliest novels in U. S. Hispanic literature, written in Spanish by the Cuban exiled prelate, Felix Varela, stands as a symbol of Cuba. The author offers as evidence an historical overview of Varela's life and times and compares it to a critical reading of the novel.

All of the essays in this volume confirm the existence and magnitude of an Hispanic literary tradition that did not burst forth in the trendy heat of multiculturalism or pluralism or increased immigration as many scholars would have us believe. Such frameworks have always characterized the Hispanic/Latino(a) experience in the United States. The historical precedents and longevity of this heritage can no longer be in doubt. The intellectual range of these essays demonstrates that we are indeed grappling with the fine points of an Hispanic literary heritage expanding our understanding of gender, class and ethnicity; diversity within and across the Hispanic experience; innovative criticism; new literary genres and the parameters of the American literary canon.

Part I

Rewriting the Present:
Nineteenth-Century Historical Novels

Es Necesario Mirar Bien: Nineteenth-Century Letter Making and Novel Writing in the Life of María Amparo Ruiz de Burton

Amelia M. de la Luz Montes

Sñr, q.[uien] aprecio[1]

Como el correo sale muy temprano mañana y ahora ya es tarde, solo tengo corto tiempo para escribir esta; tampoco tengo mucho q. *decir,* y lo q. quiero *decir,* no sé como *decir,* ¡pobre [C]alifornita! Si no me animara el pensamiento q. estoy hablando con un buen compatriota seguramente acabaria por decir nada, pero el título de paisana vale demasiado para no hacer uso de él; conozco q. no debo hablar á u. con rodeos, "Entre soldados y amigos, cumplimientos son perdidos" dejaremos pues para con los estranjeros, el uso de todas esas bagatelas, y para entre nosotros los paisanos la franqueza. . .

Esteemed Sir

Because the post goes out very early tomorrow morning and because today it is late, I only have a short time to write this; I also do not have much to say, and what I want to *say,* I do not know how to *say,* poor little California! If the thought of speaking with a fellow compatriot does not cheer me, I would end saying nothing, but the title of fellow compatriot means too much to me not to make use of it; I know not to speak in roundabout ways. "Among soldiers and friends, compliments are unnecessary." We shall put aside then what is spoken between strangers, the use of all those trifles, and between us, the compatriots[:] frankness . . . (Ruiz de Burton, 23 November 1851)[1]

"How to Say": Fashioning Narrative Windows

Who were the California writers of the nineteenth century? Open a literary or history schoolbook and you may find pastel textbook pictures: Large-boned horses gallop in a whirl of raw sienna. Dusty riders hurl lariats at runaway steers. Turn the page: Burnt umber hands grasp rusted pans half filled with sand. Ashen faces peer out calico covered wagons to survey a brown rocky valley. The impression may be that no one had time to write while searching for gold, homesteading lands, or later fretting over the Civil War. However, if we close the schoolbooks and open the doors to various archive libraries today, we

16

will find many Californians who participated in oral autobiographical testimonials or wrote letters, diaries, histories and novels: Doña Apolinaria Lorenzana, Mariano Guadalupe Vallejo, Antonio María Osio, María Amparo Ruiz de Burton and others.[2] These Californians, many of whose writings are now republished, remain in the margins of popular imagination. Helen Hunt Jackson, whose novel *Ramona* continues to fascinate, infuriate, and entertain readers, is often marked as the popular voice for nineteenth-century California. The novel has had such an unwavering popularity that today, tourists flock to Hemet, California to see the novel performed as melodrama.[3] This famous writer, however, cannot claim a California heritage. She hails from the eastern seaboard, home to John Smith, William Bradford, and other American literary historians. In fact, if we open schoolbook pages about the east we will not find ruddy pastels but translucent watercolors: red cherry blossoms, viridian patterned farm lands, and ebony ink wells empty from the activity of writing. New England literary names come to mind quite quickly: Hawthorne, Melville, James. These names and images have become synonymous with American canonical literary history.

These impressions, however hyperbolized, serve an important purpose: first to remind us how literary history and literary canons have been constructed to privilege an Anglo-American experience, and to further explore current reconstructions of American literary history which focus upon literary historians/writers who have been silenced or forgotten. Their "recovered" words gift us with a more thorough understanding and appreciation of our literary past.[4] The focus of my work, then, concerns one California writer: María Amparo Ruiz de Burton. Her work is pertinent in today's efforts to revisit nineteenth-century American literary history because she brings yet another perspective in which to investigate the nineteenth century from its domestic to its public sphere, from California writings which mythologize the Mexican to her own writings which demythologize stereotypes of herself and her culture.

Her letters, like the one excerpted above, reveal a writer struggling to establish her voice within a newly arrived Anglo-American presence. Implicit in the writings is her desire to publicly represent herself, her beliefs, and to be accepted in a male Mexican and Anglo-American culture. As a woman, an upper class elite, an author and dramatist, she sought the arena of American literature for such validation. Therefore, she purposely wrote her fiction in English in order to seek American publishers and reviewers. Studying her fiction alongside her personal letters, which are primarily in Spanish and addressed to her closest Mexican/Californio acquaintances, allows for a fascinating juxtaposition of bilingual and bi-racial identity. Her letters and fiction whisper between U. S. and Mexican land issues, nudge border constraints, and violate old and newly established cultural boundaries. Ruiz de Burton travels sometimes with ease and sometimes with much difficulty through these partitions and it is her struggle and her perception of United States' society and culture which begs the reader to take another look at who we were and who we have come to be. Because Ruiz de Burton does not fit neatly delineated nineteenth-century canonical descriptions, she belongs there in order to explode conventions. Most importantly, her letters shatter western definitions and constructions of the Mexican both in the nineteenth and twentieth centuries. In other words, she complicates and deepens literary and historical discourse about Mexican Americans.[5]

There are over one hundred personal letters as well as formal letters and documents belonging to the Mission Santa Barbara Archives and The Huntington Library's collection of Ruiz de Burton manuscripts. Most of the personal letters are in Spanish. Those letters written in English are addressed to lawyers, businessmen, or are legal documents she drew up without the aid of an attorney. Eighty-one of these are personal letters to Mariano Guadalupe Vallejo, wealthy Californio landowner who, like Ruiz de Burton, lost his lands by the end of his life. Other letters are addressed to Vallejo's wife as well as to Ruiz de Burton's husband, Col. Henry S. Burton, and other family members. About twelve of these letters are directed to Samuel L. M. Barlow, a wealthy attorney, landowner and entrepreneur in New York. The Barlow letters are more formal and in English, and they reveal how Ruiz de Burton negotiated and conducted herself within the Anglo-American upper class society. Finally, there are the legal documents. At first glance, they may not seem important for purposes of autobiographical data, but because Ruiz de Burton more than once took it upon herself to write her own legal statements and forms, they become yet another aspect to her narrative.

A general overview of the letters uncovers descriptions of California, most notably her beloved Ranch Jamul *"con mi jardincito en frente de la ventana á donde yo me sentaba á leer ó escribir"* [with my garden in front of the window where I used to sit to read or write] (June 23, 1860). She also describes the eastern part of the United States where her husband was stationed during the Civil War. Of Vermont she says, *"Durante el verano el Campo es mucho mas agradable p* [para] vivir q. [que] las ciudades, y casi la mitad de la gente se viene á los campos á vivir"* [During the summer the country is much more agreeable to live in instead of the cities, and almost half the people come to the country to live] (June 23, 1860). Because of her marriage to Col. Henry S. Burton, she is able to observe and comment upon New England upper class society and compare the state of the union with the state of Mexico as well as of California. She decries the California Land Commission as well as the *Comision de Mejico* because both contribute to her eventual loss of lands. The letters also entreat Mariano Guadalupe Vallejo to come to Washington and participate in Washington's governmental process. Ruiz de Burton also wants him to meet Abraham Lincoln: *"No deje de venir, y yo quiero tener el placer de presentarlo á Mr. y Mrs. Lincoln. Ella y yo somos muy buenas amigas y yo sé muy bien q. si yo lo presento será muy bien recibido . . . Venga pronto"* [Do not hesitate to come, and I want to have the pleasure of presenting Mr. and Mrs. Lincoln to you. She and I are very good friends and I well know that if I present you, you will be well received] (March 8, 1860[1]).[6] Nine years later, she writes a dark, painful letter announcing the death of her husband and follows this letter with many others decrying the overwhelming amount of squatters occupying and filing claims upon her California lands. She repeatedly writes that she is alone in the fight to save her lands: *"Que es posible Dios mio. . . q[ue] soy tan miserable q[ue] no tengo un solo amigo . . ."* [Is it possible my God . . . That I am so miserable, that I have not one friend . . .] (Nov. 23, 1869). Her years of struggle to keep her lands push her to seek new ways to acquire money. At one point, she writes to Samuel Barlow, a prominent New York lawyer, hoping to begin a partnership to patent a talc substance which may yield money:

> It is called 'folliated talc' and used for ornamenting cabinets, boxes, fans, [etc.]. It looks like enamelling, or mother of pearl. It makes also, beautiful wall paper. I will send you a small specimen for you to see . . . If you will help me get the Patent we can do so, but I alone, I cannot. (Sept. 5, 1883)

Although she participates within a male Anglo-American business environment, she continually feels, *"pisoteada bajo el pie del Sajón"* [trampled under the foot of the Saxon] (August 26, 1867). Letters such as these allow for a recovery of autobiography which resists and reconfigures Anglo-American stereotypes of the Californio in the nineteeth century.

Her letters are what Genaro Padilla has observed in Mexican American narratives: "a set of responses that mediate the nascent national and existential realities imposed upon the daily lives of Mexican (American)s by a regime that mouthed a rhetoric of democratic ideals but practiced unrelenting hostility in its relations with them" (158). Because her novels fictionalize these "responses," the letters then serve as another set of "intentions" alongside her recently published novels. Ruiz de Burton fashions a narrative window through which we can observe a discursive process of cultural negotiations both within her own racial and gender group as well as outside of these spheres. In this sense she parallels the early Chicano narratives of acculturation.[7] I say this cautiously because of Ruiz de Burton's elite military background. She was clearly not a subaltern in the sense of belonging to the Mexican subordinate class. However, her transformation into American society subsumes her into an American subordinate class as both Hispana *and* a woman. Critic José David Saldívar rightly sees Ruiz de Burton "as a subaltern mediator who is simultaneously an insurgent critic of monopoly capitalism and a radical critic of Anglocentric historiography" (170). Therefore, her colonialist lineage should not deter readers and critics from her writings which confront and challenge stereotypes of the Mexican in the United States. They should be studied alongside Mexican (American) writings of the subaltern, writings of all peoples of color from a variety of backgrounds, as well as Anglo-American writings in order to broaden our perceptions of nineteenth-century literary history. Rosaura Sánchez, for instance, explores similar experiences of disenfranchisment using Ruiz de Burton's *The Squatter and the Don* and the contemporary Chicano novel *Reto en el Paraíso,* by Alejandro Morales.[8] If we ignore Ruiz de Burton's writings within the Chicano/American literature arenas, we are only perpetuating further stereotypes of our literary historical past and reconstructing old monochromatic idealizations of the west. Ruiz de Burton was able to enter various American political structures reserved for Anglo-Americans and what she did within those constructs is also my focus of this work. Ruiz de Burton writes within a Mexican American literary landscape as well as writing upon it because she incorporates and intersects what is perceived as American nationhood with Mexican considerations (albeit Californio ones).

"This Yankie Nation": Negotiating Gender and Race in Washington

... Fuí á varias de las *"receptions"* del [P]residente, x Miss Lane, algunas de las esposas de Senadores y miembros del Gabinet. Tambien fuí al Capitólio á oir los discursos de los Srs. Davis, Douglas, Sumner, Hammond x. x. x. No puedo decir q.[ue] su eloquencia me hizo imaginar q.[ue] estaba oyendo á Demóstenes cuando Philip amenazaba á Atenas, *not a bit of it—*, pero como llevaba mi ópera glass, me divertia mirando la concurrencia en las galerias.

... I went to many of the [P]resident's *"receptions"*: Miss Lane, one of the senator's wives and members of the cabinet. I also went to the Capital to hear the speeches of the gentlemen: Davis, Douglas, Sumner, Hammond x. x. x. I cannot say that their eloquence made me imagine that I was listening to Demosthenes when Philip threatened Athens, *not a bit of it*, but since I had brought my opera glass, I amused myself by looking at the audience in the galleries (June 23, 1860)

Perhaps in our fictional imaginations, we can place Ruiz de Burton at her desk writing speeches, and on the floor of the senate speaking on behalf of the Californios. From her balcony seat and gazing through opera glasses, perhaps she looked down and imagined herself there as well. In truth, however, she did not remain immobile in her desires to be politically active. The excerpted letter above displays a woman who was busy attending functions *and* actively aware of the political milieu. The nagging caveat she had to obey was to be present but silent among the crowd of Washington ladies, to attend a number of congressional hearings, speeches, and balls while on the arm of her husband, Col. Henry S. Burton. Although Ruiz de Burton had no choice but to remain outwardly obsequious to the societal manners expected of Anglo-American women married to politicians and military elite, she subversively rejected the decorous role with her pen.

Consider the balcony scene excerpt above. Her words give voice to keen observations. Her cutting allusions turn American patriotic reverence for government leaders on its head. She is satisfying her desires in two ways which again link her epistolary concerns to her fictional writing. In the first, she continually epistolizes her impressions which then serve as preliminary sketches. Consider the following two letter excerpts: *"La salá esta llena de gente y casi ni sé lo q.[ue] escribo. Anoche fuimos á la 'reception' de Mr. y Mrs. Lincoln y de allí a un baile y no v[e]nimos sino hasta despues de las tres . . ."* [The parlor is full of people and I hardly know what I write. Last night we went to Mr. and Mrs. Lincoln's "reception" and from there to a dance and we did not return until after three . . .] (March 8 186[1]). Later that year, she writes: *"Y tambien es necesario q.[ue] se venga á dar una paseada, q[ue] pase un invierno en Washington y vea q.[ue] gran humbug es esta* Yankie nation. *Un humbug tan sistemado y bien sostenido q.[ue] aun ellos mismos casi lo creen."* [And it is also necessary that you come for a visit, to stay a winter in Washington and see what a great humbug is this *Yankie nation.* A humbug so methodical and well supported that they even *almost* believe it.] (June 23, 186[1]). Her penchant for continually recording her experiences is apparent in the first excerpt. Even with a minimum amount of sleep and a parlor full of people, she sits down to write and in the next fragment her cutting sarcasm and humor emerge. She is an American military wife by marriage but a sharply critical Mexican observer in her heart, refusing to completely assimilate herself in "their" culture. She then transforms these rudimentary sketches into fiction.

In her first novel, *Who Would Have Thought It?,* she creates the character of Lavinia, who nurses the sick and dying soldiers of the Civil War. Critic Anne Goldman, accurately points out that "Lavinia is as much condescended to as lauded by Ruiz de Burton . . ."(76) In this scene, Lavinia resembles the hotheaded aristocrat somewhat familiarly akin to Ruiz de Burton. Lavinia goes to Washington to plead for the exchange of her brother Isaac Sprig. She announces herself upon arriving and realizes that in these hallowed halls, "her name had never sounded to her ears so insignificant, so unaristocratic as at that moment when uttered in the now historical palace, before so haughty a personage" (the officer at the door) (105). Later, when she is in the waiting area, she contemplates:

> [T]hat no matter how much a woman, in her unostentatious sphere, may do, and help to do, and no matter how her heart may feel for her beloved, worshipped country, after all she is but an insignificant creature, whom a very young man may snub, simply because he wears very shiny brass buttons and his uncle is in Congress. "What a miserable, powerless thing woman is, even in this our country of glorious equality! Here I have been sitting up at night, toiling, and tending disgusting sickness, and dressing loathsome wounds, all for the love of our dear country, and now, the first time I come to ask a favor— a favor, do I say? No. I come to demand a right—see how I am received!" (106)

Lavinia's headstrong temperament embodies many of the qualities Ruiz de Burton exemplifies in her letters to Vallejo. Lavinia's feelings of alienation and betrayal mirror Ruiz de Burton's frustrations. The novels and letters, then, become the primary avenue to voice her desire to be recognized on an equal footing in Washington. They also become an indirect way to be active. In her letters, she repeatedly asks for Vallejo's assistance because he is a man. She can only give advice, she says, and even that is not valued. In the following fragment, Ruiz de Burton criticizes Vallejo for failing to appear in Washington to sway congress to vote in favor of the Californios land rights:

> Para manejar ese negocio se necesita mas de un diplomático q[ue] de un politician, y le aseguro á u.[sted], q[ue]. . . su "influjo moral" es de hablar personalmente con Senadores q.[ue] dentro de media hora van á votar en contra ó en favor de u.[sted] sabiendo q[ue] u.[sted] está sentado en la galeria oyendolos.
>
> Todavia creo q.[ue] si u.[sted] hubiera seguido mi consejo y venido á Washington en '60 o '61, otro habria sido el resultado de este negocio. Pero u.[sted] es hombre, y no me creyó con la suficiente seguridad para darle un buen consejo.

> To negotiate that business, one needs more a diplomat than a politician, and I assure you that your moral influence is to speak personally with senators who, in a half hour will be voting for or against you, knowing you would be sitting up in the gallery hearing them.
>
> I still believe that if you had listened to my advice and come to Washington in '60 or '61, the result of the negotiation would have been different. But you are a man, and you didn't believe with sufficient certainty that I could give good advice. (March 18, 1863)

Her literary efforts to be heard within her own Mexican community on American soil are potent and compelling actions. She is similar to American women writers such as Margaret Fuller who challenge the state of woman: "If there is a misfortune in woman's lot, it is in obstacles being interposed by men . . ." (Fuller 28) or novelist Catharine Maria Sedgwick, who created unconventional female characters in her fiction.[9] Yet Fuller and Sedgwick's circumstances in the nineteeth century are privileged when compared to Ruiz de Burton's situation. They publish widely within the Anglo-American society and are economically stable. When Ruiz de Burton's husband dies, her sole and direct link to American upper class society and economic stability is severed. She becomes a widow in financial straits with a growing number of squatters laying claim to her lands, and she must forge a readership who is willing to accept the views of a western Mexican Californio voice. Sometimes the burden becomes overwhelming, as is apparent in this letter fragment:

> . . . ¡Ah! Si yo fuera hombre! . . . Qúe miserable cosa es una mujer!

Decididamente la providencia debe recompensarme de alguna manera por haberme hecho muger! . . . .y fea . . . y pobre! . . . va! Como si ser mujer no fuera suficiente Calamidad sin añadir otras. No, es necesario q.[ue] yo no me entusiasme por el progreso del Continente. ¿Para que? Ni mi raza ni mi sexo mejora.

. . . Ah! If I were a man! . . . What a miserable thing is a woman! Verily, providence needs to compensate me in some manner for having made me woman . . . and ugly . . . and poor! . . . oh! As if being a woman were not sufficient calamity without adding others. No, it is necessary that I do not become enthusiastic over the progress of the Continent. Why? Neither my race nor my sex can improve. (February 15, 1869)

Her lament deftly links the word *race* with gender, a personal concern not belonging to nineteenth-century Anglo women's circles. In this aspect, Ruiz de Burton is similar to Doña Apolinaria Lorenzana who lost a twenty-five year battle for her lands to a Captain Magruder, one of many Anglo-American squatters. Lorenzana's narrative mirrors Ruiz de Burton's anguish:

Así es que despues de haber trabajado tantos años, de haber poseido bienes, de que no me desposié por vento ni de otro modo, me encuentro de la mayor pobreza, viviendo de fabor de Dios y de los que me dan un bocado de comer.

So, that's the way it turns out, that after working so many years, after having acquired an estate, which I certainly didn't dispose of by selling or by any other means, here I find myself in the greatest poverty, living only by the grace of God and through the charity of those who give me a mouthful to eat. (1878)

Where there may be some evidence of similarity among the aforementioned women's intents and writings, it is in the subject of race and Mexican/Californio usurpation which separates Ruiz de Burton from her Anglo female counterparts. She is writing against a powerful wave of publishers, critics, and political bodies interested in establishing an American nationhood whose Puritan/Protestant principles are quite different from her Mexican Catholic heritage. The remarkable characteristic about Ruiz de Burton is her unfailing determination to publish despite the overwhelming odds against her in an Anglo-American publishing industry. She leaves behind literary works that record a woman's racial, gender and political struggles. It is important to note as well, that within these literary stories and letters, she is also working toward refining her writing stylistically. She plays with a number of genres within her letters which later appear in the novels (such as refining her classical metaphors and allusions). Readers may observe familiar features of naturalism, muckraking scenes, and realism. *Who Would Have Thought It?* and *The Squatter and the Don* resemble American women's novels of the time, such as Stowe's *Uncle Tom's Cabin* and Warner's *The Wide, Wide World* which were highly popular in the 1850s. However, Ruiz de Burton also takes risks. She confidently takes more stylistic leaps with narration combining rural (western) and urban (eastern) settings.[10] Her experiments make her work pertinent for today's discussions concerning canon formation.

"I Shall Write": Experimenting in Genres, and Expanding the Literary Canon

Mucho hay que ver en E.U., y mucho q. pensar, particularmente si uno empieza á hacer comparaciones. Realmente para apreciar bien una cosa es necesario mirar bien otra. Creo q. lo mejor q. yo pueda hacer es escribir un libro, ¿Que tal? . . . las escenas deben ser en Califa. el [contento difinitivo] de las dos razas es un gran tema.

There is much to see in the U.S., and much to think about, particularly if one begins to make comparisons. In reality, to truly appreciate one thing it is necessary to look well at another.

I think the best that I can do is to write a book. What do you think? the scenes should be set in California and the definitive topic of two races is a grand theme.   (Ruiz de Burton, 23 June 1860)

In the above letter excerpt written to Mariano Guadalupe Vallejo, Ruiz de Burton begins to construct ideas for her work *The Squatter and the Don,* a California romance. The letter hints at a setting and plot: an appreciative but critical look at two races. However, the final draft of her novel really traces the demise of a Californio family. It is her perspective of a Mexican Californio ranch family struggling to keep their lands after 1848. It is also her perspective of an Anglo New England family coming to California to settle on those lands. She is *looking well* (as she says in the letter above) at both the west and east: her own people and those usurping her lands. Through their written correspondence, Vallejo helped her develop the initial ideas for the book. In a letter fragment which is not dated, she writes, *"En respuesta de su segunda [carta] diré q.[ue] con mucho gusto escribiré una relacion de el efecto q.[ue] la proclama esa tuvo sobre los Californios y como influyó su destino."* [In response to your second (letter) I say with much pleasure that I shall write a story of the effects that the proclamation had upon the Californios and how it influenced their destiny] (October 10, ?).[11] The novel is not only a romance (or Sentimental Romance) but it is apparent that Ruiz de Burton experiments with aspects of various genres such as realism and naturalism. These genres surface in her letter writing as when she sympathizes with Vallejo due to a death in his family:

Y por mas negro que esté el corazon de dolor y el alma toda enlutada tambi-

en, los árboles tan verdes, y las flores tan brillantes! . . . Y el cielo tan azul, y
el sol y la luna y las estrellas siguen su marcha luminosa como jactándose de
su insensible immortalidad . . . Así refleccionaba yo cuando Enrique murio! y
sé bien que u.[sted] tambien mi pobre amigo, he de estar sintiendo y pensan-
do así.

And the more my heart blackens with pain and the soul in mourning as well,
the trees are so green, the flowers so brilliant! . . . And the sky so blue, the sun
and the moon and the stars follow their luminous course as if boasting of their
unfeeling immortality . . . That is what I considered when Henry died! [A]nd
I know well that you, my poor friend, are also feeling and thinking similarly.
(May 18, 1878)

Her keen descriptions, her political protests, and her awareness of human limitations (including her own and those of the Californios) are preliminary
sketches of these various genres. It is important to note that contemporary critics as well as textbook publishers have attributed these genres to later novels
and novelists, categorizing each genre into separate headings and chronological
ordering. These genres surfaced earlier in the nineteenth century by writers such
as Rebecca Harding Davis.[12] Davis and Ruiz de Burton published more than
thirty years before William Dean Howells, Frank Norris, or Stephen Crane.
Their earlier works move in and out of realism, naturalism, romance. Because
Ruiz de Burton's letters are linked within the construction of these genres we
can further trace and investigate her stylistic development. From epistolary
prose to structured scenes, her style is one which consistently breaks fictional
narrative for various reasons: to achieve a direct authorial voice, to provide realistic focus, to create a mood. In addition, Ruiz de Burton's works also contain
literary aspects attributed to a later American group of writers known as the
muckrakers.[13] When learning about the writers leading the muckraking movement, we are often guided to the early 1900s and Upton Sinclair. Theodore
Dreiser and Frank Norris are also placed under the category of naturalism. All
of these writers are indeed significant. However, contemporary readers are at a
disadvantage without having access to cross-class, multi-racial literatures from
nineteenth-century authors who became Americans or were born in the United
States and who experimented with a myriad of genres.

Consider Ruiz de Burton's first chapter of *The Squatter and the Don* with
Chapter Nine of Stowe's *Uncle Tom's Cabin*. Ruiz de Burton creates the scene
in the home of a New England family. The wife is admonishing her husband for
being a squatter and taking land that legally is not his but that of the Alamar
Californio family. "I beg of you, do not go on a Mexican grant unless you buy
the land from the owner. This I beg of you specially, and must insist upon it"
(57). Note how the scene also mirrors her letters to Vallejo. Chapter Nine in
Uncle Tom's Cabin also begins within the home. Senator John Bird, a member
of Ohio's legislature, and his wife Mary are sitting at the table. From this

domestic sphere, it is Mary who admonishes the senator after he tells her he supports "a law forbidding people to help off the slaves that come over from Kentucky . . . I never could have thought it of you, John . . . You ought to be ashamed . . ." (142-144).

At the conclusion of both novels, the discursive structure changes from what began as a romance to a realistic mode which seeks specific ends toward reform. Beecher Stowe calls for an end to slavery and delineates how legislation is violating human rights. Ruiz de Burton calls for an end to Californio harrassment and delineates how the Treaty of Guadalupe has not been honored and discusses the need for new legislation. They both prove their points with copious quotations from published legislation, treaties, and political figures of the time. Ruiz de Burton ends her novel by pointing out that: "Our representatives in Congress, and in the State Legislature, knowing full well the will of the people, ought to legislate accordingly. If they do not, then we shall—as Channing said "kiss the foot that tramples us!" and "in anguish of spirit" must wait and pray for a Redeemer who will emancipate the . . . slaves of California" (372). Twenty-one years after Ruiz de Burton's publication, Upton Sinclair's 1906 publication of *The Jungle* ends like this: "the rallying of the outraged workingmen of Chicago . . . we shall organize them, we shall drill them, we shall marshal them for the victory! We shall bear down the opposition, we shall sweep it before us—and Chicago will be ours . . ." (346). Sentimentalism is a mode that has designs upon the world.[14] If writing has an ideological (and historical) base (and I look to Bakhtin's theory of dialogisms here as well as nineteenth-century constructions/reviews of fiction) then we must look at the ways discourse shapes the ranges of perspectives. In this case, what ends does the realism and muckraking mode seek to achieve upon the larger world? What kind of textual work does it try to achieve? When Ruiz de Burton writes "I slander no one but speak the truth" (364), which parallels Theodore Dreiser's own words when he writes in *Sister Carrie* that "the needle of understanding will yet point steadfast and unwavering to the distant pole of truth" (Dreiser 57), both authors rupture fictional narrative to appropriate a more direct authority. True their intentions or "truths" differ, but to investigate such considerations is what broadens the discussion of literature and literary history.

These examples reveal an attempt at a restructuring of American literature which has unlimited possibilities in the number and kind of text and genre. These examples untie the stringent, exiguous textbook lists that have kept readers in unnecessary corsetry. As Jane Tompkins points out, "'[L]iterature' is not a stable entity, but a category whose outlines and contents are variable (190)." Other critics such as Paul Lauter, Henry Louis Gates, Jr., William Spengemann, Toni Morrison, Rafael Pérez-Torres, and Ramón Saldívar have also called for reconsiderations of American literary history. In 1995, Annette Kolodny appealed for a new kind of American literary canon which "frees American literary history from the persistent theories of continuity that have made it virtually impossible to treat frontier materials as other than marginalia or cultural mythology" (10). Treating lesser known works as unimportant or simply calling them marginal furthers a mythology of those whose voices have been labeled as "other." In Ruiz de Burton's case, her marginalization was not solely a literary one but one of personal identity. After the Treaty of Guadalupe was signed, and especially after her husband died, Ruiz de Burton fought a daily battle against becoming an exotic or mythologized figure in Californio history.

"Los Malos y Falsos Informes": Fighting Marginalization

No creo que deb[e]mos omitir ni un solo papel, puesto que pa. [para] el "ape[l] y deslinde" la copia del título tiene que ser "facsimile". Así pues, perdóneme que le suplique de no dejar fuera nada, sino compiarlos en orden cronológico así como se lo espliqué. La venta esa en [I]ngles fue hecha por mi mamá y mis tias, y debe seguir el título de mi abuelita, es decir, la posesion dada por Salgada. No cambie nada, hagame favor de solo cambiar lo q.[ue] le dije y lo demas déjelo como está.

Ya u. verá que despues de la venta en [I]ngles siguen la Patente y los documentos ó derechos del gobierno ratificando mi título.

Este orden cronológico me parece mejor que poner "apéndices" para evitar confusion (in the American mind) al leer tanto documento.

I do not believe we should omit not one paper since for the "appeal and demarcation of land" the copy of the title needs to be a "facsimile". So forgive me if I implore you not to leave anything out, but instead copy them in chronological order as I have explained it to you. The sale is in English and was prepared by my mother and my aunts, and should follow my grandmother's title, I mean the possession given by Salgada. Do not change anything(.) (D)o me the favor of only changing what I told you and leaving the rest as is.

You will see that after the sale in English(,) the Patent and the documents or rights of the government ratifying my title follow.

It appears to me that this chronological order is better than an appendix to avoid confusion (in the American mind) at reading so many documents.

(January 12, 1886)

Perhaps it is easier to envision a nineteenth-century American woman tying a crinoline bow around her satin covered cinched waist or a woman newly arrived in California, standing on her veranda listening to the rhythmic music of the haymakers in the barn. I was raised with such textbook images rather than pictures of Mexican American women sitting at a table writing detailed descriptions of legal documents. Ruiz de Burton had the multi-faceted gift of negotiating cross-cultural affairs which included advising Californios on legal documents. The excerpted letter above provides much more than Ruiz de Burton's knowledge of legal documents. It informs the reader that she was acutely aware of American ideology and creative in her methods to work within/against their system. Unlike the Californios, whose lives were primarily spent on California ranches far away from Anglo-American congressional assemblies, Ruiz de Burton had first-hand experience of both worlds. Rosaura Sánchez notes that, "The Californio . . . did not have her [Ruiz de Burton's] English-language skills and by 1875 were much older than she and totally impoverished. As a marginalized, dispossessed, and disempowered minority, the Californios had come to believe that anything they said would carry little weight and find no acceptance from the American public" (25). However, with all of Ruiz de Burton's proficiencies, after Col. Burton's death, she continually lost battles to keep her lands and in the end also died impoverished. What endured were her letters and fiction, which would resurface in the 1990s.

Before then, her written production was kept hidden while stereotypes of the Californios were exploited and perpetuated. Why? Despite her connections to the Lincolns, eastern social circles, and connections with Hubert H. Bancroft, the powerful force underway was the United States' settling of California lands. Ruiz de Burton may have been aware of American ideology but her knowledge was not going to deter the construction of a carefully wrought historical myth forged upon the Mexican heritage.[15] Before California erased the Californio, they were denigrated in various ways. In Frank Norris' novel *The Octopus,* for example, Norris' descriptions of the Californio transform them into "decayed, picturesque, vicious, and romantic" stereotypes (20). And for publisher and book collector Hubert H. Bancroft, his appropriations of Californio testimonials helped further the disappearing voice of the Mexicano. Bancroft was determined not to allow another voice to share his literary landscape. Philip Fisher has said of Bancroft: "Bancroft's volumes defined the standard colonial history, the pre-history of the political entity called the United States" (23). By defining the west and writing Californio history, Bancroft was essentially writing the conquest and erasing the voices he was collecting. Ruiz de Burton was aware of such power and her limitations as a woman. She wrote in defiance:

> Si yo pudiera creer en el "Manifest Destiny" dejaria de creer en la justicia ó la sabiduria divina. No amigo mio, el Manifest Destiny no es otra cosa q.[ue] "Manifest Yankie trick" como sus "wooden hams & wooden nuttmegs" del Connecticut.

> If I could believe in "Manifest Destiny", I would stop believing in justice or in divine wisdom. No my friend, Manifest Destiny is no other thing except "Manifest Yankie Trick" like their wooden hams and wooden nuttmegs of Connecticut.   (February 15, 1869)

For every letter Ruiz de Burton wrote in a desperate attempt to sustain what she believed to be the Californio identity, hundreds of pages were printed and widely distributed by Anglo Americans propagandizing their brand of

Californio/Mexican American identity.[16] Illinois lawyer and travel writer, Thomas Jefferson Farnham, published *Travels in California and Scenes in the Pacific Ocean* in 1844. He wrote:

> [T]he Californios are an imbecile, pusillanimous race of men, and unfit to control the destinies of that beautiful country . . .The ladies, dear creatures, I wish they were whiter, and that their cheekbones did not in their great condescension assimilate their manners and customs so remarkably to their Indian neighbors . . . a pity it is . . . that they have not stay and corset makers' signs among them, for they allow their waists to grow as God designed they should, like Venus de Medici, that ill-bred statue that had no kind mother to lash its vitals into delicate form . . . (148)

These are just some of the voices with which Ruiz de Burton had to contend. If one looks through the San Francisco *Argonaut* of 1885, one will not find Ruiz de Burton's books mentioned. The now established canonical writers are present: Henry James and William Dean Howells. Helen Hunt Jackson is also mentioned numerous times as the official writer of the Indian and Mexican romance. On September 12, 1885 under "Literary Notes" in the San Francisco Argonaut, a notation reads: "Mrs. Helen Hunt Jackson's novel, *Ramona,* has now reached its eighteenth thousand" (The Argonaut 10). All of the above writers were in one way or another supported monetarily and professionally by Hubert H. Bancroft. To Ruiz de Burton (as well as the other Californios) he offered to romanticize them in an account he entitled, *California Pastoral.* Making Ruiz de Burton a passive character which he called "The Maid of Monterey" denied any possibility for the public to visualize her as a serious writer. Even a ballad was written about her which was inspired from the brief insurrection at La Paz in the 1840s:

> The moon shone but dimly/ Beyond the battle plain/ A gentle breeze fanned softly/ O'er the features of the slain/ The guns had hushed their thunder/ The guns in silence lay/ Then came the señorita/ The Maid of Monterey.
>
> She cast a look of anguish/ On the dying and the dead/ And made a pillow/ For those who mourned and bled/Now here's to that bright beauty/ Who drives death's pangs away/ The meek-eyed señority/ The Maid of Monterey
>
> Although she loved her country/ And prayed that it might live/ Yet for the foreign soldier/ She had a tear to give/ And when the dying soldier/In her bright gleam did pray/ He blessed this señorita/ The Maid of Monterey. . . (Davidson)

As late as the 1930s, the romanticization of Ruiz de Burton continued. Biographer Winnifred Davidson wrote in *1931 Notes:* "Those who used to know her remember her lovely, small feet with their high curved arches and her grace that was perfection itself in the dance. Her good nature overcame her native hauteur" (Davidson). Ruiz de Burton's letters differ greatly from the published descriptions of Californianas as either loose and out on the street or veiled within the domestic sphere. Of course none of the stereotypes describe Ruiz de Burton's complex identity.

Therefore, the choice to write in the nineteenth century becomes a subversive act for Ruiz de Burton. It is doubly subversive for her because she clandestinely depicts actual Anglo-American acquaintances in her novels. In her letters, she is more forthright. For example, in a letter to Vallejo, she writes:

> . . . los Americanos son y seran siempre los enemigos mortales de mi raza, de mi Méjico.
> No digo esto con odio; ellos no hacen mas q. seguir la ley de su ser. Las naciones, los individuos, los animales, todos hacen lo mismo.
> Sin odio, los tiburones se comen las sardinas; sin rancor los lobos se comen los borregos. . . Todos todos siguen *"la ley de su Ser."*
> . . . pero ni los tiburones, ni los lobos . . . deben esperar ser amados de sus victimas. . .

> . . . the Americans are and will be the mortal enemies of my race, of my Mexico.
> I don't say this with hatred; they don't do anything except to follow the laws of nature. The nations, individuals, the animals, everyone does the same.
> Without hatred, the sharks eat the tuna, without rancor the wolves eat the sheep . . . Everyone follows *the laws of nature.*
> . . . But neither the sharks, nor the wolves should wait to be loved by its victims . . . (August 26, 1867)

By this time in 1867, Ruiz de Burton is beginning to assess these written criticisms to cull them for her novel *Who Would Have Thought It?* later to follow with the *Squatter and the Don.* The bulk of the Vallejo letters are written before and during the writing of *Who Would Have Thought It?* which leads one to surmise, when considering the planning and drafting of a novel, that much of it came from years of writing letters, especially to Vallejo. Upon finishing *The Squatter and the Don,* she writes her friend George Davidson: "I have been writing a book, so I hope you won't scold me for being indolent. I don't know whether I shall publish it under my own name, so I want to keep the matter quiet yet. Only two or three friends know I am writing it. I want to publish it this fall, in September" (July 7, 1890). Like the dissemination of her beliefs in epistolary form, she also works tirelessly to disseminate her novels to a wider audience. Through her New York connections, specifically the New York lawyer Samuel Barlow, who knows prominent Philadelphia publisher J. B. Lippincott, she is able to imagine a larger audience for her writing. "I will write today to Mr. Lippincott telling him to send you a copy. . . I would like so much to know what you think of it, you must tell me. The title of it is—*Who Would Have Thought It?* I hope you will give me all the benefit of your influence with the New York Press . . . I did not write for glory" (Sept. 9, 1872).

Today the extent of her readership is not known and reviews of her books are difficult to find. However, inside a Lippincott volume titled *Entertaining Novels* (1874–1875) which features works by Rebecca Harding Davis, Sarah Winter Kellogg, and Francis Asheton, one will find a very brief review of *Who Would Have Thought It?* It reads: "A bright and attractive romance, with an interesting plot, well sustained throughout" (Entertaining Novels). In 1885, when *The Squatter and the Don* was published, she wrote to Vallejo and said, *"El libro ya salio a luz. Pobre feito mio!"* [The book has now been born. My poor ugly one!] (1885). *The Squatter and the Don,* under the pseudonym C. Loyal, *Who Would Have Thought It?*, and Ruiz de Burton's letters and documents, become for contemporary readers a recovery of a Mexican American literary presence mostly ignored if not headed for complete erasure. Because of the complexities inherent in her letters and novels, Ruiz de Burton cannot be cornered into a type. Instead, Ruiz de Burton's works help to reopen the multiple and varied volumes which can only point away from ruddy pastel pictures and toward a better understanding of the Mexican American of the nineteenth century. The recent re-publication of Mexican American and Latino writing also continues to expand the literary canon to achieve a more heterogeneous nineteenth-century American literary history.

Notes

I thank Noelle Arrangoiz, José Aranda, Mary Kelley, Susan Johnson, J. Alemán, Anne E. Goldman and Rik Knablein for their comments on drafts of this essay. I am also grateful to the Santa Barbara Mission Archive Library and The Huntington Library for their support toward this research and for permission to use and quote from the Ruiz de Burton letters in the De La Guerra Collection. My research and translation work has also been supported and funded through the Rocky Mountain Modern Language Association (RMMLA) in conjunction with the Huntington Library Fellowship and a grant through the Recovery Project in Houston.

[1] I am currently finishing, for publication, a bilingual translation of Ruiz de Burton's letters which cover roughly thirty-five years of her life: 1851-1887. The letters in this essay will be included in my book. To remain true to her writing, I have not corrected some of her misspellings or grammatical errors.

[2] Like Ruiz de Burton, Doña Apolinaria Lorenzana, Mariano Guadalupe Vallejo, and Antonio María Osio were all Californios who were disenfranchised after the Mexican American War. All four either independently wrote or had their testimonials recorded either by Bancroft or another biographer. See Lorenzana's testimonial, "Memorias de la Beata" recorded in Bancroft's

narratives; Vallejo's "Recuerdos Históricos y Personales;" and Osio's *History of Alta California: A Memoir of Mexican California.* There are other writers as well. See Genaro Padilla's *My History Not Yours;* Rosaura Sánchez' *Telling Identities* and collected testimonials in *Critica: A Journal of Critical Essays,* edited by Rosaura Sánchez, Beatrice Pita and Bárbara Reyes.

[3] Helen Hunt Jackson's *Ramona* is the narrative romanticization of Spanish Mexican stereotypes: the once noble Mexicans, now decayed and extinct. The novel still enjoys widespread popularity. And since 1923, Hemet, California, produces an elaborate *Ramona Pageant* (mainly attended by hundreds of Anglo-American tourists) every spring which celebrates the nostalgic "Spanish" days and at the end of the melodrama, the Californio characters all march back to Mexico. Hemet calls its pageant the "Official California State Outdoor Play."

[4] Efforts to recover archival or privately owned Latino works are currently underway. Various universities are placing emphasis in such projects. University of Houston's ten year Recovery Project is one as well as Texas A&M's efforts which have recently recovered González and Raleigh's historical novel, *Caballero.* These projects have also led to critical analysis of newly recovered works. So far, María Amparo Ruiz de Burton's writings have been given cursory attention in a number of scholarly texts concerning Chicana(o) writing and Mexican American testimonials: Genaro Padilla's work, *My History, Not Yours: The Formation of Mexican American Autobiography;* Rosaura Sánchez, *Telling Identities: The Californio Testimonials;* Tey Diana Rebolledo, *Women Singing in the Snow: A Cultural Analysis of Chicana Literature;* Lisbeth Haas, *Conquests and Historical identities in California 1769-1936;* José David Saldívar, *Border Matters: Remapping American Cultural Studies.* In these texts, she is introduced as one of the early writers who wrote fiction and was influential in Californio society. These writings do the important work of theorizing her place within a cultural nineteenth-century context and the impact she has upon recovery work today. The next step is to take up the project of analyzing Ruiz de Burton's work with her letters in an American literary context. Most recently, Volume II of *Recovering the U.S. Hispanic Literary Heritage* features three essays on Ruiz de Burton's novels by Anne Goldman, John M. González, and Manuel M. Martín Rodríguez. The only recent biography on Ruiz de Burton is a Masters Thesis written in 1992 by Frederick Bryant Oden from The University of San Diego's History Department. The thesis includes translations of some of her letters. The new editions of her novels, published by Arte Público Press, do include introductory analysis (by Rosaura Sánchez and Beatrice Pita) but again do not focus on her letters or her place within canonical American literary traditions.

[5] See José F. Aranda Jr.'s essay, "Contradictory Impulses: María Amparo Ruiz de Burton, Resistance Theory , and the Politics of Chicano/a Studies" in the journal, *American Literature.* Here, Aranda opens the door to further in-

depth analysis with Ruiz de Burton's writings by arguing for "historicizing Ruiz de Burton and her Californio peers as products of competing colonial enterprises in Alta California" (573). Taking this perspective, Ruiz de Burton's efforts to publish in English for an American audience only emphasizes her wish to partake and resist within American *and* Mexican literary traditions.

[6] Although Ruiz de Burton clearly wrote 1860 in two letters which contain information concerning the inauguration and receptions of President Lincoln, the date is incorrect. It should read 1861. To remain true to her letters, however, I simply add a [1] next to her date.

[7] See Ramón Saldívar's evaluation of Ernesto Galarza's *Barrio Boy*. It provides interesting parallels to Ruiz de Burton despite differences in class. It is important to keep in mind Ruiz de Burton's racism and adherence to colonialist aristocracy. However, Ruiz de Burton's letters, like *Barrio Boy,* are not one-dimensional accounts. Her identity unfolds through her struggles to assimilate and to resist. But even this type of evaluation becomes reductive and therefore needs further analysis using Bakhtin's ideas of the dialogic. J. Alemán (University of Kansas) says that Ruiz de Burton's letters are situated in a dialectical socio-historical context that she then dialogizes through her narrative strategies of irony, parody, reported speech, and letter writing form. Also, see Bakhtin's "Discourse in the Novel" where Bakhtin argues against a stylistic analysis in the novel and argues for an understanding of "each language's socio-ideological meaning" in order to be open to all genres/narratives (heteroglossia). Ruiz de Burton's letters are part of and inform narrative/novel making. It is clear that in many instances, the content of her letters is incorporated into her novel writing: "from one genre to another" (Bakhtin 418).

[8] See Rosaura Sánchez' *Telling Identities* where she compares Morales and Ruiz de Burton's writings. For Sánchez, "In Morales's novel lunacy becomes a trope for displacement and dispossession" (296).

[9] Mary Kelley notes that Sedgwick's characters, especially those in her story "Cacoethes Scribendi" were in many ways reflecting her own struggles of a woman's place in nineteenth-century America. "Cacoethes Scribendi" gave Sedgwick the opportunity to explore these struggles. "Thus did Sedgwick write," says Kelley, "more than in any other of her fictions, about all of her selves" (214). Ruiz de Burton, like Sedgwick, continually plays with various self-referent female characters which at times embody both the colonialist as well as the oppressed voice struggling against an Anglo-American colonization.

[10] See Nina Baym's *Novels, Readers, and Reviewers: Responses to Fiction in Antebellum America.* She notes that in the 1850s, "critics were separating out two forms of the [narrative] mode, the New England novel and the western. New England stories were invariably "quiet"; their settings were rural, their scope domestic. It is clear from the reviews that western stories were extremely popular, and it is difficult not to suppose that the basis of that pop-

ularity was the action rather than their fidelity to details of western life" (117). In both Ruiz de Burton's novels, she combines the New England or eastern settings with that of the western to create comparative perspectives.

¹¹ This letter fragment is a partial letter contained in a packet of loose and torn letters. No date is recorded. There were numerous proclamations which the California Land Commission placed upon Californio properties and which eventually cost them their lands.

¹² Tillie Olsen revised Davis' works in 1985. Davis' "Life in the Iron Mills" is sophisticated in its development of what we call today realism and naturalism. In its entirety it also is an example of muckraking—uncovering the injustices of life in the iron mills.

¹³ The term *muckraking* did not exist during Ruiz de Burton's literary lifetime. Yet, I mention "muckraking" here because the term (coined by President Theodore Roosevelt) originates from John Bunyan's allegory, *Pilgrim's Progress: From This World To That Which Is To Come,* published in 1678 and 1684 (part I and II respectively). Christian, Bunyan's main character, must flee his city which is to be burned. Ruiz de Burton's Californios in *The Squatter and the Don* experience colonization—a burning which dislocates and melds the Alamar family into hod carriers and an inevitable invisibility. Her writing is no allegory due to the naturalist and realist modes she incorporates in her works. However, her intent is similar to the later muckraker writers. Theodore Roosevelt used this term to demean American writers whose aim was to expose business, city, state, and national corruption. Ruiz de Burton's work could easily be placed under this category. Interestingly, in Holman and Harmon's *Handbook to Literature,* they place muckrakers "between 1902 and 1911 . . . [they] worked to expose the dishonest methods and unscrupulous motives in big business and in city, state, and national government" (303).

¹⁴ See Jane Tompkins' *Sensational Designs:* "When one sets aside modernist demands . . . and attends to the way a text offers a blueprint for survival under a specific set of political, economic, social, or religious conditions, an entirely new story begins to unfold, and one's sense of the formal exigencies of narrative alters accordingly, producing a different conception of what constitutes successful characters and plots" (xvii-xviii). In this sense, sentimentalist literature offers us (or one could say, "designs" for us) a way to see and discuss narrative on a multiplicity of levels or dialogisms (Bakhtin). Tompkins also points out that throughout the years, anthologies have repeatedly reorganized and restructured standards of aesthetics in an effort to codify a method of literary analysis. "[E]vidence of the anthologies demonstrates not only that works of art are not selected according to any unalterable standard, but that their very essence is always changing in accordance with the systems of description and evaluation that are in force. Even when the 'same' text keeps turning up in collection after collection, it is not really the same text at all" (196).

[15] In fact, as late as 1985, McGraw Hill's American Literature text ("a chronological approach") contains no record of Mexican American writers in the nineteenth century, nor any mention of the Mexican American War.

[16] See Benedict Anderson's *Imagined Communities* in which he writes that "the convergence of capitalism and print technology on the fatal diversity of human language created the possibility of a new form of imagined community, which in its basic morphology set the stage for the modern nation" (46). Anderson argues that the establishment of nationhood occurs with the production and distribution of vernacular literacies which define an agreed upon idea of community. In this case, Ruiz de Burton's two novels resist American stereotypes and ideals of nationhood. This could therefore be one reason why her novels were not mass produced or well distributed and why she had to partly finance and "market" her works by asking influential friends to send them to newspapers in order to get reviewed. The fact that Ruiz de Burton writes and publishes at all (a Mexican American in the nineteenth century) is an act of resistance against erasure of the Californio.

Works Cited

Aranda, José F. Jr., "Contradictory Impulses: María Amparo Ruiz de Burton, Resistance Theory, and the Politics of Chicano/a Studies." *American Literature.* 70 (September 1998): 551-579.

Bakhtin, M. M. "Discourse in the Novel." *The Dialogic Imagination: Four Essays.* Trans. Michael Holquist. Ed. Michael Holquist. Austin: University of Texas, 1994.

Bancroft, Hubert Howe. *The Works of Hubert Howe Bancroft, XVIII-XXIV, XXXIV.* San Francisco, 1888.

Baym, Nina. *Novels, Readers, and Reviewers: Responses to Fiction in Antebellum America.* Ithaca: Cornell University, 1984.

Crawford, Kathleen. "María Amparo Ruiz de Burton: The General's Lady." *The Journal of San Diego History* 30 (1984): 209.

Davidson, Winifred. *1931 Notes.* San Diego Historical Society Research Archives.

―――. Letter from Winifred Davidson to Eugene Divan Buchanan. *Burton Biographical File.* San Diego Historical Society.

Davis, Rebecca Harding. *Life in the Iron Mills and Other Stories.* Ed. Tillie Olsen. New York: Feminist Press, 1985.

Dreiser, Theodore. *Sister Carrie.* Ed. Donald Pizer. 2nd ed. New York: Norton, 1991.

Entertaining Novels. Philadelphia: J. B. Lippincott & Co., 1875.

Farnham, Thomas Jefferson. *Travelers in California and Scenes in the Pacific Ocean.* 1844. Reprint. Oakland: Biobooks, 1947.

Fisher, Philip. *Hard Facts: Setting and Form in the American Novel.* New York: Oxford University Press, 1987.

Fuller, Margaret. *Woman in the Nineteenth Century and Other Writings.* Oxford: Oxford University Press, 1994.

Goldman, Anne E. "'Who ever heard of a blue-eyed Mexican?': Satire and Sentimentality in María Amparo Ruiz de Burton's *Who Would Have Thought It?" Recovering the U.S. Hispanic Literary Heritage, Vol. II.* Ed. Erlinda Gonzales-Berry and Chuck Tatum. Houston: Arte Público, 1996.

Holman, Hugh and William Harmon, eds. *A Handbook to Literature.* 6th ed. New York: Macmillan, 1992.

Kelley, Mary. *Private Woman, Public Stage: Literary Domesticity in Nineteenth-Century America.* Oxford: Oxford University Press, 1984.

Kolodny, Annette. "Letting Go Our Grand Obsessions: Notes Toward a New Literary History of the American Frontiers." *Subjects and Citizens.* Ed. Davidson and Moon. Durham: Duke University, 1995.

Lorenzana, Apolinaria. "Memorias de la Beata." 1878. MS. Bancroft Library, University of California, Berkeley.

Osio, Antonio María. *The History of Alta California: A Memoir of Mexican California.* Trans., Ed., Rose Marie Beebe and Robert M. Senkewicz. Wisconsin: University of Wisconsin, 1996.

Norris, Frank. *The Octopus.* New York: Penguin, 1986.

Padilla, Genaro M. "Recovering Mexican-American Autobiography". *Recovering the U.S. Hispanic Literary Heritage.* Ed. Ramón Gutiérrez and Genaro Padilla. Houston: Arte Público, 1996.

Reynolds, David S. *Beneath The American Renaissance: The Subversive Imagination in the Age of Emerson and Melville.* Cambridge: Harvard University, 1988.

Ruiz de Burton, María Amparo. Letter to Mariano Guadalupe Vallejo. MS. FAC667(1135). 10 October ? De La Guerra Papers, The Huntington Library, San Marino.

———. Letter to Mariano Guadalupe Vallejo. MS. FAC667(1135). 23 November 1851. De La Guerra Papers, The Huntington Library, San Marino.

———. Letter to Mariano Guadalupe Vallejo. MS. FAC667(1135). March 8, 1860[1]. De La Guerra Papers, The Huntington Library, San Marino.

———. Letter to Mariano Guadalupe Vallejo. MS. FAC667(1135). June 23, 1860[1]. De La Guerra Papers, The Huntington Library, San Marino.

———. Letter to Mariano Guadalupe Vallejo. MS. FAC667(1135). March 18, 1863. De La Guerra Papers, The Huntington Library, San Marino.

———. Letter to Mariano Guadalupe Vallejo. MS. FAC667(1135). August 26, 1867. De La Guerra Papers, The Huntington Library, San Marino.

———. Letter to Mariano Guadalupe Vallejo. MS. FAC667(1135). February 15, 1869. De La Guerra Papers, The Huntington Library, San Marino.

————. Letter to Mariano Guadalupe Vallejo. MS. FAC667(1135). November 23, 1869. De La Guerra Papers, The Huntington Library, San Marino.

————. Letter to Mariano Guadalupe Vallejo. MS. FAC667(1135). September 9, 1872. De La Guerra Papers, The Huntington Library, San Marino.

————. Letter to Mariano Guadalupe Vallejo. MS. FAC667(1135). July 8, 1877. De La Guerra Papers, The Huntington Library, San Marino.

————. Letter to Mariano Guadalupe Vallejo. MS. FAC667(1135). May 18, 1878. De La Guerra Papers, The Huntington Library, San Marino.

————. Carta a Hubert Howe Bancroft (15 de Julio de 1878). Savage documents, 2:121-23.

————. Letter to Mariano Guadalupe Vallejo. MS. FAC667(1135). September 5, 1883. De La Guerra Papers, The Huntington Library, San Marino.

————. Letter to Mariano Guadalupe Vallejo. MS. FAC667(1135). 1885. De La Guerra Papers, The Huntington Library, San Marino.

————. Letter to Mariano Guadalupe Vallejo. MS. FAC667(1135). July 7, 1890. De La Guerra Papers, The Huntington Library, San Marino.

————. Letter to George Davidson. 7 July 1890. The Bancroft Library, Berkeley.

————. *The Squatter and the Don.* Eds. Rosaura Sánchez and Beatrice Pita. Houston: Arte Público, 1 1992.

————. *Who Would Have Thought It?* Eds. Rosaura Sánchez and Beatrice Pita. Houston: Arte Público, 1995.

Saldívar, José David. *Border Matters: Remapping American Cultural Studies.* Berkeley: University of California, 1997.

Saldívar, Ramón. *Chicano Narrative: The Dialectics of Difference.* Wisconsin: University of Wisconsin, 1990.

Sánchez, Rosaura. *Telling Identities: The California Testimonios.* Minneapolis: University of Minnesota, 1995.

————. Beatrice Pita and Bárbara Reyes, eds. "Nineteenth Century Californio Testimonials. *Critica: A Journal of Critical Essays.* University of California, San Diego (Spring 1994).

Sinclair, Upton. *The Jungle.* New York: Bantam, 1981.

Stowe, Harriet Beecher. *Uncle Tom's Cabin, Or, Life Among the Lowly.* Ed. Ann Douglas. New York: Penguin, 1982.

Tompkins, Jane. *Sensational Designs: The Cultural Work of American Fiction 1790-1860.* New York: Oxford University Press, 1985.

The Argonaut. Vol. XVI. No. 6. San Francisco, February 7, 1885.

————. September 12, 1885.

Vallejo, Mariano Guadalupe. "Recuerdos históricos y personales tocante a la alta California." 5 vols. 1875. MS. Bancroft Library, University of California, Berkeley.

Novelizing National Discourses: History, Romance, and Law in *The Squatter and the Don*

Jesse Alemán
University of New Mexico

I

As Genaro Padilla explains in *My History, Not Yours*, the war of 1846-48 and the westward expansion that followed "set off social, political, economic, linguistic, and cultural shock waves that generated a rhetorical situation in which Mexicans—now Americans—struggled to reconcile themselves to loss while also marking their resistance to that loss" (15). But unlike her Californio contemporaries, such as Mariano G. Vallejo, María Amparo Ruiz de Burton did not register her opposition to Anglo colonization through a nostalgic, or in our case, romantic (re)configuration of the past. Instead, she wrote *The Squatter and the Don*, a narrative that challenges the dominant discourses of U.S. colonization—history, romance, and law.

Undoubtedly, Ruiz de Burton's writing marks a level of socio-discursive resistance quite novel to her Hispana and Anglo contemporaries. As Tey Diana Rebolledo puts it, "It is a wonder that [Hispanas] wrote at all," considering the gender, genre, and language roles/rules to which Hispanas, and nineteenth-century American women in general, were limited (135). In fact, "[b]earing the imprint of female marginality, the domain of women's fiction is any place but history," according to Emily Miller Budik (xi), and the aim of those women who did write historical romances, Nina Baym explains, "was not to challenge received history . . . [but] to participate in the patriotic work of establishing and affirming national origins, characters, and values" (153–55). To paraphrase the title of Ruiz de Burton's first novel, who would have thought a nineteenth-century Hispana would publish for an Anglo readership a narrative in English that exposes the racism, class oppression, and dubious legal maneuverings that underlie Anglo America's romantic conception of the nation's history?

It is likewise significant that *The Squatter and the Don*'s subtitle reads: "A Novel Descriptive of Contemporary Occurrences in California." As Sánchez

38

and Pita point out, the subtitle "anticipates the historical subtext" of the narrative (14), but when it is placed within its socio-literary context, the subtitle also foregrounds the narrative's *novelness*, indicating *The Squatter and the Don*'s main discursive strategy of resistance. After all, even though it recounts contemporaneous events in California, the text is not subtitled "a historical account," nor is the narrative subtitled a "romance," despite the romance plot between Clarence Darrell and Mercedes Alamar; finally, the narrative is not subtitled a "historical romance" like much of its Anglo literary counterparts.[1] Rather, as a novel, *The Squatter and the Don* consists of a variety of socio-literary discourses that interact to create a dialogized structure in which the ideological underpinnings of each discourse is contested, challenged, and exposed. All this suggests that Ruiz de Burton's narrative, like the novelistic discourse Bakhtin describes, "begins by presuming a verbal and semantic decentering of the ideological world . . . [I]t is a consciousness manifesting itself in the midst of social languages that are surrounded by a single [national] language" (367).

So, even though the terms "romance" and "novel" may have been used synonymously in the nineteenth century (Baym 60), the ideology of their forms are quite different. As a genre, the romance insists on social cohesiveness by solving historical conflicts, but as a modern modality, the multiple discourses of the novel rupture social unity and instead register the conflict of heteroglot discourses interacting, undermining, and contradicting each other. In terms of how the nation is narrated, this is an important distinction. As an Anglocentric construction, nineteenth-century American history is the stuff of romance; it is thus not surprising that, as the most productive period of Anglo nation-building, the nineteenth century is also the most productive period for the development of the American historical romance.

After the 1814 publication of Walter Scott's *Waverley*, scores of similar narratives flourished in the United States, including James Fenimore Cooper's Leatherstalking Tales (1823-41), Lydia Maria Child's *Hobomok* (1824), Catharine Maria Sedgwick's *Hope Leslie* (1827), Nathaniel Hawthorne's *The House of Seven Gables* (1851), Harriet Beecher Stowe's *Uncle Tom's Cabin* (1852), and Helen Hunt Jackson's *Ramona* (1884), to name only a few. These "foundational fictions" were directly involved in building American national identity. In fact, despite her attempt to distinguish between the two, what Doris Sommer says of nineteenth-century Latin American romance writers seems to hold true for North America's own romancers: "The writers were encouraged both by the need to fill in a history that would help establish the legitimacy of the emerging nation and by the opportunity to direct that history toward a future ideal" (7). In other words, innocuous as they may seem to contemporary readers, the American historical romance "provided the technical means for 're-presenting' the *kind* of imagined community that is the nation" (Anderson 25). And that nation was imagined as white.

The correlation between the discourses of history and romance, then, is neither accidental nor ideologically innocent. Instead, it registers a socially symbolic act that turns the complexity of real socio-historical tensions into a simple good versus evil dichotomy in order to resolve social conflict, since good always triumphs over evil in the romance (Jameson 117). As its form solves the conflicts of America's historical content, the romance creates a unified master narrative in which historical fiction legitimates fictional social history.[2] That is, romance whitewashes history by collapsing the difference between the two as social discourses to build a monologic national discourse of Anglo goodness and purity destined to triumph over the evil of darkness. Even the most socially progressive historical romances contribute to this Anglo nation-building. For instance, George Harris, the rebellious slave in *Uncle Tom's Cabin*, indeed finds his freedom in Canada, but he refuses to return to the United States, opting instead to take his family to Africa, where they can find "a nation of [their] own" as colonial missionaries (375), while Harris's Anglo foil, George Shelby, "liberates" his own slaves by giving them the option to work on his plantation for wages (379). In effect, the narrative strategically eliminates the subversive elements of the slave debate by sending the rebellious slaves back to Africa; at the same time, it resolves the problem of slavery itself by subsuming its form of paternalism into the Anglo capitalistic paternalism of George Shelby. The romance thus concludes with a whitewashed social history palatable to Anglo readers.

It is also no coincidence that, even though The Fugitive Slave Law frames the narrative of *Uncle Tom's Cabin*, Stowe's romance avoids representing the racism African Americans experienced in the North, suggesting that there is an intimate connection between history, romance, and legality. Indeed, as Hayden White explains, "we cannot but be struck by the frequency with which narrativity, whether of the fictional or factual sort, presupposes the existence of a legal system against or on behalf of which the typical agents of a narrative account militate. And this raises the suspicion that narrative in general . . . has to do with the topics of law, legality, legitimacy, or, more generally, *authority*" (13). Clearly, law legalizes the romantic construction of Anglo authority in the national narrative of American history. In order to continue its "quest" westward, for example, the United States passed the 1851 Land Law, which not only called into question Spanish-Mexican land grants but legalized the romantic notion of Manifest Destiny in general. So when it appears in nineteenth-century historical romances, Manifest Destiny, as a legally sanctioned event, legitimates the romantic "progress of civilization and the heroic founding of a new *patria* and a new national character" (Dekker 42). Insofar as romance resolves historical conflict, then, legislative acts legalize these national romantic resolutions to create a "single [national] language," as Bakhtin puts it, that re-frame history in a "factual" discourse instead of a fictional one.

As a novel, however, *The Squatter and the Don* makes it clear that the nation is anything but unified; rather, it is a hodge-podge of genres, geographies, and peoples, all of which see the world through competing social and literary discourses. Truly, the nation is novelistic in this sense, and it is exactly its novelness that foregrounds how socio-literary discourses interact to challenge each other's view of the world. As Bakhtin explains, "The internal social dialogism of novelistic discourse requires the concrete social context of discourse to be exposed" (300). So if romantic narratives of the nation seek to suppress the ideological relationship between history, romance, and law, *The Squatter and the Don*'s novelistic discourse does just the opposite: it dialogizes history, romance, and law to expose their complicit "concrete social context" in the making of a romantic American national history. Challenging the discursive apparatuses of Anglo colonization, the narrative subverts the traditional boundaries of discourse through forms of parody and reported speech that historicize the romance, represent history through legal discourse, and fictionalize legality in a socially symbolic process that turns the narrative of United States history into a novelistic site of social rupture instead of a nationalistic site of romantic closure. In this sense, *The Squatter and the Don*'s oppositional narrative strategies work against mainstream Anglo American literary history and fit within a Chicano/a paradigm of social resistance.

II

As Sánchez and Pita have adequately explained, romance functions ideologically in *The Squatter and the Don*. On an allegorical level, the romance constructs a series of historical contradictions—Squatter *vs.* Don; monopoly capitalism *vs.* individual entrepreneurship; government *vs.* laborer—that it then resolves symbolically through a "mediating" narrative act, such as the marriage of Clarence Darrell and Mercedes Alamar (31). What is striking, however, is the degree to which the romance narrative adheres so closely to mainstream American historical romances and yet concludes without offering a symbolic resolution to the historical conflict that frames the romance.

In fact, history is not just a backdrop of the narrative's romance plot. History is a discourse that challenges the romance's narrative authority, suggesting that the romance plot itself is a generic parody that fulfills the socio-literary expectations of an Anglo readership without legitimating a romantic configuration of Anglo social history.[3] Instead of presenting history as romance, then, *The Squatter and the Don* uses parody to historicize romance, which deconstructs the narrative's romantic conventions, since the ideological effectiveness of romantic closure depends on the degree to which it suppresses its fictional revision of history.

For instance, as a romance proper, the marriage between Clarence and Mercedes affirms the national symbolic act of romantically representing American history: Clarence is the Anglo hero who rescues the Alamar family from certain destitution. Insofar as it affirms Anglo history, this romance remains palatable to an Anglo readership by contributing to the Anglo national myth of dominance. But because the romance between Clarence and Mercedes calls attention to itself as a fiction, it undercuts its ideological function as a romance. "'It isn't half so romantic to love a plain gentleman as to love a brigand, or, at least, a squatter . . . I think our romance is spoiled,'" George Mechlin tells Mercedes after Clarence reveals that he did indeed pay Don Mariano for his land (141). George's self-reflexive parody "spoils" the romance plot by foregrounding it as a fiction, but his parody also opens up a space for history to intrude on the romance's conventions and historicize them to the point of actually replacing them. The marriage between Clarence and Mercedes, after all, is less a culmination of their romance and more a pragmatic response to the family's historical conditions.

Clarence and Mercedes "marry right away" in a rather anti-climactic wedding so that Mercedes can help take care of her brother Gabriel, who seriously injures himself when he falls from a ladder while helping to build "the houses of the railroad millionaires" (343). Gabriel's social displacement from being a member of the landed Californio gentry to being a member of the rising class of Hispanic laborers allegorizes the historical shift in the material conditions of Californios in general. As Ruiz de Burton puts it, "In that hod full of bricks not only his own sad experience was represented, but *the entire history* of the native Californians *of Spanish decent* was epitomized" (352). This historical condition, and not the convention of the romance plot, determines the marriage between Clarence and Mercedes, thus undermining the narrative's romantic closure while emphasizing the historical rupture the romance was meant to solve. Of course, by incorporating the romance plot, the novel draws on a narrative tradition that is not only familiar to American readers but part of their national consciousness, but by radically historicizing the romantic closure, the narrative strategically contains the ideology of the romance's form. Instead of presenting history *as* romance, the narrative grounds romance *in* history in a dialogic process that uses historical discourse to register the social conditions romance cannot resolve. As George Mechlin says, "'[O]ur romance is stripped of its thrilling features'" (142).

The double-voicedness of the narrative's historicized romance is perhaps most apparent in the final scene of the romance plot. After Clarence and Mercedes finally marry, Doña Josefa witnesses a mock marriage in San Francisco that self-reflexively undercuts and historicizes the romantic trope of marriage as an allegorical solution to historical conflict. Next door to Doña Josefa's new home, "one of the railroad kings, who had killed the Texas pacific . . . was giving a 'silver wedding' party to the elite of San Francisco" (361). This collective wedding of California's new rich is their celebration of the national romance narrative that claims anything is possible, despite real historical conflict, but as the narrative makes quite apparent, this national myth is a mockery: "Mr. Millionaire" leads his wife to the "mock altar" where their "mock marriage ceremony was to be performed" (362). After the ceremony, Mr. Millionaire decides to offer his own romance of sorts, so, speaking "to those who have yet their fortunes to make," he advises, "'Be not discouraged if you meet with hardships and trials. Go ahead and persevere. Look at all these luxurious appurtenances surrounding us! I might well say, look at this wealth!'" (362).

If Clarence and Mercedes marry out of historical necessity, the mock marriage of the millionaires is out of romantic luxury, which foregrounds the ironic distance between the romantic closure of these two marriages. The fact that Doña Josefa witnesses the wedding is thus quite important, since the collective romance the wedding celebrates also represents the nationalist ideology that displaced Doña Josefa, killed her husband, and led to the large-scale dispossession of other Californios. So once again, parody opens up a space for historicity as Doña Josefa's position outside the "silver wedding" party ironically highlights her own social condition and the limitations of her daughter's marriage as a symbolic resolution to the narrative's historical conflict. Finally, the scene itself undercuts the romantic closure of Mr. Millionaire's speech: "'Be plucky and persevering, and go ahead, as I did,'" he says, espousing the romantic myths of Manifest Destiny and individual success. A young man in the audience, however, quietly exposes the real historical conditions underneath the American myth of success as he responds, "'Yes, I would be plucky and persevering if I had an associate in Washington with plenty of money to bribe people so that no other railroad could be built to start competition in California'" (362).

As if to legitimate the novel's own representation of historical events, though, legal discourse, such as the young man's response, informs the narrative's historicity, so even as history dialogizes the narrative's romance, legal discourse dialogizes the narrative's history. Gabriel's historical condition as a laborer, for instance, is a direct result of a racist legal process that displaced Californios in the first place. George and Clarence, the narrative explains, "reviewed the *history* of the Alamares, and feelingly deplored the *cruel legislation* that had ruined them" (352). Legal discourse thus competes with history for narrative authority, creating the impression that there would be no historical narrative if there were no legal discourse "against or on behalf of which" the characters act (White 13). So just as history refuses to be the "subtext" of the romance, legal discourse refuses to be the "subtext" of the novel's representation of history. Instead, the language of law crosses into the boundaries of the narrative's historical critique, dialogizing it in a way that allows the narrative's novelistic discourse to highlight the social discontinuities of the nation.

Don Mariano's forms of reported speech, for example, ironically emphasize the duplicitous legalese of The Treaty of Guadalupe Hidalgo and the 1851 Land Act. "How could Mexico have foreseen then that when scarcely half a dozen years should have elapsed the trusted conquerors would, '*In Congress Assembled*,' pass laws which were to be retroactive upon the defenseless, helpless, conquered people, in order to despoil them?" he asks (67). Because "In Congress Assembled" is at the center of Don Mariano's historical critique, the legal phrase becomes reaccented through his discourse, making it a double-voiced phrase that signifies in two directions at once.

On the one hand, it represents the official stamp of a democratic government's laws, and on the other hand, Don Mariano uses the phrase against itself to account for the social and economic oppression of Californios under those laws. He thus "legalizes" his own historical critique by using the language of law to foreground what the Californios were legally promised and what was illegally taken from them. By appropriating the phrase, Don Mariano exposes the ideological underpinnings of congressional legislation to show that the legalization of the American romance resolves historical conflict for one group, Anglo Americans, while it exacerbates social strife for another, Mexicans. He clearly makes this point when he refers to the 1851 Land Law:

> Then, as a coating of whitewash to the stain on the nation's honor, a 'land commission' was established to examine land titles. Because, having pledged the national word to respect our rights, it would be an act of despoliation, besides an open violation of pledged honor, to take the lands without some pretext of a legal process. (67-68)

Deconstructing the national narrative of American history, Don Mariano unravels the ideological relationship between history, romance, and legality in the building of the nation. In order for the United States to colonize Mexico, it first had to resolve the socio-historical conflict between Americans and Mexicans, so it constructed the romantic notion of Manifest Destiny, but in order to "conceal its stain," the United States then legalized Manifest Destiny with the 1851 Land Law. As Robert Clark explains, "terms such as 'natural right to the land,' 'freedom,' 'civilisation,' 'savagery,' 'providence,' 'manifest destiny,' appear in political rhetoric at those points where the contradictions of social experience are too acute to allow further ideological elaboration" (14). The result of such discourse is a legal romantic history free of social conflict, so Don Mariano's appropriation of legal discourse re-emphasizes the historical rupture at the heart of American national history.

What Carl Gutiérrez-Jones says of contemporary Chicano/a cultural production, then, is also true for *The Squatter and the Don*: it "build[s] on legal ideals in order both to critique the shortfalls of the legal process and to offer [its] own revised processes" embedded within the "formal structure" of the narrative (42). Because the "formal structure" of *The Squatter and the Don* is essentially dialogic, though, legal discourse itself undergoes a novelistic transformation as it gets incorporated into the narrative. That is, legalese indeed functions to legitimize the narrative's historical critique, but the very act of incorporating the language of law into a novel crosses the boundaries of legal discourse's own function as an "objective" set of principles meant to maintain social order. In fact, the wholesale parodies of legal documents in the narrative emphasize just the opposite by revealing the congressional and judicial corruption underneath legal rhetoric. Gasbang and Roper's legal claim of the Mechlin's house and land, for instance, legitimates the form and discourse of legal rhetoric, but the contents of the claim undermine its "objectivity" as the "innocent purchasers," Gasbang and Roper, deny that James Mechlin ever purchased the land (338-39). Encapsulating the double-voiced complexity of the narrative's oppositional strategies, the parodied legal document allegorizes the "legal" process by which Californios were displaced of their land, but the document also exposes the Anglo legalization of Manifest Destiny as a self-consuming process, since the Mechlin's are not Mexican; they are Anglo.

So the legal document also works dialogically. In the process of legitimating the narrative's historical critique, it de-legitimates the social function of legal rhetoric in general by emphasizing its pliability as a fictional discourse. Perhaps this is no where more apparent than in the narrative's wholesale incorporation of the language of the 1851 Land Act. The voice of the narrator in particular uses the law's language not only as a way of reading history but also as a way of writing fiction: "'No. 189. *An act to ascertain and settle the private land claims in the State of California,*' says the book. And by a sad subversion of purposes, all the private land titles became *unsettled*. It ought to have been said, 'An Act to *unsettle* land titles, and to upset the rights of the Spanish population of the State of California'" (88). The irony of the passage alone performs a form of subversion as the narrator highlights the distance between what the law "says" and what it actually allows people to do. More importantly, though, the narrator's ironic revision of the law turns the 1851 Land Act into a fictional trope for the entire narrative. What is *The Squatter and the Don*, after all, if not a story about how the land titles in California became "unsettled" and the rights of Californios "upset" in the process? As with Gasbang and Roper's claim, the law becomes the foundation of fiction writing as the narrative uses legalese against itself to show that the language of law is just as fictional as the novel. However, by placing legalese in the context of fiction, and fiction in context of legalese, the narrative shifts the social value of each discourse and reconfigures their ideological significance to affirm the discourse of the novel while it undercuts the legitimacy of legal rhetoric.

III

Such double-voiced gestures fill *The Squatter and the Don*, making it a highly dialogized narrative in which "an utterance that belongs, by its grammatical (syntactic) and compositional markers, to a single speaker . . . actually contains mixed within it two utterances, two speech manners, two styles, two 'languages,' two . . . belief systems" (Bakhtin 304). It is in this sense that Ruiz de Burton's novel is subversive. As the discourses of history, romance, and law challenge each other for the narrative's authority, their novelistic discourse undermines the formation of a unified nation and highlights instead the historical and discursive rupture that makes the nation a site of conflict without resolution. "If the problematic 'closure' of textuality questions the 'totalization' of national culture," Homi K. Bhabha explains, "then its positive value lies in displaying the wide dissemination through which we construct the field of meanings and symbols associated with national life" (3).

Certainly, as a "disseminated" narrative, *The Squatter and the Don* stands in opposition to mainstream Anglo American socio-literary history: it resists the tendency for romance to whitewash history and laws to legalize romance. In this context, the work of Ruiz de Burton's Anglo contemporary, Helen Hunt Jackson, is instructive. A native northerner, Jackson became an advocate for Indian rights with her 1881 publication of *A Century of Dishonor*, which is a collection of government records exposing their "double dealings" with Native American tribes (Dorris ix). As Commissioner of Indian Affairs, Jackson went to California in 1883 to report on the conditions of the California Indians and published another scathing document, *Report on the Conditions and Needs of the Mission Indians of California*. In 1883, Jackson also began *Ramona*, a romance between Ramona Ortegna, the daughter of an Indian woman and Scotch immigrant, and Alessandro Assis, a California Indian laborer. As Michael Dorris puts it, "*Ramona* was propaganda. It was meant to have a political as well as a literary impact, and it succeeded on both fronts" (xvii). Compared to *The Squatter and the Don*, however, the ideology of that success is questionable.

For instance, despite her access to political rhetoric and legal discourse, Jackson refrains from using them dialogically in her narrative. Unlike Don Mariano's reported speech, the narrative of *Ramona* refers to the 1851 Land Law as an unproblematic part of (naturalized) history. The Land Commission "undertook to sift and adjust Mexican land titles" (12). Of course, Señora Moreno's references to the Land Commission are acerbic: "Once a thief, always a thief. Nobody need feel himself safe under American rule," she says. But then again, Señora Moreno is the evil, Catholic-ridden, widowed stepmother in this romance. Thus, even though the legislation that caused the hardships of California Indians and Hispanas frames the historical romance, Jackson's narrative suppresses the relationship between the two. As her two previous publications suggest, politics is one thing, and romance is another. What her narrative does not interrogate is how the legalization of romance itself led to the colonization of California.

Undoubtedly, Jackson's narrative effectively deconstructs a dominant paradigm of American colonization. Alessandro, who at the beginning of the narrative is a noble savage, is driven into madness by the narrative's historical conflict; eventually, he is killed after being wrongly accused of stealing a horse. But the narrative must still resolve the historical dilemma that Ramona and her Californio step-brother, Felipe, represent. After all, now that the noble savage has vanished from the frontier, the national romance narrative must also clear away the cultured Californios. Not surprisingly, "[Felipe] was beginning to yearn for Mexico,—for Mexico, which he had never seen, yearned for like an exile. There he might yet live among men of his own race and degree" (359). So indeed, he and Ramona marry and leave the country. In this light, *Ramona*, as with *Uncle Tom's Cabin*, must be considered a romance proper instead of a novelization of it, which means that the text contributes to the building of an Anglo national identity, perhaps in spite of Jackson's own intentions.

Its subtextual nationalist "propaganda" might explain why *Ramona* was immediately successful, "has since been through more than three hundred English-language editions, and many more abroad," and has been adapted for film a few times (Dorris v). *Ramona*'s success in American culture suggests that its narrative propaganda is quite different than the narrative strategies of *The Squatter and the Don*, which calls the romantic narrative of United States history into question by novelizing those national discourses that seek to resolve the nation's social conflicts symbolically. Ruiz de Burton's novel thus works against its contemporaneous American historical romances and perhaps even prefigures the oppositional narrative strategies of contemporary Chicano/a literature, since it also incorporates a variety of discourses that dialogize each other to create a narrative of socio-discursive conflict. Along with the interlingualism of English and Spanish, our narratives incorporate oral, mythic, historical, legal, academic, literary, and political discourses as well. "Rather than discard," Rafael Pérez-Torres reminds us, Chicano literature "recasts. Rather than reject, it affirms the reality that things do not coalesce in neat packages of personal identity, national identity, cultural identity" (270). *The Squatter and the Don* is the same type of hybridized narrative. It "recasts" the romance plot in a way that radically historicizes it, and it likewise refigures legal discourse in a way that exposes it, in the words of Gutiérrez-Jones, "as a set of structuring principles for performance in which Anglo society's racist actions may cloak themselves in postures of judicial neutrality" (169). With this, *The Squatter and the Don* novelizes the nation, so to speak, in a social and literary act of resistance to the dominant discourse of U.S. colonization.[4]

Notes

[1] It is unclear whether Ruiz de Burton, her publisher, or the publisher's printer subtitled *The Squatter and the Don*. But this uncertainty only highlights my point that the text is novelistic: multiple voices reverberate beneath the subtitle of *The Squatter and the Don*, each of them competing for the ownership of the text as a socio-literary product. "In such duplicity begins America's first novel and American fiction," Cathy N. Davidson writes in her discussion of the marketing strategies of publishers and printers in the late eighteenth century (91).

[2] Here and throughout the essay, I am using *form* to refer to what Jameson explains in *The Political Unconscious* as the ideology of form: "What must now be stressed is that at this level 'form' is apprehended as content. The study of the ideology of form is no doubt grounded on a technical and formalistic analysis in the narrower sense, even though, unlike much traditional formal analysis, it seeks to reveal the active presence within the text of a number of discontinuous and heterogeneous formal processes . . . [B]ut a dialectical reversal has taken place in which it has become possible to grasp such formal processes as sedimented content in their own right, as carrying ideological messages of their own, distinct from the ostensible or manifest content of the works" (99).

[3] In their introduction to *The Squatter and the Don*, Sánchez and Pita offer a strong reading of the novel's romance plot; they take it "seriously," so to speak, without considering the possibility that it is a parody. Ironically, in their introduction to *Who Would Have Thought It?*, Sánchez and Pita cogently analyze how Ruiz de Burton deploys parodies of sentimental novels and novels of domesticity as a narrative strategy of resistance. So, for a full analysis of Ruiz de Burton's parodic style, please see Sánchez and Pita's introduction to *Who Would Have Thought It?*

[4] I have learned much about Ruiz de Burton, her personal and public life, as well as California history from José F. Aranda Jr. and Amelia María de la Luz Montes and would like to thank them for their engaging and enlightening discussions. I would also like to thank Randéll Elizabeth Caffejian for reading several drafts of this essay and offering her valuable comments.

Works Cited

Anderson, Benedict. *Imagined Communities: Reflections on the Origin and Spread of Nationalism.* 2nd ed. London: Verso, 1991.

Bakhtin, M. M. "Discourse in the Novel." *The Dialogic Imagination: Four Essays by M. M. Bakhtin.* Trans. Caryl Emerson and Michael Holquist. Ed. Michael Holquist. Austin: University of Texas, 1990. 259-422.

Baym, Nina. *American Women Writers and the Work of History, 1790-1860.*

New Brunswick, N. J.: Rutgers University, 1995.

———. "Concepts of the Romance in Hawthorne's America." *Feminism and American Literary History.* New Brunswick, N. J.: Rutgers University, 1992. 57-70.

Budick, Emily Miller. *Fiction and Historical Consciousness: The American Romance Tradition.* New Haven, Conn.: Yale University, 1989.

Clark, Robert. *History, Ideology, and Myth in American Fiction, 1823-52.* London: Macmillan, 1984.

Davidson, Cathy N. *Revolution and the Word: The Rise of the Novel in America.* New York: Oxford University, 1986.

Dekker, George. *The American Historical Romance.* New York: Cambridge University, 1987.

Dorris, Michael. Introduction. *Ramona.* By Helen Hunt Jackson. New York: Signet, 1988. v-xvii.

Gutiérrez-Jones, Carl. *Rethinking the Borderlands: Between Chicano Culture and Legal Discourse.* Berkeley: University of California, 1995.

Jackson, Helen Hunt. *Ramona.* 1884. New York: Signet, 1988.

Jameson, Fredric. *The Political Unconscious: Narrative as a Socially Symbolic Act.* Ithaca, N.Y.: Cornell University, 1981.

Padilla, Genaro. *My History, Not Yours: The Formation of Mexican-American Autobiography.* Madison: University of Wisconsin, 1993.

Pérez-Torres, Rafael. *Movements in Chicano Poetry: Against Myths, Against Margins.* Cambridge, Mass.: Cambridge University,1995.

Rebolledo, Tey Diana. "Narrative Strategies of Resistance in Hispana Writing." *Journal of Narrative Technique* 20 (1990): 134-46.

Sánchez, Rosaura and Beatrice Pita. Introduction. *The Squatter and the Don.* By María Amparo Ruiz de Burton. Ed. Rosaura Sánchez and Beatrice Pita. Houston: Arte Público, 1992. 5-51.

———. Introduction. *Who Would Have Thought It?* By María Amparo Ruiz de Burton. Ed. Rosaura Sánchez and Beatrice Pita. Houston: Arte Público, 1995. vii-lxv.

Sommer, Doris. *Foundational Fictions: The National Romances of Latin America.* Berkeley: University of California, 1991.

Stowe, Harriet Beecher. *Uncle Tom's Cabin.* 1852. Ed. Elizabeth Ammons. New York: Norton, 1994.

Ruiz de Burton, María Amparo. *The Squatter and the Don.* 1885. Ed. Rosaura Sánchez and Beatrice Pita. Houston: Arte Público, 1992.

———. *Who Would Have Thought It?* 1872. Ed. Rosaura Sánchez and Beatrice Pita. Houston: Arte Público, 1995.

White, Hayden. "The Value of Narrativity in the Representation of Reality." *On Narrative.* Ed. W. J. T. Mitchell. Chicago: University of Chicago, 1981. 1-23.

Como dios manda:
Political Messianism in Manuel C. de Baca's
Noches tenebrosas en el condado de San Miguel

Erlinda Gonzales-Berry
Oregon State University

With the arrival of the railroad in New Mexico in 1877, Las Vegas became a boom town overnight. And with the economic boom came trouble in the form of gunslingers and outlaws of every ilk. Many of the latter have gone on to form the subject matter for colorful narratives in Western history books. But for many years, mainstream historians had little to say about the havoc that progress and displacement wreaked on the local *Nuevomexicano* population. This does not mean, however, that the native inhabitants remained indifferent or silent regarding the changes that so dramatically threatened their way of life. In fact, scores of *Nuevomexicanos*, the majority of them educated by Christian Brothers in Santa Fe and the Jesuits in Las Vegas, took advantage of recently arrived presses to record the events of daily life, to sway public opinion—particularly at the election polls—but, more important, to disseminate an agenda which clearly addressed issues crucial to *Nuevomexicano* cultural survival and self-determination. The products of their labor were to become the motherlode for contemporary scholars who have finally turned their attention to the forgotten or ignored facets of Western history.[1] Of special interest to literary scholars is the fact that the Spanish-language newspapers of the nineteenth century also provided propitious avenues for the dissemination of creative literature.

One literary piece which has come to light in recent years is Manuel C. de Baca's *Noches tenebrosas en el condado de San Miguel [Dark Nights in San Miguel County].*[2] This brief text appeared between March and February, 1892, in *El Sol de Mayo*, a newspaper owned and edited by the very author of the piece under discussion. Because the subject matter of this serialized narrative is the historically verifiable organization that called itself Los Gorras Blancas, or the White Caps, it would seem appropriate to treat it as a historical chronicle. However, a moralistic impulse compelled the author to approach his subject through a literary discourse that relies primarily upon the terminology of Medieval Christian orthodoxy.

The Gorras Blancas

While little was known about the Gorras Blancas in the first half of the twentieth century, Chicano activists were quick to add them to the growing list of "social bandits" whose lives and actions were held up as models of revolutionary activity during the heyday of the Chicano movement. Scholars of Chicano history were likewise eager to give the Gorras Blancas their due in emergent revisionist histories.

Anselmo Arellano, a devoted researcher of the history of the region, supplies details regarding the organization's emergence:

> Las [*sic*] Gorras Blancas were organized early in April 1889 by Juan José Herrera and his younger brothers Pablo and Nicanor, with support from other poor people in the area of El Salitre, El Butto, Ojitos Fríos and San Gerónimo. Eventually, all the settlements which fell within the boundaries of the Las Vegas Grant and other northern New Mexico communities joined the organization. On April 3, 1889, the *Las Vegas Daily Optic* carried an article on the destructive activities of the White Caps in Tuscola, Ill. White Caps in that state destroyed the barn and contents belonging to one of the commissioners of an unpopular drainage canal that was being built. Twenty-three days later, Las Gorras Blancas made their first appearance in San Miguel County. The masked riders destroyed four miles of new fenceline belonging to two Englishmen who were ranching near San Gerónimo. (16)

Robert Rosenbaum's study of the Gorras Blancas in his 1972 dissertation was a watershed chapter in the history of this period. He writes of the group's motives:

> Building on a sense of ethnic and class identification that grew stronger in the face of racial slurs and economic threats, Herrera forged a movement out of the traditional materials of Hispanic culture. To 'las masas de los hombres pobres,' the issues were clear. Traditional use of land led their list, followed by fair and dignified treatment of wage labor. The two specters of hunger and change motivated most. Maybe, on the border between the conscious and the subconscious, glimmered a hope that they could drive los extranjeros from their land and reunite with Mexico. But they would settle for traditional land tenure and fair treatment of labor. (217)

A more intimate perspective on the Gorras Blancas is rendered by 92-year-old Rosa Herrera de Adams, the daughter of one of the leader of the Gorras Blancas, in an oral history recorded by Arellano:

> Porque estaban los estos tejanos, agarrando todos los ranchos de los mexicanos y cercándolos, y por eso mi papá hizo esta sociedad, pa' tumbales sus cercos. Porque estaban cercando lo que no era de ellos. Y les tumbaron todos los cercos y los echaron fuera. Habían dejao a los pobres mexicanos tiraos . . . sin propiedades.[3]

[Because there were these Texans, grabbing all the ranches from the Mexicans and fencing them in, that's why my father formed this society, to tear down their fences. Because they were fencing what was not theirs. And they cut down the fences and they threw them out. They had left the poor Mexicans abandoned . . . without land.]

For those of us scholars of Southwest culture who cut our teeth on versions of history such as those cited above, Manuel C. de Baca's intractable diatribe against historical agents whom we have come to see as *héroes del pueblo* is indeed a surprise. Our disbelief is exacerbated upon learning that M. C. de Baca was the brother of Ezequiel C. de Baca, whose involvement with *La Voz del Pueblo*, a newspaper with strong links to both the progressive Partido del Pueblo and Los Caballeros de Labor, is well known. El Partido del Pueblo, an independent third party, was organized in Las Vegas in 1890 with hopes of drawing *Nuevomexicano*s away from the Republican Party, thereby weakening its stronghold on the Territory. Its platform was informed by a populist ideology that promoted, among other things, the protection of communal land grants. Los Caballeros de Labor was a local chapter of the nationally active Knights of Labor whose primary agenda was anti-capital and pro-workers' rights. Its organizer in Las Vegas was also the leader of the Gorras Blancas. The identity of the two organizations was frequently conflated, though there is evidence that not all members of the Caballeros de Labor were associated with the Gorras Blancas.

Ezequiel's brother, on the other hand, was a staunch Republican. His newspaper, *El Sol de Mayo*, did not miss an opportunity to cast barbs such as the following at *La Voz del Pueblo*:

The *Voz* says that "it will not lend itself for no man's tool." No, we presume it prefers selling. (May 1, 1891)

Muy cortos se nos han hecho los días durante el tiempo que hemos estudiado y contemplado un panorama: Nuestro colega *La Voz*, nadando denodadamente en un charco sin agua. Después de reproducir un razgo de nuestro periódico, *El Sol de Mayo*, encabeza una respuesta *Otra vez le burra al trigo*. Pero son efluvios de su exquisita lógica y pleno conocimiento en gramática. Nosotro después de un serio estudio no hemos podido sondear la aplicación vaga y obtusa y vulgar de ese artículo, excepto que tiende a defender cosa que no le va ni le viene. (20 August, 1981, pr. 2)

[The days have seemed quite short during the time that we have studied and contemplated a panorama: our colleague, *La Voz* boldly swimming in a dry pool. After copying a passage from our newspaper, *El Sol de Mayo*, it writes a response under the title "Once Again the Donkey to the Wheat." But these are effluvia of its fine logic and deep grammatical knowledge. After serious study, we have not been able to fathom the vague, obtuse and vulgar intent of this article, save that it tends to defend a cause that is none of its business.] (August 20, 1981)

The feelings of antagonism between the two periodicals were mutual, and, whereas *La Voz del Pueblo* demonstrated a thinly veiled empathy towards the Gorras Blancas, *El Sol de Mayo* patently declared its hostility in weekly denunciations and it sang the organization's requiem with the publication of *Noches tenobrosas en el condado de San Miguel* in 1892.

A Messiah for Stormy Seasons

A close reading of *Noches tenebrosas* reveals that the central concern of C. de Baca's narrative is burnished with messianistic overtones that hearken back to a medieval scatological design, one shored up by a hierarchical framework that erases the boundaries between sacred and secular agendas.[4]

In a fashion typical of messianistic writing, the introduction to the series presents a peace-loving people—beset by a series of woes—who are entreated by the narrator to rise against the enemy:

> La ilustración o diseño que encabeza nuestra historia, representa con exactitud el retrato de los Gorras Blancas en pleno uniforme, y en la manera y forma en que han cabalgado repetidas veces, por las calles de las villas y plazas del Condado de San Miguel, y como cabalgarán en las de otros Condados del Territorio, si el pueblo pacífico no se prepara para ponerles freno y evitar que sigan adelante con sus infernales escaramuzas. (Cited in Arellano's mss., no p.)

> [The illustration or design which heads our history represents, with exactness, a true picture of the White Caps in full uniform and the manner and form in which they have repeatedly marauded through the streets of the villages and towns in San Miguel County on horseback. They will continue to ride in other counties in the Territory in such a manner, if the peaceful people do nothing to prepare themselves to stop them and prevent them from continuing their infernal skirmishes.]

The vertical orientation of the narrative is set immediately through reference to the "infernal" nature of the Gorras' activities and is further elaborated with an epithet which leaves no doubt regarding which pole of the spatial continuum their leader occupies:

> ¡Ahí va! La milicia infernal según enlistada y habilitada por el antecristo que tenía en vista levantar una grande cosecha del fruto y resultado de los actos de los Gorras Blancas, en el Condado de San Miguel.

> [There it goes! The hellish militia, recruited and enlisted by the Antichrist, whose vision was to reap a big harvest from the fruits and labor of the engagements of the White Caps in San Miguel.]

Implicit in this introduction is, if not the call, then certainly the desire for the appearance of a messiah empowered to cleanse the land and deliver the people from the Antichrist. Said messiah, however, does not appear until a full description of the enemy's wicked transgressions is presented in detail for the reader.

The first chapter opens in the style of high *sturm und drang* Romanticism with a tempest that renders the peaceful village the very image of infernal chaos. The narrator's allusion to the biblical flood establishes the superior pole of the narrative structure'a vertical bearing and provides the parameters for a reading of the text as Christian mythopoesis.

> Cerraba la noche del 28 de abril de 1889 con una fuerte lluvia casi compara-ble con la primera noche de las cuarenta del diluvio universal. El copioso aguacero diseminado en menudísimas gotas, por la violencia de un furioso vendaval formaba una espesa nublina, que impedía ver desde un extremo a otro la extensa y desmantelada plaza de Las Vegas.

> [The night of April 28, 1889, was coming to a close with a rainstorm almost comparable to the first night of the forty which occurred during the universal flood. A furious windstorm brought a thick cloud cover, and the pouring rain spread violently. Such was the storm and the swirling wind that one could barely see from one side of the plaza in Old Las Vegas to the other.]

The three sinister figures who make their appearance in this ominous open-ing scene, El Gran Capitán, the village barber, and "un estranjero" [a stranger], meet in the shadows of a building which formerly served as a church. In his role as the Antichrist, the Gran Capitán, usurping the space which formerly belonged to Christ, introduces himself as a worldly man who has traveled throughout the western states, acquiring experience and knowledge of anarchist societies. He informs his interlocutors that he has a plan for launching "una guerra cruel en contra del rico." Playing his role by the book, the Antichrist knows full well that it is within his power to delude God-fearing people with exotic ideologies (i.e. "de los Nihilistas de Rusia, la de los Mafias de Italia, la de los Gorras Blancas de Indiana, la de los Anarquistas de Chicago"). The gen-eral populace, he informs his interlocutors, can with little effort be bamboozled into accepting his program provided it is presented under the veil of the popu-lar Caballeros de Labor. The stranger is eager to begin the dirty work of the Gorras Blancas under the auspices of what the narrator facetiously refers to as la "Caballada de Labor" [the labor horses]. The village barber, however, though a believer in the reformist precepts of the Knights of Labor, resists El Gran Capitán's plan, for his good conscience—and, we must speculate, his Christian conscience—will not allow him to engage in illicit activities. Nonetheless, he resolves to follow along to spy on the group.

At the end of the first chapter, the narrator resorts once again to a Romantic treatment of nature as a device for portending bad times. This strategy, used throughout the text, contributes to the allocation of value to the binary paradigm which bolsters C. de Baca's mythological matrix.

The chaotic squall that opens the first chapter gives way to a pure and beautiful star-studded sky, but presently an enormous comet makes its appearance announcing the disruption of Order:

> En el fondo de aquel cielo purísimo y bello se dejaba ver un cometa enorme. Aquel viajero fenómeno anunciaba una época de infortunios y vicisitudes para el Condado de San Miguel.

> [A large, streaking comet could also be seen across the lower end of that pure and beautiful sky. That traveling phenomenon announced the arrival of a new epoch of misfortune and unfavorable events brought to San Miguel County by chance.]

Allocation of value to the structuring binary paradigm follows a logic that goes something like this: storm/comet equals Chaos; Chaos is instigated by the Antichrist; the Antichrist is Evil; therefore Chaos is Evil. Its reverse rendition reads: Calm skies equal Order; if the Antichrist disrupts Order, Order must be ordained by God; if Order is ordained by God—the fountainhead of Good— then Order is Good. We can take this logic a step further and conclude that if Order is ordained by God, Order must be natural. Thus, the equation of the State's public order to Natural Order, the tenet that undergirds C. de Baca's text, is not only made possible but, as we presently shall see, it justifies C. De Baca's class ideology.

In the chapters that follow, the author's invective against the Gorras Blancas swells with descriptions of an intricate web of maneuvers through which the Antichrist secures the cooperation of the local sheriff, the complicity of the Knights of Labor, and the manipulation of the common people with promises of retribution against their oppressors:

> . . . de reyes, emperadores y amos. Anconsejaba al pueblo, que las malas leyes, que las malas administraciones y las persecusiones en contra de algunos existían por razón de que En otros lugares lavantaba la cuestión política, la question que el pueblo pobre no se unía y escojía sus oficiales de entre las masas de los pobres.

> [In other localities he brought up political issues and the question of kings, emperors and bosses. He counseled the people that bad laws, poor political administrations, and the persecution against certain people existed for the simple reason that poor people did not organize themselves to choose their own officials from among the masses of the poor.]

Chapters three through eight are devoted to descriptions of the Gorras Blancas' midnight forays, which include fence cuttings, barn burnings, and a spate of additional violent activities against landowners, the railroad company, and those who refuse to collaborate. Chapters six and seven comprise the dramatic peak of the narration.

In keeping with the religious orthodoxy that influences C. de Baca's Christian vision of the world, sins of the flesh are added to the list of grievances against the Gorras. The rape of Guadalupe Bernal's fifteen-year-old daughter by a "tropa infernal de bribones" [an infernal troop of scoundrels] represents the Gorras' ultimate manifestation of barbarian behavior. If any doubt remains regarding the Gorras' morally reprehensible nature, it is summarily dispelled with the following description:

> Tomaron a Braulia, y la arrastraron a un zaguán contiguo en donde aquellos hombres de la gorra, sin corazón, le robaron y pisotiaron aquella joya preciosa, despojándola de su mejor adorno, ¡su virginidad![5]

> [They grabbed Braulia and dragged her outside to the porch. There, those heartless men of the hood stripped her of her most precious jewel and adornment, her virginity!]

Braulia's rape, contrary to the narrator's words, is not just one more act in a long chain of dishonorable deeds. It is, in fact, incontrovertible proof of the Gorras Blancas' total disregard for a hierarchical scheme ordained by God:

> Esta horrible escena añade un acto más a la historia de los gorras blancas y prueba lo que los hombres una vez asociados con malos fines pueden hacer más y más cuando son capitaneados y aconsejados por hombres que jamás conocieron la existencia de un Dios inexorable ante cuya presencia de cada detalle de estas acciones se les tomará rigurosa cuenta.

> [This horrible scene adds one more act to the history of the White Caps. It demonstrates what men are capable of doing whenever they are led and counseled by men bent on evil intent and who never accept the existence of an inexorable God. They will be punished rigorously for each and all of the actions they have committed before His presence.]

But cannot the proponents of law and order act in God's stead? Can they not punish the transgressors, and, in the process, release the county's peace-loving citizens from the Antichrist's stronghold?

Enter the figurative messiah. Collectively taking on the role of the state, which has all but abdicated its duties ("tanto quebranto sufrían las instituciones a que estamos sometidos" [all the institutions to which we belonged had suffered gravely]), a group of citizens forms a law-and order society:

> . . . los hombres que tenían a pecho los intereses del pueblo, su bienestar, alumbrados de un sentimiento heroico y patriótico, pusieron mano a la obra. El día 8 de noviembre de 1890, era día grato para la historia de nuestra novela, en medio de los más ruidosos aplausos y el pueblo altamente conmovido comprometiendo sus más ávidos sentimientos y cooperación, sellaron bajo un solemne compromiso establecer la noble organización de Caballeros de Protección Mutua.

[These men who seriously took the best interests and welfare of the community to heart were enlightened by heroic and patriotic feelings. November 8, 1890, was truly a memorable day for the historic purpose of this novel. Amidst the loudest cheers and applause possible, the people were emotionally moved by their growing sentiments and spirit of cooperation. Together they solemnly swore to seal a pact and establish the new and noble organization Knights of Mutual Protection.]

Under the banner of the Orden de Caballeros de Protección Mutua de Ley y Orden del Territorio, its members rise to the challenge as they declare nothing less than a holy war against the Antichrist and his followers:

La Orden de Caballeros de Protección Mutua, muy sigilosamente se preparó para esperar de una manera prominente a aquel elemento de bandidos hechos y derechos. El sol por fin se ofuzcó y comenzó una constlación en el cielo.

[The Order of Knights of Mutual Protection soon made secret preparations to wait for that perfect element of bandits. After the sun had finally set, a constellation of stars appeared in the heavens.]

Said war is waged under the vigilant eye of God himself:

La luna se escondía entre densas nubes y las estrellas se dejaban ver transparentemente, pero no suficiente para aclarar los escondrijos de aquellos transgresores que creían que el ojo de Dios no los alcanzaba a penetrar, porque tal es su ceguedad y tal es su mala fe.

[The moon hid among some dense clouds. A few transparent stars could be seen, but they were not bright enough to illuminate the hideouts of those transgressors who thought the eye of God would never catch up to them. Such was their blindness and such was their bad faith.]

When the Gorras Blancas are finally rooted out, the majority of them flee from battle in a most cowardly fashion, and those who do stick around to engage their enemy are soundly trounced. The battle closes with the triumphant imagery of angels and seraphim on the verge of raising their voices in song.

Will the Real Messiah Please Stand Up?

While C. de Baca convincingly delineates the collective character of his messiah, I wish to suggest at this point that his tack was but a subterfuge. The informed reader of his times would have known that one of the two individuals responsible for organizing the Caballeros de la Sociedad de Protección Mutua was none other than Manuel C. de Baca.[6] As such, the cunning reader would have understood that when angels and seraphim finally raise their heavenly voices in praise of the victors, it was, in fact, in honor of Manuel C. de Baca that they sang. For it was he, the author of this tale of redemption, who was the true Messiah of El Condado de San Miguel; it was he who was responsible for turning *noches tenebrosas* into starlit nights of peace and order.

Who Profits from Redemption?

The mythological imagery which undergirds *Noches tenebrosas* bears testimony to Manuel C. de Baca's ideological stance *vis-a-vis* the Gorras Blancas and the politics of his day, a stance that not disinterestedly reduced a complex political and class struggle to an essentialist battle between the forces of Good and Evil. The constituents of this struggle, as mapped out by C. de Baca in descending order of abstractness, are: God, Order (Natural and State), and Virtue on the side of Good. Symbolic representations of these abstract concepts are the Church alluded to at the beginning of the tale, private and corporate property, and Braulia's virginity. In the antithetical column, the forces of Evil are the Antichrist, Chaos (in the form of vigilante violence against private property), and failure to respect Virtue. Standing in for these concepts are the Gran Capitán and the Gorras Blancas—depicted as nocturnal animals—fence cutters, axes and torches, and the men who defile Braulia. The Romantic descriptions of nature highlight the difference between Order and Chaos, and, clearly, the Gorras Blancas represent chaos, disharmony, and the transgression of all that is Good and Natural.

And who represents the real threatened element in this binary construct? Is it an undifferentiated group of "rational citizens" of the Condado de San Miguel who finally unite under the banner of the Caballeros de Protección Mutua as the narrator would have us believe? Or is it the members of the landed class to which Manuel C. de Baca belongs, the "ricos" which the narrator announces early in the text as the target of the Gorras' attacks? That the author may have been moved by an abiding commitment to Law and Order is commendable, particularly in view of the fact that as County Prosecutor he certainly must have had his fill of blatant disregard for the laws of the land. However, we cannot ignore that Order—Divine and therefore "Natural," as well as State-sanctioned Order—has been the proverbial pillar that throughout the centuries has permitted the landed gentry to maintain their privileged position. "Exotic" ideas such as those imported by El Gran Capitán, a disenchanted adventurer from the peripheral tiers of San Miguel society, represented a very real threat to Manuel C. de Baca's social position. On the other hand, the following words, uttered by the barber in *Noches tenebrosas*, suggest a clue to Manuel C. de Baca's infatuation with what turns out to be not only a Christian but a colonial discourse of civilization versus barbarianism:

> Esto [las acciones de los gorras blancas] atraería la más horripilante mala fama
> al pueblo neo-mexicano a quien marcaría con el sello de la incivilización, con-

firmaría los anteriores informes de poca delicadeza.

[This the actions of the White Caps) would cast the most horrifying ill repute upon the *Nuevomexicano* town, marking it with the stamp of barbarism and confirming its previous reputation as being a place of little gentility.]

In fairness to Manuel C. de Baca, we must point out that denigrating discourses uttered against *Nuevomexicano*s were very real indeed, and that numerous educated Hispanos joined him in scripting a counter discourse designed to highlight the dignity of the native population and the worth of their culture. Few of them, however, inveighed against members of their own population as a means to achieving this end. One might say that Manuel C. de Baca occupies a unique position among his peers of creative writers with his public condemnation of the Gorras Blancas.

Fact, Fiction, or Self-Righteousness?

To conclude my reading—which, of course, is marked by my own ideological position—of this nineteenth-century narrative, I would like to point out that although Manuel C. de Baca's text was written one hundred years ago it is very timely if considered within the contemporary discourses on the relationship between history and fiction. C. de Baca, in fact, deliberately blurs the line between "the hard facts of history" and the stuff of fiction by drawing on the mythical imaginary to emplot his narrative and by explicitly referring to it as a novella. Given that readers of his time would have been familiar with the "hard facts" which had just recently taken place, did C. de Baca not risk being faulted by readers for taking gratuitous poetic license? I would suggest that C. de Baca was willing to take that risk because his concern was less about accusations than it was about pragmatics; what truly mattered to Manuel C. de Baca was to sway his readership to agree that, after all was said and done regarding Los Caballeros de Labor, Los Gorras Blancas, and Los Caballeros de Protección Mutua, it was the latter who held the high moral ground. A mythic scatological discourse, the weight and authority of which still had the potential for influencing his predominantly Catholic readership, was an ideal medium proving his point.

Notes

[1] For interesting studies of the Spanish-language press in New Mexico, see Doris Meyer, *Speaking for Themselves: Neomexicano Cultural Identity and the Spanish-Language Press, 1880-1920*; Gabriel Meléndez, *So All Is Not Lost: The Poetics of Print in Nuevomexicano Communities, 1834-1958*, both issued in the

Pasó Por Aquí Series of the University of New Mexico Press.

²I wish to thank Anselmo Arellano for allowing me to use his unpublished compilation of this serialized novella.

³Interview with Anselmo Arellano, *Las Vegas Grandes on the Gallinas, 1835-1985*, p. 104. While this descendent of Juan José Herrera claims that the activities of the Gorras Blancas were directed primarily toward Anglo encroachers, the organization played down the issue of ethnicity in their platform: "Nosotros estamos opuestos a distinciones de razas, pues todos somos hermanos del género humano protejidos por la misma bandera gloriosa." [We are opposed to distinctions based on race, as we are all brothers of the human family, protected by the same glorious banner.] Cited in *Noches tenebrosas.*

⁴I am indebted to Frank Graziano, whose ideas and language in his analysis of Argentina's "dirty war" have influenced my reading of *Noches tenebrosas.*

⁵The scatological conflation of sacred and secular agendas is accentuated if we read Braulia's body as an emblem for the County of San Miguel. Such a reading is not unwarranted if we consider that it is common practice to portray homelands, nations and contested territories in general as the female body incarnate. Thus, in this tale of political messianism, the battle between the champions of Natural Order and those who openly contest that order and the economic and political structures that it sustains, is waged over the "patria chica," El Condado de San Miguel, depicted here as the defiled female body.

⁶*El Sol de Mayo*, in its first issue announced itself as the mouthpiece for *La Sociedad de Protección Mutua de Ley y Orden*: "Periódico comprometido a los intereses del pueblo de Nuevo México—y órgano de la Orden de Caballeros de Protección Mutua de Ley y Orden del Territorio." [Newspaper devoted to the interest of the people of New Mexico—and organ of the Order of Knights of Mutual Protection of Law and Order of the Territory] (*El Sol de Mayo*, 1 mayo, 1891, p. 1.)

⁷C. de Baca's strong Christian leanings frequently are expressed in *El Sol de Mayo*, and they lead his writerly hand in his second novella, *Vicente Silva y sus cuarenta bandidos*. He states in the introduction: "If man were to strictly obey the holy precepts of love and quality that are contained in the Ten Commandments, that sublime code of love and justice that was given to Moses on the summit of Mount Sinai in the midst of thunder and lightning, the world would be a paradise; we men would truly be brothers, and human laws, courts of justice, gallows and prisons, would be completely unnecessary." (p. 2)

Breaking All The Rules: María Amparo Ruiz de Burton Writes a Civil War Novel

José F. Aranda, Jr.
Rice University

> I feel . . . a true hatred and contempt (as a good Mexican) for this certain "Manifest Destiny." Of all the wicked phrases invented by stupid people, there is not one more odious for me than that, the most offensive, the most insulting; it raises the blood in my temples when I hear of it, and I see it instantly in photographs, all that the Yankees have done to make us, the Mexicans, suffer: the robbery of Texas, the war, the robbery of California, the death of Maximilian. If I were to believe in "Manifest Destiny," I would cease to believe in justice or Divine wisdom. No, friend of mind, this Manifest Destiny is nothing more than "Manifest Yankee trash". . .
>
> M. A. Ruiz de Burton, letter to M. G. Vallejo, February 15, 1869[1]

María Amparo Ruiz de Burton could simultaneously decry the effects of Manifest Destiny on Mexico but also lament the death of Maximilian, an Austrian imperialist who crowned himself emperor of Mexico.[2] Why? The answer to this question is actually rather startling. So I like to proceed with biography, because it is a biography of Ruiz de Burton that is critically needed if we are going to contextualize and historize perhaps the most important Mexican-American writer of the nineteenth century. Because of her status as a "recovered" author, no textual analysis can proceed without some attention to biography. While this admission may seem reasonable, even logical, as Jesse Alemán has reminded us, the relationship between textuality and biography must be assiduously negotiated to avoid a reductive privileging of one over the other.[3] And yet, because of the obvious pitfalls involved with archival research on minorities and women in the United States, biographical and textual analyses will inevitably feed off each other in tandem and uneveningly, until all possible resources are exhausted.

The purpose of this essay is thus to examine María Amparo Ruiz de Burton's "imagined intervention" in the U. S. colonization of North America in her novel *Who Would Have Thought It?* (1872) and to delineate, as best as possible, her contradictory biographical responses to the post-1848 realities of the Treaty of Guadalupe Hidalgo. The basic argument is as follows: María Amparo Ruiz de Burton is a tremendously complex person and writer, a person who easily broke stereotypes in her own day—stereotypes that she continues to break today because of the history of racism and discrimination directed at people of Mexican descent since 1848. And yet she is not a Dolores Huerta of the United Farmer Workers Union nor a Gloria Anzaldúa of the borderlands in nineteenth-century clothes. But this still leaves wide open the question who she is. The biography I reconstruct here will enable us to consider Ruiz de Burton in the context of her own times, thereby historicizing the complexities of *Who Would Have Thought It*? This task is crucial, especially now that the novel's entry into Chicano/a literary canon is itself inaugurating a full scale reevaluation of the foundations of Chicano/a Studies.

Since 1992, the most prominent biography of Ruiz de Burton has been the one written by Rosaura Sánchez and Beatrice Pita in their introduction to *The Squatter and the Don*. Of note is the manner in which Sánchez and Pita read Ruiz de Burton's biography within established critiques of patriarchy, capitalism, eighteenth-century liberal ideology, Western colonialism, and U. S. imperialism. This is to say that Ruiz de Burton's biography lends itself to an analysis currently deployed by resistance theorists and postcolonial critics. Sánchez and Pita read Ruiz de Burton as part of a collectivity they identify as "subaltern," arguing that Californios represent a conquered people, conquered as much by the U. S. military as capitalist ideology itself, a collectivity held to a subordinated legal status for reasons of race, class, and political disenfranchisement.[4] This latter treatment is especially egregious given the provisions of the Treaty of Guadalupe Hidalgo that insured Mexican nationals the rights of citizenship and property if they remained in the newly conquered territories.

While I wholeheartedly agree that these critiques are available to us via Ruiz de Burton's writings, her biography, as acknowledged by Sánchez and Pita, also indicates that she saw herself as part of a white, educated elite—aristocratic in its origins and with a prior history in Alta California as colonizers, not as colonized. Further, even Sánchez and Pita, argue that the central story told in *The Squatter and the Don* is not the illegal dispossession of lands held by Californios, but rather a criticism of corporate monopoly and political corruption: "It is this monopolistic power and the government-monopoly collusion, not the capitalist system *per se*, that Ruiz de Burton's novel attacks. This anti-monopolistic stance is simultaneously also a defense of entrepreneurial competitive capitalism" (29). In short, Ruiz de Burton did not see herself exclusively within agrarian, feudal terms. The economic ventures as cited by Sánchez and Pita, from cattle raising to a cement plant, indicate her inclination towards capitalism. Not withstanding those exceptions, Sánchez and Pita nevertheless retain the "subaltern" thesis as a major characterization of Ruiz de Burton.

By contrast, historian Lisabeth Haas reads Ruiz de Burton's biography, as supplied largely by Sánchez and Pita, in a slightly different manner. In a section entitled "Gender Stories of Conquest," Haas compares Ruiz de Burton's biography with that Apolinaria Lorenzano, who, unlike Ruiz de Burton, did not to belong an aristocratic, educated elite class:

> The lives of Ruiz Burton and Lorenzano illustrate the social differences among Californio landowners and the potential meaning of those differences in the American period. Ruiz Burton was from a colonial military elite family and married an American in 1849. She continued to accumulate land in the early American period, modernized the production of cattle and other procedures on her ranchos in the 1860s, and fought vigorously and tirelessly against the laws and persons that threatened her properties. Lorenzano, in contrast, represents the relatively poor landowners of the colonial and Mexican periods who worked with their hands or labored for others . . .
>
> They were vulnerable as women in U. S. society, where women were not accorded equal status in law or custom, and they were vulnerable to the anti-Mexican prejudices of Anglo-American migrants. Ruiz Burton was aware of these vulnerabilities when she set her elite California characters apart from the world of business and landownership and asserted Californios' European lineage, despite the contradiction of such a portrayal with the actual order of the time.[5]

Haas refers here to Ruiz de Burton's characters in *The Squatter and the Don*. Haas' conclusion that Ruiz de Burton was well aware of the vulnerabilities that her U. S. status cost her is echoed by Sánchez and Pita. In fact, with regards to *The Squatter and the Don*, Sánchez and Pita observe that the "identity of the novel constructs of the Californio is itself class-based (aristocracy), but collective rather individual ('We, the conquered'), regional ('native Spaniards' or 'Spanish Californians' and 'Mexican'), religious (Catholic), political ('the conquered natives' or 'the enemy') and racial ('my race')" (39). Given the general agreement on analysis found here, what is the difference between Sánchez and Pita's and Haas' biographical readings? In fact, Professor Sánchez is particularly adept in differentiating the class differences among Californias in her book *Telling Identities* (1995).

The difference lies, I argue, in what is being privileged. Sánchez and Pita construct Ruiz de Burton's biography, as they construct her literary career, as emblematic of "the counter-history of the sub-altern, the conquered Californio population" (5). In contrast, Lisabeth Haas privileges the class differences that existed among women like Ruiz de Burton and Apolinaria Lorenzano before and after 1848. The Ruiz de Burton that emerges from Haas' metanarrative is thus an individual who was in a position to secure for herself and her family certain advantages due to her marriage to Henry S. Burton, due to her white skin, and due to her aristocratic class background. There's no moral judgment here about Ruiz de Burton's character, ethnic loyalties, or the opportunities that life presented her—she was who she was.

This brings me back to my own original question. Who was she? To answer that, I offer two new additional glimpses into the life of María Amparo Ruiz de Burton. In following up Lisabeth Haas' contention that Ruiz de Burton socialized with Abraham Lincoln, I discovered, in the collected works of Lincoln, a printed record of a meeting between them. It reads as follows:

To Simon Cameron
Hon. Sec. of War   Executive Mansion
My dear Sir: June 1. 1861

Mrs. Capt. Burton is very desirous that her husband may be made a Colonel. I do not know him personally; but if it can be done without injustice to other officers of the Regular Army, I would like for her to be obliged.
Yours truly   A. Lincoln.[6]

Current readers of *Who Would Have Thought It?* will recognize this meeting's resemblance to that fictional meeting between Julian Norval and Abraham Lincoln, and for that matter Miss Lavinia's attempt to gain an audience with Capitol Hill officials who might free Isaac Sprig from a Confederate prison camp. In itself, Lincoln's memo to the Secretary of War is an interesting footnote for literary criticism. It ties Ruiz de Burton's satirical treatment of Washington, D. C. and Lincoln concretely to her own historic presence in the nation's capitol during the Civil War. But this a secondary matter. What's really interesting is the person, Mrs. Capt. Burton, who successfully negotiates her spouse's promotion with no less than the President of the United States. Six months later the Senate formally approves of the promotion. This memo alerts us that Ruiz de Burton was not only formidable in person but that she was also at the center of history itself. Given the mythic regard that mainstream history and popular culture showers on Abraham Lincoln, is it not amazing to know that Ruiz de Burton created her own history with the President? In this meeting, where is her liminality, her marginality, her lack of historical agency? And yet, we must keep in mind that her own personal empowerment is not representative of the Californio in 1861, not by a long shot.

Some five years after this meeting, Ruiz de Burton will once again be at the center of history but with decidedly different players. On November 27, 1865, Bvt. Brig-General Burton will take command of Regiment headquarters, Ft. Monroe, Virginia.[7] This was an important duty, given that he was in charge of the nation's most notorious prisoner of war at the time, the ex-Confederate president, Jefferson Davis. In fact, General Burton made it possible, notwithstanding some political risk to himself, that Jefferson Davis' wife, Varina Davis, be able to join her husband at the camp in a respectable manner. Varina Davis' gratitude for the General's gentlemanly treatment of her spouse is recorded in a letter to William Preston Johnston, former aide-de-camp to Davis, a family friend and son of Confederate General Albert Sidney Johnston. Along the way, Ruiz de Burton appears in an interesting manner:

> Mr Davis is not so strong as he was during the last few weeks—I am afraid his health is permanently injured. He is always calm and quiet. Since Genl Burton came into position here, he has been very civil and kind to me and to him. His wife is a sympathetic warm-hearted talented Mexican woman who is very angry with the Yankees about Mexican affairs, and we get together quietly and abuse them—though to say truth since Miles' departure all here are kind to us, and considerate.[8]

Reading this letter makes you wonder about the content of these "quiet conversations." Certainly, it is clear that Ruiz de Burton's anger against the Yankees is a nationalistic one.[9] But how curious it is that Varina Davis identifies Ruiz de Burton as Mexican. Is this a racialized identification? A regional one? Is this an identity that Ruiz de Burton herself promoted? If so, what of her position as the General's spouse? Prior to the Civil War, General Burton was a "veteran of both Seminole and Mexican wars [and] had also been a professor at West Point."[10] This man was deeply involved in the United State's territorial acquisitions and displacement of Native Americans. And what role did the fact that Jefferson Davis was the ex-president of the Confederacy and de facto champion of states' rights and slavery play in her relationship with Varina Davis? And finally what, if anything, does this letter suggest about Ruiz de Burton's own politics with regard to race, class, nationhood, U. S. foreign policy, etc.?

Together, these two biographical glimpses are provocative and highly suggestive, but not conclusive. On the one hand, Abraham Lincoln, a Yankee, is someone Ruiz de Burton ably persuades to advance her husband's career. On the other, Varina Davis, the ex-Confederate first lady, takes comfort that Ruiz de Burton and she share their enmity of the Union. Varina Davis's letter suggests an odd collusion between the vanquished South and the defeated Mexico. This is all the more curious given the moral support Abraham Lincoln and Benito Juárez exchanged with each other over their respective wars. There's a complexity in all this that defies easy explanation. Friends, foes, loyalties, histories, are all, in helter-skelter fashion, set loose from their traditional moorings. The only thing to be said is that there exists a more extensive biography of Ruiz de Burton somewhere out there in dusty archives of libraries waiting to be written. She is a complex figure. Her writing attests to this. Historicizing her complexity will be a cautious affair for years to come. If indeed Chicano/a Studies comes to accept Ruiz de Burton as a "subaltern," it will have to be conceded that she is such a sophisticated one as to require redefinition of the term.[11]

If we read Ruiz de Burton's biography as complex, aristocratic, white European creole, educated, and elitist, how do we then proceed to read her novels, especially *Who Would Have Thought It?*, her first and the more complex of the two? I argue for the need to understand her rendering of Mexico as central to any study of *Who Would Have Thought It?*'s cultural politics. Furthermore, I argue that Ruiz de Burton's "imagined intervention" in the U. S. domination of

North America is constrained by the very same cultural and historic forces that allow her to negotiate her newly emerging status as Mexican-American within Anglo society. What this means is that even as she imagines her intervention, it is already circumscribed rhetorically, militarily, and ideologically by Anglo-American hegemony. While there are no utopias in Ruiz de Burton's text, there is also no lack of political idealism fueling her narrative strategies. This is no doubt a contradictory stance on her part, but nevertheless very telling of the forces that impinged on her as writer and citizen. In this regard, her text, like her biography, provides a powerful glimpse into the social and political transformations that were acutely felt by all people of Mexican descent in the United States—all the more drawn out in Ruiz de Burton's case, given her access to the hegemonic discourses of her time.

Ruiz de Burton's "imagined intervention" takes the form of a satire that unmasks several of the most endeared mythologies of the United States in the nineteenth century.[12] The novel's title, *Who Would Have Thought It?*, is in fact a phrase that is used several times to underscore complete surprise at the state of affairs that have sullied the pristine image of the United States.[13] With the intent of de-mystifying the United States and its cultural institutions, Ruiz de Burton pits the rhetoric of politicians against their deeds of avarice, cowardice, and duplicity. In her novel, political representation is a farce played out on the backs of the illiterate and working class. Ruiz de Burton equally lashes out at notions of constitutional inequality that bar women from elected office and social norms that infantilize the potential of women's social worth. She wastes no time in depicting the hypocrisy among white abolitionists who maintain racist views of blacks while simultaneously championing their cause, and finally she ridicules savagely the pretense of respectability and republican patriotism associated with Anglo American women who fiercely attempt to embody the "cult of domesticity" popular at the time.

Given this summary, it should be evident that Ruiz de Burton satisfies many of our current expectations of "resistance literature." As Sánchez and Pita point out:

> *Who Would Have Thought It?* satirizes American politics, an emerging consumerism, and dominant representations of the nation itself, often through a mocking of divisive political discourses and practices of the period set against the backdrop of idealized constructs of domesticity and nationhood. (xv-xvi)

> Class, gender and race, here interconnected, reveal cultural constraints on women and their consent to norms that subordinate them significantly, the novel shows, as much in Mexico and in the United States; the novel also counters stereotypical notions of Mexicans with a construction of upper-class Latino/as as white, a perhaps defensive—though not defensible—move on Ruiz de Burton's part, in view of the fact that Congressional records of the period refer to Mexicans in the Southwest as a "mongrel race." (xix-xx)

. . . [In the course of the novel, slavery becomes] a metaphor for disempowerment and disenfranchisement. It is the meaninglessness of "citizenship," the
fragmentation of the union and with it any illusions of national identity, as well
as the glaring discrepancies in the social contract, ably concealed by ideological discourses, that most concern the novel. (xliii)

From these quotes it would seem self-evident that Sánchez and Pita had recovered a major "resistance" novel. But then the unexpected occurs.

In the course of the novel, Ruiz de Burton conceives of her main protagonist and narrator in white, European, educated terms. Once again I quote from
Sánchez and Pita: "In spite of its acerbic critique, Ruiz de Burton's novel is not
all populist" (xlix). This observation is an important discrepancy our editors
note, because in contemporary Chicano and Chicana criticism a working class
ideology is central to the whole construction of Chicanismo in the late 1960s
and early 1970s. This observation is as threatening to any "resistance" labeling
of *Who Would Have Thought It*? as Ruiz de Burton's implicit racism towards
Native Americans and blacks in the novel. But to continue: "On the contrary,
[the novel] favors an elitist standard, that of an intellectual "aristocracy," that is,
of an enlightened professional class, a perspective akin to that of the Liberals of
1872 who supported rule by the "best men [Foner, 1990, 214]" (xlix). Sánchez
and Pita contend that this position by Ruiz de Burton aligns her with an
"'American intelligentsia' who saw abroad the mass uprising of the Paris
Commune [1871] as a harbinger of things to come in the United States and was
particularly upset with the likes of the Democratic machine of 'Boss' William
M. Tweed" (li).

In *Who Would Have Thought It*?, Ruiz de Burton's liberal politics achieve
their most complicated rendering when the plot shifts to Mexico during its own
turbulent 1860s. The switch in settings provides Ruiz de Burton the opportunity to ruminate about Mexico's crisis in the 1860s: the French invading army and
the Austrian, Maximiliano, sent by Napoleon III, to be emperor of Mexico. But
rather than focusing on how best to expel the invading French, Ruiz de Burton's
narrative line is occupied by Mexican nationals, supporters of Benito Juárez's
government in exile, contemplating the political viability of monarchy's return
to Mexico in the figure of Maximiliano. Their discussion is driven by a shared
perception that Mexico's attempts to emulate U. S. democracy since its war of
independence in 1821 has resulted in a series of civil wars, depopulation of the
country, destruction of commerce and lands, and the terrible defeat at the hands
of "norteamericanos." In short, electoral politics has left Mexico weak, its sovereignty in debt to foreign nations, and defenseless against armed invasion.
Maximiliano's aristocratic pedigree at least assures a claim on behalf of the
Spanish Bourbons, an ethnic tie that is commensurate with these men as the
minimum requirement for recognition of Mexico as a prior extension of Spain
and therefore European.

Sánchez and Pita are judicious scholars; they review a section of five pages out of a 300-page novel in all its complexities and potential controversy because it deals with Mexican history and politics. And what they find disturbing in this section is that Ruiz de Burton's upper-class Mexican characters "support a liberal economic policy" that would welcome the Austrian Archduke Maximiliano as emperor of Mexico in a constitutional monarchy. In effect, Ruiz de Burton reenacts in hindsight a political crisis in Mexico during the French invasion, reproducing the debates "between pro-capitalist, anti-clerical Liberal and pro-monarchy, pro-oligarchy conservatives (church and landowners)" (liii). As Sánchez and Pita observe, Ruiz de Burton seemingly sides with those, who in the course of a long drawn-out war with the French, concluded that a republican form of government was not in Mexico's best interests. Sánchez and Pita write:

> Whether Ruiz de Burton herself favored a liberal monarchy is not clear nor really at issue. What is clear is that by 1872, having lived in the United States for about 25 years—about two-thirds of her life—she had a highly developed sense of self as a Latina in opposition to Anglo-dominant society. What particularly concerned her was, on the one hand, the perceived misrepresentations of the U. S. as regards its democratic and egalitarian principles, and on the other, the subordinate status of Mexicans, especially Californios in the United States, and U. S. imperialist policies towards Mexico. (liii-lvi)

One can see that having brought up this episode in Mexico, the Chicana editors nevertheless go to great pains to remind their audience of Ruiz de Burton's resistant character. There is an anxiety about Ruiz de Burton that her editors find difficult to resolve. Sánchez and Pita finally admit that the novel's critique of the United States is "circular in its argument, for its critique of the U. S. government, as has been noted, revolves precisely around the transgression of guarantees protected by the Constitution and Congress. In many cases it is the government's failure to follow its own precepts that is criticized . . . [Ruiz de Burton's] perspective is reformist and ultimately in good measure elitist" (p. lvii).

The predicament that Sánchez and Pita find themselves when evaluating Ruiz de Burton's political affiliations is an institutional problem, not Ruiz de Burton's. It is the way that Chicano/a Studies has conferred canonical status on writers of Mexican descent that is the obstacle.[14] Meanwhile, Sánchez and Pita make it clear that this Mexican episode has the potential to be "very insightful in its reconstruction of [the political debates in Mexico during the French invasion] and its constructed distinction between economic and political liberalism and democracy" (liii). I agree, and I think this is the place to go to get an enhance understanding of Ruiz de Burton's politics in 1872. Ruiz de Burton's figuring of a new monarchy for Mexico contextualizes, I argue, the critiques she launches against the United States and the New England culture she associates with American Manifest Destiny. For her, what's at issue is not colonialism per se, or even which European group becomes the majority, but whether or not a certain genteel, educated, white middle-class can become the moral authority of the country; the final form of government, representative or monarchical, is the least of her concerns.[15] Ultimately, I would argue she was some kind of Pan Americanist interested in any form of government that would guarantee intellectuals a leading role. This government would also provide for a system of checks and balances that would undermine populist movements but nevertheless discourage political corruption and nepotism. Her "imagined intervention" aims towards a universalist position on nationalism, citizenship, and democracy. In this regard, she echoes the politics of the Spanish-language newspaper, *El Nuevo Mundo*, and its Californio readership, who subscribed to a politic of universal democracy that they perceived was in keeping with U. S. culture and ideology.[16]

The question remains, why would this appeal to her sensibility as an irreparably dispossessed California? I would argue that Ruiz de Burton has a stake in this brand of political idealism. It is precisely because Spanish/Mexican colonialism has failed her that Ruiz de Burton ends her novel by forecasting the future marriage of Lola Medina and Julian Norval. This marriage suggests a union between two colonial enterprises; here Mexican colonialism and its material wealth is merged with U. S. colonialism and its promises of representative democracy. The anticipated marriage therefore imagines a parallel movement in the geopolitical governance of North America, implicitly placing individuals like Ruiz de Burton at the center of a new nationalism. Thus, in 1872, she is cautiously optimistic/hopeful about the role that upper-class Hispanics will play in the reformation of the United States. This is despite the loss of Texas in 1836 to Anglos, despite the loss of the Southwest from Texas to California in 1848, despite the de facto second-class citizenship already apparent by the 1850s, and despite the many Anglo stereotypes of Mexicans that continue even in today's political arenas.

Given all this, how could she be optimistic? The answer to this lies in the much larger issue that this novel hints at in its portrayal of the United States as the Colossus of the North—the dominant influence in North America. Let me return to a key moment in the Mexican episode. One of the Mexican characters laments the following:

> Of course the ideas of this continent are different from those of Europe, but we all know that such would not be the case if the influence of the United States did not prevail with such despotic sway over the minds of the leading men of the Hispano-American republics. If it were not for this terrible, the fatal influence—*which will eventually destroy us*—the Mexicans, instead of seeing anything objectionable in the proposed change, would be proud to hail a prince who, after all, has some sort of a claim to this land, and who will cut loose from the leading strings of the United States. (198)

Sánchez and Pita read this section as a declaration against the imperialism of the U. S., a fact more terrible and problematic than the occupation army of the

French (p. lv). Although I don't dismiss this reading, what I would argue in addition is that this quote admits the degree to which the United States had become a model of nationhood, capitalism, and democracy in Latin America. It was a U. S. model of democracy that was clearly implied in the Mexican Constitution in 1824, and once again reaffirmed in the Mexican Constitution of 1857. Her reinvention confirms that there were political forces in Mexico during the nineteenth century that saw themselves as participating in a tradition of liberal ideology that had made the United States a success.[17]

What this reinvention also dramatizes is the quandary that Mexican intellectuals found themselves in when a liberal ideology failed to take hold in Mexico. It should have worked, but it didn't. By Ruiz de Burton's generation, the perception of this influence has enlarged to encompass all of South America. That the novel can not offer a better resolution is, of course, not the fault of Ruiz de Burton. Significantly, Mexico's liberal ideology was severely shaken after the French crisis, and prepared the way for Porfirio Díaz's seizure of the government in 1877. Porfirio Díaz, for many reasons—too many to list here—will reinscribe Mexico under the shadow of the United States. His dictatorship will set up, in essence, the political forces that will culminate in the Mexican Revolution of 1910. Ruiz de Burton's treatment of Mexico prefigures not only Díaz's rise to power but liberal ideology's ultimate collapse at the hands of peasant revolutionaries.

Overall, Ruiz de Burton's novel will have a major impact on Chicano/a and American studies because it documents Mexican American writers as participating in discourses on literature, aesthetics, and the nation in the nineteenth century. Indeed, Ruiz de Burton's perspective on a variety of issues confronting the nation, from slavery to sexuality, is so different, I would argue, because she brings to her writing a different colonial tradition. Her observations and judgments about New England society and U. S. politics are informed by the memory of her prior status as a Mexican citizen. Few American writers of this century share such a distinction as Ruiz de Burton's.

Who Would Have Thought It? will also significantly help to clarify the role that postcolonial theory may play in Chicano/a criticism. Chicano/a Studies' recent adoption of postcolonial criticism overlaps institutionally with its past applications of poststructural theory as vehicles for developing and sustaining anti-imperialist, anti-colonialist, "resistance" strategies of reading Chicano/a texts. Unfortunately, the adoption of postcolonialism in Chicano/a Studies has been awkward, a victim of institutional forces that consistently reduce the field of analysis to only one colonialism, that promulgated by the United States. What is often mentioned but quickly relegated as a non-topic is a Spanish/Mexican colonial past. Chicano/a scholars consistently mark the Mexican-American War of 1846 and the treaty of Guadalupe Hidalgo of 1848 as that geopolitical and psychic rupture that made possible the internal colonization of a 100,000 Mexican citizens. While this assessment is irrefutable, what is ironically lost upon most Chicano/a scholars is the prior colonialist status of these same 100,000 Mexicans citizens. The complexities of Ruiz de Burton's life and writings alone argue that much work remains to be done.

In closing, I would like to return to whole idea of constructing María Amparo Ruiz de Burton as a subaltern and her biography as an unproblematized counter-imperialist history. I would prefer not to identify her as a subaltern. I would be more comfortable with historicizing her, and her Californio peers, as products of competing colonial enterprises in Alta California. I would prefer to think that *Who Would Have Thought It?* is her exploration of the two colonial legacies in North America that until 1848 were more openly in earnest competition with each other. Despite good cause to see the United States negatively given her prior status as a Californio, Ruiz de Burton would have her readers understand that she has an equal stake in reforming U. S. democracy.

Notes

A special thanks goes to Jaime Mejía, assistant professor of Chicano Literature at Southwest Texas State University, for our provocative conversations, extremely helpful editing and his friendship.

[1] See Frederick Bryant Oden, "The Maid of Monterey, The Life of María Amparo Ruiz de Burton, 1832–1895," ms. thesis (San Diego: University of California, San Diego, History Department, 1992), 77. My gratitude to Amelia M. de la Luz Montes for sharing this important material at a critical moment.

[2] This essay is an abbreviated and edited version of a larger treatment titled "Contradictory Impulses: María Amparo Ruiz de Burton, Resistance Theory, and the Politics of Chicano/a Studies"; see "No More Separate Spheres," special issue of *American Literature*, special issue ed. Cathy N. Davidson, September 1998.

[3] Here I am grateful to Jesse Alemán's comments directly after our joint panel on Ruiz de Burton at the Fourth Conference of Recovering the U. S. Hispanic Literary Heritage, Interpreting and Contextualizing the Recovered Text, University of Houston, November 1996.

[4] For more, see the introductions by Sánchez and Pita in *Who Would Have Thought It?* (Houston: Arte Público, 1995) and *The Squatter and The Don* (Houston: Arte Público, 1992). For a more extensive treatment of the Californios as "subalterns," see Rosaura Sánchez *Telling Identities: The Californio testimonios* (Minneapolis: University of Minnesota, 1995).

[5] See Lisabeth Haas, *Conquests and Historical Identities in California*, 1769–1936 (Berkeley: University of California, 1995), 77–86.

[6] See *Collected Works of Abraham Lincoln*, Vol. IV, ed. Roy P. Basler

(New Brunswick: Rutgers University, 1953), 392.

⁷ See Hudson Strode, *Jefferson Davis: Tragic Hero, The Last Twenty-Five Years,* 1864–1889 (New York: Harcourt, Brace, & World, Inc., 1964).

⁸ See "Letters" ed. Arthur Marvin Shaw, *The Journal of Southern History*, 16.1 (1950), 75–6.

⁹ Amelia María de la Luz Montes' research on Ruiz de Burton's letters at the Huntington Library adds an interesting twist to this anger. In the paper she delivered at the Fourth Conference of Recovering the U. S. Hispanic Literary Heritage, "Es necesario mirar bien: María Amparo Ruiz de Burton as a Precurso to Chicana(o) Literature in the American Landscape," De la Luz Montes read letters from Ruiz de Burton to her long time friend and prominent Californio, Mariano G. Vallejo. These letters make clear that she felt she was living among the enemy during her time out East. And yet, this view did not prevent her from making associations with prominent Anglo-Americans. Kathleen Crawford notes in her article that the Burtons attended Lincoln's inaugural ball, and that Ruiz de Burton became friends with the First Lady soon after. See Kathleen Crawford, "María Amparo Ruiz de Burton: The General's Lady," *Journal of San Diego History*, 30.3 (1984), 198-211.

¹⁰ *See Who Was Who in the Civil War, ed.* Stewart Sifakis (New York: Facts on File, 1987), 94.

¹¹ We can see how problematic the use of "subaltern" is here when the historical context is enlarged to consider other groups that meet two essential criteria: one, that they were conquered by a Western European nationalist group, and two, that the conquered were themselves prior colonialists. Under these conditions, French Canadians could be counted among the "subalterns" because of British colonialism, and even more distressing, we would have to agree that Dutch Afrikaners qualify as "subalterns" under British colonialism. This is an untenable use of "sub-alterity" and postcolonialism.

¹² For a more developed summary, see the introduction by Rosaura Sánchez and Beatrice Pita.

¹³ This title, as strange as it is, has a precursor in John Day's 1608 play, *Law-Trickes, or who would have thought it.* The whys and wherefores of Ruiz de Burton's connection to this English play is unclear, but the link could be a critique of law and is its relation to justice. If so, this is yet another indication of Ruiz de Burton's command of Western literature and discourses.

¹⁴ In fact, Ruiz de Burton's second novel, *The Squatter and the Don* (1885), which is a humorless indictment of the illegal dispossessions of Mexican landowners in California after Reconstruction, although recovered simultaneously with *Who Would Have Thought It?*, was published first. And I argue, it was because its "resistant" character was not ambiguous at all.

¹⁵ Throughout this scene there is definitely a displacement of the elected president, Benito Juárez. His indigenous roots and dark skin may very well be at the heart of this displacement. And this is despite having received a patent

for a land grant (Rancho Ensenada) in Baja California from Benito Juárez on December 31, 1859; see Oden (169).

[16] For this connection, I am beholden to Nancy Hernández's research in her conference paper, "The Lynching of Mexican American Identities." She writes: "The writers involved in *El Nuevo Mundo* were firm believers in the universal ideals of democracy, freedom and separation from monarchy. These writers were firmly convinced that all people in the Americas could get along because they all wanted one thing—freedom from the crown. It made perfect sense to the writers of *El Nuevo Mundo* that the Americas would become one land full of people who held the same ideals" (2). Delivered at he Fourth Conference of Recovering the U. S. Hispanic Literary Heritage, Interpreting and Contextualizing the Recovered Text, University of Houston, November 1996.

[17] Rodrigo Lazo's research on nineteenth-century Cuban exiles in New York suggests a similar pattern of collusion with U. S. institutions of colonialism. In his paper "A Man of Action: Cirilo Villaverde as American Revolutionary Journalist," delivered at the Fourth Conference of Recovering U. S. Hispanic Literary Heritage, Lazo notes that certain Cuban exiles, in their desire to rid themselves of Spain, actively promoted U. S. annexation of Cuba.

Part II

**Women's Voices:
The Construction of
Ethnic Gender Identities**

Los textos narrativos
y su importancia historiográfica:
Las memorias de Leonor Villegas de Magnón

Martha Eva Rocha Islas
Dirección Estudios Históricos—INAH

La historiografía sobre la Revolución Mexicana privilegió el mundo de la política, las acciones de guerra y los hechos trascendentales como su objeto de estudio, permaneciendo las mujeres en la bruma de la historia. Recientemente y cada vez más, la exploración sobre la actuación femenina en el periodo revolucionario ocupa la atención de los investigadores preocupados por desentrañar el papel de las mujeres como sujetos políticos y participativos, en la primera revolución social del presente siglo.

El reconocimiento de Veteranas de la Revolución que ostentaron a partir de los años cuarenta algunas de las mujeres que participaron en el movimiento armado de 1910–1917, me llevo a explorar en los papeles militares del Archivo de Veteranos de la Revolución, en la Secretaría de la Defensa Nacional, los motivos y significados que llevaron a las veteranas a escribir sus historias ¿Por qué y cómo escriben sus relatos? El hecho de escribir autobiografías, memorias, cartas o narraciones—géneros literarios distintos—, plantea una cuestión importante sobre el proceso del recordar, los usos de la memoria, y las formas de escritura.

La autobiografía proclama la dignidad de los destinos singulares, tiene la intención de registrar para sí mismo, pero también para los demás, los acontecimientos que merecen salvarse del olvido, en esta escritura los impulsos personales se ocultan en aras de la aparente objetividad del relato. Por el contrario, en las cartas personales podemos apreciar la libre voluntad de quien las escribe, la espontaneidad y frescura que contienen las correspondencias personales, particularmente las escritas por mujeres en una prosa rápida, coloquial y alejada de formalismos —ya que la temática es casi siempre de índole privada—, describe las preocupaciones más constantes, las emociones más íntimas, las anécdotas y noticias compartidas, en general constituyen un registro único de vida cotidiana.

Cuando nos referimos a la escritura de memorias, en ellas está siempre presente la intención de dejar registro del cúmulo de experiencias trasmisibles y sólo se realiza en el momento en que el autor piensa en sus lectores y diseña la trama de su relato. Los recuerdos pero también los olvidos intencionales o generadores de silencios en la narración, pasan por el tamiz de la memoria.

Fue precisamente el manuscrito en español de las "memorias noveladas" de Leonor Villegas de Magnón, además de la versión en inglés publicada bajo el título *The Rebel*,[1] los provocadores de algunas reflexiones que intentaré desarrollar a lo largo del artículo, así como destacar la importancia que tiene para la historiografía de la Revolución la tarea de recuperación de escritos surgidos de plumas femeninas. El género de autobiografía/memoria señala Clara Lomas en su excelente estudio introductorio al libro *The Rebel* "encarceló el relato de Villegas de Magnón en una forma narrativa que históricamente era privilegio de la autoridad, autoría y discurso masculinos, y que ignoraba o devaluaba esas mismas cualidades femeninas".[2]

El período revolucionario fue generador de múltiples relatos que intentaron explicar el significado y esencia histórica de las diversas acciones de sus protagonistas. Narraciones históricas, novelas, diarios y sobre todo memorias personales se transformaban en la novela de la Revolución Mexicana que como señala Marta Portal "imprecisamente encuadra la más importante narrativa mexicana del dieciseis al cuarenta y que se inscribe temporal y semiológicamente en el momento primero de la metáfora".[3] En esta narrativa se refleja la realidad de manera inmediata, el argumento lo constituyen los sucesos revolucionarios, las vivencias y experiencias compartidas, los personajes son los propios intérpretes, confundidos o no con el narrador, pero aún vivos y reconocibles. Es la llamada novela documental de la revolución. Tal género narrativo privilegió la publicación de textos surgidos de plumas varoniles.

La Rebelde, "versión novelada" de las memorias escritas por Leonor Villegas de Magnón deja ver dos preocupaciones presentes y constantes en el texto narrativo. Primero el testimonio escrito y aun fotográfico de la presencia y participación de las mujeres en el movimiento armado de 1910, las vivencias personales de la protagonista, su relación con los principales caudillos constitucionalistas y su compromiso con el Primer Jefe de escribir sobre los acontecimientos vividos en el México convulsionado por la guerra, pero sobre todo, llama la atención su preocupación por dejar constancia para la posteridad del trabajo realizado al lado de tantas mujeres que se involucraron en las tareas de guerra como enfermeras, cuya labor fue más allá de atender y curar heridos tanto en los campos de batalla como en los improvisados hospitales de sangre en casas particulares y con los recursos de los que simpatizaron con la causa constitucionalista. Y la segunda preocupación que se advierte ya en las últimas páginas del texto, es referir los esfuerzos de Leonor Villegas por conseguir el reconocimiento de veteranía para sus compañeras de lucha, en tanto lo consideraba un acto de justicia, así como conseguirles una pensión económica a la que creía firmemente tenían derecho.

La muerte del Primer Jefe, Venustiano Carranza, puso fin al arduo trabajo organizativo y político desempeñado por Leonor Villegas durante una década de lucha armada que enfrentó a los diversos grupos revolucionarios que se disputaban la dirección y el control del país. Así, 1920 significó la cancelación de los proyectos sustentados por el constitucionalismo y de las espectativas del grupo de colaboradores leales a Carranza, grupo al que también pertenecía la Rebelde.

La historiografía oficial sobre la participación femenina en el período de guerra sólo se ocupó en un principio de la creación mítica de mujeres valientes y aguerridas recogidas y popularizadas en los corridos, de la imagen idílica y heroica de las soldaderas[4] y de ciertas heroínas como Carmen Serdán, Juana Belén Gutiérrez de Mendoza, Dolores Jiménez y Muro. Una mayoría anónima y olvidada permanecía en los repositorios de archivos familiares, oficiales y aún en textos que escritos al fragor de la lucha armada y preparados como libros apenas concluida la guerra, esperaron inútilmente el interés de editores o bien de las instituciones gubernamentales, como fue el caso del manuscrito de *La Rebelde*. Los Talleres Gráficos de la Nación bajo el gobierno de Venustiano Carranza pudieron ser el espacio para la publicación del texto en español escrito en 1919. Como leemos en las propias memorias de Leonor Villegas, Carranza le confirió tal empresa y ella aceptó la responsabilidad: "Usted estará cerca de mí, dijo el Jefe, sabrá muchas cosas, observará más y algún día escribirá".[5] Sin embargo el manuscrito tuvo un fin trágico como la propia muerte de Carranza. No ocurrió lo mismo a la obra de Hermila Galindo, joven e inquieta feminista y también cercana colaboradora del Primer Jefe a quien en ediciones del gobierno[6] le fueron publicados sus libros, aunque también se retiró del escenario político en 1920.

¿Por qué motivo Villegas de Magnón no logró dar a conocer su relato al público de México y Estados Unidos entre 1920 y 1955? Se pregunta Clara Lomas y nos explica en la introducción de *The Rebel* que "las numerosas lecturas del texto otorgaron una evaluación crítica que de manera significativa selló el destino de su relato. [...] Las lecturas se hicieron en el interior de dos diferentes tradiciones "literarias" nacionales: las memorias posrrevolucionarias mexicanas y la tradición de la escritura de autobiografías en el mundo de habla inglesa. Varios procesos de marginalización colocaron el relato de Villegas de Magnón en las fronteras precarias, en particular en la situación marginal de las autobiografías de mujeres."[7]

Al inicio de la década de los sesenta, dos años después de rechazar el manuscrito de *La Rebelde,* el Instituto Nacional de Estudios Históricos de la Revolución Mexicana (INEHRM), publicó el primer libro de historia de la participación de las mujeres en la Revolución, de Angeles Mendieta Alatorre. Ironía de la vida, en él se omite el activismo de Leonor Villegas aun cuando la preocupación central del libro es:

Hablar de la mujer como heroína, de la que participó valerosamente en las causas nacionales, la que callada y con profunda abnegación colaboró con su dulzura en los hogares de aquellos que se entregaron a la violencia [...] de quienes impulsadas por su ingénita bondad de mujeres mexicanas, sus sentimientos humanitarios y nobilísimos y su amor a la causa que habían abrazado los padres, hermanos o parientes de algunas de ellas, actuaban varias señoritas y señoras de honorables familias de Monclova, cuyos nombres santificados por la caritativa tarea que se impusieron de cuidar y atender a los heridos, deben figurar en estas líneas como un homenaje merecido y como un recordatorio a su valor y altruismo . . .[8]

La historia de las mujeres lleva un largo camino recorrido y las líneas de investigación se mueven entre la búsqueda de los orígenes históricos de la opresión, el rescate del protagonismo femenino y los más recientes y novedosos estudios que abordan la problemática de las mujeres desde la perspectiva de género.[9] Los libros escritos en la posrrevolución sobre la participación femenina en la etapa armada (1910–1920) se inscribieron en la línea del protagonismo. En ellos quedó en evidencia la preocupación por el rescate y la recuperación del quehacer de las mujeres en la Revolución y por este motivo los textos comparten una estructura similar: la de los relatos biográficos, que cumplen la función de resaltar acciones "heroicas" realizadas por mujeres, rastrear su invisibilidad en los registros del pasado y mostrar su presencia en la historia.[10] Sin embargo las ausencias todavía son notorias, de ahí la importancia que reviste la aparición de relatos históricos como *La Rebelde*, que no sólo implican la recuperación de protagonistas que permanecían en el anonimato, sino que permiten adentrarnos en un proceso histórico-social, desde la mirada femenina. [11]

La singularidad de la producción historiográfica escrita por plumas femeninas sobre el movimiento armado de 1910 es que muestra individualidades cuyo protagonismo pareciera que se desarrolló en el aislamiento. La gran aportación de narraciones como *La Rebelde* radica en que contribuyen a partir del género biográfico a revelar la presencia de una generación de mujeres intelectuales que actuó con gran compromiso político desempeñando funciones de liderazgo. A partir de las vivencias del personaje de la rebelde se recupera en el relato una participación múltiple y colectiva.

Articular las redes, vínculos, posturas ideológicas y niveles de injerencia de las mujeres en el desarrollo de los acontecimientos políticos del país está aún por hacerse. Rebasar el nivel de la heroicidad como explicación de la actuación femenina (propia del pensamiento de la época y de los "naturales" atributos de la mujer: fragilidad, abnegación, dulzura que la mantenía en la pasividad y el aislamiento), ayudará en el análisis y comprensión de la rebeldía de las mujeres como agentes del cambio histórico y como objeto de consideraciones políticas.[12]

La vida privada poco se expresa en el texto de Leonor Villegas. El amor y la pasión, los afectos, los sentimientos, las tristezas y nostalgias, la separación de sus hijos (a los que deja en Laredo al cuidado de su hermano primero y más tarde, cumpliendo el ritual de las familias burguesas, los envía a internados americanos para su educación); los recuerdos de sus años formativos, del hogar y la familia, del apego al terruño, de una infancia feliz a la vez que dolorosa por la pérdida de su madre, aparecen en el relato como evocación y añoranza. Su escritura es, ante todo, el testimonio del compromiso político que establece con la revolución; su impulso y energía entregados al trabajo organizativo y colectivo constituyen los ingredientes de su historia novelada.

> Yo también amo . . . dijo la Rebelde . . . pero antes que el amor es el deber. ¿Por fin que es el amor? ¿Quién puede decirlo? ¿Quién puede descifrar ese incomparable sentimiento del alma que a un mismo tiempo es dicha y dolor? Esa fuerza poderosa que transforma el corazón humano, que purifica, que regenera a toda la humanidad . . . los destinos de mi vida han cambiado bruscamente, al ver estos heridos caer ante las balas de sus propios hermanos me he sentido conmovida.[13]

Los personajes revolucionarios en la narrativa de Villegas parecen tener objetivos más urgentes que el de enamorarse. La rebelde no fue la excepción, el sentimiento amoroso se expresa en la entrega piadosa y en el servicio al prójimo.

Las memorias de *La Rebelde* están escritas desde la percepción de una mujer burguesa, originaria del estado norteño de Tamaulipas, que vivió en ambos lados de la frontera, que realizó estudios profesionales en los Estados Unidos graduándose de profesora. Desde muy joven participó de las ideas democráticas y, ya casada y en la ciudad de México se involucró en los círculos de oposición que pugnaban por un cambio político para el país. Leonor Villegas pertenece a esa minoría de mujeres ilustradas formada en las últimas décadas del siglo pasado que desempeñaron un papel de liderazgo en las organizaciones que promovieron, que realizaron tareas peligrosas en la clandestinidad, que hicieron labor de proselitismo, que participaron en distintos ámbitos y con diferentes grados de responsabilidad, que colaboraron estrechamente con caudillos y jefes militares contribuyendo al éxito de la guerra con acciones propias; mujeres, en fin, que adquieren el carácter de excepcionales en tanto su participación coadyuvó en el largo plazo a modificar costumbres, actitudes, hábitos, es decir, las relaciones entre los géneros.

La historia personal y familiar de Leonor Villegas narrada en las memorias, muestra el rostro de una mujer inquieta y, en efecto, rebelde frente a las costumbres y prescripciones de moralidad religiosa que impregnaban la atmósfera porfiriana. Normas y comportamientos que establecían la separación de los ámbitos público y privado y la inserción de las mujeres en el espacio doméstico del hogar y la familia, que pretendía eternizarla en la inmovilidad de su función maternal sin concederle capacidad de acción e iniciativa. La rebeldía de Leonor no es fortuita sino que responde en parte al espíritu liberal imbuido en la sociedad norteamericana en la que se educó y que reconocía la importancia de la formación escolar de la mujer pues, al rebasar los límites estrictos del hogar, la libraba de la ignorancia. Al mismo tiempo en la capital mexicana, ideólogos y educadores porfiristas aún sostenían un debate sobre la pertinencia y nivel de educación que debía impartirse a las mujeres. Persistía la idea de que la preparación intelectual las alejaría de sus funciones atávicas de esposas y madres.

La herencia de la Ilustración y el positivismo como ideología sustentadora del Estado porfirista, bajo los paradigmas de modernidad, urbanización, crecimiento y progreso, concibió a la educación como una forma de ascenso social. El reconocimiento de la capacidad intelectual formalizó para la mujer la posibilidad de acceder a una educación escolarizada en condiciones de igualdad. Esta política educativa comenzó poco a poco a dar frutos. Tanto en la capital como en la provincia mexicana se abrieron escuelas para niñas y la creación de la Escuela Normal de Profesoras en 1889, dio a la profesión de maestra una importancia formal de la que hasta entonces carecía; con ello el magisterio se convirtió en la gran oportunidad de profesionalización para las mujeres. Otras opciones eran las carreras cortas impartidas en la Escuela de Artes y Oficios y la de enfermería, considerada también propia del sexo femenino por sus "naturales dotes maternales". Las profesiones universitarias aún se mantenían en la división de varoniles y propias para mujeres; sin embargo, en esta etapa se traspasan las barreras genéricas y reconocemos a las primeras profesionistas en el campo de la ciencia y la cultura.

La prensa fue el espacio desde donde, en la última década del siglo XIX, el grupo de mujeres ilustradas empezó a cuestionar la función social femenina. Profesoras, periodistas y escritoras fundaron revistas y periódicos dirigidos a mujeres para expresar su inconformidad frente a las desigualdades entre los sexos y la separación de los ámbitos privado y público que les negaba la oportunidad de participar en las esferas del poder y la política.[14]

Los movimientos feministas europeos y el sufragista norteamericano, y más concretamente la presencia de mujeres extranjeras en el país que habían bebido en otros veneros, se deja sentir en los escritos de las nuevas portavoces de las ideas emancipadoras, de los derechos y prerrogativas de las mujeres mexicanas convirtiéndose en la vanguardia dedicada a identificar las reivindicaciones más urgentes y a pugnar por la dignificación de la mujer en la sociedad acorde con el espíritu progresista e innovador de la época.[15]

La guerra como período de excepción, funciona como un detonador de lo aprendido y propicia en sus protagonistas un acelerado proceso de cambio que las va involucrando en una lucha social en la que influye el contacto con realidades que rebasan el ámbito inmediato de la vida cotidiana contribuyendo a modificar conductas tradicionales. No fue entonces la Revolución de 1910 el parteaguas que cuestionó la subordinación femenina, si bien es cierto que el período de lucha armada acentuó la participación de las mujeres en el escenario político frente al deterioro cada vez mayor de las condiciones sociales y económicas del país.

A lo largo de su relato Leonor Villegas se propone hacer explícito el trabajo que realizaron las enfermeras, rendir tributo al valor y abnegación con el que lo desempeñaron. Soporte indispensable en la guerra, además del cuidado y atención de los heridos—labor humanitaria y por extensión femenina—, adquirieron

diversos niveles de compromiso y responsabilidad. Involucrarse como enfermeras significó para estas mujeres la alteración de su vida cotidiana que transcurría
en la quietud de la provincia mexicana, y en no pocas ocasiones provocó la dis-
gregación familiar. En los campos de batalla enfrentaron los riesgos de tiroteos,
asaltos y tomas de plaza, aventura llena de avatares en su constante desplaza-
miento por diversos lugares del país, amores abandonados en aras de las propias
convicciones políticas.terminada la guerra fueron olvidadas, en la medida en
que la historia de su participación proviene menos del relato femenino y más de
la mirada de los hombres centrada en el recuento de los grandes acontecimientos. Leonor Villegas rubrica así su manuscrito: "la historia relatará los hechos
militares, aquí solo toca hacer vivir y recordar a las heroicas olvidadas".[16] Su
propia percepción de lo público/privado, masculino/femenino es paradójica. Las
acciones militares competen a los hombres, las realizadas por las mujeres son
actos heroicos y merecen el reconocimiento de la sociedad. Su manuscrito se
ubica en la década de los veinte, si bien es cierto fue a partir de estos años de rea-
comodo de la sociedad en general, que las mujeres experimentaron una serie de
cambios resultantes de sus experiencias durante la lucha armada, no obstante su
concepción del mundo, las representaciones de la masculinidad y de la feminit-
dad, los papeles génericos: actitudes y conductas no corresponden a la vorágine
de los veintes. La construcción de los géneros refuerza o modifica las formas
simbólicas en cada etapa histórica; de ahí que el relato de Villegas insista en res-
catar a las mujeres como actores sociales. Cumple una función ontológica al
reconstruir y exaltar sus acciones realizadas en el pasado, para expresar su
estructuración del mundo identificada con un sistema de valores y significados
provenientes del patriarcado.

La segunda preocupación de la autora de *La Rebelde*—como ya se señaló—
fue lograr el reconocimiento oficial para sus compañeras como Veteranas de la
Revolución y conseguir para ellas una pensión del ejército, actividad a la que
dedicó el esfuerzo de sus últimos años hasta su muerte ocurrida en 1955.

El gobierno de Lázaro Cárdenas (1934–1940) fue, en muchos sentidos, la
culminación de los procesos político-sociales originados en la Revolución.Trató
de hacer efectivas las demandas por las que hombres y mujeres habían luchado
en la guerra civil. En el aspecto militar abrió un espacio de reconocimiento para
todos aquellos revolucionarios sobrevivientes de 1910 y para llevar a efecto tal
disposición se formó la Comisión Pro-Veteranos de la Revolución,[17] dependient-
te de la Secretaría de la Defensa Nacional. Esta comisión fue la encargada de
estudiar, dictaminar y entregar las condecoraciones al mérito revolucionario y las
recompensas estipuladas en el decreto presidencial de octubre de 1939. [18]

Presentaron documentación ex combatientes hombres y mujeres[19] de distint-
ta condición social y que ostentaron diversos grados militares en los ejércitos
revolucionarios. Amnistiados o bien retirados, viejos en su mayoría, sobrevivían
con muchas dificultades en el México de los años cuarenta. Algunos de los veteranos militaban en las filas del nuevo Ejército Mexicano. El Instructivo de la

Comisión no es explícito en lo relativo a las recompensas económicas, pero es de suponer que el interés de quienes acudían era conseguir la protección económica mediante una pensión o jubilación además de ser reconocidos como veteranos, hecho que los colocaría en una situación de prestigio.

El reconocimiento de veterano se otorgaba—según señala el Reglamento— a quienes hubieran participado en la lucha durante los períodos determinados oficialmente como revolucionarios. El primero, el maderista, cubría los servicios activos, militares o civiles, prestados contra la dictadura porfirista, dentro del lapso comprendido entre el 19 de noviembre de 1910 y el 15 de mayo de 1911. El segundo, el constitucionalista, comprendía los servicios civiles o militares encaminados a combatir a la usurpación huertista, dentro del lapso de 20 de febrero de 1913 al 15 de agosto de 1914,[20] fecha en que Carranza se levantó en armas, seguido por viejos y leales maderistas que enarbolaban la bandera de la legalidad constitucional.

La derrota del ejército federal el 14 de agosto de 1914 y la firma de los *Tratados de Teoloyucan*, pusieron fin a la Revolución desde la mirada oficial. Se inicia el licenciamiento de tropas que en la realidad no operó. El divisionismo al interior del constitucionalismo motivó la lucha de facciones. Los movimientos populares continuarían en pie de lucha porque no veían satisfechas sus demandas.

La participación revolucionaria de quienes solicitaban el reconocimiento de veteranía debía ser calificada como "importante" por dos o más personas que ya tuvieran acreditada su personalidad militar.Debían además llenar un formulario y anexar los documentos originales—en caso de conservarlos—que comprobaran su actuación: nombramientos y grados militares alcanzados, hojas de servicio, fotografías, nombramientos de puestos administrativos en el gobierno de la Revolución, correspondencia intercambiada con los principales jefes, entre otros.

A la muerte de Carranza, la lealtad y admiración al *Varón de Cuatro Ciénegas*, llevaron a Leonor Villegas a retirarse de la actividad revolucionaria y a refugiarse por un tiempo en la tarea magisterial. La casa paterna de Laredo, Texas, fue el sitio donde establececió un colegio de niñas para ayudarse a mitigar el dolor de la derrota, mientras las pugnas entre los grupos políticos reconocían aguas más tranquilas que le permitieran reanudar su tarea de justicia.

La recepción en Laredo, Texas, de un telegrama de las compañeras de lucha Trini y Evita Flores Blanco motivaron su traslado a la ciudad de México. "Véngase, traiga consigo sus documentos, preséntelos para que le den sus correspondientes condecoraciones y se acuerden que algo le deben".[21] Leonor Villegas presentó sus papeles a la Comisión Pro-Veteranos de la Revolución el primero de enero de 1940 y se quedó a vivir en la ciudad de México hasta su muerte.

El expediente de Leonor Villegas de Magnón registra su ingreso a la Revolución en 1910 con Juan Sánchez Azcona, Emeterio Flores y Melquiades

García. En 1910 este último era secretario de la Junta Insurreccional del movimiento maderista en Laredo, Texas, en 1913 agente comercial de la revolución constitucionalista y de 1914 a 1920 cónsul de México en Laredo. Fue García quien certificó las actividades revolucionarias de Leonor Villegas en diciembre de 1939.

> En 1910 y 1911 se distinguió como activa propagandista de las ideas libertarias. En abril de 1913 cuando el Corl. Jesús Carranza atacó la ciudad de Laredo, Tamps., la señora Magnón organizó la brigada Cruz Blanca; en enero de 1914 cuando el Gral. Pablo González atacó la misma ciudad de Laredo la señora auxiliada por un grupo de damas y caballeros estableció en dos amplios salones de la propiedad de la familia Villegas, el hospital de sangre en donde varios jefes, oficiales y cientos de soldados de la Revolución fueron atendidos. Colaboró inteligentemente en las columnas del periódico revolucionario *El Progreso* del cual el suscrito fue uno de los editores y redactores.[22]

El general de brigada Arnulfo González Medina expidió el segundo comprobante el 10 de noviembre de 1939, en ese entonces director de Justicia y Pensiones de la recién creada Secretaría de la Defensa Nacional.

La profesión magisterial y el trabajo periodístico realizado por Leonor Villegas fueron compartidos por algunas de las veteranas reconocidas, lo que confirma la presencia de una generación de mujeres ilustradas que se involucraron activamente en la lucha armada.

> Las señoritas profesoras Blacayer, [sic] hermanas del ferrocarrilero del mismo nombre ellas nos ayudan en Monterrey, en Saltillo la señorita profesora Rosaura Flores [. . .] culta joven profesora de la facultad de Saltillo, alentó la causa maderista con su brillante oratoria . . . La señorita Trini había sido jefe de telégrafos durante la campaña maderista y había pasado los primeros telegramas del señor presidente Francisco I. Madero y más luego los del Gral. Pablo González, muchas veces estuvieron en peligro sus vidas, permanecieron en sus puestos hasta el triunfo del señor Francisco I. Madero y ahora amenazadas a cada rato abandonan su puesto y vienen en camino a Laredo, deben llegar de un día a otro, todos tenemos la contraseña Constitución C.B.C.[23]

No fue fortuita la incorporación casi inmediata de las profesoras en tareas propagandísticas y sobre todo en actividades no visibles pero necesarias para el triunfo de la Revolución. Las cualidades características de este grupo de veteranas: aplomo, audacia, sagacidad—aunque por tradición identificadas con lo masculino—, hacían falta en las tareas de proselitismo, en las más concretas de reclutamiento voluntario y en las más delicadas de trasmisión de información confidencial. De tal suerte que su desempeño implicó para ellas grandes riesgos. El miedo a ser descubiertas, los cateos en sus domicilios, la vigilancia y persecución policíaca e incluso la agresión y encarcelamiento que algunas de ellas padecieron no las amedrentaron, por el contrario, hicieron de su trabajo revolucionario el motivo mismo de su existencia.

De los papeles que comprueban estar en poder de la señora Magnón, aunque algunos fueron destruidos al verificarse un cateo en su domicilio en Laredo, Texas, el mes de febrero del presente año en vista de una orden expedida por las respectivas autoridades.[24]

Para otorgar las condecoraciones debidas a las mujeres que realizaron tareas de guerra dentro de estos períodos, sus acciones fueron medidas a partir del rango en que se les clasificó y por el que fueron reconocidas como: "servicios civiles" prestados a la Revolución, no obstante que los niveles de responsabilidad en la lucha, el desempeño en la jerarquización de las tareas, el involucramiento y compromiso adquirido, a más de los riesgos a los que estuvieron expuestas rebasaban ese rango de "servicios civiles" según se desprende de los relatos.

El estudio de los expedientes de mujeres veteranas en el archivo militar, supone de entrada el encuentro con todas aquellas mujeres que, combatiendo fusil en mano y bajo la presión de tiroteos, emboscadas, asaltos, persecuciones, cercos, incorporadas con jerarquía militar en los distintos ejércitos revolucionarios, adquirieron sus grados y ascensos por méritos en campaña. El mito de todas aquellas guerrilleras inspiradoras de corridos y leyendas populares cobraría un rostro en los papeles del archivo militar. Sin embargo, sargentos, subtenientes, capitanas y coronelas fueron las excepciones en el universo de veteranas reconocidas. A todas ellas guerrear les significó adoptar una conducta viril que empezaba desde el atuendo: cambiar las enaguas por los pantalones.

Tal fue el caso de María de Jesús González, también veterana reconocida y que el relato de *La rebelde* rescata y describe como una valiente y aguerrida mujer, profesora de Monterrey, constitucionalista, correo, agente confidencial que realizó tareas delicadas y peligrosas. Leonor Villegas pugnó para que el Primer Jefe le diera nombramiento de teniente coronel de caballería pues era excelente jinete y no conocía el miedo.[25] María de Jesús siempre vistió como hombre hasta el triunfo de la Revolución porque un soldado empuñando armas sólo como hombre podía sobrevivir. La guerra destruye las rígidas diferencias entre los géneros. Los límites en las conductas y actividades de las mujeres se desmoronan y con ello se subvierte aunque por tiempo breve, el ordenamiento genérico de la sociedad.

El rango militar que habían alcanzado las mujeres durante la lucha armada fue desconocido casi de inmediato, como lo expresa la circular #78 expedida por la Secretaría de Guerra y Marina el 18 de marzo de 1916. "Se declaran nulos todos los nombramientos militares expedidos en favor de señoras y señoritas, cualesquiera que hayan sido los servicios que éstas hayan prestado".[26] Tal disposición les cerraba la posibilidad de reingresar al ejército, de pertenecer a la Legión de Honor en su calidad de militares y finalmente les negaba el beneficio de una pensión de retiro. Llegados los tiempos de paz, la institución castrense no sólo soslayó, sino que ignoró la participación femenina en los ejércitos pues reconocer su presencia significaba violentar una institución por excelencia patriarcal. Una reforma al reglamento de la Legión de Honor Mexicana creada en 1949, abrió las puertas a los civiles, consecuentemente a las mujeres. Algunas de ellas fueron reconocidas como legionarias, sin que esto expresara el reconocimiento de su jerarquía militar y menos el derecho a una jubilación.

El 14 de febrero de 1941 Leonor Villegas fue reconocida Veterana de la Revolución por los dos períodos oficiales certificando también sus servicios el Lic. Miguel Alessio Robles, los generales Felipe Zepeda, Pablo González, Eduardo Hay, Felipe Aguirre, Antonio I. Villarreal y el Ing. Federico Cervantes, recibió las condecoraciones respectivas el día 22 de febrero, aniversario luctuoso de Francisco I. Madero.

Las vivencias personales de Leonor Villegas cobran sentido en el conjunto de experiencias de las veteranas, que nos permite armar esa historia de minucias, basada en la muy particular percepción de cada una de ellas. Esta historia se enriquece con la aparición de relatos como el de Leonor Villegas, que no sólo registra las tareas desempeñadas por las mujeres en la guerra sino que les da un significado: agitador, conspirador, espía, propagandista, correo o enlace. Así se explica ese protagonismo femenino tan ninguneado y se hace visible la presencia de las mujeres como actores sociales comprometidos con el devenir histórico y los problemas de su país.

> María se levantó de la mesa e hizo sus últimos arreglos, en un zapato una navaja, en la cintura la cartuchera y una pistola, una bolsa de provisiones y dinero suficiente para llegar al primer campo rebelde.[27]

Una primera reflexión sobre el carácter de la información contenida en los expedientes de mujeres en el archivo militar revela que en sus páginas coexisten dos historias que se enlazan entre sí: la historia oficial e institucional contenida en el llenado del formato (solicitudes presentadas entre 1940 y 1954) y la historia personal construida con los recuerdos de las protagonistas o bien de los compañeros de lucha, jefes o caudillos que extienden los comprobantes para avalar la actividad revolucionaria de las solicitantes. Las descripciones son un relato retrospectivo en prosa que refiere la participación de las mujeres en el conflicto armado, en las narraciones se entretejen los recuerdos personales con la cronología de los acontecimientos revolucionarios consignados en la historia oficial; así encontramos entreverado lo realmente vivido con la recreación hecha a distancia de un pasado que en su momento—un presente intensamente vivido—significó para ellas la defensa de un objetivo común.

En la lectura de los relatos de las veteranas se advierte lo que Marta Portal denomina: tiempo histórico y tiempo narrativo.[28] En las narraciones hay una concepción del tiempo, posterior al acontecimiento y anterior al tiempo narrativo. Las historias escritas narran acontecimientos vividos entre 1910–1915, pero en el momento en que las escriben—el del tiempo narrativo—hay un distanciamiento y un proceso de recreación. La Revolución es el referente porque fue el tiempo de tránsito que hizo posible el nuevo presente, desde el que ahora se narra y se acompaña de la valoración de personas y acontecimientos. Los recuerdos llevados a la escritura registran las experiencias de lucha compartidas pero también las adquiridas a posteriori, los relatos se vuelven críticos y expresan tanto la satisfacción del deber cumplido en la Revolución como un reclamo por el olvido en que quedaron sus protagonistas.

El relato de Leonor Villegas rescata particularmente el trabajo organizativo desempeñado en la Cruz Blanca Nacional. Cuando se separó del ejército era Presidenta de la benéfica institución, nombramiento expedido por el propio Carranza que anexa a su expediente como documento probatorio.[29] Incluye además un detallado informe de los gastos efectuados en la organización de la Cruz Blanca y las actividades realizadas al frente de la institución; cubre de abril de 1913 al 20 de agosto de 1915 y fue entregado al Primer Jefe en Veracruz.

La historia oficial corresponde a la información que las mujeres registran en la solicitud de estudio. El llenado del formato entrega una confesión, un testimonio que apunta al reconocimiento de "revolucionaria" en términos oficiales y que por lo mismo debió adecuarse a un formulario pensado primero en función de ex combatientes concebidos como hombres y como militares. Preguntas como: "fecha de su ingreso a la Revolución y grado con el que se inició. Nombre de los jefes con los que militó. Regiones donde operó. Contra que fuerzas enemigas combatió. Grado con el que se separó del ejército", son preguntas que difícilmente pudo contestar la mayoría de profesoras y enfermeras que con justicia esperaban ser reconocidas como veteranas. Las mujeres respondieron elaborando mentalmente las preguntas del cuestionario y adecuándolas a las actividades que realizaron, a los grupos revolucionarios en los que participaron y a las organizaciones femeniles a las que se adscribieron.[30]

Cuando se les pregunta el grado con el que se iniciaron, las mujeres responden señalando el carácter de su participación: espía, correo, enlace, propagandista, agente confidencial, enfermera, etc. Estas actividades implicaron diversos niveles de compromiso: la preparación, escritura y distribución de propaganda, de proclamas y manifiestos; la agitación en mítines de protesta; la introducción al país de armas y pertrechos de guerra; la trasmisión de información confidencial y el espionaje en los campos enemigos, la atención y curación de heridos y la colaboración en tareas de reclutamiento.

Como integrantes de la Cruz Blanca Constitucionalista realizaron sus miembros importantes trabajos como la conducción de parque y municiones, dar asilo a los soldados de la Revolución proporcionando medios a muchos de ellos para su incorporación al ejército libertador . . . Desde que los constitucionalistas atacaron Nuevo Laredo los instalamos provisionalmente en los Hospitales de sangre establecidos en Laredo, Texas. 150 heridos los trasladamos al hospital en casa de la señora Magnón. Permanecieron por 3 meses los soldados al cuidado de la Cruz Blanca Constitucionlista en diferentes establecimientos, 25 fueron llevados a casas particulares encargándose nuestra asociación del cuidado de 125 soldados. Todos los gastos por enfermería, asistencia, lavado, etc. pagado durante estos 3 meses, la cantidad reunida por donativos, festivales de caridad, contribuciones del comercio y de otras varias partes del Estado de Texas que espontánemanente ayudaron. Prestaron su servicio como 50 señoras y señoritas quienes asistieron eficazmente a los siguientes médicos: Halsell, Suavignet, Cook, Wilcox, Garloc, Leal, Lowry y De la Garza. Conforme los soldados se iban aliviando, las enfermeras y los partidarios de nuestra causa proporcionaban los medios conducentes a la reincorporación del Ejército con peligro de ser descubiertas.[31]

Para contestar el formulario hubo que poner a trabajar, más que la memoria, la imaginación: había que destacar aquellos episodios que la historia oficial había determinado como "importantes" y olvidarse de los que la Revolución institucionalizada mantenía en descrédito .

Leonor Villegas en su carácter de organizadora de los servicios médicos del constitucionalismo militó en varias divisiones: Nordeste, Centro, División del Norte, que dependía del Noroeste pero que actuó como fuerza independiente. Las regiones de operación. Prácticamente la República Mexicana. Tamaulipas, Chihuahua, Coahuila, Zacatecas, Nuevo León, San Luis Potosí, Querétaro, la Capital, Durango, Veracruz. Los jefes con los que militó: con los principales caudillos revolucionarios, desde el propio Carranza, Francisco Villa, Felipe Angeles, Pánfilo Natera, Maclovio Herrera, Jesús Carranza, Pablo González, Gustavo Espinosa Mireles, Antonio I. Villarreal, Eulalio Gutiérrez.[32]

El expediente en el archivo militar de Leonor Villegas resulta lacónico: cuando presenta su solicitud de veteranía en los años cuarenta ya hacía dos décadas que había escrito sus "memorias noveladas" tanto en español como en inglés y había buscado inútilmente editor para el manuscrito. La aparición editorial de *La Rebelde* enriquece a los papeles oficiales localizados en el archivo militar; en su conjunto constituyen una historia amalgamada por múltiples experiencias y una contribución al rescate de voces olvidadas, descubre otro nivel de colaboración femenina en la transformación del México de 1910.

Finalmente la recuperación de escritos biográficos inéditos representa una contribución historiográfica en la medida en que permite explicar la presencia femenina en la historia desde la producción escrita por ellas. No sólo hacer visible la actuación de las mujeres—como señala Joan W. Scott—sirve a un proceso compensatorio: insistir en su activa participación en el pasado, sino "preguntarse el por qué y cómo las mujeres se vuelven invisibles para la historia, cuando de hecho fueron actores sociales y políticos en el pasado".[33]

La historia de Villegas como la de muchas veteranas cuyas vivencias rebasaron el estricto mundo femenino reducido al espacio cerrado del hogar y la familia, de la cotidianidad de la vida privada, muestran cómo a partir del desempeño de una actividad tradicional femenina, trascendieron las barreras genéricas y propiciaron la construcción de nuevas identidades que en el largo plazo contribuyeron a modificar su propia visión del mundo.

Notas

[1] Leonor Villegas de Magnón. *The Rebel.* Ed. Clara Lomas. Houston: Arte Público, 1994.

[2] *Ibidem*, p. 31.

[3] Marta Portal. *Proceso narrativo de la Revolución Mexicana*, Espasa-Calpe, 1980, p. 297.

[4] Martha Eva Rocha. "Presencia de las mujeres en la Revolución Mexicana: Soldaderas y revolucionarias" en: *Memoria del Congreso Internacional sobre la Revolución Mexicana.* México, Gobierno de SLP/INEHRM, 1991, T. I.

[5] Leonor Villegas de Magnón, *La Rebelde*, Manuscrito, p.151.

[6] Hermila Galindo. *La doctrina Carranza y el acercamiento indolatino.* México, Talleres Gráficos de la Imprenta Nacional, 1919. *Un presidenciable, el general Pablo González.* México, Talleres Gráficos de la Imprenta Nacional, 1919.

[7] Leonor Villegas, *The Rebel, op.cit.* p. 31.

[8] Angeles Mendieta Alatorre. *La mujer en la Revolución Mexicana.* México, Talleres Gráficos de la Nación, 1961, pp. 17, 83. (Biblioteca del INEHRM, No. 23)

[9] Mary Nash. *Presencia y protagonismo. Aspectos de la historia de la Mujer.* Barcelona, España. Ediciones del Serbal, 1984. Carmen Ramos, compiladora. *Género e Historia.* México, UAM/Instituto Mora, 1992. (Antologías Universitarias)

[10] Martha Rocha. "Nuestras propias voces. Las mujeres en la Revolución Mexicana" en *Historias 25*, México, Dirección de Estudios Históricos/INAH, octubre 1990–marzo 1991. Y Ana Lau Javien. "Las mujeres en la Revolución Mexicana. Un punto de vista historiográfico." *Secuencia*, 33, sept.-diciembre 1995.

[11] El problema de la invisibilidad ocupa un lugar importante en los estudios historiográficos sobre las mujeres. Lo más novedoso en materia biográfica sobre el período revolucionario es la aparición del *Diccionario Histórico y Biográfico de la Revolución Mexicana*, publicado por el INEHRM en 8 tomos entre 1990 y 1994. Uno de sus méritos es precisamente el registro de mujeres que participaron en la lucha armada: 2000 perfiles biográficos recogen sus páginas.

[12] Joan Wallach Scott. "El problema de la invisibilidad" en Carmen Ramos. *Género e Historia, op. cit.*

[13] Leonor Villegas. *La Rebelde, op. cit.* pp. 103, 104.

[14] Martha Rocha. "Nuestras propias voces . . . ." *op. cit.* pp. 112, 113.

[15] Laureana Wright de Kleinhans, dirigió la publicación *Violetas de Anáhuac* en 1887, espacio dedicado a la participación, reflexión y discusión de los problemas de las mujeres. Ella se mostraba partidaria de la emancipación femenina y pugnaba por la regeneración de su sexo, en ello iba la convicción de que la mujer podía y debía recuperarse como mujer en el plano intelectual por medio de la instrucción y la educación. "La emancipación de la mujer por el estudio" en *La Mujer Mexicana*, 1905. *Apud.* Martha Rocha . *El Album de la mujer. Antología ilustrada de las mexicanas.* V. IV, pp. 214–221.

[16] Leonor Villegas. *La Rebelde, op. cit.* p. 162.

[17] El Gral. de Div. Jesús Agustín Castro, en su calidad de secretario de la Secretaría de la Defensa Nacional, forma la Comisión Pro-Veteranos de la Revolución, así como el Instructivo con el cual se regirá dicha Comisión y que deberá empezar a operar a partir del 1o. de marzo de 1939. Archivo Histórico de la Secretaría de la Defensa Nacional. Sección Veteranos. En lo sucesivo haremos referencia al archivo bajo las siglas AHSDN.

[18] Decreto #659 expedido por el presidente Lázaro Cárdenas el 5 de octubre de 1939 que crea la condecoración al Mérito Revolucionario y el reglamento a que deberá sujetarse.

[19] Una lista de 395 mujeres con expediente en el Archivo de Veteranos de la Secretaría de la Defensa Nacional registra el libro de Angeles Mendieta. *La mujer en la Revolución Mexicana.* Sin embargo no todos los expedientes pudieron localizarse, dos de ellos corresponden a hombres: Nieves Brindis de la Flor y Matilde Chavarría Rey, hecho muy común en el período ya que el mismo nombre se usaba indistintamente para ambos sexos. También fueron localizados otros expedientes no incluidos en la relación de Mendieta.

[20] Instructivo de la Comisión Pro-Veteranos de la Revolución. Artículos 3o. y 4o. AHSDN.

[21] Leonor Villegas. *La Rebelde, op. cit.* p. 296.

[22] Exp. Leonor Villegas. AHSDN.

[23] Leonor Villegas. *La Rebelde, op. cit.* pp. 101, 102.

[24] Exp. Leonor Villegas. AHSDN.

[25] Leonor Villegas. *La Rebelde, op. cit.*

[26] Véase en expediente D/112/365 María Teresa Rodríguez. AHSDN.

[27] Leonor Villegas. *La Rebelde, op. cit.* p. 102.

[28] Marta Portal, *op. cit.* p. 319.

[29] Nombramiento de autorización expedido a la Sra. Leonor Villegas de Magnón como Presidenta de la Cruz Blanca Constitucionalista para que organice la benéfica institución en todos los estados de la República con la nueva designación de Cruz Blanca Nacional reconociendo los trabajos anteriores a esta fecha. Constitución y Reformas. Saltillo, Coahuila, 8 de junio de 1914. Rúbrica: Venustiano Carranza. Exp. Leonor Villegas. AHSDN.

[30] El estudio de antecedentes revolucionarios contiene los siguientes datos: Nombre, Ser natural de, Edad, Fecha de su ingreso a la Revolución y Grado con el que se inició. Nombre de los jefes con los que militó. Regiones donde operó. Contra que fuerzas enemigas combatió. Si tiene expediente en la SDN. Si se encuentra separado del servicio activo de las armas, decir los motivos y fecha de su separación. Lugar y fecha. Firma del interesado. Dirección actual. AHSDN.

[31] Exp. Leonor Villegas. Cruz Blanca Constitucionalista. Informe de sus trabajos. Nuevo Laredo, Tamps., marzo 17 de 1916. AHSDN.

[32] *Ibidem.*

[33] Joan W. Scott. "El problema de la invisibilidad*", op. cit.* pp. 46, 47.

Bibliografía

Diccionario Histórico y Biográfico de la Revolución Mexicana. 8 tomos. México, INEHRM, 1990-1994.

Galindo Hermila. *La doctrina Carranza y el acercamiento indolatino.* México, Talleres Gráficos de la Imprenta Nacional, 1919.

————.*Un presidenciable, el general Pablo González.* México, Talleres Gráficos de la Imprenta Nacional, 1919.

Mendieta Alatorre, Angeles. *La mujer en la Revolución Mexicana.* México, Talleres Gráficos de la Nación, 1961. (Biblioteca INEHRM 9, 23)

Nash, Mary. *Presencia y protagonismo. Aspectos de la historia de la mujer.* Barcelona, España, Ediciones del Serbal, 1984.

Portal, Marta. *Proceso narrativo de la Revolución Mexicana.* España, Espasa-Calpe, 1980.

Ramos, Carmen (comp.). *Género e Historia.* México, UNAM instituto Mora, 1992. (Antologías Universitarias).

Rocha Islas, Martha Eva. *El Album de la mujer. Antología Ilustrada de las mexicanas.T. IV El Porfiriato y la Revolución.* México, INAH, 1991.

————. Nuestras propias voces. Las mujeres en la Revolución Mexicana, en *Historias 25.* México, Dirección de Estudios Históricos/INAH, octubre 1990-marzo 1991.

————. Presencia de las mujeres en la Revolución Mexicana. Soldaderas y revolucionarias. *Memoria del Congreso Internacional sobre la Revolución Mexicana.* México, Gobierno de SLP/INEHRM, 1991, T. I.

Representing Mexico: María Cristina Mena's Short Fiction in *The Century Magazine*, 1913–1916

Amy Doherty
University of Chicago

Born in Mexico City, María Cristina Mena (1893–1965) was sent to New York City by her family in 1904 at the age of fourteen, before the Mexican Revolution of 1910 (Simmen 39). There, she lived with family friends, continued her education, and published short stories in *The Century Magazine* between 1913 and 1916. As a writer for *Century*, Mena was working within a system of pre-existing literary and visual images of Mexico. As I compare three of Mena's short stories, "John of God, the Water-Carrier" (November 1913), "The Birth of the God of War" (May 1914), and "The Vine-Leaf" (December 1914) with *Century*'s representations of Mexico, I will analyze the trope of vision in a magazine devoted to images.[1] Like today's late twentieth-century Chicana writers, Mena turns to Guadalupe, Coatlicue, and La Malinche[2] to revive the spiritual and the truth that can't be seen. Mena recognized that the holder of the gaze had the power in the early twentieth century, and she responded with her own vision of Mexico.

Like many marginalized authors, Mena broke into publishing through the genre of the short story. Mary Louise Pratt's analysis of the relationship between the short story and "marginal subjects" is pertinent to Mena's position as a writer in the United States. Pratt writes:

> Obviously, whether a given subject matter is central or peripheral, established or new in a literature has a great deal to do with what is central and peripheral in the community outside its literature, a great deal to do, that is, with values, and with socioeconomic, political and cultural realities. In some cases at least, there seem to develop dialectical correspondences between minor or marginal genres and what are evaluated as minor or marginal subjects. (188)

Although short stories have traditionally been considered minor works, this genre allowed Mena to present many aspects of life in Mexico, including folktales or, more accurately, *cuentos*. As Gloria Velásquez-Treviño writes, "The word 'tale' may indicate make believe while the word *cuento* implies knowledge and experience in Mexican oral tradition" (27). As Pratt writes, the short story is not a lesser version of a literary genre, but "the form best-suited to reproducing the length of most oral speech events" (190). Through the short story, then, Mena influenced the representation of Mexico in *Century*, and gained a measure of authority for herself. She was eventually recognized as "the foremost interpreter of Mexican life" in *The Household Magazine*,[3] and as her *New York Times* obituary states, she "dedicated her work 'to bringing to the American public the life of the Mexican people'" ("Mrs. Henry Chambers").

To contextualize the climate in which Mena wrote her first short stories, it is necessary to examine the audience and purpose of *Century Magazine*. Targeting a genteel audience, the publication attempted to strike a balance between pleasing its "cultivated readers," "lovers of artistry and subtlety,"[4] and presenting a variety of cultural experience in its fiction. Through a careful composition of travel narratives, political articles, fiction, and poetry, the publication played on the readers' desires to travel and experience the foreign, as well as their fears of infiltration. As the magazine struggled to maintain a "common quality" in its fiction ("Topics of the Time" 951), Mena was commissioned to contribute to *Century*'s literary project, which, in inviting her, opened the doors to a wider variety of fiction but still sought to appeal to a "cultivated" white audience.

Century Magazine reflected U. S. society's ambivalence toward immigration during World War I and the Mexican Revolution. The articles that appeared in *Century* along with Mena's work were biased against immigrants. For example, in "American and Immigrant Blood: A Study of the Social Effects of Immigration," Edward Alsworth Ross, a noted sociologist, lists such threats to Anglo-Americans as "illiteracy," "peonage," "insanity among the foreign born," and "social decline" (December 1913, 225-32), indicating a desire to maintain a division between "the domestic" and "the foreign." When the Mexican Revolution further threatened U. S. borders, the editors turned to essays which struggled with the question of U. S. intervention in Mexico. For example, in "The Mexican Menace" (*Century*, January 1914), W. Morgan Shuster questions whether the United States should aid in deposing Huerta, who seized power from President Madero. Fearing that the United States could incite a "war between the Mexican and the American peoples" (599), Shuster argues that the United States should intervene in Mexico—but only with outside help: "Acting alone in Mexico, the American nation will only soil its hands in a useless, aimless, inglorious struggle with a weaker, if misguided, people" (602). Working against a stream of paternalism and racism in *Century Magazine*, Mena searched for a perspective from which to portray life in Mexico as her commission requested, and, at the same time, to comment on U. S. intervention, which was close to her personal experience. Representing Mexico to an Anglo-American audience, she wrote from both sides of the border.

In her short stories, Mena presents a mirror to her *Century* audience, confronting them with their assumptions and prejudices. In *Borderlands/La Frontera*, Gloria Anzaldúa describes the mirror as an "ambivalent symbol." She writes, "Not only does it reproduce images (the twins that stand for thesis and antithesis);[5] it contains and absorbs them" (42). Mena uses mirroring in "John of God, the Water-Carrier," "The Birth of the God of War," and "The Vine Leaf" to reproduce images which counter those in *Century*. Although seeing may construct barriers ("Subject and object, I and she"), Anzaldúa emphasizes that "in a glance also lies awareness, knowledge" (42). As Mena unsettles the distinction between subject and object for her characters and her readers, she introduces knowledge to those who demanded difference.

The trope of mirroring in Mena's short stories is relevant to the visual atmosphere in which she wrote. A mirror to its subjects, photography played a strong role in *Century*'s representations of Mexico. In *The Magazine in America: 1741–1990*, Tebbel and Zuckerman write that *Century,* as one of the last magazines to shift from engravings to photographs, "treated the pictures primarily as art rather than as conveyors of information or reflections of reality" (229). However, photographs haunt the space between illusion and reality (Freedberg 439), presenting an image which is "real," even authoritative, yet subject to the vision and framing of the photographer. In the early twentieth century, photography gave the Anglo-American viewer a sense of ownership of the foreign image, and by extension, the subject. As David Freedberg writes in his description of the photograph, "The reality of the image does not lie, as we might like to think, in the associations it calls forth; it lies in something more authentic, more real, and infinitely more graspable and verifiable than association" (439). For an audience seeking a packaged version of another country, these photographs offered the immediacy and authority which television provides today, affecting the imagination in a similar way. As Tebbel and Zuckerman note, "It needs to be remembered, too, that in this period from 1891 to the end of the Great War, magazines enjoyed a time when they were not rivaled by radio, motion pictures, or television. They were the only national communications medium, and their audience was unlimited" (77). In this period, travel was increasingly possible for Anglo-Americans, and they were curious about all areas of the world, but especially those people and places tantalizingly close to them. By capturing the foreign in photographs and in print, *Century* responded to this interest. Through the establishment of difference, the publication presented an aura of authority in a quickly changing society.

In the photographic essay "Unfamiliar Mexico" (*Century*, September 1915), F. F. McArthur seeks to familiarize his audience with Mexico, to arrest images and "bring them home," so to speak, thereby domesticating the foreign. However, the distanced view of the photographer perpetuates the unfamiliarity of his subjects. No relationship exists between photographer and subject: The Mexicans he views are surprised by, hidden from, and turned away from the camera. These images, then, especially of the cloaked, inscrutable Mexican woman, suggest the seduction of the foreign country, the secrets Mexico holds. Framed within the title "Unfamiliar Mexico," the photographs give the audience a sense of familiarity, but they maintain the boundaries between the "imagined communities" of the U. S. and Mexico (Anderson 7).

Besides photography, the fiction and illustrations in *Century* also presented distancing, even demeaning, images of Mexicans. As in the photographic essay presented above, Mexican women were of particular interest to the Anglo-American reader and viewer, symbolizing seduction or subservience, depending on the desires of the author, photographer, or illustrator. For example, in "The Transformation of Angelita López" (*Century* August 1914), a story by Anglo-American writer Gertrude B. Millard, the Mexican woman symbolizes servitude: Angelita, the servant of a wealthy family in California, is deferential, dependent on the "Puritan, common-sense, ex-New Englander" (547) Miss Jane for her livelihood and advice concerning her unmotivated husband, Antonio, whom she portrays as unwilling to work and unable to hold down a job or maintain his family. As an Anglo from the northeastern United States, Miss Jane represents the perspective of *Century*'s readers and editors, and her paternalistic attitude toward Angelita and Antonio demonstrates the magazine's negative portrayal of Mexican immigrants in the United States.[6]

The pieces described above represent the choices of *Century*'s editors, and Mena was subject to editorial control of her topics as well as the length of her stories. Her letters to *Century*'s editors demonstrate Mary Louise Pratt's observation: "Magazine stories are made to order, their tone, subject matter, language, length controlled in advance by the other more powerful discourses in whose company they appear" (192). Upon acceptance of her first story, "John of God, the Water-Carrier," Mena wrote to editor Robert Underwood Johnson of her thrill in being published: "Still your wonderful praises ring in my ear, and the afternoon I passed in your office remains in my memory as a moment of enchantment in a life that has not always been as happy as it is now."[7] In this letter, Mena alludes to her own experience of immigration and settling in the northeastern U. S., certainly a lonely struggle for acceptance. However, her struggle is not over; she must argue to maintain the integrity of her first published story. She writes, "I felt as if I had foisted a white elephant upon an amiable friend, who now begged my permission to make the creature more conformable by amputating its legs, trunk and tail—not forgetting its ears." She accuses the editors of wanting to de-emphasize her story because of its focus on a Mexican Indian, and she makes this criticism in their terms. She asks, "Could it be that the water carrier's lowly station in life made him a literary undesirable? Then what of Maupassant's Norman peasants, Kipling's soldiers and low-caste Hindoos, Myra Kelly's tenement children, and many other social nobodies of successful fiction?" (Letter to Robert Sterling Yard, [March 1913]). Mena's statement calls attention to a racialized literary hierarchy, which includes a corresponding caste system of "literary undesirables," and her arguments with her editors show her struggle for representation, both of her own work and of Mexico.

In Mena's first short story, "John of God, the Water-Carrier," she challenges the stereotypical portrayals of Mexicans in *Century*, as is evident on the opening page (39). The artist, F. Luis Mora, illustrated all of Mena's stories in *Century* except "The Emotions of María Concepcíon" (January 1914) and "The Vine Leaf." In a letter to *Century*, Mena mentions looking for "an artist of my country" (20 March 1913); indeed, the choice of an illustrator was very important to her representation because, as Tebbel and Zuckerman explain, "the artists' names had become as familiar to the reading public as those of the contributors" (72). In comparison to the portrait of the solitary Mexican in McArthur's photo-essay, Mora depicts a Mexican community; it is a more spontaneous, interactive scene of people going about their daily lives, and it accompanies a story which provides a view of Mexico as a community apart from the "framing" of Anglo-American writers and photographers.

Through the juxtaposition of John of God with his brother Tiburcio, Mena presents the supposed threat of capitalism to the Mexican community. John of God migrates to Mexico City to carry water to the city's wealthy residents but he experiences competition from Tiburcio, who uses the "highly painted and patented American force-pumps" (44) to service John of God's customers in Mexico City. In this story, Mena alludes to the infiltration of capitalism during the Díaz regime (Acuña 126-7), and figures the Virgin of Guadalupe as a vital, centering force. In contrast to Tiburcio, John of God leaves behind worldly concerns to become an *aguador* for the pilgrims to Guadalupe, where his spiritual, communal role recuperates Mexican tradition, community, and religion.

The Virgin of Guadalupe figures strongly in this short story, challenging the images of subservient Mexican women presented in such works as "The Transformation of Angelita López." As Tey Diana Rebolledo explains, the Virgin of Guadalupe "represents the merging of European and Indian culture since she is, in some senses, a transformation or 'rebirth' of the native goddesses" (50). In "John of God, the Water-Carrier," the Virgin of Guadalupe is also a figure of mediation between brothers, and Mena argues to keep the details of their pilgrimage in order to translate its significance to her readers. Writing to her editors, Mena emphasizes the importance of these scenes:

> Another passage marked for cutting out was the one telling of the pilgrims eating blessed earth and drinking blessed water and buying blessed tortillas with chile sauce, and tortillas of the Virgin, which are small and sweet and dyed in many colors—a passage that I would almost defend with my life! (Letter to Johnson, 4 April 1913)

Although Mena's retort may sound "picturesque," she argues to save the signs of her culture; she will not let these important details be lost in translation. Finally, the editors allowed Mena to keep the details of the pilgrimage which they had suggested she strike from her copy. Significantly, in the final version of the story, Mena suggests that the indigenous Mexicans' faith in the Virgin of Guadalupe provides strength. As a translator, Mena presents several incarnations of the goddess in Mexico, offering new models to Anglo and Chicana readers alike.

As Mena becomes more comfortable with her audience, she turns to the *cuento* in a more personal way. In "The Birth of the God of War," for example, Mena narrates in the first-person, as a granddaughter recalling her grandmother's story of the birth of Huitzilopochtli. This story depicts a fusion between the Mexican upper class and the Mexican Indians, a connection missing in her earlier stories. Furthermore, as compared to "John of God, the Water-Carrier," women play a more central role in this story. Mena focuses on the goddess Coatlicue, emphasizing her life-giving, spiritual qualities. As Rebolledo explains, "Coatlicue is an extremely complex goddess of many aspects, transformations, and features, and she is considered to be probably the most ancient of the Nahuatl deities."[8] Her role could be considered analogous to Mena's in her shape-shifting among her audience, her editors, and her culture as she variously represents the Aztec, *mestiza*, and upper-class perspectives.

In a story which mirrors *Century*'s figurative conquest of Mexico, Mena returns to a past before Christianity, before the capitalism and technology which *Century* represents. In a dialogue between grandmother and granddaughter, Mena reminds the reader of Coatlicue's foundational role in Mexican culture before Christianity, as the grandmother recalls the past buried beneath the signs of conquest:

> Such, attentive little daughter mine, is the legend narrated to the Aztec priests by the forests, the waters, and the birds. And on Sunday, when *papacito* carries thee to the cathedral, fix it in thy mind that the porch, foundation, and courtyard of that saintly edifice remain from the great temple built by our warrior ancestors for the worship of the god Huitzilopochtli. Edifice immense and majestic, it extended to what to-day is called the Street of the Silversmiths, and that of the Old Bishop's House, and on the north embraced the streets of the Incarnation, Santa Teresa, and Monte Alegre. (49)

Here, Mena's recounting of Aztec legend is not distancing, picturesque, or "superstitious." As she writes, "It was not mythology to me" (45); instead, it was her cherished heritage. In her series of stories, she works tirelessly to dispel myths about Mexican culture, ending "The Birth of the God of War," for example, with the grandmother's admission, "I am a little fatigued, *chiquita*. Rock thy little old one to sleep" (49). Perhaps tired herself, like the grandmother, Mena becomes the ancestral voice which perpetuates the Aztec legend in *Century Magazine.* Stories such as "John of God, the Water-Carrier" and "The Birth of the God of War," based on oral tradition,[9] represent the conflicts, values, and legends of her culture.

This recovery of an Aztec past is a strong element of the Chicana project of re-imagination. Late twentieth-century readings of Guadalupe, Coatlicue, La Malinche, and La Llorona recuperate these women as powerful and heroic (Anzaldúa, 30-31). Writing decades before these revisionist readings, Mena also imagines these figures as central to her Mexican heritage. As Tiffany Ana López notes in "María Cristina Mena: Turn-of-the-Century La Malinche, and Other Tales of Cultural (Re)Construction," Mena's narration of the marquesa's unexpected power in "The Vine Leaf" recalls the legend of La Malinche and also suggests Mena's role as translator for an Anglo-American audience. López states that Mena "revises the La Malinche reading to depict women as sexually assertive and communally productive—rather than destructive—individuals" (34). The fiction received *Century's* editorial praise: "It is an exquisite thing, worthy of de Maupassant, both for style and treatment" (Doty, letter to Mena, 28 September 1914). Mena replied that "The Vine Leaf" was "a great favorite of my own, between you and me!" (Letter to Doty, [October 1914]). Certainly, this story represents her desire for linguistic and artistic control in her publishing career. Similar to Mena's conversations with her editors, in this story, the marquesa craftily resists the surgeon's demand of "confession," as well as her husband's desire to capture her, like her portrait, in a domestic frame. In a close reading of this short story, I will examine the relationship between the main character, the marquesa, and the men she outwits in her life: the doctor, the marqués, and the artist. Finally, I will discuss the "framing" of the marquesa in *Century Magazine* as indicative of Mena's position as a writer for the publication.

In "The Vine Leaf," Mena artfully portrays the marquesa's rebellion against the European doctor, Dr. Malsufrido, and her husband, the marqués. She visits Dr. Malsufrido to have a birthmark in the shape of a vine leaf removed from her back. Dr. Malsufrido insists on confessions from women whose bodies are literally in his hands. However, Mena plays on his authority, and, through inversion, displaces his class position. The narrative voice builds on Dr. Malsufrido's inflated identity: he knows the "family secrets of the rich," he had been "dosing good Mexicans for half a century," and he was "forgiven for being a Spaniard on account of a legend that he physicked royalty in his time" (289). However, in response to Dr. Malsufrido's pompous treatment of "good Mexicans," the marquesa asserts: "'To you I come, Señor Doctor, because no one knows you'" (290). In Mena's artful narration, Dr. Malsufrido's self-created reality becomes *incredible*. He represents those Europeans and Anglo-Americans who separate themselves from "bad Mexicans"—in other words, those who may not believe in his medicine nor accept his appropriation of their "secrets." As López notes in her reading of "The Vine Leaf," the marquesa plays the role of trickster (30-33), outwitting the self-absorbed doctor, the dominant figure in this narrative.

As the marquesa resists Dr. Malsufrido's proprietary and violating perspective, Mena's narrative plays on the importance of science and the visible to her audience. The doctor says of the vine leaf, "'My science tells me that it must be seen before it can be well removed'" (290). "My science" suggests an imperialistic relationship to the "foreign" body; the demand that the object "must be seen" illustrates the importance of the empirical to modern science. Instead of confirming the doctor's possession of her secret, the removal of the marquesa's vine leaf suggests a reality beyond the doctor's empiricism. The vine leaf is magically removed: "'Neither the cutting nor the stitching brought a murmur from her'" (290) and no scar remains. As in "The Birth of the God of War," Mena contrasts Dr. Malsufrido's religion based on confession and his science founded on the visible, with a reality beyond empirical proof. The magic of the vine leaf unravels the doctor's colonializing logic, his association of touching with knowing, seeing with controlling, hearing with possessing. In "The Vine Leaf," the marquesa's power operates outside the grasp of the reader who would claim interpretive mastery.

The concealed power of feminine sexuality, the unexpected potency of the regenerative vine leaf, arises again in the "story within the story" of the artist and the marquesa. In this framed story, the marquesa possesses the sexual and interpretive power of La Malinche. In her relationship with the artist, Andrade, the marquesa leads a double life outside of her relationship with the marqués. Andrade had painted a portrait of her back, which the marqués, ironically, wanted to present as a "betrothal gift" (292) to the Señorita Lisarda Monte Alegre, the future marquesa. He wants to add the painting to the "curiosities he had collected in various countries" (291), a description which suggests the images of Mexicans presented as "curiosities" in *Century*. Like the doctor and the marquesa's husband, the European artist Andrade also objectifies the marquesa. Although the artist refuses to relinquish his work, the marqués obtains the piece when he finds the artist murdered, and he interprets the sign of the artist's murderer to be the vine leaf painted on the woman's back in the portrait. Andrade attempts to mirror her image in the portrait of her back, in the mirror of her face, and in the "excrescence" (292) of the vine leaf. However, the artist's portrait of the marquesa's face in the mirror is effaced: "'the mirror was empty of all but a groundwork of paint, with a mere luminous suggestion of a face'" (291). The woman will not be bound to his image of her. Finally, the artist mirrors the marquesa: the knife sticking between Andrade's shoulders reflects the "stain" on Monte Alegre's back. Like La Malinche, the marquesa seizes control of those who attempt to make her, a feminine and Mexican subject, their mirror.

Mena suggests the marquesa's almost supernatural powers in this story, in her ability to sustain the removal of the vine leaf without a sound, in her eerie presence, veiled at the doctor's office, and, in a sense, "unveiled" in her husband's "museum." Mena mirrors the gaze of the conqueror in the doctor's surgery, the marqués's collections, and the artist's portrait, then undermines their perspectives. Writer, narrator, and protagonist merge in the marquesa's rhetorical question, "'Can you blame me for not loving this questionable lady of the vine-leaf, of whom my husband is such a gallant accomplice?'" (292). This "questionable lady of the vine leaf" resists interpretation. The reader never knows if the marquesa or her husband actually murdered the artist, whether the marquesa was having an affair with the artist, or the extent of her husband's knowledge of their relationship. The plot leads in many directions simultaneously; it refuses to be captured in a single interpretation. In a succession of "frames," Mena's story builds outward from Dr. Malsufrido, to his female patient, to the marquesa, and finally, to Mena; each character overlaps and pushes the interpretation a little further. *Century* also frames the story with a nude portrait facing the title page, objectifying the marquesa and sensationalizing Mena's story. However, even in *Century's* "portrait," the marquesa's identity, concealed from the mirror, is not revealed to the viewer. By shifting the tensions of the romance to the woman who holds the key to the mystery, Mena mediates between text and reader, image and viewer. Mena plays on the false view of the "conquerors" and collectors who attempt to capture the marquesa's identity.

In "John of God, the Water-Carrier," "The Birth of the God of War," and "The Vine Leaf," Mena challenges *Century's* representations of Mexico with images derived from Mexican tradition. The Virgin of Guadalupe, Coatlicue, and La Malinche play important roles in Mena's narratives and help her to define her role as a writer for *Century*. Besides bearing power as mediators and possessors of "secret stories," these figures symbolize Mena's position as a translator between cultures. Writing of Mexico for an Anglo-American audience, Mena uses her borderland position to inform her readers of a reality beyond the images of Mexico portrayed in *Century Magazine*.

Notes

[1] For a more extensive discussion of Mena's works, please see *The Collected Stories of María Cristina Mena*, ed. Amy Doherty (Houston: Arte Público, 1997).

[2] For a revisionist reading of La Malinche in relation to Mena's "The Vine Leaf" and "The Sorcerer and General Bisco," see Tiffany Ana López, "María Cristina Mena: Turn-of-the-Century La Malinche and Other Tales of Cultural (Re)Construction." Ammons and White-Parks, *Tricksterism in Turn-of-the-Century Literature*.

[3] This descriptor appeared on the first page of Mena's short story, "A Son of the Tropics" (January 1931), which Mena published under her married name, María Cristina Chambers.

[4] "Topics of the Time," *Century* Oct. 1913: 951–952. Although the edi-

tor's name is not included in the essay nor the index of *Century*, the description of the Century Company Records indicates that Hewitt H. Howland was the editor from 1912–30, and thus would have written "Topics of the Time." Valerie Wingfield, Rare Books and Manuscript Division, New York Public Library.

⁵ Marius Schneider, *El origen musical de los animales-símbolos en la mitología y la escultura antiguas* (Barcelona, 1946), cited in Anzaldúa 42.

⁶ For further examples of stereotypical images in *Century*, see López 27–32.

⁷ Letter to Robert Underwood Johnson, 20 March 1913. All correspondence with Mena is included with permission from Century Company Records, Rare Books and Manuscript Division, New York Public Library, Astor, Lenox, and Tilden Foundations.

⁸ Ferdinand Anton, *Women in Pre-Columbian America* (New York: Abner Schram, 1973), 58, cited in Rebolledo 50.

⁹ Gloria Velásquez-Treviño notes that "John of God, the Water-Carrier" is "based on a religious folktale" (29).

Works Cited

Acuña, Rodolfo. *Occupied America.* 2nd ed. New York: Harper, 1981.

Ammons, Elizabeth and Annette White-Parks, eds. *Tricksterism in Turn-of-the-Century American Literature: A Multicultural Perspective.* Hanover: University Press of New England, 1994.

Anderson, Benedict. *Imagined Communities: Reflections on the Origin and Spread of Nationalism.* New York: Verso-New Left Books, 1991.

Anzaldúa, Gloria. *Borderlands/La Frontera.* San Francisco: Aunt Lute Books, 1987.

Chambers, María Cristina. "A Son of the Tropics." *Household Magazine* Jan. 1931: 4+.

Doty, Douglas Zabriske. Letter to María Cristina Mena. 28 September 1914.

Freedberg, David. *The Power of Images: Studies in the History and Theory of Response.* Chicago: University of Chicago, 1989.

López, Tiffany Ana. "María Cristina Mena: Turn-of-the-Century La Malinche, and Other Tales of Cultural (Re)Construction." Ammons and White-Parks 21–45.

McArthur, F. F. "Unfamiliar Mexico." *Century Magazine* Sept. 1915: 729-36.

Mena, María Cristina. "The Birth of the God of War." *Century Magazine* May 1914: 45-9.

———. "John of God, the Water-Carrier." *Century Magazine* Nov. 1913: 39-48.

————. "The Vine Leaf." *Century Magazine* Dec. 1914: 289-92.

————. Letter to Robert Sterling Yard. [March 1913].

————. Letter to Robert Underwood Johnson. 20 March 1913. Century Company Records.

————. Letter to Robert Underwood Johnson. 4 April 1913. Century Company Records.

————. Letter to Douglas Zabriske Doty. [October 1914]. Century Company Records.

Millard, Gertrude B. "The Transformation of Angelita López." *Century Magazine* Aug. 1914: 547–57.

"Mrs. Henry Chambers, 72, Short-Story Writer, Is Dead." *New York Times* 10 Aug. 1965: 29.

Pratt, Mary Louise. "The Short Story: The Long and the Short of It." *Poetics* 10 (1981): 175-94.

Rebolledo, Tey Diana. *Women Singing in the Snow: A Cultural Analysis of Chicana Literature*. Tucson: University of Arizona, 1995.

Ross, Edward Alsworth. "American and Immigrant Blood: A Study of the Social Effects of Immigration." *Century Magazine* Dec. 1913: 225–32.

Shuster, W. Morgan. "The Mexican Menace." *Century Magazine* Jan. 1914: 593–602.

Simmen, Edward, ed. *North of the Rio Grande: The Mexican-American Experience in Short Fiction*. New York: Penguin, 1992. 39–84.

Tebbel, John and Mary Ellen Zuckerman. *The Magazine in America: 1741-1990*. New York: Oxford University, 1991.

"Topics of the Time." *Century Magazine* Oct. 1913: 951–52.

Velásquez-Treviño, Gloria Louise. "Cultural Ambivalence in Early Chicana Prose Fiction." Diss. Stanford University, 1985.

Confronting *la Frontera,* Identity and Gender: Poetry and Politics in *La Crónica* and *El Demócrata Fronterizo*

Louis Mendoza
University of Texas at San Antonio

We need newspapers that awaken the public spirit; the patriotism of the people is entangled in a terror with no name. —Sara Estela Ramírez, *El Demócrata Fronterizo* (9/25/1903)

As a journalist her reputation was such that a Mexican writer, on learning of her premature death, exclaimed: "The most illustrious Mexican woman of Texas has died." —*La Crónica* (08/ 27/1910)

I have often proposed to my *colegas* our need to seek out the precursors to contemporary Tejana writers . . . If we continue to remain indifferent to them, the world will never know their words, nor will they know the contentment of their literary companionship as Tejanas. —Teresa Acosta, "Tejana History as a Poem"

This essay re-examines the work of Sara Estela Ramírez, a transborder poet, journalist and feminist activist who lived in Laredo from 1897 until her death in 1910 at the age of 29. My objectives are multiple: I am particularly interested in viewing the writings of this exemplary intellectual as a point of departure for further study on the relationship between culture and power in turn-of-the-century South Texas. By examining how a politicized cultural identity was articulated in two important newpapers in Laredo in the first decade of the century I hope to illuminate strategies of subversion and containment surrounding gender and national identity. Another objective is invested in launching a critique of how early Chicano studies scholars have shaped our understanding of the period with paradigms that perpetuate analytical blind spots. This essay is grounded in research I conducted for my 1994 dissertation (UT–Austin) and subsequent work supported by a 1995 Recovery Project Grant in which I sought to expand the scope of Ramírez's recovered works. My work is deeply indebted to and follows the important groundbreaking recovery work of her letters, journalism, and poetry that originally appeared in *La Crónica* and *El Demócrata Fronterizo* by

Emilio Zamora, Jr. and Inés Hernández Tovar, whose 1984 dissertation is the most extensive analysis of Ramírez yet to be performed. Hoping to expand the known corpus of Ramírez's work, I followed their lead. It is clear from their work that a large body of Ramírez's pre-1908 journalistic and artistic endeavors are yet unrecovered. I concentrated on trying to locate those editions of newspapers in which Ramírez was writer and/or publisher (pre-1910 issues of *La Crónica, La Corregidora, Vesper*), her literary journal (*Aurora*), and any book or pamphlet length editions of her poetry or stories—all of which continue to be unavailable. Unfortunately, despite extensive research of archives in Austin, San Antonio and Laredo (The Barker Texas History Center–UT and the Texas State Archives, and numerous conversations with archivists at the Laredo Public Library, Texas A&M International, Webb County Heritage Foundation, Los Caminos Del Rio (Laredo), Texas Women's University, and the Institute of Texan Cultures) very little new information was recovered. In re-examining available issues of *El Demócrata Fronterizo* and *La Crónica,* I was able to locate an advertisement for a heretofore unmentioned publication of Ramírez, titled *La Estatua de Paz: Cuento Gitano,* that was being sold out of the offices of *El Demócrata Fronterizo.* Although my archival searches for unaccounted writings by Ramírez yielded little success, in perusing *El Demócrata Fronterizo,* the newspaper responsible for publishing the bulk of known writings by this author, I did survey a substantial body of work by poets upon whom little has been written, and who published their work in the literary pages of these important periodicals along-side Ramírez's. Although I will have occasion to refer to some of these poems later in the essay, a more extended survey and analysis are needed.

In my re-examination of her work, I argue that Ramírez's articulation of the relationship between her art and her politics allow us to reconsider traditional notions of "Mexican" identity in this region and period. As a transborder activist and writer Ramírez's identity defies the reductionism of national identifiers. Indeed, as someone who had a demonstrated commitment to literary production and social change in Mexico *and* South Texas, Ramírez expands and complicates our understanding of the formation of Mexican identity in the United States. Not only does her literature help broaden our understanding of the scope of U.S. and Mexican literatures, it also productively problematizes a longstanding tension in Chicano historiography. The period in which Ramírez lived is often referred to as the Migrant Generation by Chicano historians who utilize a generational par-adigm. This periodization framework, initially proposed by Rodolfo Alvarez in the early 1970s but which has endured a long, rich life,[1] has been subsequently problematized by labor and feminist revisionists, whose work has helped expose the ideological, class and gender biases which inform the generational paradigm. In her work Ramírez articulates an identity that was adaptable to the socio-polit-ical realities of her life on the border. In her literature she is cognizant of a dual audience of a common Mexican origin. Her insurgent activites and gendered deconstruction of political and social power are not contained by the U.S.-

Mexican border, nor can they be understood as part of a "pre-political and socially passive" Migrant Generation.

The prevailing scholarship on the Migrant Generation characterizes them as a group whose primary intentions were to live and work outside of the turbulent political and social climate of the Mexican Revolution.[2] According to historians, the political sentiments of this generation, whether they intended to return to Mexico or not, were negligible to non-existent; their chief concern was to survive, not to actively participate in political life. Such a perspective characterizes them as politically passive, meek, naive and isolated. The generational labels given to the "creation" generation and the "migrant" generation are both problematic. The former illustrates the problems associated with defining a community of people from the perspective of the dominating social group, while the latter *defines* a people's history based on the experiences of only one sector of that community. The designator "Creation Generation" refers to the making of Mexicans into a subordinate ethnic group and the concomitant rise of anti-Mexican sentiment in Southwestern United States. In this schema, history prior to the 1848 Treaty of Guadalupe Hidalgo is insignificant; consequently, any understanding of Mexican-descent communities in the United States is bound to a subjugated socio-economic and political status. The application of labels that are reflective of social and political processes to an entire generation of people fails to take into account elite elements of this ethnic national group who were complicit with and benefited from the change in citizenship status, as well as many other situations in which social relations were different. Similar problems are inherent within the category of Migrant Generation. The most obvious is that a focus on this group during the first two decades of the twentieth century neglects to examine the activities of Mexican-descent people who were native to the region prior to the conquest and the Mexican Revolution. This is one problem that is inherent in the generational approach to history: it privileges the experiences of one sector of the community at the expense of others.

This is not to say that Chicano historians have shied away from the significance of conflict in their material approaches to history; writing from within a Chicano Movement perspective, however, their assessment of *mexicano* resistance to economic, political and cultural domination has often been overdetermined. The following quotation from Rodolfo Alvarez exemplifies this:

> During the period designated as the 'Migrant Generation,' there were many isolated instances of great conflict between groups of Mexican Americans trying to alter their lower caste-status, but they were locally over-powered, and *a general state of acquiesence became the state of collective consciousness.*
>
> (*MA* 41, emphasis mine)

This attitude towards pre-Chicano Movement political history prevails in the historical literature; indeed, even though the generation that follows the Migrant Generation, the Mexican American Generation, is commonly perceived as assimilationist, it is also known as the first overtly political generation of Mexican Americans. In explaining his approach to the Mexican American Generation, Mario García reveals something of his perception of the Migrant Generation:

> The problem . . . for this study concerns the role that ethnicity plays in the transition from either first-generation immigrants or those Mexican Americans native to the Southwest *who had been mostly isolated from mainstream currents* to a second, U.S. born generation . . . that on the whole began to understand that it was part of U.S. society and that it had to compromise between its ethnic roots and full incorporation and assimilation into American society.
>
> (*MA* 10, emphasis mine)

Political practice is thus defined only in relation to U.S. electoral politics. Little effort is made by proponents of the generational approach to understand diverse forms and directions of political identity. Consequently, Mexico-oriented political practices are often ignored or effaced, as well as other non-electoral political struggles, such as the cultural politics of domestic and communal space. Both formal and informal cultural forms are particulalry salient sites for examining these negotiations of power relations.

There is, however, another school of thought that has a very different interpretation of the Migrant and Mexican American generations' interaction with mainstream U.S. society. Chicano labor historians such as Juan Gómez-Quiñones, Emilio Zamora and Luis Leobardo Arroyo have contributed to a more complex understanding of the role of Mexican workers in labor organizing during these periods. Their research presents Mexican workers as active agents, not as passive and submissive laborers.[3] Gómez-Quiñones' essay on Chicana/o labor history, written in 1972, marks an important moment in Chicano historiography because it examines the significance of labor as a site of resistance that illuminates intracultural as well as intercultural divisions and alliances.[4] Furthermore, by critiquing and expanding the field of labor history, feminist historians, such as Antonia Castañeda, Adelaida R. del Castillo, Vicki Ruiz, and Emma Pérez among others, have successfully integrated an analysis of gender, labor, ideology and culture which eschews elitist notions of power, space and political participation by writing a subaltern history of those excluded from political institutions and leadership positions.[5]

The Migrant Generation is, by definition, characterized by geographical movement across national borders. For the thousands of Mexicans who migrated northward during the first two decades of the twentieth century, their movement across geopolitical boundaries helped them gain relief from the social and economic upheaval that preceded, accompanied, and followed the Mexican Revolution. It is commonly acknowledged by historians and sociologists that many of these migrants viewed their move into the United States as a temporary hiatus from the military and economic turmoil of Mexico.[6] Mexicans in the United States are able to maintain their national identity with relative ease. This has been primarily due to the proximity of their nation-of-origin and the formation of close-knit communities that have reinforced their cultural and national identity. The consequences of their move across an arbitrary national border and their interactions with a decisively different economic, political and social life were not determined or homogeneous. Their experiences, responses, and reactions to U.S. society varied widely. Unlike the settler community of the eighteenth and nineteenth centuries, these migrants voluntarily entered into a relationship with the United States. Their complex motivations and intentions and the effects of these on their national and political orientation are left unexamined by a generational approach which, notwithstanding its resistance to a particular national identity, universalizes their experiences across ideological and gender axes. The generational approach to political and social history thus needs to be interrogated for its "blind spots" and generalizing tendencies.

The historiography on Mexican-descent women is one such blind spot that has been created by the racialist and sexist paradigms of historians and the institutions that have produced and supported them. A lack of analysis of the impact of gender in political, social and intellectual history exists in both canonical and revisionist historiography. This lack of analysis is usually explained as a result of insufficient data or primary materials. What has often resulted is what Gayatri Spivak has elsewhere labeled "cognitive failure," which, in the case of revisionist histories, produces an ethnic version of elite historiography: a history which assumes a "great man" approach to writing Chicana/o history. The effect of dominant methods of organizing knowledge and the contradictions it entails for subalterns can be seen in the emergence of the field of Chicana/o history. In its early years much effort was devoted to searching for a proper paradigm or periodization schema. While new modes of analysis were tested with the intention of producing a subaltern history of Chicanos, they often contained limitations that were inherited from traditional paradigms. Much Chicano history privileges conflict with and resistance to domination as a means of moving away from a modes of production master narrative. The benefit of this analytical approach, as Spivak has pointed out, is that "the agency of change is located in the insurgent or 'subaltern'" (3). Both within and outside of the framework of elite historiography, the gender, ethnic, class and immigrant status of Mexicanas in the U.S. have conspired to leave their history ignored and suppressed. One way to overcome the supposed lack of evidence of subaltern history is to examine the production and definition of evidence, its management as elements of truth and its interpretation. The process of uncovering Chicano/a history is still underway. The point to be made here is that many Anglo and Chicano histories have neglected Chicanas' active participation in the making of history.[7] An analysis of the discursive representations about and by women of Mexican descent is one of the ways in which we can read against the grain of established histories.

The historical literature produced by and about the "Migrant Generation" foregrounds problematics that continue to inform the production and critical analysis of Chicano literature because a material analysis is inextricably bound to an historical understanding of this period of both "Mexican" and "American" history. A dialectical approach to history and culture should disallow any effort to separate neatly the impact of one nation-state and its people upon another. Under close scrutiny, the contentious relationship of these two bordering nations can potentially have a profound effect on our notions of nationality, nationalism, labor, leadership and political engagement. What scholars have often overlooked is that migrants were not, and are not, an homogeneous class of people who necessarily share a common identity, ideology, degree of education or vision of the future. The life and work of Ramírez illustrates that *mexicanos* of this period can not be so easily classified.

While Ramírez should be seen as an exemplary figure of this era, she was not an anomaly. In the U.S. context, many Mexicans at the turn of the century maintained the national identity of their country of origin in their cultural and political practices. For many, this entailed political involvement and support of one or another political faction of the anti-Díaz *revolucionarios*. Mexican political activists used a nebulous international boundary to their advantage. Aware that residency in the United States was in many cases perceived as a temporary condition of exile by the Mexican population north of the border, some political activists exploited the border by establishing organizational bases that were, initially at least, out of the reach of Mexican officials who were trying to crush resistance against the Díaz regime. Organizations such as the Partido Liberal Mexicano (PLM) tapped into the nationalist sentiments of Mexicans residing in the Southwestern United States. Sara Estela Ramírez was one such organizational representative who became an important spokesperson for the PLM in Texas. Furthermore, chain migration from Mexico resulted in the maintenance of communal ties across the border and also provided the groundwork for labor and political organizing.

Ramirez's Poetics and Praxis

In her last known poem, "Rise Up!: To Woman," (*La Crónica,* 04/09/10) Ramírez urges women to action with words that echo contemporary gender analyses and establish her as a precursor to politically engaged Chicana feminist writers. In the following excerpt from "Rise Up!" she urges action that is based on an awareness of one's agency and informed by a demystified sense of self, one not limited by constructions of gender that privilege or empower either males or females.

> One who is truly a woman is more than goddess
> or queen. Do not let the incense on the altar, or
> the applause in the audience intoxicate you, there
> is something more noble and more grand than all
> of that.

> Gods are thrown out of temples; kings are
> driven from their thrones, woman is always woman.
> . . . Only action is life; to feel that one
> lives is the most beautiful sensation.
>
> (qtd. in Tovar 194)[8]

Ramírez does not specify an objective to which women should aspire; what she privileges is action as an end in itself. In "Sara Estela Ramírez: Una rosa roja en el Movimiento," Emilio Zamora suggests that based on Ramírez's life and writings we might conjecture that she is urging women to "struggle for democratic rights," and certainly there is ample basis for this. Tovar, on the other hand, links Ramírez's purpose in this poem with the philosophy of life proclaimed by Ricardo Flores Magón. Magón says that in addition to basic needs of food, shelter and clothing, "the man of our times [needs] intellectual sustenance that will illuminate his understanding" (qtd in Tovar 255). Tovar points to Ramírez's feminist critique of the narrow pre-conceived roles allowed women. Of Ramírez's encouragement to women to "be a mother, be a woman" Tovar says that this is possibly "a compensation for her own lack of maternal guidance as well as her own realization that women can be 'mothers' for their sisters and fellow human being [*sic*] by caring for and sustaining them" (256). Zamora's and Tovar's interpretations of this poem are not mutually exclusive. The poem urges activity: "Only action is life; to feel that one lives is the most beautiful sensation." The poet's own life was a model of political, social and intellectual activity. At times, she, in the company of other women, adopted a gender specific strategy for addressing the concerns and problems particular to women involved in political movements in South Texas and northern Mexico. In this way, these women were able to impact the political activity and program being developed. Ramírez's poetics must be seen as intimately linked to her political practice as an important means of intervention within the popular discourses on gender, nationality, and class.

In addition to the feminist critique in "Rise Up!" which rejects the position of the pedestal as objectifying, Ramírez also comments on the constructions of other forms of power which hierarchize human relations in the social and political realm. Her admonition that there is a choice to be made and that "before Goddess or Queen, be a mother, be a woman" is a call to embrace those positions which are more innately human rather than positions of relative power. Goddesses are seen in relation to Gods, Queens in relation to Kings. A woman in one of these positions is dependent upon a relationship to a male for her power. She does not see woman as a function of the position of man. Despite the fact that her call for women to be mothers is a valuation of a social position that might be seen as limiting by some contemporary feminists, it may also be read abstractly as a call for individual and collective regeneration, a continual process in the struggle for social change.

Born in Coahuila, Mexico in 1881, Ramírez moved independently to Laredo at the age of sixteen. The eulogies written in her honor upon her death in 1910 testify to the impact of her work over a thirteen-year period. *La Crónica* published two eulogies on August 27, 1910, and the funeral oration given by Clemente Idar on September 5. The first two paragraphs of one of the eulogies are dedicated to establishing her relationship with *La Crónica:*

> With profound grief we deliver the news of the death of our collaborator and beloved friend Sarita . . .
> *La Crónica* has more than enough reason to dress this page in mourning, since the gentle and spiritual poet was a constant collaborator of our weekly and in these same columns her first poetic essays appeared, some twelve years ago, as well as her beautiful literary articles. (qtd. in Tovar 200)

We learn from this eulogy that *La Crónica* published her "first poetic compositions and literary articles which she produced when she was barely fifteen or sixteen years old," and of her editorship of "the strong literary newspaper *La Corregidora,*" which was published in Laredo and Mexico City, as well as the founding of *Aurora,* a literary journal whose publication she was forced to suspend due to her illness in 1910. *La Crónica* asserts her significance as a binational border poet and journalist in the following lines:

> As a profound thinker and forceful writer, she deserved the respect and admiration of the entire Texan press and a large part of the Mexican press, especially in the states along the border, where she was considered the most noble, most sentimental and first of the woman poets of the region.
>
> (qtd. in Tovar 201)

These eulogies, probably written by Jovita and Clemente Idar, celebrate her dedication, creativity and intelligence; and, as Tovar reminds us, these are most important when we consider the role of the alternative press movement for the Mexican community in Texas (211).

In her dissertation, Tovar points out the multiple reasons why there were hundreds of Spanish language and bilingual newspapers established in the Southwest after the Mexican War: "Experiencing linguistic and cultural alienation from the dominant society's media organs, finding its reality misrepresented or omitted completely from those organs . . . the Mexican community had ample reason to initiate its own means of journalistic efforts" (110). The alternative press fulfilled a variety of needs, both general and specific. As Tovar has said, Mexican owned newspapers served as a "cultural arm by which to respond to historical circumstance" (108). Unlike English language newspapers, many of the publications in Spanish commonly offered a literary page.[9] According to Richard Valdés, Mexican communities developed literary associations and debate societies to encourage and refine their linguistic skills and maintain their culture, as well as providing a means for in-group education in response to exclusion from the Anglo-dominated educational system (qtd. in Tovar 111-12).

The significance of writing, in all forms and genres, at the turn of the century cannot be overstated here. In *Sembradores, Ricardo Flores Magón y El Partido Liberal Mexicano: A Eulogy and Critique*, Juan Gómez-Quiñones has pointed out the important role that newspapers played as organizing vehicles in the Southwest between 1904 and 1910 (23). Furthermore, the bi-national leader-ship of the PLM found it important to foster transregional solidarity between Mexicans in the United States and Mexicans in Mexico as well as with Anglos. This strategy stemmed from a refusal to accept the legitimacy of national borders or corrupt nation-states. The role of the alternative press in turn-of-the-century South Texas was significant and is a necessary context for our specific discussion of Sara Estela Ramírez. In turn of the century South Texas these newspapers fomented a cultural nationalism that transcended national borders by creating a sense of community that extended wherever Mexicans resided—in this instance the idea of the nation was *not* geographically bounded but culturally and linguis-tically specific, as well as cognizant of the widely shared experience of political, economic and racial domination.[10] The role of the Spanish language, bilingual and Mexican-owned newspapers that reported on and to the Mexican communi-ty was crucial in facilitating the imaginable alternatives to a different social order. Benedict Anderson has claimed that, by creating a unified field of exchange and communication, print-language has historically helped lay the bases for a nation-al consciousness (44). Mexicans' place in the shifting social order of the first decade of the twentieth century, along with a common language and culture, defined their sameness, and newspapers provided them with a sense of commu-nity. By engaging and fulfilling the needs of a specific audience, Mexican-oriented journalism in the United States participated in what Anderson calls a new way of linking "fraternity, power, and time" because it encouraged large numbers of people to think about themselves and others in new ways.

Ramírez's role in advancing the alternative press movement points to her recognition of the power of the written word. Indeed, given the paucity of bio-graphical information on her, it is primarily through her contributions to and associations with various journalistic enterprises that we know anything of her at all. From available issues of *La Crónica* and *El Demócrata Fronterizo,* we know that from 1908 until her death in 1910, Ramírez was a regular contributor, pub-lishing essays, poetry and literary articles frequently. However, from her letters to Magón we know that she began writing for them soon after she arrived in Laredo in 1897. In her first letter to Magón in 1901, Ramírez thanks him for "undeserved praises" that she had received in the PLM's official newspaper for her work in *La Crónica*. Ramírez also wrote for *Vesper: Justicia y Libertad,* a four page weekly with a circulation of 8,000, published by Juana Gutiérrez de Mendoza.

Besides being revealing about the tense political climate of Laredo in 1901, which made it difficult to organize, Ramírez's first letter to Magón makes an explicit link between political and journalistic work and how these are informed by gender constructions:

> . . . there are faint hearted spirits, conquered by terror, who refuse to support a cause, no matter whether they understand that cause to be just and noble. That is happening right now here in Laredo, where the woman is the mobile and the most powerful lever of [change]. . .

As Ramírez alludes to in this letter, the hostile social conditions at the turn of the century situated women in a unique position to facilitate social change. According to Zamora, harassment of political organizers by local police often forced the men to be less conspicuous and prompted women to fulfill the more public roles. Gómez-Quiñones quotes a woman observer as saying that, in Texas at least, "women had to continue the work men were now too intimidated to do" (*Sembradores* 36). Police repression only further highlights the risks assumed by and the dedication of women like Ramírez. This was not an activity that went unnoticed by the PLM leadership who, in a time and place when it was rare, actively solicited the participation of women in political and social change. This is not to say, however, that the PLM's gender politics were unproblematic, as Emma Pérez has noted in her critique of the PLM.[11] One instance of the PLM's invocation of gender was the manner in which women's strong participation was used as a means of highlighting men's weaknesses, in an obvious attempt to shame men who would be bothered by this "unusual" reversal of roles. An example of this is the praise given to Juana Gutiérrez de Mendoza by *Regeneración* upon the appearance of *Vesper:*

> Now when many men grow feeble and through cowardice withdraw from the struggle, considering themselves insufficiently strong to recover our liberties . . . there appears a spirited and valiant woman, ready to fight for principles which the weakness of many men has permitted to be trampled and spat upon .
>   . . .   (qtd. in Mirandé and Enrique 204-5)

Ironically, these women activists appealed to popular notions of masculinity to incite shame for what they perceived as political irresponsibility. In her 1977 dissertation on the participation of women in the Mexican Revolution, Shirlene Soto reports another instance of this rhetorical strategy directed toward the national patriarch. A tactic they hoped would gain women dissidents relief from repressive measures being taken against them. In July, 1903 issue of *Vesper,* Gutiérrez de Mendoza and Elisa Acuña y Rosetti "scorned Díaz's fear of them and taunted him as being the first man afraid of women" (qtd. in Tovar 20).[12] Seeking to realize an aesthetics of agency that would help change the course of history, these women activists, journalists, and *compañeras* in struggle penned their words to a culturally and nationally specific audience with a specific purpose.

In this letter, dated September 25, 1903, Ramírez further elaborates on her role as a journalist:

> We need newspapers that awaken the public spirit . . . We need to educate the people and awaken their energy. Our race is a race of heroes, a worthy race and it will know how to make itself respected.   (qtd. in Tovar 121)[13]

Besides pointing to the significance of newspapers as an organizing medium, this passage also illustrates the racialized climate of the turn of the century which characterized social and political relations and promoted cultural nationalism as a viable organizing strategy. In their writing and organizing PLM proponents depended upon a *mexicano* identity to promote awareness of shared struggle. And yet Mexican nationalism in the U.S. had a dual focus that makes it idiosyncratic. The rallying cry around a national identity, exemplified by Ramírez's invocation of a "race of heroes," is not directed solely at those interested in transforming the Mexican state, but also at Mexicans in the United States. As an ideology, Mexican nationalism need not be Mexico specific, but, rather, a response to a transborder capitalism that simultaneously prompted migration to the United States and forced *mexicanos* into a new relationship with capital in a land that was both foreign and familiar.

Ramírez's active membership in feminist organizations like *Hijas de Cuauhtémoc* and *Regeneración y Concordia,* as well as the liberal anti-clerical organization *Club Redención,* show her to be aware of the value of using multiple and specialized organizational strategies to address different ideological problems. It is through the work of scholars like Tovar, that the contributions of these intellectuals are not lost and through which Chicana feminists can discover their intellectual antecedents throughout the United States.

Ramírez's letters to Magón give us insight into many aspects of her political and literary work in Mexico. Although most of the letters convey questions and explanations regarding organizational logistics or news, they also contain reflections on the social climate and political situation in which she lived. In a letter dated October 21, 1903, Ramírez asks Magón if he would be willing to undertake the sale of some of her pamphlets of poetry to an editorial house in Mexico. In the next known letter to him we learn more about her poetry and Magón's response to it. She writes,

> Was my little volume of poetry a bundle of memories for you? I find in each page a memory and sometimes it hurts me to remember the beloved period of heroic struggle. Why did it end? eh? When will it return? (qtd. in Tovar 132)

Although Ramírez's words suggest that the poems she refers to are about an earlier period of Mexican political history, it is difficult to tell from these lines whether her poems are about their present struggle or a different era altogether. In this same letter Ramírez refers to what sounds like another collection of poems: "My 'Rhymes' have suffered, like their author, a series of unspeakable contrarieties. It is time they rested in a sealed box. As soon as they come I will send you the promised gift; . . . my little volume will accompany your favorite books" (qtd. in Tovar 133). The limited circulation of Ramírez's poetry and her own diminutive adjectives in the above two references to her "little" volumes of poetry refer to an economy of production and consumption that not only reveals her humility in regards to her creative work, but is also, perhaps, indicative of material limitations.

At this point a brief discussion of Ramírez's poetry that appeared in *El Demócrata Fronterizo* will yield further insight into her poetry of praxis. Of her surviving poems few address overtly political themes, they divide into three general categories:

1) occasion pieces dedicated to friends or family on their birthdays;
2) poems of unrequited love, and
3) philosophical poems about beauty and nature.

It is primarily but by no means exclusively in her philosophical poems that Ramírez embeds explicitly political critiques and in which she conveys her understanding of Mexican history and her vision for social change. Given her role as an activist and organizer and the intensely political nature of her letters to Magón, one might expect Ramírez's writings to be more overtly political calls to action and explicit criticisms of oppressive conditions. Keeping in mind that many of her journalistic and creative writings remain unavailable to contemporary readers, we are left, however, with the task of interpreting the form, style and content of those writings that are available.

Ramírez's writings on nature, love and philosophy share qualities of the romance style. The political relationships she comments upon are masked by references to nature. In one way this acts as a geographical strategy of containment through which she can articulate her ideas. Given the intense repression that her political affiliates experienced, she may have utilized this style as a means of deflecting the attention of authorities. The repressed content is, nevertheless, still there as an allegory to be interpreted by the discerning reader. In *The Political Unconscious,* Fredric Jameson states that ideology, production and style interact to create multiple levels of meaning and a reader must see through these interactions before one can discern the ostensible subject of a literary artefact and its ideology (214). Thus far, much detail has been provided to help us interpret Ramírez as an historical figure and, following Jameson, what I would like to suggest is that her style and form of writing also needs to be historicized, with the understanding that she was aware of her own poetic strategies.

In her poetry and essays Ramírez utilizes a rhetoric of pathos to inspire sympathy for her subjects. For instance, the following lines are taken from a poetic essay titled "The Kiss of an Angel," a eulogy for an eight-year-old girl named

María.

> María was an orphan and very poor,
> so poor, that her humility made a pain-
> ful contrast beside the other educated
> girls with rich clothes, sovereign
> haughtiness, smiling cheeks and looks
> always lively and mischievous.
>
> More than once I accompanied
> María to her house. Such humility, such
> poverty, better said, such misery!
>
> The little work her mother did was
> barely enough to prolong the agony of
> the life of four little ones.
> (qtd. in Tovar 172)

Tovar suggests that in this essay María symbolizes "Mexico, the nation. the people, the poor and suffering masses whose liberation was so urgent for these [PLM] revolutionaries" (Legacy, 14). Much of Ramírez's writing bears strong stylistic resemblance to essays in *Regeneración* written by Enrique and Ricardo Flores Magón. The following excerpt is from a piece titled "Bread!" by Enrique Flores Magón in the February 28, 1913 issue of the party newspaper.

> Don't cry my child. Some day a good man will give you bread. . . His mother, a young woman, with pale and trembling lips from hunger and brilliant eyes with the fever of weakness, walked the streets of the city of Mexico, searching in vain for work.
> Nobody wanted to employ her. Of what good was a weak girl? . . . The night now had been closed a long time, and still the unhappy woman, with her feet sore from the unceasing walk, still hunts a piece of bread for the hungry child. Such is the life in Mexico.

Sentimentality in their writings subsumes class consciousness with nationalist sentiment. Tom Nairn suggests that political mobilization of people of underdeveloped nations often resorts to commonplace sentiment as well as cultural and racial identities because the insurgent group does not have access to economic and political institutions or "high" literature. Accordingly, though nationalism exploits difference it is also invariably populist. Nairn says: "For kindred reasons, [nationalism] has to function through highly rhetorical forms, through a sentimental culture sufficiently accessible to the lower strata now being called to battle" (340). The claim that nationalism has a cultural base which can be manipulated rhetorically, as in the above excerpts by Flores Magón and Ramírez, is buttressed by Benedict Anderson's assertion that nationalism is a cultural artefact (4).

As Ramírez's membership in an anti-clerical association attests, she is an opponent of institutional religion, yet much of her poetry utilizes the rhetoric of faith, if only to subvert it. Her faith is secular, it is linked to the lived experiences and material reality of people. She believes in people's ability to overcome adversity. To this end, those experiences which strip people of their illusions are seen as valuable, even when they are painful. Her aesthetics regarding beauty and nature are often informed by power dynamics. These concerns are apparent in the opening lines from "Reef."

> If the reef does not cause anger, if it does
>   not discourage
> To be wounded twice on the same rock;
> If not two times, then not a hundred; the
>   arena of combat
> Provokes triumph and not surrender.

The anarchist tendency toward martyrdom, or the "heroic stance" as Gómez-Quiñones calls it, is also apparent in the above lines. Tovar compares Ramírez's views on traditional religion and spirituality with Ricardo Flores Magón's expressed in an essay titled "Vamos Hacia la Vida" (July 1907). In these writings, both Ramírez and Magón express a philosophy of praxis in which combat and opposition solidify and clarify one's determination. As is apparent in the above lines, "Reef" begins by privileging adversity. The last four lines, however, suggest that the struggle is a learning process in which metaphysical illusions must be overcome:

> Blessed be the reef that relieves pain!
> Blessed be Lucifer for the rude assault!
> Blessed be the obstacle that teaches us
> To struggle and always to climb higher!
>   (qtd. in Tovar 183)

In firm opposition to the church, Ramírez aligns the struggle for good with Lucifer, the rebel angel thrown out of Heaven for not accepting his place in the hierarchy. Written in 1908, her lines echo Magón's 1907 essay, where he proclaims: "Submission is the cry of the vile; Rebellion is the cry of men! Lucifer, rebel, is more dignified than the henchman, submissive Gabriel" (qtd in Tovar 234). Tovar notes that in their writings both Magón and Ramírez claim resistance as a sacred act which demonstrated that "The spirituality of the Magonista and other revolutionary movements (like Zapata's) was grounded in a faith in the people and in the possibility of radical change" (234). In positing secular change in spiritualist terms the Magonistas sought to engage the imagination of its audience in culturally familiar forms. Flores Magón's essay grounds revolutionary practice in the material world and aligns the Mexican Revolution with democratic struggles occurring elsewhere.

Nations no longer rebel because they prefer to adore one god in place of another. The great social commotions that had their genesis in religions, have been left petrified in history. The French Revolution gained us the right to think; but it did not gain us the right to live, and the winning of this right is what the conscious men of every country and every race intend to do.

Here is why we revolutionaries are not in pursuit of a chimera. We do not struggle for abstractions, but rather for material things. We want land for everyone, and for everyone bread. Since perforce blood must be shed, may the conquests gain benefits for all and not just for a particular social caste. (*Sembradores* 100)

As one of the chief propagandists for the PLM, Magón's writings were more lengthy and developed than Ramírez's essays in *El Demócrata Fronterizo* or *La Crónica*. Although her own writings often remained abstract and less explicit in their analysis, Magón's influence upon Ramírez is evident. By no means should Ramírez's style be seen as merely derivative of her cohorts; her poetry is always explicitly grounded in the context from which she writes. In "Reef" Ramírez writes of pain as a metaphor for the measure of that which all people must be willing to give to forge a new life. By inverting a spiritual epic and making it applicable to the harsh conditions of war and social conflict faced by *mexicanos* on both sides of the border, Ramírez widens the terrain for discussing who was affected by and involved in the Revolution. It is not, after all, only soldiers and statesmen who suffer the material effects of war.

One occasion poem of Ramírez's is an explicit call to political action. "21 of March: To Juárez", written during a trip to Mexico in the Spring of 1908, is an explicit call to political action.[14] This poem is one of four poems dedicated to Juárez published by various poets in *El Demócrata Fronterizo* and *La Crónica* from 1906 to 1910. In these poems the authors praise Juárez's traits as a "true" leader of the people for the political reforms he initiated. This poetic tradition, imbued with nostalgia for better social and political times, I would argue, is informed by a critique of the Díaz regime, for all that it is not.[15]

In Ramírez's tribute to Juárez her nationalism is clear, as are her beliefs in the ultimate liberation of Mexico and the long, painful nature of political struggle as well as and the human frailties that impede social progress. Ramírez celebrates the history of resistance to domination that is Mexico's legacy. According to the poet, Mexico's redemption will lie in the fulfillment of its destiny, a destiny to which past wars of liberation have only served as a "prologue sublime and irresolute." And though the poem is in honor of an historical figure, Ramírez wants his invocation to rouse political action in the present. Ever the pragmatist, Ramírez knows that victory is not easily won, but is the culmination of a long process which requires dedication.

All those feats,
Cheers that the mountains repeat

> Like an echo of the Creator, drive us mad:
> And it is for this that on going from mouth to mouth,
> From heart to heart, it is forgotten
> That the glory of the present is little,
> And the work for the good is unfinished.
> . . . It is only the fault of human effort
> Which will forgive me if I find it to be the culprit.

Although written on March 21, 1908 during a visit to Castaños, Mexico, "21 of March: To Juárez" was not published in *El Demócrata Fronterizo* until May 9, 1908, after her return. A planned revolt against the Mexican government was scheduled for June 25 and involved forty to sixty-four PLM groups. The signal for the different PLM groups to begin their revolt was to be an attack on Ciudad Juárez launched from El Paso, Texas. Six days before the scheduled rebellion the El Paso headquarters were raided by U.S. authorities.[16] It cannot be unmistakably proven, but it seems quite probable that the proximity of the publication of Ramírez's "21 of March: To Juárez" to the date and location of this offensive was not entirely arbitrary. The call to action and the prophesy in the poem anticipate future actions even while commemorating a glorious past:

> I am happy, because I feel my heart
> Shout like a prophet:
> You, the indomitable Mexican people,
> Look at the past and think of tomorrow,
> You are yet most distant from your goal.
> (qtd. in Tovar 159-61)

The intersection of Ramírez's poetry and politics is nowhere more evident than in the above lines. A devout nationalist who believed that Mexico could only win self-determination through a popular revolution, Ramírez also believed that inspiration for the future must be drawn from the past: "Oh pages of yesterday, blessed, holy, / You are the pedestal of glory / To which our feet direct us." Her "21 of March: To Juárez" is an exemplary poem of Ramírez because in it she utilizes the natural and the metaphysical to buttress her explicit political call to action.

As an eloquent and outspoken woman struggling for social and political justice, Ramírez can be seen as an intellectual and ideological precursor to Chicana feminism and Chicano literature. Austin-based writer Teresa Acosta has written an essay that investigates the relationship between herself as a contemporary Chicana poet and Ramírez as one of her most significant political and poetic precursors. This essay, "Tejana History as a Poem: Sara Estela Ramírez and Me," explores the relationship between the political and the personal in both Ramírez's and Acosta's poetry. Writers like Ramírez serve as inspiration and reminder to the contemporary Chicana poet of the significance of "historical foundations."

Acosta's identification with Ramírez is based not only upon gender and ethnicity, but upon shared notions of justice and resistance, and a common way of responding—through the written word. Acosta's sense of affiliation and camaraderie with Ramírez thus symbolically and materially connects contemporary Chicanas/os to past and present Mexicans on both sides of the border. This poetic essay on Ramírez reminds us that the legacy of racism and land dispossession still affects *mexicanos*. Government sponsored corporate transnationalism negatively impacts lives along the U.S. border today, and reminds us that there is a continuing need to practice a politics that transcends the border.

Conclusion

In focusing on the international dimension of labor, the PLM transcended the limitations of the nation state, despite their acknowledgment of the value of nationalism as an organizing strategy. As an intermediary of the PLM leadership, a devoted activist, and teacher, Ramírez must be seen as part of a political avant garde which refused to accept or respect restrictive notions of gender roles, national identity, national borders or citizenship status. She viewed nationalism as a strategem for living with the contradictions produced by class struggle in the racialized context of the United States.

Ramírez's writings belong to a literature of political and social movement that anticipated the need to counter narrow notions of identity. For her, geographical movement across national borders was strategic, as part of a larger purpose of political education and propagandizing. The Mexican diaspora into the United States has been spurred by the economic, political and physical violence that accompanies capitalism and colonialism, and it should be seen as part of the continuing legacy of transnationalism. In an idosyncratic manner, the insurgent activities and gendered deconstructions of power and politics that Ramírez articulates defies notions of the Migrant generation as pre-political and passive. The activities and concerns she wrote of are still germane for comprehending the cultural and national identity of Mexicans in the United States. In her work, Ramírez demonstrates that history is neither a phenomenon of any single nation that can be contained by national borders, nor can it be understood in segmented, discrete and otherwise arbitrary periods of historical generations in which a given national and political identity is asserted to be universal.

Finally, though my own search for the "lost" texts of Ramírez was not fruitful, no archival work is unproductive. We must continue to seek out Ramírez's unrecovered work in those pre-1910 issues of *La Crónica,* in *La Corregidora*, in her contrbutions to *Vesper,* and in *Aurora,* the literary journal she founded in 1909, as well as her various collections of poems and stories which were circulated in limited numbers in Mexico and Tejas.[17] Clearly, much work remains to be done in order to fully comprehend the complexity of this astute thinker and writer. Though very little advance has been made in the recovery of her work, a

clearer picture of what needs to be done has been drawn as well as a better understanding of the socio-political context in which she and her fellow "Mexicanos"
wrote. Even as we continue to search for the remainder of her work, however,
there is an ongoing need to make her writings available to the general populace
and especially to the community of Mexican descent in the United States, which
grows in readership and continually acquires new critical perspectives as well as
deeper historical knowledge. Though we can never predict with precise accuracy what will be recovered in archives that contain our literary heritage, doing
such work enables us to explore that beautiful mystery.

Notes

[1] Several book-length studies of Chicano history attest to this. Mario García's
Mexican Americans: Leadership, Ideology and Identity, 1930-1960 (1989) and
Carlos Muñoz's *Youth Identity & Power: The Chicano Movement* (1989) are but
two examples.

[2] Many scholars acknowledge that some of these migrants viewed their relocation into the U.S. as a temporary condition. For these people, a return to their
native country was imminent as soon as more peaceful conditions emerged.
Among migrants are people who see their relocation as a temporary inconve-
nience, others who may consider their move as permanent, those who are worried
about their immediate survival and who have no pre-determined long term goals
and others who, in the first quarter of the century especially, may consider themselves political exiles. This last group, political exiles, are often not considered
official migrants because they are still oriented to their nation of origin. However,
I would argue that this orientation is always mediated and affected by the specific context in which they are living and working. Just as those migrants who saw
their move to the U.S. as a temporary hiatus, so too, did exiles believe that they
would return to Mexico when conditions improved. For a variety of reasons,
many people who once thought they would return, did not.

[3] See Luis Arroyo's "Notes on Past, Present, and Future Directions of
Chicano Labor Studies," in *Aztlán*, 6.2 (1975) for a discussion of the various
approaches to Chicano labor history.

[4] "The First Steps: Chicano Labor Conflict and Organizing, 1900-1920."
(13-45). *Aztlón*. 3.1 (1973).

[5] See *Between Borders: Essays on Mexicana/Chicana History*, Ed. Adelaida
R. Del Castillo; *Women's Work and Chicano Families*, Patricia Zavella; *La
Chicana: The Mexican-American Woman*, Alfredo Mirande and Evangelina
Enríquez; *Cannery Women, Cannery Lives*, Vicki Ruiz; *Building With Our Own
Hands: New Directions in Chicana Studies*. Eds. Adela de la Torre and Beatriz
M. Pesquera.

[6] See Ricardo Romo's, *East Los Angeles* (31-59) and Mario García's, *Desert*

Immigrants, for two examples.

[7] De León's *They Called Them Greasers: Anglo Attitudes Towards Mexicans in Texas, 1821-1900,* both writes against this problem and perpetuates it. De León notes how early Anglo histories of Texas only referred to Tejanas as objects of Anglo men's fancies (9-10). However, he limits his own discussion of them to familial and cultural practices. In contrast, Chicana history foregrounds agency by women in the public and private sphere.

[8] Ramírez's poetry was originally written in Spanish. Tovar provides a complete translation of Ramírez's work in her study. I utilize her translations.

[9] Valdés, in Tovar 111. *Punto Rojo* and *El Amigo del Pueblo* are two other socialist oriented Spanish language papers mentioned by Zamora in "Chicano Socialist Labor Activity in Texas, 1900-1920."

[10] The proliferation of politically oriented alternative newspapers in the Southwest at the turn of the century can also be seen as yet another organizing practice carried over from Mexico. In Mexico, anti-Díaz propagandists were frequently jailed and opposition presses shut down by the Mexican government in efforts to silence resistance. Cockcroft reports that in 1901 and 1902 at least forty-two anti-Díaz newspapers were shut down and fifty journalists imprisoned (*Intellectual Precursors* 102). The threat to the nation-state posed by journalism was not unique to Mexico, but it does point to the powerful role of the press in facilitating a national vision that was at odds with the state apparatus and ideology. In the U.S. context, however, the form that popular Mexican nationalism assumed was of a different sort, requiring an "imagined community" that, in contrast to Benedict Anderson's definition, was not inherently limited and sovereign (6).

[11] "'A La Mujer': A Critique of the Partido Liberal Mexicano's Gender Ideology on Women." See Works cited for full citation.

[12] In the construction of the Migrant Generation as we know it, the work and lives of these women have not found a place. It is only in the specialized histories of labor, journalism and "women" that their work is acknowledged. That people like Sara Estela Ramírez are not included in historical narratives attests to the limited notions of identity and leadership which inform that genre of historical literature.

[13] Tovar has suggested that the name Ramírez chose for her independent newspaper, *La Corregidora,* signifies her commitment to fostering feminist ideas by acknowledging the important role that Doña Josefa Ortíz de Domínguez played in the 1810 Mexican War for Independence.[1] Doña Josefa is one of the few, if not the only, women in the pantheon of heroes of Mexican independence. Although no known copies of *La Corregidora* still exist, Ramírez's second letter to Magón informs us that she is going to suspend its publication in order to collaborate with two other PLM supporters to publish another paper, *La Verdad,* which would be produced in Austin.

[14] Benito Juárez was the indigenous populist President of Mexico in 1861

and again from 1867 to 1872. He was instrumental in leading the fight against French occupation. His tenure marked the beginning of the Liberal Reform Movement, which was to end with the ascension of Díaz to power. In 1899, on the anniversary of Juarez's death students in San Luis Potosí marked the date by staging an anti-Díaz demonstration (Cockcroft 73). Thus there was a recent precedent for using the anniversary of his death to protest political and social conditions.

[15] These poems, "A Juárez" by Nina Ernestina Flores, "Remitido: En Defensa 'A Juárez' y Homenaje al Igniniero Bulnes" by Pedro Leal Cortés, and Constancio Peña Idíaquez's "A Juárez" deserve closer readings as individual poems than I can give here. They also signal the extent to which Ramírez's poetry was indicative of the social and political times as well as the aesthetic sensibility to which they gave rise. This is even more evident when a broader examination of the poetry published in these papers is taken into account. The range of subject matter is evident in a selection of titles to the poems: "La Creación: Poema Indio," "Horas Tristes: A Mi Esposa," "El Cometa del Halley," "Raza Impura," and "Triptico" are but a few examples. Many of these poets names appear only once, but there are some important exceptions of names that appear numerous times. Of these, Ernesto Siliceo Martínez appeared to be a prolific poet who consistently published his work in the papers.

[16] The raid seriously impeded the effectiveness of the overall rebellion, although it did not stop it completely (*Sembradores* 33). The raid at El Paso was a result of infiltration by the U.S. government (MacLachlan 18). It was particularly damaging—a large cache of dynamite that had been provided by the miners of Arizona was captured.

[17] The next phase of recovery work on Ramírez should perhaps be conducted in Mexico—in the border states and in México City where her work was distributed. Also, an extensive search for her work in the archives of others, especially a family like the Idars, might prove fruitful. Another avenue of inquiry could be a closer analysis of the articles in *La Crónica*. Although Ramírez is consistently listed as a collaborator until the announcement of her death appears, she never received bylines. And while many of the other collaborators did not receive bylines, it is clear from those that did that the male writers were much more likely to have their authorship identified.

Works Cited

Acosta, Teresa. "Tejana History as a Poem: Šara Estela Ramírez and Me." Thomas Barker Collection, University of Texas, Austin.
Anderson, Benedict. *Imagined Communities: Reflections on the Origin and Spread of Nationalism*. 1983. Rev. ed. London: Verso, 1991.
Cortés, Pedro Leal. "Remitido: En Defensa 'A Juárez' y Homenaje al Inginiero

Bulnes." *El Democrata Fronterizo.* 7 June 1906; 2.

Cockcroft, James. *Intellectual Precursors of the Mexican Revolution, 1900-1913.* Latin American Monographs 14. Austin: University of Texas, 1976.

de la Torre, Adela and Beatriz M. Pesquera. *Building With Our Own Hands: New Directions in Chicana Studies.* Berkeley: University of California, 1993.

de León, Arnoldo. *They Called Them Greasers: Anglo Attitudes Toward Mexicans in Texas, 1821-1900.* Austin: University of Texas, 1983.

Flores. Ernestina. "A Juárez." *El Democrata Fronterizo.* 14 April 1906; 2.

García, Mario. *Mexican Americans: Leadership, Ideology, & Identity, 1930-1960.* New Haven: Yale, 1989.

Gómez-Quiñones, Juan. *Sembradores, Ricardo Flores Magón y El Partido Liberal Mexicano: A Eulogy and Critique.* Los Angeles: Aztlán Publications, 1973. 114-16.

Hernandez, Inés. "Sara Estela Ramírez: Sembradora." *Legacy: A Journal of Nineteenth-Century American Women Writers.* 6.1 (1989): 13-26.

Idíaquez, Constancio-Peña. "A Juárez." *La Crónica.* 19 August 1910; 5.

MacLachlan, Colin M. *Anarchism and the Mexican Revolution: The Political Trials of Ricardo Flores Magón in the United States.* Berkeley: University of California, 1991.

Magón, Ricardo Flores. "A La Mujer (To Women)." *Regeneración* [Los Angeles] 24 Sept. 1910. Rpt. in *Mexican Women in the United States: Struggles past and present.* Ed. Magdalena Mora and Adelaida R. Del Castillo. Occasional Paper 2. Los Angeles: Chicano Studies Research Center Publications, University of California, 1980. 159-62.

———. "Bread!" Trans. Mary F. Winnen. *Regeneración* [Los Angeles] 28 Feb. 1913: 8.

Mendoza, Louis G. "Making History: Generational Constructs, National Identity, and Critical Discourse in 20th Century Chicana/o Literature." Diss. University of Texas, 1994.

Mirandé, Alfredo, and Evangelina Enríquez. *La Chicana: The Mexican American Woman.* Chicago: University of Chicago, 1977.

Muñoz, Carlos. *Youth, Identity, and Power: The Chicano Movement.* London: Verso, 1989.

Nairn, Tom. *The Break-Up of Britain: Crisis and New-Nationalism.* 2nd ed. London: Verso, 1977.

Pérez, Emma M. "'A La Mujer': A Critique of the Partido Liberal Mexicano's Gender Ideology on Women." *Between Borders: Essays on Mexicana/Chicana History.* Ed. Adelaida R. Del Castillo. La Mujer Latina Series. Encino: Floricanto Press, 1990. 459-82.

Spivak, Gayatri Chakravorty. Introduction. *Selected Subaltern Studies.* Eds. Ranajit Guha and Gayatri Chakravorty Spivak. New York: Oxford, 1988. 3-32.

Tovar, Inés Hernández. "Sara Estela Ramírez: The Early Twentieth Century Texas-Mexican Poet." Diss. University of Houston, 1984.

Zamora, Emilio, Jr. "Sara Estela Ramírez: Una Rosa Roja en el Movimiento." *Mexican Women in the United States: Struggles past and present.*

Mediating the Desire of the Reader in Villegas de Magnón's *The Rebel*[1]

Andrea Tinnemeyer
Rice University

The republication of *The Rebel* by the Recovering the U.S. Hispanic Literary Heritage Project marks a turning point in Mexican-American letters and criticism. Prior Chicana/o representations of the Mexican Revolution privileged a version which was agrarian based, and peopled by members of the lower class. This is especially true in such texts as José Antonio Villarreal's *Pocho* and Ernesto Galarza's *Barrio Boy*. More recently, Sandra Cisneros' "Eyes of Zapata" from *Woman Hollering Creek* tempers the heroic aura of Emiliano Zapata through a narrative that recenters the efforts of Mexican women as the silenced bodies that sustained the Revolution. Likewise in criticism, Chicana/o scholars have tended to apply Marxist, structuralist, and poststructuralist theories to better understand and promote the histories of working-class Mexican-Americans in the United States. In contrast, Leonor Villegas de Magnón narrates a little understood version of the revolution and her relationship with Venustiano Carranza, a member of the upper-class that led a segment of the revolution often at odds with Emiliano Zapata and Pancho Villa.

The distance which Villegas de Magnón bridges with contemporary Mexican-American readers in terms of providing a new perspective on the Revolution likewise existed for her immediate audience. Despite the socialist orientation of the revolution, Villegas de Magnón makes clear the various obstacles she faces as a woman born in Mexico, but also claiming U. S. citizenship, and as a member of an upper-class family which benefited under the *porfiriato*. Augmenting this condition was the U. S. perception of the war. For this perception, Villegas de Magnón rewrote *La Rebelde*, a text originally intended for a pro-nationalist, Mexican reader, into *The Rebel*, a text that characterized, presupposed, and anticipated an Anglo-American reader. Like René Girard's exploration of the dynamics of mediated desire in *Deceit, Desire, and the Novel*, Villegas de Magnón deduces and then mediates the desires of an Anglo-American audience in the rewriting of her book. In his text, Girard explores mediation's capacity to supplant the "normal" discourse of desire, generally considered to be mutual, through the distorting influence of conjecture.[2] What occurs, then, is a triangle of desire predicated on the supposed desire of the other for the object; the object itself is therefore void of intrinsic meaning, but is rather defined by the conjectured desire which each rival supposes the other to possess for it. This essay explores the dynamics of reading that transpire in Leonor Villegas de Magnón's *The Rebel* between an Anglo-American reader and a Mexican-American author.[3]

How does a mediated discourse of desire translate into an interpretive model for the interactions between an Anglo-American reader and a Mexican-American author? In "Interaction between Text and Reader," Wolfgang Iser cites R. D. Laing's *The Politics of Experience* to explain the degree to which invisibility, what I will term unknowability because it implies the absence of shared experience, constitutes the gap between individuals which must always be arrived at through mediation. In other words, because we cannot know the experience of others, this difference in knowledge (invisibility) results in the repeated formation of views to account for the disparity of knowledge and mutually shared experience. Hence, each dyadic interaction, "will contain a view of others and, unavoidably, an image of ourselves" (Iser, 22). Iser states that the absence of a "face-to-face situation" in reading, meaning that a text cannot adopt itself to each reader, generates a series of questions in which the partners in the dyadic interaction interrogate each other to determine the success of their projected images to fill this gap of unknowability and lack of mutual experience.

For the sake of this argument, cultural, linguistic, and historical differences comprise the gap between Anglo-American readers and the Mexican-American author. Since the text takes up the Mexican Revolution as its subject matter, this gap occurs along lines of national history and racial understandings; and since the United States intervened in the conflict, it is at least possible that the reader as well as the author come to the text with preconceptions. This is not to say that the text's intentionality is entirely didactic or merely that the reader learns about Mexico and its history; it is also, and more importantly, to say that the reader must learn how to bridge the gap of differences caused by unknowability. In short, it is by reading *The Rebel* that one must learn how to read it.

If the text can mediate between the experience of the reader who expresses a desire to know and the object which occupies the desired position, then the author can likewise offer an interpretation which can replace the reader's experience outside of the text. Further, the novel can provide a textual experience that can then be substituted for the actual previous experience of the reader. The text itself, as Villegas de Magnón has constructed it, stands in as the site of mediation between the desires of the reader and those of the author. One can trace metatexual moments where the author's desire supplants that of the reader. These moments include narrative ruptures of the genre and the choreography of Lily Long, the only Anglo-American character in the text.

Within *The Rebel* are textual moments functioning as cultural or social markers to make a spectacle of the Mexican-American to the Anglo-American reader. These moments occur early in the narrative and primarily involve Julia and Pancho, two members of the lower social class who are the loyal servants of Leonor and her father's family. These two figures become the representatives of the lower class in Mexico, of the *indios* and all their gestures and words are mediated with textual commentary that provides a reading of them as such. They are flat figures created by the one-dimensionality of the colonizing gaze either of the Spaniard *conquistador* or the American reporter/tourist.[4]

When Leonor's father remarries and the family decides to reside on the American side of the river, Julia and Pancho move with them and thus become subject to the narrative of bordercrossers. They survey the process of assimilation of Leonor and her brother, Lorenzo, whose step-mother has declared that she will make Americans of them.[5] These two indigenous servants whose identities are inextricably tied to notions of class, are continually enclosed in and surrounded by houses and huts whose depictions reflect a very American accounting of indigenous Mexicans and echo stereotypical portrayals of Mexicans as simple-minded people. Julia and Pancho are seen in tableau: fixed, immobile, and on display.

Before the Villegas family travels across to the other side of the river, Julia and Pancho make plans to remain in close proximity to the family and to report to the grandmother, Doña Damiana: "We can sell candy on the streets. Each of us can have a *little* candy box trimmed with gay tissue paper, the box covered with a screen. We can stand on the corners of the busy streets selling our candy" (47, emphasis mine). Such a trade as selling candy on the streets would hardly feed the two and yet this entrepreneurial prospect is presented in such innocent terms almost reminiscent of Horatio Alger novels that it seems aware of previous American propaganda literature. What the reader takes away from Julia's plan is a visual image, as are all other depictions of the two of them, rather than a deep, textual sense of their thoughts or troubles. They are presented primarily on a two-dimensional plane and become three-dimensional only as a picture might—that is, when the reader imagines it.

After crossing the river into the United States, Pancho and Julia remain diminished caricatures: "When [they] arrived in Laredo, they went to the friend's house nearby. They rented a *little* hut close to the landing. Here, spreading a sarape on the hard clay floor, they were soon asleep in each other's arms" (49). Later, "Pancho made a *little* shed around the house, walling it with branches and vines. Big earthen jars of water on the crude table and benches in the shade soon attracted weary travelers" (51). From these descriptions, Mexicans emerge as simple, rural people who are content with the most basic pleasures and are happiest when they are serving other people. Further, Villegas de Magnón's emphasis on the space which Julia and Pancho occupy serves as a metonymy to trite representations of Mexicans which also restrict them, confine their movements and their possibilities for breaking free from rhetorical constraints. However, Villegas de Magnón carefully addresses the stereotype and subverts this very reading by making it an almost hyperbolic intrusion into the text and, therefore, discloses its falseness or bankruptcy. Pancho's active participation in the revolution by ferrying rebel soldiers across the river serves as one instance in which the character explodes formulaic depictions (87-90). Pancho's courageous and patriotic acts exceed the previous racist descriptions of him and his wife.

The descriptions of Julia and Pancho are in direct contrast, particularly with respect to class, with Leonor and early depictions of her own family. Hence, there is an implicit contrast between what Americans stereotypically conceive of as Mexicans (Julia and Pancho) and the upper-class Villegas family, educated in the United States and, therefore, more closely aligned with American attributes and appealing to the Anglo-American reader. In fact, the confluence of race and class is further problematized by the presence of national difference. The prosperity of the Villegas family coincides with Leonor's education in the United States, which can be read as a correlation between financial success and American assimilation. However, a reading of the relationship between Leonor's mother and father echoes and queries trite notions of *machismo*. On one page we read, "She adored her husband and lived only to please and serve him," (10) on the next, we encounter passages that disrupt such a reading by recounting how the mother saves her husband's life. Further, what appears in the quote to be one-sided, self-sacrificing devotion emanating from the wife only is later qualified by the actions and emotions of Don Joaquín when Doña Valerianna, his first wife, is on her deathbed: "Don Joaquín took his wife's hand, bending over her to hear her voice. He could not speak. She was the braver" (36). Here we have two instances of the mother's actions and then the narrator's interpretation which run counter to the original stereotypical portrayal of a Mexican wife/mother. What makes this series of citations metatextual is the authoritative discourse turning against itself and therefore positioned to critique itself.

The text labors in a similar vein when addressing Native Americans, a race perhaps even more subject to racism than Mexicans at the time. When Leonor and her family encounter Comanches on their way to another part of Mexico, cries like, "Only God can save us," rise up at the first sight of the approaching Native Americans. Such responses do not seem far removed from the religious rhetoric that permeated early Puritan texts such as Mary Rowlandson's captivity narrative. However, also absent from these early American narratives, closely following a stereotypical reading of Native Americans, is a counter speech addressing commonalities between the Mexicans and the Native Americans:

Yes, I admit, they appeared fierce, yet they gave us many beautiful things, fine

furs, beads, and moccasins. They are the last of a noble race that once owned
Mexico. Now they are wanderers in their own land. These men are good at
heart, just like all of us. If they are approached in a friendly manner, they
quickly respond. The world is not actually against anyone. It is fear and misunderstanding that make people fight. (22)

Don Joaquín's speech is a perfect instance of the multi-voiced heteroglossia that
permeates this novel and allows it to both speak to and against the Anglo-
American reader. Unpacking the various voices that speak at this particular
narrative moment reveals first, the stereotype (Native Americans appear fierce),
then a counter voice (they are good at heart), then a didactic voice (It is fear and
misunderstanding that make people fight). In the sequence of these voices is the
very structure that on a macroscale informs *The Rebel*. Villegas de Magnón
begins her narrative with formulaic renditions in keeping with racist stereotypes, then counters them with fuller representations that are psychologically
rich, and ultimately supplants them with a didactic statement that instructs.
Statements like Don Joaquín's form a definitive conclusion working directly
against the primary supposition, spoken from the voice of "fear and misunderstanding."

The passage also performs a secondary function, which is to indirectly
address misconceptions about Mexicans, here textually coded as Native
Americans. Further, the statement, "the last of a noble race that once owned
Mexico" speaks to the issue of the loss of Mexican territory to North Americans
after the 1848 Treaty of Guadalupe Hidalgo. Following the hands through
which Mexican territory was exchanged, we note that Native Americans and
Spanish were former possessors of the land. The fact that Native Americans are
referred to as "the last of a noble race" indirectly indicts current owners by placing them after this age.

Chapter VIII is primarily devoted to enlarging the reader's familiarity with
Mexico and the events prefiguring the Revolution—knowledge vital to our
understanding of Leonor's entrance into the war as the organizer of *La Cruz
Blanca* and as a supporter of Carranza. In particular, Villegas de Magnón supplies a version of Mexican history leading to the revolution against Madero that
runs counter to that held by Americans who base their conception of the revolution on America's alliance with General Huerta. She again creates a dialogical
moment in the narrative by allowing oppositional voices, those loyal to Huerta
and those loyal to Madero, to speak against each other. Driven by her implicit
awareness of the American narrative of Mexican Revolution, she provides her
reader with a carefully scripted account of Huerta's actions against Madero
predicated on a characterization of Huerta as a villain.

The vilification of Huerta marks a rhetorical turn in the narrative which
flies in the face of the point of view commonly held by Americans who favored
Huerta over Madero. Villegas de Magnón uses the text as a site of mediation by
creating a dialogue between the oppositional voices that speak to different read-

ings of the political struggle between the two men:

> The *coup d'etat* that overthrew Madero in early 1913 was in no way a popu-
> lar revolution. It was a barracks plot, a conspiracy of a few army officers
> financed by *científicos* living in exile and a few Spanish reactionaries. It was
> attended by circumstances of treachery so depraved, of villainy so fantastic, of
> cruelty so barbaric that the story is one which the mind has difficulty in accept-
> ing as credible. (83)

This cited passage marks a shift from what M. M. Bahktin terms as an authoritative discourse to one that is internally persuasive. What at first would appear
to be a colonizing narrative moment is in fact similar to heteroglossia because
it presupposes another voice that exists in its absence and its inability to narrate
this historical event. Villegas de Magnón brings about this discursive change by
undermining the voice's authority through the presence of the voice in its
absence, in its negation. The authoritative voice dialogues with the narrative
one and is signaled inversely in its negation, "in no way a popular revolution."
Such a phrase presupposes another voice which would speak of the *coup d'etat*
as a popular revolution. Hence, the novel reveals the extent to which it enters
into a dialectic with other voices, here particularly focused and struggling
against two terms for labeling the same event where the use of one word, *coup
d'etat,* necessarily signals the negation of the other, "revolution." She also provides the reader with a discursive space that can accommodate their original
reading of the event by couching the horrors that surround the death of Madero
as difficult to believe, or incredible.

At this narrative moment, Villegas de Magnón does not specifically identify this other voice aligned with Huerta as American. However, the following
paragraph implicates the national identity behind this voice that speaks of the
assassination of Madero as "revolutionary" through the visual image of Huerta
with American Ambassador Wilson (83). For the Anglo-American reader who
arrives at this scene of camaraderie between Huerta and Wilson, Villegas de
Magnón has successfully created a dissonance between him/her and the
American government which, by its friendship with Huerta, sanctions these acts
of treachery, villainy, and cruelty, even if indirectly. Perhaps this narrative
moment marks the initiation of the reader into a loyal alliance with the author
in direct defiance of a nationalistic authority, here represented by Ambassador
Wilson, therefore freeing them from an unexamined dependence on American
interpretations of the Mexican Revolution. Paragraphs like these which are
interspersed throughout the novel represent the very accommodating gestures
that Villegas de Magnón makes to first satiate the reader's desire to know and
then to provide them with the correct information that supplants extant narratives and myths of Mexico. The awkwardness of these metatextual moments
becomes a locus where the reader recognizes the multi-voiced nature of the text.
However, unlike other moments previously discussed, here one of the voices is

represented by its silence, its absence.

Accommodations to the reader such as these weave a metatextual narrative of disparate knowledge and experience even as they function to ameliorate difference, whether cultural or otherwise. Some of these metatextual moments are what I term "anthropological," where the narrator disrupts the present action in order to fill in the cultural or historical background. The author breaks her narrative voice to interject necessary historical information, much like a guide at a museum who points out a figure and then proceeds to give a brief account of it. This occurs with figures and with historical events related to the Revolution. Clara Lomas, the editor of the novel, seems to echo these passages by extending her introduction beyond the text proper into appendices that give brief biographies of central characters.

The penetration of the narrative by a historian at various moments in the novel is not unlike the glossaries of Spanish terms that appear in the back of books of Chicana/o poetry or fiction. But these moments go beyond what amounts to dictionary entries because they are tied to individuals, to historical events, and to cultural practices. There are moments when the narrator steps in and informs the reader that the meal just catalogued is a typical frontier meal (164) or that Julia and Pancho's duties are typical of servants in the *hacendado* system. What occurs at these sites of interruption is two-fold: there is an implicit acknowledgement of the reader's lack of knowledge of these cultural, historical practices and events, and there is an almost exaggerated effort to make the reader culturally conversant. In other words, because these moments exist at all testifies to the distance between narrator and reader. Taken as such, these moments can be read backwards, undone, and shown to indicate a reading of the reader. They are anticipations of the sites of knowledge which remain unbridged. Villegas de Magnón builds this bridge through metatextual passages.

The ruptures in narrative voice which seek to overcome difference not only react to a perceived absence of knowledge, but also to a perceived present knowledge hostile to that held by the author. Americans did in fact intervene in the Mexican Revolution, yet they were allied with the *federales*, the very entity against which Carranza, and therefore Villegas de Magnón, were fighting. American involvement in the war reflected its economic investments in Mexico.[6] General Blackjack Pershing invaded Mexico by permission of the Mexican government, hoping to capture Pancho Villa and retaliate against his attacks on U.S. in border towns and trains.[7] Thus, the Anglo-American reader previously conversant with the Revolution will most likely arrive at the text with a preconceived notion of the troops under Carranza and Villa. The American reader enters into the war via the narrative guide who places him/her not only against the ruling American government, but more significantly, against the Americans involved in the Revolution.

Under the rubric of rebellion, the Americans have a scripted role that not only allies them with the Mexicans, but places them against their own nation's interest and alliance. This shift in allegiance functions in the reading of the text as a pledge of loyalty and more closely aligns the reader with the narrator who has also had to tear away from the government and its alliances in order to work for a higher cause of justice.

Villegas de Magnón mentions the U. S. government in passing, but focuses mainly on the Red Cross, who fail to maintain a neutral stance in the revolution by only treating the wounded federales and ignoring or denying medical treatment to the rebel soldiers. Villegas de Magnón amends this problem easily not only by pointing to the sites of similarity between the two nations, but also by presenting Lily Long who comes from the other side of the bridge to dedicate her time and her energy to curing wounded Mexican soldiers. Those moments where the Red Cross and the Red Cross come together are telling. At first, the Red Cross is found to be selectively treating wounded soldiers. Despite their duty or their pledge to serve all Mexican soldiers, they are only helping Federal soldiers (90). It would appear by default that the White Cross is founded to fill the void left by the Red Cross and treat the soldiers loyal to Carranza. This politicization of the wounded is indicative of the difference between American involvement in the war and that of Villegas de Magnón and the Americans whom she recruits into the White Cross.

Genre Rupture

The political merges with the personal and it is on this conflated field that Villegas de Magnón sets her third person autobiography. The text begins with her birth and then chronicles the life of her family until the moment when she marries and travels to live with her husband in Mexico City. Marriage becomes the occasion for her shift in narrative from chronicling the life of herself and her family to the history of her country and its turmoils related to the end of Porfirio Diaz' reign of tyranny. There is a significant break in the narrative voice at this point in the novel where the reader is being educated in Mexican history and given a dramatis personae that will carry through the drama of the Mexican Revolution. It is interesting that the moment of her political activism and her nationalistic sentiments occurs after her marriage—she is now inscribed within the patriarchy and therefore her actions would not seem as dangerous or as rebellious. However, this is far from the truth. In fact, her marriage can be seen as a veil which covers over her true spiritedness and sanctions her actions. It is also interesting to consider the roles that she plays in the Revolution itself. She organizes the White Cross which administers to the wounded soldiers of the Revolution and thus works within the paradigm of feminine behavior, that of nurturing and caring for others. The fact that she does this on a volunteer basis and that she recruits other women who also dedicate their time and talents to caring for wounded soldiers likewise remains within gender specific scripts.

Within this role, Villegas de Magnón carries out her own rebelliousness in a time of rebellion.

Her rebellion extends to the genre of autobiography, traditionally written in first person. Writing in third person thus divorces her from giving a more personal account of herself and more closely aligns her with the perspective naturally held by an American audience—that of an outsider. But before she relinquishes herself to utter objectification, she dedicates the first several chapters to a more conventional autobiographical trajectory and subject matter, which follows the marriage plot. However, even this section of the text deviates from the conventional genre because it abandons the protagonist to address the relationship between her father and step-mother while Leonor is further distanced from her family. The wedding becomes a metaphor for the union between the personal and the political and it is after this moment in the text that the reader follows the movements of the Rebel rather than those of Leonor. There is an interesting distinction in the terms used to refer to her because they indicate not only a projected version of the self, but also a type of self-authoring which permits her the same degree of freedom in her narrative as that afforded a rebel.

This anxiety about writing and producing a text and a series of meanings related to one's life story becomes even more problematic when the author is Mexican-American and the primary frame of meaning is Anglo-American. Outside of writings about the particular individual, the author of a Mexican-American text must also wrestle with the stereotypical representations historically and culturally in place which generate their own discourse of meaning regarding Mexican-Americans. For *The Rebel*, these other discourses of meaning center on pre-conceived notions of a Mexican-American female and include particular readings of members of the social elite as well as members of the community who side with Villa, Carranza, or the *federales* during the Mexican Revolution. Like current Chicana poets and writers, Villegas de Magnón is faced with the potential for dual betrayal—a siding with Anglo-Americans ideals in the writing of her own story and in her class relations, or, more specifically, a siding with Anglo-American women in her desire to write a story about herself which does not figure her into the patriarchy. In other words, by taking up the subject of women's potential for positive affect in Mexico, Villegas de Magnón is openly flouting *machismo* and Mexican patriarchy so that any liberating moment is at once seen as a betrayal to the Mexican heritage in general and to the Mexican men in particular.[8] A liberating act becomes one of betrayal of one's patrilinear ancestry and an alignment with Anglo-American culture which has preconceived notions of Mexicans.

Villegas de Magnón appears aware of the ruling interpretive communities that would impose their systems of meaning onto a reading of her text. Accordingly, her text not only contains a foil for the ideal American reader through the character of Lily Long, but also a textual account for a chracterization of herself that unites the textual bifurcation represented by autobiography and history into the characters of Leonor and Rebel respectively. This character who can encompass both is María de Jesús who cuts her hair, joins the troops, and places herself on the battlefield to fight for the Revolution (108-9). Unlike the female-gendered role of nurse which seems to cover and mask the liberating actions of the Rebel, María de Jesús participates in the transfer of secret communication between generals. She is captured, thrown into jail, and is able to escape by donning the attire of a servant woman who brings meals to the prisoners. Her cross-dressing back into the patriarchal system and into the costume of a patriarchally sanctioned role allows María de Jesús to escape from the very world whose clothing she temporarily wears. There are accounts before the Mexican Revolution, namely those of the Spanish Conquest, in which women wore the battle costume of men and engaged in combat. Hence, there is an historical precedent already operating with its own system for reading female participation in battle.

The Rebel itself makes several sacrifices that may be construed as textual gestures toward the inclusion of Anglo-American readers. Shifting the narrative from first to third person constitutes one such act. Much like the collective narrative voices collapsed into the protagonist in Tomas Rivera's *. . . y no se lo tragó la tierra,* who not only forgets the name that he is called, but whose narrative is itself intersected, interrupted, and ultimately compromised by the various communal voices originating from the migrant workers, Villegas de Magnón defies narrative convention of autobiography (also employed by Henry Adams in *The Education of Henry Adams*) by shifting from first to third person. There is a textual gesture which aligns the author with the reader by making an object out of the self which can then be read. This narrative move, marked by the shift in voice, places the self outside of the self and then comments, reads, and projects meaning onto it in much the same way that the Anglo-American reader looks at the text and at the Mexican-American as spectacles.

The novel opens with conventionally recognizable methods of identifying and characterizing Mexicans and then promptly disrupts these narrative structures and rebels against them. In other words, the text begins with characterizations that follow a shared system of reading conventions, namely those of biography. We follow the conventional chronology of the main character from her birth to her marriage. It is at the moment of her marriage where the text deviates from literary convention and inserts, and then operates on, its own structure of meaning.

All deviations from the standard literary convention of autobiography gesture to the colonization of the reader whose reading of the novel is carefully orchestrated by Villegas de Magnón to ensure against misreading. This is similar to the layering of identities—Leonor and Rebel—which together weave a tapestry that first lays down a more conventional telling of the life of a Mexican-American woman and then on top of that framework embellishes with a rebellious account of her participation in the Mexican Revolution and her dual loyalty to both Mexico and the United States. She begins in much the same way as a tour guide in a museum who has trained his/her own eye to see the same way as the tourists and to anticipate the same wonder and interest with which they will look upon something or someone representative of Mexico. And this is the initial position of the reader at the novel's beginning when presented with a social account of the *mozos*, "caretakers of the rich" (4).

Lily Long as the Ideal American Reader

Some of these metatextual passages bridging the reader and author are accomplished through the choreography of Lily Long, the woman who accompanies the Rebel during her time with Carranza. "Mrs. Lily Honeycutt Long, wife of a doctor, was the Rebel's secretary, capable friend, and companion. A good shot, skillful equestrienne, a perfect nurse, she did not speak a word of Spanish" (106). She appears or is introduced at the end of a long list of women, mostly upper-class Mexicans, who have volunteered their time and efforts for the White Cross. But despite being an American woman, Lily pledges her loyalty to the Rebel just pages after, stating: "I shall not leave you one single moment" (108). Within the span of two pages, Villegas de Magnón has set up what would conventionally be Other and then absorbed it into the ranks of the White Cross which does not make such distinctions. This is not a singular event—Lily becomes the character through which the author can negotiate differences in culture and language and overcome them.

When the Rebel and Lily meet Carranza for the first time, Lily's blond hair and blue eyes set her apart from the others who automatically read her as a stranger. However, the body is also the site of sameness. The scar on the Rebel's hand links her to Carranza. Mention is made of the conversations which occur in English—they are singled out because of their rarity and because they signal inclusion. There is a choreography of Lily's body which also echoes the rhetoric of inclusion and of a bond between Mexico and the United States. During the numerous dinners that the Rebel and Lily have with Carranza, occasioned by his arrival into a new state in Mexico, seating arrangements are mentioned—Carranza is flanked by Lily and Leonor. These gestures of inclusion, read through the character of Lily, do not only make this alliance on a political ground, but rather extend it based upon a female bond, articulated through the rhetoric of motherhood.

Maternal affection not only informs the actions of the women of the White Cross, but also the relationship between Lily and the Rebel. There is a way in which the American women caring for Mexican soldiers could be read as infantilizing the men and making them subordinate to the care of the women of the White Cross. The text counters this stereotypical reading by framing the relationship between Lily and the Rebel in familial terms. On several occasions,

Lily is worried for the Rebel. Not only that, but she remains loyal to her and stays with her in much the same way that a child clings to a parent. When Lily is stricken with a high fever, the only person that she calls out to is the Rebel (111). In a text where disease is a major trope for the healing of difference between Americans and Mexicans, this is the conversion or the performance of the love and loyalty that Lily has for the Rebel.

Lily could easily represent the ideal Anglo-American reader—she is sympathetic to the Mexican cause and willing to volunteer to help it. However, she is American and it is some time into the narrative before she encounters someone who speaks enough English to inform her of the historical background leading up to the Revolution. In consideration of the commonalities between Lily and the Anglo-American reader, she can be a model for the reader. The reader becomes informed of the key players and of past historical events which give rise to the Revolution just as Lily is—through a gradual process which occurs only once the character has professed a certain affinity to Mexico, whether volunteering for the White Cross or reading the text.

As with Lily Long, Villegas de Magnón is at times hyper-conscious of the differences between her originally intended audience and her English-speaking one. Anthropological moments in the text, an awareness of her own class bias, and a heightened sense of the different nationalities of the members of the White Cross all form a characterization of the reader based on a disparity of shared culture, knowledge, and history. Villegas de Magnón has a very difficult task in writing *The Rebel*. What she does to establish herself and what she interjects throughout the narrative to maintain a sense of community with audiences on both sides of the Rio Bravo marks her narrative as distinctive, as somewhat self-conscious, and as helpful as an early example of Mexican-American literature. As an autobiography told in third person, the text is already mediated and it is mediated specifically at the site of the individual subject. Perhaps this is because she knew that a woman taking on such a role would be difficult for readers, particularly Mexican readers. But even for Anglo-American readers, there is no point of connection with a Mexican-American author, particularly one who is relating the events of her own life and of the Mexican Revolution, a war fought on other land by other people. Villegas de Magnón seems hyper-aware of the different levels on which her text must bridge the gap created by difference. First, she must accommodate an audience's predisposition to read an autobiography by a Mexican-American. This is accomplished by shifting from first to third person, and thus objectifying a personal account. In this way, the narrator places herself more on the level of the reader. She tells us about herself. One trope that seems to permit her to deviate from hegemonizing structures is self-evident in the title—*The Rebel*. She is placed in this trope of rebellion by her father, who names her his rebel from the night of her birth. During the majority of the novel, she refers to herself as such.

Habermas talks about the emergence of the bourgeois public sphere, which creates its own reading public united in their common experiences of reading, experiences which are directed by the author. Villegas de Magnón must take into account the experiences and cultural and social identities of the readers. Which concepts will be readily acknowledged, accepted, and promulgated? The dialectic involved in the reading and writing process involves the simultaneous confirmation of the discrete subjectivity of both author and reader, at times quite evident in the direct authorial address. Villegas de Magnón does make gestures which could loosely fall into the category of authorial address, because of their indication of the self-conscious nature of the text. The novel must necessarily be self-conscious for the various problems that it must overcome in order to be a text in the first place. In the shift in intended audience or readership, Villegas de Magnón must necessarily have amended her text to accommodate the differences in readership which did not possess the same characteristics or cultural beliefs of her original, intended audience, Mexican nationals. This accommodation takes the form of excess—the novel expands and breaks from its original voice at times in order to create a landscape of mutual understanding and experience between narrator and reader. In order for Leonor Villegas de Magnón to create a dialogical structure to her novel, she must necessarily begin with not only an awareness of the voices on the American side of the river and their system of meaning, but she must give way to these voices. In admitting the voices of Americans into her text, in including metatexual and anthropological moments into her text, she opens her novel up to the Anglo-American reader. By making all of these textual maneuvers, Villegas de Magnón could be read by contemporary Mexican-American scholars as an early predecessor of Anzaldúa and others who rupture conventional narratives in order to disrupt and therefore control the process of textual mediation.

Notes

[1] *The Rebel* was serialized in *The Laredo News* in 1961. Originally entitled *La Rebelde*, and intended for a Mexican audience, the text chronicles the Mexican Revolution through the eyes of the founder of *La Cruz Blanca* (The White Cross), a volunteer organization of men and women who administered medical aid to the wounded soldiers of Venustiano Carranza's troops.

[2] Girard explains this mediated desire in Stendahl's *The Red and the Black* by showing how two men triangulate a maid into their discourse of desire strictly because Julien believes or projects the desire of Valenod toward the maid and therefore fuels his own desire for the maid in direct proportion to the supposed desire of his now rival.

[3] In her introduction to the novel, editor Clara Lomas refers to Villegas de Magnón's dual national identity as a native-born Mexican who also claimed

U.S. citizenship (xxii).

⁴ See John Reed's *Insurgent Mexico* as an example of a text which takes the Mexican Revolution as its subject, but which approaches said topic through the gaze of the American reporter and thus unwittingly provides a commentary on the author's paucity of knowledge as well as on his preconceived notions of Mexico.

⁵ Villegas de Magnón, Leonor. *The Rebel.* Ed. Clara Lomas. Houston: Arte Público Press, 1992, p. 48. Note: further references to this book will appear parenthetically in the text.

⁶ "By 1910, according to figures published by the Mexican government, total foreign capital amounted to over 2 billion pesos, of which 1.2 billion pesos (or over $500 million U.S.) was American. By 1914, the figure had grown to $580 million" Raat, W. Dirk. *Revoltosos: Mexico's Rebels in the United States, 1903-1923.* College Station: Texas A&M Press, 1981. p.13.

⁷ See John Mason Hart's *Revolutionary Mexico.* Villa attacked a U.S. Army garrison town, Columbus, and killed eighteen Americans. General John J. "Blackjack" Pershing entered Mexico with 12,000 soldiers in vain in search of Villa.

⁸ For a more in-depth discussion of how feminism and lesbianism specifically are read as acts of cultural betrayal equivalent to *malinchismo*, see Cherrie Moraga's "From a Long Line of Vendidas."

Works Cited

Bakhtin, M. M. *The Dialogic Imagination.* Trans. Michael Holquist. Austin: University of Texas, 1981.

Girard, René. *Deceit, Desire, and the Novel.* Trans. Yvonne Freccero. Baltimore: Johns Hopkins, 1965.

Habermas, Jurgen. *The Structural Transformation of the Bourgeois Public Sphere.* Trans. Thomas Burger Cambridge: M.I.T., 1994.

Hart, John Mason. *Revolutionary Mexico.* Berkeley: University of California, 1989.

Iser, Wolfgang. *The Act of Reading: A Theory of Aesthetic Response.* Baltimore: Johns Hopkins, 1980.

———. *The Implied Reader.* Baltimore: Johns Hopkins, 1974.

Raat, W. Dirk. *Revoltosos.* College Station: Texas A&M, 1981.

Framing the Female Voice: The Bancroft Narratives of Apolinaria Lorenzana, Angustias de la Guerra Ord, and Eulalia Perez

Virginia M. Bouvier
University of Maryland at College Park

In the 1870s, Hubert Howe Bancroft, an entrepreneur and historian of the U.S. West, set to the task of writing the history of California. For this purpose, he employed five scribes, or reporters, to interview some 160 elderly residents of California. Half of the subjects interviewed were "of Spanish blood."[1] The other half were foreign pioneers (mainly Anglo-Europeans) from a wide range of classes who came to California before 1848. In the aggregate, those interviewed included a fair cross-section of the Californian people, although certainly not a proportionally representative sample.[2]

The time spent by Bancroft's scribes with each interviewee ranged from a few days to twelve months, and yielded from a few pages to five volumes of manuscript. The length of the interview, according to Bancroft, was determined by the "prominence, memory, and readiness to talk of the person interviewed."[3] Likewise, the scribe's (and Bancroft's) sense of history and determination of the importance of the interviewee's status and story, the interviewee's willingness to participate in the constructed dialogue, and the content of the interviewee's narration, all influenced the length and nature of the narratives.

The interviews were done in both Spanish and English, and include at least eleven which were conducted with Spanish-speaking women. I will analyze three of these female narratives, given over a four-month time period from 1877 to 1878 to Thomas Savage. In particular, I am interested in the struggle for interpretive power between the interviewer and the interviewees as it is seen in the narratives of three women of diverse backgrounds—Eulalia Pérez, Apolinaria Lorenzana, and Angustias de la Guerra Ord. In the contest for narrative authority, which may be seen on one level as a struggle between orality and text, what discursive strategies did the interviewer and the interviewees employ?

Eulalia Pérez, Apolinaria Lorenzana, and Angustias de la Guerra Ord were born in Baja California, Mexico City, and San Diego, respectively, although all spent their entire adult lives in California. The women varied in age, marital status, economic background, and occupation.

Eulalia, rumored to be the "oldest woman in the world," claimed to be some 139 years of age. She was twice married and twice widowed, had six children plus at least two other sons who died in infancy. Her narrative of some 35 manuscript pages (including notes) is the shortest of the three.

Both Eulalia Pérez and Apolinaria Lorenzana worked at the Franciscan missions, which were set up from 1769-1823 along the California coast from San Diego to Sonoma as part of the cultural and economic vanguard of Spanish conquest. Apolinaria came to California around the age of seven in 1800, which means that she was approximately 84 years old at the time of the interview with Savage. She worked at the missions as a *curandera*, or healer, and teacher, never married, and had no children. Angustias de la Guerra was born in 1815. At age 62, she was the youngest of the three women interviewed, and her narration is the longest at 156 pages. The daughter of the wealthy Santa Barbara Presidio commander and treasurer for the missions, Angustias was an active participant in the social circles in which political rebellions and revolutions were hatched and nurtured. Like Eulalia, she was twice married and twice widowed. While she mentions the names of two of her children in passing, she does not say how many children she had.

Thomas Savage, the interviewer of these three women, was born in 1823 in Havana, Cuba to New England parents. By the age of nine, Savage spoke Spanish better than English, and French better than either language.[4] He studied law and then served as a clerk in the U. S. consulate in Havana for more than two decades before coming to work for Bancroft in 1873 as the resident authority on Spanish American affairs at the Bancroft Library, then located in San Francisco (now at the University of California at Berkeley).

The contest for narrative authority between the narrator and the interviewer was played out on a number of fronts. An important element in this contest was the framing of each narrative. Savage introduced each Spanish interview with an introductory statement. Despite his fluency in Spanish, each of these introductory statements were written in English. This linguistic juxtaposition privileged English as the language of authority, and is a dramatic metaphor for the Anglo appropriation and attempted control of Hispanic literary production, particularly in light of the U.S. conquest of Mexican California in the mid-nineteenth century. Like the silver from the mines of Potosí, these oral histories were extracted from the native population for foreign consumption.[5] The narratives were recorded, sorted, sifted for the larger nuggets, copied onto index cards, labelled, and retrieved at a later date. Yet one of the ironies of history is that we would have that many fewer voices to recover today if Bancroft and his scribes had not written down these oral narratives.

Savage conducted these interviews to facilitate the writing of a history of California, a project which was completed in seven volumes some twenty years later under Bancroft's guidance. Thus, the interviews had an explicitly pragmatic purpose. Although the narratives were written as autobiographical statements in the first person with no indication of the interviewer's interventions, it is clear that Savage used a formal question and answer format for his interviews, as the interviews share a number of common themes related to political events of the late Spanish and Mexican periods.

Within the interviews themselves, there was a contest over the topics to be addressed. As the women would be heard, and their voices recorded, only insofar as what they had to say was of interest to the interviewer, the women clearly negotiated rhetorical strategies of self-empowerment.

Pérez used the advantages of her age to control the themes of her conversation with Savage. The ways in which she exercised domination in the selection of her topics can be surmised from Savage's remarks of introduction to Pérez's narrative. "Her memory is remarkably fresh on some things and much clouded on others, particularly on her age," wrote Savage. He found Pérez to be "flighty" at times, and he noted that "by asking her questions only upon such matters as she could be conversant with," he was able to obtain "intelligible answers."[6]

Responding only to the questions which interested her, Pérez dwelled upon the details of life at the San Diego and San Gabriel Missions where she served. Pérez's long period of service at these missions gave her an opportunity to experience the shift of the mission system from an institution dedicated to the acculturation of the Indians to a flourishing economic system which depended on the organized labor of the mission residents.[7] Her narrative illustrates how women's roles changed from teachers to participants in light manufacturing and industry. Just as Mexico gained independence from Spain, in 1821, Perez's duties at the mission were dramatically expanded. From chief cook and teacher, Pérez was suddenly called upon to be the *llavera*, or housekeeper, a job which entailed the organization, production, and distribution of food, clothing, and suppplies to thousands of Indian neophytes, and the oversight of the production of soap, wine, and olive oil. In her story of mission life, Pérez discloses considerable information about the social hierarchy existing between and among Indians and Spaniards at the missions, paying particular attention to relations among women and between men and women.

In addition to answering only those questions which interested her, Pérez also feigned deafness where she did not want to discuss certain topics. In these cases, Savage was forced to rely on Pérez's daughter to ask the questions, he complained, "because the centenarian lady is quite deaf, tho.' not to the extent of needing to be addressed in an excessively loud tone."[8]

Yet Eulalia's hearing appears to have been exceptionally good. In another interview conducted some months earlier, a female interviewer, Mrs. Frank Leslie, wrote that Pérez "kept up the conversation in an eager and animated manner and with a strength of voice and quickness of hearing quite extraordinary, accompanying her words with marked gesticulations."[9] Such testimony highlights the extraordinary power of the interviewer to represent static images of his or her subjects. It also underscores the dynamic quality of the subjects themselves, who could adopt persona that varied with the interviewer, and depending upon their relationship with the interviewer, could reveal or conceal aspects of their lives and personalities.

Many in this conference have echoed Hayden White's conclusions that history is subordinate to narrative perspectives.[10] In the same way that Vincent Pérez recognized that the Pérez family history narrative was changed by the recuperation of the voices of the Robles women,[11] or that Luis Leal,[12] John-Michael Rivera[13] and A. Gabriel Meléndez[14] showed how a wide variety of writers claimed Joaquín Murieta, Billy the Kid, and Casimiro Varela as their own, I would caution that every historical narrative is conditioned to a varying degree by considerations of race, class, gender, nationality, generation, geography, and a wide range of variables that make it difficult to classify any history as *mine* or *yours*. To a great extent, Eulalia Pérez chose when she would speak, how she would speak, and upon which themes she would speak based on such considerations. Savage, on the other hand, had the power to limit the interview or to extend it, and it is noteworthy that Pérez's narration is only 35 pages long.

We do not have a record of the questions which caused Pérez to change the subject, thus appearing "flighty" to Savage. Yet Savage's introduction to the testimony by Angustias de la Guerra Ord provides some clues as to his expectations. Savage wrote of his interview with Angustias:

> I had hoped to obtain from her much information on manners & customs of the Californians, which would, no doubt, have been interesting & reliable, as proceeding from a lady of her intellectual and social standing, but a regard for her distressed condition of mind, deterred me from occupying her attention any longer.[15]

Here we see Savage's disappointment that Angustias's narrative failed to address what he considered to be appropriate topics for women, namely "information on manners and customs of the Californians." What Savage received in its stead from Angustias was a narrative which is blatantly political. Her discussion challenges the public-private dichotomy which purportedly characterized male and female spheres in the nineteenth century. Savage's efforts to steer the conversation to more so-called "feminine" topics failed, as Angustias de la Guerra related 156 manuscript pages of an often rather dry and minutely detailed account of the political highlights of early nineteenth-century California. In her narrative, Angustias recalled the attack of an Argentine ship commanded by the Frenchman Hippolyte Bouchard who hoped to provoke the revolt of California against Spain; the political infighting, revolts, and revolutions headed by the Californios; the secularization of the missions in the 1830s, and her opposition to the U.S. conquest of California.[16]

Thomas Savage seemed surprised at Angustias's interest in these events. Women were not supposed to be the repositories of such details of public life. One cannot help but note Savage's ambivalence at the detailed observations made by Angustias de la Guerra. While the subject matter might not have been considered appropriate for a woman, it was certainly useful for writing the political history of California. Bancroft himself would observe about Angustias's narrative that it compared "favorably in accuracy, interest, and completeness, with the best in my collection."[17]

Savage's reluctance to grant Angustias de la Guerra complete affirmation warranted a caveat, however, that "the accompanying pages were dictated to me by Mrs. Ord at a time when her mind was very uneasy," due to a relative's illness.[18]

The third woman whom Savage interviewed, Apolinaria Lorenzana, was also clearly interested in national politics. In her 48-page narrative, Lorenzana gave her opinions on the inner workings of mission life, the secularization of the missions, the American takeover of California, and Indian activities at the missions. Like Angustias, Apolinaria voiced her strong opposition to the American conquest of California in the late 1840s. She was so greatly saddened by that event that she wanted to leave San Diego, hoping that if she left, so too might the Americans. "Yo estaba encalavernada con la cosa de los americanos," she recalled.[19]

As with the other narratives, Savage seemed reluctant to validate Lorenzana's right to have political opinions. The pertinence of Lorenzana's commentary on political happenings of the day were thus minimized by Savage, who underscored Lorenzana's age and the isolation of her life at the mission. He wrote:

> Considering her advanced age and feeble condition, her memory is quite fresh. But it is evident that she passed her life in the mission, and had but little opportunity of ascertaining what happened of a political nature around her.[20]

Savage's comment that Lorenzana had "little opportunity of ascertaining what happened of a political nature around her," is blatantly false. She not only had the opportunity to ascertain what was happening, but she commented on it openly in her narrative. The missions were extremely political institutions, which saw their rise and fall from power during Lorenzana's lifetime. Furthermore, Lorenzana was in a particularly good position from which to comment, having been greatly affected by government policies throughout her life. She came to California sponsored by the Spanish government in 1800, and in the 1840s, she was the beneficiary of two land grants from the Mexican government; she later bought a third.[21] In the wake of the Mexican-American War, Lorenzana lost her land to speculators.[22] In her narrative, Lorenzana tells how an American "borrowed" one of her *ranchos* for the use of the U. S. cavalry and never gave it back, leaving her virtually destitute.

Savage's introduction to Lorenzana's narrative downplayed the effects that the American takeover had had on Lorenzana's life. He wrote:

> She appears to be a good old soul—cheerful and resigned to her sad fate, for in her old age and stone blind, she is a charge on the county and on her friends, having by some means or other lost all her property. She was loath to speak on this subject, assuring me that she didn't want even to think of it.[23]

In addition to the contest over the topics to be addressed, both the narrator and the interviewer engaged in the rhetorical negotiation of authority. Each of the women interviewed established her authority to speak based on a number of considerations, the first of which was family ties. Family connections in Californio society were extremely important, especially among the more elite Spanish. Angustias de la Guerra emphasized these connections when she began her narration:

> Yo, María de las Angustias de la Guerra, nací en San Diego el once de Junio de 1815, siendo mis padres el Ten[te]. (despues Capitan) D[a]. José de la Guerra y Noriega, que entónces estaba haciendo servicio allí, y D[a]. María Antonia Carrillo, hija del Capitan D[a]. Raimundo Carrillo y de D[a]. Tomasa de Lugo.[24]

Throughout her narrative, it was her relationships with her blood relations and fictive kin, particularly her father, an upright Spanish military officer, that appeared to have shaped Angustias's involvement in the minutiae of California politics. Her narration underscored her ties to three of the earliest elite Spanish families, whose names, De la Guerra, Carrillo, and Lugo, are immediately recognizable to students of California history, and whose elite status are marked by Angustias's use of the titles, Don and Doña. During the 1870s, when these interviews were conducted, there was already an effort among early Spanish-speaking settlers on the California frontier to emphasize their status as the prominent first families, in order to differentiate themselves from the newly arriving "Mexican" immigrants.

Unlike Angustias, Eulalia in referring to her family members did not use the title "Don" or "Doña," suggesting that she came from a more modest economic background. Although Eulalia Pérez was not tied to well known or landed Spanish families, she too initiated her statement by asserting her family connections. She was particularly interested in asserting her identity as white. She began:

> Yo, Eulalia Perez, nací en el presidio de Loreto en la Baja Cal. Mi padre se llamaba Diego Perez y era empleado en el departamento de marina de dicho

presidio; mi madre se llamaba Antonia Rosalía Cota — ambos eran blancos puros.[25]

Savage challenged by inference Pérez's claim of racial purity. At a time and place of fluid racial boundaries, Pérez's claim that her parents were "blancos puros" did not require that they actually be pure white. As though to cast doubt upon Pérez's assertion, in a singular move, Savage attached to his manuscript interview a photograph of Eulalia Pérez, in humble dress, with high cheekbones and wispy hair, looking very "Indian," as well as a newspaper article with a sketch of Eulalia.[26] In addition, his introduction to Eulalia Pérez's narration seemed more novelistic than journalistic; his style shared characteristics of the natural realism vein of writing in vogue at the time. Savage wrote of Pérez:

> She sat by me upon a chair a while yesterday; but her usual set is on the floor, and when flies or mosquitoes annoy her, she slaps & kills them with her slipper on the floor. When wishing to rise, she places both palms of her hands on the ground before her, and lifts herself first on four feet (so to speak) and then with a jerk puts herself on her two feet—for this she needs no assistance. After that she goes abt. the house without difficulty. She did it in my presence yesterday, and saying that she felt chilled, walked out and sat on the stoop to sun herself a while—then came back and resumed her former seat.[27]

Savage's description of Pérez as though she were a "primitive" or animal reinforced the possibility that Pérez was not really from "blancos puros," as she claimed. Likewise, in an article titled "Eulalia Perrez [*sic*], The Oldest Woman in the World," interviewer Mrs. Frank Leslie noted that Eulalia's skin was "almost as dark as a mulatto's." (*Frank Leslie's Illustrated newspaper*, Jan. 12, 1878, n.p.)

Savage countered each narrator's statements of familial identity with a focus on marital relationships, giving the latter considerably more weight than the women themselves did. Although Eulalia Pérez and Angustias de la Guerra were each widowed twice, for example, neither of them used any of their spouses' names to refer to themselves. In fact, the husbands were virtually overlooked in Angustias's narrative. In the course of 156 manuscript pages, Angustias mentioned Edward Ord, her second husband, a U. S. army surgeon, only once in passing (and without identifying him as her husband!). Manuel Jimeno Casarín, Angustias's first husband, a prominent statesman in Mexican California whom she married at age 16, figured only slightly more often in her narrative. Eulalia Pérez mentioned her two husbands in a rather negative light: Eulalia married her first husband, Miguel Antonio Guillén, at the age of fifteen, and she complained that when the couple came to San Diego, he refused to accompany her to visit her relatives; she mentioned her second husband, Juan Mariné, in the context of her reluctance to remarry. Pérez recalled:

> Después que se casaron todas mis hijas . . . el Padre Sánchez se empeñó mucho conmigo para que me casara con el Teniente de premio Juan Mariné, español catalán, que había servido en la artillería, y que era viudo con familia. Yo no quería casarme, pero el Padre me dijo que Mariné era muy bueno, como en efecto resultó serlo — además, tenía alguna fortuna en dinero, pero nunca me dio posesión de la caja. Accedí a los deseos del Padre porqe. no me hallaba con ánimo pa. negarle nada cuando el Padre Sánchez había sido pa. mí y toda mi familia, como padre y madre.[28]

But Eulalia told a slightly different version of her marriage choices to a female interviewer some months earlier. Mrs. Leslie wrote that Pérez

> had been married twice, and said that in her youth she had many lovers, but could not decide which of them to marry until the *padre* interfered and insisted that she must make a choice, which she accordingly did; but was left a widow, and again she made a selection, and one based on maturer judgment, and she had been even happier in her second nuptials than in her first.[29]

Mrs. Leslie noted that the priests compelled Eulalia to marry for the first time before she was ready; she credits Eulalia with making a better marriage for herself the second time round. In the Savage interview, on the other hand, Eulalia noted that she really did not want to remarry, but she gave in to the priest's desires.

· What are we to make of the different versions? Did the centenarian confuse her two marriages? Did the priests influence both of her decisions to marry? Was Eulalia's account different in each interview? Or did each interviewer put their own spin on Eulalia's narrative? In speculating on these questions, it is interesting to note that the female interviewer was the one who gave greater agency to Eulalia and credited her with the ability to make a mature decision, one that surpassed the priest's, about a suitable marriage partner.

The women's reluctance to emphasize their marital connections perhaps relected their lack of enthusiasm about marriages which had been arranged or prodded by others. Thus they married more in response to perceived social obligations or to fullfill their parents' desires, than on their own initiative. A poem from early California reflects this attitude:

> Levántese niña
> Barra la cocina
> Atice la lumbre
> Como es su costumbre.
>
> Yo no sé barrer
> Yo no sé tizar
> Yo no me casé
> Para trabajar.[30]

Yet despite the relative lack of attention which the women gave to their spouses in their narratives, Savage chose to emphasize the women's marital affiliations rather than their paternal or maternal lineages. Although she called herself Angustias de la Guerra, Thomas Savage insisted on calling Angustias by her married name of Mrs. Ord, subtly underscoring Angustias's connections to the Americans.[31] While Eulalia Pérez emphasized her genealogical origins, Savage focused on her widowhood. Pérez, he declared in his first sentence of introduction, was a "widow, first of Miguel Anto. Guillen, and next of Juan Mariné."[32]

Apolinaria Lorenzana, born in Mexico, was less concerned than the other two women with establishing her ethnic background or blood ties, although she was clearly of Spanish descent. As a woman with no children, she emphasized her ties to a broader society. Savage undermined this effort to establish narrative authority, however. His introduction to Lorenzana instead portrayed her as an aged orphaned child, an adopted ward of the Spanish (Mexican) state. Savage wrote:

> This old lady residing in Santa Barbara, was one of the foundling children sent to California by the Viceroy of Mexico in the early part of this century . . . She was known by many as Apolinaria la Cuna (the foundling) & by most as la Beata (the pious).[33]

Lorenzana defied such labelling in her opening statement. She had a mother, and she had no loyalties to the State, which had distributed the children "como perritos" among the California families.[34] Lorenzana described her arrival in Monterey in 1800 with her mother, who shortly thereafter remarried, abandoned her daughter to return to Mexico with her new husband, and died, probably, Lorenzana claimed, of a broken heart at leaving her seven-year-old daughter behind. She recalled:

> Mi madre . . . casó con un artillero y cuando vino relevo de artilleros, le tocó a mi padrastro volverse a Mexico, y se llevó a mi madre consigo. Así quedé yo separada de mi madre, y no volví a verla más. Ella murió casi a su llegada a San Blas, talvez del sentim[to]. de haberme dejado a mí.[35]

As a young teenager, Lorenzana was placed in the home of Angustias de la Guerra's grandparents, Lt. Raymundo Carrillo and Doña Tomasa Lugo. There, Lorenzana, who had taught herself to write, began to teach other girls catechism and to read and write.[36] After she moved in with Sargeant Mercado and Doña Josefa Sal, she continued to teach, and she recalled that after the Sargeant died, his widow opened a girls' school. As Josefa's time was consumed with running her large estate, Apolinaria was given virtually exclusive custody of the school, where girls were taught reading, catechism, and sewing. Once at the mission, she taught both boys and girls to read, but she seems to have always taken a few girls under her wing.[37]

Lorenzana established her narrative authority on the basis of her adoptive families' connections, as well as her connections with the broader society. Although she had no children of her own, Lorenzana underscored her relationships caring for the priests and educating the mission Indians. She emphasized her role in teaching many children to read and write, and noted that she was godmother to some 200 *ahijados*, or godchildren, of all backgrounds.[38] Lorenzana's emphasis on her role as both baptismal and confirmation godmother to these youngsters was her way of justifying her existence as a woman before a society which belittled women who did not fulfill their reproductive capacities. Furthermore, Lorenzana's teaching and mission work brought her in contact with a large cross-section of frontier society and enabled her to develop a knowledgeable position on politics, defined in a broad sense.

In an effort to portray her as an isolated spinster solely devoted to affairs of the church, however, Savage wrote that Apolinaria "never married, preferring to devote herself to the care of the church missionaries at San Diego."[39] In her narrative, Apolinaria underscored that it was not for lack of opportunity that she did not marry. She recalled:

> Cuando era muchacha, hubo un joven que se empeñó mucho en que yo me casara con él. No me llamaba la inclinación al estado del matrimonio (a pesar de conocer los méritos de una institución tan santa) y rehusé su oferta.[40]

Lorenzana's devotion to the church and the missionaries at the San Diego Mission, where she worked most of her life, earned her the "highest terms of praises" from both sexes, according to Savage.[41] Yet Lorenzana's narrative reveals that at the mission, Lorenzana was not simply dedicated to obeying her superiors, but was a talented *curandera*, who, practicing her art in spite of the priests' efforts to check her, earned herself the title of "La Beata." She narrated:

> Los tres años que tuve la mano tullida no podía trabajar. Pero en el hospital de la misión lo que hacía era curar los enfermos. Aunque el Padre Sánchez me había dicho que no lo hiciera yo misma sino lo mandara hacer, y estuviera presente para que las sirvientas lo hiciesen bien. Pero yo siempre, como podía, metía mano, y asistía a las enfermas.[42]

Here we see how, when given the opportunity, Apolinaria subverted the authority of the priest to make her own choices at the mission. And, given the opportunity, Apolinaria narrated examples which underscore this struggle for control over how she would live her life.

What emerges from these autobiographical narratives is a contest for narrative authority and credibility, in which the interviewer is an invisible, but very present participant. I have not discussed here other aspects of control which

Savage exercised as interviewer, transcriber, and editor.[43]

Focusing instead on the written transcripts of the narratives, I have shown how women were often successful in establishing the parameters for the topics to be included in the interview. Women used oral strategies of digression, dissimulation, and selective hearing to bring the conversation around to the issues they were most interested in discussing. In their narratives, we find a continual affirmation of self in relation to others; a recognition of the societal and familial pressures which affected their decision-making, particularly regarding marriage; an insistence that women made their own choices to go along with or to defy such traditions; and varying degrees of interest in the political affairs being played out in the public arena.

Nonetheless, the interviewer, still had the first and last word. We must remember that Savage, as transcriber and editor, as well as interviewer, wrote his introductions after the interviews had been completed. Thus his words of introduction are actually conclusions, calculated to frame the female voices in a particular way. Savage used his opening statements to prepare the reader for the accounts which followed, or indeed, to discourage readers seeking specific kinds of information from reading any further. Often, Savage's opening statement challenged or undermined the credibility and authority of the women themselves, based on the woman's age, mental or physical condition, marital status or ethnicity.

These narratives are not only the site of a struggle over discourse, but a site of struggle for female agency. In them, women, confronted by, indeed, invited by writers of history to flesh out the dominant social customs of the time, took the opportunity to assert their presence as actors in the making of history. Each side—interviewer and interviewee—used the rhetorical and discursive strategies available to support his or her own view of history and women's place in that history.

Notes

[1] Hubert Howe Bancroft, *The Works of Hubert Howe Bancroft*, Vol. 18, *History of California*, Vol. 1, 1542-1800 (San Francisco: The History Co., Publ., 1890), 55.

[2] Indians were certainly underrepresented in the sample. In one case, a narration by Lorenzo Asisara, a Christianized neophyte Indian, appears in the middle of an interview with the elderly Spanish soldier, José María Amador. His fascinating tale is thus included in the series of interviews by apparent happenstance. See José María Amador, "Memorias sobre la historia de California," dictated to Thomas Savage, Whiskey Hill (San Luis Obispo), 1877. Bancroft Library, Hubert Howe Bancroft Collection. Pioneers of African descent were noticeably absent among the interviewees. See Jack Forbes,

"Black Pioneers: The Spanish-Speaking Afro-Americans of the Southwest," *Phylon* 27 (1966): 233-46; and Kenneth G. Goode, *California's Black Pioneers: A Brief Historical Survey* (Santa Barbara: McNally & Loftin, 1974).

[3] Bancroft, *History of California*, 1:55.

[4] Hubert Howe Bancroft, *The Works of Hubert Howe Bancroft*, Vol. 39, *Literary Industries* (San Francisco: The History Co., Publ., 1890), 255.

[5] The historical narratives themselves, as Rosaura Sánchez has pointed out, "interested no one except as raw material to be appropriated by U.S. historians manufacturing California history." Rosaura Sánchez, "Nineteenth-Century Californio Narratives: The Hubert H. Bancroft Collection," in *Recovering the U.S. Hispanic Literary Heritage*, ed. Ramón Gutiérrez and Genaro Padilla (Houston: Arte Público Press, 1993), 280.

[6] Thomas Savage, "Una Vieja y Sus Recuerdos: Dictados por Doña Eulalia Perez que vive en la Mision de San Gabriel a la edad avanzada de 139 años," December 11, 1877, Bancroft Library, iv. Edited version in *Three Memoirs of Mexican California*, trans. Vivian C. Fisher (Berkeley: The Friends of the Bancroft Library, 1988).

[7] On this topic, see Robert Archibald, "The Economics of the Alta California Mission, 1803-1821," *Southern California Quarterly* 58 (summer 1976): 227-40.

[8] Savage, "Una Vieja," iv.

[9] Mrs. Frank Leslie, *California: A Pleasure Trip from Gotham to the Golden Gate* (New York, 1877), cited in *Frank Leslie's Illustrated Newspaper*, January 12, 1878, n.p.

[10] Hayden White, *Tropics of Discourse: Essays in Cultural Criticism* (Baltimore: The Johns Hopkins University Press, 1978). Citations to the conference refer to the Recovering the U.S. Hispanic Literary Heritage conference held at the University of Houston on November 8-9, 1997; some of the proceedings have been published in this volume. See especially Erlinda Gonzales-Berry, "'Como Dios manda': Manuel C. de Baca's *Noches tenebrosas en el condado de San Miguel*"; and Lynn E. Rice Cortina, "The Construction of the Feminine Object and the Reconstruction of the Female Subject: *The Story of Evangelina Cosío y Cisneros*."

[11] Vincent Pérez, "Reading Mexican American History: Genealogy, Cultural Memory, and Testimonial Narrative."

[12] Luis Leal, "En torno a Joaquín Murieta: Historia y literatura."

[13] John-Michael Rivera, "Miguel Antonio Otero's Biography: *The Real Billy the Kid with New Light on the Lincoln County War*."

[14] A. Gabriel Meléndez, "Recovering Nuevomexicano Life Narratives: The Biography of Casimiro Barela in Historical and Cultural Context."

[15] María de las Angustias de la Guerra Ord, "Ocurrencias en California," Santa Barbara, April 1, 1878, Bancroft Library, Hubert Howe Bancroft

Collection, n.p.

[16] De la Guerra opposed the American conquest of California in no uncertain terms. She narrated, "La toma del país no nos gustó nada a los Californios y menos a las mugeres. Pero debo confesar que California estaba en el camino de la más completa ruina. Por un lado, los indios estaban desbordados, cometiendo robos y crímenes en los ranchos, y poco ó nada se hacía pa. contener las degradaciones. Por otro lado, estaban las desavenencias entre la gente del norte y la del Sur, y de ambas contra los Mexicanos de la otra banda. Pero el peor cáncer de todo era la rapiña que se había hecho general." Ibid., 143. A published English translation may be found in Francis Price and William E. Ellison, ed. and trans., *Occurrences in California related to Thomas Savage in Santa Barbara by Mrs. Ord (Ma. Angustias de la Guerra), 1878* (Washington, D.C.: Academy of American Franciscan History, 1956), 67-68, n.9. For a discussion of problems with this translation, which indicated Angustias's support of the U.S. takeover, see Genaro Padilla, "'Yo sola aprendí': Contra-patriarchal Containment in Women's Nineteenth-century California Personal Narratives," *Americas Review* 16 (Fall/Winter 1988): 91-109.

[17] Bancroft, *History of California*, 1:55.

[18] De la Guerra, "Ocurrencias," n.p.

[19] "I was livid about what happened with the Americans." Thomas Savage, "Memorias de Doña Apolinaria Lorenzana 'La Beata' Vieja de unos setenta y cinco años," Santa Barbara, March 1878. Bancroft Library, Hubert Howe Bancroft Collection, p. 20.

[20] Ibid., n.p.

[21] J.N. Bowman, "Prominent Women of Provincial California," *Historical Society of Southern California Quarterly* 36 (June 1957): 149-66.

[22] Richard Griswold del Castillo, "Neither Activists Nor Victims: Mexican Women's Historical Discourse—The Case of San Diego, 1820-1850," *California History* (Fall 1995): 235.

[23] Savage, "Memorias," n.p.

[24] "I, Maria Angustias de la Guerra, was born in San Diego on June 11, 1815. My parents were Lieutenant (and later Captain) Don Jose de la Guerra y Noriega, and Dona Maria Antonia Carrillo, daughter of don Captain Raimundo Carrillo and Don Tomasa de Lugo." De la Guerra, "Ocurrencias," 1.

[25] "I, Eulalia Pérez, was born in the Loreto presidio in Baja California. My father's name was Diego Pérez, and he was employed in the Navy section of that presidio; my mother's name was Antonia Rosalia Cota. Both were pure white." Savage, "Una Vieja," 1.

[26] Ibid., i-ii.

[27] Ibid., iii-iv.

[28] "After all of my daughters got married . . . Father Sánchez pushed me a lot to marry the prize Lieutenant Juan Mariné, a Spanish Catalán who had

served in the artillery, insisting that I was a widow with a family. I did not want to get married, but the priest told me that Mariné was a very good man, as in effect he turned out to be, and besides, he had some fortune in money, but he never gave me possission of the cash box. I gave in to the wishes of the Priest because I did not find myself with the spirit to deny him anything, since Father Sanchez had been for me and all of my family, like a father and mother." Savage, "Una Vieja," 13.

[29] "Eulalia Pérez, the Oldest Woman in the World," *Frank Leslie's Illustrated Newspaper*, January 12, 1878, n.p.

[30] Theresa Morehouse, ed. *Singing Gold: Songs and Verses from Early California* (Sacramento: The Sacramento Bee, 1977), 77.

[31] For a literary interpretation of Angustias de la Guerra Ord and her relationships, see Gertrude Atherton, *The Splendid Idle Forties* (N.Y.: The Macmillan Co., 1902).

[32] Savage, "Una Vieja," iii.

[33] Savage, "Memorias," n.p.

[34] Ibid., 1.

[35] "My mother . . . married an artillery man, and when he was relieved of his artillery duties, my stepfather had to return to Mexico, and he brought my mother with him. Thus I remained separated from my mother, and I never saw her again. She died almost upon her arrival in San Blas, perhaps from the feeling of having left me." Ibid., 1-2.

[36] Lorenzana had learned catechism and to read at a very young age, before she left Mexico, and she taught herself to write when she got to California. She recalled, "Desde muy niñita antes de venir de Mexico, me habían enseñado a leer, y la doctrina. Ya cuando era mugercita en California, yo sola aprendí a escribir, valiéndome para ello de los libros que veía. Imitaba las letras en cualquier papel que lograba conseguir. Tales como cajillas de cigarros vacías, o cualquier papel blanco que hallaba tirado. Así logré aprender lo bastante pa. hacerme entender por escrito cuando necesitaba algo." Ibid., 4-5.

[37] Ibid., 5.

[38] Ibid., 44-45.

[39] Ibid., n.p.

[40] "When I was a little girl, there was a young man who insisted strongly that I marry him. I was not inclined toward the state of matrimony (despite knowing the merits of such a holy institution) and I refused his offer." Ibid., 45-46.

[41] Ibid., n.p.

[42] "For the three years that my hand was mangled, I could not work. But in the mission hospital, what I did was cure sick people. Although Father Sánchez had told me that I should not do it myself, but should order to have it done, and I should be present to ensure that the servant girls did it well. But,

as much as I could, I always pitched in, and helped the sick." Ibid., 6-7.

[43] Another layer of interventions exists here as well, namely, my own selection and interpretations of these texts. However, all spellings, abbreviations, and accentuations here reflect the original manuscripts and have not been modernized. Citations in the original text are in the original language; translations provided in these notes are by the author unless otherwise indicated.

Part III

Chroniclers, Ethnographers, and Historians

New Approaches to Old Chroniclers: Contemporary Critical Theories and the Perez de Villagrá Epic

María Herrera-Sobek
University of California at Santa Barbara

The Gaspar Pérez de Villagrá's epic *Historia de la Nueva México* (1610) lends itself well to the application of contemporary critical theories in spite of its being a document that has its origins in the early sixteen-hundreds with the advent of the Spanish conquerors into New Mexican territory. In this study I apply contemporary cultural studies theories, mythic studies theories as well as more established methods of anlysis in the hermeneutics of Villagrá's work. In particular, I focus on the ancient myth of Aztlán extant in Villagrá's epic. The soldier-poet's epic presents a pair of twins dividing the territories of the Southwest and Mesoamerica under the edict of a female deity (most likely Coatlicue). This is one of the earliest instances where we find a written Spanish literary rendtion of the Aztlán myth. My study provides insights into the nature of the myth and its use in "imagining" a new community and nation.

In an earlier work, "The Rhetoric of the *Memorial*: An Analysis of the Discursive Strategies of a Colonial Genre,"[2] I applied the principles of Aristotelian rhetoric to the analysis of Villagrá's 1614 *Memorial* to the King of Spain. My principle findings indicated Villagrá was probably familiar with Aristotelian rhethoric and had made ample use of it in his defense against the charges leveled at him by the court in Spain after the Acoma massacre in New Mexico. This findings underscored the important fact that writers from the colonial period often had university training and thus the literature written during that period in New Spain and its territories reflected such a training. The Chicano colonial literary heritage is therefore firmly rooted in the medieval and Golden Age tradition of Spanish letters as well as the renaissance literary tradition of the period in Europe.

In a more recent study I presented at the XXXI Congreso de Literatura Iberoamericana in Caracas, Venezuela in June 1996 titled "Episodios novelísticos en la épica de Gaspar Pérez de Villagrá: Hacia una teoría sobre los orígenes de la novela latinoamericana" I explored several theories related to the origins of the novel and came to the conclusion that these theories reflected an

Anglocentric optic and did not take into consideration the literature produced during the colonial period in Latin America and the Southwest. The Villagrá epic contains important information that can be applied to the construction of theoretical paradigms for the origins of the novel.

Aside from the seminal studies done by Don Luis Leal on Villagrá, the epic poem *Historia de la Nueva México, 1610* has not been extensively studied. Scholars in the United States have viewed the work as pertaining to a Mexican or a Spanish literary heritage since it is written in Spanish and dates to the colonial Spanish period. Mexican academics, on the other hand, have relagated this literary gem to the United States or have viewed it as a marginal work of little import and literary relevance. There is only one edition in existence in Mexico dating to the 1900. In a similar manner, Spain has paid scant attention to the work. There are two relatively new editions published in Spain, one from Madrid (1989) edited by Mercedes Junquera and another edition edited by Augusto Quintana Prieto, *et al* in León, Spain in 1991.

More recently, the critical bilingual edition edited by Miguel Encinias *et al* and published by the University of New Mexico Press in 1992 has stimulated new interest in the work. Don Luis Leal, as mentioned earlier, has witten at least two important articles. The literary and historical richness of the work, nevertheless, allows a multitude of critical perspectives.

In this study I focus my analysis on the myth related to the origins of the Aztecs in the land known as Aztlán (the present southwestern part of the United States) included in Villagrá's epic. One of the interesting aspects of this particular myth is its antiquity since Villagrá's history was written in 1610. The Spanish soldier-poet recounts the well-known myth related to the origins of the Aztecs and has inscribed it in his epic. Our interest in the Villagrá myth is further piqued when we notice that it is a variant of the more traditional one since it differs in both plot and structure. My study seeks to highlight those points of convergence and divergence between the myth cited by Villagrá and the more canonical Aztec myth found in the Aztec Codices and in the chronicles written by the missionary friars from the sixteenth century. More importantly, my study explores Frederick Jackson Turner's thesis expounded in his book *The Frontier in American History* (1920) which seeks to explicate the character and development of North American civilization. According to Turner, the existence for several decades of a "frontier" in the United States has been instrumental, and indeed, the primary factor in the formation of the psychology, the sociology, and the cultural and economic development of the United States. Turner underscores how the frontier, for exemple, aided in the assimilation process of the new immigrants and was important in carrying out the national project. Other historians, however, reject Turner's thesis regarding the effects of the frontier on the formation of a national character and cultural production in the United States. Some historians go so far as to assert that in reality the frontier had little or nothing to contribute to the cultural development of the United States since the U. S. population had their cultural formation in Europe. According this opposing view, European settlers retained their cultural specificity in America and in fact promulgated it in the new lands.

Daniel Weber, on the other hand, laments the fact that Turner has been marginalized by both United States historians and Mexican scholars. He underlines the importance Turner's theories have in helping to explain the development and formation of frontier culture and the significant importance this has had in United States and Mexican history.

In fact, Turner's fundamental thesis regarding the frontier's impact on the cultural formation of civilizations with such frontier experiences is of the outmost importance in my study. I posit that both colonizers and colonized suffered extensively by the encounter and clash of the coming of two opposite and radically different cultures. That is to say, I differ from Turner's position in granting the frontier experience a totalizing force in the formation of cultural and character traits. But I also differ in granting this experience a negligible impact. The study of the first two cantos in Villagrá's *Historia de la Nueva México* provides us with a clear view of the immediate sincretization process the two cultures underwent upon contact with each other. The Villagrá variant of the legend of the origins of the Aztecs underscores the penetrating force of European elements in an Aztec myth.

The Aztlán Myth

In the *Crónica de Mexicayotl*, edited by Fernando de Alvarado Tezozomoc around the 1600s, the text provides us with a version of the myth of Aztlán. This version is included in Angel M. Garibay K's anthology titled *La literatura de los azteca* and cites Cuaucohuatl and Axolohua as the Aztec leaders who undertook the pilgrimmage south: "Cuaucohuatl y Axolohua fueron pasando y miraron mil maravillas allí entre las cañas y las juncias." (p. 43). The edict given by their god Cuaucohuatl or Huitzilopochtli was that they should migrate south until they were to see the signal: "Id y ved un nopal salvaje: y allí tranquila veréis un Aguila que está enhiesta. Allí come, allí se peina las plumas, y con eso quedará contento vuestro corazón." And later on Huitzilopochtli amplifies:

> Allí les haremos ver: a todos los que nos rodean allí los conquistaréis!
> !Aquí estará perdurable nuestra ciudad de Tenochtitlan!
> !El sitio donde el Aguila grazna, en donde abre las alas;
> el sitio donde ella come y en donde vuelan los peces,
> donde las serpientes van haciendo ruedos y silban!
> !Ese será México Tenochtitlan y muchas cosas han de suceder!
>
> (Garibay K. 1991:44-45)

According to the version cited by Juan de Torquemada in his chronicle *Los 21 libros rituales y monarquía indiana* a bird commanded the leaders Huitziton and Tecpatzin to leave their present abode and to initiate a pilgrimmage to the promised land. They wandered for fifty years until they arrived and "entraron en la Laguna; y como tenían su Oráculo, y Respuesta de su Sitio, fuéronlo buscando, por entre los Carrizos, y espesura de Juncias, y otras Yervas, que en la dicha Laguna dulce, se criaban como en el Libro de su Peregrinación." The two leaders Axolohua and Cuauhcoatl advance ahead of the others in order to locate the most propicious place to found their empire. Axolohua enters the swamp and sinks to the bottom. He reappears the next day informs his people that Tlaloc "Señor de la tierra" spoke to him in this manner:

> Sea bien venido mi querido Hijo Huircilopuchtili (que era el Dios que avían traído los Mexicanos consigo, y los avía guiado hasta aquel lugar) con su Pueblo: diles a todos esos Mexicanos, tus Compañeros, que este es el lugar donde han de Poblar, y hacer la Cabeza de su Señorío, y que aquí verán ensalsadas sus Generaciones. (Torquemada, 1979)

The highly respected chronicler Fray Bernardino de Sahagún has provided us with yet another version. Sahagún indicates how the ancient Mexicans wandered for many years:

> Y antes que se partiesen de Colhuacán dicen que su dios les habló, diciendo que volviesen allí donde habían partido y que les guiaría mostrándoles el camino por donde habían de ir. Y así volvieron hacia esta tierra que ahora se dice México, siendo guiados por su dios; y los sitios donde se aposentaron a la vuelta los mexicanos todos están señalados y nombrados en las pinturas antiguas, que son sus anales de los mexicanos. (Sahagún, 1981:71-72)

The most commonly known Aztlán myth narrates how the Aztecs inhabited the lands of the Southwestern United States. One day their God, Huitzilopochtli adivises them to leave their present abode and travel south where he promises them to make them lords of the universe. The Mexica-Colhua are to travel until a sign appears. The sign is an eagle perched on a cactus devouring a serpent. This would be the place where the Mexica were to found their new empire.[1] The myth cited by Villagrá includes two brothers who leave on a pilgrimmage toward the south. Suddenly a "demon" appears in the form of a woman and informs them that she will divide the lands in two empires between the brothers. The "demon" places a mass of iron on the ground and indicates the south portion of the land will be for one brother and the northern portion of the land will be for the empire of the other brother. The sign encompassed by the eagle devouring a serpent remains the same. Villagrá's myth, however, is completely impregnated by myths, legends, characters and literary allusions gleaned from European sources.

First of all Villagrá structures his historical poem using the renaissance epic format; Canto I, for example, imitates Virgil's *Aeneid,* as can be seen in the following strophe:

> Las armas y el varón heroico canto
> El ser, valor, prudencia y alto esfuerzo
> De aquel cuya paciencia no rendida,
> Por un mar de disgustos arrojada,
> A pesar de la envidia ponzoñosa
> Los hechos y prohezas va encumbrando
> De aquellos españoles valerosos
> Que en la Occidental India remontados,
> Descubriendo del mundo lo que esconde,
> "Plus ultra" con braveza van diciendo
> (Villagrá 1992:3)

Villagrá orients the European reader, to whom the work is addressed, regarding the geographic location where the deeds that will be recounted transpired. He does this by linking the American geographic space to a more accesible European one—Jerusalem:

> Debajo el polo Artico en altura
> De los treinta y tres grados que a la Santa
> Ierusalem sabemos que responden
> (Villagrá, 1992:4)

Upon approaching the Aztec myth, Villagrá will compare the two Aztec brothers who are the founders of Tenochtitlan and Aztlán with the two Roman brothers Romulus and Remus:

> Desta nueva Región es notorio,
> Pública voz y fama que decienden
> Aquellos más antiguos Mexicanos
> Que a la Ciudad de México famosa
> El nombre le pussieron porque fuesse
> Eterna su memoria perdurable,
> Imitando aquel Rómulo prudente
> Que a los Romanos muros puso tassa,
> Cuya verdad se saca y verifica
> Por aquella antiquísima pintura
> Y modo hieroglíphico que tienen,
> (Villagrá 1992:6)

Romulus and Remus are the two legendary brothers credited with the foundation of Rome. According to the legend Amulio usurped the throne of the twins' grandfather, Numitor, and ordered the twins to be killed. The twins were placed in a basket and left on the waters of a river. A wolf discovered the twins and raised them. When Romulus became an adult he kills Amulius and takes the throne. Together with Remus he founds Rome (*Encyclopedia Brittanica,* 1953).

As can be seen in the passage quoted above, Villagrá cites the Aztec codices stating they are: "Antiquísima pintura y modo hieroglíphico que tienen" and compares them to European writing:

> Por el qual tratan, hablan y se entienden,
> Aunque no con la perfección insigne
> Del gracioso coloquio que se ofrece
> Quando al amigo ausente conversamos
> mediante la grandeza y excelencia
> Del escribir illustre que tenemos.
> (Villagrá 1992:6)

The superiority of European ways of being and doing things as compared to the Native Americans is frequently alluded to in the epic.

The variant offered by Villagrá is composed of elements from both American and European cultures. The editors of the critical edition of the *Historia de la Nueva México* Miguel Encinias, *et al*, point to the possible influencias of *La Tebaida* written by Estacio and the work by Martín del Barro Centenera *Argentina y conquista del Río de Plata* published in1602 which includes the famous Tupi and Guaraní brothers in the legend. The motif of the division of the land between the two brothers appears in the Martín del Barro Centenera text. Keeping in mind the theoretical postulates on reception theory promulgated by Wolfgang Iser we can assert that Villagrá was addressing a European public which was not knowledgeable about America. In order to make his text more accesible to this audience the author had to make use of various strategies. One of these strategies was to incorporate mythological and historical characters within the epic's structure. In this manner, he Europeanized and universalized his Aztecs. On the other hand, the poet-soldier wanted to elicit the interest and the wonder of his European readership. He therefore sought to compare and contrast the European and the American culture. The work set out by Villagrá was not easy. His vast literary knowledge and the fact that he had university training since he had been a student at the University of Salamanca, aided him in the construction of his epic and achieving the desired effect. His epic is adorned with erudite images taken from the Greco-Latin literary tradition. He incorporates the mythological figures of Andromeda, Perseo, Venus, and Mecury in citing the celestial constellations; Boreas, when referring to the northern wind, Romulus and Remus, two protagonists from the historical Roman legend, and Dido from the mythic history of the founding of Carthage. All of these European mythological and historical figures he relates to the founding of the Aztec empire.

The legend offered by Villagrá differs from the traditional legend of the founding of the Aztec empire known by most Mexicans. In the traditional version the origins of the ancient Mexicans is attributed to the appearance of their god Hitzilopochtli and commanding them to migrate south in order to found their empire and become the rulers of the universe. In Villagrá's version it is a demon—for the Spanish conquistadors all the Aztec gods were demons—in the figure of a woman.

> Delante se les puso aquel maldito
> En figura de vieja rebozado
> Cuya espantosa y gran desemboltura
> Daba pavor y miedo imaginarla.
> Truxo el cabello cano mal compuesto
> Y, qual horrenda y fiera notomía,
> El rostro descarnado, macilento,
> De fiera y espantosa catadura;
> Desmesurados pechos, largas tetas,
> Hambrientas, flacas, seca, y fruncidas,
> Nerbudos pechos, anchos y espaciosos,
> Con terrible espaldas bien trabadas;
> Sumidos ojos de color de fuego,
> Disforme boca desde oreja a oreja,
> Por cuyos labios secos, desmedidos,
> Quatro sólo colmillos hazia fuera
> De un largo palmo, corbos, se mostraban.
>   (Villagra 1992:10)

The portrait delineated by Villagrá seems to resemble that of Coatlicue and not of Huitzilopochtli, God of War who in the traditional more commonly known legend appeared to the Aztec leaders giving them instructions to their new homeland.

The linkage to Europe is structured through the image of Circe from Greek mythology. Other linkages with Europe are given through the parallelism seen in the division of the territories between the two Aztec brothers and the division of the Roman empire into Western and Eastern parts. The image of the imperial eagle with two heads is in reference to the House of Hapsburg, and the emblem of the Sacred Roman Empire. In a similar manner the mass of iron implanted by the Aztec Goddess parallels the Egyption obelisk that is found in Rome.

Villagrá intends to make the inaccesible accesible in his epic through rhetorical strategies that link European entities with Aztec ones. The interesting aspects of the Villagrá version of the Aztlán legend is its antiquity, its historical-literary function within the work and the originality of this particular variant. The feminine deity perhaps dates to an ancient matriarchy although the patriarchal system is already firmly implanted in the epic.

Benedict Anderson as well as Homi Bhabha have amply written regarding the importance of a literary tradition in nationalist projects of imagining a nation. Anderson provides us with the definition of a nation as "a political community imagined . . . (p. 6) and offers the different vectors through which we can see how this imaginary construction of a nation or a community is accomplished. Bhabha, on the other hand, asserts that "Nations, like narratives, lose their origins in the myths of time and only fully realize their horizons in the mind's eye. Such an image of the nation—or narration—might seem impossibly romantic and excessively metaphorical, but it is from those traditions of political thought and literary language that the nation emerges as a powerful historical idea in the west." (Bhabha 1990:1).

The Aztlán myth was a cornerstone of the Chicano Movement, particularly during the 1960-1970 years. Since Chicanos had been perceived as strangers, as foreigners in their own land right after the Mexican American War of 1848, the myth aided in legitimizing the historical role of the Chicano people as founders and as indigenous people of the Southwest. That is to say, the myth reiterated the fact that Chicanos were not Johnny-come-latelys, foreigners or colonizers but could trace their roots to the first settlers of the Southwest. Chicanos of the 1960s were not cognizant of the existence of the Aztlán myth found in Villagrá's epic. This myth would have certainly appealed to the early Chicano Movement leadership since it not only reiterates the origins of the Aztecs in Aztlán but indicates that a group of Aztecs actually did not migrate south towards the founding of Tenochtlitlan but in fact stayed on to settle and populate the Southwest.

Notes

[1] This variant of the Aztlán myth was told to me by my grandmother, Susana Escamilla de Tarango when I was a little girl growing up in south Texas (Rio Hondo) and in Reynosa Tamaulipas, Mexico. I also heard the same verison from various other educators and Mexican acquaintances when I was young.

[2] See special issue of *Genre,* "Chicano/a Studies: Writing into the Future," Vol. 8 (Fall 1999).

Works Cited

Anderson, Benedict. *Imagined Communities.* New York: Verso, 1991.

Becco, Horacio Jorge. *Historia Real y fantástica del Nuevo Mundo.* Caracas, Venezuela: Biblioteca Ayacucho, 1992.

Bhabha, Homi K. *Nation and Narration*. New York: Routledge, 1990.

Encyclopedia Brittanica. New York: Americana Corporation, 1953.

Garibay K, Angel M. *La literatura de los aztecas*. México: Editorial Joaquín Mortiz, 1991.

Godoy, Roberto y Olmo, Angel, eds. *Textos de cronistas de indias y poemas precolombinos*. Madrid: Editora Nacional, 1979.

Herrera-Sobek, María. "Aproximaciones teóricas sobre los orígenes de la novela latinoamericana: Villagrá y *la Historia de la Nueva México*." Paper presented at the Congreso de Literatura Iberoamericana. Caracas, Venezuela, June 24-29, 1996.

————. "Los gemelos Rómulo y Remo en Aztlán: El mito azteca aztlanense-verisón Pérez de Villagrá (1610)." Paper read at the Seventh International conference on Latino Cultures in the United States. Taxco, México, August 7-11, 1996.

Leal, Luis. "Poetic Discourse in Pérez de Villagrá's *Historia de la Nueva México*." In *Reconstructing a Chicano/a Literary Heritage: Hispanic Colonial Literature of the Southwest*. Edited by María Herrera-Sobek. Tucson: University of Arizona Press, 1993. Pp. 95-117.

————. "The First American Epic: Villagrá's *History of New Mexico*." In *Pasó Por Aquí: Critical Essays on the New Mexican Literary Tradition 1542-1988*. Edited by Erlinda Gonzales-Berry. Albuquerque: University of New Mexico Press, 1989. Pp. 47-62.

Sahagún, Bernardino de. *El México antiguo*. Caracas, Venezuela: Biblioteca Ayacucho, 1981.

Torquemada, Juan de. *Los 21 libros rituales y monarquía indiana*. In *Textos de cronistas de indias y poemas precolombinos*, Roberto Godoy y Angel Olmo eds. Madrid: Editora Nacional, 1979.

Turner, Fredrick Jackson. *The Frontier in American History*. 1920. Introd. Ray Allen Billington. New York: Holt, Rinehart and Winston, 1962.

Villagrá, Gaspar Pérez de. 1610. *Historia de la Nueva México*. 1610. Alcalá de Henares: Luis Martínez Grande.

————. *Historia de la Nueva México*. 2 Vols. Ed. Luis González Obregón. Mexico City: Imprenta del Museo Nacional, 1900.

————. *History of New Mexico*. Trans. Gilberto Espinosa. Los Angeles: The Quivira Society, 1933.

————. *Historia de la Nueva México, 1610*. A Critical and Annotated Spanish/English edition translated and edited by Miguel Encinias, Alfredo Rodríguez, and Joseph P. Sánchez. Albuquerque: University of New Mexico Press, 1992.

Virgil. *The Aeneid*.

Cantaron la victoria: Spanish Literary Tradition and the 1680 Pueblo Revolt

Barbara De Marco
University of California at Berkeley

The uprising known as the 1680 Pueblo Revolt took place simultaneously and by prearranged signal in several pueblos in northern New Mexico on August 10, 1680. The revolt was not entirely unexpected; nonetheless, the swift ferocity of the 1680 attack took the Spanish completely by surprise. The effect of the rebellion was to drive the Spanish colonists out of New Mexico and into the far remove of El Paso del Norte, at the southern extremity of the province.

The eyewitness testimony to the Revolt and its aftermath makes compelling reading. A selection of original documents was published in English translation in 1942 as part of the "Coronado Cuarto Centennial Celebrations" (see Hackett and Shelby 1942). The preparation of Spanish editions of the manuscripts pertaining to the Revolt is now in its first stages.[1] The intellectual justification for such editions has been argued elsewhere (Craddock 1996; Craddock and De Marco 1997); in what follows I discuss the documents of the Pueblo Revolt, not as a neglected record of the early history of the American Southwest, but as a reflection of a Spanish literary tradition that goes back to the earliest vernacular texts. One particular feature of interest, especially from the perspective of a medievalist, is the extent to which the official documents and correspondence which comprise the historical record contain echoes of hagiographic narratives which are so integral a part of the literary history of Spain.

By way of illustration, I compare the eyewitness account of a particularly dramatic episode of the 1680 Pueblo Revolt to two other examples of Spanish narrative style. The first is made up of a representative sample of the thirteenth-century compilation, Alfonso el Sabio's *Cantigas de Santa María*, a collection of some four hundred songs to the Virgin. The second is the work of the twentieth-century New Mexican historian, novelist, and poet Fray Angélico Chávez.

The specific episode of the Pueblo Revolt to which I refer, the siege of Santa Fe, is taken from the eyewitness account sent by the governor, Antonio Otermín, to the Franciscan *procurador general*, Fray Francisco de Ayeta. Ayeta, thrust by circumstance into the role of the "real savior of the New Mexican refugees" (see Hackett and Shelby 1942, 1:lxxix), figures prominently in the extensive correspondence among civil and ecclesiastic authorities that ensued as a result of the Revolt.

In a letter to the Viceroy, written in 1693 (after having received news of Vargas's successful re-entry into New Mexico), Ayeta presents a retrospective account of the 1680 Pueblo Revolt, its consequences, and its implications for maintaining a Spanish presence in New Mexico. Ayeta writes with a keen attention to style and a breathlessness of pace that belies the decade intervening between the events and their recounting. He explains in his prologue (the letter itself, numbering twenty-seven folia, is supplemented with nearly five-hundred folia of official documents and related correspondence)[2] that he is taking advantage of both time and distance to reveal certain details upon which his earlier discretion enjoined silence:

> [D]esde aquellos reinos no debía hablar hasta que se le requiriese, e inter-pelase; reconociendo ahora que negocios más graves pueden haber suspendido el cuidado de éste, como quiera que para con el suplicante, no haga otro mayor; tubiera como tiene por de grave escrúpulo, si tanto tiempo se entregara al silencio y no representara a Vuestra Magestad lo que vió, el estado en que estas conversiones quedaron, y lo que, de orden de vuestro Virrey Marqués de la Laguna, propuso, sobre si era o no conveniente continuar con la guerra de estos indios (fol. 987r).

In the episode of the siege of Santa Fe, Spanish survivors from the north-ern Pueblos have gathered in the Villa with Governor Otermín. Events of the previous days have warned them to expect no mercy at the hands of the rebel-lious Pueblo Indians. Holed up in the Villa, outnumbered by the ever-growing enemy forces, weakened by hunger and thirst, the Spanish refugees are in a truly desperate situation. Ayeta sketches the scene which confronts the besieged occupants of the Villa:

> Llegada la noche en esta forma, la pasaron como las demás, con el cuidado y desvelo que se reconoce, y muy fatigados de la sed por falta de el agua, y al otro día, sábado al amanecer, empezaron los yndios con más aprieto y ahinco a flechar y a tirar piedras a los españoles, diciéndoles que ya no se habían de librar de sus manos porque demás de su gran número esperaban socorro de los Apaches a quienes habían convidado, y este día se fue en pelear, y sobre todo fatigaba mucho la sed a los españoles, porque ya al anochecer, se ahogaban; y por el peligro evidente en que se veían, de que no les ganasen los dos quartos de cañón que estaban en las puertas de las casas reales, asestados a las bocas calles para entrarlos dentro, se vió muy apretado el gobernador, por las pocas fuercas con que se hallaba, porque reconoció que el intento de los indios era quitárselas, y luego que éstos vieron que las retiraba, cantaron la victoria, con alaridos de guerra, quemando todas las casas de la Villa, en que se ocuparon toda la noche, con el susto que se puede considerar causaba a los españoles

verla hecha un volcán de fuego, y lo que es más, el tremendo dolor que les aquejaba de ver el desprecio con que trataban el santo nombre de Dios, oraciones de la iglesia, y decoro de las imágenes (fol. 990v-991r).

Governor Otermín determines that the only recourse is to last out the night, battle to the death, and if victorious, escape somehow to the southern border. To prepare for this grim last-ditch effort, he enjoins the people to prayer and repentance, to make peace with each other and with God. In this manner they pass the night:

> Y viéndose en este estado el Gobernador, quemado el templo y la Villa, con pocos caballos y algún ganado menor y vacas sin comer ni beber en tanto tiempo, y que ya se le había muerto mucha parte e iba pereciendo la demás, y lo principal con gran número de gente, todos los más niños y mugeres (que con poca diferencia llegarían a mil personas), cercado de tanto llanto y conflicto, determinó salir por la mañana a pelear hasta morir o vencer, y considerando que las mejores fuerzas y armas son las oraciones, para aplacar la ira divina (aunque en los días antecedentes las pobres mugeres las habían ejercitado con fervor), aquella noche las encargó lo hiciesen con mucho más, y al guardián y otros dos religiosos de los que allí se hallaban que les dijesen misa al amanecer, y exhortasen a todos tanto el repentimiento de sus pecados como la conformidad con la voluntad divina, y que les absolviesen a culpa y a pena en cuyas diligencias de confesar, comulgar, pedir perdón a Dios y despedirse los padres de sus hijos y las mujeres de sus maridos, llenos por todas partes de pavor y estruendo, batallando con las agonías de la muerte por la cercanía del fuego, pasaron la noche hasta el amanecer (fol. 991r).

The next morning, after a serious battle and against considerable odds, they manage to escape south, where they later join with a second band of refugees.

Songs of siege are common in tales of the medieval *reconquista*: A castle is besieged by the Moorish King of Granada. Within this castle, the frightened Spanish inhabitants resort to desperate but effective measures: they take the statue of the Virgin from the chapel, set her on the castle walls, and enjoin her to defend them from the Moors, who would burn her image ("E os que dentro jazian ouveron tan gran pavor / que fillaron a omagen da madre do Salvador / que estava na capela e fórona a põer / Ontr' as ameas, dizendo: 'Se tu es Madre de Deus / deffend' aqueste castelo e a nos, que somos teus, / e guarda a ta capela que non seja dos encreus / mouros en poder, nen façan a ta omagen arder'. / E leixárona dizendo: 'Veremo-lo que farás'," *Cantiga* 185, vv. 71-80). As events in the *Cantigas* are wont to transpire, the inhabitants of the castle are saved.

A similar tale, set in Jérez de la Frontera, recounts the episode of some *almogávares* who have tried—repeatedly and unsuccessfully—to defeat the Moors. These *almogávares* are mercenary raiders, bordering, it would seem, on *desperados*, for the *Cantiga* clearly states that they finally come to understand it is their own sins that keep them from victory ("Mais depois que entenderon que esto per seus pecados / era, logo mantinente se teveron por culpados, / e en correger cuidavam muyto depois en sa vida," *Cantiga* 374, vv. 18-20). They repent and decide to keep vigil in a chapel dedicated to the Virgin, praying for eventual victory. Being mercenaries, they also promise her a reward—they will bring her a vestment of gold and purple-dyed cloth ("E ouveron seu acordo que fossen t er vegia / ena fremosa capela da Virgen Santa Maria / e logo en caval- gada movessen en outro dia, / e se gãassem, a Virgen ouvess' en de sa partida / A cousa que mais fremosa e mais rica y fillassen. / E porend'a Gloriosa lles fez que desbaratassen / h a recova mui grande de mouros, e que achassen / a pur- pura muy rica, feyta d'ouro muy velida," vv. 22-30).[3]

We are not surprised, in a collection of *Cantigas de Santa María*, to see full prominence given to the efficacious power of the Virgin, and the investment of that power in some manifestation of her image.[4] A striking feature of these medieval hagiographic tales, however, is the preference given to mercy over justice, with the Virgin offering legal aid to her devotees. Thus, lascivious monks, wayward nuns, thieves, drunks, and ill-doers of all kinds may rely on the unstrained quality of her mercy because, whatever their failings, they nonetheless remain devoted to her. For those who defame her, however, pun- ishment is swift and effective.[5]

In this respect, narratives of the Pueblo Revolt contrast sharply with the hagiographic expectations recounted in the *Cantigas*. We do not read, in the chronicles of the New Mexican frontier, that the Christian forces, besieged by infidels and heretics, sustained by prayers and aided by divine intervention, are brought to ultimate triumph—though this is always the lesson in the *Cantigas*. Nor do we read of any punishment immediately descending upon the *yndios* for their desecration of holy images and artifacts.[6] Ayeta tells us, rather, of a ter- rorized band of settlers who somehow escape certain death only to make an uncertain trek southwards. Yet the practice of hagiographic narrative, with its expectations of immediate reward or punishment, does nonetheless make it appearance in the historical accounts, as in this episode, which Ayeta tells in the first person, of finding a necessary source of water:

> Y por la noche sobrevino la noticia de la ninguna seguridad con que se que- dava en el pueblo de el Passo. . . y con el dolor, señor, de que el agua que teníamos distaba una legua corta, y las noticias eran que los indios sólo aguardaban a privarnos de ella para acabar con la gente que quedaba, en cuyo estrecho, y en el de quedar todos dentro de el circuito de el convento amural- lados y peltrechados para defendernos de los asaltos de los indios, enprehendió el suplicante la faena de que, a 25 pasos de la frente de el con- vento se cavase para ver si Dios nos socorría con agua, y quiso su divina providencia que a diez brazas la hallásemos tan abundante y dulce que con ella pudimos mantenernos y asegurarnos de las hostilidades que nos amenazaban de los indios (fol. 988v).

A second account of the siege of Santa Fe, written by the Franciscan Angélico Chávez, derives its dramatic effect from those same historical documents sent by Ayeta to the Viceroy. Though this twentieth-century narrative of New Mexico is written in English, by theme, author, and narrative technique, it clearly places itself within the Spanish literary tradition.

In *My Penitente Land*, a book of strange and beautiful musings over Hispanic history and identity in the American Southwest, Chávez recounts the following story: "There lived a little girl in Santa Fe . . . who had been crippled since childhood by some illness. Suddenly she found herself cured, as she herself told about her experience, by a little statue of Nuestra Señora del Sagrario which she had by her bed" (183).[7]

Stories of miraculous cures—especially of children—are the very stuff of miracle tales.[8] In the *Cantigas* healing, and even restoration from death, is due almost exclusively to the intercession of the Virgin. Even if the child does not live, it is clear that he or she is under the protection of the Virgin. In perhaps the most extreme variation on this theme, the child dies for very love of the Virgin: the parents discover from the autopsy that an image of the Virgin is inscribed on the child's heart ("Esta donzela tan muito Santa Maria amou / que, macar no mund' estava, por ela o despreçou / tanto, que per asteença que fazia enfermou, / ... / O padr' e a madre dela, quando a viron f ir, / cuidaron que poçon fora e fezérona abrir; / e eno coraçon dentro ll' acharon y sen mentir / omagen da Groriosa, qual x' ela foi fegurar," *Cantiga* 188, vv. 17-19, 32-35).

The life or death of the child, however, is a secondary focus in the *Cantigas*; what is primary is the special relationship which exists between the child and the Virgin. This is also true of Chávez's young girl in Santa Fe. To her story, however, he adds an unusual detail, which he ties directly into the 1680 Pueblo Revolt:

> The girl said that the Virgin had prophesied that the Kingdom would soon be destroyed by the Indians, chiefly because the settlers themselves had often proven themselves irreverent toward the missionaries. . . As a direct result of the alleged prophecy, the colonists prevailed on the new governor to proceed on an overall destruction of *kivas* and other shrines. . . and in the suppression of *catzina* ceremonials and the punishment of the 'witches' who were behind them all. Ironically it was the most effective means of making the prophecy come true (1974:183-184).

Chávez rounds out his episode with his own version of the siege of Santa Fe, the very story that his Franciscan counterpart, Francisco de Ayeta, told some three hundred years earlier, in the *cantaron la victoria* episode cited previously:

> Since the larger statue of La Conquistadora. . . had been taken from the church before the siege began, the women and the children and the aged now prayed

before her for deliverance while all the men able to bear arms kept the enemy at bay. They were sure their prayers were answered when the defenders managed to put the Indian warriors to rout temporarily, and this allowed enough time for the Lord Governor and his people to flee three hundred miles southward to the newest mission of the Kingdom at Guadalupe del Paso (1974:184).

That "their prayers were answered" at all is a matter entirely of interpretation. Recounting the events of 1680, Francisco de Ayeta made no such claim, nor did his eyewitness, Governor Antonio Otermín, and neither makes any mention of a statue of the Virgin. In fact, the details of Chávez's account have more in common with the tale of the Spanish occupants of the castle in Granada, recounted above (*Cantiga* 185) than with the historical record of the siege of the Villa of Santa Fe. Clearly, Chávez has consciously created the context—and even invented the details—for his version,[9] and of course he was not setting out to write a history of New Mexico, at least not in this work: the subtitle of *My Penitente Land* is *Reflections on Spanish New Mexico*.[10]

Chávez's re-telling of the siege of Santa Fe becomes more compelling when read in the light of the historical record of events set down by eyewitnesses; both Ayeta's historical account and Chávez's dramatic narrative take on a new dimension when viewed in the context of hagiographic narratives, a literary tradition which is as old as Spanish vernacular literature itself.

Notes

[1] The intention of this project, supported in part by a Collaborative Research Grant from the National Endowment of the Humanities (1997-1999) is to make available reliable editions *in Spanish* of a series of documents of the Spanish exploration and settlement of the American Southwest. In many cases, the Spanish edition will be the first published record of the document. With regard the 1680 Pueblo Revolt, even the major historical studies of the period acknowledge their reliance on the Hackett and Shelby 1942 English edition (see, for example, Weber 1992:415-416, n. 76). Ayeta's 1693 letter to the Viceroy, cited extensively in this paper, has never, to my knowledge, been published, although a transcript was found among the Bolton papers in the Bancroft Library (H. E. Bolton Papers, C-B 840, Carton 30, Folder 435). Possibly because of its date, the document was filed in among the Vargas papers in AGI Guadalajara, *legajo* 139, and thus escaped notice; the central corpus of documents regarding the 1680 Pueblo Revolt are contained in AGI Guadalajara, *legajo* 138.

I wish to express my appreciation to the Recovering the U. S. Hispanic Literary Heritage Project of the University of Houston, for the 1996 grant-in-aid that made possible the transcription of the Ayeta document cited herein.

Unless otherwise indicated, all citations are from my own transcription of MS Archivo General de Indias (AGI), Audiencia de Guadalajara, *legajo* 139, ff. 984r-1012v (see De Marco 1997b), *presented here with modernized spelling and punctuation*. All citations of the *Cantigas* are taken from the authoritative Mettmann edition (1959-1972). My interest in documents of the Hispanic Southwest was first inspired by a reading of the Vargas correspondence, published under the auspices of the Vargas Project at the University of New Mexico; see Kessell 1989; Kessell et al. 1992, 1995.

My thanks also to Jerry R. Craddock (University of California, Berkeley) for initially suggesting the project, for advice and assistance with paleographic methods, and for a critical reading of successive versions of this article.

[2] Ayeta mentions to the viceroy that he encloses with his letter four sets of supplementary documents bearing on the Revolt (f. 1011v): the first (357 folios) contains eyewitness testimony ("testimonios de autos") and describes the events which succeeded immediately upon the Revolt ("lo que sucedió en el, recursos que se aplicaron, providencias y socorros que en México se resolvieron"); the second (33 folios) consists of Ayeta's own reports and requests for immediate aid, delivered personally in Mexico; the third assembles reports by Otermín (81 folios); the fourth is an account of the *entrada* (28 folios), that is, the first—unsuccessful—attempt of the regrouped settlers to subdue the rebellious Pueblo Indians and regain their foothold in northern New Mexico.

[3] I pursue the theme of the parallels with medieval literature in "*La Conquistadora*: Hagiographic Elements in don Diego de Vargas's Narrative of Reconquest" (De Marco 1997a). Vargas, writing what purports to be both an official record of military expeditions and a deliberate maneuvering for favors and accolades, shows no hesitation in attributing his victory to the intervention and protection of the Virgin Mary; nor does he shun the efficacious use of images of the Virgin, especially the standard of *Nuestra Señora de los Remedios*. Similarly, in the narrative of *reconquista* which is clearly one of the themes of his *Cantigas*, Alfonso el Sabio, like Vargas, openly attributes his various successes to the intervention of the Virgin. Thus, just as Alfonso el Sabio, in a determined effort to create a corpus of hagiographic poetry, included verifiable elements of history, so Vargas, in his unabashed attempt to write a self-glorifying history of the reconquest, laces his narrative with details that form part of the hagiographic repertoire.

[4] In addition to numerous stories of healing effected by a pilgrimage to one of her many churches, (the *Cantigas* mention local cults at, *inter alia*, Cordova, Montserrat, Porto, Rocamadour, Tocha, Tuda, and Vila-Sirga; see also n. 8), the power of the Virgin may also be made manifest in a statue (e.g., *Cantiga* 38: "Esta é como a omagen de Santa Maria tendeu o braço e tomou o de seu Fillo, que queria caer da pedrada que lle dera o tafur, de que sayu sangui") or other image (*Cantiga* 264: "Como Santa Maria fez pereçer as naves

dos mouros que tiin[n]am çercada Costantinopla, tanto que os crischãos poseron a ssa ymagen na rriba do mar"). To a much lesser extent, other *Cantigas* likewise refer to relics (*Cantiga* 257: "Como Santa Maria guardou sas relicas que se non danassen entr' outras muitas que se danaron"), specifically, a type of amulet (*Cantiga* 299: "Como Santa Maria veo en vision a un freire e mandou-lle que désse a ssa omagen que tragia a un rey"), and even a linen shift believed to have belonged to the Virgin (*Cantiga* 148: "Como un cavaleiro guareceu de mãos de seus eemigos por h a camisa que chaman de Santa Maria, que tragia vestida").

[5] Those who play at dice seem particularly susceptible to blasphemy: *Cantiga* 72: "Como o demo matou a un tafur que deostou a Santa Maria porque perdera"; *Cantiga* 154: "Como un tafur tirou con h a baesta h a seeta contra o ceo con sanna porque perdera, porque cuidava que fi[ri]ria a Deus ou Santa Maria"; *Cantiga* 163: "Come uun ome d' Osca, que jogava os dados, descre[e]u en Santa Maria e perdeu logo a fala; e foi a Santa Maria de Salas en romaria e cobró-a; *Cantiga* 174:"Como un cavaleiro servia Santa Maria, e aveo-lle que jogou os dados, e porque perdeu deostou Santa Maria; e arrepentiu-se depois, e do pesar que ende ouve tallou a lingua; e são-lla Santa Maria, e falou depois muy ben."

[6] The desecrated image of the Virgin found among the charred ruins of the mission church in the Pueblo of Sandía motivated a separate article (see Craddock and De Marco 1997). The relevant passage from Ayeta's letter reads: "Y en el 17 siguiente, habiendo arrasado el tiempo, viéndose el Governador dos leguas de el Pueblo de Sandía, mandó prevenir 20 soldados, y una esquadra de indios amigos, y marchó con ellos para el dicho Pueblo, entró en él, y halló la iglesia y convento quemado y demolido, registróse el Pueblo, y se hallaron dos campanas quebradas en cinco partes, una salvilla de plata, una vinagera, una naveta de incienso, una coronita quebrada, y vistas todas las casas, se halló en una, por trofeo de los apóstatas, pintada en una tabla, la imagen de la purísima concepción de Nuestra Señora, con un dragón a los pies, cuya pintura servía de remate al colateral del altar mayor de la iglesia, y la imagen de Nuestra Señora tenía desbaratados los divinos ojos y boca [y] en las demás partes del cuerpo, señales de haberla apedreado y la maldita figura que estaba a sus pies, sana y buena" (f. 1003r). The same episode is also described, in somewhat less circumspect terms, in a report from the *cabildo*. This is contained in two copies in the "autos tocantes al alzamiento de los indios de la provincia de la Nueva México" (AGI Guadalajara legajo138, fols. 391v-399r, 728v-737v), a full transcription of which is included in the article.

[7] The same story is used as the centerpiece of Chávez's *The Lady from Toledo: An Historical Novel Set in Santa Fe*. The revised edition of the 1960 novel includes as an addendum Chávez's 1959 article on the cult of *Nuestra Señora de la Macana*, which he himself calls "a most curious mixture of legend and history."

[8] Children saved from sickness or death, and even brought back from death, are the subject of numerous *Cantigas*. The small sample given here also mentions several of her pilgrimage sites. *Cantiga* 21: "Esta é como Santa Maria fez aver fillo a h a moller man a e depois morreu-lle, e ressocitou-llo"; *Cantiga* 43: Esta é de como Santa Maria resucitou un men o na ssa eigreja de Salas"; *Cantiga* 269: "Como un menino que era sordo e mudo resuscitó-o Santa Maria per rogo de sa madre do menino e fez-lle cobrar o falar e o oyr"; *Cantiga* 321: "Esta é como Santa Maria guareceu en Cordova h a moça d a grand' enfermidade que avia"; *Cantiga* 343: "Como Santa Maria de Rocamador guariu h a manceba demoniada de demonio mudo e fez que falasse"; *Cantiga* 347: "Esta é como Santa Maria de Tudia resorgiu u menynno que era morto de quatro dias"; *Cantiga* 381: "Como Santa Maria do Porto resuscitou un menino que morrera, fillo dun ome bõo que morava en Xerez."

[9] In his edition of short stories, Genaro Padilla ranks Angélico Chávez among New Mexico's leading men of letters (Padilla 1987:vii). Regarding's Chávez's narrative technique, Padilla observes: "Although his work may incorporate structural elements from the *cuento* tradition, as Chávez himself warns, his stories are not a 'rehashing of old folk tales'. What makes Chávez original is that his stories locate themselves somewhere between the allegorical *cuento* and historical fiction" (xi).

[10] Chávez's competence as a professional historian, completely familiar with the historical documents of Spanish New Mexico, is amply attested to by numerous studies and editions; see, for example, Chávez 1954, 1957, 1968; Adams and Chávez 1976.

Works Cited

Adams, Eleanor B., and Fray Angélico Chávez, eds. 1976. *The Missions of New Mexico, 1776: A Description by Fray Francisco Atanasio Domínguez with Other Contemporary Documents*. 2d ed. Albuquerque: University of New Mexico.

Chávez, Fray Angélico. 1954. *Origins of New Mexico Families in the Spanish Colonial Period*. Santa Fe: Historical Society of New Mexico.

———. 1957. *Archives of the Archdiocese of Santa Fe, 1678-1900*. Washington, D.C.: Academy of American Franciscan History.

———. 1959. "Nuestra Señora de la Macana." *New Mexico Historical Review* 34 (2):81-97.

———. 1993. *The Lady from Toledo: An Historical Novel in Santa Fe, New Mexico*. Rev. ed. with a foreword by Thomas E. Chávez. Santa Fe: Museum of New Mexico. lst ed., Academy Guild Press, 1960.

———. 1968. *Coronado's Friars*. Washington, D.C.: Academy of American Franciscan History.

————. 1974. *My Penitente Land: Reflections on Spanish New Mexico*. Santa Fe: Museum of New Mexico.

Craddock, Jerry R. 1996. "Philological Notes on the Hammond and Rey Translation of the *[Relación de la] Entrada que hizo en el Nuevo Mexico Francisco Sánchez Chamuscado en junio de [15]81* by Hernán Gallegos, Notary of the Expedition." *Romance Philology* 49:351-363.

Craddock, Jerry R., and Barbara De Marco. 1997."La profanación de lo sagrado: modalidades medieval y novomexicana." *Anuario de Letras* 35:193-213.

De Marco, Barbara. In preparation. *Documents of the 1680 Pueblo Revolt: Edition and Catalog*. Archivo General de Indias, Audiencia de Guadalajara, legajo 138.

————. 1997a. "La Conquistadora: Hagiographic Elements in don Diego de Vargas's Narrative of Reconquest." Paper delivered at panel on "*Beatos y beatas* in Colonial Latin America," Conference on Colonial Latin American History, annual meeting of the American Historical Association, January 1997.

————. 1997b. "Fray Francisco de Ayeta and the 1680 Pueblo Revolt: Spanish Documents of the Period." Edition of AGI Guadalajara 139, ff. 984r-1012v. Submitted to the American Academy of Franciscan History.

Hackett, Charles W., and Charmion C. Shelby, trans. and eds. 1942. *Revolt of the Pueblo Indians of New Mexico and Otermin's Attempted Reconquest, 1680-1682*. Coronado Cuarto Centennial Publications, 8-9. 2 vols. Albuquerque, New Mexico: Univ. of New Mexico.

Kessell, John L., ed. 1989. *Remote Beyond Compare: Letters of don Diego de Vargas to His Family from New Spain and New Mexico 1675-1706*. Vargas series, 1. Albuquerque: University of New Mexico.

Kessell, John L., and Rick Hendricks, eds. 1992. *By Force of Arms: The Journals of don Diego de Vargas, 1691-1693*. Vargas series, 2. Albuquerque: University of New Mexico.

Kessell, John L., Rick Hendricks, and Meredith D. Dodge, eds. 1995. *To the Royal Crown Restored: The Journals of don Diego de Vargas, New Mexico, 1692-1694*. Vargas series, 3. Albuquerque: University of New Mexico.

Mettmann, Walter, ed. 1959-1972. Afonso X, o Sábio, *Cantigas de Santa María*. 4 vols. Coimbra: Universidade.

Padilla, Genaro M., ed. 1987. *The Short Stories of Fray Angélico Chávez*. Albuquerque: University of New Mexico.

Weber, David J. 1992. *The Spanish Frontier in North America*. New Haven and London: Yale.

Los Comanches: Text, Performance, and Transculturation in an Eighteenth-Century New Mexican Folk Drama[1]

Enrique R. Lamadrid
University of New Mexico

El comanche y el apache	El cumanche y la cumancha
se citaron una guerra	se fueron a Santa Fe,
el apache no se raja	pa' vender a sus hijitos
el comanche se le aferra.	por azúcar y café.
—"Coplas comanches"	—"Arrullo comanche"[3]

The performance tradition of the *Nuevomexicano* folk play *Los Comanches* spans more than two centuries and several revivals, from its inscription in the late 1770s to early 1780s to the present. In a seminal essay, Genaro Padilla thoughtfully questions the forays of Chicano criticism into the colonial period in search of roots, wondering:

> Is this a move to invent continuity between colonial Hispanic and Chicano literary discourse—the first a hegemonic discourse of possession and domination, the second a counterhegemonic discourse generated by dispossession and subordination? (32)

In the case of *Los Comanches* there is no need for invention, or critical artifice because the record of transculturation (Harris, Pratt) from the discourse of power to one of resistance is complete, if an ethnographic gaze is cast beyond the play as published text to the play as cultural enactment and socially symbolic performance. The evolution of the play's range of meaning offers a fascinating glimpse into the dynamic process of cultural *mestizaje*, what postcolonial theory terms "a rethinking of the forms and forces of 'identification' as they operate at the edge of cultural authority (Bhabha: 149)." The context of historic and contemporary Comanches celebrations is broad and intercultural.

The waxing of the first autumn moon, New Mexico's "Comanche Moon," lights the beginning of a unique cycle of traditional feasts which unites the region in carnavalesque celebration of cultural otherness. From the San Gerónimo Fiesta at Taos Pueblo on September 30 until Lent, Hispanos and Pueblos dressed and singing as Comanches may be found somewhere along the Río Grande del Norte at every major feast, including Christmas, New Years and *Funciones* or Patron Saint's Days.[4] Hispano placitas and Indian pueblos alike come alive with colorful processions, heroic historical drama, religious morality plays, and boisterous ceremonial dancing (Hurt, Campa 1979, Cavalio-Bosso, Hurt, King, Lamadrid 1992, Martínez, Sweet); all in mixed defiance and emulation of a much-admired former foe—those Yamparicas, Yupes, Cuchanecas, Cotsotecas, and Ietanes known collectively to themselves as Nuhmuhnuh, the people, and to their enemies as *los Comanches*. Exuberant and ambiguous, the cross-cultural image of the Comanche is unified under a sign of anarchic individualism, the explanation for legendary prowess as formidable warriors and prodigious traders. In the Indo-Hispano imagination, this compelling image of Comanches has animated a process of subjectification and transculturation which in New Mexico folk traditions encompasses all points on the scale from cultural self to other.

This is the bioregional festival context of the spectacular folk play known in the scholarly record as *Los Comanches*. To distinguish it from the other "Comanches" celebrations, the people sometimes call it *Los Comanches de Castillo* in reference to the "castle" or base area the Spanish Mexican soldiers use in the play (Gonzales). In an equestrian display equaled only by the New Mexican *Moros y Cristianos,* the play is an ambivalent celebration of the defeat of the great chief Tabivo Naritgante (brave and handsome) in the final campaign of the Comanche wars of the late eighteenth century. Famous for his distinctive battle headdress, Cuerno Verde is known by the name the Spanish Mexicans gave both him and his father, whose death he avenged in a series of raids until his own defeat in September of 1779. He and most of the Spanish Mexican opponents can be found on the pages of chronicles and letters from the period (John, Thomas: 62, 99, 309). In the play, the cast of mounted braves and soldiers meet on the field of battle to taunt each other and exchange fierce *arengas* or military harangues in a dazzling verbal display. Two *Pecas,* or captive children from Pecos pueblo, are rescued in a skirmish. A messenger from another group of Comanches with a peace treaty with the government arrives at the last minute, but is unable to intervene in the inevitable conflict at hand. In the final scene the battle rages, ending in a rout of the Comanches. In some versions Cuerno Verde dies, and others he remains. A disturbingly enigmatic and burlesque character named Barriga Dulce watches the captives, robs the dead on the battlefield, and ridicules the entire spectacle.

Although five generations of scholars acknowledge that *Los Comanches* is a folk play which several actually witnessed, there are no performance studies to date. The majority of the scholarship concerns itself with the play's origins and the plethora of tantalizing historical references (Austin 1927 &

1933, Brown 1939, Campa 1942 & 1979, Englekirk 1940 & 1957, Espinosa 1907 & 1976). Four more recent scholars have examined the literary structure of the play (R. Anderson, Dahlberg, Lamadrid 1993, Roeder).

The scholars' agreement on the historical record is that the play combines or conflates two distinct campaigns against the Comanches. In September 1774, following a violent summer of raiding and retaliation, Governor Mendinueta implemented his zero-tolerance policy of extermination above diplomacy, and dispatched Don Carlos Fernández with a rag-tag force of six hundred poorly equipped presidial soldiers, militia, and Pueblo auxiliaries. A large encampment composed of Comanche families was surprised east of Galisteo, and over four hundred were captured or slaughtered. For the next five years, the Comanches exacted their vengeance on *Nuevomexicano* settlers, who paid a terrible price for this controversial victory and failed policy (Noyes: 62-65). In August of 1779, newly appointed Governor De Anza was faced with bringing closure to the genocidal policies of his predecessor before initiating his own ultimately successful diplomacy efforts. He captured an even larger camp of Cuerno Verde's people and all their winter supplies, southwest of the present site of Colorado Springs, while the warriors were off raiding in northern New Mexico. Returning from the raid, forty Comanches desperately charged the Spanish Mexican army of eight hundred, and Cuerno Verde, his son, and all his chiefs were annihilated (Noyes: 74-79).

The absence of the victorious De Anza as a character in the play has puzzled scholars. Early scholarship attributes the presumed inaccuracy to a folk aesthetic more interested in dramatic spectacle than in historic fact (Espinosa 1907, Campa 1942). Those more interested in dating the play have speculated that it may have been written between 1774 and 1779, adding Cuerno Verde's death as a codicil (Englekirk 1957). Recent scholarship has noted that the exclusion of the newcomer De Anza actually adds to the drama of the play, since Cuerno Verde was familiar with veteran Carlos Fernández, and yearned for the opportunity to avenge himself personally for the Galisteo atrocities of 1774 (R. Anderson). The Comanche losses were more dreadful and desire for vengeance stronger than historians imagined, since many of the victims died by drowning, which in the Comanche belief system prevents the soul from properly exiting the body (Gelo).

This writer has wondered if the author of the play was troubled with De Anza's emerging policy of diplomacy and was yearning for vengeance and the more extreme and intractable policy of the previous governor. In any case, the name that resounds to this day in the popular memory is that of Don Carlos Fernández, while the name of De Anza lives on only in books. If the play's intent was to erase him from the popular consciousness, it succeeded. "Native son" sentiment is also a factor in northern New Mexico, especially in the area of Alcalde, New Mexico, where the only surviving performance of *Los Comanches* is staged. Unnoticed by scholars is the marriage of Don Carlos

Fernández to one of the daughters of Sebastián Martín, the original settler of the Alcalde area, whose descendants are still present (Brown 1936).

Sandra Dahlberg, the newest critic to join the debate, uses careful textual scrutiny to posit De Anza's exclusion from the play as a clever and calculated protest of government Indian policy and a personal objection to the flamboyant style of De Anza:

> Fernández is not only personifying the Anza administration's lack of regard for the Comanche people and the Spanish intent to conquer the Indians . . . he is also reflecting authorial disapproval of Anza's personal involvement in the war with Cuerno Verde's Comanches. The use of the personal pronoun rather than relying on the established empirical power, exposes Anza's self-pride, his need to flaunt his power, a tendency supported by Anza's own notes on the engagement (140).

The hilarious but disturbing speeches of the comic character Barriga Duce take on new significance in this critical light. He is much more than a stock *gracioso* providing humorous relief from the heroic action, but rather veils and reveals the author's cynical view of the cruelty of the Comanche campaigns and the complicity of the *Nuevomexicano* settlers as they divide up the booty of war.

The other critical dilemma of *Los Comanches* concerns authorship. All scholars but one (Englekirk 1957) agree that, based on the wealth of cultural and historical detail in the text, the author of *Los Comanches* was in all probability a participant observer of the Comanche campaigns of the 1770s. Critical speculation as well as oral historical sources indicate that the author may have been none other than Don Pedro Bautista Pino of Galisteo, the New Mexican representative to the Cortes de Cádiz of 1810. Amado Chaves, the donor of the first manuscript to be published, reported to Aurelio Espinosa that descendants of Pino by family tradition claim him as the author (Chaves). Pino was a participant in the campaigns and his ranch was attacked several times by Comanches. Two family members were taken captive and others perished in the Tomé massacre of 1777. Despite these personal tragedies, he writes favorably, even admirably about Comanche culture in his 1812 *Exposición sucinta y sencilla de la provincia del Nuevo México*, which he personally delivered to the Cortes. The most convincing case for Pino's authorship is provided by Dahlberg's close reading of the opinions expressed in the *Exposición* and the opinions implicit in *Los Comanches*.

In terms of literary origins, there is unanimous critical agreement concerning the dramatic lineage of *Los Comanches* with its parent, *Moros y Cristianos*. The analogous dramatic action and staging is evident to anyone who has seen both plays in New Mexico. Opposing mounted armies face each other across the battlefield, then enter into combat to rescue the *Santa Cruz* in one case and the Pecas captives in the other. However, the ideological differences stand in sharp contrast. In *Moros y Cristianos* the symbolic action progresses from challenge, to conflict, to defeat, and culminates with forgiveness, conversion, and inclusion. The irony of *Los Comanches* is that it truncates the dramatic paradigm of heroic folk theater. The play ends abruptly with utter defeat and no mention or possibility of redemptive closure, the moral sanction for *guerra justa* or justified violence. This lack of symbolic resolution supports the analysis of the play as a political protest cloaked in the familiar and popular guise of the heroic equestrian play (Dahlberg).

What is evident in performance is that the ancient paradigm of heroic drama fulfills itself beyond the ambivalent climax of *Los Comanches de Castillo*. It is in the other manifestations of Comanches and *Matachines* celebrations in the larger bioregional context where the values of forgiveness, redemption, and inclusion are not only realized, but surpassed in a process of trans-culturation which proceeds through emulation to identification.

Like other literary phenomena of frontier and borderlands areas, *Los Comanches* occupies a space defined by inscription but contiguous with oral tradition. Testimonial accounts from both the nineteenth and twentieth centuries suggest that *Los Comanches* has led a dual existence: one in the careful conservation, circulation, and hand copying of manuscripts; the other in the more dynamic and subjective process of oral transmission, revivals, and actual performance. The trail of paper has many branches but can be traced to two sources, both published in the *University of New Mexico Bulletin*: the copy one J. J. Vigil made "*Verbatim et Literatim*" sometime between 1840 and 1850, given by Amado Chaves of Santa Fe to Aurelio Macedonio Espinosa (1907); and the more complete 1864 copy by one Miguel Sandoval, given by Rafael Lucero of El Pino to Arturo Campa (1942), which adds opening speeches by Barriga Duce, a burlesque character, and Cuerno Verde's death scene at the end. Unpublished manuscripts gathered by Mary Austin, Lorin Brown, Frank M. Bond, Lorin Brown, Lester Raines, and John D. Robb are close copies of these two.[5]

The popularity of the play undoubtedly enhanced its oral transmission. In his memoirs, Rafael Chacón recalls spirited performances prior to the U.S. military conquest of 1846 (Meketa 76). Aurelio Espinosa also testifies to its popularity, then its decline by the turn of the century. In 1907 he declared that:

> Up to some twenty years ago, it was produced in many parts of New Mexico, during the Christmas holidays or other important feast days. The popularity of the play during the last century is confirmed by the fact that very few New Mexicans over fifty years of age are not able to recite portions of *Los Comanches* from memory (19).

Additional substantiation of the play's dual literary and oral existence is suggested by the skepticism of John Englekirk as to the antiquity of the play. He noticed that Espinosa's and Campa's manuscripts show little textual evidence of having been in the oral tradition at all (1957: 238n7).

After the global trauma of World War I and the cultural shock of the returning troops, the decline noticed by Aurelio Espinosa in the performance tradition turns into a lapse corroborated by oral history accounts (Vialpando 1991). In subsequent years two kinds of revivals of *Los Comanches* would surface: promotional and authocthonous. By the 1920s, the emerging Anglo art colonies in Taos and Santa Fe had noticed the "primitivist" vitality of *Nuevomexicano* folk art as well as folklore. An undated manuscript of *Los Comanches* appeared in Mary Austin's collection of folk plays about the same time she and the Spanish Colonial Art Society began encouraging the work of traditional *santeros*. Then in the summer of 1929 (Roeder), Taos attorney and history buff Francis T. Cheetham promoted a performance spectacular enough to attract the attentions of tourists and folklorist Arthur Campa:

> *Los Comanches* . . . was staged in the open spaces, where a battle on horseback could be enacted, and the plains of Galisteo and the high mesas around Taos were favorite sites where both audiences and participants could enjoy the drama. Real Indians often took the parts of the Comanche braves, and as the battle that is the climax of the play opened, both sides became caught up in the action. When the summer tourists visiting Taos in 1929 witnessed the drama on the mesa between Taos village and Ranchos de Taos to the south, hundreds of warriors and soldiers took part on both sides. They presented such a realistic scene, to the accompaniment of rifle shots and arrows, that the visitors took cover, thinking that real warfare had broken out (1979: 232).

The role of Cheetham in encouraging the 1929 Taos performance and the initial 1935 Galisteo staging is unacknowledged by Campa. After the initial Anglo promotion and validation of the plays in the writings of the Spanish Colonial Arts Society members (Barker), subsequent performances in these communities undoubtedly took on a life of their own as evidenced by their reincorporation into the usual Christmas time performance slot. John D. Robb reports an impressive December 1955 performance in Taos, but doesn't mention the participation of Indian actors, an aspect that would not have escaped his attention (602). Whatever the popular interest that was generated with these promotional revivals, none seems to have survived the cultural impact of World War II, which was the relinquishment of traditional culture and folkways in the postwar boom.

The revival of *Los Comanches* that has survived into the present is an authoctonous one from Alcalde, New Mexico. As in other villages, the performance tradition was interrupted by the world wars and the intervening economic turmoil, which forced many families to leave the community to seek work in migrant labor and distant mines. A vital link in the transmission of the play was a few performances staged immediately following World War II. Returning *Nuevomexicano* veterans had suffered the harsh conditions of the

Pacific theater and horrific episodes such as the Bataan Death March. Many made personal *promesas,* or solemn vows, to rededicate themselves to their religion and the traditions of their community. However the pressures of the 1950s created another yet another lapse in the observance of cultural traditions which lasted into the 1960s.

In response to the requests of a curious new 1960s generation of Chicano cultural activists, a teacher named Roberto Vialpando Lara, his associate Adelaido Chacón, friends, and neighbors became instrumentally involved in reviving the two Indo-Hispano folk celebrations traditionally previously observed in tandem in Alcalde: *Los Matachines* an Indo-Hispano ritual dance drama; and *Los Comanches* (Vialpando 1991, Montoya, Sánchez).[6] Relying on childhood recollections and the memories of aging musicians and actors, texts, choreography, and music were reconstructed to reintroduce these traditions into a community eager to reestablish its cultural roots. Since performances of *Los Matachines* could still be observed in neighboring pueblos and placitas, and since the Alcalde melodies were still in living memory, the revival mostly involved the training of new dancers and musicians. The restaging of *Los Comanches* was more of a challenge, because the community's script had been lost. Despite the availability of the two published texts of *Los Comanches* (Espinosa 1907, Rael 1942), a painstaking effort was made to recover the authoritative Alcalde version from memory and oral tradition.

Vialpando and his cousin Feliberto López conducted extended interviews at Medina's Cantina and at private homes with Elfido Gonzales, Eduardo Edmons, and others who had acted in turn-of-the-century productions directed by Macedonio Chávez and his associate Noé Martínez. Adelaido Chacón's childhood memories of the play were clear enough to reconstruct the stage directions. Everyone remembered how carefully the horses were trained and rehearsed. Vialpando recalls a particular sorrel horse, an *alazán tostado* of his uncle, that would gracefully kneel before the image of San Antonio to pay reverence before the play began.

An almost primal sense of authenticity is reclaimed for the Alcalde production, given its proximity to San Juan de los Caballeros and San Gabriel, the very first settlements of Españoles Mexicano in the land. Vialpando was always told that the very first Comanches and *Matachines* celebrations came from Abiquiú, the *genízaro* town just up the Chama river valley from Alcalde. From there he traces their spread to Ojo Caliente, Alcalde, Ojo Sarco, Chamisal, Las Vegas, Belén, and Socorro. One of the current performers is from Canjilón, where performances were staged when he was a child (Montoya).[7]

Vialpando attributes his knowledge of these traditions to Bozor Lara, an ancestor of his grandmother. A key person in his paternal lineage was his grandfather Mónico Vialpando, a captive raised with Indians. Mónico's father Juan Antonio Vialpando was himself a Navajo raised by Españoles

Mexicanos. Since so many children were lost to raids, the colonial authorities gave the settlers permission to capture and raise Indian children as their own.

Vialpando believes that the Comanches are celebrated because they were fiercer than the Navajo and their 1779 defeat was earlier and more definitive. The final victory over the Navajos did not come until 1865, well into the American period. He claims each community performed their own distinct versions of *Los Comanches.*

Matachines and Comanches celebrations were performed together in Alcalde because the costumes and mystery of the *Matachines* served to attract the attention of the Indians, while the purpose of the Comanches was to "pacify" the Indians.

In Alcalde, *Los Comanches* is staged immediately following the *Matachines* dance, which is organized yearly by *mayordomo* sponsors as a part of the *Función* or patronal feast day, which in Alcalde is December 27 (Sánchez).[8] Participants in *Matachines* are motivated by strong personal faith, the hope for blessings, and devotional *promesas.* Actors in *Los Comanches* are motivated by a deep sense of cultural pride and dedication to community, whose original spirit is expressed in the play. All are young and middle aged *Nuevomexicano* men involved in everything from ranching to work at the National Laboratory in Los Alamos. Performances are given for the *vísperas* celebrations in the early evening of December 26 at the old plaza and San Antonio chapel, and twice on December 27—after morning mass in front of the new church, and again in the afternoon, either at the house of the mayordomos, the old plaza, or in front of a community dance hall. Although the feast day of San Antonio de Padua is June 13, a priest moved the fiesta many decades ago. On the morning of December 27, the saint is taken in procession to a vantage point where he too can watch the festivities.

The spirit of the Alcalde *Matachines* is devotional, yet festive. The twelve masked spirit captains dance in graceful rows and crosses in a series of movements, all to the accompaniment of violin and guitar music. The Monarca directs the dance drama and the interactions of the other characters, which include the spirit guide Malinche dressed as a little bride and the Torito with horns and cowhide, both played by children. On the periphery, the masked Abuelo monsters tease the crowd, fight, and subdue the Torito, which they kill with a rifle and castrate at the end of the dance. *Los Matachines* is a conquest drama which in its most universal interpretation represents the Encounter and Conciliation of European and Indigenous spirituality. Like the Comanches celebrations, it is a regional Indo-Hispano celebration with a range of meanings from sacred to burlesque, depending on the particular performance contexts of Hispano *placitas* and Indian pueblos (Rodríguez, Romero). Many of the actors of *Los Comanches de Castillo* are also *Matachines* dancers, and occasionally participate in both.

After the *Matachines* finish and retire, the musicians and the Abuelos remain on the scene to provide the music and crowd control for "Los Comanches." Still clowning with the crowd, the Abuelos with their short *chicote* whips, help clear the crowd from the performance space to be used by the horses and riders. The musicians are called on later in the play, after the Comanche war council, when Cuerno Verde calls our for music. As the action begins, they play a short prelude to focus the attention of the crowd.[9] The Indio Embajador comes racing in at a full gallop, shouting that an armed confrontation between Comanches and Españoles is at hand.

Close examination of the earliest video recording made in Alcalde in 1978 and several made in the 1990s reveals performances which stay well within the parameters of the Vialpando text of 1963. There are several moments which lend themselves to *ad libertum* improvisations, but all the major *arengas* are delivered in similar style. Through the years, roles are circulated and new actors join the group, although several such as Alfredo Montoya, Galento Martínez, and Tomás Sánchez have been performing for more than two decades and have played all the parts. There seems to be no particular role that could be deemed director, since the more experienced actors take the lead.

The oral recovery of the Alcalde text reveals a fascinating process of reduction, realignment, and modification that permits the play to reflect the social desires of its performance community. The script is reduced to 273 octosyllabic verses, as compared to the 515 in the Espinosa and the 714 in Rael. In the original cast as in the historical battles, Españoles significantly outnumber Comanches. As might be expected the list shrinks from fifteen to ten characters, but the reduction is not proportional. In Alcalde the Indians become the majority. Both versions have six Comanches, but Alcalde eliminates the two Pecas children[10] and four Españoles: Don Salvador Ribera, Capitán, Sargento, and most importantly, Barriga Duce, the battlefield buffoon. His Rabelaisian excess and repugnant antics cast a disparaging, even cynical light on the gallantry of the events. Although he follows the Spanish camps, neither his name nor his behaviour conforms with Spanish standards. He apparently represents the common settlers, including *genízaros*, who are Hispanicized Indians. With time Barriga Duce's critique is blunted and finally eclipsed by the comic function of the character. In Alcalde, the presence of the *Matachines* Abuelo clowns at the edges of the performance may have subsumed Barriga Duce.

Another notable revision in the Alcalde text is the virtual disappearance of the rhetoric of empire and its twin ideological pillars of dynasty and religion. The abundant allusions to imperial dominion and invocations of divine right and miraculous intervention all but vanish. The only direct mention of the king is ironically on the lips of Cuerno Verde:

Esta el Rey en su lugar
Como todo el Cristianismo. [*sic*.] (l. 45-46)

Only one of the Españoles, Toribio Ortiz, mentions the regent in passing, taking pride in his own financial independence:

> El Rey le sirvo a mi costo,
> Con un esmero especial. (l. 176-177)

In the original play, the Españoles boasted swore allegiance to the crown with almost every other breath. In Alcalde, only Toribio Ortiz invokes Christian divinity:

> Santiago, La concepción de María,
> Sean mi norte y guía. (l. 200-201)

It might be argued that this attrition is merely a factor of the economy of orality. What is more probable is the shift in what Benedict Anderson calls the imagined community, an abandonment of the discourse of imperial power, and the emergence of a *Nuevomexicano* identity formation consonant with the shifting political landscapes of nineteenth- and twentieth-century New Mexico.

Perhaps the most celebrated aspect of *Los Comanches* beyond the prodigious equestrian display are the stirring *arengas,* in which the opponents match their rhetoric and wits. What Espinosa noticed at the beginning of the century is still true at the end. Older folks in northern New Mexico can still quote Cuerno Verde's stirring invocation, which is also a prayer to the four directions (Leyba):

> Desde el Oriente al poniente,
> Desde el Sur al Norte frío,
> Suene el brillante clarín y
> Brille el acero mío. (l. 17-20)

No "Indian Spanish" or pseudo-pidginized forms here or on the lips of any of the other warriors. Only the Indio Embajador or lowly messenger of the first scene speaks in dialect:

> Dende tan lejo yo vene
> Oh tata Gobernado!
> Vengo a traete esta noticia
> Que alla en mi pelbo paso [*sic.*] (l. 1-4)

All the other Comanche speeches use the same diction, imagery, and elocutionary figures as their Español opponents. All liken their ferocity to the wild animals of the sierra and link their strength and fury to the forces of nature. Only chief Cabeza Negra briefly transgresses the decorum of heroic discourse when he threatens to cut of the head of his opponent. Even though warriors and soldiers contest each other on stage, they do so with the same voice. Is the author's aim to ennoble himself by elevating the discourse of his enemy? Michel de Certeau reminds us that "The written discourse which cites the speech of the other is not, cannot be, the discourse of the other (78)." If dialogue is the communication of difference, then monologue is the contemplation of identity.

One of the moments of highest drama in *Los Comanches* is the confrontation of the two antagonists, the brash challenge of Cuerno Verde and the seasoned response of Don Carlos Fernández. In Rael's manuscript, Cuerno Verde delivers 108 verses and Don Carlos 76. In Alcalde, the exchange is composed of 45 and 38 verses respectively. What is most extraordinary about Don Carlos' Alcalde response is that it is a total appropriation and adaptation of the second half of Cuerno Verde's speech in the longer manuscript. Don Carlos calls out to his troops with the very words of Cuerno Verde on his lips:

> Ea, nobles capitanes!
> Que se pregone este grito!
> Que yo como General
> he de estar aprevenido. (l. 76-80)

There is no disjunction in the discourse or in the action. The only break is in the distinction between cultural self and cultural other. Cuerno Verde doesn't die in the skirmishes of Alcalde. In the display of valor and resistance, a new cultural sign is forged for the battles of the twentieth century. The old differences and oppositions dissolve into a new synthesis in the edifying spectacle. At the play's conclusion, Comanches and Españoles ride off together.

Cultural othering is part of the ideology and psychology of warfare. But the conflict between the Comanches and Spanish Mexicans created sociological consequences that blurred the category of otherness. By the census of 1776, fully one-third of the population of New Mexico were *genízaros* (Gutiérrez). A sizeable portion of the *genízaro* population of New Mexico comes from Comanche stock, originating with the orphans and captive children that were raised by Spanish Mexican families. The colonial notion of Comanches as cultural others becomes ambiguous and obscured. An implicit recognition emerges that they are also a part of the extended cultural family.

> Al Santo Niño de Atocha
> le encargamos por favor,
> cuide de sus comanchitos
> que no olvide cuántos son.
> Yana, jeyana, jeyana, je yo.
> —"Los Comanchitos"
>   Bernalillo, NM

> Españoles y cumanches
> todos en armonía,
> se juntaban a cantar
> y a bailar con alegría,
> je ya, je ya, je ya, ha.
> —"Indita de la Nacioncita de
>   la Sangre de Cristo,"
>   Cleofes Vigil[11]

Notes

[1] Forthcoming in the *Pasó por aquí* series of the University of New Mexico press is a critical, annotated edition of the secular folk plays of New Mexico, including *Los Comanches*.

[2] This essay is dedicated to the memory of the two people who guided me to this project: "mi querida tía política" Fermilia "Phyllis" Domínguez Wood, of Chamisal, New Mexico, archival secretary at the New Mexico State Records Division who gave me a manuscript copy of *Los Comanches* in 1976; and the late Don Roberto Vialpando Lara, Ph.D., "el maestro de Alcalde," gracious friend and author of the first literary history of New Mexico and the community scholar behind the revival of the Matachines and Comanches of Alcalde, New Mexico.

[3] The first couplet in the popular style is sung by the family of Francisco Gonzales of Ranchos de Taos and dates to the late eighteenth century, the peaceful Jicarilla apaches were mercilessly persecuted by the Comanches. They complained to colonial authorities for protection (Lamadrid 1992). The second burlesque couplet sung by Leota Frizzell is used as an "arrullo" or lullaby in many New Mexican communities (Lamadrid 1994).

[4] In New Mexican Spanish, "hispanos, mexicanos, nuevomexicanos, and manitos" are synonymous terms of self designation for the people the state government refers to as "Hispanic New Mexicans." The analogous term found in colonial era documents is "españoles mexicanos."

[5] Translations include Mary Austin (nd.), Gilberto Espinosa, and I.L. Chávez.

[6] All this data and opinions are taken directly from personal interviews with Roberto Vialpando Lara, Tomás Sánchez, and Alfredo Montoya, of Alcalde, New Mexico.

[7] Other communities where performances have been witnessed include: Taos, Ranchos de Taos, and Llano (Campa 1979, Jaramillo, Robb); Galisteo (Campa 1979), Roeder); El Rancho (Brown 1978); Rainsville and Mora (Rivera), and the villages of the Purgatoire Valley in southern Colorado (Taylor).

[8] All this data and opinions are taken directly from personal interviews with Tomás Sánchez, Española, New Mexico, January 28, 1991. The chronology of performances dating to the beginning of this revival is currently being reconstructed from ongoing oral histories.

[9] Also played on violin and guitar, Alcalde Comanches music closely resembles the Matachines tunes, since the same musicians play them both. In contrast, Comanche music used in past performances of *Los Comanches de Castillo* in Ranchos de Taos is unaccompanied pentatonic, vocable singing; a completely Native American sound.

[10] A performance update: Beginning in 1996, one of the Pecas, or captive children, reappeared in the play.

[11] The first verse is from the music of Comanches Nativity Play from western New Mexico. It is sung on Christmas Eve in Bernalillo as the little "Comanchitos" follow the "Las Posadas" procession and dance for the Holy Child (Lamadrid 1992, Smithsonian-Folkways). The second verse is from the "Himno a la Nacioncita de la Sangre de Cristo" of the famed late folk poet and singer Cleofes Vigil, of San Cristóbal, New Mexico (Lamadrid 1994).

Works Cited

Primary Sources

Austin, Mary. "Los Comanches" (three Spanish and one English typescripts, Mary Austin Collection). San Marino, California: Huntington Library, nd.

Bond, Frank M., ed. "Los Comanches" (typescript and notes). Santa Fe: Museum of International Folk Art, 1972.

Brown, Lorin W. "Los Comanches" (typescript) in W.P.A. Files, File 5, Drawer 5, Folder 45 #1. Santa Fe: New Mexico Historical Library, 1937.

Brown, Lorin W. "Los Comanches" (typescript) in W.P.A. Files, File 5, Drawer 5, Folder 45 #2. Santa Fe: New Mexico Historical Library, 1939.

Campa, Arthur L. "Los Comanches: A New Mexican Folk Drama." University of New Mexico Bulletin, Modern Language Series 7, 1 (April 1, 1942).

Chávez, Clemente. "1908 Guerra Entre los Comanches y los Españoles." (Notebook) in John D. Robb Archive of Southwestern Music. Alburquerque: University of New Mexico, copied December 6, 1925, collected by Robb in 1963.

Chávez, I. L., trans. "Los Comanches." Translation of M. Celso E. Aragon manuscript, Ranchos de Taos, December 24, 1900. (typescript) in W.P.A. Riles, File 5, Drawer 5, Folder 45 #2. Santa Fe: New Mexico Historical Library, nd.

Espinosa, Aurelio M. "Los Comanches, A Spanish Heroic Play of the Year Seventeen Hundred and Eighty." Albuquerque: University of New Mexico Bulletin of the University of New Mexico 1, 1 (December 1907).

Espinosa, Gilberto "Los Comanches." New Mexico Quarterly, I, 2 (May, 1931), 133-146.

Leyva, Macario, "Indio Comanche." In John Donald Robb. Hispanic Folk Music of New Mexico and the Southwest: A Self-Portrait of a People. Norman: University of Oklahoma Press, 1980. 599-602.

Martínez, Paul G. "Los Comanches, a play celebrated yearly." (typescript) in W.P.A. Files, File 5, Drawer 5, Folder 45. Santa Fe: New Mexico Historical Library, nd.

Raines, Lester. "Los Comanches" (typescript) in W.P.A. Files, File 5, Drawer 5, folder 45. Santa Fe: New Mexico Historical Library, 1936.

Vialpando, Roberto. "Antiguo Juego Dramático del Folklore Nuevo Mexicano: Los Comanches." (typescript) Acto de Preservación, 1963. Author's mss. collection.

Interviews

Gonzales, Francisco. "Personal Interview with Author." Ranchos de Taos, January 28, 1992.

Montoya, Alfredo. "Personal Interview with Author." Alcalde, December 27, 1993.

Rivera, José. "Personal Interview with Author." Albuquerque, October 3, 1987.

Sánchez, Tomás. "Personal Interview with Author." Alcalde, January 28, 1991.

Vialpando Lara, Roberto. "Personal Interview with Author." Alcalde, New Mexico, January 1, 1991.

Secondary Sources

Anderson, Benedict. *Imagined Communities.* 1983. London: Verso, 1991.

Anderson, Reed. "Early Secular Theater in New Mexico." In *Pasó por Aquí: Critical Essays on the New Mexican Literary Tradition.* Ed. Erlinda Gonzales-Berry. Albuquerque: University of New Mexico Press, 1989.

Austin, Mary. "Native Drama in Our Southwest." *The Nation,* CXXIV, 3224 (April 20, 1927), 437-440.

Austin, Mary. "Folk Plays of the Southwest" in *Theatre Arts Monthly,* Vol XVII, 1933, 299-606.

Barker, Mrs. Ruth Laughlin. *Caballeros.* New York: D. Appleton and Co., 1931.

Bhabha, Homi K. "The other question: Difference, Discrimination, and the Discourse of Colonialism." In *Literature, Politics, and Theory.* Eds. Francis Baker, Peter Hulme, Margaret Iversen, and Diane Loxley. London and New York: Methuen, 1986, 148-172.

Brown, Lorin W., with Charles L. Briggs and Marta Weigle. *Hispano Folklife of New Mexico: The Lorin W. Brown Federal Writers' Project Manuscripts.* Albuquerque: University of New Mexico Press, 1978. 40-41.

Campa, Arthur L. *Spanish Folk Poetry in New Mexico.* Albuquerque: University of New Mexico Press, 1946. 220.

Campa, Arthur L. *Hispanic Culture in the Southwest.* Norman: Oklahoma University Press, 1979. 230-232.

Cavallo-Bosso, J. R. "Kumanche of the Zuñi Indians of New Mexico: An Analytical Study." BA Thesis, Wesleyan University, Middletown, Connecticut, 1956.

Certeau, Michel de. *Heterologies: Discourse on the Other.* Trans. B. Massumi. Manchester: Manchester University Press, 1986.

Chaves, Amado. *The Defeat of the Comanches in 1716.* Historical Society of New Mexico, Publications in History N. 8. Santa Fe: 1906.

Dahlberg, Sandra. "Having the Last Word: Recording the Cost of Conquest in Los Comanches." In Erlinda Gonzales-Berry and Chuck Tatum, eds. *Recovering the U. S. Hispanic Literary Heritage,* Vol. II. Houston: Arte Público Press, 1996: 133-147.

Englekirk, J. E. "Notes on the Repertoire of the New Mexico Spanish Folk Theatre." *Southern Folklore Quarterly* 4 (1940): 227-237.

Englekirk, J. E. "The Source and Dating of New Mexico Spanish Folk Plays." *Western Folklore* 16 (1957): 232-55.

Espinosa, Aurelio M. *The Folklore of Spain in the American Southwest.* Ed. J. Manuel Espinosa. Norman: University of Oklahoma Press, 1976.

Gelo, Daniel. "Comanche Belief and Ritual." Ph.D. dissertation. New Brunswick, N. J.: Rutgers University, 1986.

Gutiérrez, Ramón. "The Politics of Theater in Colonial New Mexico." *Reconstructing a Chicano/a Literary Heritage: Hispanic Colonial Literature of the Southwest.* Ed. María Herrera-Sobek. Tucson: University of Arizona Press, 1993.

Harris, Max. *The Dialogical Theater: Dramatizations of the Conquest of Mexico and the Question of the Other.* New York: St. Martin's Press, 1993.

Hurt, Wesley R. "The Spanish-American Comanche Dance." *Journal of the Folklore Institute* 3, 2 (August 1966): 116-132.

John, Elizabeth A. H. *Storms Brewed in Other Men's Worlds: The Confrontation of Indians, Spanish, and French in the Southwest, 1540-1795.* College Station, Texas: Texas A & M University Press, 1975.

King, Scottie. "Los Comanches de la Serna." *New Mexico Magazine* January 1979, 26-27, 42.

Lamadrid, Enrique R. "Los Comanches: the Celebration of Cultural Otherness in New Mexican Winter Feasts" (46 pp. report, 8 audio tapes and transcripts, 1 video tape, 39 transparancies), 1992 New Mexico Festival of American Folklife Archive, Smithsonian Center for Folklife and Cultural Studies.

Lamadrid, Enrique R. "Entre Cíbolos Criado: Images of Native Americans in the

Popular Culture of Colonial New Mexico." *In Reconstructing a Chicano/a Literary Heritage: Hispanic Colonial Literature of the Southwest.* Ed. María Herrera-Sobek. Tucson: University of Arizona Press, 1993.

Lamadrid, Enrique R. *Tesoros del Espíritu: A Portrait in Sound of Hispanic New Mexico.* Alburquerque: Academia/El Norte Publications, 1995.

Meketa, Jacqueline Dorgan, ed. *Legacy of Honor: The Life of Rafael Chacón, a Nineteenth-Century New Mexican.* Albuquerque: University of New Mexico Press, 1986.

Mendoza, Victente T. y Virginia R. R. de Mendoza. *Estudio y clasificación de la música tradicional hispánica de Nuevo México.* México: Universidad Nacional de México, 1986.

Noyes, Stanley. *Los Comanches: The Horse People, 1751-1845.* Albuquerque: University of New Mexico Press, 1993).

Padilla, Genaro. "Discontinuous Continuities: Remapping the Terrain of Spanish Colonial Narrative." In *Reconstructing a Chicano/a Literary Heritage.* María Herrera-Sobek, ed. Tucson: University of Arizona Press, 1993: 24-36.

Pino, Pedro Bautista. *Exposición sucinta y sencilla de la provincia del Nuevo México.* Cádiz: 1812.

Pratt, Mary Louise. *Imperial Eyes: Travel Writing and Transculturation.* London: Routledge, 1992.

Robb, John Donald. *Hispanic Folk Music of New Mexico and the Southwest: A Self-Portrait of a People.* Norman: University of Oklahoma Press, 1980. 599-602.

Rodríguez, Sylvia. *Los Matachines Dance in Northern New Mexico.* Alburquerque: University of New Mexico Press, 1996.

Roeder, Beatrice A. "Los Comanches: A Bicentennial Folk Play." *Bilingual Review* 3 (1976): 213-220.

Romero, Brenda. "The Matachines of Alcalde, New Mexico." Ph.D. dissertation, University of California at Los Angeles, 1991.

Sweet, Jill D. "Ritual Play, Role Reversal, and Humor: Symbolic Elements of a Tewa Pueblo Navajo Dance." Paper presented at the CORD/ADG Conference, Honolulu, 1978.

Smithsonian-Folkways. Music of *New Mexico: Hispanic Traditions.* Washington, D. C.: Smithsonian Center for Folklife Programs, 1992.

Thomas, Alfred Barnaby. *Forgotten Frontiers: A Study of the Spanish Indian Policy of Don Juan Bautista de Anza, Governor of New Mexico, 1777-1787.* Norman: University of Oklahoma Press, 1932.

A Portrait of the Spanish Conquistador in *La Florida del Inca*

Shannon L. Moore-Ross and José B. Fernández

The Spanish conquistador has been the subject of controversy ever since he set foot in the New World. The enemies of Spain's conquest of the New World have portrayed the Spanish conquistador as an armed medieval knight riding on his horse, ready to cut a defenseless native in half with his sword. The advocates of the Spanish *conquista*, on the other hand, have depicted him as being a kind of militant saint ready to offer his life in the conversion of barbarous infidels (Fernández 115).

What kind of man was the Spanish conquistador? What motivated him? Was he a superhuman or simply a man of flesh and bones who was a product of his times? The answers to these questions are difficult, for the Spanish conquistador was a very complex man. Nevertheless, an attempt must be made to offer a general portrait of this individual.

The Spanish conquistador, like all Europeans, was a product of his time, constructed and conditioned by the co-existing impacts of his environment. If, in retrospect he appears archaic, excessively cruel and romantic, it is only because he reflects more than other Europeans the period in which he lived (Leonard 6).

Portrayed as a complex individual, he was a product of the Reconquista and the New World. He lied, abused, cheated, ransacked, raped, murdered, destroyed Indian civilizations and committed atrocities. On the other hand, he brought his religion, fresh plants, and new tools to all the places he conquered. He extinguished the practice of human sacrifices, constructed hospitals and schools and was willing to deliberate the rights and wrongs of what he considered a justified war. The conquistador displayed constant loyalty to his King and Church. He despised the coward and the man without *pundonor* (personal honor). He could face obstacles beyond human comprehension, but at times he would cry like a child. He could battle and destroy one of his own, but yet respect and honor one of his enemies (Blacker 13–14).

Once Spain began to expand its empire in the New World, an old medieval genre, the chronicle, was revived. The need to narrate the Spaniards' deeds and the idea of historical truth became important. In most cases, the principal pro-

189

tagonists of this great enterprise were the writers and chroniclers of the *conquista*. Strongly trained by the ethical and collective tradition of the Middle Ages, these men were also representative of Spanish individualism (Crow, Leonard and Reid 10). As a result, they decorated their narratives in fancy rhetorical language that attested to their personal dignity, honesty and complete familiarity with the events in question (Zamora 39).

Among the chroniclers of the *conquista*, there was the Inca Garcilaso de la Vega (1539–1616), the first *mestizo* writer of the New World. Unlike his predecessors and contemporaries, he was not a participant in the conquest and colonization of the New World. His three chronicles, *La Florida del Inca* (1605), *Los Comentarios reales* (1609), and *La historia general del Perú* (published posthumously in 1617), were dependent on the oral testimony of eyewitnesses of the *conquista*.

La Florida del Inca, which incidentally was his first original work, appeared in Lisbon in 1605 and was published by Pedro Craasbeck. In it, the Inca traces the steps of Hernando de Soto's ill-fated expedition through North America (1538–1543).

Even though the De Soto expedition was considered to be a failure for Spain, it was nevertheless one of the most incredible journeys in North American history. De Soto's odyssey provided valuable information into the lifestyles and culture of the native population in the southeast and the interaction between the natives and Spaniards. It was also a source of inestimable data for conquistadores that had yet to dare to adventure into the mysterious interior of La Florida.

La Florida del Inca is an organized narrative divided into six books, one for each year of the expedition. Book I serves as a general introduction to the history. In it, the Inca narrates the genesis of De Soto's expedition, its departure from the port of San Lúcar de Barrameda in 1538, its arrival in Cuba and the final departure for La Florida in 1539. The Inca also provides information concerning the previous expeditions of Juan Ponce de León, Lucas Váquez de Ayllón and Pánfilo de Narváez.

Book II is divided into two parts. The first part begins with the expedition's arrival in Florida on May 25, 1539 and chronicles its march from Tampa Bay to Osachile, west of the Suwannee River. The second part traces the expedition's trek from Osachile to Apalachee—present-day Tallahassee—where De Soto decided to winter.

While in Apalachee, De Soto heard tales of the supposedly gold-laden province of Cofitachequi, north of Apalachee. The march from Apalachee to Cofitachequi, serves as the point of departure for Book III. After its arrival in Cofitachequi and its subsequent disappointment—there was neither gold nor silver in such province—the expedition moved towards present-day South Carolina. From there it marched towards Tennessee and Alabama. Book III also narrates De Soto's battle with Chief Tuscaluza and ends with the Spaniards' arrival in present-day Mississippi in 1540.

Book IV concentrates on narrating De Soto's attack on the Indian strong-hold of Alibamo, his march to the Mississippi River and subsequent crossing on makeshift barges and his wintering at Utianque—present-day Arkansas.

Divided into two parts, Book V describes De Soto's return to Mississippi and his death in 1542. The second part narrates the expedition's turn to the west under the command of Luis de Moscoso de Alvarado, De Soto's successor. Moscoso's men reached Texas, only to return to the Mississippi.

The last book of *La Florida del Inca* chronicles the Spaniards' departure down the Mississippi and culminates with their arrival in Mexico on September 10, 1543.

In examining any piece of literature, it is always necessary to know the author's purpose on writing his or her work. One of the Inca's purposes in writing *La Florida del Inca* was to record the deeds performed and the hardships suffered by conquistadores "for the honor and renown of the Spanish nation" (xxxviii). In this study, we shall examine several aspects of the life of the men who came to conquer "La Florida" as they are portrayed in *La Florida del Inca*. The author comments directly on the qualities of the soldiers of what was once the most powerful nation in the world. Typical characteristics of the conquista-dores such as courage, stoicism, individualism, chivalry, religious zeal, greed and cruelty will be treated in order to present the conquistador for what he was, a complex man of flesh and bones.

In his chronicle, the Inca devotes an inordinate number of pages to exalt the courage of the men that came to conquer the mysterious province of La Florida. The Spaniards courage is best depicted in their innumerable battles against the indomitable "savages," their crossings of the mosquito-infested swamps and swollen rivers of Florida; their marches through the mountains of North Carolina and their hardships amidst the scorching heat of summer and the cold north wind of winter. According to the Inca, it was the Spaniards' courage and determination that enabled them to undertake the conquest of the New World, for as he comments in his chronicle full of pride:

> So from this little we have told in our history and shall tell to the very end of it, any judicious person will be able to deduce the innumerable and never ade-quately or even moderately extolled hardships which our Spaniards have suffered in the discovery, conquest and settlement of the New World — expe-riences so without profit to themselves or to their sons, a fact to which I, as the offspring of one of them, can certify well (561).

Perhaps one of the greatest portrayals of the conquistadores' courage is found after the Battle of Mabila. The Spaniards had taken heavy casualties yet the Inca attributes this victory to the "invincible spirit" of Spain, for he com-ments:

Therefore from the bottom of their hearts and in loud voices they called upon God to shelter and assist them in their affliction, and our Lord, as a compassionate Father, did come to their aid by bestowing upon them in that hardship, an invincible spirit, a spirit which has always enabled the Spanish nation, above every other nation of this world, to succor itself in its greatest necessities, just as these Spaniards did in their present want (375–376).

Of all of the Spaniards mentioned in the chronicle, none match the courage and bravery of Hernando de Soto. While the Fidalgo de Elvas, one of the chroniclers of De Soto's expedition, attest that the *Adelantado* was a courageous man, he, however, describes his bravery in rather subdued terms.[1] The Inca, on the other hand, makes De Soto the paradigm of courage and valor. In *La Florida del Inca*, Hernando de Soto is treated as a hero and phrases like "the very valiant soldier he was"(204), "he always prided himself on being first in all things"(400), and "as a good captain, he gave courage to his men"(204) are abundant. While no one can doubt De Soto's courage and valor, he was no saint full of goodness and gentleness. As Paul Hoffman points out:

A close reading of the available record shows us a man who delighted in his skill with a horse and lance when used against other human beings, was ambitious and greedy, and, in the view of contemporaries who knew him well, passionate and curt in his behavior toward others. Such a person would not be welcomed in the dens of many (459).

One of the principal reasons why many of De Soto's men managed to survive and return from their ill-fated expedition was due to their stoicism. In *La Florida del Inca*, the reader will find several pages with words such as "hunger," "cold," "sigh," "death," "pain," "exhaustion," "thirst," "groan," "misfortune," "calamity," "sorrow," "blood," "hardship," and "suffering," which clearly depict their trials and tribulations in La Florida. Yet, in spite of their misfortune, they were able to survive because of their stoicism.

In no other part of *La Florida del Inca* does the reader better come into contact with the sense of Spanish stoicism than the passage in which the Inca narrates the wretched state of the Spanish soldiers after the Battle of Mabila:

The least wounded hastened at once and with great diligence to aid those who had received the most injuries . . . Others brought straw on which to place the sick and some took the shirts from their deceased companions as well as from their own selves to make bandage and splints . . . In this manner, they aided each other that night, all forcing themselves to bear with good spirit the hardship in which evil fortune had thrust them (376).

Not only were these men through their stoicism able to conquer the cruelty of war, but also the hardships of nature. Many authorities, such as the French historian Jean Descola, are of the opinion that the conquistadores were a group of individuals incapable of cooperation. As Descola states:

> The people of Spain, whatever may be her political regime, are the least pos-
> sible "community-minded." They do not believe in the "collective soul," that
> invention of sociologists, useful sometimes as a propaganda theme but as ster-
> ile as it is theoretical . . . Pride and privation: that was the Spaniard of the
> sixteenth century (359).

It is true that the conquistadores were known for their individualism and
lack of cooperation but in *La Florida of the Inca*, the Spaniards were able to set
aside their individual pride and rivalries and became cooperative. One has but
to turn to the passages in the chronicle in which the Inca narrates the construction of the brigantines that would eventually deliver them from their ordeal. In
the entire history of *La Florida*, few are the episodes that better illustrate the
cooperative spirit of the conquistadores. A number of the *hidalgos* worked with
others of less ranks at the forges, while others ripped up their shirts to make
sails. Several of the stronger ones carried their sick and wounded companions
to the brigantines so they would not perish in a strange land.

Luis de Moscoso, De Soto's successor, as commander of the expedition
was able to guide the Spaniards to safety, not because of his leadership qualities, but because of his men's cooperative spirit. They shared their meager
rations, their blood sweat and tears, but in the end they survived because they
worked as a unit, not as individuals.

The conquest of La Florida by Hernando de Soto was a constant battle
between the indomitable natives of North America and the invaders from
Castile. Despite the carnage there existed acts of chivalry among them. On
many occasions, the Inca censures the Spanish cruelty against the Indians but
in many instances this is offset by the Spaniards magnanimity towards the
natives. The Inca states how the Spaniards treated their native prisoners with
respect and even gave them food after their encounter at Mabila:

> In each of the settlements within a radius of four leagues, they encountered
> many wounded Indians who had escaped from the battle, but there was not a
> single man or woman among them to treat their injuries. It was believed, there-
> fore, that the Indians came at night with supplies for the wounded and then
> returned to the forests during the day. Instead of maltreating such of them as
> were afflicted, the Castilians regaled them and share with them the food they
> carried (384).

At times, the scarcity of food was one of the greatest enemies of De Soto's
expedition. Yet, according to Garcilaso, it also gave the Spaniards the opportunity to practice their *hidalguía* (chivalry). On one occasion, the Inca comments
on De Soto's *hidalguía* towards his Indian captives when

> he commanded that they kill some of the swine and dole out eight ounces of
> this meat to each Spaniard as a fresh ration. Even so, the Spaniards shared

their food with the natives to make it clear that they desired no advantage over them in any respect, but wished rather to endure the hardship with them equally (288).

Another chronicler of De Soto's expedition, Rodrigo Rangel, cites very few examples of Spanish *hidalguía* towards the natives.[2] He, for example, is more interested in narrating how De Soto and his men plundered and ravaged Indian villages and how they cast Indians to dogs than how they shared their meager rations with them, for he narrates:

Therefore, continuing his conquest, he [De Soto] commanded that General Vasco Porcallo de Figueroa should go to Ocita, because it was said that there was a gathering of people there. And this captain having gone there, he found the people gone, and he burned the town, and he set the dogs on [*aperrear*] an Indian he brought as a guide. The reader must understand that to set the dogs on [an Indian] is to make the dogs eat them or kill them, tearing the Indians to pieces (257).

According to the Inca, the Spaniards' *hidalguía* was also directed towards the natives in view of their courage. The Inca devotes an entire chapter to a lengthy oration delivered by four young Indian captives who had held the Spaniards at bay for more than thirty hours and gives the Spaniard reaction to their words:

And when many Spaniards, well-read in history, heard them, they asserted that the captains appeared to have been influenced by the most famous officers of Rome when that city dominated the world with its arms, and that the youths, who were lords of vassals, appeared to have been trained in Athens when it was flourishable in moral letters. Consequently, as soon as they responded and the governor had embraced them, there was not a captain or a soldier of any importance who did not embrace them likewise, with very great rejoicing and enthusiasm at having heard them (160–161).

The Fidalgo de Elvas narrates the encounter between the natives and the Spaniards but there is no mention of De Soto embracing the Indians as he simply reports: "They were all put in chains and on the day following were allotted among the Christians for their service" (68). Rangel does not mention this oration given by the Indians and states that once the Indians surrendered they "were taken to be put in a hut, their hands tied behind" (265).

Hernando de Soto is also portrayed by the Inca as the prototype of a Spanish *hidalgo*, full of chivalry and magnanimity towards the enemy. The Inca comments that De Soto ordered the rescue from a lake of seven Indians who had been fighting the Spaniards because "it was inhuman to permit men of such magnanimity and virtue (which even in enemies inspires our admiration) to perish" (150).

Spanish chivalry was not reserved for Indian males; it was also directed towards Indian women. The Inca narrates the encounter between Hernando de Soto and the *cacica* of Cofitachequi. When the lady *cacica* of Cofitachequi was hesitant to present De Soto with a pearl strand because she was a woman and he was a conqueror, the Inca states that the Spanish leader asked Juan Ortiz, his interpreter, to inform her that "I shall esteem the honor of having received the pearls from her own hands more than the value of the jewels themselves" (302). Once she presented him with the strand, "he in like manner arose to receive them, taking from his finger a gold ring set with a ruby, which he now bestowed upon her as a symbol of the peace and friendship they were now discussing" (302).

Luis Hernández de Biedma, a member of De Soto's expedition, does not mention any meeting between Hernando de Soto and the lady *cacica*.[3] The Fidalgo de Elvas reports that when the *cacica* came to meet De Soto, he took her hostage and forced her to march with the Spanish army. She, however, managed to escape to the woods with "a slave of Andrés de Vasconcellos who refused to come with them [the Spaniards]; and it was very certain that they [the *cacica* and the slave] held communication as husband and wife" (87). Rodrigo Rangel is the one chronicler who comes the closest to Garcilaso's description of De Soto's encounter with the *cacica*, although there is hardly a trace of chivalry, for he states that "she removed a string of pearls that she wore about the neck and put it on the Governor's neck, in order to ingratiate herself and win his good will" (278).

In another instance, the Peruvian *mestizo* describes an example of Spanish chivalry when two Spaniards in a scouting foray reached an Indian village and were presented with two beautiful Indian maidens to "sleep with them and divert them during the night" (340). The Spaniards, however, claimed that "they had not dared touch these women" (340). It simply seems incredible in that instance, that chivalry would have triumphed over the conquistadores' famous voracious sexual appetites!

If one carefully examines the other chronicles of Hernando de Soto's expedition, as well as other documents of Spain's conquest of the New World, one can discern that the Inca exaggerated the concept of Spanish chivalry in his chronicle, though this is not to state that the conquistadores of La Florida did not possess it.

One of the principal objectives of the Spanish conquest of the New World was the conversion of the natives and the propagation of the Catholic faith. The Catholic religion, the bond that united so many conquistadores, is present in *La Florida del Inca*. In his preface, the Inca indicates that one of his reasons for writing his chronicle was to urge Spain to colonize La Florida to convert the natives to Catholicism, as he states:

Neither would I fail to displease gravely the Eternal Majesty (who is the one we should fear most), if with the idea of inciting and persuading Spaniards by my history of acquire the land of Florida for the augmentation of Our Holy Catholic faith, I should deceive with fictions and falsehoods those of them who might wish to employ their property and life in such an undertaking. For indeed, to tell the truth, I have been moved to labor and to record this history solely by a desire to see Christianity extended to that land which is so broad and so long (xliii).

Throughout *La Florida del Inca*, Garcilaso presents the natives in a favorable light and takes pains to demonstrate to the reader that the Indians are worthy of conversion. He also, in a very subtle manner, blames the Spaniards for not placing the immediate conversion of the natives on their priority list. This is best exemplified when the Spaniards had no intention of converting Mucozo, the friendly and noble *cacique* who came out to greet them when they first landed on the Florida shores:

> Thus it was a great pity that the Curaca Mucozo was not invited to accept the waters of baptism for because his good judgment, few persuasions would have been necessary to turn him from his paganism to our Catholic faith. And the conversion of this man would have been a fine beginning, since one can expect such grain to produce many ears of corn . . . And let this be said here in order to exonerate these Castilians for exercising the same carelessness in similar instances which we shall see later; for certainly very propitious occasions were lost for the Gospel to be preached and received. And let those who forfeit such opportunities not be surprised that they are lost (226–227).

Although the Inca chastises the Spaniards for not converting the natives to the Catholic faith, he comments extensively on the religious spirit of the conquistadores. On almost every page of his chronicle there are references to God and Jesus Christ. The Peruvian chronicler constantly employs phrases such as "Thanks to the King of Kings and Lord of Lords" (xliii), "we gave thanks to God our Lord" (116), "it was God's blessing" (209), "thanks to Jesus Christ our Lord and Redeemer" (383), "they would pray to God our Lord, the Father of mercy, to grant them this grace" (432), and "we render our thanks to God, the Creator of Heaven and Earth" (433).

In times of war, the Spaniards turned to divine intervention to assist them. It also appears that in times of tribulation and suffering, the conquistadores turned to religion for comfort, while in fortunate times, the Spaniards attributed to divine mercy and goodness anything positive that occurred.

The Spanish conquistador was notorious for his greediness. Bernal Díaz del Castillo made the statement that finding riches was one of the primary motives for the Spaniards conquest of the New World. In his *True History of the Conquest of New Spain*, he states: "We came to serve God, to gain glory and to get rich" (69). Francisco Pizarro, for example, when reprimanded by a young priest for mistreating an Indian, turned to him in anger and replied: "I have come here for just one reason, to take away their gold" (Blacker 22). Francisco de Aguilar, a conquistador who accompanied Hernán Cortés during his conquest of Mexico, wrote the following: "When we became discouraged, Cortés gave us a very good talk, leading us to believe that gold and silver each one would become a count or duke. With this, he transformed us from lambs to lions and we went out against the large army of Indians without fear or hesitation." (Fuentes xiv-xv)

These passages are irrefutable proof that the conquistadores were a selfish group of men and there is no doubt that many sailed across the ocean for no other purpose than to get rich as quick as possible and sail back to Spain with their fortune.

While the Inca devotes more pages to praise the admirable qualities of the Spaniards such as courage, stoicism, and *hidalguía*, he nevertheless condemns their greed. From their very beginning of their landing in Florida, he points out that:

> The first idea in the minds of these cavaliers was to conquer that kingdom and seek gold and silver, and they paid no attention to anything that did not pertain to these metals. Thus they failed to accomplish other things of more import such as tracing out the limits of the land (103).

The Fidalgo de Elvas and Rodrigo Rangel blame the failure of De Soto's expedition on Hernando de Soto's greediness. The Fidalgo de Elvas, for example, who was no friend of the Spanish commander, reports that some of De Soto's men welcomed his death and the change of leadership and states that:

> There were some who rejoiced at the death of Don Hernando de Soto, considering it as certain that Luis de Moscoso (who was fond of leading a gay life) would rather prefer to be at ease in a land of Christians than to continue the hardships of the war of conquest and discovery, of which they had long ago become wearied because of the little profit obtained (139).

The Inca also blames the failure of settling La Florida on Hernando de Soto and his companions. De Soto and his men were so blinded by their greed in the pursuit of gold and silver—neither of which they found—that they spent their efforts in futility. The Inca praises De Soto, and describes him as "so courageous that wherever he entered a battlefield fighting, he cut a path through which ten of his men could pass" (500). On the other hand, he subtly condemns his greediness and comments "in like manner, he forfeited the honor of having given origin to a very great and beautiful kingdom for the Crown of Spain, and what he must have regretted most of all, of having augmented the Holy Catholic faith" (388). Had De Soto and his Spaniards attempted to colonize La Florida instead of being overcome by their lust for gold and silver, they would have met a better fate.

Much has been written about the cruelty of the conquistadores towards the natives during their conquest of the New World. The Inca mentions this evil in his chronicle. Early in his narrative, the Inca indicates that De Soto's men found the Indians around Tampa Bay to be extremely unfriendly towards them. He attributes this attitude on the part of the natives to a number of atrocities committed by Pánfilo de Narváez during his expedition to La Florida in 1528, and states:

> When Pánfilo Narváez had gone to conquer that province, he had waged war with Hirrihigua and later he had converted the Indian to friendship; then for some unknown reasons, he had committed certain abuses against the *cacique* which are of too odious a nature to be told here (60–61).

The Inca, however, does tell some of the cruelties suffered by the natives in Chapter three of his chronicle, which included the cutting off of Hirrihigua's nose. As the Inca comments:

> Each time that Hirrihigua recalled that Spaniards had cast his mother to the dogs and permitted them to feed upon her body, and each time that he attempted to blow his nose and failed to find it, the Devil seized him with the thought of avenging himself on Juan Ortiz, as if that young man personally had deprived him of his nostrils. The very sight of this Spaniard always brought past offenses before his eyes, and such memories increased each day his anger and lust for retributions (68).

Like Narváez, De Soto was known for his cruelty towards the Indians. Even though the Inca seems to minimize De Soto's cruelties towards the natives of La Florida, other chroniclers of the De Soto expedition, such as Fidalgo de Elvas, did not. De Soto used to cut off the hands and noses of Indians and cast them to the dogs. He also used to cut off their lips and chins, leaving their faces flat. In addition, he beheaded Indian carriers who had fainted, rather than bother to untie the collars by which they were led. One of the weapons used by the Spaniards in fighting the natives of the New World were the Spanish greyhounds. The Indians had never seen such beasts and were terrified of them. In *La Florida of del Inca*, the Inca narrates the pursuit of natives by Spanish greyhounds and gives an account of the importance of greyhounds to the Spaniards. As he states:

> In the conquest of the New World, greyhounds have accomplished feats that are worthy of great respect. For instance, on the island of San Juan de Puerto Rico, the Spaniards manifested their admiration for a dog named Becerrillo by giving him a part of their winnings, or rather by leaving the dogs portion with his master, a crossbowman, who as a result, received a share and a half of the amount due a man of his profession. Furthermore, Leoncillo, a son of Becerrillo, received five hundred pesos in gold as his share in one of the divi-

sions made after the famous Vasco Núñez de Balboa had discovered the sea of the South (126–127).

The use of dogs proved of such great value to the Spaniards that it led to the coining of a new word in the Spanish language, *aperrear* (to cast to dogs).

De Soto and his men not only used greyhounds to pursue and dismember natives as a form of punishment but at times they would have their horses trample them. The Inca narrates how the Spaniards surrounded an Indian sniper with their horses "and then they trampled him in an effort to overcome him before he could regain his feet" (252).

Cultural perception was another key factor the conquistadores of the New World used in their struggle to subdue the Indians. The conquistadores viewed war differently than the Indians. For example, for the Aztecs, war was just a way to obtain tribute and prisoners for their human sacrifices. In contrast with this ceremonial concept of war, the Spanish conquistadores practiced total warfare that left no room for any outcome other than full victory or death. For the Indians, a conference with a Spanish conquistador was a tactful formality, but for the conquistador it meant an ideal chance to capture the enemy chief and use him as a hostage to insure them that all demands would be met (Céspedes 16). The Inca, along with all of the chroniclers of De Soto's expedition, reports examples of this most dastardly form of treachery, yet no one condemns it.

A true portrait of the conquistador of La Florida would not be complete without mentioning his constant companion, the horse. The Spaniard, white-faced, bearded and armored, came as a shocking surprise to the Indian, but nothing added to that surprise more than the conquistadores' horse (Morison 2:247). As Pedro Castañeda de Nágera, chronicler of Franciso Vázquez de Coronados expedition wrote: "After God, we owed the victory to our horses" (Fuentes xiv). The horse was a pivotal factor in the conquest of the Indians. Not only did it give the Spaniards unmatched mobility, but it provided them with a psychological advantage. Many Indians believed the horse to be immortal, while others perceived him as cannibalistic because he supposedly feasted on human flesh. It was not uncommon for the Indians to beg forgiveness of the horse under the conquistador (Morison 2:247).

In his ill-fated conquest of La Florida, De Soto brought three hundred and fifty horses. Although the swampy terrain of the peninsula and the Mississippi basin rendered the horse less effective than other parts of the Western hemisphere, the animal, nevertheless, proved to be a valuable weapon for the Spaniards. In some instances the Inca narrates that the Indians on many occasions "out of fear of the horses, dared not to attack or even await them" (242). In other instances, he comments that "the Indians themselves were more pleased to kill one horse than four cavaliers, for they felt that it was solely on account of the horses that their enemies had any advantage over them at all" (409).

The Inca claims that the conquistadores regarded horses "as the nerve and sinew of our army" (327). According to him, these animals were so necessary that when they were lost "everyone mourned their loss more than if they had been their own brothers" (303). One of the most pathetic descriptions found in *La Florida del Inca* appears towards the end of the Spaniards' ordeal in La Florida when they were forced to unload their horses from their makeshift brigantines to lighten their weight and escape the Indians. The Fidalgo de Elvas unemotionally relates the incident by indicating that the Spaniards had to leave the horses behind "because of the slowness with which they sailed on account of them" (158). Garcilaso, on the other hand, narrates the incident in a manner sure to provoke the readers empathy:

> And now the enemies, on perceiving that the Spaniards had reached safety, turned their fury upon the horses that had been left ashore. Removing their headstalls, and halters to prevent their being hindered in running, and taking off their saddles to leave them unprotected from arrows, they set them loose in the open countryside. Then as if these animals were deer, they hurled arrows at them with great fiesta and rejoicing, continuing to do so until they saw them all fallen. Thus came to an end on this day those three hundred and fifty horses which had entered Florida for its discovery and conquest; and on none of the expeditions which to date have been made in the New World have so many and such fine horses been seen together. Beholding their mounts pierced with arrows and being unable to go to their assistance, the Castilians experienced extreme sorrow, weeping for these animals as if they were their sons (581).

The chroniclers of the *conquista* had a tremendous impact on the Hispanic colonial heritage of the United States. The interesting fact about *La Florida del Inca* is that it was written by an erudite who depended almost exclusively on the oral testimony of an "anonymous" eyewitness (Gonzalo Silvestre). Handicapped in that he was not a participant in Hernando de Soto's expedition to La Florida, and cognizant that he was a *mestizo* who was proud of his Spanish blood, the Inca appears somewhat overzealous and romantic in his portrait of the man who came to conquer La Florida. The Spanish conquistador, nevertheless, is portrayed in *La Florida del Inca* for what he was: A man of flesh and blood with both virtues and vices, who was the product of his times.

Notes

[1] The first chronicle of Hernando de Soto's expedition to appear was the *Relaçao Verdadeira dos trabahos que O Governador D. Fernando de Souto e certos fidalgos portugueses passaram no descobrimiento da provincia da Florída*. It was published in Portuguese in 1557 by an anonymous Portuguese

survivor of the expedition known as the Fidalgo de Elvas. See Fidalgo de Elvas, *True Relations of the Hardships Suffered by Governor Don Hernando de Soto and Certain Portuguese Gentlemen in the Discovery of the Province of Florida*, trans. James A. Robertson, *The De Soto Chronicles*, eds. Lawrence A. Clayton, Vernon James Knight, Jr., and Edward C. Moore, vol. 1 (Tuscaloosa: University of Alabama, 1993).

[2] Rodrigo Rangel was De Soto's private secretary. His account given to Gonzalo Fernández de Oviedo, "Official Chronicler of the Indies," shortly after the expedition's return, is a detailed diary of the expedition. It appears in Gonzalo Fernández de Oviedo's *Historia general y natural de las Indias*, which was not published until 1851, some three centuries after Fernández de Oviedo's death. See Rodrigo Rangel, *Account of the Northern Conquest and Discovery of Hernando de Soto*, trans. John E. Worth, *The De Soto Chroniclers*, eds. Lawrence A. Clayton, Vernon James Knight Jr., and Edward C. Moore, Vol. 1 (Tuscaloosa: University of Alabama, 1993).

[3] Luis Hernández de Biedma, *factor* of the expedition—a *factor* was an official who collected taxes and tributes for the Spanish Crown—presented a brief testimony concerning the expedition to the Council of the Indies in 1544. This testimony, however, was not published until 1841. See Luis Hernández de Biedma, *Relation of the Island of Florida,* trans. John E. Worth, *The De Soto Chronicles*, eds. Lawrence A. Clayton, Vernon James Knight Jr., and Edward C. Moore, vol. 1 (Tuscaloosa: University of Alabama, 1993.)

Works Cited

Blacker, Irwin R. *The Golden Conquistadores.* Indianapolis: Bobbs-Merrill, 1960.

Céspedes, Guillermo. *Latin America: The Early Years.* New York: Knopf, 1974.

Crow, John, A., Irving A. Leonard, and John T. Reid. *An Anthology of Spanish-American Literature.* Ed. John E. Englekirk. New York: Appleton-Century-Crofts, 1965.

Descola, Jean. *The Conquistadors.* New York: Viking,1957.

Díaz del Castillo, Bernal. *Historia verdadera de la conquista de la Nueva España. Historiadores primitivos de Indias.* Ed. Enrique de Vedia. Biblioteca de Autores Españoles. Tomo 26. Madrid: Ediciones Atlas, 1947.

Fernández, José B. *Alvar Núñez Cabeza de Vaca: The Forgotten Chronicler.* Miami: Ediciones Universal, 1975.

Fidalgo de Elvas. *True Relations of the Hardships Suffered by Governor Don Hernando de Soto and Certain Portuguese Gentlemen in the Discovery of the Province of Florida.* Trans. James A. Robertson. *The De Soto*

Chronicles. Eds. Lawrence A. Clayton, Vernon James Knight, Jr., and Edward C. Moore. Vol. 1. Tuscaloosa: University of Alabama, 1993.

Fuentes, Patricia de. *Conquistadores.* New York: Orion, 1963.

Hernández de Biedma, Luis. *Relation of the Island of Florida.* Trans. John E. Worth. *The De Soto Chronicles.* Eds. Lawrence A. Clayton, Vernon James Knight Jr., and Edward C. Moore. Vol. 1. Tuscaloosa: University of Alabama, 1993.

Hoffman, Paul E. "Hernando de Soto: A Brief Biography." *The De Soto Chronicles.* Eds. Lawrence A. Clayton, Vernon James Knight, Jr., and Edward C. Moore. Vol. 2. Tuscaloosa: University of Alabama, 1993.

Leonard, Irving A. *Books of the Brave.* New York: Gordian Press, Inc., 1964.

Morison, Samuel. *European Discovery of America.* Vol. 2. New York: Oxford University, 1971.

Rangel, Rodrigo. *Account of the Northern Conquest and Discovery of Hernando de Soto.* Trans. John E. Worth. *The De Soto Chronicles.* Eds. Lawrence A. Clayton, Vernon James Knight, Jr., and Edward C. Moore. Vol. 1. Tuscaloosa: University of Alabama, 1993.

Vega, Garcilaso Inca de la. *The Florida of the Inca.* Trans. John Grier Varner and Jeanette Johnson Varner. Austin: University of Texas, 1962.

Zamora, Margarita. *Language, Authority, and Indigenous History in the Comentarios reales de los incas.* Cambridge: Cambridge University, 1988.

El exilio cubano del siglo XIX:
La leyenda negra y la figura del indio

Marcela W. Salas
University of Houston

Varela/Sellén: la construcción de una identidad
y la formación de una conciencia nacional

Tanto Félix Varela como Francisco Sellén fueron protagonistas de dos de las transiciones más importantes de la Cuba decimonónica. Uno estuvo en la apertura y el otro en el cierre de un período signado por los esfuerzos por desprenderse de la metrópoli. Del mismo modo que sus textos toman escenas del primer capítulo histórico de la relación entre América y España, al mismo tiempo los autores protagonizan el último.

Al padre Varela le correspondió ser el más indiscutible formador de opinión y maestro de la juventud cubana que plantaría las semillas de la revolución en la etapa en la que se daban los primeros sacudones para desasirse del poder de España. Varela es partícipe de la transformación que va desde la factoría a la colonia en el período que corre entre 1790 y 1834.

Para ser patriota hay que encontrar una identidad nacional y para ello hay que separarse de España. El primer paso que Varela da en ese sentido, es alejar a la filosofía del escolasticismo. A través de una tesis lingüística Varela se enfrenta con un aparato conceptual que define al español y que ya no es eficaz. Para construir una identidad cubana separada de lo español les deja a ellos el latín (desvalorizándolo de alguna manera como lengua lógica) y se adueña del castellano. Si Calibán maldijo a Próspero por haberle dado el lenguaje, Varela por el contrario, para "calibanizar" a los cubanos, agradece la donación y se apropia de la lengua del conquistador para hacerla materia del pensamiento cubano. Todavía no se utilizará una lengua "cubanizada" en los documentos escritos, pero se ha iniciado el camino.

Varela representó a Cuba en las Cortes del 22 al 23 pero sus propuestas reformadoras no le valieron más que el exilio. Leal y Cortina apuntan que las actividades en las Cortes durante 1823 demostraron que Varela era un gran patriota y un profeta y citan al mismo Varela "No importa lo que suceda, España perderá lo que no puede retener . . . pero si no reconoce su independencia perderá su amistad... Si España espera, solo podrá beneficiar a otros países absteniéndose así de toda cooperación con Hispanoamérica".[1] Mientras estuvo en España, Varela no abogaba por la independencia sino por la autonomía, pero su vivencia en las Cortes lo hizo cambiar de rumbo. Tuvo que marchar al exilio, se volvió promotor del ideal independentista y publicó en Filadelfia *El habanero*, primer periódico revolucionario cubano. Cuando publica *El habanero* está separado de España física e ideológicamente. Ya no es un "español de ultramar" como solía definirse a sí mismo Arango y Parreño, (economista de la época al que luego Varela ficcionalizará en la figura de Magiscatzin), es un cubano exiliado que trata de definir su "otredad". Ser cubano en principio es no ser español pero también es no ser estadounidense.

Evidentemente, las publicaciones de Varela que se han estudiado son sus escritos filosóficos y periodísticos ya que nadie lo consideraba autor de ficción. En los manuales de literatura cubana tradicionales aparece o bien como figura histórica en cuanto a la evolución del pensamiento o se encuentra algún análisis superficial de sus *Cartas a Elpidio*. Sólo desde hace poco tiempo, se ha comenzado a ver a Félix Varela como autor de *Jicoténcal*, según Anderson Imbert, "la primera novela histórica escrita en castellano".[2]

En esa crisis revolucionaria presentada por Varela tuvo concreta participación Francisco Sellén. Sellén (1836-1907) nació en Santiago de Cuba y compartió con sus hermanos, especialmente con Antonio, el gusto por la actividad literaria y las lenguas además del credo separatista. Francisco pasó en Nueva York casi la mitad de su vida ya que emigró a esta ciudad apenas comenzada la guerra de los diez años y sólo retornó a su patria cuando se instaló la República. Fácilmente podríamos decir que es un post-romántico, influido principalmente por autores alemanes e ingleses a los que traduce. En casi todas las Antologías y notas biográficas, el nombre de Francisco Sellén aparece asociado al de su hermano Antonio y esto resulta lógico porque tuvieron un destino común tanto literario como político. En 1862 se dieron a conocer publicando un semanario bilingüe (español-inglés) llamado *El Heraldo Cubano*, de breve duración. En 1863 publicaron *Estudios Poéticos*, un volumen de "imitaciones y traducciones" de distintos poetas extranjeros entre los que figuran autores como Goethe, Uhland, Heine, Müller, Schiller, etc., muchos de ellos aún desconocidos en castellano. Ambos colaboraron en *Revista de la Habana*, *Floresta Cubana*, *Aguinaldo Habanero*, *Siglo*, *Opinión* y otras revistas literarias. Casi todas ellas eran órganos de manifestación política hasta 1968. En esta década previa a su exilio, Francisco Sellén tuvo intensa actividad como escritor público. Su gusto por las lenguas, además de afirmar su transculturalismo lo lleva a publicar varias traducciones. Fundó con Saturnino Martínez *La Aurora* de La Habana. Este periódico semanal estaba dedicado y concebido (como decía su título) a los artesanos del tabaco, el primer grupo de trabajadores cubanos que generó una conciencia de clase y reclamó sus derechos. *La Aurora* además de tener intenciones educativas, comentaba los problemas de los trabajadores.

También fue el disparo inicial para que comenzaran las famosas lecturas en las fábricas de cigarros. Finalmente las presiones políticas, especialmente la de la oligarquía, más los conflictos bélicos que se avecinaban obligaron al cierre del periódico que se hizo efectivo en 1868. Además de esta importartante labor que lo orillaba cada vez más al conflicto político que desencadenaría en su largo exilio, en 1865 publicó como obra original *Libro íntimo* y entregó en folletines la novelita *Una temporada lírica* de muy escaso mérito según la crítica de la época.

Involucrado por completo en la tormenta política, preso, prófugo y finalmente exiliado a partir de 1968, en pocos años se volverá a oír su voz en periódicos hispanos del exilio. Trabajó como redactor de *El Educador Nacional* que fundó y dirigió con Néstor Ponce de León y también en *El Nuevo Mundo*, *América Ilustrada*, *El Museo de las Familias*. Algunas de estas colaboraciones provocarán el comentario risueño de Rubén Darío: "el poeta Sellén, el celebrado traductor de Heine y su hermano fueron a Nueva York a hacer almanaques para Lemman y Kemp, si no mienten los decires"[3], posiblemente un comentario un poco frívolo teniendo en cuenta las duras necesidades del exilio. Sin embargo, Martí lo reconoce como maestro. Dice éste describiendo la residencia neoyorquina de Sellén ". . . el poeta modesto a cuya casa llena de libros y flores, acude el joven que busca guía, el versificador en apuros, el bibliómano a caza de curiosidades, el literato menesteroso de consejo. El poeta acompaña hasta la puerta al visitante como si fuera él quien recibiera el favor"[4]. Esto confirma la influencia que tenía Sellén en la comunidad literaria que lo rodeaba en Estados Unidos. Sus libros originales serán publicados en Nueva York, a partir de 1889 por A. Da Costa Gómez, editor de otras obras en español. En 1890 se publica su primer libro, *Poesías*, una refundición de su primer *Libro íntimo* y los poemas compuestos en el exilio. La edición tiene dos partes bien diferenciadas llamadas "Primeras Poesías" y "Nuevas Poesías". En 1891 publica *Hatuey,* poema dramático en cinco actos y en 1900, *Cantos de la Patria,* otro libro de poemas que también mezcla poemas ya publicados, textos corregidos y nuevos poemas. En 1901 otro editor, M. M. Hernández publica *Las apuestas de Zuleika*, una obrita en un acto basada en una anécdota de Balzac.[5] Max Henriquez Ureña, historiador de la literatura cubana, prologó y publicó el último libro de Sellén *La Muerte de Demóstenes*, poema dramático, de manera póstuma en 1926 por encargo del autor. Ureña nos confirma que la única obra de Francisco Sellén que subió al escenario fue su obrita en prosa *Las apuestas de Zuleika* traducida al inglés y representada en el Berkeley Lyceum el 28 de abril de 1893.[6] La totalidad de las obras de Sellén confirman que su obra original, a pesar de parecer completamente dedicada a Cuba, estaba teñida por su propio transculturalismo. Su desenvolvimiento en múltiples lenguas y su exilio fueron el agente entre estas culturas, específicamente entre la cultura anglo y la cultura hispana. Probablemente era éste su camino hacia la desespañolización. Lo mismo parece haber pasado con Varela que, después de tantos años en el exilio, comunicándose permanentemente en otro idioma que llegó a dominar, y con otras preocupaciones como la educación de las mujeres, por ejemplo, se acercó también a esta transculturación. Sin embargo, ninguno de los dos perdió en ningún momento el objetivo. Decididamente ambos autores se habían propuesto construir una literatura nacional cubana a partir de la definición de su identidad. Desde el exilio escriben y publican en el contexto de la leyenda negra (aunque en diferentes circunstancias) dos piezas fundamentales de la literatura cubana .

La leyenda negra y la figura del indio

Fray Bartolomé de Las Casas afianzó la leyenda negra creando la imagen de un indígena atropellado. La edición holandesa de De Bry de la *Brevissima relación de la destrucción de indias* dio la vuelta al mundo innumerables veces desde el siglo XVI y todavía hoy recordamos o manipulamos los grabados que ilustraron el relato de Las Casas. En este punto Juderías sostiene que si fue injusta la campaña de difamación sostenida a causa de su acción en Europa, más injusta lo fue la sostenida a causa de su acción en América. Afirma además que Las Casas hizo un terrible daño a su patria reduciendo la conquista a dos puntos: crueldad implacable e insaciable sed de riquezas.[7]

Es importante mencionar dos puntos alrededor de Las Casas, el sermón de Montesinos que es el primero que denuncia las crueldades cometidas en contra de los indios y la disputa legal que sostuvieron el padre Las Casas y Ginés de Sepúlveda en cuanto al derecho de España a las tierras conquistadas y a la situación legal de los indios. Sepúlveda se fundamenta en la supuesta "inferioridad" de los indios diciendo que lo superior debe dominar sobre lo inferior, lo racional sobre lo irracional. Las Casas distingue entre tres tipos de bárbaros: las fieras irracionales, los que no pueden expresarse y los que son capaces de gobernarse a sí mismos. En realidad se trata de un proceso de "descosificación" del indígena que tomarán los patriotas como eje para sus propios reclamos.

Las cuestiones fundamentales en el debate que protagonizó Las Casas eran si el indio americano debía ser tratado como un ser dotado de raciocinio y por lo tanto se debía emprender una conversión pacífica o era lícito y justificable con tal objetivo el empleo de métodos violentos. Los partidarios de la primera tesis entre los que se contaba Las Casas llegaron a poner en duda el derecho de la corona a gobernar esas tierras.

Colón identifica sin duda indígena y bestia, ya que en algún momento habla de "cabezas de mujeres" exactamente como si hablara de cabezas de ganado. Desde Colón, criticado por Las Casas a causa de esto, la asociación indígena/cosa es un hecho. Fray Bartolomé de Las Casas intenta redefinir al indígena americano para devolverle la identidad de persona que le había sido arrebatada desde las primeras descripciones colombinas. Vale la pena citar a Las Casas.

Todas estas universas e infinitas gentes, a todo género crió Dios los más simples, sin maldades ni dobleces, obedientísimas, fidelísimas a sus señores naturales y a los cristianos, a quien sirven, más humildes más pacientes, más pacíficas y quietas, sin rencillas ni bullicios, no rijosos, no querulosos, sin rencores, sin odios, sin desear venganzas que hay en el mundo.(...) Son eso mismo de limpios y desocupados y vivos entendimientos, muy capaces y dóciles para toda buena doctrina y aptísimos para recibir nuestra santa fe católica y ser dotados de virtuosas costumbres (...). En estas ovejas mansas y de las calidades susodichas, por su hacedor y criador así dotadas, entraron los españoles, desde luego que las conocieron como lobos y tigres y leones crudelísimos de muchos días hambrientos.[9]

Las Casas considera rasgo esencial del indígena la inocencia edénica y por ende la falta de interés en lo material que por supuesto opondrá a la figura del conquistador, caracterizado por la corrupción y la codicia. Este es el mismo esquema que utilizarán los escritores independentistas del siglo XIX alimentando la imagen del "buen salvaje" afianzada durante la Ilustración. La corriente llamada indigenismo basada en esta imagen y a la que Powell se refiere irónicamente, tuvo vigor en toda América Latina y cobró diferentes formas que van desde el indianismo hasta el siboneyismo, pasando entre otras por la literatura gauchesca.[10] En Cuba, el tema del indio y también el de la naturaleza "edénica" que lo circunda fue constante a lo largo del siglo. Ya Heredia ponía su atención en la figura del indio pero recurriendo al indígena azteca como en "En el teocalli de Cholula". Plácido toma justamente a Jicoténcal como protagonista de un romance, Domingo Delmonte propone teóricamente la utilización del indio como figura literaria. Más tarde la corriente siboneyista, en la que algunas veces incluyen a Sellén, retoma esta tradición especialmente en la poesía. El siboneyismo florece en la década del 50, buscando siempre una forma de expresión típicamente cubana. Las autoridades españolas censuraron los intentos más arriesgados. Cuando José Fornaris, uno de sus máximos cultores, publica *Cantos del Siboney,* fue llamado por un general que le dijo "Aquí somos españoles y no indios, ¿está usted?, todos españoles".[11]

En prácticamente todos estos casos, la figura del indio en nada se acerca a la del verdadero indígena, ni aboga por sus derechos, ni está volcada a describirlo como una parte integrante del sistema social. En Cuba, los indios habían casi desaparecido y ese lugar vacío había sido ocupado por el negro. Esta figura del indio, celebrada en la corriente indigenista no es otra cosa que la nueva identidad del criollo, la manera estilizada de verse como héroes en los textos, el método más eficaz de la desespañolización. Claro que cuando se halla algún capítulo sobre la indigenista en Cuba encontramos que su primera manifestación es el breve relato "Matanzas y el Yumurí" de 1837 y se menciona también a Gertrudis Gómez de Avellaneda con *Guatimozin* y *El cacique de Turmeque.* En realidad, la primera novela histórica escrita en lengua castellana, en 1826, es cubana aunque fue publicada en los Estados Unidos y de tema indigenista, como lo prueba *Jicoténcal* del padre Varela. Lo mismo sucederá medio siglo más tarde con *Hatuey* de 1891, esta vez una obra dramática, que insistirá en este tema indigenista, en el contexto de la leyenda negra y en la búsqueda de una identidad cubana que comience por la desespañolización.

Jicoténcal/Hatuey: alegoría y desespañolización

Jicoténcal (1826) y *Hatuey* (1891) están separadas por medio siglo y aunque lo que comenzaba a ser un intento de forcejeo y de conciencia nacional en época de Félix Varela era ya desesperación y estallido revolucionario en época de Francisco Sellén, es factible observar que ambas trabajan casi con el mismo ideologema. Las oposiciones conquistador/conquistado, colonizador/ colonizado, español/ criollo se revierten (como así también la oposición civilización/barbarie) para revalorizar el segundo término. Los detalles de la leyenda negra aparecen atenuados en *Jicoténcal* y exacerbados en *Hatuey*.

Para tomar un ejemplo y comenzando por las fuentes, Varela utilizará la historia de Solís (1684), un texto más bien racionalista que renuncia a los detalles fantásticos y que pertenece de alguna manera a la leyenda blanca (aunque recurre para algún episodio a Las Casas).

Sellén no sólo utiliza a Las Casas, cuya publicación era reciente en los Estados Unidos (proyectando un doble efecto propagandístico) sino que incluye su documentación en la edición del drama. No tenemos noticia de la representación de *Hatuey* pero es más que probable que haya sido representada en uno de los tantos círculos patrióticos que se reunían para recaudar fondos para la causa. Sin duda los medios audiovisuales (y ya se tenía conciencia de esto en el Barroco) tendrían un mayor efecto propagandístico.

Varela publica la novela de manera anónima. Ya estaba bastante comprometido, inclusive había sido víctima en el exilio de un intento de asesinato a causa de la publicación de *El habanero*. Era el momento de elegir una máscara y no sólo se esconde en el anonimato sino que elegirá también al indígena mexicano y no al cubano. Tampoco podía mostrar a sus discípulos sus dudas y opiniones acerca de la iglesia. *Jicoténcal* es un texto más catártico que consciente de la creación de una literatura nacional. De hecho se ha "escapado" de formar parte de la literatura cubana durante muchísimo tiempo.

Por el contrario, sellén no sólo firma el texto sino que lo propone en el prólogo como primer monumento del teatro nacional. Además lo documenta tratando de infundirle cierta verosimilitud histórica con intenciones obviamente efectistas y de propagación de la leyenda ya que parte de esta documentación será el texto de Las Casas.

> Mientras pluma de mejor temple que la mía no erija a Hatuey monumento más digno de su memoria, queden estas páginas siquiera como tentativa , y acaso al mismo tiempo principio de lo que un día, cuando tengamos patria, llegue a

ser nuestro teatro nacional. Aunque no he pretendido hacer obra de arqueología, me ha parecido conveniente, agregar algunas citas y notas por vía de documentos justificativos.[9]

Ambos autores toman un episodio de la conquista para generar la alegoría pero Varela se remonta a México y Sellén prefiere ser más directo y referirse a Cuba. En cuanto a la elección del personaje, en ambos casos y dada la lectura alegórica, ésta responde a necesidades concretas. "Desespañolizarse" era el objetivo y por eso estos liberales ilustrados eligen la figura del "noble salvaje", ensalzado por Las Casas como un ser manso pero inteligente y además productivo. Sin embargo en estos textos el indígena que se presenta es mezcla de inocencia y sabiduría, hábil político y mejor guerrero, justo y medido, generoso con los suyos y con los otros si estos lo merecen, pero siempre atento al deber. A pesar de que éste es el modelo europeo del caballero virtuoso para los criollos significaba "americanizarse" o en este caso específicos "cubanizarse". Pero de ninguna manera en estos textos hay una propuesta consciente de mestizaje ni se buscan las verdaderas raíces indígenas. Sencillamente se genera una figura idealizada, no española (aunque el modelo se le parezca como los mismos criollos) con la que identificarse. El criollo está buscando la humanización, el dejar de ser "cosa", situación a la que lo relegaba su condición de colonia, y debe identificarse con alguien que haya sostenido la misma lucha. En los extremos, estas figuras indígenas heroicas se oponen a los "bárbaros españoles". Jicoténcal a Cortés, Hatuey a Velázquez. La oposición civilización-barbarie, queda así trastocada convirtiendo a los supuestos civilizadores en bárbaros y viceversa. De todos modos ambos autores dejan un rezago de "barbarie" en el indígena, pero esta clase de indio está ausente en el texto y en ambos casos es sólo una amenaza. En *Hatuey*, concretamente el caribe es el enemigo. Al pensar en "Calibán" de Fernández Retamar se concluye que no es el indianismo verdadero lo que se acepta, como luego podrá hacerlo Martí, sino sólo la figura "civilizada" del indígena pacífico y no el bárbaro "caníbal". Todavía los antecesores idealizados de los independentistas latinoamericanos se parecían más al modelo del Cid Campeador. Jicoténcal y Hatuey son modelos de oratoria, ecuanimidad y tácticos geniales en cuanto a lo militar y no parecen estar muy cerca de las verdaderas raíces indígenas que en realidad ya casi no existían.

En este punto se puede ver la alegoría general que proponen ambas obras. Los indígenas que habitan en este "paraíso" son los patriotas que representan a los criollos habitantes de Cuba. La llegada de los españoles que trae barbarie y desolación, representa al gobierno de España, descomedido y opresor. La lucha de resistencia a la conquista se relaciona, lógicamente con la lucha por la independencia de los patriotas. La traición que padecen en ambos casos representa las luchas internas (autonomistas, anexionistas, independentistas). El sacrificio de ambos héroes está relacionado con todas las formas de martirio que sufrieron los patriotas, como la censura, el exilio o la misma muerte. Todavía podríamos proponer una tercera cadena de signos menos general y referirnos a las "biografías" de cada autor y en ambos casos se correspondería. La lectura alegórica de Leal y Cortina identifica ciertos personajes literarios con personajes históricos: Jicoténcal/ Varela, Maxiscatzin/ Arango y Parreño, Cortés/ Fernando VII, etc.[13]

En el caso de Sellén podríamos establecer un paralelo identificando a Hatuey con alguno de los mártires de la revolución, casi todos ellos cercanos a Sellén o relacionar la traición de Atabaiba con la de aquella mujer que traicionó el primer intento del "Grito de Yara" a instancias de su confesor.[14] Pero lo importante es que indio-héroe-patriota-intelectual-autor se vuelven eslabones de la misma cadena. Esta figura del indígena representa ese nuevo sentido de cubanidad nacido con el comienzo del siglo y profundamente arraigado en época de la publicación de *Hatuey*. Es tan clara la identificación del protagonista indígena con el intelectual/escritor que en ambos casos, tanto Jicoténcal como Hatuey se presentan con un discurso que profetiza la tragedia. Su primer papel es el de voceros, son transmisores antes que luchadores, profetas como lo han sido los dos autores en su época correspondiente.

Otro de los ejes de alimentación de la leyenda negra es el concepto de la edad de oro o la visión del paraíso perdido que será recurrente en la poesía patriótica de este siglo. Esta idea parece menos sensacionalista en *Jicoténcal* que en *Hatuey*. Es cierto que se plantea un antes y un después de la llegada de los españoles pero en el antes se describe también esa paz cargada de peligros y amenzada por otros tiranos como Moctezuma. En *Hatuey*, a pesar de que se presenta la cercanía del caribe como enemigo, la primera escena muestra a los indígenas en una especie de estado de beatitud, danzando y haciendo ofrendas hasta que aparece Hatuey con el anuncio de la llegada de los españoles a interrumpir el rito. De todos modos en ambos casos se insiste en que todo fue peor después de la llegada de "esas gentes cuya venida se perpetúa en el vaticinio y tarda en el desengaño".[11] según dice Jicoténcal, el joven, en su primer discurso.

Consecuentemente con la pérdida del paraíso se produce la pérdida de la inocencia. Teniendo en cuenta que la descripción "humanizada" del indio, es decir la de Las Casas, se centra en la inocencia, ésta es una forma de la pérdida de la identidad. Sin embargo, a diferencia del concepto tradicional, en estos casos no hay estricta responsabilidad personal sino que la reponsabilidad recae en el agente externo: la serpiente, el demonio, los españoles. De todos modos aquí estriba uno de los puntos de lucha ya que para los patriotas la identidad es el tema fundamental. El perder la inocencia, es decir el "entregarse" a los españoles se paga con la muerte como en el caso de Atabaiba o Magiscatzin.

Los personajes femeninos que en ambos textos son los únicos personajes ficticios, tienen mucho que ver con la pérdida del paraíso o por lo menos cargan con parte de la culpa. Culpa por adaptarse, por sobrevivir a la nueva cultura, por pretender y apreciar cosas diferentes de la nueva situación. Se erigen en traidoras, son siempre la Malinche. Según la lectura de Leal y Cortina , Teutila representa el amor a la patria y a la libertad. Pero en esta lectura no se menciona a Doña Marina que sería una especie de otro yo, sombra o figura complementaria de Teutila. Si Teutila es el patriotismo, Marina es la traición al mismo, si una es la inocencia, la otra es la experiencia, si una la virtud, la otra el vicio y la corrupción. Teutila no rinde esta virtud hasta la muerte. Marina, hacia el final, se regenera y se funde con Teutila. Son ella y su hijo quienes quedan para representar a los indígenas (o a los cubanos), esa patria entregada pero que sigue clamando ante los oídos sordos del tirano por la independencia.

Atabaiba representa al indígena de inocencia ciega (ese que también inventó Las Casas). Esta inocencia la lleva a la entrega inmediata y a la traición inconsciente. A diferencia de la traición de Marina la de Atabaiba en ningún momento se considera maliciosa, por el contrario otra vez se cargan las tintas en la leyenda, Atabaiba y Teutila representan la inocencia de la que se aprovecha el español bárbaro codicioso. Atabaiba paga con la muerte cuando los suyos, representados por Hatuey, la desprecian, Teutila nunca rinde su virtud pero se destruye en el afán de conservarla.

Estas mujeres, fundidas en una sola, parecen representar la relación de los criollos con la patria pero no solamente con Cuba sino también con España. De este modo se presentan no solamente el amor, sino también la traición, no solo la fe ciega sino también las dudas, no solamente la virtud inconmovible sino la posibilidad de regeneración. En esta historia interna de los dos autores y a lo largo del siglo se verifica la relación que va desde el extremo de no permitir la violación hasta el extremo de entregarse ciegamente y por completo, o como Marina que siendo esclava de Cortés, representante de "la mala España", está siempre deseando a "la buena España" representada en ese caso por Ordaz. Esta relación constatemente en tensión lleva al aniquilamiento. La figura de la violación también apunta a la alimentación de la leyenda ya que en múltiples documentos que la fomentan a través de los siglos, se insiste con las violaciones despiadas de los bárbaros españoles. La lujuria de Cortés y de Ordaz tiene parentesco directo con la figura de Felipe II en los términos de la leyenda. Es decir que, apuntalándose en la lujuria que propaga la antigua leyenda, se desata una cadena de símbolos que representa el hecho histórico de la "violación" de Cuba con las cosecuentes imágenes de resistencia, entrega, etc.

Configurada la pareja edénica, el patriota se halla reflejado en la figura del héroe indígena y su relación tanto con la isla como con la metrópoli está representada en los personajes femeninos. Este es el camino a la "desespañolización" ya que identificándose con el tlaxcalteca o con el siboney se consigue el negativo exacto de estos indígenas idealizados en la figura de los españoles. En este punto los dos textos están separados básicamente por el tiempo y la historia que corre entre uno y otro. Vale la pena insistir en un detalle: Varela, guardando algo de condescendencia hacia España trabaja con una serie de opuestos complementarios como se ha visto en el caso de Teutila/ Marina, india-virtuosa/

india-traidora, Jicoténcal, el viejo/Magiscatzin, que presentan la misma oposición, Ordaz/Cortés, representando la buena y la mala España, etc. En *Hatuey*, en cambio, Sellén trabaja con dos líneas en espejo, indios buenos, virtuosos, leales, desinteresados y españoles malos, corruptos, traidores, codiciosos. El único nexo entre ambas líneas es el padre Las Casas convertido en personaje, único representante de una España buena pero al mismo tiempo su más grande detractor. En Jicoténcal existe todavía una España buena y admirable representada por Diego de Ordaz. Este personaje histórico que encarna todas las virtudes en este texto será la representación del mal en Hatuey. En *Jicotencal* además entre los indígenas también existe traición, codicia, lujuria y todos los vicios enumerados por la leyenda para los españoles. La figura de Cortés se equipara a la de Moctezuma, tanto Magicatzin como Marina, venden a su patria para beneficiarse personalmente. Ordaz, en cambio, está totalmente colocado del lado de los virtuosos y "toma partido" por los indígenas.

Cuando Francisco Sellén edita su texto ya había corrido demasiada historia y habían sido numerosos los sacrificados, ya no teóricos, en aras de la independencia, por lo tanto ya no quedan españoles salvables. Todos están extraídos directamente del modelo lascasiano.

En realidad carece de importancia el "cambio de personalidad" que una figura histórica padece de uno a otro texto. Bajo el molde de la leyenda devienen modelos repetidos, traición, lujuria, barbarie, aprovechamiento de la inocencia más indefensa, fraticidio, etc.

El cainismo es una de las consecuencias más nefastas de la pérdida del paraíso bíblico. Cuba no sólo enfrentó una guerra contra España sino que sus habitantes tuvieron que librar entre sí muchas batallas ideológicas, algunas armadas. Anexionistas, reformistas, separatistas, esclavistas o abolicionistas fueron grupos aliados o enemigos que hicieron avanzar o retroceder la revolución. También la relación entre naciones especialmente en tiempos de guerra genera alianzas fraternales o antagonismo. *Jicoténcal* es de alguna manera un texto que trata de expiar el sentimiento de traición. Varela se sentía traicionado por sus "hermanos", su período de representación en las Cortes fue una amarga experiencia. El temor a una guerra civil es una de las cosas que mantiene al cacique Jicoténcal bajo control. Pero, en general, en *Jicoténcal* las relaciones fraternales son más bien metafóricas (por ejemplo Magiscatzin "vendiendo" a sus hermanos). En *Hatuey* en cambio son claramente carnales. Sellén mismo se vio estrechamente ligado a sus propios hermanos en la patria y al mismo tiempo debió reencontrar relaciones de ese tipo en el exilio. Varias relaciones fraternas se exponen en este texto. Las relaciones entre hermanos (elegidos o reales) son positivas mientras existe el paraíso, una vez perdido el Edén son cainistas. Los hermanos Pedro y Diego de Ordaz representando a los españoles, son la versión más cruel de esta vertiente. Pedro deja a su hermano abandonado, muriéndose en una ciénaga, mientras él huye para salvar su vida. Pagará su traición con la muerte. Sin embargo los indios no están exentos por completo del mismo mal. Atabaiba, sin saber que su hermano carnal ha sido asesinado por aquellos a quienes ella protege, traiciona a los suyos y provoca la aprensión y luego la muerte de Hatuey. También Atabaiba morirá para pagar su culpa. La única relación fraterna de signo positivo, la de Hatuey-Macorijes, se da también entre algunos de los pueblos y sus jefes, ambos justamente por no traicionarse sucumbirán en la hoguera. Todas las relaciones fraternales en el texto tienen como destino último la muerte. Otra vez la metáfora de un país en una guerra permanente. En algunos de los poemas de Sellén este tema se repite.[12]

El tema del cuestionamiento de los valores religiosos o por lo menos de los eclesiásticos, alrededor de esta literatura y de la leyenda negra, es uno de los más controvertidos. Es, sin duda, una viga fundamental de la leyenda negra en dos sentidos: en principio reflota la España inquisitorial y en segundo lugar aparece el tema de los falsos valores religiosos, estos falsos valores en general se encuentran determinados por otros intereses. Pero si los patriotas pretendían "desespañolizarse" de ninguna manera pretendían "descristianizarse" porque significaba renunciar a sus propios valores. Más complicado resultaba en el caso de Varela que representaba esos mismos valores. Aunque el exilio había colocado a ambos autores en un mundo anglosajón y protestante y aunque la ideología liberal conlleva una cuota de anticlericalismo, Varela ejerció su sacerdocio en Nueva York y en Filadelfia.

Sellén no renunció, por lo menos no tenemos noticia, a su religión católica. De modo que en base a estos cuidados la alimentación de la leyenda no pasa por reflotar a la España inquisitorial (aúnque ambos personajes mueran en la hoguera), esas responsabilidades las carga la política aunque se ejecute en nombre de Dios. Se acusa a este poder político de enarbolar falsamente la religión. Esta es la porción de la leyenda que sale a relucir en estos textos: anteponer la codicia y disfrazarla de valores religiosos es el peor acto que cometen estos conquistadores. Codicia es una palabra que se repite largamente en ambos textos, sobre todo en *Hatuey*, y esto está perfectamente enunciado en los discursos iniciales de ambos protagonistas. Dice Jicoténcal:

> En cuanto a esa benignidad que tan pomposamente se ostenta, yo la tengo por un artificio para ganar a menos costa los pueblos; en una palabra la tengo por una dulzura sospechosa de las que regalan el paladar para introducir el veneno porque no conforma con lo demás que sabemos de su codicia, soberbia y ambición. Estos hombres, si ya no son algunos monstruos que arrojó la mar en nuestras costas, roban nuestros pueblos, viven al arbitrio de su antojo, sedientos de oro y de la plata y abandonados a las delicias de la tierra; desprecian nuestras leyes, intentan novedades peligrosas en la justicia y en la religión, destruyen los templos; destrozan las aras, blasfeman de los dioses...¡Y se les estima de celestiales![13]

Algo muy similar sostiene Hatuey:

Otra causa hay mayor, proviene todo
del Semí de los pérfidos cristianos
Que llaman oro, el oro es lo que adoran
su religión: el oro. Han observado
Que hay oro entre nosotros y obtenerlo,
es su afán, su ambición: ved en mis manos
Su Dios, lo que los mueve, lo que buscan."[14]

En *Jicoténcal* la iglesia católica está representada por Fray Bartolomé de
Olmedo y a pesar de ser ésta una figura histórica y además la creación de otro
fraile, no es precisamente una figura halagüeña. Olmedo, que aparece como el
confesor de Ordaz y tratando de convertir a todos los personajes principales del
texto, es un personaje prácticamente inofensivo pero al mismo tiempo timorato
y poco apto para las confrontaciones. Los sucesos de ese mundo nuevo parecen
ser demasiado para él y su estrecha visión. Huye en general a las confrontaciones y sostiene la más agria relación con Doña Marina (probablemente fueron
las fuertes opiniones sobre la iglesia en boca de los indígenas las que provoca-
ron que Varela se escondiera en el anonimato). El clérigo no sale airoso de la
misma pero reclama para sí al hijo de la mexicana. Probablemente esto sea un
símbolo ya que la América hispana, hija de este mestizaje, también fue recla-
mada para la fe católica, la religión a la que se había convertido y con la que
había mezclado su propia religión. En *Jicoténcal* resulta sorprendente la forma
en que Doña Marina conserva constantemente un último reducto para sus propios valores.

Probablemente Varela se encuentre frente a la necesidad de adaptación de
los valores religiosos al comprobar que en la Isla, en la metrópoli y en los
Estados Unidos, las cosas funcionan en este sentido de manera muy diferente y
que esta fuera la misma necesidad en la que se encontraban los indígenas en el
momento de la conquista. Esta dicotomía religiosa hará surgir un fenómeno de
"diglosia": frente a los representantes del poder colonial se "hablará" cristiano,
mientras que en la comunidad indígena se sigue practicando el idioma ancestral"[15] Esta dicotomía confunde al personaje del padre Olmedo, representante
del poder colonial. Varela, oponiéndose a él, busca en el cuestionamiento una
solución. Sabemos que Varela fue un reformador en varios campos, entre ellos
el de la filosofía, a la que alejó tanto del latín que la hacía inaccesible como del
dogma religioso. En Olmedo, Varela identifica a la iglesia cerrada y timorata,
incapaz de comprender esa nueva realidad.

En el caso de Sellén como ya dijimos, el nivel de tolerancia había dismi-
nuido enormemente. La representación de la iglesia se sincretiza con la única
representación de la "buena España" en la figura de Bartolomé de Las Casas.
Los tibios atisbos de leyenda blanca que encontramos en *Jicoténcal* desapare-
cen por completo en *Hatuey* convirtiendo en figura protagónica al mayor
promotor de la leyenda negra en América.

Desde todos estos flancos que hemos enumerado tanto esta novela como este drama histórico sostienen la leyenda negra. Se genera un perfecto paralelo entre la América de la conquista y la de la colonia siguiendo a su promotor americano hasta el punto de convertirlo en fuente y personaje. Jicoténcal muere silenciado, Cortés tiene que emplear los recursos más bajos para vencerlo. Lo privará de su mujer primero y de víveres para su tropa después, probablemente esto tenga que ver con la abolición de las Cortes, y la sentencia que sufre Varela. Hatuey rechaza al español inclusive en el último momento. Un fraile franciscano le ofrece la conversión y el paraíso, ni el indio ni el patriota quieren ir allí si tambien van españoles. Lo sugerente es que en la *Brevissima* de Las Casas el relato es el siguiente:

> Atado al palo decíale un religioso de San Francisco, un santo varón que allí estaba, algunas cosas de Dios y de nuestra fe; el cual nunca jamás las habia oído, lo que podía bastar aquel poquillo tiempo que los verdugos le daban, y que si quería creer aquello que le decía que iría al cielo, donde había gloria y eterno descanso y si no que iría al infierno a padecer eternos tormentos y penas. El, pensando un poco preguntó si iban cristianos al cielo, el religioso le respondió que sí pero que iban los que eran buenos. Dijo luego el cacique que no quería ir allá sino al infierno por no estar donde estuvieren y por no ver tan cruel gente. [16]

En cambio en *Hatuey* la escena cambia claramente sosteniendo la tesis de que desespañolizarse no era necesariamente descristianizarse. Hatuey pregunta en primer lugar "¿Van al cielo españoles?" y solo después "Y cristianos al cielo van también?"[17] Sellén no volvió a Cuba hasta que ésta fue completamente libre en 1902.

Ni siquiera hace falta mencionar el interés que durante el Siglo XIX pone Estados Unidos en Cuba, convirtiéndose no sólo en centro de refugiados y base de operaciones, apoyando económicamente a la revolución o tratando de comprar a Cuba. Pero al mismo tiempo, estos patriotas cubanos residentes allí durante tanto tiempo, influyeron definitivamente en su historia tanto nacional como literaria. Publicando en español se hacía propaganda antiespañola.

Aunque de ninguna manera esto hubiera cabido en la intención de estos hombres, un siglo más tarde se transformaría en propaganda anti-hispana. Los movimientos políticos generaban nuevas publicaciones como en el caso tardío de los textos de Las Casas. La leyenda negra, que en aquellos momentos debía difundirse para conseguir los ideales independentistas, ayudó a alimentar una mala imagen de lo hispano.[18] En *Hatuey* y en *Jicoténcal* se reúnen la historia de la conquista, la historia cubana del Siglo XIX y la leyenda negra. Todo esto publicado en los Estados Unidos formará por un lado la idea de una literatura culta en español, filosófica y preocupada por altos ideales y al mismo tiempo, reforzará los estereotipos que luego se utilizarán con otros fines políticos.

Notas

[1] Varela, Félix. *Jicoténcal.* Ed. Leal, Luis, y Cortina, Rodolfo. Houston: Arte Público Press, 1995. XII.

[2] Anderson Imbert, Enrique. *Literatura Hispanoamericana I.* México: Fondo de Cultura Económica, 1962. p. 189. A pesar de que Anderson Imbert desconoce la autoría de *Jicoténcal*, la supone mexicana. Luis Leal fue el primero que propuso la autoría de Varela. La tesis está sustentada en el estudio introductorio de Luis Leal y Rodolfo Cortina de la edición de 1995.

[3] Estenguer, Rafael. *Cien de las mejores poesías cubanas.* La Habana: Ediciones Mirador, 1948. 203.

[4] Estenguer 204.

[5] En realidad el librito dice en su tapa M. M. Hernández Impresor Venezolano y su última página incluye una lista de obras del autor publicadas y con precios (*Libro Intimo* y *Estudios poéticos* figuran como agotados). El distribuidor sigue siendo A. Da Costa Gómez a quien además va dedicado el libro.

[6] Henríquez Ureña, Max. *Panorama histórico de la literatura cubana.* New York: Las Américas Publishing Co., 1963. 322-23.

[7] Juderías y Loyot, Julián. *La leyenda negra.* Madrid: Editora Nacional, 1954. 255.

[8] Las Casas, Bartolomé de. *Brevissima relación de la destrucción de las Indias.* Chile: Biblioteca Popular Nascimento, 1972. 28-29.

[9] Las Casas 29.

[10] Foner, Philip S. *A History of Cuba and its Relationship with the United States.* New York: International Publishers, 1962. 171. "Almost immediately after the October 3 meeting, another event occurred which forced the revolucionist to disregard previous plans and take immediate action. A telegram from Captain General Lersundi to Colonel Udaeta, governor of Bayamo, was intercepted by a telegrapher friendly to the revolutionaries. It read: *Cuba belongs to Spain and for Spain she must be kept no matter who is governing. Send to prison D. Carlos Manuel de Céspedes, Francisco Vicente Aguilera, Pedro Figueredo, Francisco Maceo Osorio, Bartolomé Masó, Francisco Javier de Céspedes* . . . The conspiracy had been discovered. The wife of one of the rebels, Trinidad Ramírez, had revealed the plan in confession to her priest who had convinced her that it was her religious duty to inform the authorities."

[11] Varela 8.

[12] En algunos de los poemas de Sellén este tema se repite. Veánse sus poema "Los dos hermanos" publicado en *Libro Intimo* y en *Poesías* y también "A ciertos cubanos degradados" de *Cantos de la Patria* cuya estrofa final sentencia:

...
Id y besad la mano que chorrea
sangre de los que hermanos nuestros son
Y el mundo entero en vuestra frente vea
De Caín la tremenda maldición.

[13] Varela 8.

[14] Sellén, Francisco. *Hatuey*. New York: A. Da Costa Gómez, 1891.

[15] Lienhard, Martín. *La voz y su huella*. Hanover: Ediciones del Norte, 1991. p.116.

[16] Las Casas 43-44.

[17] Sellén 134.

[18] Fernández Retamar, Roberto. *Caliban and other Essays*. Minneapolis: University of Minnesota Press, 1989. "It is nor surprising, given its origin, that the black legend should find a place among the diverse an unacceptable forms of racism. We need only mention the sad case of the United States, where the words 'Hispanic' or 'Latino' as applied to Latin Americans, to Puerto Ricans and Chicanos in particular, carry a strong connotation of disdain . . ." (p. 43)

Negating Cultures, Saving Cultures: Franciscan Ethnographic Writings in Seventeenth-Century *la Florida*

E. Thomson Shields, Jr.
East Carolina University

In 1604, Pedro de Ibarra, the new governor of *la Florida*, that is, Spain's territories in what is now the southeastern United States, wrote to King Philip about his first experiences with the region's Native American peoples:

> After I had spread the news of my arrival in these provinces, there came to pay me allegiance in the name of Your Majesty more than 50 chiefs from different areas: I entertained and looked after them as well as I could, both because Your Majesty ordered me to and because they are living as Catholics, and are show-ing very clear signs of the fruit being produced in them by the teaching missions[1]. . . . (105-106)

Ibarra's idea of what was important to record concerning the Native Americans of *la Florida* reflects a typical twentieth-century idea of how Europeans viewed the people they encountered upon coming to the New World. Ibarra gives importance to Native Americans only in terms of how Christian these people have become, a sign of their political acquiescence to European power. In other words, from Ibarra's secular viewpoint, the most important feature of *la Florida's* Native American culture was its ability to assimilate to Spanish cul-ture. In fact, whether or not conversion to Christianity meant the same as assimilation to Spanish culture is an important question in studying the mission work of *la Florida*. One aspect of Franciscan missionary philosophy, incultur-ation, or the idea of blending one culture's practices with another's, implies that ethnographic differences can and should be encouraged between Roman Catholics from different cultural backgrounds. However, the practice does not always bear out the theory.

To the end of converting *la Florida*'s Native American population to Roman Catholicism, Spanish authorities brought in a series of missionaries dur-ing the sixteenth and seventeenth centuries. With the founding *of San Augustín*[2] in 1565 came Jesuit missionaries, but by 1572, Native American rebellion in missions outside of *San Augustín* helped push the Jesuits out of *la Florida* altogether to emphasize the order's work in the seemingly more fertile ground of Mexico. In the Jesuits' stead came Franciscan missionaries. Despite the death in 1595 of several missionaries at the hand of the Guale Indians along the present-day Georgia coast, the Franciscans stayed in *la Florida*, becoming a major force in the region until at least the last years of the seventeenth century.[3]

Interestingly, while the purpose of the Franciscan missionaries was to effect the conversion of Native Americans to Roman Catholicism, some of the very processes used to abolish those parts of Native American culture most offensive to Roman Catholic theology and sensibilities actually helped preserve the very same cultural practices they attempted to eradicate. The interplay of conversion, assimilation, and inculturation ended up developing a complex system of evangelization. As an evangelizing tool, the act of writing played a major role. Some Franciscan missionaries not only taught the Native Americans they were trying to convert to Roman Catholicism to recite the important elements of religious practice; they also taught some of their converts to read and write.[4] Just as important, though, was the Franciscan use of writing to show people not in the mission field, such as their religious superiors, why certain aspects of Native American culture in *la Florida* were not able to be kept synchronically with Roman Catholicism. It is in many of these writings that some Franciscan missionaries end up creating significant records of the cultural practices they wanted to abolish. As much as in works which emphasize the inculturation of Native American practices into Roman Catholicism, works which emphasize the abolition of certain practices become significant ethnographic studies of the very cultures being changed.

It needs to be emphasized, however, that not every description of Native American culture by a seventeenth-century Franciscan missionary in *la Florida* emphasizes practices that the friar believes should be abolished. In fact, inculturation has long been an important feature of Franciscan and Roman Catholic missiology, the philosophy of missionary work. Inculturation has two components: the adaptation of the missionary to local culture and, more to the point of this discussion, the adaptation of local cultural practices to the church. Roman Catholic missiology promoted inculturation even before the founding of the Franciscan order in the thirteenth century. As early as AD 601, during the evangelization of England by the Roman Catholic church, Pope Gregory sent Abbot Mellitus the following instructions:

> Since they have a custom of sacrificing many oxen to demons, let some other solemnity be substituted in its place, such as a day of Dedication or the Festivals of the holy martyrs . . . . They are no longer to sacrifice beasts to the Devil, but they may kill them for food to the praise of God, and give thanks to the Giver of all gifts for the plenty they enjoy. If the people are allowed some worldly pleasures in this way, they will more readily come to desire the joys of the spirit. (Bede 87)

Taking an act that has traditionally been used for non-Christian rituals and imbuing it with Christian significance—such as turning the sacrifice of an ox to a non-Christian deity into a feast celebrating the Christian God's bounty—has a long history. This same belief in integrating local cultural practices with Roman Catholic religious practice can be found in seventeenth-century Franciscan missiology. The "Instruction for the Guidance of Vicars Apostolic Leaving for the Chinese Kingdoms of Tomkin and Cochinchina," issued May 10, 1659, makes the following point:

> Do not make any effort or offer any argument to convince these people [the Chinese] to change their rites, their manners, or their customs, unless they are obviously contrary to religion and morality. What would be more absurd than to transport France, or Spain, or Italy or some other country of Europe to China? Do not bring them our countries, but the Faith, that Faith which neither rejects nor offends against the rites and usages of any people, provided these practices are not completely objectionable. Quite to the contrary our Faith insists that local usages be maintained and protected. (Considine 57-58)

The missiology that Franciscans were to use in the field, then, included the idea of inculturation—the synchronic use of native cultural practices along side and even as part of Roman Catholic religious practice.[5]

Some Franciscan writing from seventeenth-century *la Florida* does reflect the idea of inculturation. One of the most interesting works which offers the possibility of synchronic use for some of the cultural acts described is Francisco Alonso de Jesús's 1630 "Memorial." Written while Alonso de Jesús was in Spain recruiting friars for the *la Florida* mission field, the "Memorial" is a piece filled with geographic and ethnographic descriptions, all used to promote the missionary work being done in the region. One Native American cultural practice that Alonso de Jesús describes is dancing. Because it does not necessarily conflict with the tenets of Roman Catholic doctrine, dancing can be synchronically incorporated into a newly Roman Catholic Native American society:

> They have their songs[6] that they sing and they have certain little tambourines[7] that they beat and sing along with in complete unison,[8] to which the women, placed in a crescent and standing up, respond, dancing with the same rhythm.[9] During their heathen days, these dances were very lengthy and drawn out[10]; that they lasted for entire days and nights. On [their][11] becoming Christians, they became more moderate and shorter and not so continuous. And they have abandoned them in many areas where the sacraments are frequented despite their being decent and licit. (97)

Even though Alonso de Jesús accepts Native American dancing as an unobjectionable cultural practice, he ends up portraying it as a leftover element of a pagan past, not a Christian future. This mixed sense of inculturation defines much of the positive ethnographic description by seventeenth-century Franciscan missionaries in *la Florida*. The practices described can be, but don't necessarily have to be, brought into the new Roman Catholic Native American culture through inculturation. Alonso de Jesús finds it interesting, but not sad, that some newly Christian Native Americans give up their dancing altogether. Even though this cultural act seems to be fading in importance—and perhaps because he believes dancing's importance in Native American culture will continue to decline—Alonso de Jesús records its existence.

However, when the cultural practice being described is one that cannot fit into the rubric of Roman Catholic theology, or when a Franciscan friar because of his own sensibilities assumes that a practice cannot fit into a Roman Catholic society, the act of writing takes on an ironic twist. The very act of writing, meant to show why a particular practice needs to be abolished, often becomes the sole means by which we still know about that practice.

Alonso de Jesús's description of funeral practices illustrates well the desire to eliminate exactly what the writer records. About these rituals, Alonso de Jesús writes:

> They are a most pious people toward their deceased, and thus they practice various ceremonies and superstitions relative to them, which they renounce and abandon with great ease on receiving our Holy Catholic Faith. In some provinces, as soon as the one who is ill expires, they all cry with great tenderness for the time of 30 days, the women with high and doleful[12] tone, the men in silence, without having a set time. In some provinces, when the principle cacique[13] died, they buried some children from the common and plebeian people along with his body. For this benefit, their father and mother are held and esteemed as leading people from then on and enjoy their privileges . . . . In other provinces, all the blood relatives, both men and women, cut themselves with sharp flints on the upper arms and thighs[14] until they shed a great amount of blood. (99)

Alonso de Jesús goes on to tell about the disposal of the corpses, writing how once the flesh is gone, the bones are packed into leather trunks and placed in little houses, where they are visited "every day and they offer them a small amount of everything they eat" (99). Alonso de Jesús is definitely pleased that once the Native Americans of the region accept Christianity, they stop such practices. Even so, it should be noted that the tone of Alonso de Jesús's piece makes it interestingly problematic. The friar writes with a respectful understanding about the seriousness with which these people treat death. In this way, Alonso de Jesús develops the possibility that while the cultural practices of *la Florida's* Native Americans cannot be redeemed, their sense of seriousness about death can be integrated into the Roman Catholic culture that is to be adopted.

However, very few of the other Franciscan missionaries who write about the cultural practices of *la Florida's* native peoples include the sense of possible inculturation that Alonso de Jesús does. This is not to say that these writers reject the philosophy of inculturation. Instead, the implication is that those elements of Native American culture which the writers find unobjectionable are quietly inculturated while the practices which the writers feel are objectionable within a Roman Catholic world view are those that need presentation and discussion. For this reason the very process of recording cultural acts in order to tell why they need to be banned preserves the objectionable practices while other aspects of *la Florida's* native culture never become part of the written record.

Luís Gerónimo de Oré's *Relación de los mártires que ha habido en las Provincias de la Florida (Relation of the Martyrs Who Have Been in the Provinces of la Florida)* illustrates just such a principle.[15] Most likely written sometime soon after the Franciscan friar's two visitations to *la Florida* in 1614 and 1616, Oré's *Relación* gives the history of all missionary work in *la Florida*, Jesuit and Franciscan, from the arrival of Juan Ponce de León in 1513 to the time of Oré's second visitation.[16] For the most part, Oré's *Relación* tells more about the missionaries of *la Florida* than about the people being evangelized. However, throughout the work, elements of Native American ethnography do enter in, particularly in the sections where Oré presents the stories of various missionaries in their own words. One such section is the story of Francisco de Avila, who was taken captive by Native Americans during the late sixteenth-century revolt among the Guales of what is now the Georgia coast.

In describing his ordeal, Avila gives two types of ethnographic information, that describing the everyday culture of his captors and that describing the practices specifically related to his captivity. The first type of ethnographic description is sketchy at best. For example, telling about the clothing he was given to wear after his robe was taken away, Avila is quoted by Oré as saying, "In the meanwhile I wore a small coat[17] which he left with me. This is the clothing in which the Indians go about" (87). Nothing more is said about the clothing Avila is given, leaving readers with only a vague idea of what the clothing of *la Florida's* Native Americans is like.

On the other hand, when describing how he is to be tortured, Avila is much more specific. As Oré relates Avila's words, the torture is described as follows:

> Many Indians, men and women, came out to meet me, all of whom were painted, and who made a great show[18] and mockery of me. In this manner they took me to their hut where they made me sit down on the ground, while they all stood around me laughing at me and ridiculing me . . . . A little before arriving [at the town I was being taken to], we encountered a great number of painted Indians, their faces smeared with red earth, and fitted out with bows and arrows. They seemed numberless and looked like demons. They all came out to receive me, and amid great mockery and fun, led me to their habitation. When I arrived at the door of the hut, I found a great quantity of dry palm.

They told me that the palm was to make a fire to burn me. And on entering, I found they had erected a large cross, while on the one side there was a large whip which was a green rod with many branches which they use when at first they make the blood flow. On the other side of the cross was a rod to be used as a firebrand having a pine branch before it with the head-skin of a small animal. (88-89)

The greater detail in Avila's description of his impending torture than in his description of the clothing he was given is understandable. After all, the torture is a much more immediate concern. (Luckily for Avila, the torture is carried out only in part because his captors realize that the friar, if left alive, might be exchanged for a boy, the heir to the chief, who is being held in *San Augustín*.) Even though the balance in detail is understandable, the effect is that the more troubling aspects of Native American culture for the Franciscans are preserved while a written record of the everyday aspects of the culture is lost to posterity.

That the circumstances under which ethnographic details are presented skew what will be recorded and what will not can be seen further in two examples from Avila's story in Oré's *Relación* that describe similar subject matter as found in Alonso de Jesús's *Memorial*. In the part of his narrative during which he is still a captive, though after his life has been spared, Avila tells about the Native Americans' treatment of corpses:

They tried to make me serve in cleaning the house of the demon, for such we call it. They, however, call it a tomb. There they place food and drink for the dead which the dead are supposed to find at the morning meal. The Indians believe that the dead eat this food. However, they are already persuaded that the dead do not eat it, because the wizards eat it themselves, as they know by experience, for we have made this known to them. The same wizards themselves have confessed this and we have made good Christians of them. (91-92)

Like Alonso de Jesús, Avila records in some detail a practice that he would like to see eliminated from *la Florida's* native culture. However, unlike Alonso de Jesús, Avila shows no sympathy for even the reasons why the practice might be used, that is, the sense of seriousness about death in the Native American community. The situation through which Avila's ethnographic information is filtered, his capture and torture, allows it to be seen only in a negative light, without any hope for inculturation.

Even more biased by the situation of its presentation is Avila's description of Native American dancing, given as part of the story of his torture. Oré quotes Avila, writing, "Soon the Indians began to dance around me as if they were passing in review before me, and if it struck someone's fancy, he gave me a heavy blow with a macana.[19] In this manner they danced for three hours while they made a thousand incantations" (91). Avila's description of dancing is not as full as Alonso de Jesús's, but it is as descriptively powerful. However, despite the fact that each of the friars tells how the dances could continue for long periods of time, the differences are even more striking. Alonso de Jesús describes a practice which has possibilities for inculturation, with the "songs that they sing and . . . certain little tambourines that they beat and sing along with in complete unison, to which the women, placed in a crescent and standing up, respond, dancing with the same rhythm." The practice Avila describes includes beating him on the head with *macanas*, stone hatchets, rather than beating on tambourines; and in the place of songs and rhythms are "a thousand incantations." In this manner, the ethnographic descriptions tell as much about the concerns of the individual ethnographers as they do about the people being described. Ultimately, when one of *la Florida's* Franciscan friars finds a cultural practice among the Native Americans he is trying to convert that will not fit within the parameters of Roman Catholic theology, those practices get the most powerful ethnographic descriptions. The concerns of each individual friar give bias (though often understandable, as in Avila's case) to the type of ethnographic information presented.

Perhaps even more interesting than the way Avila's captivity affects how his ethnographic material is developed is the work of Francisco de Pareja, because Pareja's ethnographic biases come from significantly less stressful concerns. Instead of captivity, it is Pareja's work as a successful evangelist that affects his ethnographic writing. Pareja came to *la Florida* in 1594 to work in the mission field. He was the priest at various *doctrinas* in the area where the Timucua people lived in what is now the northern part of Florida, from the region of present-day Jacksonville, Florida, west to where the Apalachee lived in what is now the Florida pan handle. In 1610, Pareja left *la Florida* and went to Mexico, where he wrote and published a series of four books on using the Timucuan language to teach Roman Catholic doctrine to the Timucuan people: *Confessionario en lengua Castellana y Timuguana* (1613), *Grammatica de la lengua Timuquana* (1614), *Catecismo de la doctrina cristiana en lengua Timuqua . . .* (1617), *Catecismo en lengua Castellana, y Timuqua, en el qual se contiene lo que se les puede enseñar a los adultos que han de ser baptizados* (1617).[20]

At first glance, Pareja's linguistic and doctrinal works seem to be simply lists of confessional questions in both Spanish and Timucua used to help priests learn Timucua. However, by reading the list of questions, a portrait of the concerns Pareja had about his Timucuan converts comes across. For example, one question and response from the 1613 *Confessionario* reads:

> Did you search [for] any object lost by the Demon's artifice?
> What you are doing to make reappear what is lost and that you say: "It is here, or it is in such and such a spot, or he stole it?" All this the Demon tells you in order to get hold of your soul; do not believe in him, let it go, for this is a great sin. (Gatschet [1877] 500)[21]

Such an exchange, given in the work in both Spanish and Timucua, reveals very little ethnographically. Instead, it illustrates Pareja's belief in an incarnate Satan more than revealing a Timucuan belief in such a power.

However, at times Pareja's concern about "demonic" cultural practices among the Timucua does influence what material he includes in such a manner that his doctrinal questions reveal elements of Timucuan culture. The following three examples of such statements appear in the *Confessionario*:

> After being cured by the doctor and having become reconvalescent, did you prepare food of a sort of cakes or fritters[22] or of other things and did you halloo to the doctor "that he cured you," supposing that if you did not do so, the disease would reappear?
>
> Did you order that the bones of the game must not be thrown away, unless the game would no longer enter into the snare or trap, but that they must be hung up or placed upon the roof of the house?[23]
>
> Before hunting some antelope did you take the antlers of another antelope and pray over them the Demon's prayers? (Gatschet [1877] 501)

Even though Pareja condemns these acts—"You must abandon with the force of your will all (pagan) ceremonies, superstitions, auguriums, dreams, sortileges, cursings, maledictions, visions, and lies, for all these things have been taught by the Devil" (Gatschet [1877] 501)—in his very act of condemning them, he preserves them. Because of his own concern about creating a Roman Catholic culture (though not necessarily a Spanish culture) among the Timucua, he often ends up recording the very practices he would like the Timucua to give up.

The same irony of saving in writing what the authors wish to eliminate from the native culture can be found in Oré's *Relación* when he cites Pareja's testimony about the success of evangelizing among the Native Americans of *la Florida*. Describing his Native American converts, Pareja, as cited by Oré, states:

> Among them I have never found a trace of idolatry or witchcraft or superstition. For instance, they never say: "By means of this you will be healed; if you do not cure yourself with this herb, you will die"; or "if the owl hoots, it is a sign that some disgrace must overtake me"; or, "do not cook the fish in warm water if it was the first that entered the fishing grounds where no other fish enter"; or "do not eat maize of the cultivated land where lightning struck for you will be sick with such a sickness."
>
> When a woman gives birth, she does so apart, but she no longer places a laurel at the door of her house saying that the devil should not strike her, as she used to do. (106)

Pareja's testimony as given by Oré ends up this litany of former cultural practices by noting, "All these things and others has the word of the Gospel extirpated so much that the Indians do not even remember them" (106). While the Christian Timucua may no longer remember these acts, they continue to exist in Pareja's writing and in Oré's citation of Pareja. Perhaps the major irony is that the acts Pareja, as well as many other Franciscans, find the most objectionable are also those they end up recording the most completely.

In an interesting twist, though, Pareja's testimony as given by Oré also presents one of the best examples of inculturation—respect for the dead being shown through offerings of food. While both Alonso de Jesús and Avila record this practice in order to condemn it, Pareja records it as a positive cultural practice well within the acceptable bounds of Roman Catholic theology. To the question of whether the converted Native Americans he has encountered are truly Christians, Oré gives as part of Pareja's response:

> They show great reverence for the dead, for not only the General Commemoration of the Dead[24] do they bring them an offering, such as pumpkins or beans or a basket of maize or a hamper of toasted flour, but also during the year they have Mass said for them with some offering of the afore-mentioned articles which they offer as an alms. On Monday, at the procession for the Departed Souls, they come to be present at it and to hear mass. (105)

What makes this example of inculturation fascinating, aside from the very different treatment Pareja gives to the same cultural practices that Alonso de Jesús and Avila believe need to be abolished, is that Pareja never indicates that the practices he describes are an instance of inculturation. Without knowing Alonso de Jesús and Avila's ethnographic descriptions, Pareja's audience would assume that the practices he describes come solely from a Christian tradition rather than from a blending of pre-Christian Native American cultural practices with Roman Catholic rites. Within his works, then, not only does Pareja best describe ethnographically those practices he would like to see abolished, but he suppresses the ethnographic importance of those practices which have been inculturated into Roman Catholic rites.

But perhaps the most interesting case of saving in writing the very thing that one wants to eliminate from the culture of *la Florida*'s Native Americans is Juan de Paiva's 1676 manuscript "Origen y principio del juego de pelota que los Indios Apalachinos y Yustacanos an estado jugando desde su infidelidad asta el año de 1676" ("Origin of the Game of Ball That the Apalachee and Yustagan Indians Have Been Playing Since Pagan Times Until the Year of 1676"). Paiva's description of the ball game played by the native peoples in what is today western Florida—similar to that played in pre-Columbian Mexico and by various peoples throughout the New World—uses as its framing device the local myth of how the ball game came into being. Because he describes not only how the game is played, but also the myth that gives the game ritualistic significance, Paiva's text is both one of the most complete extant descriptions of the game as a cultural practice and an interesting literary work. The very quality of Paiva's writing makes his attempt to discredit the ball game all the more attractive.

Reading even the opening lines of Paiva's manuscript illustrates this point. Paiva begins the work in this manner:

> In the pagan times of this Apalachee nation there were two chiefs, whose experiences I am going to recount, who in their [time of] blindness[25] lived close to one another as neighbors. One was named Ochuna nicoguadca, whom they say is Lightning Bolt. And the other Ytonaslaq, a person of banked fires. And in his understanding both [are] the names of demons, which they have held as such, especially Ytonanslalaq.
>
> The latter had an orphaned granddaughter named nico taijulo, woman of the sun. The leading men, who are those in charge of the place, the aldermen, as we would say, sent her out for water every day. She became pregnant in this employment and gave birth to a son and hid him among some bushes, where the panther, the bear, and the jay found him. And they brought him to Itonanslac,[26] his great-grandfather. (331)

The story goes on from there to tell how this child is raised and, upon reaching young manhood, is suspected by Ochuna Nicoguadca of being the man prophesied to kill him; therefore, Ochuna Nicoguadca gives the young man three dangerous tasks which appear impossible to fulfill, but which he actually does complete with the help of his great-grandfather, Ytonanslaq. Because the young man survives, Ochuna Nicoguadca realizes that he cannot kill the young man and orders that the ball game be played, a game that ends up being filled with rituals based on the young man's daring. The rest of Paiva's manuscript is taken up with describing how the ball game is played, emphasizing what Paiva calls the "abuses and omens and superstitions" behind every element of the game (338), from the way the pole is raised to the rules of "this bedeviled game" (340). Each of these practices in the ball game, including a few that are dangerous to the point of sometimes turning fatal, reflects an aspect of the story of the young man challenged by Ochuna Nicoguadca.[27]

The interesting feature of Paiva's storytelling style is that it mirrors what we would recognize today as the oral storytelling style of much Native American literature. Especially in the manner that he presents the fantastic elements of the Apalachee myth as historical events—"She became pregnant . . . and gave birth to a son and hid him among some bushes, where the panther, the bear, and the jay found him. And they brought him to . . . his great-grandfather"—Paiva ends up giving credibility to the very myth that develops and transmits the belief system the friar is trying to discredit. While Paiva tells this story and describes the rules of the game in hopes that his superiors will recognize that "this game was invented by the devil" (349), in the process he ultimately gives the most complete extant description of this Apalachee ritual game.

Overall, then, the inclusion of ethnographic materials in Franciscan writing from seventeenth-century *la Florida* reflects the complex interaction of conversion, assimilation, and inculturation that occurred in the mission field. Among the most interesting features of these works, though, is the manner by which some of the texts being used to help explain the need to expunge various cultural acts from a newly Roman Catholic Native American society actually end up preserving those same acts. In this manner, what are set up as doctrinal and historical writings end up serving equally as well or better as ethnographic writings. In the wonderful way that writing often works, the ironic distance between the intended theme and the effective theme becomes a defining feature of many Spanish-language ethnographic works about Native Americans in seventeenth-century literature of southeastern North America.

Notes

Work on this project was begun as part of a 1993 National Endowment for the Humanities Summer Seminar on "Colonial North America: New Approaches to Its Hispanic Past," directed by David J. Weber of Southern Methodist University. A grant-in-aid from the Recovering the U.S. Hispanic Literary Heritage Project at the University of Houston greatly assisted with further work. I would also like to thank Fr. Capistran Hanlon, O.F.M., of Siena College for assisting me with materials concerning Franciscan missiology, the philosophy of mission work. Finally, many of these works are available in print only as English translations; therefore, for consistency, I have used English translations throughout, checking the translations against the Spanish originals whenever possible.

[1] David B. Quinn indicates that the word used here is *doutrinas*, a variant (or misspelling?) of the word *doctrinas*. *Doctrinas* were missions set up with resident friars as opposed to *visitas*, missions set up without resident friars but which a friar would regularly visit. The missionaries used the *doctrinas* to instruct Native Americans in religious doctrine, thus the name.

[2] Modern-day Saint Augustine, Florida.

[3] Two good short overviews of the mission projects aimed at converting the Native Americans of *la Florida* to Roman Catholicism are Chapter Four, "Christianizing the Indians," of Charlton W. Tebeau's *A History of Florida* (43-56) and Jerald T. Milanich's "Laboring in the Fields of the Lord." On the seventeenth-century missions in particular, see Charles W. Spellman, "The 'Golden Age' of the Florida Missions, 1632-1674." A good overview that places the Franciscan missionary work of *la Florida* within the context of Roman Catholic missionary work and Spain's exploits throughout North America is David J. Weber's *The Spanish Frontier in North America*, espe-

cially Chapters 4 and 5, "Conquistadors of the Spirit" and "Exploitation, Contention, and Rebellion" (92-146).

[4] Very little has been written about Native American literacy in the Spanish colonies of what is now the United States. However, there are sources that indicate such learning went on. Mention of Native American Spanish literacy in *la Florida* dates to at least 1630, at which time Francisco Alonso de Jesús mentions in his "Memorial" that many of the native peoples who have been baptized also know how to read and write (100). As for examples of Native American writings, the earliest works now available in print are from the late seventeenth century. In 1699, Patricio Hinachuba, the leader of the Apalachee town of Ivitachuco, wrote at least two letters, one authored with Andrés Usunaca, the leader of the town of San Luis, addressed to the King of Spain, and one to Antonio Ponce de León, a chaplain at *San Augustín* (Boyd, Smith, and Griffin 24-27).

At least two historians of *la Florida* cite documentary materials written by Native Americans of the region during the seventeenth century. See Amy Bushnell's "Patricio de Hinachuba: Defender of the Word of God, the Crown of the King, and the Little Children of Ivitachuco" and "Ruling 'the Republic of Indians' in Seventeenth-Century Florida" as well as John H. Hann's *Apalachee: The Land between the Rivers.* Additionally, there are records of mission schools in *Nuevo México*, the other major seventeenth-century Spanish colony in what is now the United States (Gallego 21).

[5] The theory of inculturation continues to be an important part of modern Franciscan missiology; in fact, the very term *inculturation* is a contemporary one and is applied a bit anachronistically to pre-twentieth-century missiology. For a good overview of how contemporary Franciscan missiology explains inculturation, see Hermann Schalück's *"To Fill the Whole Earth with the Gospel of Christ": The Minister General to the Friars on Evangelization: From Tradition to Prophecy.* Among the most interesting ideas that Schlück presents is that Jesus Christ, by becoming flesh in the Incarnation, left heaven and used inculturation to preach the gospel on earth (41). Schalück's definition of inculturation states that the process "involves much more than simple adaptation to the style of life, speech, dress, dwelling and food of a particular region or culture." Instead, he says, "What it does involve is a process of rooting, insertion and incarnation which will enable the local culture [to] share in the process of evangelization, starting from its own cultural roots, identity and ethos" (41).

A continuing example of inculturation begun during the seventeenth century can be found in the western United States where within some of the Pueblo peoples' villages (Zuñi, Hopi, etc.), Roman Catholic churches are decorated on the inside with not only European religious iconography, but with paintings of Kachinas, figures depicting traditional Pueblo spirits.

[6] John H. Hann, the work's translator, inserts *músicos* in brackets after

"song" to indicate the original Spanish word. Hann and Albert S. Gatschet, whose translations of Francisco de Pareja's combined linguistic and doctrinal works are used below, insert the original Spanish word following translations that might have more than one reading; however, I have replaced all such parenthetical insertions with notes.

[7] Hann inserts *atavales*.

[8] Hann inserts *con toda proporción*.

[9] Hann inserts *mismo concierto*.

[10] Hann inserts *muy largos y prolijos*.

[11] The square brackets are Hann's own.

[12] Hann inserts *lastimosa*.

[13] *Cacique*: chief.

[14] Hann inserts *molledos de los brazos y muslos*.

[15] All citations from Oré's *Relación* are given from the Maynard Geiger translation. The only modern Spanish-language edition of the work is that edited by Atanasio López, against which Geiger's translations have been compared.

[16] The full title of Oré's *Relación* shows the ecumenical breadth of his work, at least within the Roman Catholic church: *Relacion de los martires qve a avido en las Prouincias de* la Florida; *doze Religiosos de la Compañia de IESVS, que padecieron en el Iacan, y cinco de la Orden de nuestro Serafico P. S. Francisco, en la Prouincia de Guale. Ponse asi mesmo la discripcion del Iacan, donde se an fortificado los Ingleses, y otras cosas toca[n]tes a la conuersion de los Indios,* which translates into English as *Relation of the Martyrs that Have Been in the Provinces of* la Florida, *Twelve Religious of the Company of Jesus, that Suffered in Jacan, and Five of the Order of Our Seraphic F[ather] S[aint] Francis, in the Province of Guale. Also Given is the Description of Jacan, Where the English Have Fortified Themselves, and of Other Things Touching on the Conversion of the Indians.* The Jacan mentioned in the title is a mission the Jesuits established in the Chesapeake Bay region of what is now Virginia and the English fort is most likely Jamestown.

[17] Oré's term is *gamucilla vieja* (1:97), which more literally than Geiger's "small coat" means "old chamois shirt."

[18] Oré's word is *fiestas*, which implies as much a celebration as a show (1:98).

[19] *Macana*: Oré has defined this Guale word earlier in his text as "a stone hatchet" (73).

[20] It is interesting that Pareja and Juan de Paiva, who will be discussed below, identify their ethnographic writing with specific groups of native Americans in *la Florida* while Alonso de Jesús and Oré do not. The effect is that Alonso de Jesús and Oré create images of a monocultural Native America while Pareja and Paiva develop the possibility of a multicultural Native

America. Oré describes many different groups, from the Algonquin people of what is now Virginia to the Guale, Timucua, and others of what is now Florida and Georgia. It is most likely that Alonso de Jesús uses the Timucua as his main model, though it may have been the Guale. Alonso de Jesús describes and delineates practices from different cultures; however, he does not identify any of the cultural groups by name.

[21] This translation, and perhaps the original Spanish, are clearly awkward here, a regrettable necessity: All quotations from Pareja's linguistic and doctrinal works come from Gatschet's two articles, both titled "The Timucua Language." The only modern edition of Pareja's doctrinal writing is *Francisco Pareja's 1613* Confessionario*: A Documentary Source for Timucuan Ethnography*, translated by Emilio F. Morán and edited by Jerald T. Milanich and William C. Sturevant. However, while it contains facsimile pages and transcriptions of the Spanish/Timucuan edition of Pareja's 1613 work along with English translations of the facsimile pages, the complete *Confessionario* is not included. Gatschet is used here because he includes selections from Pareja that the Milanich and Sturevant edition does not, though knowing how literal Gatschet's translations are is difficult for while he gives the original Timucuan for each question and response, he gives the English translation without the original Spanish.

[22] Gatschet inserts *de tortas ó gacha.*

[23] Gatschet inserts *en las palmas de la casa.*

[24] The Commemoration of All Souls, November 2 (Geiger's note).

[25] *Time of blindness*: before their conversion to Roman Catholicism. All square brackets in this selection are Hann's own. The unusual capitalizations and multiple variant spellings of names are from Hann's translation.

[26] A variant spelling of *Ytonanslaq.*

[27] Good sources on the ball game are Hann's *Apalachee: The Land between the Rivers*, in which Hann's translation of Paiva's manuscript appears, and Amy Bushnell's "'That Demonic Game': The Campaign to Stop Indian Pelota Playing in Spanish Florida, 1675-1684."

Works Cited

Alonso de Jesús, Francisco. "1630 Memorial of Fray Francisco Alonso de Jesús on Spanish Florida's Missions and Natives." Trans. John H. Hann. *The Americas* 50 (1993): 855-105.

Bede. *A History of the English Church and People*. Trans. Leo Sherley-Price. Rev. by R. E. Latham. Middlesex, UK: Penguin, 1968.

Boyd, Mark F., Hale G. Smith, and John W. Griffin. *Here They Once Stood: The Tragic End of the Apalachee Missions*. Gainesville: University of

Florida, 1951.

Bushnell, Amy. "'That Demonic Game': The Campaign to Stop Indian Pelota Playing in Spanish Florida, 1675-1684." *The Americas* 35 (1978): 1-19.

———. "Patricio de Hinachuba: Defender of the Word of God, the Crown of the King, and the Little Children of Ivitachuco." *American Indian Culture and Research Journal* 3.3 (1979): 1-21.

———. "Ruling 'the Republic of Indians' in Seventeenth-Century Florida." *Powhatan's Mantle: Indians in the Colonial Southeast*. Ed. Peter H. Wood, Gregory A. Waselkov, and M. Thomas Hately. Lincoln: University of Nebraska, 1989. 134-50.

Considine, John Joseph, ed. *The Missionary's Role in Socio-Economic Betterment*. Proc. of the Fordham-Rural Life Socio-Economic Conference, Maryknoll Seminary, 1958. Westminster, Md.: Newman, 1960.

Gallego, Bernardo P. *Literacy, Education, and Society in New Mexico, 1693-1821*. Albuquerque: University of New Mexico, 1992.

Gatschet, Albert S. "The Timucua Language." *Proceedings of the American Philosophical Society* 16 (1876-77): 626-43.

———. "The Timucua Language." *Proceedings of the American Philosophical Society* 17 (1877): 490-505.

Hann, John H. *Apalachee: The Land Between the Rivers*. Ripley P. Bullen Monographs in Anthropology and History 7. Gainesville: University of Florida–Florida State Museum, 1988.

Ibarra, Pedro de. "April 12, 1604. Pedro de Ibarra to Philip III." *New American World: A Documentary History of North America to 1612*. Ed. David B. Quinn. Vol. 5. New York: Arno P. and Hector Bye, 1979. 105-106.

Milanich, Jerald T. "Laboring in the Fields of the Lord." *Archaeology* 49.1 (Jan.-Feb. 1996): 60-69.

Oré, Luis Gerónimo de. *The Martyrs of Florida (1513-1616)*. Trans. Maynard Geiger. Franciscan Studies 18. New York: Joseph F. Wagner, 1936.

———. *Relación histórica de la Florida, escrita en el siglo XVII*. 2 vols. Ed. Atanasio López. Madrid: Ramona Velasco, 1931.

Paiva, Juan de. "Origin of the Game of Ball That the Apalache and Yustagan Indians Have Been Playing Since Pagan Times Until the Year of 1676 [Origen y Principio Del Juego De Pelota Que Los Indios Apalachinos y Yustacanos an Estando Jugando Desde Su Infidelidad Asta El Año De 1676]." Trans. John H. Hann. Hann 331-53.

Pareja, Francisco de. *Confessionario en lengua Castellana y Timuquana*. Mexico: Diego Lopez Davalos, 1613.

——— .*Francisco De Pareja's 1613* Confessionario: *A Documentary Source for Timucuan Ethnography*. Trans. Emilio F. Moran. Ed. Jerald T. Milanich and William C. Sturevant. Tallahassee: Division of Archives, History, and Records Management, Florida Department of State, 1972.

————. *Catecismo de la doctrina cristiana en lengua Timuqua* . . . . Mexico: n.p., 1617.

————. *Catecismo en lengua Castellana, y Timuqua, en el qual se contiene lo que se les puede enseñar a los adultos que han de ser baptizados*. Mexico: La Viuda de Pedro Balli, 1617.

Schalück, Hermann. *"To Fill the Whole Earth with the Gospel of Christ": The Minister General to the Friars on Evangelization: From Tradition to Prophecy*. English Speaking Conference on the Order of Friars Minor, St. Louis, Missouri, 1996. N.p.: n.p., 1996.

Spellman, Charles W. "The 'Golden Age' of the Florida Missions, 1632-1674." *Catholic Historical Review* 51 (1965): 354-72.

Tebeau, Charlton W. *A History of Florida*. Rev. ed. Coral Gables, Florida: University of Miami, 1980.

Weber, David J. *The Spanish Frontier in North America*. New Haven, Conn.: Yale, 1992.

The Nogales Dispute of 1791-92:
Texts and Context[1]

Charles A. Weeks
St. Paul's School

In January, 1791, the Spanish captain general in Havana, Cuba, approved the establishment of a post on bluffs along the east bank of the Mississippi River some eighty-five miles north of Natchez.[2] The site, which had been called Walnut Hills by the English because of a stand of black walnut trees there, lay close to the mouth of the Yazoo River, the western end of what the Spanish regarded as the northern boundary of the Natchez District within the province of West Florida. On February 12, an expedition headed by Elias Beauregard, who had been appointed by the governor-general of Louisiana, Estevan Miró, to be the commandant of the new post, began the long trip up the Mississippi from New Orleans to begin work on the fort and other buildings.[3] By April work was well along.[4]

In May of the same year, the governor of Natchez, Manuel Gayoso de Lemos, to whom Beauregard was directly responsible, received a letter from two chiefs of the Choctaw Nation, Franchimastabé and Taboca, protesting what they described as an usurpation of lands belonging to the Choctaws and their "brothers" the Chickasaws. Written in English, the letter was short and blunt. Not only did it accuse the Spanish of taking the land by force, it said that it was not theirs to occupy, that fifteen villages "of our nation" wanted it, and that the Chickasaws and the Choctaws were united on this matter. They begged the Spanish to leave.[5]

What followed was a year of active diplomacy directed by Gayoso to sort out the issues in this conflict and resolve them. Such resolution came in May, 1792, during a lengthy congress in Natchez where Gayoso and the major native-American parties and their intermediaries agreed on a treaty of friendship that allowed the Spanish their post and made possible two more negotiations and treaties within a year that ceded additional land for another post and secured the confederation and alliance of important Indian nations in the Gulf South, thereby enabling the Spanish to move forward with other projects of frontier defense and the Indians to feel more secure before aggressive expansion coming from the newly independent United States.[6]

The documents that were generated by this conflict and provide its historical record contain evidence of a remarkably sophisticated culture of diplomacy that enabled the Spanish and the principal native-American groups to pursue interests and work out differences in a peaceful manner. Beginning with the arrival of the French in the region in the late seventeenth century and continuing with the British and the Spanish, this culture developed over the course of a century of commercial, social, and political interaction. The discussion that follows will provide a narrative context for these documents by reviewing the European encounter with this region and its peoples and highlighting the principal events of the Nogales episode. In addition, it will seek to identify some of the key features of a diplomacy that made possible peaceful resolution of conflicts such as this one, and, I hope, present a strong case for making these and other documents more accessible in bilingual form, so that more knowledge and better understanding can be had of an area dubbed the Spanish borderland by the early twentieth-century historian Herbert Bolton, a geographical and historical region that remains even today neglected in historical writing about the United States.[7]

The initial contact of Europeans and native-Americans in the area dates to the early sixteenth century and the arrival in the Gulf South of a number of Spanish exploring expeditions. The contact with natives was only initial, for the Spanish did not stay. For natives, however, it proved to be of great consequence, for disease bought by the Europeans inflicted havoc on their societies and influenced population decline, movement, and amalgamation. The best known of these contacts and the most important and violent at that time was the Hernando de Soto *entrada* of the early 1540s.[8]

A period of sustained contact began toward the end of the seventeenth century, and out of it emerged a culture of exchange that the Spanish endeavored to sustain after they became the dominant European powers in the region in the last quarter of the eighteenth century. Two developments mark the beginning of this contact: the incursion of English slavers from South Carolina, who, with the help of Chickasaw, Yamasee, and Creek allies, attacked the Choctaws; and the establishment of permanent French settlements along the Gulf coast and the Mississippi River following Sieur de La Salle's claim of the whole of the Mississippi valley for the French in the early 1680s. The French established posts along the Gulf coast including Mobile Bay and eventually the Mississippi River, building a fort in 1716 where present-day Natchez, Mississippi is located and founding New Orleans two years later. They remained the dominant European group until the end of the so-called French and Indian War in 1763, when they relinquished their holdings on the North-American continent to the British and the Spanish.[9]

During the American Revolution the Spanish took control of what the British had organized as the provinces of East and West Florida as a consequence of the successful military campaigns of the governor-general of Louisiana, Bernardo de Gálvez, between 1779 and 1781.[10] After the Treaty of Paris of 1783 ending the war and confirming these conquests, Spanish authorities began to forge close ties with the native-American groups, particularly the Choctaws, the Chickasaws, the Creeks, the Cherokees, as a way to secure their holdings and to provide a defense for the natives from pressures from the newly independent United States. Major congresses were held in Pensacola and Mobile in 1784 that produced treaties of friendship and commerce, and steps were taken to continue sustain an economy of trade that had begun during the French period and had come to assume economic and political significance for all parties.[11] In addition, the Spanish sent Diego de Gardoqui as its first minister to the United States to seek a treaty of commerce and to defend Spain's boundary claims and control over river traffic on the Mississippi.[12]

Successful diplomacy was recognized as a way to establish some kind of order in this region inhabited by diverse peoples, and for a short time it seemed that both the Spanish and natives were were succeeding in working out a stable political and economic order. Before I examine the elements of this diplomacy as revealed especially well in the documents of the Nogales controversy, some points should be made about the major native group with whom the Spanish dealt in this particular episode, the Choctaws. Even though throughout the negotiations the Choctaw leader repeatedly insisted that he would defer to the views of "the Chickasaw king," it was the Choctaws, their many chiefs, and the traders who had settled among them who played the major role.

It must be stressed that, although referred to in the documents as a nation, the Choctaws were no more than a loose confederation of chiefdoms or villages. Grouped into three broad divisions defined by cultural, geographical, and political ties, each village had at least one chief. Over all was a titular chief, who, as this episode amply demonstrates, had only limited power. These villages were centered in the watersheds of the Pearl, Tombigbee, and Pascagoula rivers. Their total population was about fifteen thousand at the middle of the eighteenth century. Allied with them were former enemies, the Chickasaws, a smaller group living in the northwestern part of the present state of Mississippi but similar socially and politically.[13]

In dealing with the Choctaws, the Spanish found that divisions among the Choctaws could work to their favor, but they realized that they had to understand and respect certain native cultural traditions and institutions. The Choctaws, along with other groups, may have allowed themselves to become dependent on the Europeans for goods, but Europeans, in turn, as this episode illustrates, had to know native culture, its practices and expectations, and its key leaders and their interests for successful diplomatic and other relations.[14] Such sensitivity facilitated the creation of a kind of cultural "middle ground" for all parties in this region, as it had in other parts of North America.[15]

A major cultural factor defining the diplomatic relation throughout this century of French, British, and Spanish contract was a gift-kinship system that assigned roles to mothers, fathers, and brothers unlike those with which Europeans were familiar. This system attached great value to generosity. Only imperfectly understood by Europeans early in the period, confusion sometimes resulted with respect to European perception of the roles of fathers and mothers and the use of those terms by the natives in diplomatic language. The father within the conjugal family, for example, had little authority over his children; rather, he was perceived as one who should be indulgent and kind toward his children.[16] The letters exchanged by Gayoso and various native leaders provide a good example of natives using the structure and language of this kinship system. The latter referred to Gayoso as "father" and themselves as "sons" or "children," and the Chickasaws as "brothers." Brothers of wives assumed far more important and active roles with regard to the children of those wives than did the fathers. It is uncles who usually merited deference, not fathers.

The language of kinship and the generous use of gifts were two components of a culture of diplomacy that emerged over a century of contact.[17] Gayoso's letters to native chiefs reflect an understanding of both, and he tried to use them to his benefit. He knew the importance of gifts and the generosity they symbolized; they kept the diplomatic machinery running smoothly. He and his adjutant made every effort to reassure the natives with whom they dealt that there were gifts available for them in Natchez or in New Orleans, and he constantly requested his superior in New Orleans to send gifts to have on hand for visiting Choctaws or Chickasaws. He won great favor among the native chiefs and essentially convinced any doubters among them during the Natchez congress of May, 1792, by giving them the keys of the royal warehouse and including in the final treaty a statement that "he [the governor] hands over at the present time to the mentioned chiefs the keys to these royal warehouses in which the goods are [stored] so that they may take from them whatever they wished to be satisfied."[18] In addition, his willingness to take "sons"—in fact, they may have been nephews—of the Choctaw chiefs to further their education marked an innovation in European-native relations in the region and contributed significantly to his high status among native counterparts, so much so that during the Nogales congress of 1793, during which a treaty of confederation among the Spanish and the principal native groups in the Gulf South was approved, Gayoso was enthusiastically proclaimed "King of the Choctaws."

Another significant aspect of this diplomatic relationship was trade and the role of traders as intermediaries. From the very beginning, when the French began to settle, an exchange economy emerged. The English in the late seventeenth century, as mentioned above, had established contact with the Chickasaws and the Choctaws and tried to manipulate both in their quest for slaves to send back to the Atlantic coastal region. More important, the French along with the English developed a substantial commerce in deer skins, to such an extent that by the time of Spanish rule in the 1780s the deer population had declined drastically, and native hunting parties were forced to cross over the Mississippi River in their search for game. Traders took up residence among the Choctaws and Chickasaws, acquired native sexual partners, and produced a significant number of children and thereby became a part of native society and played a major role in it.[19] The Spanish threatened their position by granting a monopoly on trade with the natives to a group of Scottish traders based in Pensacola and organized as the Panton-Leslie Company, which in time developed an interest in opening posts in such locations as Nogales. These conflicts provided an added dimension and challenge to the diplomatic process undertaken by Gayoso to construct the new military post.[20]

The conferral of patents and medals was a practice the French began as a way to acknowledge and even define political relationships. Both the British and the Spanish continued it as an important constituent of the diplomatic process. Whether or not a chief was a small or a great-medal chief, was something of considerable importance in conducting relations, and, as one of the final documents in this episode reveals, the granting of medals was a way for the Spanish to reward those chiefs who played a major role in achieving a peaceful resolution of the conflict.[21]

As in any diplomatic procedure, adherence to protocol in public meetings was also very important, yet it was balanced by attention to personal characteristics and interests. The diaries that Stephen Minor submitted to Gayoso at the conclusion of his two trips to the Choctaws and Gayoso's final report describe in detail meetings that were successful because they followed what had been established as protocol. Major meetings were conducted with great ceremony, enhanced by displaying such important symbols as flags and making use of a very important part of any native diplomatic encounter, the calumet and pipe. Seating arrangements reflected careful attention to the location of authority within groups, and speeches followed what by the 1790 was well-established and understood order and form. At the same time, however, private meetings and conversations occurred that allowed attention to very personal interests and even whims. Both Minor and Gayoso report instances of such informal and private encounters and deals in their reports.

With these general points in mind, we can now take a look at this episode that reveals so much about a way of life that heretofore has been so little known and understood. What lay back of the decision of the Spanish to establish a post at Nogales? A simple answer is the Yazoo affair and all it portended, an attempt by American land speculators to secure land along the east bank of the Mississippi River. In response to their interest and pressure, the Georgia assembly in early 1785 created a county called Bourbon on the east bank of the Yazoo River south of the thirty-first parallel, the line Americans regarded as the southern boundary of the United States.[22] Commissioners were sent by Georgia to organize a county government, and the land speculators secured company charters from various state governments. The one that focused particularly on

Bourbon County was the South Carolina Yazoo Company.[23]

For both natives and the Spanish these actions were clear evidence of a major political, economic, and demographic challenge to their land and future. Even before the overt challenge posed by the creation of a Georgia county, Spanish authorities had begun to develop policy and take action to strengthen their position in the Mississippi Valley. The two congresses of 1784 endeavored to lay the basis for good relations with Choctaws, Chickasaws, and others. Then in 1787, the government of the Natchez District was reorganized and strengthened and a governor appointed, Manuel Gayoso de Lemos, who had already gained considerable experience in the Spanish government and was fluent in English.[24] In addition, as this episode so amply demonstrates, he was a very skilled diplomatist. In addition, the Spanish worked with Americans who were moving west and south. Self-interest motivated these Americans much more than any kind of loyalty to the United States, and the Spanish and even natives were able to appeal to this motive to protect themselves or advance their own objectives.[25]

The governor-general of Louisiana used the Yazoo schemes as the occasion to request authority from his immediate superior, the captain general in Havana, Cuba, to move. He even said that if the Yazoo schemes went forward before he got specific instructions, he would undertake the establishment of a fort and post at the mouth of the Yazoo River.[26] By January, 1791, authorization came; even before it, Miró issued instructions that individuals associated with the South Carolina Yazoo Company should not be allowed to settle in territory claimed by Spain.[27] By then Gayoso had already made a trip to the site that produced specific suggestions as to location and design of a post.[28] In this context, a letter to Gayoso from an American, John Williams, reported a plan by the South Carolina company to establish a settlement at Walnut Hills.[29] Miró appointed Elias Beauregard of the Louisiana Infantry to be the commandant of Nogales and on February 12 instructed him to depart for the site to begin work and "uniformly contribute to the respect for the territory of the King."[30] Gayoso arranged for supplies and appointed an interpreter for the post.[31]

Gayoso accompanied Beauregard, and the expedition arrived on April 1. Work began immediately.[32] Gayoso maintained a diary of the trip and stay, which he later submitted to Miró as a report. In it he described visits by Choctaws, both of which were friendly. The first included the chief, Itelagana, from the village of Boucfouca, and it provided an opportunity for Gayoso to try to impress the natives by taking the chief with him on a boat, going about a league upstream, and then on the return witnessing the firing of cannons and shouts of "Long live the King!" from the crew and from people on shore. A few days later, another group of Choctaws arrived, and, according to Gayoso, they presented themselves "with all the pomp of which they were capable and dancing the calumet," an important ritual symbolizing peace.[33]

Gayoso's gestures of hospitality and his efforts to impress the Choctaws failed to secure the support of some of their leaders, including Franchimastabé, the chief of the nation, for the project. The next month, the letter of Franchimastabé and Taboca protesting the Spanish enterprise arrived. Using the language of the native kinship system, the two chiefs established at the outset an important parameter of discussion, that of the Spanish governor as father (weak with respect to authority but nevertheless generous) and the natives as children: "I have heard that my Father, the Father of the Choctaws and the Chickasaws, without knowing the reason why takes our lands."[34] Gayoso suspected that the letter was probably written by some "white rogue" (*pícaro blanco*) living in the nation; nevertheless, he took it seriously, prepared a response, began to collect gifts, and decided to send his adjutant, Estevan Minor (Stephen Minor), who had come from Pennsylvania to Natchez during the American Revolution and remained, to carry the letter of response and determine the native's motives and concerns.[35]

Minor's trip began in late May and concluded in the middle of June. It was to be the first of two trips made to gather information, argue the Spanish case, and to lay the basis for the final congress and treaty. During this first trip, Minor was told that the British had never paid for the land, which the Spanish assumed was theirs by virtue of conquest and the treaties concluding the American Revolution. Encouraging the Choctaws in this view were traders living in their midst. These men were concerned that a Spanish post at Nogales would include a branch of the Panton-Leslie Company to challenge their commercial interests. One of them, Turner Brashears, Minor discovered, had written the letter sent by Franchimastabé and Taboca. Minor assured the Choctaws and those they described as their "brothers," the Chickasaws, that the Spanish governor desired no more than "to protect the land of his beloved red people so that it would not be taken by the Americans." The natives, as reported by Minor, remained adamant in their opposition; as a result, other matters were discussed and resolved, at least verbally, namely the theft of horses and slaves from the Natchez district and the movement of Natchez people without appropriate passports through the Choctaw Nation.[36]

Before Minor's next trip almost a year later, events moved in favor of the Spanish. Divisions within the Choctaw Nation surfaced as various chiefs visited Natchez to tell Gayoso that they supported the Spanish position. One was Itelagana, whom Minor identified in his second diary as a possible successor to Franchimastabé. The visits to Natchez were so numerous that Gayoso complained of the difficulty of dealing with so many people. Nevertheless, he acknowledged the need to be patient and always to have on hand gifts for the visitors.[37]

Still, opposition continued, the most important from Franchimastabé, convincing Gayoso of the need for another letter and trip by Minor. While he was visiting New Orleans in January, 1792, to greet and confer with the new governor-general, François Luis Hector, Baron de Carondelet, Franchimastabé and a number of both great and small medal chiefs accompanied by some eighty men and women arrived in Natchez to protest the establishment of the post.[38] Upon his return Gayoso prepared two letters apologizing for his absence. Addressed to "my dear friend and brother Franchimastabé and to Tascahetuca, usually referred to in the documents as "The King of the Chickasaws," the governor expressed both his great affection and that of the King of Spain for the native peoples and asked that unity be maintained among the Choctaws, Chickasaws, Talapuches (Creeks), Cherokees, and "other Indian nations that are in our vicinity." He extended to both Tascahetuca and Franchimastabé a welcome to Natchez but asked them to advise him in advance so that they could be received appropriately.[39]

Minor carried the letters and was given elaborate instructions outlining objectives and detailing procedures and the kinds of information he should try to secure about the natives: their population, the location of villages, and the white men living among them and extent of their influence. Above all, Minor was told to use all of the resources at his disposal to assure the natives of Spanish friendship and to tell them once again that the purpose of the fort was to help them defend their lands from incursions by the Americans.[40]

As reported in the second Minor diary, the trip was a success. Minor finally won the support Franchimastabé, in part by meeting with him privately and suggesting that it could be arranged that "the greater part of the gifts that are destined for the chiefs" could be appropriated by Franchimastabé without the others knowing. Franchimastabé, by now a skilled hand at dealing with Europeans, replied, "I always thought that at the end you would find the true path to my heart." The leaders of the Choctaws agreed to come to Natchez to conclude the whole matter by means of a treaty and, as always, accept gifts.[41] In response to continued opposition to commercial activity at Nogales, Gayoso ordered that all trade with the natives there be suspended and that Turner Brashears, whom Minor had identified as the white man having the greatest influence on Franchimastabé, be received there and treated well.[42] More opportunity for personal diplomacy on the part of Gayoso came that month when the Choctaw chief, Taboca, and his oldest "son" arrived in Natchez to spend several days in the governor's house and engage in lengthy talks.[43]

The culmination of the affair came in May with a congress in Natchez lasting several days. Gayoso's lengthy and detailed report provides a wealth of insight into the extent to which matters of protocol, language, generous use of gifts, and personal contact responded successfully to the needs and expectations of all parties. A treaty was prepared authorizing the Spanish to go ahead a build their post. Although nothing was said about it in the treaty document, an understanding was reached whereby the Choctaws and the Chickasaws could continue to use that land in conjunction with their hunting interests. In addition, it clarified boundaries between the Choctaw, Chickasaw nations and the Spanish Natchez District, and in three articles it stipulated that the Spanish would provide the natives with substantial gifts, including the privilege of taking from the royal warehouses "whatever they wished to be satisfied" and that the Choctaw and Chickasaw nations would be "constant friends of the Spanish Nation."[44]

Further successes came the next year, with yet another major gathering, this time at the new post of Nogales. The Treaty of Nogales of 1793 brought about a confederation of the Spanish, the Choctaws, the Chickasaws, the Creeks, the Cherokees, the Alibamones, and the Talapuches, that might have evolved into a successful form of confederation government binding together natives and Spaniards.[45] Instead, in 1795 Spain gave up her claim to much of this region in the Treaty of San Lorenzo with the United States, and the course of history, particularly for natives, took a decided turn for the worse.[46]

Notes

[1] The texts selected for this project, which was supported in 1996 by a grant from the Recovering the U.S. Hispanic Literary Heritage Project, translated by Professor Sarah J. Banks of Jackson State University, annotated and introduced by Charles A. Weeks, were: (1) Diary of Gayoso's Trip to Nogales (Manuel Gayoso de Lemos to Estevan Miró, Natchez, May 10, 1791, Archivo General de Indias [hereafter cited as AGI], Papeles procedentes de la Isla de Cuba [hereafter cited as PC], legajo [hereafter cited as leg.] 2352, #84); (2) Letter of Franchimastabé and Taboca to Gayoso (Franchimastabé and Taboca to Manuel Gayoso de Lemos, May 14, 1791, AGI, PC, leg. 2352); (3) Letter of Gayoso to Franchimastabé and Taboca (Manuel Gayoso de Lemos to Franchimastabé and Taboca, May 28, 1791, AGI, PC, leg. 41, #108); (4) Diary of Minor's First Mission to the Choctaws (Estevan Minor to Manuel Gayoso de Lemos, Natchez, June 13, 1791, transcript copy, Mississippi Department of Archives and History [hereafter cited as MDAH], Mississippi Provincial Archives, [hereafter cited as MPA], Spanish Provincial Transcripts [hereafter cited as SPT], vol. III, 715-39); (5) Gayoso to Franchimastabé, March 12, 1792, Archivo Histórico Nacional [hereafter cited as AHN], Estado, leg. 3885bis, expediente [hereafter cited as exp.] 7; (6) Diary of Minor's Second Trip to the Choctaws (Diario que executó Don Estevan Minor Ayudante de la Plaza de Natchez en el viaje que acaba de hacer por comisión a la Nación Chacta) Natchez, April 3, 1792, AHN, Estado, leg. 3898, exp. 5); (7) Franchimastabé to Gayoso, Choctaw Nation, March 28, 1792, AHN, Estado, leg. 3898, exp. 5, #2, copia; (8) Gayoso to Tascahetuca, Natchez, March 28, 1792, AGI, PC, leg. 2353; Gayoso's Account of the Natchez Congress (Manuel Gayoso de Lemos to Baron de Carondelet, Natchez, May 29, 1792, AHN, Estado, leg. 3898, exp. 5); (9) The Natchez Treaty (Treaty of Friendship

Between the King of Spain and Tascahetuca, King of the Chickasaws, and other Indian Chiefs, Natchez, May 14, 1792, AHN, Estado, leg. 3885bis and leg. 3898, exp. 5).

[2] Manuel Gayoso de Lemos to Estevan Miró, Natchez, Feb. 1, 1791, AGI, PC, leg. 41. Hutchins, Thomas. *An Historical Narrative and Topographical Description of Louisiana and West Florida. A Facsimile Reproduction of the 1784 edition*, intro. and index by Joseph G. Tregle, Jr. Gainesville: Florida, 1968. 53. Elliott, Jack D. "The Fort at Natchez and the Colonial Origins of Mississippi." *The Journal of Mississippi History* 52 (Aug. 1990): 183-84.

[3] Estevan Miró to Elias Beauregard, New Orleans, Feb. 12, 1791, AGI, PC, leg. 17.

[4] Manuel Gayoso de Lemos to Estevan Miró, Natchez, Aug. 9, 1791, AGI, PC, leg. 41.

[5] Franchimastabé and Taboca to Manuel Gayoso de Lemos, Choctaw Nation, May 14, 1791, AGI, PC, leg. 2352; trans. and copy enclosed with Manuel Gayoso de Lemos to Estevan Miró, Natchez, May 28, 1791, AGI, PC, leg. 41. See a discussion of the importance of kinship terms in diplomatic language: Galloway, Patricia. "'The Chief Who is Your Father': Choctaw and French Views of the Diplomatic Relation," *Powhatan's Mantle: Indians in the Colonial Southeast*. Ed. Peter Wood, Gregory W. Waselkov, and M. Thomas Hatley. Lincoln: Nebraska, 1989. 254-78.

[6] Gayoso set down on paper his reactions to the negotiation and recommendations for policy in an essay entitled "Political Condition of the Province of Louisiana." *Louisiana Under the Rule of Spain, France, and the United States. Social, Economic, and Political Conditions represented in the Louisiana Purchase as portrayed in hitherto unpublished contemporary accounts by Dr. Paul Alliot and various French, English, and American Officials*. Trans. ed. and annotator: James Alexander Robertson. 2 vols. Cleveland, 1911. vol. 1. 271-89. See also Holmes, Jack D. L. "Spanish Policy Toward the Southern Indians in the 1790s." *Four Centuries of Southern Indians*. Ed. Charles Hudson. Athens: Georgia, 1975. 65-82.

[7] Two volumes of Spanish documents for this period and place were compiled early in the century by Serrano y Sanz, Manuel. *Documentos históricos de La Florida y La Luisiana Siglos XVI al XVIII*. Madrid: 1912. *España y los indios cherokis y chactas en la segunda mitad del siglo XVIII*. Sevilla: 1916. Lawrence Kinnaird translated and edited a collection in the 1940s. *Spain in the Mississippi Valley, 1765-1794. Annual Report of the American Historical Association for the Year 1945*. 4 vols. Washington, D. C: U. S. Government Printing Office, 1946-47. For the original discussion of the borderland concept, see Bolton, Herbert. *The Spanish Borderland: A Chronicle of Old Florida and the Southwest*. New Haven: Yale, 1921 and a more recent elaboration in Weber, David J. *The Spanish Frontier in North America*. New Haven: Yale, 1992.

[8] The terms "initial," "marginal," and "sustained" are useful terms to distinguish the character of the major chronological divisions of the European encounter with America in this region before 1800: 1492-1541, 1541-1699, 1699-1800. Galloway, Patricia, ed. *Native, European, and African Cultures in Mississippi 1500-1800.* Jackson: MDAH, 1991. Galloway, Galloway. "The Emergence of Historic Tribes in the Southeast," *Ethnic Heritage in Mississippi.* Ed. Barbara Carpenter. Jackson: University Press of Mississippi, 1992. 21-44. Henry Dobyns, *Their Number Became Thinned.* Knoxville: Tennessee, 1983. Galloway, Patricia. *Choctaw Genesis.* Lincoln: Nebraska, 1995. 137-43. Duncan, David Ewing, *Hernando de Soto: A Savage Quest in the Americas.* Norman: Oklahoma, 1996. 215-84.

[9] *Fleurs de Lys and Calumet: Being the Pénicault Narrative of French Adventure in Louisiana.* Ed. and trans.: Richebourg Gaillard McWilliams. Baton Rouge: Louisiana State University Press, 1953. 159. *La Salle and His Legacy: Frenchmen and Indians in the Lower Mississippi Valley.* Ed.: Galloway, Patricia. Jackson: University Press of Mississippi, 1982.

[10] Caughey, John Walton. *Bernardo de Gálvez in Louisiana 1776-1783.* Berkeley: University of California, 1934. 135-214.

[11] Estevan Miró to Martín Navarro, New Orleans, April 15, 1784, AGI, Audienca of Santo Domingo (hereafter cited as SD), leg. 2611, #216; Martín Navarro to José de Gálvez, New Orleans, April 16, 1784, AGI, SD, leg. 2611, #216; Artículos de convenio, trato y pacificación estipulados y acordados por la Nación Española con los Indios Talapuches en el Congreso celebrado con este objeto en la Plaza de Panzacola Capital de la Florida Occidental, en los días treinta y uno de Mayo, y primero de Junio de mil setecientos ochenta y cuatro, AGI, SD, leg. 2611, #239.

[12] Cava Mesa, María Jesús y Begoña Cava Mesa. *Diego María de Gardoqui. Un bilbaíno en la diplomacia del siglo XVIII* (Bilbao, 1992); Whitaker, Arthur Preston. *The Spanish-American Frontier: 1783-1795: The Westward Movement and the Spanish Retreat in the Mississippi Valley.* Lincoln: Nebraska, 1969.

[13] Galloway, Patricia. "Choctaw Factionalism and Civil War, 1746-1750," *The Journal of Mississippi History*, 44 (Nov., 1982): 289-327; "'So Many Little Republics': British Negotiations with the Choctaw Confederacy, 1765," *Ethnohistory*, 41 (Fall, 1994) 513-37. Hutchins. *Historical Narrative and Topographical Description*, 54. Holmes, Jack D. L. "The Choctaws in 1795," *Alabama Historical Quarterly*, 30 (Spring, 1968): 33-49. St. Jean, Wendy. "Chickasaws: Firm Friends of the English?", *The Journal of Mississippi History*, 68 (Winter, 1996): 345-58.

[14] Richard White describes in detail a "play-off" system that the Choctaws used to deal with the newcomers: *The Roots of Dependency: Subsistence, Environment, and Social Change among the Choctaws, Pawnees, and Navajos.* Lincoln: Nebraska, 1983. 34-69.

[15] The metaphor is Richard White's. See *The Middle Ground: Indians, Empires, and Republics in the Great Lakes Region, 1650-1815.* Cambridge: Cambridge University Press, 1991, especially 50–79.

[16] Galloway, "'The Chief Who is Your Father.'"

[17] An early assessment of the importance of gifts by a new Spanish governor came in the context of the transfer of Louisiana by the French to the Spanish in the 1760s. Antonio de Ulloa to Marqués de Grimaldi, New Orleans, March 9, 1766, AGI, SD, leg. 2585.

[18] Manuel Gayoso de Lemos to Baron de Carondelet, Natchez, May 29, 1792, #86, copy. Annex to letter #3, Baron de Carondelet to Conde de Aranda, New Orleans, June 11, 1792, AHN, Estado, leg. 3898, exp. 5.

[19] Francisco Bouligny to Estevan Miró, Natchez, August 28, 1785, in Kinnaird. *Spain in the Mississippi Valley, 1765-1794. Post-War Decade, 1782-1791.* 143-45. Kidwell, Clara Sue. "Indian Women as Cultural Mediators." *Ethnohistory.* 39 (Spring, 1992): 102. See Usner, Jr., Daniel H., *Indians, Settlers, & Slaves in a Frontier Exchange Economy: The Lower Mississippi Valley Before 1783.* Chapel Hill: University of North Carolina Press, 1992 for a discussion of the economy that emerged in the lower Mississippi valley in the early eighteenth century.

[20] A history of the activities of this company is Coker, William S. and Thomas D. Watson. *Indian Traders of the Southeastern Borderlands. Panton, Leslie & Company and John Forbes & Company, 1783-1847.* Pensacola: Florida, 1986.

[21] Ewers, John C., "Symbols of Chiefly Authority in Spanish Louisiana," *The Spanish in the Mississippi Valley 1762-1804.* Ed.: John Francis McDermott. Urbana: University of Illinois Press, 1974. 272-84; Manuel Gayoso de Lemos to Baron de Carondelet, Natchez, May 29, 1792, AHN, Estado, leg. 3898, exp. 5, #4.

[22] "An Act Creating Bourbon County," Feb. 7, 1785. Kinnaird. *Spain in the Mississippi Valley, 1765-1794. Post-War Decade, 1782-1791.* 120-22.

[23] A significant collection of documents, many in Spanish and left untranslated, pertaining to the creation of Bourbon County was compiled by Edward C. Burnett and published as "Papers relating to Bourbon County, Georgia, 1785-1786," *The American Historical Review.* 15 (Oct. 1909 to July, 1910): 66-111, 297-353. See also Din, Gilbert. "War Clouds on the Mississippi: Spain's 1785 Crisis in West Florida," *Florida Historical Quarterly,* 60 (July, 1981): 51-76; *Francisco Bouligny: A Bourbon Soldier in Spanish Louisiana.* Baton Rouge, Louisiana State University Press, 1993. 141-56. See also Whitaker, *Spanish-American Frontier,* 122-39.

[24] Holmes, Jack D. L. *Gayoso: The Life of A Spanish Governor in the Mississippi Valley 1789-1799.* Baton Rouge: Louisiana State University Press, 1965. 49-50.

[25] James Wilkinson was perhaps the best-known. He advised the Spanish

as to activities of Yazoo speculators. James Wilkinson to Estevan Miró, Lexington, Ky., Jan. 26, 1790, AHN, Estado, leg. 3898, exp. 4.

[26] Estevan Miró to Domingo Cabello, New Orleans, May 19, 1790, AHN, Estado, leg. 3898, exp. 4.

[27] Luis de las Casas to Estevan Miró, Havana, Nov. 20, 1790, AGI, PC, leg. 1446.

[28] Manuel Gayoso de Lemos to Baron de Carondelet, Natchez, Jan. 17, 1792, AGI, PC, leg. 2352.

[29] John Williams to Manuel Gayoso de Lemos, Natchez, Jan. 16, 1791, enclosed in Manuel Gayoso de Lemos to Estevan Miró, Natchez, Jan. 17, 1791, AGI, PC, leg. 41.

[30] Estevan Miró to Elias Beauregard, New Orleans, Feb. 12, 1791, AGI, PC, leg. 17, #1.

[31] Manuel Gayoso de Lemos to Estevan Miró, Natchez, Feb. 13, 1791, AGI, PC, leg. 41, #12; March 12, 1791, AGI, PC 41, #41.

[32] Elias Beauregard to Estevan Miró, Nogales, April 7, 1791, AGI, PC, leg. 17, #5.

[33] Manuel Gayoso de Lemos to Estevan Miró, Natchez, May 10, 1791, AGI, PC, leg. 2353, #84.

[34] Franchimastabé and Taboca to Manuel Gayoso de Lemos, Choctaw Nation, May 14, 1791, AGI, PC, leg. 2352.

[35] Manuel Gayoso de Lemos to Estevan Miró, Natchez, May 28, 1791, AGI, PC, leg. 41, #108; Holmes, Jack D. L. "Stephen Minor: Natchez Pioneer," *The Journal of Mississippi History*, 42 (Feb., 1980): 17-26.

[36] Diario de Don Estevan Minor Ayudante de la Plaza de Natchez relativo a la comisión que el Señor Don Manuel Gayoso de Lemos, Gobernador de dicha Plaza la encargó para Franchimastabé Principal Jefe de la Nacióm Chacta, May 30 - June 14, 1791, enclosed with Manuel Gayoso de Lemos to Estevan Miró, MDAH, SPT, vol. 3, 715-39.

[37] Manuel Gayoso de Lemos to Elias Beauregard, Natchez, July 7, 1791, AGI, PC, leg. 41; Manuel Gayoso de Lemos to Baron de Carondelet, New Orleans, Jan. 17, 1792, AGI, PC, 2353;

[38] Carlos de Grand-Pré to Estevan Miró, Natchez, Jan. 31, 1792, AGI, PC, leg. 17.

[39] Manuel Gayoso de Lemos to Franchimastabé, Natchez, March 12, 1792, AHN, Estado, leg. 3885bis, exp. 7; Manuel Gayoso de Lemos to Tascahetuca, Natchez, March 21, 1792, AHN, Estado, leg. 3883. Reprinted in Serrano y Sanz, *Documentos históricos de La Florida y La Luisiana*, 414-15.

[40] Manuel Gayoso de Lemos to Estevan Minor, "Instrucciones," Natchez, March 13, 1792, AHN, Estado, leg. 3883. Reprinted in Serrano y Sanz, *Documentos históricos de La Florida y La Luisiana*, 414-15.

[41] "Diario que executó Don Estevan Minor Ayudante de la Plaza de

Natchez en el viaje que acaba de hacer por comisión a la Nación Chacta," Natchez, April 3, 1792, AHN, Estado, leg. 3898, exp. 5; AGI, PC, leg. 2352.

[42] Manuel Gayoso de Lemos to Elias Beauregard, Natchez, April 10, 1792, AGI, PC, leg. 41.

[43] Manuel Gayoso de Lemos to Baron de Carondelet, Natchez, April 19, 1792, AHN, Estado, leg. 3898, exp. 5. The word "hijo" as recorded here and in other documents may in fact mean nephew, given the nature of the Choctaw kinship system mentioned earlier.

[44] Manuel Gayoso de Lemos to Baron de Carondelet, Natchez, May 29, 1792, #86, copy, annex to letter #3, reserved, enclosed with Baron de Carondelet to Conde de Aranda, New Orleans, June 11, 1792, AHN, Estado, leg. 3898, exp. 5.

[45] Manuel Gayoso de Lemos to Baron de Carondelet, Natchez, Dec. 6, 1793, copy, AHN, Estado, leg. 3899, exp. 1; December 7, 1793, AGI, PC, leg. 42, #389; "Tratado de amistad, y garantía entre S.M.C. Rey de España y Emperador de las Indias, por una parte, y por la otra las Naciones Chicachas, Creek, Talapuche, y Alibamones, Cherokee, y Chactas, copy, enclosed with Luis de las Casas to Conde del Campo Alange, Havana, Jan. 9, 1794, SD 2563, #364.

[46] Whitaker. *Spanish-American Frontier*. 201-22.

Part IV

Identity and Affirmation: Contextualizing U. S. Hispanic Literature

Before the Diaspora:
Early Dominican Literature in the United States

Silvio Torres-Saillant
City University of New York
Dominican Studies Institute

I. Cultural Invisibility

The state of knowledge about the cultural life of Dominicans in the United States is dismal. Most reference publications that purport to account for the ethnic groups that make up the American people, including those dealing specifically with the Hispanic portion of the U. S. population, leave Dominicans out. Over four decades ago, a book titled *Spanish-Speaking People in the United States* made no mention of Dominicans. It focused on Mexican-Americans, Hispanos of New Mexico, Puerto Ricans, and Filipinos (Burma 1954). Nearly twenty years later, the Hispanic chapter of a guide to media and materials covering American ethnic minorities still omitted Dominicans, limiting the survey to Cubans, Puerto Ricans, and Mexican-Americans or Chicanos (King 1976: 189-239). In the same year, the bibliographic compendium *A Comprehensive Bibliography for the Study of American Minorities* carried a section entitled "From the Islands," which included the "Puerto Rican-American Experience" and the "Cuban American Experience" but said nothing of Dominican life in the United States (Miller 1976, II: 757 *et passim*). Still in the 1990s the place accorded to Dominicans in reference sources remained so meager that it seemed possible to compile a voluminous *Hispanic Almanac* covering virtually every field of endeavor and to give under five pages to Dominican personalities and events (Kanellos 1994).[1]

The invisibility of Dominicans in the reference sources seems difficult to explain in light of their numerical presence in the population of many cities in the Northeast. In New York, for instance, people from the Dominican Republic have outnumbered all other immigrant groups in their rate of arrival as well as in school enrollment and naturalization, evincing the community's desire to integrate into the larger American society. But, as has so often happened with disempowered communities in the United States, the wielders of cultural discourse have found it difficult to see Dominicans despite their massive presence.

The expression "out of sight, out mind" takes on a bitter turn when applied to Dominicans, who have remained generally "out of mind" even while being visibly "in sight". The complaint against the omission of Dominicans, particularly from literary histories, anthologies and compilations, has been articulated in public fora at least since the start of the 1990s (Torres-Saillant 1991:139-40). However, still in 1997 major panoramic vistas of U. S. Latino literature appeared, such as *The Latino Reader* (Augenbraum and Fernández Olmos 1997) and *The Hispanic Literary Companion* (Kanellos 1997), which failed to include a single Dominican literary figure.

II. The Literary Productivity of the Diaspora

At present excluding Dominicans from the literary history of U. S. Latinos seems hardly defensible given the visibility enjoyed for over a decade now by Julia Alvarez, a poet and fiction writer born in New York to Dominican parents in 1950. Alvarez spent her early childhood in her parents' homeland, where she attended Carol Morgan, an American school, coming back to New York in 1960, when the family felt the need to flee the Trujillo regime. For many years a resident of Middlebury, Vermont, Alvarez is a professor of English at Middlebury College. Her literary career began in full force in 1984 when Grove Press published her book of poems *Homecoming*, which garnered attention in the realm of American poetry. Combining narrative with lyrical verse, the volume features a speaker who searches for her identity as a woman through an exploration of her mother's teachings about the craft of housekeeping and through an understanding of the worldview informing her mother's culture. The last poem in the second section, "Orchids," explores the theme of the woman artist who achieves self-realization through her craft but loses touch with her creativity when marriage occurs. The second section of *Homecoming*, titled "33," uses the sonnet form to examine the angst of a childless, divorced woman, confronting solitude, sexual desire, the trials of womanhood in an androcentric world, and the awareness of aging.

Alvarez has continued writing verse, publishing *The Other Side* in 1995 and *Homecoming: New and Collected Poems* in 1996, both under Penguin Books. The importance attributed to her verse may be illustrated in her selection for inclusion in the exhibition "The Hand of the Poet," a display of "original manuscripts by 100 masters" at the New York Public Library. The second part of the exhibit, which displayed manuscripts of poets from E. E. Cummings to Julia Alvarez, remained open to the public from August 16, 1996 through February 15, 1997. Interestingly, her poetry had already received canonical treatment in a 1987 anthology, edited by Robert Bender and Charles Squier, entitled *The Sonnet: An Anthology*, which surveyed practitioners of the sonnet from Sir Thomas Wyatt in the English Renaissance to Julia Alvarez in contemporary American verse. But it was truly her fiction that propelled

Alvarez to the international plane she now occupies. Her first two books as a storyteller, *How the García Girls Lost Their Accents* (1991) and *In the Time of the Butterflies* (1994), became best-sellers. The third, *¡Yo!*, earned favorable reviews since it first appeared in 1997. The first was named Notable Book of 1991 by the *New York Times Book Review* and by the ALA, apart from receiving the PEN Oakland/Josephine Miles Award for excellence in literature. The second was nominated for the 1995 National Book Critics Circle Award. Alvarez's work has received national and international prizes, having been translated into other languages.

Coming a generation earlier than Alvarez, another Dominican writer who uses English as her medium of expression is Rhina Espaillat, who was born in La Vega in 1932, and came to this country in 1939. Though she writes primarily in English, she has retained her Spanish and has published poems in newspapers of the Dominican Republic. Espaillat studied at Hunter College, of the City University of New York. For her graduate work, she attended Queens College, also in New York City's municipal higher education system. After receiving her MA, she worked as an English teacher in the city's public high schools. Currently, she lives with her husband in Newburyport, Massachusetts. Though not well-known among Dominicans in the United States, probably due to her delaying the publication of her book-length texts until later in life, Espaillat has had some 280 poems published in literary magazines and journals.

At sixteen, Espaillat became the youngest member ever to have been inducted into the Poetry Society of America. Decades later, the Poetry Society of America would honor her twice, in 1986 and 1989, with its Gustav Davidson Memorial Award. The British magazine *Urbis* also gave her two awards (Fernández 1994: 79). In 1992 she published her collection of poems *Lapsing to Grace*, which includes her own line drawings as illustrations. The compilations and anthologies that have published Espaillat's poems include: *Looking for Home: Women Writing about Exile* (1990), *Sarah's Daughters Sing: A Sampler of Poems by Jewish Women* (1990), *A Formal Feeling Comes: Poems in Form by Contemporary Women* (1994), and *In Other Words: Literature by Latinas of the United States* (1994). Many of her poems evoke memories of childhood and wrestle with distant images of Dominican life, conjuring the complex interaction of contemporary poetic diction with often traditional forms.

The most striking literary development in the Dominican community in recent times has been the current stardom of Junot Díaz, an author who was born in Santo Domingo in 1969. He came to the United States at the age of seven, spending the rest of his childhood and his adolescence in New Jersey, where he attended high school and college. A graduate of Rutgers University, he went on to study at Cornell University's prestigious Creative Writing Program. When he left Cornell with a MFA degree in hand, he had already published a short fiction text in the prestigious literary magazine *Story*. Within a month, between the end of 1995 and the beginning of 1996, *The New Yorker* published two short stories by him. The January 15, 1996 issue of *Newsweek* carried a story on the "overnight success" of the young Díaz, celebrating his impressive "six-figure" contract with Riverhead Books, a division of Putnam, for a collection of stories and a novel. Stories by Díaz have earned inclusion in *The Best American Short Stories: 1996* (Houghton Mifflin Co., 1996) and in the *The Best American Short Stories: 1997*. Named a Notable Book of 1996 by the *New York Times Book Review*, the collection of stories *Drown* established Díaz as a vigorous new voice in American fiction.

Drown appeared in mid-1996, immediately earning the enthusiastic critical reception of reviewers in *The New York Times*, *The Village Voice*, *Publishers Weekly*, and even in fashion and entertainment magazines such as *Elle* and *Mirabella*. Showing a keen intellectual sensibility, the author of *Drown* delves piercingly into the Dominican chapter of the human experience. His characters, whether in the Dominican Republic or in their U. S. immigrant locus confront misery and uprooting. With an exceptional command of words, Díaz communicates emotions and states of mind through concrete images and vivid scenes. The grown ups in *Drown* vie with unfriendly destinies. Their children, diasporic creatures, have the awe of the American dream thrust upon them by their parents' despair. We come upon the stress inherent in the interaction between the individual and the collective that frames social identity.

Certainly, successful Dominican writers working in the United States do not abound. Few indeed have transcended the limitations inherent in the social marginality that has typified their community in general. The majority of Dominican authors write predominantly in Spanish for the virtually exclusive consumption of small literary circles in Dominican neighborhoods. These literary artists have practically no publication opportunities. They normally have to finance, supervise the production of, and distribute their own books. They have hardly any chance of becoming inserted in mainstream literary markets or at least of attaining a level of prestige outside of their immigrant enclaves. Yet, they have proven tenacious in their persistent dedication to their literary production and have continued to publish against all odds. A mere listing of the authors who in the 1990s have committed their poems, novels, and short fiction to print illustrates their dynamism: Carlos Rodríguez, Marianela Medrano, Alexis Gómez Rosa, Franklin Gutiérrez, Miriam Ventura, León Félix Batista, Rei Berroa, Juan Rivero, José Carvajal, Josefina Báez, Tomás Modesto Galán, Julio Alvarado, Maitreyi Villamán Matos, Norberto James Rawlings, Juan Torres, Teonilda Madera, Diógenes Abreu, Yrene Santos, Felix Darío Mendoza, Juan Matos, José Segura, Ynoemia Villar, and Dagoberto López, to name only the most active. Whether or not their works prove enduring, the community will remain in their debt for assuming the task of bearing witness to the traumatic immigrant experience of their people.

The glaring exception to the fate of literary works written in Spanish by writers from the Dominican community is the remarkable case of Viriato Sención's *They Forged the Signature of God* (1995) published in English by the Connecticut-based publisher Curbstone Press. The Spanish edition, *Los que falsificaron la firma de Dios,* written by Sención in the South Bronx, broke the Dominican Republic's sales records in the country's literary history since it appeared there in 1992. Dominican readers, including people who had shown no interest in literature before, took to the bookstores in massive numbers. A tale of intrigue, corruption, and deceit set in contemporary times, the novel features characters bearing an unmistakable resemblance with Rafael L. Trujillo and his political heir Joaquín Balaguer, the best known of the country's military chiefs, and Balaguer's influential relatives and associates, representing the whole gamut of the political scene in the Dominican Republic during the last decades. The novel shows the mendacity of the country's ruling class and government officials. Its indictment proved so biting that President Balaguer himself publicly supported the Minister of Education's decision to revoke the 1993 National Award for Fiction that a panel of experts had awarded to the work.

The English version of the novel, translated by Asa Zatz, has received noteworthy reviews in *Publishers Weekly*, *The Washington Post Book World*, *Choice*, and the *Latino Review of Books*, among others. During the 1996 presidential election in the Dominican Republic, *The New York Times* quoted various fragments from *They Forged the Signature of God* to illustrate the behavior of some of the contenders in the political contest. Sención wrote the novel after living in New York for nearly fifteen years. Though the book deals with political situations of the homeland, its scathing indictment of the Dominican power structure reflects a diaspora perspective in that inside the country such representation would be inconceivable in light of the government's virtual control of the media, the publishing industry, and the venues of intellectual discourse. It was arguably the distance from the native land that sharpened the author's memory and activated his critical sense. This book constitutes an important stage in the Dominican community's coping with the political events that caused its migration.

III. The Case for a New Chronology

Given the small place accorded by current Latino literary historiography to Dominican authors, despite the achievements of Alvarez, Díaz, Sención, and Espaillat, one can easily imagine the state of knowledge about U. S. Dominican writing prior to the settlement of large Dominican neighborhoods in Northeastern cities over last four decades. Indeed, the prevailing assumption appears to be that the cultural and artistic presence of Dominicans in this country is an all too recent phenomenon. Suffice it to mention a recent essay by the scholar William Luis on Cuban, Puerto Rican, and Dominican writing in the

United States written for Volume 2 of *The Cambridge History of Latin American Literature*. Luis begins his account of Puerto Rican writers with literary figures who visited but did not stay in the United States in the first half of the century, namely authors such as René Marqués and José Luis González (Luis 1990:538-39), just as he opens the Cuban part of his chronicle with prominent visitors such as José María Heredia (1803-1839), Cirilo Villaverde, and José Martí throughout the nineteenth-century. As Luis gets to Dominicans, however, he radically shortens the temporal reach of his account: "Dominicans are the most recent group of Hispanic Caribbean authors to write in the United States. The Dominican Republic and its writers have been marked by two important events: the end of the Trujillo dictatorship and the U. S. invasion of the island" (Luis 1996:554). Guided by that chronology, Luis naturally could only cite references to Dominican literary artists in the United States beginning in the mid-1970s.

However, the chronology adopted by Luis fails to account for a long history of interaction between Quisqueya and North America prior to the 1965 U. S. invasion. It is that interaction which explains the emergence of large Dominican settlements in this country. When one considers that background, which includes a legacy of political and also cultural exchange between the two sovereignties, it becomes possible to trace the literary activity of Dominicans in the United States back to the founding of the Dominican nation. Actually, prior to the proclamation of the Dominican Republic on February 27, 1844, Juan Pablo Duarte, the ideological architect of Dominican independence, spent time in New York, where, according to his sister Rosa, he studied English (Duarte 1994: 40). Duarte regularly produced verse, prose, and plays—some now lost, some still extant—and no evidence exists to rule out his having added to the bulk of his writings during his North American sojourn. It seems fit to conjecture, in other words, that Duarte did not refrain from writing during his stay in this country. But no conjecture is really needed to show the literary presence of Dominicans in the United States during the nineteenth century. Following the official beginning of the Dominican Republic as an independent state, the Dominicans who came to this side of the Atlantic were likely to have literary interests and aptitudes since they generally belonged to the educated class. They normally came from the ruling élite, which often made them indistinguishable from the literati. Illustrative of that interrelationship is the book entitled *Los próceres escritores* (Balaguer 1947), in which the author surveys the literary activities of most of the well-known political leaders in nineteenth-century Dominican history.

IV. U. S.-Dominican Relations

Contact between Dominicans and the United States began as soon as Santo Domingo's creole élite succeeded in implementing the juridical emancipation of their country—roughly two-thirds of the island known as Hispaniola—which had for the preceding twenty years been politically unified under Haitian rule. The leaders of the incipient nation-state found it necessary to seek the recognition of their neighbor to the North. The newly born republic urgently needed commercial and diplomatic credibility in order to meet the challenge of surviving in the world economic system. As a result, the Dominican government sent an emissary to Washington in December 1844, the same year of the independence, to secure the establishment of formal relations between the two countries. John C. Calhoun, then Secretary of State, espoused the recognition of the small Caribbean country (Welles 1966: 76). But nothing further happened because the issue had come up at the very end of President John Tyler's administration.

Tyler's successor, President James K. Polk, who came to the White House in March 1845, took some concrete steps. Polk's Secretary of State, James Buchanan, appointed a man named John Hogan as American agent in Santo Domingo and sent him there to assess the country. Two other American envoys would arrive there before the end of President Polk's term in office: Francis Harrison and Jonathan Elliot. In a letter to Secretary Buchanan, dated May 2, 1849, the American agent would report enthusiastically about a conversation with Dominican President Manuel Jimenes regarding the possibility of annexing the country to the United States. After Polk, virtually every new American chief of state—Zachary Taylor, Millard Fillmore, Franklyn Pierce, and James Buchanan—dealt in varying degrees with the need to articulate a policy toward the Dominican Republic. The administration of President Abraham Lincoln, immersed in the throes of a heart-rending internecine war, could not afford to tackle the Dominican question. However, the context of the war and the prevailing sense of national despair that ensued, created an emotional ambience that favored the enterprise of William Cazneau and Joseph Fabens, who hoped to make money by selling land to their troubled compatriots in the Dominican Republic. The two American adventurers, having obtained sizable land concessions from the Dominican government, set up an American colony in Santo Domingo and sought to promote migration to that country as an escape from the sorrows of the war and a safe pathway to prosperity and wealth.

After the war, President Andrew Johnson, upon the advice of Secretary of State William H. Seward, renewed the U. S. government's interest in the Dominican Republic. This time Washington had its eyes trained on the acquisition of Samaná Bay to install there a naval base that would serve to ward off the danger of European aggression in the Caribbean. Johnson even worked the Dominican question into his fourth annual message to Congress on December 9, 1868. At that point, on his way out, as it were, he plainly urged the annexation of Santo Domingo (Welles 1966: 355). This occurred less than twenty years after the Guadalupe Hidalgo Treaty (Feb. 2, 1848). The United States had not yet ceased to expand territorially. Thus, when President Ulysses S. Grant came to the White House, he embraced Johnson's exhortation with a vehemence that bordered on obstinacy. He sought by various means to deflect the opposition posed by given political sectors in the Dominican Republic and in the United States. Due to the effective challenge of vigorous voices in Congress, such as that of Senator Charles Sumner, Grant failed to receive congressional approval for the annexation of Santo Domingo to the U. S. territory. Pleading his case insistently with the legislature, he finally prevailed upon the Senate to authorize his appointing a Commission of Inquiry to visit Santo Domingo and prepare a report on the condition of the country for the benefit of the Congress. With the young Frederick Douglass as a recording secretary, the Commission featured three U. S. Senators: Benjamin F. Wade, Samuel G. Howe, and Andrew D. White, who would subsequently move on to serve as Cornell University's founding president.

The Dominican Republic did not become a territory of the United States. However, the decades that followed witnessed the growing influence of the Northern neighbor continuously and progressively on the country's economic, social, political, and cultural spheres. The United States by the end of the nineteenth century had become the predominant foreign influence in the nation, having displaced "European interests that had traditionally dominated Dominican commerce" (Moya Pons 1995: 272). The trend took a momentum of its own, and by 1905 Washington found it necessary to assume control of all fiscal transactions in the land via the establishment of a customs receivership under direct supervision by American officials. In 1916 the management of Dominican life by the United States escalated further, with the formal declaration of a U. S. military occupation whereby Washington would rule the small republic until 1924. When they withdrew after eight years of governing Dominicans, the occupying forces left a radically Americanized country. They had created many social and political institutions, including a National Guard, one of whose most clever graduates, Rafael Leonidas Trujillo, would perpetrate 30 years of the most ruthless tyranny against the Dominican people. The rest is history. Trujillo meets his death in 1961. Democracy raises its hopeful head in 1962. The old Trujillo oligarchy overthrows the constitutional government in 1963. The people revolt demanding democracy in 1965. The United States intervenes militarily to quell the popular uprising. And in 1966, the elusive Joaquín Balaguer, Trujillo's craftiest servant, becomes the President of the Republic. The great exodus of Dominicans to the United States thus begins, remaining unabated until the present day.

V. Nineteenth-Century Dominican Presence in the United States

The foregoing overview of U. S.-Dominican relations crams many decades into a few paragraphs merely to provide a historical framework within which it might appear reasonable to assert that there must have been a Dominican presence in the United States just as there was an American one in the Dominican Republic since 1844. When channels of communication between two countries open, the movement that follows normally occurs in both directions. One thinks, for instance, of Tomás Cocco y Alum, born in New Orleans, Lousiana in 1843, who settled in Puerto Plata, where he in time achieved distinction as a Dominican patriot. No less meaningfully, Federico Lithgow, born in Puerto Plata in 1842, had parents who were themselves natives of the United States. His father, Arturo Lithgow, came from Augusta, Maine, and his mother, Ana María Pellegrín, was a native of New Orleans (Rodríguez Demorizi 1963: 72, 173).

The United States was important to Dominican statesmen and entrepreneurs no less than Santo Domingo was to American ones. The North was a place where prominent Dominicans could come when expelled from their country by powerful political rivals. For instance, on June 13, 1866 we find the dictator Buenaventura Báez in St. Thomas writing to his brother Damián Báez and asking him to arrange a meeting for him in New York with some potential business associates (Rodríguez Demorizi 1969: 459). In a February 5, 1867 letter to a friend's daughter named Corinne, the exiled statesman speaks about his having just arrived in Curaçao from New York (p. 203). On December 25, 1875, writing from Curaçao to Damián Báez, the shrewd caudillo complains about his having been detained "in New York when I was there having my eye illness treated" (p. 465). But political rivalry was not the only motive for people from the Dominican Republic to venture across the Atlantic. A different example of a Dominican presence in the United States is suggested by Captain Jose Gabriel Luperón, the older brother of General Gregorio Luperón, probably the most venerated of nineteenth-century Dominican patriots. According to the testimony of his younger brother, Captain Luperón participated in the American Civil War on the side of the North and received from President Lincoln the rank of Captain: "He was," says the source, "the courageous soldier who cut the chain that had blocked the way of the North's naval vessels at the entrance of the Mississippi" (Rodríguez Demorizi 1963: 185).

The awareness that Dominicans traveled to the United States as political exiles or as individual talents in search of wider horizons in the nineteenth-century may help to overcome the faulty chronology that has hampered the dissemination of knowledge about the Dominican contribution to the U. S. Hispanic literary heritage. A modification of that chronology would put us closer to historical truth, enabling us to see a long Dominican literary presence in the United States prior to the massive immigration that began in the mid 1960s. I would venture to affirm, further, that the Dominican portion of the U. S. Hispanic literary heritage is ample and significant enough to warrant its inclusion in recovery efforts of the kind marshaled by Nicolás Kanellos at the University of Houston. In the sections ahead, I will simply try to map, in a necessarily schematic fashion, some of the areas of research that can prove fruitful for the scholar interested in reconstructing the thus far neglected Dominican presence in the United States prior to the formation of Dominican enclaves and in this country.

I would begin by looking closely at the Dominican presence in New York in connection with the independence movement of the Antilles. Dominicans were invariably at the center of the movement. We have the testimony of the most prominent Hispanic Caribbean thinkers Ramón Emeterio Betances, Eugenio María de Hostos, and José Martí themselves to support this affirmation. Once nineteenth-century Dominican Antilleanists are identified, one needs to examine their writings, including their correspondence, to isolate the portion pertaining to their stay in North America. A salient example is fiction writer and essayist Alejandro Angulo Guridi (1822-1906), who arrived in the United States in the 1840s and stayed here continuously until 1852. He became a U. S. citizen and had his second marriage in Charleston, Virginia. Subsequently, Angulo Guridi returned to the Dominican Republic, where he became reintegrated to political life, although he retained contact with North America. On December 31, 1863, he went to Washington as an assistant to Dominican Secretary of State Pablo Pujol. His pamphlet against the annexation of the Dominican land to the Spanish empire, *Santo Domingo y España* (1864), appeared in New York under a printer identified as "Imprenta de M.W. Siebert" (Vallejo Paredes 1995:65). Also, at that time he was "writing a lot in English" as a "correspondent for the *New York Herald* and the *Daily News,*" as he says in a letter dated March 10, 1865 addressed to Don Ulises Francisco Espaillat, an intellectual who would years later become President of the Dominican Republic (Rodríguez Demorizi 1963: 21-23).

Many prominent Dominicans came to the United States in the nineteenth century simply to comply with diplomatic assignments, as did General José Billini, Dr. José Caminero and the aforementioned Pablo Pujol, while others, like General Matías Ramón Mella, one of the three patriots generally recognized as founders of Dominican nationhood, used the U. S. territory as a stepping stone to return to their home country's political arena. Having been exiled to Liverpool by dictator Pedro Santana, Mella made his way back via the United States, from where he went to Puerto Rico, before reaching Santo Domingo in 1848 (Rodríguez Demorizi 1963:40-41, 203, 269). Still others succeeded at building alliances in the North American territory with Cuban and Puerto Rican counterparts who were also devoted to the cause of national liberation. In 1865 the Sociedad Democrática de los Amigos de América printed the pamphlet *Las Colonias españolas y la República Dominicana* penned by the Cuban nationalist Juan Manuel Macías. Founded by Macías, the Sociedad included the Puerto Rican physician José J. Basora and the Cuban novelist Cirilo Villaverde among its prominent members. By the same token, on December 15, 1870, the New York-based periodical *El Demócrata* featured a long obituary authored by Cuban patriot J.M. Ferregur in homage to one of the original leaders of the Dominican independence movement, Pedro Alejandrino Pina, who had died several months before. Ferregur's ardent appraisal highlighted not only Pina's devotion to Dominican causes but also his invaluable support of the Cuban struggle for independence which was consistent with the spirit of regional solidarity that characterized the typical attitudes of nineteenth-century Antillean leaders (Rodríguez Demorizi 1963:186, 259-60).

In addition to political motives, some nineteenth-century Dominicans had personal reasons for settling in the United States. I think, for instance, of Juan de Dios Tejada, a Dominican who in 1897 lived in New York where he occupied an appartment at 49 East 99th Street. Earlier that year, on traveling to Santo Domingo from New York, Tejada's beloved wife and four children had died in a shipwreck accident. Yet, despite his bereavement, he undertook to marry again only a few months after the tragedy. Mindful of the heavy baggage of reproach elicited by his action, he writes a letter on December 24, 1897 to Ramona Ureña, an old family friend, in a clear effort to plead for sympathy with someone whose moral judgement he fears or respects. In a telling passage, he gives the following rationale for rushing to remarry: "The life one leads here is pitiful or extremely risky for a man in my condition. I am still young, and in order to avert the cold dryness of an old bachelor or the unnatural temptations that here one is besieged by every minute, I decided to marry"/La vida aquí se hace penosa o en extremo expuesta para un hombre en mis condiciones. Soy joven aún, y con el objeto de evitarme la sequedad fría del solterón o las tentaciones bastardas que aquí a cada paso se presentan, me casé" (Tejada 1994: 281-83). The interest of Tejada's letter lies not only in that it presents us with the all too human drive to seek justification from others for decisions we have made on our own to satisfy ourselves, but also in that it documents the personal drama of an individual Dominican who had made his home in New York in the late nineteenth century.

IV. The Twentieth Century: The Henríquez Ureña Family

The twentieth century, of course, offers the most fertile ground for the excavation of Dominican literary artifacts buried in North American soil. At the very beginning of the century, one finds distinguished Dominicans who came to this country in pursuit of personal objectives, namely the Henríquez Ureña family. The young Pedro Henríquez Ureña and his brothers, upon completing their secondary education in their native city of Santo Domingo, traveled to New York on February 19, 1901. Their father, Francisco Henríquez y Carvajal, had sent them there for their college education. As he acknowledges in a 1902 letter to his son Pedro, their father wanted them to "become acquainted with the American spirit" before moving on to complete their graduate studies in Europe (Henríquez y Carvajal 1994: 291). During their stay in New York, the young men attended Columbia University and lived in the vicinity of the campus: 326 West 113ᵗʰ Street to be exact. They spent the whole month of August 1901 in Buffalo, New York, in the company of a Dominican writer from Puerto Plata named Mercedes Mota. In 1902, Pedro and his brothers received word from their father about the loss of his government position. His economic condition having thus changed, he could no longer afford to provide for them in New York and regretfully asked them to return home. However, with a temerity befitting their youth, the young men chose to stay and fend for themselves. Pedro got himself a sales job in a retail store, and his younger brother Max found a spot playing the piano in a restaurant. Pedro worked long hours, studied hard, and wrote assiduously (Lara 1975: 25).

It was arguably in New York that Pedro Henríquez Ureña, the Dominican literary figure with far the most international recognition, began writing regularly. In that respect, one could contend that it was in the context of his New York experience that he, devoid of paternal supervision and protection, made the serious decision to become a professional writer and literary scholar. Many of the earliest of Henríquez Ureña's extant compositions come from his New York years. The poems written in his youth appeared posthumously in a slim volume entitled *Poesías juveniles* (1949). The book includes 22 poems, out of which eight from the first and earlier half give New York as their place of composition. Written between 1901 and 1904, they appear in the following order: "Flores de otoño," "En la cumbre," which bears a dedication to the aforementioned Mercedes Mota, "Mariposas negras," "Intima," "Música moderna," "Frente a las 'Palisades' del Hudson," whose reference to New York could not be more obvious, "Ensueños," and "Escorzos." Not only did Henríquez Ureña affirm his commitment to writing at the time of these early poetic texts, but from his correspondence it becomes clear that in New York he and his brothers did not live in isolation from other important Dominicans. In a letter dated July 5, 1902 to his maternal aunt Ramona Ureña, he names many friends from his social circle back home, including writers, who were also in the city, some having paid him a visit already (P. Henríquez Ureña 1994: 289-90).

According to Pedro's testimony, they found "various Dominicans" upon arriving in New York: "the ex President D. Alejandro Woss y Gil, a man of subtle intelligence and good friend of my father as well as of my cousin Enrique, the Consul Leonte Vásquez, brother of the then Vice President Horacio; the students Floricel Rojas and *Niño* Alfonseca; that remarkable character Abelardo A. Moscoso, an energetic man, not entirely uncouth but of somewhat bizarre ideas and feelings on account of his long years of struggle in exile; and many more whom we had less to do with" (cited in Roggiano 1961: xiii). Pedro and his brothers frequented the libraries as well as the theaters of the city. As a regular feature of their social life, they also visited, in addition to educational and cultural institutions, "the hotels and houses that lodged the Dominicans who came to New York for their summer vacation, whose number increased every year" (Roggiano 1961: xxviii). The young men's decision to stay in New York provides us with a case of Dominican youths fending for themselves in the big city at the very beginning of the present century. In 1903 they ventured into renting their own flat, one located on West 15th Street in Manhattan, where other compatriots would board as well: Virgilio Ortea, a family friend who had come to New York "to work in commerce," and his brother Julio, whose parents had sent him so that he could "become Americanized" (Roggiano 1961: xxix). They lived in a neighborhood that "teemed with Dominican exiles who now increasingly headed for New York" (p. xxxi).

For the next decade Pedro and his brothers moved from New York to Cuba to Mexico to Cuba again. Only in 1914 did Pedro return to the United States. He went to Washington, first, as a correspondent to the newspaper *Heraldo de Cuba*, for which he wrote under the pen name E. P. Garduño. He kept his column until April 1915, when he relocated to New York to join the staff of the periodical *Las Novedades*, which the Dominican intellectual and entrepreneur Francisco José Peynado had founded there. Pedro wrote abundantly for *Las Novedades* until mid 1916 (Lara 1975: 38). New York at the time appears to have been a sight of much intellectual activity for many Dominicans who enjoyed positions of privilege. A letter from his father during Pedro's second sojourn in the United States refers to meetings in the city with other well-known Dominican writers such as Tulio M. Cestero. His father's eager inquiry about the possibility of "developing in New York the publication of books in Spanish" gives ground for supposing that the hispanophone cultural life that he came across in the city must have been considerable (Henríquez y Carvajal 1994: 657).

El nacimiento de Dionisios (1916), a dramatic piece in prose in which Henríquez Ureña aims to reconstruct the form of Greek tragedy "during the period immediately before Aeschylus," appeared in New York in 1916 through the press of *Las Novedades* (P. Henríquez Ureña 1976: 63). Though probably written in Mexico, as biographer Juan Jacobo Lara claims, the text waited until the author returned to New York to be committed to print (Lara 1975: 38). In Mexico, Pedro had studied law. Now back in the United States, beginning on September 27, 1916, he began teaching in the Romance Languages Department of the University of Minnesota, Minneapolis, while he pursued a graduate degree in the same University. In June 1917, he received his Master of Arts degree in Spanish, having produced a thesis entitled "The Irregular Stanza in the Spanish Poetry of the XVI and XVII Centuries" (Lara 1975: 40). Immediately after receiving his MA, Henríquez Ureña proceeded to enroll in the doctoral program at the University of Minnesota. Obtaining permission to write his dissertation in Spanish, he proposed to conduct a more advanced and in depth study of the topic of his MA thesis. The outcome of this effort was a major scholarly product that subsequently earned the praise of the eminent Spanish humanist Ramón Menéndez Pidal and the cadre of distinguished philologists then associated with Madrid's Centro de Estudios Históricos. Entitled *La versificación irregular en la poesía castellana*, and published in 1920 in the Spanish capital precisely under the imprint of the Centro de Estudios Históricos, this rigorous investigation by Henríquez Ureña surveys poetry written in Spanish from the medieval epics and romances through the twentieth century with an eye on metrical arrangements. His panoramic quest abundantly confirmed the premise that "metrics in Spanish poetry is a lot less simple than scholars have thus far noted" (P. Henríquez Ureña 1978: 13).

In 1921 Henríquez Ureña left Minnesota to settle in Madrid, subsequent to which professional engagements would also take him to Mexico, Argentina, and, for a period of less than two years, to his native Dominican Republic. The last time he came to the United States was to occupy the Charles Elliot Norton Visiting Professorship at Harvard University during academic year 1940-1941 (M. Henríquez Ureña 1984: xlix-l). During this third stay in North America, Henríquez Ureña continued to be the prolific writer that he had been since 1901. In addition to his other output, his lectures at Harvard, which he delivered in English, would appear in book form in 1945 from Harvard University Press under the title *Literary Currents of Hispanic America*. A literary and cultural survey of Latin America from the conquest to the present, the book carried on the inside flap of the cover a biographical error, saying that "these lectures by a South American scholar mark a real milestone." I have often mused about the gloomy symbolism evoked by that editorial oversight at Harvard University Press that changed the author's nationality. In a strange way, it presaged the invisibility that Dominican writers would have to endure in later accounts of Hispanic literatures in the United States.

After his visiting professorship at Harvard, Henríquez Ureña would leave the United States never to return again. Yet it is clear from the foregoing overview, swift and sketchy though it is, that the writings he produced during his three prolonged stays in this country constitute a major Dominican contribution to the U. S. Hispanic literary heritage. The anthological selections contained in Alfredo Roggiano's *Pedro Henríquez· Ureña en los Estados Unidos* (1961) bear witness to the fruit that an effort of recovery of the eminent humanist's texts could yield. An extensive search into the annals of *Heraldo de Cuba, Las Novedades, El Fígaro, Romanic Review, Revue Hispanique*, and other periodical publications, plus those books in his total *oeuvre* whose composition, regardless of place of publication, can be traced to the years he spent in American cities, could reveal a sizeable body of work by an author who is ranked among the top essayists in twentieth-century Latin-American literature.

When Pedro Henríquez Ureña received his Ph.D. from Minnesota in June 1918, another Dominican was also graduating in the same commencement exercises, namely, his sister Camila Henríquez Ureña (1894-1973), who got an MA degree (Lara 1975: 41). She, like her brother, became a literary scholar and essayist. Upon graduating from Minnesota, she went back to Cuba, where she had lived prior to pursuing graduate studies in the United States. There she spent most of her productive years, except for a span of 17 years, between 1941 and 1958, when she lived and worked in the United States. She taught in the Spanish Department at Vassar College, in Poughkeepsie, New York, also offering courses occasionally at Middlebury College, in Vermont. The work of recovering the literary texts produced by Camila during her 17 years of life and work in North America has yet to begin. The voluminous compilation *Estudios y conferencias* (1982), published posthumously in Cuba under her name, comes strictly from sources found in the archives of the Cuban Academy of Science's Institute of Literature and Linguistics. I look at that important collection and cannot help but wonder longingly about the rich potential of undertaking a comparable search for Camila's texts with a focus on her North American years.

V. Dominican Writers in New York through the 1950s

I would now just like to list a few other of the Dominican literary artists who wrote and published work in the United States, primarily in New York, early in the twentieth century. José M. Bernard (1873-1954), a highly regarded poet in his lifetime, published his book of poems *Renuevos* in 1907 in New York through a firm called Imprenta Hispano-Americana. In 1908, also in this city, appeared the volume of short fiction *Cuentos frágiles* (1908 Braeunlich) by Fabio Fiallo (1866-1942), a poet and short story writer who enjoyed great renown in Latin America. He was a close friend of Rubén Darío and other towering literary figures of the continent. Another important name among those Dominican writers being mapped here is Manuel Florentino Cestero (1879-1926). This author lived in the United States with his family since early in the century when the sudden loss of privilege caused by the fall of a government that had favored him made him leave his native country never to return again (Martínez 1971: 119). In New York he published a book of poems, *El canto del cisne*, in 1915, printed at *Las Novedades* , and in 1920 a prose fiction work entitled *El amor en Nueva York*.

There is also an intense period of Dominican literary productivity in the United States connected with the large presence of middle class exiles who lived here during the thirty years of the ruthless dictatorship of Rafael Leónidas Trujillo. Jesús de Galíndez, the Basque writer whose murder at the hands of Trujillo's henchmen on March 12, 1956, caused international uproar, attested to the numerical significance of anti-Trujillo Dominican exiles active in New York during the 1940s (Galíndez 1973: 252). The year 1946 witnessed the publication in the city of the tract *¡Yo también acuso!*, by Carmita Landestoy, a former collaborator of the regime who later became an opponent. Andrés Requena, a well-known fiction writer who fell from grace with the dictatorship and ended up joining the opposition in exile, wrote in New York the novel *Cementerio sin cruces* (1951), published by Editorial Veracruz in México (Silfa 1980: 332).

This novel, plus his other writings in the anti-Trujillo paper *Pluma y Espada*, published occasionally in New York by its editor José R. López Cestero, as well as in the periodical *Patria*, which Requena co-edited with Juan M. Díaz, cost the author his life (Galíndez 1973: 279). The Consul General of the Dominican Republic in New York, Felix W. Bernardino, an angel of death whom Trujillo appointed specifically to silence a few opposition voices then active in New York, supervised his murder.

The fiction writer Angel Rafael Lamarche (1899-1962) lived also in New York in the 1940s. Here he wrote *Los cuentos que Nueva York no sabe* (1949) and *El Nueva York de un iberoamericano* (?), which were published elsewhere—the first at Talleres Gráficos La Carpeta in Mexico—earning considerable praise in the literary circles of Santo Domingo. Lamarche is not known to have joined the opposition to the Trujillo regime in New York, but it is clear that most of the writings and publications of Dominicans here from 1930 through 1961 emanate from a reaction to the deeds of the dictatorship. In addition to the Dominican-led periodicals cited above, it is important to note the prominent presence of Dominican authors in the pages of widely known Hispanic publications such as *Visión*, *La Prensa*, and *El Diario de Nueva York* (Galíndez 1973: 136-37). Significantly, Stanley Ross, who was the editor of *El Diario de Nueva York* in the 1950s, had lived in the Dominican Republic where he had founded the daily *El Caribe* (Silfa 1980: 426). A search for Dominican texts in those invaluable sources can prove rewarding. Hector J. Díaz (1910-1952), the Dominican poet whose work is most often recited by non-literary audiences, spent the last years of his life in New York. It would be useful to look into the totality of his verse production to determine whether a meaningful portion of his work can be isolated as dating from his years in the city.

VI. Recovering Early U. S. Dominican Texts

With Héctor J. Díaz, as with the other writers referred to in this brief sketch, whether they wrote verse or prose, whether they produced creative or expository texts, one needs to determine how much of their work falls within the conceptual parameters that we deem valid in the configuration of what we have agreed to call the U. S. Hispanic literary heritage. I believe that once one accepts the idea that there was a Dominican literary presence in the United States during the one hundred and fifteen years prior to the great exodus that began in the mid 1960s, it becomes automatically plausible to chance upon texts by Dominican authors worthy of being recovered. The point of my remarks here, ultimately, is that when the literary activity of Dominicans in the United States began to be noticed in the late 1970s, as part of a given ethnic community of recent immigrants, leading up to the successful careers of Julia Alvarez, Rhina Espaillat, Viriato Sención, and Junot Díaz, they already had forerunners in compatriots of earlier generations. For the most part, today's Dominican writers in the United States know very little of an earlier history of Dominican writing in this country. An important question to ask, in a future exploration of this topic, would be whether one can identify any resonance between present and past Dominican writers in the United States across the large divide of class origins, generations, and historical circumstances.

Note

[1] This paragraph and those that follow in section I and II of the essay draw extensively often borrowing sentences almost verbatim from chapter 4 ("Forging a U. S. Dominican Culture") of *The Dominican Americans* (Greenwood Press), which I co-authored with Ramona Hernández.

Works Cited

Balaguer, Joaquín. *Los próceres escritores*. Buenos Aires: Impr. Ferrari Hermanos, 1947.

Burma, John H. *Spanish-Speaking People in the United States*. Durham: Duke University, 1954.

Duarte, Rosa. *Apuntes de Rosa Duarte: Archivo y versos de Juan Pablo Duarte*. Ed. E. Rodríguez Demorizi, C. Larrazábal Blanco, and V. Alfau Durán. 2da. ed. Santo Domingo: Secretaría de Estado de Educación Bellas Artes y Cultos, 1994.

Fernández, Roberta, ed. *In Other Words: Literature by Latinas of the United States*. Houston: Arte Público, 1994.

Galíndez, Jesús de. *The Era of Trujillo: Dominican Dictator*. Ed. by Russell H. Fitzgibbon. Tucson: University of Arizona, 1973.

Henríquez y Carvajal, Francisco. "De Francisco Henríquez y Carvajal a Pedro Henríquez Ureña". *Familia Henríquez Ureña: Epistolario*. Santo Domingo: Secretaría de Estado de Educación, Bellas Artes y Cultos, 1994. 657-58.

Henríquez Ureña, Max. *Pedro Henríquez Ureña: antología*. Colección Pensamiento Dominicano. [Santo Domingo] Ciudad Trujillo: Librería Dominicana, 1950. Rept. Santo Domingo: Feria Nacional del Libro, 1984.

———. "De Pedro Henríquez Ureña a Ramona Ureña Díaz." *Familia Henríquez Ureña: Epistolario*. Santo Domingo: Secretaría de Estado de Educación, Bellas Artes y Cultos, 1994. 289-90.

———. *El nacimiento de Dionisios*. 1916. In *Obras completas*. Vol.1. Ed. Juan Jacobo Lara. Santo Domingo. Universidad Nacional Pedro Henríquez Ureña, 1976.

————. *La versificación irregular en la poesía castellana.* 1920. In *Obras completas.* Vol. 4 Ed. Juan Jacobo Lara. Santo Domingo: Universidad Nacional Pedro Henríquez Ureña, 1978.

Kanellos, Nicolás. *The Hispanic Almanac: From Columbus to Corporate America.* Detroit: Visible Ink, 1994.

————, ed. *The Hispanic Literary Companion.* Detroit: Visible Ink, 1997.

King, Lourdes Miranda. "The Spanish-Speaking American". *Ethnic American Minorities: A Guide to Media and Materials.* Ed. Henry A. Johnson. New York: R. R. Bowker Company, 1976. 189-239.

Lara, Juan Jacobo. *Pedro Henríquez Ureña: Su vida y su obra.* Santo Domingo: Universidad Nacional Pedro Henríquez, 1975.

Luis, William. "Latin American (Hispanic Caribbean) Literature Written in the United States." *The Cambrige History of Latin American Literature.* Vol. 2. Cambridge: Cambridge University, 1996. 526-556.

Martínez, Rufino. *Diccionario biográfico-histórico dominicano: 1821-1930.* Historia y Sociedad 5. Santo Domingo: Editora de la UASD, 1971.

Miller, Wayne Charles. *A Comprehensive Bibliography for the Study of American Minorities.* Vol. 2. New York: New York University, 1976.

Moya Pons, Frank. *The Dominican Republic: A National History.* New Rochelle: Hispaniola Books, 1995.

Rodríguez Demorizi, Emilio. *Próceres de la Restauración: Noticias biográficas.* Academia Dominicana de la Historia. Vol. 12. Santo Domingo: Editora del Caribe, 1963.

————, ed. *Papeles de Buenaventura Báez.* Academia Dominicana de la Historia. No. 21. Santo Domingo: Editora Montalvo, 1969.

Roggiano, Alfredo A. *Pedro Henríquez Ureña en los Estados Unidos.* State University of Iowa Studies in Spanish Language and Literature. No. 12. México, D. F.: Iowa University, 1961.

Silfa, Nicolás. *Guerra, traición y exilio.* Barcelona: n.p. 1980.

Tejeda, Juan de Dios. "De Juan de Dios Tejeda a Ramona Ureña." *Familia Henríquez Ureña: Epistolario.* Santo Domingo: Secretaría de Estado de Educación Bellas Artes y Cultos, 1994. 281-83.

Torres-Saillant, Silvio. "La literatura dominicana en los Estados Unidos y la periferia del margen." *Punto y Coma* 3.1-2 (1991): 139-149; rpt. *Brújula/Compass* 11 (1991): 16-17; rpt. *Cuadernos de Poética* 7.21 (1993): 7-26.

Torres-Saillant, Silvio, and Ramona Hernández. *The Dominican Americans.* Westport, Conn.: Greenwood Press, 1998.

Vallejo de Paredes, Margarita. *Apuntes biográficos y bibliográficos de algunos escritores dominicanos del siglo XIX.* Vol. 1. Santo Domingo: Publicaciones ONAP, 1995.

Welles, Summer. 1928. *Naboth's Vineyard: The Dominican Republic, 1844-1924.* Rept. Mamaroneck, N.Y.: Paul P. Appel, 1966. 2 Vols.

The Recovery of Salomón de la Selva's *Tropical Town:* Challenges and Outcomes

Silvio Sirias
Appalachian State Unversity

> Salomón de la Selva nació en León de Nicaragua, hace poco más de veinte y cuatro años. Cuando contaba doce, llegó la los Estados Unidos, y bien pronto, con rapidez infantil, adoptó el inglés en lugar del castellano, como lengua para sus incipientes ejercicios literarios.
>
> [Salomón de la Selva was born in León, Nicaragua, a little more than twenty-four years ago. When he was twelve, he came to the United States, and quite soon, with childlike ease, he adopted English instead of Spanish as the language for his incipient literary exercises.]
>
> Pedro Henríquez Ureña, *El Fígaro* (Havana), April 6, 1919

The Nicaraguan-born poet Salomón de la Selva poses a unique and fascinating case in the recovery of U. S. Hispanic literature. The challenge of studying de la Selva's first published collection of poetry, *Tropical Town and Other Poems*, arises as soon as we attempt to trace its literary lineage. Published in 1918 by the John Lane Company of New York, and written in English, this poetic collection remains virtually unstudied in spite of its historical and literary importance in Hispanic-American letters. Historically, Latin American critics have, for the most part, shied away from examining this significant text primarily, we can safely assume, because of the language barrier. Elena Milán and Julio Valle-Castillo at last translated several of de la Selva's English poems for Editorial Nueva Nicaragua's *Antología Mayor de Salomón de la Selva*, published in 1993. This finally has enabled the Spanish-reading public to examine de la Selva's earliest efforts. In reality, though, *Tropical Town* represents the first English-language collection of poetry by a Hispanic writer in the United States—a fact unknown to most scholars and students of Hispanic-American literature.

This lack of awareness is understandable because *Tropical Town* has fallen into the narrow gap between Latin American and U. S. Hispanic literature. Critics of Latin American literature have decided that it doesn't belong in their realm. They perceive it, for the most part, as a peculiar work, to be merely mentioned in passing when discussing the formation of this talented Nicaraguan poet. Perhaps it's time for critics in the United States to claim *Tropical Town* as part of the Hispanic-American literary legacy. The poems were the work of a poet of Latin American sensibilities who made his initial foray into the literary world in a language and an environment in which he felt, for the most part, very comfortable. The end result is an effort that is patently Hispanic-American, an enterprise that blends both the Anglo and Hispanic cultures and literary traditions.

Ever since Rubén Darío's reign over Hispanic literature, Nicaragua can rightly claim to be a land of great poets. Salomón de la Selva—"Don Sal" to his compatriots—ranks highly among that nation's most admired bards. However, many Nicaraguans are surprised to learn that de la Selva could even speak English.

The World of 1918

In 1918, the year of the appearance of *Tropical Town*, the world's attention was focused on the war in Europe. While the conflict had been raging since 1914, it was not until April 2, 1917, that President Woodrow Wilson called for a U. S. declaration of war against Germany, stating that "The world must be made safe for democracy."

Ironically, the United States had done little to make its neighbors to the south safe for democracy. Within the ten previous years, U. S. forces had militarily occupied Haiti, Panama, Cuba, the Dominican Republic, and de la Selva's homeland of Nicaragua. In addition, the United States engaged in direct interventions in the political affairs of Mexico, Honduras, Costa Rica, and Colombia. Thus, the paradox of de la Selva's political poetry is set: He admires his adoptive nation for its humanitarian vision, its technological and artistic accomplishments, and its commitment to a just war in Europe. On the other hand, the young poet is bewildered and angered at the United States' disregard for Latin American sovereignty.

On the literary front, the Spanish-speaking literary world had recently lost its leading creative genius with the death of Rubén Darío, Salomón de la Selva's fellow countryman and the leading figure of Hispanic *Modernismo*. Although *Modernismo* had been in decline for several years, the young radicals who would fully embrace the calling of the *avant-garde* movement had yet to make their full impact. *Modernismo* incorporated various philosophies along with several generations of literary creativity, and scores of approaches towards creating poetry co-existed under its banner. It was a fertile period that can be rightly compared to the Spanish Renaissance. *Modernismo* was strongly influenced by the French Symbolists and Parnassians while holding highly accomplished classical traditions in high regard (Sánchez-Romeralo XVI). Its starting point was rebellion against the aged and stagnant poetic norms of nineteenth century Peninsular literature (Max Henríquez Ureña 11). Its aim was to find original forms of artistic expression (Schulman 14). However, even though

Modernismo was known for its wide range of subject matter and style, it is still most closely associated with Rubén Darío (Kirkpatrick 6).

The remainder of the Western world was also engaged in a poetic revolution. Retrospectively called Modernism, this movement differs significantly from Hispanic *Modernismo*. The term *Modernism* is applied to a wide range of experimental and *avant-garde* trends in the literature of the early twentieth century. These include Symbolism, Futurism, Expressionism, Imagism, Vorticism, Dadaism, and Surrealism. Poets such as Ezra Pound and T. S. Eliot replaced the logical exposition of thoughts with collages of fragmentary images and complex allusions (Baldick 140). The emergence of Modernism is often linked to the change in thinking that came about as an effect of World War I. With the dissolution of outmoded political orders and the enormous casualties of war, old ways of explaining and portraying the world no longer seemed appropriate nor applicable. Alienation and isolation emerged as important themes, and even as techniques (Childers and Hentzi 192). In the United States, Carl Sandburg, Vachel Lindsay, Amy Lowell, Robert Frost, William Carlos Williams, and Edgar Lee Masters were becoming entrenched as the generation that would dominate American poetry for years to come. Some championed feminism, psychoanalysis, trade unionism, and socialism. Furthermore, and perhaps more scandalously, some practiced free love and wrote in free verse. Nineteen-eighteen, then, was a year of political and social paradoxes, of marked ironies, and of profound dichotomies. It was at this time—unknown still today by most scholars of United States Hispanic literature—that Salomón de la Selva emerged.

A Biography

Writing about Salomón de la Selva's life is a difficult task. His compatriot, the poet José Coronel Urtecho, even states, "All the [facts] available on Salomón . . . can be counted on one hand" (69). The details that do exist include a great degree of speculation and conjecture. We know that he was born on March 20, 1893, in León, Nicaragua. He was the eldest of six brothers and four sisters born to a physician, also named Salomón de la Selva, and his wife, Evangelina Escoto. A precocious young boy, Salomón de la Selva earned a scholarship from the Nicaraguan Congress, perhaps in the hope that he would become Rubén Darío's successor.[1] He left his family and his country at age eleven to live and study in the United States.[2] Virtually no information has been gathered about de la Selva's life between 1904 and 1914, his formative years in the States. It is not even known where he lived during this time except that it was somewhere in the northeastern United States. We do know, however, that he became astoundingly proficient in English. We also know that he returned briefly to Nicaragua in 1910 on the occasion of his father's death.[3] The poet's sojourn in his homeland undoubtedly served as the basis for the pictorial poems about Nicaragua that form the centerpiece of *Tropical Town*. It is not until de la Selva serves as Rubén Darío's interpreter, for the renowned poet's last visit to New York during the winter of 1914-1915, that we have any concrete news of de la Selva. This brief liaison would have a profound impact on de la Selva's work.

In 1915, de la Selva, in collaboration with the American poet Thomas Walsh, published *Eleven Poems of Rubén Darío*, a collection of poems in translation. The noted Dominican scholar Pedro Henríquez Ureña penned the introduction to the volume. Their friendship, based on a profound mutual respect for each other's knowledge and talents, would last until Henríquez Ureña's death in 1946.[4] Because of his demonstrated literary talents, de la Selva was awarded a position teaching Spanish and French at Williams College, in Massachusetts, in 1916.[5] He would remain there for two years.

Another crucial event in de la Selva's life emerges at this time: his friendship with the American poet Edna St. Vincent Millay. The two shared a love for traditional poetic form and the expression of personal emotions, rather than innovation and clinical experimentation. The two also spent much time together and developed an extremely close relationship, as evidenced in Millay's letters.[6] This friendship and its ensuing creative symbiosis would be de la Selva's greatest influence when writing in English.[7]

Also during this period, Salomón de la Selva began to let his voice be heard on issues regarding United States foreign policy. While teaching at Williams College, he gave lectures considered politically "controversial."[8] His most notable public moment took place on February 7, 1917, at the Pan American Reception of the Joint Committee of the Literary Arts, at the National Arts Club in New York. On this occasion, de la Selva gave a speech and read his poem "The Dreamer's Heart Knows Its Own Bitterness." Present in the audience was former president Theodore Roosevelt. De la Selva stated, in part:

> Nicaragua is small in extension, but powerful in its pride. My land is as great as its thoughts; as great as its hopes and its aspirations . . . . To love the United States, as I do, requires a great deal of effort when my own country is outraged by the nation to the North. No true Pan-Americanism can exist until there is justice for the weak nations.[9]

The speech garnered the enthusiastic ovation of the crowd, while Roosevelt, offended by the anti-imperialist content of de la Selva's words, abruptly left. This is far from the last time that de la Selva publicly questioned the wisdom of U. S. policies in Latin America.[10]

And yet, even while angered by the U. S. intervention in his homeland, Salomón de la Selva, at the age of 24, voluntarily enlisted in the United States Army. He trained on the campus of Williams College and earned the right to become a lieutenant. The Army, however, refused to admit him until he became a U. S. citizen. In turn, the poet refused to renounce his Nicaraguan citizenship and began to petition the military for an exception. He soon tired of his efforts and instead joined the British Army.[11]

While Salomón de la Selva petitioned the United States Army for an exception, *Tropical Town and Other Poems* appeared in print. The collection included several works previously published in magazines such as *Century*, *Harper's Monthly*, *Poetry*, and *Contemporary Verse*, among others. However, the first Hispanic to have a volume of his English language poetry published in New York did not have time to savor his success. Shortly after the book's publication, de la Selva abandoned the United States as his permanent residence and became, from that moment on, a man of many nations.

The poet's first stop was England, where he trained with the British army and was soon sent to the battlefront in Flanders, Belgium. He remained there until the end of the war. His life as a soldier makes Salomón de la Selva the only known Latin American poet to experience the First World War's "massive technological death, of a kind humanity had never known before" (Pacheco 104). After the war, he resided in London until late 1919. During this time he met and established a friendship with Ezra Pound. There are strong indications that he continued to write poetry in English. Several bibliographies of Salomón de la Selva's work suggest that while in Great Britain, he published another collection of poetry titled *A Soldier Sings*, under the auspices of The Bodley Head, in London. No one, however, has been able to produce a copy of this work. It remains, to borrow Steven White's term, a literary "ghost." [12]

After London, de la Selva returned briefly to New York, where reportedly he wrote a collection of poems in English based on his experiences in World War I titled *The Unknown Soldier,* which was never published in English.[13] Increasingly disenchanted with the continued occupation of Nicaragua by the United States Marines, he moved to Mexico, which would become his new adoptive country. There Salomón de la Selva was hired by his friend Pedro Henríquez Ureña to work for the Ministry of Education, an institution recently founded and headed by the illustrious philosopher and teacher José Vasconcelos.

In 1922, Salomón de la Selva's second, and best known, collection of poetry was published: *El soldado desconocido,*[14] a work that, according to José Emilio Pacheco, revolutionized Spanish poetry in Mesoamerica. Whether it was an entirely new work or a translation of *The Unknown Soldier* is uncertain.

De la Selva resided in Mexico until 1925. He then returned to Nicaragua and that same year married Carmela Castrillo, with whom he had two children.[15] Between 1925 and 1929 he worked ardently in favor of labor unionization in his homeland.[16] In 1927, his vocal opposition to the renewed occupation of his homeland by the U.S. Marines made de la Selva the leading Nicaraguan intellectual supporter of General Augusto César Sandino and his rebel army. In July of 1927, the poet traveled once more to the United States, this time at the head of a delegation of the Nicaraguan Workers Federation (Federación Obrera Nicaraghense) for the Panamerican Workers Conference, in Washington D.C. While in the nation's capital, de la Selva organized a forceful campaign to protest the U. S. occupation. The campaign would continue until 1933, when the Marines withdrew from Nicaragua, six years after the poet's return to his homeland.

In 1930, de la Selva, back in Nicaragua, organized a strong pro-Sandino and anti-imperialist campaign. He wrote columns in both English and Spanish protesting the American occupation of his country and exalting Sandino's cause. Because of his political activism he was twice forced into exile. The first time, from 1930 to 1931, he resided in Costa Rica; in the second instance, from 1933 to 1935, he resided in Panama, where he published a bilingual newspaper.

After 1935, Salomón de la Selva returned to Mexico and remained there for the next twenty years. His life became considerably less hectic, although he continued to write prolifically. During these years he corresponded with many influential friends throughout the world. Among these friends was Henry Wallace, Vice-President of the United States during Franklin D. Roosevelt's third term. In 1952, de la Selva was invited to become a member of the Mexican Academy of Language (Academia Mexicana de la Lengua). Imposed upon him, however, was the condition that he must become a citizen of Mexico to be inducted. De la Selva, once again faithful to his homeland, refused the invitation. Nevertheless, in 1954, the Academy made him an honorary member.

The final and perhaps most paradoxical event in de la Selva's eventful life took place in 1955, when he accepted President Anastasio Somoza García's offer to become Nicaragua's ambassador at large in Europe. His collaboration with the regime came after nearly twenty years of vociferously condemning the Somoza dictatorship.[17] De la Selva served in that position for four years. He died of a heart attack in Paris, on February 5, 1959. Although his last years were spent representing a government thoroughly dominated by the United States, Salomón de la Selva is most remembered by the Nicaraguans for his staunch opposition to foreign intervention in his country. He is still revered by his compatriots as one of the nation's greatest poets and intellectuals. In honor of his status as one of his country's most important poets, the Nicaraguan people buried him next to Rubén Darío in the Cathedral of León.

Themes

The 65 poems that make up *Tropical Town and Other Poems* are, as Henríquez Ureña states, "surprising in [their] variety of themes and forms" (16). De la Selva divides the volume into four sections, each reflecting an artistic, social, or political concern. These sections are "My Nicaragua" (19 poems), "In New England and Other Lyrics" (17 poems), "In War Time" (6 poems), and "The Tale from Faerieland" (23 poems).

"My Nicaragua" constitutes *Tropical Town's* most sterling example of transcultural transmission. Here, the Nicaraguan poet attempts to translate for the American reader his native culture and his Spanish-language poetic sensibilities, painting vivid sketches of his country in the hope that his words can convey the distant homeland stored in his memory.

The title poem opens the collection. As Valle-Castillo has asserted, the "Tropical Town" to which Salomón de la Selva refers is León, Nicaragua's second largest city and the poet's birthplace. In de la Selva's verses, León comes to represent all of Nicaragua (30). The author repeatedly invites his readers to join him on a poetic journey through his native culture. He assures them that Nicaragua possesses many virtues, emphasizing the warmth of the tropics and its people. These qualities are perhaps best illustrated by the first two lines from "Tropical House," the second poem in the collection:

> When the Winter comes, I will take you to Nicaragua,—
> You will love it there!

The poetic voice in "My Nicaragua" is nostalgic, yearning for a faraway homeland full of embracing, hopeful memories. The poet's tropical town is primitive, quaint, and colorful. At times this land is Edenic and the people who populate it (including the poet) strongly religious. Yet for all its natural beauty, what makes this country remarkable are its inhabitants. They are portrayed as loving, favoring a simple life full of music and celebration. They are also admirably strong, steadfastly maintaining their dignity in spite of the poverty that afflicts them. "Tropical Town," "Tropical House," "Tropical Park," "Tropical Morning," "Tropical Afternoon," "Tropical Life," and "Tropical Childhood" are all vivid descriptions of life in this nation. These works depict a playful dichotomy between the sacred and the profane. In "Tropical Afternoon," the fleeting yet meaningful existences of the town's inhabitants are superimposed onto the eternal, timeless quality of the tropics. In "Tropical Life," the poet ambles through the streets as he attempts to recreate his deceased father's daily routine. De la Selva's verses fill the reader with his charming remembrances of life and nature in a distant, tropical universe. The poet hopes that we will be transported into his world and share in his passion for his homeland.

De la Selva is equally enthusiastic about his country's folklore. With "Tropical Dance," "The Midget Maiden," and "The Girl that was Wise," he transforms into English three songs, or children's verses, known throughout Nicaragua. In "All Soul's Day," he describes the colorful, yet reverent, customs of the Day of the Dead. Rothschuh Tablada recognizes de la Selva as the first Nicaraguan poet to directly integrate folkloric or popular themes into his verses (VI).

The poet also acknowledges, however, that life in his Nicaragua is far from being idyllic. His fellow citizens must contend with destructive natural forces and harsh economic circumstances. In "Tropical Rain," a menacing storm threatens the lives of the poem's protagonists, women and children who huddle together to fervently invoke Jesus' name as they plead for their salvation. In "Body and Soul," de la Selva vividly describes the demanding existences of many of his compatriots. The poem concludes with the author's proclamation of his undying love for his country, in spite of the severe hardships there.

The poems in this section that have garnered critical attention are the political ones. The first to delve into politics is "The Haunted House of León." Burned by mercenary U.S. filibusters led by William Walker, the house is described as being inhabited by ghosts and demons who are in league with the spirits of the invaders. Interestingly, the evil forces can be defeated by marriage between the poet and a "Yankee girl." The merging of both peoples, the American and the Nicaraguan, constitutes a solution that de la Selva often poses to resolve many of the conflicts existent between the two nations. "A Song for Wall Street" suggests that for little money the reader can purchase a wholesome life of simplicity and music in Nicaragua. However, they can never purchase the lives of de la Selva's fellow citizens. Valle-Castillo labels this a poem of political protest in which the Nicaraguan poet rejects North American civilization (31). Similarly, White argues that:

> Salomón de la Selva was perhaps one of the most politically aware poets of his time. His perception of the unjust relationship between the United States and Latin American, especially in a poem such as "A Song for Wall Street," makes de la Selva unique among his contemporaries writing in the English language. ("Salomón de la Selva: Testimonial Poetry" 123)

The poem that provides the title for the first section, "My Nicaragua," reaffirms Valle-Castillo's claim that de la Selva rejects the imposition of alien cultural values. "My Nicaragua" describes the values treasured in the poet's country, but, perhaps most importantly, it emphatically states what his country is not:

> The *dear* hotels with palm trees in the garden
> And a self-playing piano drumming rags,
> Where you drink lemonade and rack your brains
> Thinking: What in the devil's name is Tropics?—
> This shop of German, English and French owners;
> The parlours of the ruling class adorned
> With much the same bad taste as in New York,—
> That never was my country! But the rows
> Of earthen little houses where men dwell,
> And women, all too busy living life
> To think of faking it, that is my country,
> My Nicaragua, mother of great poets!

Not only is North American civilization rejected in "My Nicaragua," but also other foreign traditions. His country is simple and sincere, remaining devoted to producing genuinely caring people and great poets.

The centerpiece of the section "My Nicaragua" is, without question, the poem entitled "The Dreamer's Heart Knows Its Own Bitterness." Subtitled "A Pan-American Poem on the Entrance of the United States into the War," it again provides the suggestion of a union, a marriage, between both nations as a solution for resolving their conflicts. As White states: "The poet creates a North-South dichotomy, characterizing the South as his mother and the North as his bride" ("Salomón de la Selva: Testimonial Poetry" 122). The poet is torn between his obligation as a son and his vow as a husband. He adores both, but feels obliged to choose one. The mother and the bride are at odds, with the bride exerting her considerable power over his mother. White summarizes: "The poet pledges his support to the United States in the war against 'Belgium's wronger,' yet urges the United States to be consistent in its sense of justice with regard to Latin America" (123). This strident yet pleading poetic creation ends the first section of *Tropical Town*.

The poems of "In New England and Other Lyrics" deal primarily with the poet's feelings towards New England, his one-time place of residence. "Deliverance" contemplates de la Selva's loneliness and desolation in a land very distant from his own: "What am I doing here, in New England?" In "The Secret," the poet expresses his desire "to pack my things and run away." Amid the beauty of the New England countryside, the poet feels sad and alone. The Nicaraguan's discomfort at being far away from his beloved country constitutes a painful current that runs through these poems.

The people of New England, however, with their gentility and goodness, provide a nurturing home for the Hispanic poet. In "Finally," de la Selva states that he has come to terms with living in New England, and he proclaims the people of New England virtuous. In a leitmotif that appears throughout *Tropical Town*, the poet hopes that he can be the bridge that brings the people of New England and the people of Nicaragua to understand, appreciate, and love one another. The poem "Confidences" portrays the Central American as an outsider with regard to New England's history and culture. Yet, in the poem's concluding stanza, de la Selva expresses his desire to be a full-fledged participant even in New England's cultural history:

> Dance, all you little children,
> And I will play with you!
> I am afraid of witches
> Also; I burn them too . . . .

In his reconciliation with life in New England, de la Selva portrays the people there as the kindest in the world. He credits them with adopting him, a foreigner, as a son.

De la Selva, in this section, also explores classical themes. "Cellini at the

Metropolitan Museum" reflects the poet's wonder at the precise and meticulous baroque artistry of Italy's most famous Renaissance goldsmith, Benvenuto Cellini. "Courtship" revolves around the classic theme of human mortality, one of the poet's primary concerns in *Tropical Town*. The themes of love and unrequited love surface in the "Sonnet" and "Three Songs." He also honors his Christian beliefs in "Song of Magdalen."

The poems of "In War Time" are conceived around de la Selva's preoccupation with the historic events that were taking place in Europe at the time of the publication. Later in the year, he would commit to his ideals in the fullest measure possible by risking his life in the "just war." His outlook, however, remains naive. The poet has yet to experience the savagery and dehumanizing effects of combat. Unbridled optimism and enthusiasm for fighting in a noble cause permeate his verses, even if his participation should end in death.[18]

In "A Prayer for the United States," the poet expresses his fear that the apocalypse foretold in the New Testament has arrived in the form of the war. In agreement with his unwavering Christian faith, de la Selva begs the Lord to deliver us from this fate.[19] In "Hatred," de la Selva delineates how hate can take control of the human soul when hunger, darkness, and sorrow surround it. The poet remains particularly fearful of how literature and art can come to serve this awful master. In "December, 1916," the world's heart is full of sadness, and there are no visible signs of peace. As the poet's eyes scan the frozen New England countryside, it acquires the look of a battlefield. De la Selva, however, foresees that peace will come in the end, achieved at a terribly high cost.

"Drill" portrays de la Selva training with other volunteers on a Williams College sports field in New England. In this piece, as White states, "the potential of violence is a quasi-mystical source of ecstatic release that illuminates the world, increasing its natural beauty" ("Salomón de la Selva: Testimonial Poetry" 127). While marching in New England, the war seems far removed. The narrator is joyful and prepared to make the ultimate sacrifice. Stunned by the beauty of the New England landscape as he prepares for war alongside other idealistic men, the poet vows to return to the countryside a happy, free, and optimistic man.

In the "Ode to the Woolworth Building," de la Selva asks the edifice, at the time the world's tallest building, if it grieves for the young men going to war. In the poet's mind, the Woolworth Building constitutes a suitable replacement for the historic French cathedral of Rheims, in occupied territory since the beginning of the war. De la Selva admires the human ingenuity which went into constructing the New York City building; in his essay "Edna St. Vincent Millay," de la Selva states that the United States had distinguished itself in only two artistic arenas: poetry and architecture (144). The building represents the heavenly glory that mankind is capable of achieving when creativity is allowed free reign. The Woolworth Building proudly stands as a monument to human redemption.

The final poem of the section, "The Knight in Gray," portrays the poet as a knight who fights for love and justice, eventually perishing in battle. The author, however, asks his friends not to lament his passing. He has lived an honest life, and thus his song will resonate for eternity. The poetry in this section, as White has noted, is full of idealism, elegance, and solemnity ("Salomón de la Selva: Testimonial Poetry" 127). De la Selva's poetic perspective regarding the war will reach its full maturity, as will the cynicism that accompanies it, with the publication of *El soldado desconocido*.

In the Manuscript Archives of Brown University resides the only known copy of de la Selva's book *The Tale from Faerieland*. According to the World Catalog library computer database, a note on its last page reads: "Cover of this book made by Rufino González. Entire lettering of the poems by the author. No other copy has been made of this volume." The place of origin listed is New York City, and the date, 1916.

This information leads to the assumption that, at one time, de la Selva considered this segment of *Tropical Town* an independent collection that in itself merited publication. Indeed, this section numbers more poems than any other: twenty-three. The narrative poem "The Tale from Faerieland" forms the section's centerpiece. In these verses, the poet portrays himself as an artisan who has weaved an extraordinary tapestry with his words. He dreams of the fame and glory that he will achieve because of his work. However, when a seed of doubt enters his mind, he sells it at far less than its value. Thus, the tapestry begins a voyage through the hands of many owners: kings, queens, Cinderella of the fairy tale, and Jason of mythological fame. All admire the tapestry's beauty. Eventually, Mary Magdalen purchases the poet's weave to wrap Jesus' body after the Crucifixion. On the day of the Resurrection, Jesus wears it around his shoulders and the poet is rewarded and blessed.

A second narrative is "The Sword of Wonder." In this work, the poet forsakes the follies allowable in his youth in favor of industry. Blinded by his narrow notions of beauty, he fails to recognize the identity of true love. Eventually, all the poet has left in his existence is to await death. He mournfully reflects on the opportunities that he missed throughout his life, urging the reader to avoid following his path and to believe fully in the mystical power of wonder.

Several poems constructed around the theme of music are included in "The Tale from Faerieland." The first is "Pastorale." This work, as the poet notes in the subtitle, is inspired by the sixteenth prelude of Johann Sebastian Bach's "Well-Tempered Clavier." It narrates the simple tale of Colin, the shepherd, who lives a peaceful and musical life in an idyllic setting. The "Aria in G," with an operatic theme, portrays the poet as encircled by darkness. His values have become contaminated and he finds himself surrounded by menacing forces without the possibility of escape. The last of the musical poems, "The Sorry Madrigal," reflects on how circumstances change throughout our lives, and the little control we have over these sometimes painful changes.

De la Selva's appreciation for classical art also emerges in this section. The poem "To a Young Man" has a portrait by the Renaissance painter Giorgione as its source of inspiration. The poet details the conflicting feelings that this painting generates within him. Although Giorgione's work is masterful, de la Selva is bewildered by the passionless "decorum" of the portrait's subject. The poet ultimately finds himself torn between loving and loathing the work.

Three poems inspired by failed loves are included in "The Tale from Faerieland." In "The Box of Sandalwood," a cycle of ten sonnets, the poet narrates a tale of lost love, an amorous relationship that wavered between sinful passion and saintly innocence. These verses are as close as the Central American comes to writing erotic poetry in English. He offers us an enigmatic ending in which the loved one's death may be metaphorical or actual. In the seven-part "First Love Revived," the poet recalls a love that had ended twelve years earlier. He had then wished to possess his subject but encountered only her disdain. She controlled his will and constituted the center of his existence. But in the poem's present, all these passions now seem like the memory of a brief afternoon fling. Although his first love has now become a woman with the grace and comportment of a queen, he longs for the naive, innocent girl of his youth.

Social concerns are present also in this section. In the "Song of the Poppy's Lover," the poet expresses his outrage at the commercialization of this flower. In "Oh Glorious Spendthrift Joy," de la Selva is overwhelmed by the poverty and suffering that surrounds him in the city. Although he wishes to assist others in need, the poet removes himself so that he may return another day with renewed energies to combat these evils.

Political concerns regarding Latin America arise once again in this section in "To Those Who Have Been Indifferent to the Pan American Movement." In this piece, de la Selva predicts a united American hemisphere. This unification will take place in spite of the apathy of the majority of the people of the United States. However, in a stern warning to the reader, the poet foresees that the cost of this unity will be much bloodshed and suffering.

As in the section "My Nicaragua," de la Selva attempts to translate his culture for American readers. In "I Would Be Telling You," the poet expresses his pain as he thinks about his distant homeland. The recent death of a loved one in Nicaragua makes de la Selva suffer, and his attempts to transmit this experience into verses for the American reader would, he believes, only increase his pain. The same theme is explored in "Her Wish Was that Myself Should Be" as the poet again laments being so distant from Nicaragua upon the death of a loved one. The final composition dealing with Hispanic culture that we encounter in *Tropical Town* is "Delgadina," a virtually uncredited translation of a Spanish ballad by the same title. In de la Selva's translation, the ballad tells of the daughter of a Spanish king who chooses death over succumbing to her father's incestuous desires.

Several of the poems in this section reflect on life and human nature. "Candle Light" deals with the eminence of death and on how the light from candles perfectly complement this solemn occasion. "Fleur D'Or" and "Song of the Poppy" focus on the slow, progressive disintegration of life. "The Modern Eve" exalts the strength of woman. Her power is portrayed as eternal, and she is unafraid of death. While the male is hungry and selfish, the woman carries deep within her immovable confidence in the future and in her status as a inexhaustible fountain of life. The poem "Joy" playfully deals with the satisfying nature of love and how the act of love could go on forever except for the human requirement to work. "Hunger in the City" credits loneliness and hunger as the agents that assist Satan's invasion of the human soul. "The Maker of Red Clay Jars," a four-part poem, details how in spite of having a perfectly good life, one always wishes to possess what someone else has. "Of Time and Song," the book's concluding poem, is perhaps the most artistically accomplished piece of the entire ensemble. It constitutes a sage treatise on the interconnectedness of all things in life and in art:

> Thus, on and on,
> All days are somehow linked, all songs are one.

Formal Aspects of *Tropical Town*

Without question, de la Selva's poetry in Spanish belongs to Latin America's literary heritage. However, *Tropical Town and Other Poems*, has yet to be claimed as rightfully belonging to the U. S. Hispanic literary heritage.

De la Selva's work poses a challenge unlike any other Hispanic-American writer's that I've encountered. Like many contemporary Hispanic-American writers (such as Julia Alvarez, Roberto Fernández, Judith Ortiz Cofer, Ed Vega, Virgil Suárez, Miguel Algarín, Pablo Medina, Tato Laviera, Gustavo Pérez-Firmat, Junot Díaz, and Esmeralda Santiago), Salomón de la Selva came to the United States at an early enough age to thoroughly adopt English as his literary language. Unlike them, though, in the early part of the twentieth century he had no examples of Hispanic-American poetry in English upon which to base his own creations. De la Selva represents an extremely isolated literary incident, a U. S. Hispanic who writes virtually in a vacuum. This brings us, then, to the most important question of this essay: To which models did Salomón de la Selva turn in order to write poetry?

Some may find the poems in de la Selva's collection highly anachronistic. At a time when poetic experimentation was already in full bloom, when American poetry was firmly on the road to Modernism, this Nicaraguan-

American poet was enamored with tradition. His poems focus specifically on the schools of American and English Romanticism. As a poet in the English language, de la Selva subscribes to Aestheticism, which promotes beauty as an end in itself and views the creation of beauty as the only proper function of the artist. The Aesthetic movement places considerable emphasis on poetic form (Chai, xi–xiii). In an era in American poetry when experimentation and free verse are in vogue, Salomón de la Selva consciously rejects the *zeitgeist*, the prevailing literary moods and attitudes of the early twentieth century. He chooses instead to create out of synchrony by favoring past models. In a letter to his friend Pedro Henríquez Ureña, de la Selva states that he adheres to the principles of good writing advocated by the English author Alice Meynell. Specifically, he cites her essay "Decivilised" as greatly influencing his *ars poetica*. Meynell reveals in that work an unmovable reverence for and devotion to the literary past:

> Evidently we cannot choose our posterity. Reversing the steps of time, we may, indeed, choose backwards. We may give our thoughts noble forefathers. Well begotten, well born our fancies must be; they shall be also well derived. We have a voice in decreeing our inheritance, and not our inheritance only, but our heredity. Our minds may trace upwards and follow their ways to the best well-heads of the arts. The very habit of our thoughts may be persuaded one way unawares by their antenatal history. Their companions must be lovely, but need to be no lovelier than their ancestors; and being so fathered and so husbanded, our thoughts may be intrusted to keep the counsels of literature. (9–10)

In addition to her specific adherence to Britain's literary past, Meynell states that the "colonial" poetic discourse of the United States "is only provincialism very articulate" (7). How did Salomón de la Selva align himself with such a traditionalist poetic stance? The answer comes to light when we look toward his intimate friendship with Millay.

The Poetic Dialogue with Edna St. Vincent Millay

Although Millay's literary prestige has significantly rebounded during the last two decades, she at one time, as Suzanne Clark writes, "courted oblivion" by concentrating on poetic form "in the era of high modernism"(3).[20] Millay's poems reject the formalist idea proposed by T. S. Eliot of "impersonal poetry." She rejects the aesthetics of the *avant-garde* and "uses the traditional forms of poetry in a productive and radical challenge to the hierarchies of modernism" (Clark 8–9). De la Selva, in his poems in the English language, is engaged in a vigorous dialogue with Millay's early poetry. He, too, adheres to tradition in his work. Henríquez Ureña describes his young friend as a literary conservative who prefers to write poetry in the "time-honored manner" rather than in the experimental spirit of his better known contemporaries (17).

In an impressive essay, "Edna St. Vincent Millay," de la Selva himself informs the reader about the preeminent role that Millay played in both his life and his poetry at the time that he authored *Tropical Town and Other Poems*. This article, written in Spanish and published in Mexico thirty-one years after de la Selva's first collection of poetry appeared in print, provides us with an affectionate glimpse into the creative relationship that existed between the two. Writing in the third person, de la Selva states that *Tropical Town* was written "at a time when Edna was the poet's constant obsession" (131–132). He restates that Millay and Alice Meynell were his guiding poetic lights during this period of his life.

Let's proceed, then, to compare a few poems in which Millay and de la Selva appear to engage in a poetic dialogue. Because of the chronology of our discussion, we shall include only poems from Millay's first collection, *Renascence*, published in 1917. We can be certain that de la Selva knew these poems well and that, moreover, as his essay on Millay indicates, he had discussed them amply with the American poet.

In "The Shroud," Millay personifies death as her mother, announcing that a red gown that she owns would be suitable for her burial:

> Death, I say, my heart is bowed
> Unto thine, —O mother!
> This red gown will make a shroud
> Good as any other!

In de la Selva's poem "Courtship," death is also personified. However, unlike Millay, he neither welcomes it nor bows to it:

> Am I too changeful, Death?
> You are too changeful too;
> Then leave me here to draw my breath
> And come no more to woo.

Clark notes that personification is Millay's favorite trope (10). The reader can easily observe that it is also de la Selva's. The poetic voice in "The Shroud," in a parenthetical statement, likens itself to a bride whose eagerness for the wedding can barely be contained:

> (I, that would not wait to wear
> My own bridal things,
> In a dress dark as my hair
> Made my answerings.
>
> I, to-night that till he came
> Could not, could not wait,

> In a gown as bright as flame
> Held them for the gate.)

De la Selva responds with a similar metaphor:

> We'd make too false a wife,
> A husband too untrue:
> Sometimes I am in love with Life
> And Life is sometimes you.

The kinship that exists between these poems is readily apparent. The primary difference resides in the poets' attitude: Millay gracefully accepts death, while de la Selva struggles against it.

Another poem from de la Selva's collection is indebted to Millay's "The Shroud." Millay's work states that a "red gown . . . / as bright as flame" would be as acceptable as any other dress for a funeral. In "Candle Light," de la Selva discusses the cloth he would create from the light of seven candles:

> Of these I'd make a banner, or a sail;
> Perhaps a tent; or else, against my death,
> A precious cerement, for this light is cool
> And would not plot against the will of Death.

De la Selva, as he does in many of his poems linked to Millay's collection, offers an antithesis to the red gown "as bright as flame." In contrast, the cloth that he offers as a burial vestment is discreet, "cool," and unwilling to "plot against the will" of a once-again personified "Death."

If we closely examine Millay's "Three Songs of Shattering," considerable evidence suggests that de la Selva responded in his own "Three Songs." In Millay's work, the abundance of spring contrast with the emptiness in the poet's heart. In Song I, Millay writes in the first stanza:

> The first rose on my rose-tree
> Budded, bloomed, and shattered,
> During sad days when to me
> Nothing mattered.

De la Selva's first song, "Tryst," replies to these verses in agreement in its second stanza:

> Do you remember—no?—
> How it was tragic there?
> Black roses all a-row
> Growing for your hair;
> And the little lake of snow,
> How it was tragic there!

Although it is winter in these verses, there are roses in the garden. However, they are black and foreboding. The reader anticipates a sad ending, as he or she also anticipates in Millay's verses. Song II is again set against the backdrop of a youthful and dynamic spring:

> Let the little birds sing;
> Let the little lambs play;
> Spring is here; and so 'tis spring;—
> But not in the old way!

Spring has returned, but something is amiss. There is a profound sadness in spite of the season and the playfulness of the birds and the lambs. De la Selva, in the second song, "Worn Toy," directly responds to the emptiness expressed in Millay's verses:

> As a child gives what it no more desires,
> With a quick gesture and avertedly,
> Grown weary of her heart, as a child tires
> Of a worn toy, she gave her heart to me.

Although the poet receives the heart of his loved one, it is devoid of feelings. His possession of it is a meaningless feat. Like Millay's verses, there is an inverse relationship between the youthful leitmotifs and the doleful outcome. Both are lacking in joy. In the first stanza of Millay's Song III, the poet's world is barren, devoid of fruit, and thus of any hope of fulfillment:

> All the dog-wood blossoms are underneath the tree!
> Ere spring was going—ah, spring is gone!
> And there comes no summer to the like of you and me,—
> Blossom time is early, but no fruit set on.

The seasons bypass summer and fall, jumping straight from spring to winter. There is no hope for a harvest that can fill the poet's heart. The poet is condemned, at least for another year, to loneliness. De la Selva's last song, "The Birch Tree," mirrors Millay's creation:

> I loved a bit of New England once
> (God knows why!),
> A white birch delicate against the snow
> Or the gray sky;
> But it was the wind that wrung its branches,
> That clasped and held and flung its branches,—
> The wind, not I.

De la Selva's verses also reflect the barrenness in Millay's heart. The primary difference resides in the Nicaraguan-American poet's struggle to win the affections of his loved one, in contrast to Millay's verses which painfully, yet passively, lament the passing of an impossible love. One poet struggled, and lost; the other simply surrendered.

Another de la Selva poem that merits comparison with Millay's "Three Songs of Shattering" is "Pastorale." Here, Colin the shepherd leads a contented existence, like the birds and the lambs in Millay's poem. Near the middle of the second stanza, de la Selva writes,

> His heart knew not as yet passion's control:
> It was the Spring for him, as for the year,
> As for the little tree he held so dear,
> As for the flowers that unhindered grew;
> And his full being gathered, like bright dew,
> A peacefulness that quieted all need,—
> Therefore he blew upon his oaten reed.

The shepherd, separated from the harsh realities of failed loves, lives an Edenic existence. The Nicaraguan-American's verses, once again, serve almost as an antithesis to Millay's painful description of an empty spring.

Of particular interest is de la Selva's creative and personal relationship with Millay's poem "Witch-Wife." In his essay "Edna St. Vincent Millay," the Hispanic poet states that Millay mailed him that poem at a time when he corresponded with her "with the frequency of a lover." He also adds that she sent him these verses "to torment him" (126). The concluding stanza of Millay's poem reveals the source of the poet's torment:

> She loves me all that she can,
> And her ways to my ways resign;
> But she was not made for any man,
> And she never will be all mine.

We can only guess if Millay and de la Selva were lovers. De la Selva's fellow countryman and poet, José Coronel Urtecho, tried to coax it out of him unsuccessfully. However, it would not be far-fetched to assume that at one time they were intimate, given Millay's strong beliefs in a woman's right to choose freely her relationships with men. Moreover, when reading de la Selva's words about Millay, one receives the impression that he is writing about the love of his life. Annie Woodbridge suggests that their relationship went beyond the parameters of friendship when she writes, "All the Millay biographies mention Salomón de la Selva, usually as the first man in her life . . ." (105). In addition, Toby Shafter states that the American poet, during the period of her friendship with de la Selva, was constantly barraged with marriage proposals (127). It would not be surprising if de la Selva were one of the most ardent suitors of this talented and attractive poet. Comparing "Witch-Wife" to several of his poems would seem to confirm this hypothesis.

In the poem "Finally," the reader encounters the poet's reflections on his life in New England. As an Hispanic poet, teaching Spanish in rural New England, de la Selva lived in cultural isolation, uprooted from the familiar world. Nevertheless, in "Finally," the poet expresses his pleasant surprise at finding that he has much in common with rural New Englanders. He finds them as kind and caring as his fellow Nicaraguans. Towards the end of the poem, though, occurs a stanza that seems out of place and out of context with the tone and theme of the rest of the composition:

> Once, when my heart went out of me, a careless rover,
> A white birch tree was growing on a New England hill
> Turned flesh, for my sake only, and let me be her lover
> Till I was sane and quiet again, having had my fill,
> Hushed with the breathless wonder that my love could move her.

The erotic overtones of this stanza are in direct opposition to what preceded it. What, then, is the source of these startling sentiments? One can only speculate that the "white birch tree" is a metaphor for Millay. (Let us recall his reference to loving an identical tree in "The White Birch Tree," discussed earlier.) Several biographies mention that at least on one occasion Millay went to visit de la Selva in New England while he taught at Williams College. The poet expresses his great delight, and even greater surprise, in finding that the "white birch tree" was responsive to his adoration. For a moment, in contrast to Millay's "Witch-Wife," the poet managed to possess the object of his affection. In this reading, New England becomes the setting for what may have been one of the most impassioned true-life encounters in American letters.

In the collection of ten sonnets titled "First Love Revived," the poet reminisces about his first love. Interestingly, when comparing it to "Witch-Wife," one finds that the fifth sonnet, "Love's Selfishness," constitutes a direct plea against the American poet's proclamation of independence:

> You say, "If I had died in the meanwhile . . . ."
> And I, "If you had married!" And you turn
> Your face to me and with a serious smile
> Dismiss the selfishness of my concern.
> I cannot help it, child. God made me so.
> And since all flesh with Death at last must bide,
> Rather than wed I wish you dead, for woe
> A man may bear who fails at wounded pride.

The Nicaraguan-American poet goes on to offer the object of his desire three alternatives: "Such beds: your maidenhood's, and Death's, and mine." The sonnet, in addition to displaying de la Selva's emphasis on traditional forms at a time of enthusiastic experimentation, allows the reader to observe a dialogue between his creation and Millay's "Witch-Wife." One cries out for independence, while the other seeks submission through marriage. In de la Selva's poem "The Sorry Madrigal," however, the poet has come to terms with losing the object of his desire:

> So like the Spring she was,—warm, not too warm,
> And sweet to smell,—
> There was no guile in her, or any harm
> In what befell
> Except the seasons change, flowers to fruit
> And fruit to seed,
> And seeds must break or ever leaf and root
> Fulfill their need.

De la Selva turns to the simile of spring, so liked by both poets, to describe his lost love, and then to the metaphor of the changing seasons to rationalize his loss. There seems to be a total acceptance on the poet's part of the loved one's need for independence ("There was no guile in her, or any harm / In what befell"). As in de la Selva's essay on Millay, time seems to have healed the wounds of his misplaced ardor. It is interesting to note that de la Selva never wrote love poetry of such amorous intensity in Spanish as he did in English in the verses of *Tropical Town* that seem devoted to Millay.

In "The Haunted House of León," de la Selva borrows the central leitmotif of Millay's "The Little Ghost" in order to create its antithesis. Millay's poem describes the ghost of a girl who walks joyfully through the poet's garden, approving of its beauty. The poet is overcome by wonder, not fear, before the ghostly presence. The closing stanza reiterates that the visitor is, indeed, of another world and another time:

> And where the wall is built in new,
> And is of ivy bare,
> She paused—then opened and passed through
> A gate that once was there.

De la Selva transposes this literary device into a landscape as familiar to him as the garden is to Millay: León, Nicaragua—his birthplace. He also transforms the solitary yet playful ghost into a host of frightening spirits. His poem acquires political overtones when he provides the ghosts with the identities of the American mercenaries who accompanied the filibuster William Walker to Nicaragua in the 1850s. These men are portrayed as:

> Sons of the Devil
> Who drank to the Devil
> All one night, and burned the house
> After the revel.

The ghosts of de la Selva's poem are capable of murdering the living. The citizenry of León shun the empty house. However, de la Selva offers an extraordinary solution to exorcise the demons: "I will marry a Yankee girl / And we will dare!" The joining of two lovers—one from each culture—will, in the poet's view, create a new beginning, a new race, a new hope for the future. The reader cannot help but wonder whether Millay was the "Yankee girl" the poet wished to marry and take to Nicaragua.

In "God's World," Millay finds the world so wondrous that she laments not being able to assimilate everything before her. In the first stanza, she writes:

> O world, I cannot hold thee close enough!
> Thy winds, thy wide grey skies!
> Thy mists, that roll and rise!
> Thy woods, this autumn day, that ache and sag
> And all but cry with colour! That gaunt crag
> To crush! To lift the lean of that black bluff!
> World, World, I cannot get thee close enough!

De la Selva responds with one of his most accomplished creations in the English language, "Guitar Song with Variations." In the eighth through the thirteenth stanzas, the Nicaraguan poet expresses a longing to capture all of God's creation in a fashion similar to Millay:

> Youth is a song, and love a song,
> Besides wide waters ringing
> When God makes music high in heavén
> And all the stars are singing.
>
> God and the stars are always
> Whispering to each other,
> Like lover and belovéd,
> Like child and mother.
>
> Youth matters little, love matters little,
> So quick to vanish away! . . . .

Both poets marvel at the perfection of the universe and fear that life shall pass by too quickly. This *carpe diem*, the identical yearning of each poet, reminds the reader to do the same. All creation is miraculous, and both poets express grief that their human limitations prevent them from capturing its glory.

In Millay's lengthy poem "Interim," the poet expresses deep sorrow over the death of a lover. The poet wanders through familiar surroundings and everything painfully reminds her of her loss. "Interim" is best summarized by the following verse, emphatically repeated twice in the poem: "I had you and I have you now no more." The lament in the poem goes as far as to question the judgement of God before it concludes with this stanza:

> Ah, I am worn out—I am wearied out—
> It is too much—I am flesh and blood,
> And I must sleep. Though you were dead again,
> I am but flesh and blood and I must sleep.

Millay's poem enjoys verisimilitude. To this poem, de la Selva responds with a collection of ten sonnets, "The Box of Sandalwood." Contained within the box are ten sonnets written to a "Friend" whom the poet once loved. In the sonnets, unlike Millay's poem, the Hispanic poet states how he never really understood the object of his love. As de la Selva attempts yet another poetic dialogue with Millay, his composition at times borders on bathos: its aim falls far from the mark. This is evidenced in the closing verses of the collection:

> Whoever reads this poem, Christian friend,
> Pray her and me good rest, for Mary's sake:—
> I loved, and she is dead: this is the end.

Like the closing of Millay's poem, the poet also seeks rest and proclaims with finality that the former object of his love is dead. The poem ends in a cliché and, furthermore, the inclusion of Mary is highly intrusive. It is not often that de la Selva falls short of his poetic goal. However, in this instance, what once again merits our attention is the ongoing creative exchange with Millay.

The poem that closes *Tropical Town and Other Poems*, "Of Time and Song," is indebted to one of Millay's works, "Ashes of Life." In it, the American poet expresses her despair at how meaningless her life is after love has left her. The reader can best observe this in the second stanza:

> Love has gone and left me and I don't know what to do;
> This or that or what you will is all the same to me;
> But all the things that I begin I leave before I'm through,—
> There's little use in anything as far as I can see.

De la Selva's response is to offer yet one more antithesis to Millay's pessimistic outlook. All the happenings of "our yesterdays . . . / Make rich the present," his poem states. The composition concludes affirming that all our efforts are for a greater purpose:

> In my arms of rhyme
> I bring a harvest of my gathering,
> Songs like pomegranates, songs like lovely fruit,
> That it was mine to pluck away, or sing.
> And these shall waste to strengthen some young root
> In days to be, as songs of singers gone
> Nourished the songs I sing.
>   Thus, on and on,
> All days are somehow linked, all songs are one.

These verses remind the reader of the interconnectedness of life, of how actions can have positive consequences far into the future. It stands in direct contrast to the despair and hopelessness in Millay's poem. Thus, the poetic dialogue that de la Selva sustains with Millay comes to an end.

Did de la Selva's poetry in turn influence Millay? At least in two cases the answer is *yes*. Millay's second volume of poetry, *Second April*, published in 1921, contains a poem with the Spanish title "Mariposa." It is known that Millay studied several languages, including French, Italian, Spanish, and Latin. It might be concluded that she merely gleaned the title of the poem from her studies. But a more direct connection arises when one examines the set of de la Selva poems titled "Three Songs My Little Sister Made." In the first of the songs, "Make-Believe," the Hispanic poet provides an introduction consisting of four "children's" verses in Spanish:

> *Mariposa, mariposita,*
> *la del ala azul,*
> *vamos a volvernos locas*
> *de tanta luz*

> [Butterfly, little butterfly
> you whose wings are blue
> let us go mad
> from so much light.]

It is likely that Millay has taken the title directly from de la Selva's poem. This becomes particularly plausible when we examine the first stanza of Millay's work:

> Butterflies are white and blue
> In this field we wander through.
> Suffer me to take your hand.
> Death comes in a day or two.

The first two lines promise a delightful outing. The tone is as playful as de la Selva's poem. But the specter of suffering and death that appears in the next two lines subverts the spirited beginning. The poem concludes by repeating the assertion that "Death comes in a day or two." It would not require much of a literary leap of faith to link her relationship with de la Selva to this poem. Millay, an ardent pacifist, could hardly have approved of her friend's decision to go fight in World War I. Her relationship with de la Selva could easily explain the poem's title, its certainty that death was merely a day or two away, and its valedictory tone.

Biographers and critics of Millay's work all acknowledge the direct link between her poem "Recuerdo," published in her collection *A Few Figs from Thistles* (1922), and the Nicaraguan-American poet. De la Selva himself, in his essay on Millay, recalls how their ferry trips together inspired the composition (147). However, another connection has never previously been explored. In his second volume of poetry, *El soldado desconocido*, published in Mexico in 1922, de la Selva includes a poem also titled "Recuerdo." In this work, written from the point of view of a soldier in World War I, the poet laments not being able to dream about the woman that he loves because the war suppresses all pleasant thoughts. Nevertheless, he states, when he marches with his fellow soldiers in circumstances of pomp, music, and glory, he can then recall her in terms of military beauty and purity:

> *¡Eres más bella, Amada, que una espada desnuda:*
> *recta y blanca y sin tacha mis ojos te recuerdan!*

> [You are more beautiful, My Love, than a naked sword:
> my eyes remember you, straight and white and without mark!]

In a letter to Marguerite Wilkinson, Millay states that she continued her correspondence with de la Selva while he resided in London. Since the two friends were in the habit of exchanging poems in their letters, it seems very likely that an English version of de la Selva's composition, which chronologically preceded Millay's, inspired her response. Furthermore, ever the pacifist, she responds to a military poem with a poem of generosity, a poem in which the two protagonists give all they own at that moment to a poor "shawl-covered" woman:

> And she wept, "God bless you!" for the apples and pears,
> And we gave her all our money but our subway fares.

The important role that Millay played in the first major volume of poetry in the English language published by a Hispanic is immeasurable. Like Millay, de la Selva looked towards the literary past for inspiration. In his letter to Henríquez Ureña, the Nicaraguan poet states that he expects that his more notable poetic contemporaries will soon tire of their literary experiments and gratefully return to the comforts of tradition. Furthermore, he proudly proclaims that among the living poets that he admires one stands out more than any other:

Edna St. Vincent Millay (17-18). De la Selva, in his essay on Millay, proclaims that his friend is descended from a refined lineage of British poets such as Blake, Wordsworth, and Shelley; and of great American poets such as Emerson, Whittier, Lowell and Whitman. It is this same noble fountain of tradition that nourishes in large part the English-language poetry of Salomón de la Selva.

The Poetic Dialogue with Rubén Darío

The works in *Tropical Town* also exhibit a strong indebtedness to Latin American *Modernismo*. De la Selva, a friend and fellow countryman of Rubén Darío, the best known and most imitated of the *modernistas*, was intimately familiar with this important Hispanic literary movement. Indeed, in *Tropical Town* de la Selva also has an ongoing dialogue with Darío's poetry. For many of his compositions with a "Hispanic sensibility," de la Selva turns to the poetic tradition engendered by his fellow countryman. Henríquez Ureña compares de la Selva's poems to those of Darío, in particular those which address U.S.-Latin American relations (19). An essay written by de la Selva, titled "Rubén Darío," confirms the important role that Darío's work exercised over his own notion of poetics. In this article, written in English, de la Selva eloquently expresses his deep respect for the work of his fellow Nicaraguan:

> Rubén Darío's work has a threefold significance: aesthetical, historical and social. As an aesthete, in the purest meaning of this term, Rubén Darío is the Spanish Keats: he taught that "beauty is truth, truth beauty," and that sincerity is the highest virtue. This message he delivered to his people, the family of Spanish-speaking countries, with such power that through his influence and that of the other poets and writers who, with him for a leader, formed the revolutionary modernist school, Spanish poetry during the last generation was changed from the rhetorical, conventional sort of thing into which it had degenerated after it had flourished gloriously in the time of Góngora, to vibrant, real, sincere song. (200)

The essay also reveals that de la Selva understood perfectly the aims and objectives of *Modernismo*. When he goes on to write about Darío's status as a universal poet, it becomes easy to imagine that this is a goal that he himself may have hoped to achieve:

> Sincerity of expression only can bring forth real poetry, and this he knew could not be attained through mere imitation. But he was eager to learn, and the Pre-Raphaelites of England, the Parnassians and Symbolists of France, Carducci among the Italians, and Poe and Whitman of the Americans, as well, of course, as the classics of all languages, had much to teach him. And the wealth of knowledge that he made his own, brought to bear upon his work, gave it that cosmopolitan bigness that made him a truly universal poet. His work, like America, as he would often say, is for all humanity. (200-201)

One can safely assume that this also expresses de la Selva's poetic beliefs. He desires the originality and sincerity of expression that he perceives to be Darío's strengths. De la Selva, like Darío, has learned much from his poetic precursors, regardless of language and culture. Also like Darío, he sees America's potential to become a land where all cultures can learn to peacefully co-exist and prosper.

Another quote from this essay becomes most enlightening if we examine de la Selva's "Guitar Song with Variations." In the essay, the poet discusses Darío's elevated stature throughout "the neo-Latin republics of America":

> To realize fully what this means we must consider the poet's position in all the Latin, and especially in the Spanish-American countries. The poet there is a prophet, an inspired, God-anointed leader of the people. He is for us the treasurer of hope, the master of the tomorrow. (202)

The refrain that recurs throughout "Guitar Song with Variations" indicates that de la Selva too aspires to achieve, the recognition awarded to Spanish-American poets:

> Beneath the stars, beneath the moon,
> Over the sands, beside the sea,
> One time in Nicaragua,
> I was a poet.

The poet looks back, full of nostalgia, to a place where he was once regarded as being important, of being that "treasurer of hope, the master of tomorrow."

The literary heritage of several compositions in *Tropical Town and Other Poems* can be traced only by comparing them to Darío's work. The first group is a series of poems that contain religious motifs and/or figures. In Darío's *oeuvre* we find this precedent. For example, Darío's poem *"Los tres reyes magos"* ("The Three Wise Men"), from the collection *Cantos de vida y esperanza (Songs of Life and of Hope)*, recreates the Kings' visit to the newly born Jesus. It concludes:

> *Cristo resurge, hace la luz del caos*
> *y tiene la corona de la Vida*
>
> [Christ rises, bringing light out of chaos
> and possessing the crown of Life]

In addition, the poem *"Spes"* ("Hope") from the same collection, constitutes a dying man's prayer. In the last two verses of this composition, the man implores Jesus both for mercy and an eternal life:

> . . . *al morir hallaré la luz de un nuevo día*
> *y que entonces oiré mi "levántate y anda!"*

[. . . upon my death I shall find the light of a new day
and then a voice shall command me to "Come forth!"]

To Darío's poems, de la Selva responds with "The Song of the Magdalen" and "Tropical Rain." In the first poem, written from Mary Magdalen's perspective, the poet states that Peter holds the keys to the kingdom, but that Magdalen holds the keys to Jesus' heart. Her relationship with Jesus is strong even at the moment of his death:

> On the Cross He lies,
> Tortured limb on wooden limb,
> But to me He turns His eyes
> And mine to Him.

Like Darío's *"Los tres reyes magos,"* de la Selva selects a theme from the New Testament that expresses great reverence for the person of Jesus. In the poem "Tropical Rain," as in Darío's *"Spes,"* the characters pray to Jesus for salvation:

> Sweet Jesu, you that stilled the storm in Galilee,
> Pity the homeless now, and the travellers by sea;
> Pity the little birds that have no nest, that are forlorn;
> Pity the butterfly; pity the honey-bee;
> Pity the roses that are so helpless, and the unsheltered corn,
> And pity me . . . .

Rather than the salvation of their soul, as the character seeks in *"Spes,"* the people caught in the storm pray for the safety of all living creatures, especially themselves. Still, what the reader finds in both poets is their firm belief in the power of prayer. Ultimately, their poems reflect both poets' faith in Jesus as savior.

Darío's poem *"A Margarita Debayle"* finds its counterpart in de la Selva's "The Tale from Faerieland." *"A Margarita Debayle"* is one of Darío's most popular compositions in his homeland. Included in the collection entitled *Poema del otoño y otros poemas (Poem of Autumn and Other Poems)*, the composition represents a story told to Margarita Debayle—a member of one of Nicaragua's most influential families. It narrates the tale of a princess who can wander throughout the cosmos at will. While traveling through the heavens she takes a star and brings it home. Alarmed because the Lord will become angry, her father, the king, prepares her punishment and orders her to return the star. The poem continues:

La princesa se entristece
por su dulce flor de luz,
cuando entonces aparece
sonriendo el buen Jesús.

Y así dice: "En mis campiñas
esa rosa le ofrecí;
son mis flores de las niñas
que al soñar piensan en mí."

[The princess becomes sad
for her sweet flower of light
when at that moment,
smiling kindly, Jesus comes to light.

And this is what he says : "From my gardens
I offered her that rose;
they're the flowers that belong to the little girls
who when they sleep dream about me."]

In "The Tale from Faerieland," Jesus also makes an unexpected appearance. This narrative poem portrays the poet as a weaver who has created a marvelous tapestry that can be worn as a robe. However, a devious critic states that it is of little value and purchases it for a pittance. The tapestry's beauty later attracts a series of legendary owners. But it is its last owner that ties the poem to Darío's "*A Margarita Debayle*":

So when the Christ was dead, who died for Love,
Magdalen brought the cloth that I had wove,

And Joseph of Arimathea dressed
The Sad Man with it, and laid Him to rest.

Thus for three days God wore it, and the third,
When at the piping of the first song bird

Sweet Jesus rose, a glorious sight to see,
Lo! round His shoulders hung my tapestry . . . .

And He will wear it on the Judgement Day,
And of it all His holy Saints will say:

"God bless the hands that wove it, and God bless
The soul of Man that dreamed such loveliness!"

De la Selva's use of the appearance of Jesus in a narrative poem can be traced to Rubén Darío. Divine intervention was never a motif that Millay employed. In fact, if anything, Millay exhibited a disregard in her poetry for the traditions of religion.

Darío's *"Primaveral"* ("Of Spring"), from the collection *Azul (Blue)*, may have served as inspiration for de la Selva's "Sonnet." In this lengthy poem, Darío describes spring as a fertile time, a time for love and the fulfillment of earthly desires. The first stanza of the poem reads:

> *Mes de rosas. Van mis rimas*
> *en ronda, a la vasta selva,*
> *a recoger miel y aromas*
> *en las flores entreabiertas.*
> *Amada, ven. El gran bosque*
> *es nuestro templo; allí ondea*
> *y flota un santo perfume*
> *de amor. El pájaro vuela*
> *de un árbol a otro y saluda*
> *tu frente rosada y bella*
> *como a un alba; y las encinas*
> *robustas, altas, soberbias,*
> *cuando tú pasas agitan*
> *sus hojas verdes y trémulas,*
> *y enarcan sus ramas como*
> *para que pase una reina.*
> *¡Oh, amada mía! es el dulce*
> *tiempo de la primavera.*

> [Month of roses. My rhymes travel
> in circles to the vast jungle,
> to gather honey and aromas
> among the half-opened flowers.
> Beloved, come. The great forest
> is our temple; there, undulating
> and floating, is the holy scent
> of love. The bird flies
> from one tree to another and it greets
> your rose-hued brow that is
> as beautiful as the dawn; and the oaks,
> robust, tall, arrogant,
> shake their green and
> tremulous leaves as you pass,
> and they arch their branches as if
> to let a queen pass through.
> Oh, my beloved! it is the sweet
> season of spring.]

To Darío's description of spring, de la Selva replies:

> Are you awake, Belovéd? Come and see
> My special garden, set and sown apart
> In the most secret corner of my heart.
> Never the butterfly, never the bee
> Has sucked a blossom there; no day too sunny
> Has dried a leaf; no wind has swept and bent
> A single careless branch: with fruit unspent
> The trees are heavy, and the flowers with honey.
>
> But I am hurt with this too rich excess:
> Come thirsty, hot and swift! Come butterfly,
> Come sun, come wind! and twist my trees awry,
> Scatter my fruit, and of this perfectness
> Leave only ruins where the Spring next year
> May say, This place is mine, love triumphed here.

Of course, spring is one of literature's universal themes. Nevertheless, the poems' common features are many. Like Darío, de la Selva invites his beloved to venture into his portrait of spring, as it will give her an idea of the abundance of his love. While Darío employs the jungle and the forest as his setting, de la Selva makes it a garden that he has locked in an untrampled spot in his heart. The gifts of nature are present in both settings, offered to the beloved for their use. The invitation is sincere, and both poets anxiously await for their offers to be accepted.

In *Cantos de vida y esperanza*, Salomón de la Selva also finds a model upon which to base another of his poems. In this collection, Darío includes the poem "*Salutación a Leonardo.*" Written in honor of Leonardo da Vinci, the Italian Renaissance painter, sculptor, architect, and engineer, the composition praises his work, stating that as an artist he has no equal. These five lines conclude the poem:

> *Por tu cetro y gracia sensitiva,*
> *por tu copa de oro en que sueñan las rosas,*
> *en mi ciudad, que es tu cautiva,*
> *tengo un jardín de mármol y de piedras preciosas*
> *que custodia una esfinge viva.*

> [Because of your scepter and sensitive grace,
> because of your golden cup in which roses dream,
> in my city, which is your captive,
> I have a garden of marble and precious stones
> that is guarded by a living sphinx.]

De la Selva, in "Cellini at the Metropolitan Museum," praises Benvenuto Cellini, a Renaissance goldsmith and sculptor, whose art the poet viewed on exhibit in New York. The work by Cellini that caught de la Selva's poetic attention was the Rospigliosi Cup. The reader can observe Darío's influence in the poem. After de la Selva describes the creature—half-turtle, half-dragon—that serves as the cup's base, he comments on the timelessness of the work:

> . . . And held an empty cup of goldenness
> To the eternal questionings. The Sphinx
> Twines calmly siren limbs—ever the call!

As in Darío's poem, there is a golden cup watched over by a living, vigilant sphinx. In saluting an artist, de la Selva attempts to emulate, in the poetic tradition of the Renaissance, his fellow countryman.

De la Selva also owes a great measure of gratitude to Darío for providing him with an example upon which to construct the compositions in *Tropical Town and Other Poems* that deal with Pan-Americanism. About Darío's personal posture towards this matter, de la Selva writes:

> Horrified by the war, he left Europe, where he had lived for some time as minister of Nicaragua, his native country, to Spain and France, and came to America, late in 1914, to preach peace, and to work for a Pan-American Union based on a community of ideals and the intellectual fellowship of the two Americas. (Rubén Darío 203)

These attitudes and ambitions can just as well be attributed to de la Selva himself. As an idealist, he instead went to Europe to try to put an end to all wars; and, certainly, he desired wholeheartedly a Pan-American Union based on the equality of all nations.

In *"Salutación del optimista"* ("Salutation of the Optimist"), from *Cantos de vida y esperanza*, Darío provides a model for de la Selva's own fervent belief in Pan-Americanism. Darío states:

> *Un continente y otro renovando las viejas prosapias,*
> *en espíritu unidos, en espíritu y ansias y lengua,*
> *ven llegar el momento en que habrán de cantar nuevos himnos.*
> *La latina estirpe verá la gran alba futura*
> *en un trueno de música gloriosa . . . .*

> [One continent and another renewing the ancestry of old,
> in a united spirit, in mind and yearnings and language,
> they see the coming of the moment when they shall sing
> new hymns.
> The Latin lineage shall see the great dawn of the future
> in a thunder of glorious music . . . .]

With Darío's poem setting a precedent, de la Selva adds to the discussion with his "To Those Who Have Been Indifferent to the Pan-American Movement." In this composition, he condemns those Americans who have paid little or no attention to their southerly neighbors. The two lines that begin the poem fully echo Darío's sentiments:

> I am the man who dreamed the new day dawned
> And so arose at midnight with a cry.

The primary difference between the poems is in the audience that they seek to address. Darío speaks with pride of all things Hispanic to a Hispanic audience, while de la Selva warns his English-speaking audience to pursue the cause of hemispheric unity before it is too late.

Darío also provides de la Selva with an example through which he can poetically criticize U.S. foreign policy. In *"A Roosevelt"* ("To Roosevelt"), also from *Cantos de vida y esperanza*, Darío firmly chastises the American president for his interventionist policies:

> *Eres los Estados Unidos,*
> *eres el futuro invasor*
> *de la América ingenua que tiene sangre indígena,*
> *que aún reza a Jesucristo y aún habla en español.*
> *Eres soberbio y fuerte ejemplar de tu raza;*
> *eres culto, eres hábil . . . .*
>
> [You are the United States
> you are the future invader
> of the naive America of indigenous blood,
> that still prays to Jesus Christ and still speaks in Spanish.
> You are a proud and strong example of your race;
> you are cultured, you are clever . . . .]

Several of de la Selva's poems echo Darío's indictment. The first composition is "A Song for Wall Street." The poet asks "What can you buy for a penny [two pennies, a nickel] there?" The first three stanzas of the poem are openly amicable. However, the closing stanza is as biting as Darío's work:

> But for your dollar, your dirty dollar,
>   Your greenish leprosy,
> It's only hatred you shall get
>   From my folks and me;
> So keep your dollar where it belongs
>   And let us be!

In "My Nicaragua," de la Selva opposes all attempts toward the cultural conquest of his homeland:

> The parlours of the ruling class adorned
> With much the same bad taste as in New York,—
> That never was my country! But the rows
> of earthen little houses where men dwell,
> And women, all too busy living life
> To think of faking it, that is my country,
> My Nicaragua, mother of great poets!

De la Selva affirms that it is the simple people, the Latin Americans of Darío's *"A Roosevelt,"* who truly represent his country's strength.

The poem that most strongly condemns United States policy towards Latin America is "The Dreamer's Heart Knows Its Own Bitterness (A Pan-American Poem on the Entrance of the United States into the War)." This composition, which de la Selva read for an audience including former president Theodore Roosevelt, personifies the South as de la Selva's mother and the North as his bride. He tries to be loyal to both, but finds his bride unwilling to compromise or to treat his mother with respect. Later in the work, the two continents are personified as the condor and the eagle, ready to become locked in combat, much to the poet's dismay. The use of the condor and the eagle derives from Darío's poem *"Salutación al aguila"* ("Salutation to the Eagle"):

> *Aguila, existe el Cóndor.*
> *Es tu hermano en las grandes alturas.*

> [Eagle, the Condor exists.
> He is your brother in the great heights.]

In "The Dreamer's Heart Knows Its Own Bitterness," the poet intervenes and manages an uneasy truce when one trespasses another's territory:

> But now a cry like a red flamingo
> Has winged its way to the Judgement gates:
> My Nicaragua and Santo Domingo
> Shorn in their leanness by the "famous States"!

The poet finds it ironic that the United States invades both his country and the Dominican Republic while calling for peace and justice on European soil:

> Will you let this thing be said of you,
> That you stood for Right who were clothed with Wrong?
> That to Latin America you proved untrue?
> That you clamoured for justice with a guilty tongue?
> Hear me, who cry for the sore oppressed:
> Make right this grievance that I bear in me
> Like a lance point driven into my breast!
> So, blameless and righteous, your strength shall be

>The power of God made manifest,
>And I pledge the South shall never rest
>Till your task is accomplished and the world is free.

The poem concludes with a pledge that, in spite of the offenses against it, the South will side with its neighbor as it undertakes a just cause in Europe.

Both Darío and de la Selva also poetically express great admiration for the United States. In *"Salutación al águila"* ("Salutation to the Eagle"), from the volume *El canto errante*, Darío writes of the positive role that the United States is capable of playing in the affairs of his continent. The poem begins:

>*Bien vengas, mágica Aguila de alas enormes y fuertes,*
>*a extender sobre el Sur tu gran sombra continental,*
>*a traer en tus garras, anilladas de rojos brillantes,*
>*una palma de gloria, del color de la inmensa esperanza,*
>*y en tu pico la oliva de una vasta y fecunda paz.*

>[You are welcomed, magic Eagle of enormous and strong wings,
>to extend your grand continental shadow over the South,
>to bring in your claws, ringed with brilliant shades of red,
>a palm of glory, the color of immense hope,
>and in your beak the olive branch of a vast and fecund peace.]

Darío's words reveal a desire for an equal partnership with the United States. The poet thinks this nation capable of bringing glory, prosperity, and peace to the entire continent. He appeals to the just and caring side of Americans. In addition, we come to see that both poets had highly mixed feelings for this country—de la Selva more so than Darío. After all, de la Selva hoped to serve as a bridge between the Americas. He expresses this clearly in the essay "Edna St. Vincent Millay": *"De la Selva estaba en vía de ser el intérprete de una y otra cultura, el lazo entre ambas, que ha hecho falta.* [De la Selva was in route to become the interpreter of one culture to the other, the link between both of them, which is what has been missing.]" Several of de la Selva's poems deal with a yearning that both cultures and peoples can some day come to understand one another.

As de la Selva, however, prepares to go to war, he turns to one of Darío's greatest poetic accomplishments, *"La marcha triunfal"* ("The Triumphal March"), from the collection *Cantos de vida y esperanza*. This poem is regarded as Darío's best by many of his fellow Nicaraguans. It describes a victorious army entering a city in a stunning parade. The rhythm of the poem is so forceful that the listener can easily imagine the thunderous sound of thousands of marching feet. The poem begins:

¡Ya viene el cortejo!
¡Ya viene el cortejo! Ya se oyen los claros clarines.
La espada se anuncia con vivo reflejo;
ya viene oro y hierro, el cortejo de los paladines.

[Here comes the cortege!
Here comes the cortege! One can hear the clear call of the bugles.
The sword is announced with a vivid gleam;
here comes gold and iron, the cortege of the paladins.]

De la Selva responds ironically to Darío's poem with the poem "Drill," which fits in perfectly with the rag-tag ranks of inexperienced American enlisted men who are beginning their preparations for their country's entry into World War I:

One! two, three four,
One! two, three four,
One, two . . . .

It is hard to keep time
Marching through
The rutted slime
With no drum to play for you.

The naiveté of de la Selva's poem is enchanting. The poet's enthusiasm and idealism are almost contagious; young men prepare for war as if going off on a great adventure. De la Selva's next collection, *El soldado desconocido (The Unknown Soldier)*, will portray a starkly different reality: that of a war weary-soldier.

De la Selva's poetry actually surpasses Darío's when it looks back nostalgically upon their shared homeland. Darío never wrote much about Nicaragua. One of his poems on the subject is *"Allá lejos"* ("Over There in the Distance"), from the volume *Cantos de vida y esperanza*. The poet starts his recollection of his birthplace with the image of an ox, laboring under the scalding sun, and proceeds to fill the remaining verses with clichés about nature and agriculture in the tropics. Another poem in which Darío looks back on his childhood in Nicaragua is "Momotombo," from *El canto errante*. The poet recalls being deeply moved as an adolescent when he caught sight of the volcano from the window of his train. Darío's rhetoric then becomes neo-classical, however, and the reader learns little of the author's country. De la Selva, on the other hand, paints startlingly vivid portraits of his birthplace. The entire section of *Tropical Town* titled "My Nicaragua" is a collection of delicate sketches designed to take to reader to the poet's homeland. For example, "Body and Soul" begins:

This cobweb of long streets is called León.
The spider Time began and left it there
To dangle in the still, tropical air
Moved in no wind but by the breathing sun.
The coloured roofs are sorry captured wings,
The churches are brown beetle carcasses;
And nothing quickens, all is loneliness,
Save when, importunate, an old bell rings.

Beside León, Subtiava sprawls. It has
No other colours but the green of trees,
The gray of huts, the zinc of dusty grass.
The Spanish city and the Indian lie,
Unmindful of the tread of centuries,
Unchangeable beneath the changeless sky.

León is portrayed as a city unchanged by the centuries—dormant, stagnant, moved only by the stifling air of the tropical sun. Wings and beetle carcasses are metaphors for roofs and churches, unmoving in time and space except for the tolling of the bells. Next to León is Subtiava, named after the indigenous tribe that inhabits it. Here, the reader finds the greenery of trees. Life flows through this native town in spite of its poverty. That is the heritage of de la Selva's Nicaragua. His portraits of his homeland are certainly more poignant than any similar work by Darío. Valle-Castillo suggests that the poetry in the section "My Nicaragua" reflects a sensibility and a thematic preference that characterizes Hispanic *posmodernismo*. It is a common preocupation of the *posmodernistas*, Valle-Castillo suggests, to celebrate the Americas, to celebrate its mestizo heritage and to reject "Yanki interventionism" (30). Thus it should not surprise us that, as Henríquez Ureña states, "My Nicaragua" is by far the most successful section of *Tropical Town and Other Poems* (19). For once, de la Selva surpasses his highly regarded master, Rubén Darío.

Salomón de la Selva After *Tropical Town*

In *Tropical Town* de la Selva took many of his creative cues from both Millay and Darío. In his next collection of poems, however, *El soldado desconocido* (*The Unknown Soldier*), he develops a voice unique in Spanish-language literature. De la Selva's *Lebenswelt*, or life-world, includes an experience shared by no other Hispanic poet of the Americas: his participation as a soldier in World War I. Stefan Baciu states that de la Selva's first collection of poetry in Spanish "announces not only a great poet, but also opens the path for the humanistic and social poetry that would arise after the War . . ." (103). De la Selva's importance has been recognized by several critics, in particular José Emilio Pacheco, who ranks him as the most important of the founders (along with his friend Pedro Henríquez Ureña, and the Mexican, Salvador Novo) of a poetic movement known as La Otra Vanguardia (The Other *Avant-Garde*). These poets are the precursors of the poetry that flourished throughout Latin America during the 1960s known as *prosaísmo* (of a prosaic nature).

As early as 1941, the Mexican poet Xavier Villaurrutia recognized de la Selva as one of the poets who introduced prosaic verse into the Spanish language. Villaurrutia postulates that this innovation reflects de la Selva's American and British poetic sensibilities (879). Rivero Ayllón notes that the *avant-garde* poets of Nicaragua, led by José Coronel Urtecho, considered Salomón de la Selva to be the bridge linking their generation to Rubén Darío's (27). De la Selva's contribution to Latin American poetry is being closely reexamined. Arellano reports that the Nicaraguan's work in Spanish is, at present, being reevaluated by several distinguished scholars (56).[21] Although de la Selva enjoys great prestige and respect in his homeland, he has yet to be awarded his rightful place in Latin American letters.

The poems in *El soldado desconocido* signal a marked departure from the formality of *Tropical Town and Other Poems*. To the optimistic playfulness in "Drill," we can contrast the war-weariness of *"Decanso de una marcha."* In this work, the poet/soldier engages in a conversation with the earth:

> *La tierra dice: "¡No me odies!*
> *Mira, soy tu madre.*
> *¿Por qué me pisoteas con dureza?*
> *Los tacones herrados de tus zapatos rudos*
> *me marcan ignominiosamente.*
> *Si soy toda suavidad para contigo,*
> *¿por qué no te descalzas? . . . . "*

> [The earth says: "Don't hate me!
> Look, I am your mother.
> Why do you trample upon me with harshness?
> The metal heels of your rough shoes
> ignominiously mark me.
> If I am nothing but tenderness toward you,
> why don't you take off your shoes? . . . ."]

In addition to a poetic stance that no longer idealizes war, de la Selva has adopted a much more conversational or prosaic tone. His views on war can at times become terribly mundane, as in these verses from "Poilu," a term used to refer to the French soldiers during the War:

> *Cuando me quite los zapatos*
> *me van a heder los pies, y tendré llagas*
> *húmedas y verdosas en las plantas.*

[When I take off my shoes
my feet will stink, and on the soles
I will have damp and greenish sores.]

The prosaic nature of these verses complement perfectly the themes of *El soldado desconocido*. De la Selva no longer finds the reality of war as heroic or noble as he did in *Tropical Town and Other Poems*.[22]

Perhaps the most stirring moments in *El soldado desconocido*, however, are when he appropriates the most successful element of *Tropical Town and Other Poems*: nostalgia for Nicaragua. In *"Granadas de gas asfixiante"* (Poison Gas Grenades), the poet stops in the midst of an attack to think about his country because the smell of the grenades reminds him of home:

El gas que he respirado
me dejó casi ciego,
pero olía a fruta de mi tierra,
unas veces a piña y otras veces a mango,
y hasta a guineos de los que sirven para hacer vinagre;
y aunque de sí no me hubiera hecho llorar,
sé que hubiera llorado.

[The gas that I have inhaled
left me almost blind,
but it smelled like the fruit of my homeland,
sometimes like pineapple and other times like mango,
and even like the bananas that are used to make vinegar,
and although that alone may not have made me cry,
I know that I would have cried.]

The poet's tenderness for home once again moves the reader. The prosaic and conversation tone of the verses, however, put it within the grasp of all readers. The formal nature of his verses in the English language have been set aside to reach out and touch all of humanity. This is de la Selva's greatest contribution to Hispanic poetry.

De la Selva, though, never forgets his two early poetic models when writing in Spanish. In the lengthy composition *"Evocación de Píndaro"* (Invocation for Pindar), from the eponymous poetic collection published in 1957, less than two years before his death, de la Selva, in several instances, reflects back on the importance of Rubén Darío in Hispanic literature:

¡Sólo Darío, Darío únicamente
renueva las latinas glorias ecuménicas
como nunca la espada: sólo él es augusto!

[Only Darío, Darío solely
renews the ecumenical Latin glories
like never the sword: only he is august!]

De la Selva goes on to recall Darío's love for and his pride in the Americas.
Then, harkening back to when he knew Darío, shortly before the great poet's
death, de la Selva laments:

> . . . *cuando murió; apenas comenzaba;*
> *¡dan ganas de llorar!*

> [. . . when he died; he was barely beginning;
> it makes you want to break into tears!]

Later, in verses that in retrospect seem particularly prescient, de la Selva
writes:

> *Donde Darío yace,*
> *bajo un triste león, en su León más triste*
> *. . . derrama miel y desparrama rosas . . .*

> [Where Darío lies,
> under a sorrowful lion, in his even more sorrowful León
> . . . he spreads honey and scatters roses . . .]

Little could de la Selva have known that less than two years from the publication of this poem he would be entombed next to Rubén Darío in the poetic
pantheon of Nicaragua, the Cathedral of León.

De la Selva neither forgets his indebtedness to Millay. In his essay on the
American poet, the Nicaraguan writes about how he has lovingly translated her
work into Spanish. Moreover, when he speaks of the translations, he argues that
they in spirit resemble a collaboration. He took considerable liberties with many
of the verses. For example, in "Witch-Wife," he translated the two opening
verses, "She is neither pink nor pale, / And she will never be all mine . . . ," as:
"Jamás ha de ser tuya la virgen / que no tiene palideces de luna ni rubores de
flor." Translated back into English, this would read: "Never shall the virgin be
yours / who does not possess the moon's paleness nor the flower's blush." De
la Selva claimed that he translated freely only when a literal translation would
fail to convey the spirit of Millay's verses. In her best-known work,
"Renascence," de la Selva's "collaboration" reaches a creative extreme when he
adds four lines not in the original:

> *Sentí cien veces la congoja*
> *de merecer, por culpa propia*
> *con pies desnudos colgar de la horca:*
> *Por culpa ajena pendí de soga.*

[I experienced a hundred times the anguish
of deserving, because of my own offenses,
to hang barefooted from the noose:
For another's offense I dangled from the rope.]

Only de la Selva's intimate familiarity with both Millay and her work can excuse such a literary transgression. The two friends, who had exhaustively read each other's verses in their youth, are now, in their latter days, once again sharing their poetic talents. Of this free translation, Woodbridge writes: "Salomón de la Selva claimed not to remember whether he heard Edna recite these lines or if he through his immersion in and understanding of the original poem composed them himself" (106). His essay and his translations of several of her poems, published only a year before Millay's death, constitutes the Nicaraguan's parting gift to his favorite poet in the English language.

The Literary Heritage of *Tropical Town*

This brings us back to our most pressing question: What, then, is Salomón de la Selva's literary heritage? The Nicaraguan poet's *Weltanschauung* is a complex one. He was divided between the experimentation that signalled the future of the continent's poetics, and his reverence for tradition. In *Tropical Town* he opted for the latter. Yet, he seemed to exist, culturally speaking, in a creative vacuum: a Hispanic poet writing in English but without any models that spoke to his unique circumstances. Thus de la Selva, in turning to traditional models, unquestionably experienced of what Harold Bloom terms the "anxiety of influence," or the attempt to create an original vision out of the poetic heritage of the past (5-10). De la Selva's English-language poetry, as well as Millay's early work, represents a *tessera*, a link to the past in which a poet tries to convince herself or himself, and the reader, of the desirability of maintaining the poetic standards set by their precursors (67). In embracing such standards, de la Selva also tries to authenticate his work: He needed to adjust his poetry to the demands of the standard marketplace (Stepto 8). Without an identifiable public to read his work, de la Selva had to try to blend into the mainstream.

In spite of these pressures, de la Selva did manage to create something new, particularly in the poems that deal with his dual heritage: the Nicaraguan and the American. He, in a term first used by W. E. B. Dubois in *The Souls of Black Folk*, exhibited the phenomenon of "double-consciousness" to a high degree. De la Selva's acute awareness of his doubleness allows him to relate playfully, at times, to the English language (Sollors 247-248). If de la Selva had continued his writings in English, as well as continued his exploration into his dual heritage, he would have undoubtedly created new poetic forms. *Tropical Town and Other Poems* certainly represents what Henry Louis Gates, Jr., has termed a "double-voiced text" (5-6). In such a work there is a strong indication of an ethnic writer's double-consciousness and, thus, of the text's dual literary heritage.

Salomón de la Selva's first collection of poetry represents a synthesis of Hispanic and Anglo literary traditions. Salomón de la Selva did, as Valle-Castillo states, express himself admirably in two vastly different poetic worlds (17). Yet, his poetic expression is also tinged with alienation. Throughout his poems, and in the subsequent actions of his life, de la Selva recognized himself as a distinct and separate entity from American society. He, for the most part, has an antagonistic relationship with the American power structure. Thus, de la Selva maintains, as White has suggested, a "highly conflictive dialogue . . . with North American verse in his evolution as a poet" ("Salomón de la Selva: Testimonial Poetry" 120). This certainly explains his refusal to continue writing in English and also his refusal to make the United States his permanent country of residence after fighting in World War I.

The compositions included in *Tropical Town* clearly reflect what Ramón A. Gutiérrez has suggested about the literature produced by American ethnic writers:

> Hispanic nostalgic literature and American ethnic literatures are not anemic versions of robust European type. They were shaped in the American continent by different forces and must be understood as such and in their relationships to the peoples and places that inspired them. (248)

Thus we have tried to understand the different forces, peoples and places that influenced de la Selva's poetry. After this exploration, we can agree with White's assessment:

> De la Selva, as a poet writing in two different languages and familiar with both literary traditions, embraces intertextuality between and within idioms. The distinction between tongues becomes, in a literary sense, nonexistent, if one accepts the idea that even works composed in one language may have been thought or felt in another. (122)

De la Selva's literary formation indeed erases the lines between languages, peoples, and cultures. He travels freely among literatures and, perhaps most importantly, he later develops an original poetic stance, engendering what Valle-Castillo terms *neo-popularismo* (neo-popularism) before it is practiced by the Spanish poets of the Generation of 1927 and beyond.

Tropical Town and Other Poems anticipates the success of today's Hispanic-American authors. Their success was arrived at only after decades of creative hardships and struggles. Sadly, it was acheived without the knowledge that a Hispanic poet had come close to succeeding in the American literary mainstream as early as 1918. The Nicaraguan poet José Coronel Urtecho suggests that American letters—and by extension Hispanic-American letters—lost an important figure when Salomón de la Selva stopped writing in English: "It is difficult to believe . . . that North American professors and critics fail to realize that Salomón de la Selva's return to his maternal tongue constituted a loss for American poetry and its development" (68). Salomón de la Selva, though, would rejoice for Hispanic-Americans if he were alive today.

Tropical Town and Other Poems, as much as Nicaraguans would like to claim it, in reality belongs to the United States Hispanic literary heritage. The hopes and visions within the pages of this poetic collection seek to move and inspire the American reader as well as reflecting the hopes and aspirations of Hispanic-Americans. *Tropical Town* constitutes de la Selva's call for all of us to build a bridge of understanding and solidarity between the continent's English- and Spanish-speaking peoples.

Notes

[1] Gutiérrez tells an anecdote in which de la Selva receives the scholarship directly from the Nicaraguan dictator, José Santos Zelaya. As a boy of nine years of age, de la Selva confronts the dictator at a public function for having imprisoned his father. Impressed by the boy's oratorical skills, Zelaya awards him a scholarship and releases his father (89). However, there are no other accounts that support Gutiérrez's story.

[2] Considerable variance exists between the accounts at hand regarding Salomón de la Selva's departure from Nicaragua. Buitrago and Tünnerman state that he left at age eleven. Wallace, writing in the *Dictionary of Mexican Literature* (630), and Pedro Henríquez Ureña (13), state that he left his country at age twelve (632). The *Oxford Companion to Spanish Literature* (537) and Ernesto Cardenal (35) place de la Selva at age thirteen when he leaves Nicaragua . Arellano seems to suggest that de la Selva was eighteen years of age when he left (*Los Tres Grandes* 57). Buitrago and Tünnerman's version is favored here because they had direct access, shortly after de la Selva's death, to his siblings, and much of the information they gathered in regard to the poet's life is the result of these contacts.

[3] According to Ernesto Gutiérrez, during his brief stay in Nicaragua, at age 17, de la Selva joined the seminary in earnest and at that time learned classical Latin (90). This account remains unconfirmed.

[4] With regard to de la Selva's enduring friendship with Henríquez Ureña, Arellano writes: "Our poet received the best lessons in his life from Don Pedro, who was the person that most influenced his formation. He would always recognize this in every instance in which he had the opportunity to do so . . ." (113)

[5] Persistent, yet unconfirmed, reports have Salomón de la Selva studying and also teaching at Cornell and Columbia universities.

[6] Salomón de la Selva is mentioned several times in Millay's letters. The first instance is in a letter dated November 26, 1916, and the last in a letter dated July 12, 1919.

[7] Coronel Urtecho tells of the time in which de la Selva related how he and Millay lost touch with one another in 1918 only to meet again more than twenty years later and spend an entire night reminiscing in laughter and in tears (75). In January of 1950, the year of Millay's death, Salomón de la Selva published the essay "Edna St. Vincent Millay."

[8] This is according to White in *Poets in Nicaragua*, p. 23.

[9] Parts of the speech were recreated in Spanish by Pedro Henríquez Ureña in his article "Salomón de la Selva." The English translation is Steven White's and can be found in "Salomón de la Selva: Testimonial Poetry," p. 124.

[10] It is particularly ironic that de la Selva offended the hero of San Juan Hill, for during the campaign to gain support for U. S. efforts in World War I, "Teddy Roosevelt was behind a movement to convert all hyphenated Americans into '100 per cent Americans.' He insisted that everyone subscribe to 'the simple and loyal motto, AMERICA FOR AMERICANS,' and roundly condemned 'those who spiritually remained foreigners in whole or in part.' To become '100 per cent Americans' it was not enough for a hyphenated American to support the government and obey the laws of his adopted land; he had to abandon all traces of the customs, beliefs and language he had brought with him from the Old Country" (*This Fabulous Century* 238).

[11] England was the country of citizenship of de la Selva's maternal grandmother.

[12] For a detailed analysis of the critical problems posed by this "ghost," see White's "Salomón de la Selva: Testimonial Poetry and World War I," pages 124-126.

[13] The poems of *The Unknown Soldier*, if they indeed do exist, have yet to be discovered.

[14] The artwork on the cover of *El soldado desconocido's* original printing was designed by the famous Mexican muralist Diego Rivera.

[15] Salomón de la Selva's son, Salomón de la Selva Castrillo, became an engineer and resided for the most part in Mexico. De la Selva's daughter died in the earthquake that destroyed Managua in 1931.

[16] Various sources state that Salomón de la Selva, at some time during his initial stay in the United States, served as secretary for the pioneer American labor leader, Samuel Gompers (1850-1924). Apparently his interest in unionization began in the United States and he carried it with him to his homeland. Exactly when, or if, he worked for Gompers is unknown.

[17] Although it is only conjecture, we can assume that de la Selva's friendship with Dr. René Schick, Nicaragua's Minister of Foreign Relations (who would later become President of the Republic), enticed him to accept Somoza's offer.

[18] The poems of "In War Time" are the ones that have received the most critical attention. Steven F. White has devoted considerable effort to explore de la Selva's "War Poetry." White, in his essay "Salomón de la Selva: Testimonial Poetry and World War I," closely examines the manner in which the Nicaraguan's war poetry parallels or contrasts with the creations of British poets who fought in the war.

[19] With regard to de la Selva's poetic stance in "A Prayer for the United States," *vis-a-vis* the creations of his British contemporaries, White writes: "This short poem is a good example of the lack of literary-historical synchronization between de la Selva and the English poets of the First World War, whose verse, by August 1917, had become deeply morbid and disillusioned" (Salomón de la Selva: Testimonial Poetry 129).

[20] Because of de la Selva's adherence to past poetic traditions, his sole work in English can be said to share the same fate as Millay's entire body of work: "Edna St. Vincent Millay has been praised extravagantly as the greatest woman poet since Sappho. She has also been dismissed with lofty forebearance as a renegade from the contemporary movement in poetry and sometimes been treated as a traitor because she never broke defiantly with the past" (Gray 43).

[21] These critics, according to Arellano, would include Alberto Hidalgo, Joaquín Pasos, Sergio Ramírez, Melvin H. Foster, José Emilio Pacheco, and Roberto Armijo (56).

[22] For a more thorough discussion on de la Selva's war poems, read Steven F. White's chapter on the Nicaraguan poet in *Modern Nicaraguan Poetry: Dialogues with France and the United States.*

Works Cited

Arellano, Jorge Eduardo. *Los tres grandes: Azarías H. Pallais, Alfonso Cortés y Salomón de la Selva.* Managua, Nicaragua: Ediciones Distribuidora Cultural, 1993.

————. *"Pedro Henríquez Ureña y Salomón de la Selva."* In *Homenaje a Salomón de la Selva: 1959-1969.* Ernesto Gutiérrez, ed. León, Nicaragua: Cuadernos Universitarios, 1969, p. 112-118.

Baciu, Stefan. *"Salomón de la Selva precursor."* In *Homenaje a Salomón de la Selva: 1959-1969.* Ernesto Gutiérrez, ed. León, Nicaragua: Cuadernos Universitarios, 1969, p. 96-109.

Baldick, Chris. *The Concise Oxford Dictionary of Literary Terms.* New York: Oxford University Press, 1990.

Bloom, Harold. *The Anxiety of Influence: A Theory of Poetry.* 1973. New York: Oxford University Press, 1975.

Bowen, Ezra, ed. *This Fabulous Century: Volume II: 1910-1920.* New York: Time-Life Books, 1969.

312 ❖ ❖ ❖ ❖ ❖ ❖ ❖ ❖ ❖ *Silvio Sirias*

Buitrago, Edgardo, and Tünerman, Carlos. *Breves datos biográficos y algunos poemas de Salomón de la Selva.* León, Nicaragua: Universidad Nacional. 1959.

Cardenal, Ernesto, ed. *Poesía nueva de Nicaragua.* Buenos Aires: Ediciones Carlos Lohlé, 1974.

Chai, Leon. *Aestheticism: The Religion of Art in Post-Romantic Literature.* New York: Columbia University Press, 1990.

Childers, Joseph, and Hentzi, Gary, eds. *The Columbia Dictionary of Modern Literary and Cultural Criticism.* New York: Columbia University Press, 1995.

Clark, Suzanne. "Uncanny Millay." In *Millay at 100: A Critical Reappraisal.* Diane P. Freedman, ed. Carbondale: Southern Illinois University Press, 1995, p. 3-26.

Coronel Urtecho, José. *"En Nueva York con el poeta Salomón de la Selva."* In *Homenaje a Salomón de la Selva: 1959-1969.* Ernesto Gutiérrez, ed. León, Nicaragua: Cuadernos Universitarios, 1969, p. 59-77.

Darío, Rubén. *Antología Poética.* Arturo Torres Ríoseco, ed. Berkeley: University of California Press, 1949.

⸻. *Poesías de Rubén Darío.* México: Editores Mexicanos, S. A., 1982.

Gates, Henry Louis, Jr. *The Signifying Monkey: A Theory of African-American Literary Criticism.* New York: Oxford University Press, 1988.

Gray, James. *Edna St. Vincent Millay.* University of Minnesota Pamphlets on American Writers, Number 64. Minneapolis: University of Minnesota Press, 1967.

Gutiérrez, Ernesto. *"Breves apuntes sobre la vida y obra de Salomón de la Selva."* In *Homenaje a Salomón de la Selva: 1959-1969.* Ernesto Gutiérrez, ed. León, Nicaragua: Cuadernos Universitarios, 1969, p. 89-95.

⸻, ed. *Homenaje a Salomón de la Selva: 1959-1969.* León, Nicaragua: Cuadernos Universitarios, 1969.

Gutiérrez, Ramón A. "Nationalism and Literary Production: The Hispanic and Chicano Experiences." In *Recovering the U. S. Hispanic Literary Heritage.* Ramón Gutiérrez and Genaro Padilla, eds. Houston: Arte Público Press, 1993, p. 241-250.

Henríquez Ureña, Max. *Breve historia del modernismo.* 1954. México: Fondo de Cultura Económica, 1978.

Henríquez Ureña, Pedro. "Salomón de la Selva." In *Homenaje a Salomón de la Selva: 1959-1969.* Ernesto Gutiérrez, ed. León, Nicaragua: Cuadernos Universitarios, 1969, p. 13-19. The article was originally published in the newspaper *Novedades*, New York, July 22, 1915.

⸻. "Salomón de la Selva." In *Homenaje a Salomón de la Selva: 1959-1969.* Ernesto Gutiérrez, ed. León, Nicaragua: Cuadernos Universitarios, 1969, p. 13-19. This article was originally published in the newspaper *El Figaro*, La Habana, 6-IV-1919, p 11-12.

Kirkpatrick, Gwen. *The Dissonant Legacy of Modernismo: Lugones, Herrera y Reissig and the Voices of Modern Spanish American Poetry*. Berkeley: University of California Press, 1989.

Lomelí, Francisco A. "Po(l)etics of Reconstructing and/or Appropriating a Literary Past: The Regional Case Model." In *Recovering the U. S. Hispanic Literary Heritage*. Ramón Gutiérrez and Genaro Padilla, eds. Houston: Arte Público Press, 1993, p. 221-240.

Meynell, Alice. "Decivilised." In *The Rhythm of Life and Other Essays*. 1896. Freeport, New York: Books for Libraries Press, 1972, p. 7-11.

Millay, Edna St. Vincent. *Collected Poems*. Norma Millay, ed. New York: Harper and Row, 1956.

———. *Letters of Edna St. Vincent Millay*. Allan Ross Macdougall, ed. New York: Harper and Brothers, 1952.

Pacheco, José Emilio. "*Nota sobre la otra vanguardia*." *Casa de las Américas* 20 (1980): 103-107.

Rivero Ayllón, Teodoro. *Tres poetas de Nicaragua: Cortés-Palláis-de la Selva*. Chiclayo, Perú: Instituto Cultural Peruano-Brasileiro, 1968.

Rothschuh Tablada, Guillermo. "*Prioridades de Salomón de la Selva*." In Jorge Arellano, ed., "*Salomón de la Selva: Antología Poética*. Managua, Nicaragua: Extensión Cultural, UNAN/Ndcleo de Managua, 1982.

Sánchez-Romeralo, Antonio. "El Modernismo y su época." In *Antología comentada del Modernismo*. Sacramento, California: Porrata y Santana, 1974, p. IX-XXXIX.

Schulman, Iván A. *Génesis del Modernismo*. 1966. México: El Colegio de México/Washington University Press, 1968.

Selva, Salomón de la. *Antología mayor*. Julio Valle-Castillo, ed. Managua: Editorial Nueva Nicaragua, 1993.

———. "Edna St. Vincent Millay." In *Homenaje a Salomón de la Selva: 1959-1969*. Ernesto Gutiérrez, ed. León, Nicaragua: Cuadernos Universitarios, 1969, p. 125-150. This article originally appeared in *América: Revista Antológica*. Published in México in January of 1950, no. 62, p. 7-32.

———. "Rubén Darío." *Poetry: A Magazine of Verse*. VIII (1916): 200-204.

———. *Tropical Town and Other Poems*. New York: John Lane Company, 1918.

Stepto, Robert. *From Behind the Veil: A Study of Afro-American Narrative*. Urbana: University of Illinois Press, 1979.

Shafter, Toby. *Edna St. Vincent Millay: America's Best-Loved Poet*. New York: Julian Messner, Inc., 1957.

Sollors, Werner. "Ethnic Modernism and Double Audience." In *Beyond Ethnicity: Consent and Descent in American Culture*. New York: Oxford University Press, 1986, p. 247-245.

Valle-Castillo, Julio. "*Acroasis sobre Salomón de la Selva y/o una poética americana de vanguardia*." In Julio Valle-Castillo, ed., *Salomón de la*

Selva: Antología mayor. Managua, Nicaragua: Editorial Nueva Nicaragua, 1993.

Villaurrutia, Xavier. *"La poesía moderna en lengua española."* In *Obras: Poesía, Teatro, Prosas Varias, Crítica.* 1953. Miguel Capistrán, Alí Chumacero and Luis Mario Schneider, eds. México: Letras/Fondo de Cultura Económica, 1974, p. 871-880. This essay originally formed the prologue to *Laurel: Antología de la poesía moderna española.* Emilio Prados, Xavier Villaurrutia, Juan Gil-Albert and Octavio Paz, eds. México: Editorial Séneca/Colección Laberinto, 1941.

Wallace, Jeanne C. "Selva, Salomón de la (1893-1959)." In *Dictionary of Mexican Literature,* edited by Eladio Cortés. Westport, Conn.: Greenwood Press, 1992.

Ward, Philip, ed. *The Oxford Companion to Spanish Literature.* Oxford, England: Clarendon Press, 1978.

White, Steven. *Modern Nicaraguan Poetry: Dialogues with France and the United States.* Lewisburg: Bucknell University Press, 1993.

————, ed. *Poets of Nicaragua: A Bilingual Anthology, 1918-1979.* Greensboro: Unicorn Press, 1982.

————. "Salomón de la Selva: Testimonial Poetry and World War I." In *Modern Nicaraguan Poetry: Dialogues with France and the United States.* Lewisburg: Bucknell University Press, 1993.

Woodbridge, Annie S. "Millay in Spanish." *Jack London Newsletter.* 11 (1978): 105-106.

"A Man of Action": Cirilo Villaverde as Trans-American Revolutionary Writer

Rodrigo Lazo
Miami University of Ohio

> He has passed into death from a long life as total patriot and valuable writer . . . the elder who gave Cuba his blood, without regret, and an unforgettable novel. José Martí, "Cirilo Villaverde"[1]

José Martí's obituary of Cirilo Villaverde, published in the New York newspaper *Patria* in 1894, challenges the dominant picture in literary history and criticism of Villaverde's life and writings. While most studies of Villaverde have framed him as a novelist and a major figure in Cuban literature, Martí brings to the forefront Villaverde's work as a political activist and journalist in the United States. What emerges in Martí's piece is a priority of deeds: Villaverde is patriot first, writer second. His willingness to sacrifice his life for Cuba takes precedence over an "unforgettable novel." Without negating Villaverde's contributions to Cuban literature, Martí calls on "others to discuss those polished works." Instead, Martí stresses how even in old age, Villaverde labored for the New York newspaper *El Espejo* and worked as a leader in the Cuban independence movement. The obituary's most captivating image recounts a "mortally cold New York night" when Villaverde took into his home a group of downcast young militants and lifted their spirits by urging them to seek new methods for bringing about Cuban independence. Martí remembered the contrast between "the gentleness of his gestures and the scourge and rebellion of his words" (Martí 5: 242) As such, Martí's piece emphasizes a part of Villaverde's life that has remained largely unexamined, his work as a political journalist and activist in the United States for forty-five years.

In 1849 Villaverde went into exile in New York and devoted himself to the intellectual and political struggle to end Spanish colonialism in Cuba. He turned away from youthful aspirations to literary success and became what he called "a man of action," a committed revolutionary intent on supporting words with military force. He edited and contributed works to a variety of newspapers and other publications, including *La Verdad* (1848-52) and *La Voz de América* (1866-67). Most of his non-fiction was deployed with the goal of bringing about change in Cuba's status as a Spanish colony. As a Cuban literary figure who established himself in New York City, Villaverde was an important precursor to Martí. While the latter has been noted as a writer of the United States and received the attention of "Americanists," Villaverde remains largely confined within the borders of Cuban national literary study.[2]

Since the publication of the final version of *Cecilia Valdés o La Loma del Ángel* in 1882, Villaverde and his novel have come to signify Cuban national heritage and culture. At the end of the nineteenth century, Manuel De La Cruz proclaimed *Cecilia Valdés* a "jewel of the fatherland's literature" and called Villaverde the creator of the Cuban novel of *costumbrismo*. ("Cecilia" 36, "Villaverde" 43). Cuban *costumbrismo* sought to capture the particularities of Afro-Hispanic customs, culture, and society, thus it represented, defined, and valorized the island as a nation rather than a Spanish colony. Because *Cecilia Valdés* recounts a doomed love affair between a mulatta and her white suitor amidst the intricacies of society in the early nineteenth century, literary critics have framed the novel as a recuperation of an epoch in Cuba's history (see R. González 21-2 and Lazo).[3] Villaverde's life-long opposition to Spanish colonialism has facilitated the critical association of his work with the Cuban nation. Such a link between literary texts and nation is not peculiar to Cuba, but the case of Villaverde is exemplary of how national literary study can limit interpretative possibilities for writers who lived in interstitial spaces between nations.[4] The ideological interweaving of author, novel, and nation in studies of Villaverde has overshadowed decades of his work in the United States and his participation in a Cuban American writing community that emerged in New York in the late 1840s.

In this essay, I will argue that Villaverde was what I call a trans-American writer, someone whose writing traveled from the United States to other parts of the Americas and back as it went through the process of composition, publication, and dissemination. Villaverde's life in the United States from 1849 to 1894 had a profound effect on his work as a writer and political activist. His move to New York marked not only a change in location but a generic shift from novels to articles published in Spanish-language newspapers that circulated both in Cuba and among U.S. Cuban communities. I will recount how Villaverde's opposition to Spanish colonialism and the alliance of Cuban emigres with US expansionists led Villaverde to a valorization of political journalism and activism that he believed were more effective than fiction for engaging political contingencies. A series of articles Villaverde wrote in 1852 for New York's *La Verdad* depict Villaverde's theory that the use of language for political purposes must be accompanied by military action and political organizing. The articles also situate Villaverde in the context of Cuban writers who settled in New York, New Orleans, and other U.S. cities. Villaverde's journalism and his theory of action challenge national literary histories both in the United States and Cuba to consider and contextualize the highly politicized writings of Cubans who published essays, journalistic pieces, and poems in the United

States for much of the nineteenth century.

I. "I Exchanged my Literary Tastes"

When Villaverde migrated to the United States he experienced a dramatic transformation that led him away from an early dedication to prose fiction and literary essays as his favored genres. Born in 1812, Villaverde devoted much of his twenties and early thirties to the prolific writing and publication in literary magazines. Most of his fiction was published in Cuba between 1837 and 1848. Among his early writings were a series of short romances that rehearsed tales of seduction, incest, and violence. Two of his stories, *El espetón de oro* (1838) and *La joven de la flecha de oro* (1840), are about young women who are forced to marry abusive men. Early success brought Villaverde into the notable literary circle of Domingo Del Monte, a literary impresario who was active in an emerging movement to prompt significant reforms in Spanish colonial rule on the island. Efforts to establish a Cuban nation distinct from Spain went back to the Latin American wars of independence, but it was in the 1830s and 1840s that intellectuals such as Del Monte as well as Creoles, Spaniards born on the island, called for greater autonomy (Poyo 4). During this period of anti-Spanish agitation among Cuba's literary and economic elite Villaverde published the first version of *Cecilia Valdés* (1839), a two-part story that contains only the most skeletal elements of the novel published in 1882. It is the latter version that has prevailed over much of the criticism on Villaverde.[5] Studies in both Cuba and the United States have left a notable gap between the early literary production and the 1882 *Cecilia Valdés*.

In the 1840s, Villaverde committed himself to fighting Spanish colonialism. A letter written to Del Monte in 1844 shows Villaverde's disgust with widespread persecution on the island. He found himself at a point in life, Villaverde wrote, where he could not longer accept the limitations placed on writers by the censors ("Letter" 70). Four years later, Villaverde joined a conspiracy to overthrow Spanish rule on the island. His involvement in the conspiracy followed a meeting at a concert in Havana with Narciso López, a Venezuela-born general who planned to lead an insurrection that he believed would lead to a provisional government and then the annexation of Cuba to the United States (Chaffin 39). When the plot was betrayed to the Spanish government by U.S. officials, López had to leave the island and some of his co-conspirators were jailed (Rauch 79).[6] Villaverde was surprised at home in the middle of the night by soldiers who threw him in jail, where he stayed for six months. A military commission convicted him of conspiracy against Spain and he was condemned to perpetual incarceration (Villaverde "Prólogo" 4). But in a daring escape worthy of one of his novels, Villaverde walked out of jail with the aid of a guard, boarded a ship for Florida, and then made his way to New York. He gave up writing fiction to focus on what he believed was a more urgent calling, Cuban separation from Spain.

Once in the United States Villaverde drew a distinction between the writing of novels and political involvement and concluded that fiction was not the most effective way to prompt political change in Cuba. In the prologue to the 1882 edition of *Cecilia,* Villaverde explained the turn away from literary pursuits after arriving in the United States: "Once outside of Cuba, I reformed my lifestyle: I exchanged my literary tastes for more noble thoughts; I passed from the world of illusions to the world of realities" (4). The distinction between "illusion" and "reality" separates literature from the field of political engagement that Villaverde envisions is necessary to change Cuba's status as a colony. On one level, Villaverde's problematic distinction is reminiscent of Marx's argument in *The German Ideology.* Just as Marx sought to overturn the idealism of Hegelian thought in favor of a practical materialism intent on "revolutionising the existing world, of practically attacking and changing existing things" (169), Villaverde abandoned (exchanged) literature for the life of a revolutionary. But like Marx's division of ideal-material, Villaverde's distinction between illusion and reality did not hold up, not even in the passage above. Villaverde explained his transformation in terms of two changes—illusion for reality and literary tastes for more noble thoughts. Given the parallels, Villaverde shows how the reality of politics was in a dialectical relationship with thought, thus his new role as a revolutionary still called for the theorizing of Cuba's political status and conceptualizing a future for the country. Villaverde's shift was not so much from illusion to reality as it was a turning away from the genre of novel.

The shift was tied to Villaverde's new role as secretary to Narciso López, who was operating in the United States. Between 1848 and 1851, López organized four separate military expeditions to take Cuba from Spain, believing that once the attack began the island's population would rise in revolt and provide a second front against Spanish military battalions stationed on the island. In the United States, López received support from expansionists who wanted to make Cuba part of the United States. Following the annexation of Texas in 1845, the acquisition of Oregon in 1846, and the end of the US-Mexico War in 1848, the growing United States debated whether it would continue to take over vast territories in the Americas. Sectors of the Democratic Party, pro-slavery Southerners, and the ideologues of manifest destiny were committed to moving into the Caribbean, and many viewed López as the one to lead the effort.[7]

But Cuban annexation had many detractors, both among Whig opponents of territorial expansionism and opponents of slavery who did not want to see another slave state enter the union. In September, 1849, the administration of President Zachary Taylor seized three of López's ships and put an end to an expedition before it even got off. Praising Taylor's response, the New York *Herald* wrote that the "the foolish attempt at revolution in that island" had failed "because the poor Cubans entrusted their cause to a set of speculators, knaves and cheats" (qtd. in Chaffin 72). The *Herald's* comment was representative of a more general view of the Cuban expeditions as the work of proslavery opportunists and soldiers of fortune who were often labeled with the denigrating appellation "filibusters." The word "filibuster" came from the Dutch *vrijbuiter,* or "free booty," and had made its way to English via the Spanish *filibustero,* another word for "pirate."[8] By charging filibusterism, opponents of the Cuba expeditions portrayed the effort as the work of pirates intent on taking over a territory to set up a slave state. While some of López's supporters were motivated by personal ambition and the desire for profits, Villaverde's main concern was a desire to see Cuba liberated from Spain.

Villaverde's work in the United States brought him into contact with John O'Sullivan, a publisher and Democratic party insider who had coined the term "manifest destiny" in an 1845 newspaper article (Pratt "Origin"). O'Sullivan was the founder of the *United States Magazine and Democratic Review,* a political-literary magazine that supported expansionism and published works by Poe, Whittier, Whitman, and O'Sullivan's good friend Nathaniel Hawthorne.[9] Allied with Cuban separatists, O'Sullivan worked tirelessly to support López and helped raise money for the expeditions. With a common goal, Villaverde and O'Sullivan collaborated on at least two pieces for the *Democratic Review.*

The English-language article, "General Lopez, the Cuban Patriot," appeared in the *Democratic Review* in 1850 and was published as a separate pamphlet the following year.[10] In the introduction to the pamphlet, Villaverde wrote,

> As we have in our possession a pamphlet which gives some brief sketches of the life of General Lopez, which we know to be faithful in their deliniations [*sic*], and the truth of which none will be found to deny, we have though [*sic*] the present an opportunity to bring them into notice by means of the public press, that they may have a wider circulation and defeat the machinations, which calumny has raised against a man destined by Providence to take a prominent part in events of the greatest importance to American history.

As the passage implies, Villaverde was aware that the Cuba expeditions were fighting public opinion in the United States. To counter criticism of López and his enterprise, the pamphlet positioned the general as a defender of liberty who had "undertaken the noble mission of emancipating Cuba from the yoke and the abomination of Spanish tyranny, with a view to her entrance to our union" (16). A biographical overview of López portrayed him as a fearless military leader, a man who was widely admired and supported by the Cuban population, and a "thorough republican in heart and conviction" (6). The article skillfully glossed over several episodes in which López showed himself to be more of an opportunist than a liberator. During Simón Bolivar's revolution to liberate Venezuela from Spain in the 1820s, López had fought on the side of Spain; this decision was justified in the article by arguing that López was responding to a massacre carried out in his town by anti-Spanish troops. A second opportunistic move, López's acceptance of a post in Cuba's colonial government as governor and commander-in-chief of the Central Department in 1839, was explained away as a "personal obligation" to a friend who had assumed the post of captain-general on the island.

Villaverde's description of López as purveyor of "Providence" and "American history" showed a willingness to use the language of manifest destiny, a theology of expansionism based on a notion that the United States had a providential right to overspread the continent; however, it is unclear whether Villaverde actually embraced that theory. His use of "American" points to a possible duplicity. Is "American" a metonymic substitution for "United States," emphasizing that López wants to bring a state into the Union? Or is Villaverde using "American" in the broader sense of the word, meaning that López will be Cuba's liberator? In other writings during this period, Villaverde does use "American" as an adjective for the Americas, particularly in opposition to Europe. The possible duplicity of Villaverde's use of "American" is part of a broader question regarding the contradictory designs of López and his supporters, who wanted to break away from their colonial ruler while advocating annexation to a growing empire. This dual purpose becomes oxymoronic in the "General Lopez" article: "His plan for Cuba has always been Independence and Annexation to the American Union" (10).

The support of annexation among Cubans in the 1850s has vexed historians for decades. Herminio Portell Vila argues that both López and Villaverde sought independence for Cuba as a primary goal but played the annexationist card as a strategic move to enlist support from the United States (1: 9). Gerald Poyo argues that Cuban whites backed annexation in part to maintain white domination of the island and stave off abolition as well what they perceived as a growing "Africanization" of Cuban society (7). Cuban Creoles believed that annexation would bring white immigration from the United States. But not all Cubans in New York agreed on why and how. Some saw annexation as a way to ensure their property rights while patriots such as Villaverde believed US intervention was necessary to defeat Spain. An alliance with the United States was appealing to a group that depicted admiration for US republicanism in their writings.

Villaverde, for one, shows a high regard for the United States in a private letter that was published in the *Democratic Review* shortly after his escape from Cuba:

> At last I am resting under the wings of the American Eagle. It may be that you are already apprised of my miraculous escape from the prison of Havana, where, as a man guilty of high treason, and accused to a

capital crime by the District Attorney (Fiscal) I was lately watched with the greatest diligence. I see myself free in the land of liberty; and I can hardly believe what I see and touch. (qtd. in "Cuba" 201)

The letter inscribes a geography of freedom, with the United States offering a space of liberty as opposed to Cuba and its system of colonial surveillance. Villaverde's use of the article "the" before "land of liberty" positions the United States as the sole guarantor of liberty in the Americas, a point emphasized by the metaphor of the eagle taking in a Cuban under its wings. Later in life, Villaverde became quite critical of the United States government's treatment of Cuban independence movements ("Revolucion"). But in the 1850s, Villaverde and Cubans in his circle admired U.S. republicanism enough to support annexation publicly as an option. Many Cubans became U.S. citizens and saw themselves under the protection of the U.S. government against the machinations of Spanish colonialism.

Ambrosio Gonzales, a general in López's command who was wounded during one of the expeditions, referred to himself as, "An American in feeling and education, a naturalized citizen of this republic, in the folds of whose sisterly embrace I long to see my native Island" (12). Gonzales published the *Manifesto on Cuban Affairs Addressed to the People of the United States* (1852) a year after López was killed in battle. Gonzales defended the López circle from attacks in the U.S. press and requested support from the U.S. public and government for ongoing efforts to establish a Cuban republic. Gonzales praised the democratic model of his "adopted country," calling U.S. citizens "heirs to the liberties won by the colonies, and to the destiny they were called to fulfill" (3). It is difficult to discern how much of Gonzales's praise of the United States is rhetoric intended to influence his audience.

Gonzales' targeting of the U.S. public in his *Manifesto* is indicative of a much wider use of pamphlets among Cubans who sought to convince members of Congress, presidential administrations, and newspaper editors that their cause was worthy of U.S. support. Gonzales, for example, gave a copy of his *Manifesto* to Caleb Cushing, a pro-slavery Northerner who served as attorney general to Franklin Pierce.[11] In other words, Cubans working in the United States viewed pamphlets and newspaper articles as textual counterparts to military plans for liberating the island. They believed publications were an avenue for creating *effects* among readers both in the United States and Cuba. The Cuban emigre who most clearly articulated a theory of writing and action was Villaverde, writing in the pages of the bilingual newspaper *La Verdad*.

Villaverde's association with *La Verdad* went back to Cuba. The newspaper had started publishing in New York in January, 1848, as a result of an alliance between Cuban Creoles and U.S. expansionists. First printed on the presses of the New York *Sun*, *La Verdad* promoted the separation of Cuba from Spain and subsequent annexation of the island to the United States. It was distributed in the United States and smuggled into Cuba aboard ships that traveled to the island. Spanish authorities banned the newspaper early in its run, and Villaverde became one of the leading clandestine distributors (Portell Vilá 2: 45). When he arrived in the United States, Villaverde contributed articles to the newspaper. After Narciso López was killed in his expedition of August, 1851, Villaverde became an editor at *La Verdad.* In a notable set of articles that appeared in the newspaper from February to April 1852, Villaverde argued that the revolutionary writer must engage in political praxis through the support and organization of armed revolt. In other words, the writer had to be a "man of action."

II. An Attack on "Literary Vanity"

In *La Verdad,* Villaverde elaborated a concept of the "man of action" as a writer for whom military and political organizing was the primary (pre)occupation. The politically committed writer should not focus on literary efforts, Villaverde argued, but follow the example of military men such as López. This notion of the writer as military operative captivated Cubans in the United States throughout the nineteenth century and culminated with Martí's death on the battlefield in 1895. For Villaverde, the model man of action was Narciso López, who had sacrificed his life for Cuba. With López's death still recent, Villaverde went to the pages of *La Verdad* to lambaste José Antonio Saco, a historian, essayist and reformer who had opposed the filibustering expeditions.

Exiled from Cuba in 1837 for publishing a tract opposed to the slave trade, Saco wielded considerable influence in Cuba's Creole community. At the time of the López expeditions, Saco was living in Europe and refused to back the annexationist cause. Unlike Cubans in New York, Saco viewed the United States as an "external threat" to Latin America and warned against U.S. expansionism. In his writings, he pointed out the U.S. "march of territorial expansion" from the purchase of Florida and Louisiana to the "infamous" seizure of Texas and the "iniquity" of the war with Mexico. Saco argued that given this trajectory, U.S. support of filibustering expeditions to Cuba and Mexico showed the depths of "the criminal ambition of a runaway democracy" (152). Saco's argument went straight to the questionable alliances of Cuban annexationists: "Two principle motives compel a part of the American public to support the acquisition of Cuba: a desire for expansion, and the interests of slavery" (151). For Saco, annexation would serve the American South, which sought to strengthen its influence in the Union with the entrance of Cuba as a slave-holding state. Saco's views, published in two separate pamphlets, prompted a flurry of responses both in Cuba and the United States, some of them published in *La Verdad.* At times, the debate became acrimonious with writers accusing Saco of being an abolitionist fanatic, a Catholic fanatic, and a retrograde. When Saco published a third piece, Villaverde stepped up to respond.

Villaverde's seven-part series, *"El Sr Saco con respecto a la revolución de Cuba,"* ("Mr. Saco's Views on the Cuban Revolution"), was a scathing and sarcastic response to Saco. At times Villaverde lapsed into *ad hominem* attack, accusing Saco of personal ambition and trying to gain favors from Spanish authorities. What is notable about Villaverde's articles is not so much the content of the attacks on Saco but his theoretical consideration of the relationship between "word" and "action." In Villaverde's estimation, words in both writing and speech were insufficient to bring about the necessary revolution in Cuba and other colonial sites.

Villaverde opened his analysis of word and action by discu.s.sing the work of the Irish leader Daniel O'Connell (1775-1846), a renowned orator who argued forcefully in the British Parliament for Irish home rule and led a series of demonstrations that energized the Irish population. Villaverde's choice of O'Connell to open an article about Cuban affairs appears unu.s.ual, but it shows the influence of New York City. Immigration from Ireland had been on the rise since the early nineteenth century, and in the wake of the potato famine of the 1840s, the Irish population in New York grew considerably. Given the rise in numbers, the Irish gained influence in the Democratic Party, the supporter of Cuban annexation. Living in New York, Villaverde is likely to have seen Irish immigrants and drawn a parallel between Ireland's colonial statu.s and Cuba's situation.

Villaverde asserted that O'Connell failed in his efforts to liberate Ireland due to a lack of military power, a point echoed by some recent historical evaluations of O'Connell (Lee 2). According to Villaverde, O'Connell relied extensively on "words" by seeking to bring about change through public speaking rather than a military option. In a turn of Spanglish, Villaverde chastised "el gran O'Connell" for not having found *"medio más expedito ni eficaz que el de los públicos* mass meetings *y los largos, interminables* speeches" ("a more effective approach than public mass meetings and long interminable speeches") ("Señor Saco" 1). O'Connell failed in his political aims becau.s.e he was a "man of the word" and not "a man of action."

In discussing O'Connell, Villaverde drew a distinction between the u.s.e of language for political purposes and the physical acts necessary to throw off oppressive regimes. This delineation between word and action was problematized within Villaverde's pieces, but he used the difference between the two to critique what he viewed as intellectual arrogance, the use of words and nothing else in attempting to bring about social change. For a writer/activist to rely extensively on language, according to Villaverde, amounted to "literary vanity." Villaverde said he did not want to offend the memory of the illustrious Irish leader, but found it necessary to point out that O'Connell's patriotism was tainted by literary vanity. The charge of "literary vanity" against O'Connell paved the way for a critique of Saco, who supposedly suffered from the same affliction.

It was Saco's vanity, Villaverde argued, that had led him to publish several pamphlets against annexation. At one point Saco had been offered the editorship of *La Verdad*. He turned it down, Villaverde wrote, but could not stand the thought of other Cubans taking a prominent role in the publishing of tracts on the political situation in Cuba. Saco also suffered from the vanity of wanting to emerge the victor in a pamphlet war with the annexationists rather than putting the interests of Cuba first. The charge of "literary vanity" is suggestive coming from someone who spent the early part of his life trying to establish himself in Cuban literary circles. But Villaverde was not referring to "literary" genres in the discussion of vanity. This vanity which emerged in O'Connell's orations and Saco's pamphlets was "literary" because like the writer who seeks success and/or self-aggrandizement in the production of literary works, an activist who relies on the spoken or written "word" has an inordinate faith in his or her own linguistic talents. In Villaverde's estimation, Saco was a man of too many words, or more precisely, "man of the pen and not of action." But that distinction is not so stable within Villaverde's articles.

Villaverde attacked Saco (and O'Connell) for relying on language, but he also conceded that oratory and writing produced certain effects. He wrote that O'Connell "delighted in watching the magical effect" that his words had "on the public masses." This implies that language can function as a form of action that can prompt certain effects in listeners and readers. At one point Villaverde pointed to *La Verdad* as a newspaper founded to "promote" the goals of annexationists in the United States and to "intercede" on behalf of the trampled interests of Cuba, thus implying that the newspaper was involved in a form of action. *La Verdad* was only one of numerous newspapers and other publications that were deployed during this period by Cubans in New York to attack Spanish colonialism.

Villaverde's critique of Saco for excessive faith in words is faced with an internal contradiction, namely Villaverde's own reliance on words by taking up the debate in *La Verdad*. Put another way, what's the difference between Saco writing a pamphlet and Villaverde responding? For one, Villaverde and Saco differed on the question of a military solution. Saco had supported negotiations with Spain to bring about reforms, whereas Villaverde worked for and wrote about "revolution." Villaverde's articles are a critique of a moderate model in anti-colonial praxis: writing without revolution. He saw himself as a participant in a military conflict that went beyond the printed page. This suggests that after his migration to the United States, Villaverde saw writing as secondary to the organizing of armed resistance. "Action" then is a signifier of military action. Spain's control of Cuba is partly a military control, and Villaverde concludes that to combat Spain the sword is needed as well as the pen.

The relationship of "action" to "words," Villaverde's terms, is analogous to the tension in *Don Quixote* between "arms and letters," a tension that informs the work of Latin American revolutionary writers throughout the nineteenth century. As Julio Ramos has pointed out, arms and letters was a great concern to Martí as well as Simón Bolivar and the Argentinean president and novelist Domingo F. Sarmiento (358). The topos of arms and letters allowed revolutionary writers and writerly revolutionaries to interrogate an anxiety that fighting on the battlefield is more valiant and/or politically utilitarian than writing and intellectual pursuits. In Don Quixote's terms, a commitment to letters entails the suffering of "time, nights of study, hunger, nakedness, indigestion," but to attain the status of "good soldier," a person has to suffer a magnified version of the commitment to letters as well as being "in peril of losing his life at every step" (343). This type of privileging of arms over letters created an anxiety in writer-soldiers such as Villaverde and Martí during the various military efforts to liberate Cuba during the nineteenth century. Echoing Villaverde, Martí wrote of the "abhorrence that I hold for words that are not accompanied by acts" (qtd. in Ramos 358). Martí ultimately turned to the battlefield. But what about Villaverde? How did he, as Martí wrote, "give his blood" for Cuba?

In the decades after his work for *La Verdad,* Villaverde conducted himself as a man of action who pursued writing and organizing as a praxis that stretched from the United States to Cuba. The engagement in more than one location was not undertaken by the writing subject but by texts that circulated in more than one place. As the struggle for Cuban independence took various turns, Villaverde continued to work for newspapers and work as a militant, publishing articles, essays, and translations. In the 1860s he turned away from annexation, becoming critical of us policy toward Cuba and called for total Cuban independence. Among the most notable of his pieces after the 1850s is the pamphlet *La revolución de Cuba vista desde New York* ("The Cuban Revolution Viewed From New York"). I will discuss this work briefly to elaborate Villaverde's position as a trans-American writer.

III. Here and There: Trans-American Revolutionary Writers

La revolución de Cuba vista desde New York (1869) is one of Villaverde's most important contributions to what I call trans-American print culture, writing that can be situated in more than one part of the Americas as it moves through the process of composition, publication, and dissemination. Villaverde's piece was prepared the year after the start of the Ten Years' War, the first significant armed rebellion in Cuba against Spain's tyranny. Revolutionary leaders had established a republic and sent a representative to Washington to negotiate for support from the administration of Ulysses S. Grant. Having suffered through the experiences of the failed 1850s expeditions, Villaverde warned revolutionary leaders of impending pitfalls in requesting support from the us government. His insights are important, but what interests me here is the pamphlet's negotiation of various audiences and locations.

La revolución de Cuba vista desde New York can be situated in various places both in terms of genre, subject, and audience. It was written as an oration and delivered before a group of Cubans in New York in July, 1869. But it was also published as a pamphlet with the goal of reaching a much wider audience, both in Cuba and the United States. It issued a critique of the revolutionary leadership that was intended to resonate in both us Cuban communities and among revolutionary leaders. The revolutionary chief, Carlos Manuel de Cespedes, had expressed support of annexation to the United States as an option, and Villaverde challenged that possibility vehemently. As the title of the pamphlet implies, Villaverde could offer a viewpoint that was not available to the revolutionary leaders, namely a us-Cuban perspective. Villaverde had firsthand experience of the machinations of us politics and the ease with which us presidential administrations could turn against a revolution. He warned that throughout the century the United States had looked out for its own interests at the expense of liberation movements in Cuba and other parts of Latin America. us investors had been willing to support various enterprises, including the López expeditions, out of a desire for profits rather than any belief in the causes, Villaverde wrote. Consistent support from the us government should not be expected:

> What we cannot understand under any circumstances is that Cubans in the United States today embrace the hope that by appealing to the greed of Americans to acquire Cuba . . . they will inspire not only sympathy but also obtain the help of the people and at least the consent of the government in Washington. (47)

Villaverde's warning anticipated the response of the Grant administration, which had initially implied it would support the Cuban revolution only to turn its back on the movement.

Given the sustained critique of us policy, *La revolución* is one of the major documents explicating us-Cuba relations in the nineteenth century. That it was written in the United States in the midst of a revolution in Cuba exemplifies how Villaverde's notion of "action" and writing crossed national borders and became trans-American. My use of trans-American is informed by contemporary considerations of transnational communities of people who retain social, economic, and political relations in more than one country. Linda Basch, Nina Glick Schiller, and Cristina Szanton Blanc discuss the transnational in relation the fluid experiences of immigrant populations that do not separate themselves from their first country and live within the United States while feeling at home in more than one place (27). As such, "transnational" is not only a designation that defines the crossing of borders as part of the capitalist agency of multinational corporations and technological innovation, it also points toward the lives of people who experience a variety of cultural and social exchanges in more than one country. This type of experience is not a twentieth-century phenomenon, as evidenced by Villaverde and his circle. However, my focus here is not the community but the print culture which stretches from the United States to Cuba and back. Throughout the nineteenth century, Cuban writers in the United States published various newspapers, poems, and pamphlets as a second front in the battle against Spanish colonialism. After the failure of the Ten Year's War to oust Spanish colonial authorities from Cuba, Villaverde recalled the efforts of Cubans in the United States. He wrote, "Here they deployed pen and word at least with as much vehemence as they did there the rifle and machete" ("Prologo" 5). The use of "here" and "there," *acá* and *allá* in the Spanish original, is indicative of the double location of revolutionary activity and the link between publishing circles in the United States and military efforts on the island.

Villaverde's view of texts as part of revolutionary action that stretched from the United States to Cuba can serve as a theoretical starting point for considering the writings of Cuban emigres in the United States. Villaverde and *La Verdad* had their antecedents and successors. The first Cuban revolutionary newspaper, *El Habanero,* was founded in 1823 in Philadelphia by Félix Varela, a priest, writer, and political activist who was exiled to the United States for criticizing the Spanish government (Leal and Cortina xv). Varela, writer of the novel *Jicoténcal,* went on to establish several English- and Spanish-language newspapers, so that by the time Villaverde arrived in New York, Cubans already had a record of publishing. In the 1850s, as we have seen, writing communities coalesced around the publications of highly influential newspapers such as *La Verdad.* Throughout the nineteenth century, the Spanish-language press in the United States prompted and responded to political developments tied to Cuban nationalist movements. At least fifty known Spanish-language publications directed by Cubans emerged in New York, Tampa, Philadelphia, Key West, and other cities in the second half of the nineteenth century. Villaverde's views on action and its link to trans-American print culture, his work in journalism as well as fiction, provide a fruitful theoretical beginning for analysis of the various forms of writing by Cubans, including highly political poetry.

Villaverde's writing in New York places him in us as well as Cuban literary history. A consideration of his entire body of work rather than just his novels calls for problematizing the association of writer and nation. In order to consider Villaverde's different locations—as well as those of other writers—the association of literature with a single nationality has to be challenged, as does the emphasis on the novel as a nationalistic genre that validates a writer's career and life.

Works Cited

Anderson, Benedict. _Imagined Communities: Reflections on the Origin and Spread of Nationalism._ New York: Verso, 1991.

Basch, Linda, Nina Glick Schiller, and Cristina Szanton Blanc. _Nations Unbound: Transnational Projects, Postcolonial Predicaments, and Deterritorialized Nation-States._ Longhorne, Pa.: Gordon and Breach Science Publishers, 1994.

Brown, Charles H. _Agents of Manifest Destiny: The Lives and Times of the Filibusters._ Chapel Hill: University of North Carolina, 1980.

Cervantes Saavedra, Miguel de. _The Adventures of Don Quixote._ Trans. J.M. Cohen. New York: Penguin, 1950.

Chaffin, Tom. _Fatal Glory: Narciso López and the First Clandestine War Against Cuba._ Charlottesville: University Press of Virginia, 1996.

"Cuba." _United States Magazine and Democratic Review_ 25 (September 1849): 193-203.

Cruz, Manuel de la. _"Cecilia Valdés" Acerca de Cirilo Villaverde._ Ed. Imeldo Alvarez. Havana: Editorial Letras Cubanas, 1982.

———. "Cirilo Villaverde." _Acerca de Cirilo Villaverde._ Ed. Imeldo Álvarez. Havana: Editorial Letras Cubanas, 1982.

"Filibustering." _Putnam's Monthly Magazine_ 9 (April 1857): 425-35.

General López, the Cuban Patriot. New York, 1851.

"General López, the Cuban Patriot." _United States Magazine and Democratic Review_ 26 (Feb. 1850): 97-112.

Gonzales, Ambrosio José. _Manifesto on Cuban Affairs Addressed to the People of the United States._ New Orleans: Daily Delta, 1853.

González, Reynaldo. _Contradanzas y latigazos._ Havana: Editorial Letras Cubanas, 1983.

Lauter, Paul, et al., eds. _The Heath Anthology of American Literature._ 2nd ed. 2 vols. Lexington: Heath, 1994.

Lazo, Raimundo. _"Cecilia Valdés:_ Estudio Crítico." _Acerca de Cirilo Villaverde._ Ed. Imeldo Alvarez. Havana: Editorial Letras Cubanas, 1982.

Leal, Luis and Rodolfo J. Cortina. Introduction. _Jicoténcal._ By Félix Varela. Houston: Arte Público, 1995.

Lee, J. J. "Daniel O'Connell." _Daniel O'Connell: Political Pioneer._ Ed. Maurice O'Connell. Dublin: Institute of Public Administration, 1991.

Luis, William. _Literary Bondage: Slavery in Cuban Narrative._ Austin: University of Texas, 1990.

Martí, José. _Obras Completas._ 21 vols. Havana: Editorial Nacional, 1963.

Marx, Karl. "The German Ideology: Part I." _The Marx-Engels Reader._ Ed. Robert C. Tucker. New York: Norton, 1978.

Portell Vilá, Herminio. _Narciso López y su época._ 3 vols. Havana: Cultural, .A., 1930; Havana: Compañía Editora de Libros y Folletos, 1952-58.

Poyo, Gerald E. *With All and for the Good of All: The Emergence of Popular Nationalism in the Cuban Communities of the United States, 1848-1898.* Durham: Duke University, 1989.

Pratt, Julius W. "John L. O'Sullivan and Manifest Destiny." *New York History* 14 (1993): 213-34.

———. "The Origin of 'Manifest Destiny'" *American Historical Review* 32 (1927): 795-8.

Ramos, Julio. "The Repose of Heroes." *Modern Language Quarterly* 57:2 (June 1996): 355-67.

Rauch, Basil. *American Interest in Cuba, 1848-1855.* 1948. New York: Octagon, 1974.

Saco, José Antonio. *La situación política de Cuba y su remedio.* 1851. *Folletos escritos por Don José Antonio Saco, contra la anexión de la isla de Cuba a los Estados Unidos de América.* New York: Roe Lockwood & Son, 1856.

Saldívar, José David. *The Dialectics of Our America.* Durham: Duke, 1991.

Sánchez, Julio C. *La obra novelística de Cirilo Villaverde.* Madrid: De Orbe Novo, 1973.

Sommer, Doris. *Foundational Fictions: The National Romances of Latin America.* Berkeley: University of California, 1991.

———. "Who Can Tell? Filling in the Blanks for Villaverde" *American Literary History* 6 (Summer 1994): 213-233.

Villaverde, Cirilo. Prólogo. *Cecilia Valdés.* Ed. Ivan A. Schulman. Caracas: Biblioteca Ayacucho, 1981.

———. Letter to Domingo Del Monte. 9 September 1844. *Cuba en la UNESCO: Homenaje a Cirilo Villaverde.* Havana, 1964. 70-72.

———. *La revolución de Cuba vista desde New York. Cuba en la UNESCO: Homenaje a Cirilo Villaverde.* Havana, 1964. 25-49.

———. "El Sr Saco con respecto a al revolución de Cuba." *La Verdad* 10 Feb. 1852: 1; 20 Feb. 1852: 1; 10 March 1852: 1; 30 March 1852:1; 20 April 1852: 1.

———. "To the Public." *General López, the Cuban Patriot.* New York, 1851.

Notes

[1] Unless otherwise noted, quotations from works by José Martí, Cirilo Villaverde, and José Antonio Saco are my translations of the cited Spanish-language editions.

[2] The Heath Anthology of American Literature includes Martí's influential "Our America." This essay, which frames inter-American relations in terms of a conflict between us imperialism and oppressed groups in Latin America, has influenced critics attempting to shift the paradigms of American literary history toward the broader context of the Americas. See Saldívar 3-22.

[3] Doris Sommer has argued that readings of *Cecilia Valdés* are dominated by a hermeneutic emphasis on how the novel inscribes the socio-historical dynamic of slavery and racial relations in Cuba. Sommer, in turn, considers the ways the novel limits the reader's ability to appropriate knowledge. See "Filling."

[4] In recent years, numerous studies have examined the role of novels in the process of nation formation. Benedict Anderson argues that the novel contributes to a sense of the nation as community by creating the perception that subjects share simultaneous time, the time of the narrative (22-36) Doris Sommer has elaborated the role of the historical romance, allegorical and romantic, in the development of nations and patriotic history in nineteenth-century Latin America. See *Foundational Fictions*.

[5] For a discussion of the differences between the three versions of *Cecilia Valdés*, see Luis 100-119.

[6] Historians have documented that the Polk Administration betrayed the first Narciso López conspiracy after Polk decided to attempt a purchase of Cuba from Spain for $100 million. As a show of good will toward Spain, Secretary of State James Buchanan informed the Spanish minister in Washington of the impending López insurrection. See Rauch 77-8 and Chaffin 35-6. Later in life Villaverde became aware that the us government had betrayed López. See Villaverde, "Revolución" 40-41.

[7] The López expeditions met with varying degrees of failure. In one case, us government officials seized a steamer and handed down indictments for violation of the Neutrality Law of 1818. López's final attempt in August, 1851 led to a rout of his forces, and the capture and execution of López himself. The most recent study of López is Chaffin's *Fatal Glory*. The authoritative Cuban history is Portell Vila's. Other discussions can be found in Brown 67-95 and Rauch 121-180.

[8] The *Oxford English Dictionary* shows that the contemporary usage of filibuster as a legislative tactic did not become common until the latter part of the nineteenth century. In 1857, for example, an article in *Putnam's Monthly Magazine* used the words "filibuster," "free booter," and "pirate" synonymously in reference to William Walker's effort to take over Nicaragua. See "Filibustering."

[9] O'Sullivan founded the *Review* in 1837 and sold it in 1846 but continued to be associated with the magazine as an editor until at least 1852. See Pratt "O'Sullivan" 225. As a result of his support of López, O'Sullivan was indicted in 1851 for violating the neutrality act of 1818, a still extant law which prevents the organizing a military expedition against a country with which the United States is at peace.

[10] The article "General López" that appeared in the *Democratic Review* in February, 1850 is identical to the pamphlet published the following year in New York under the same title. The notable difference is that the pamphlet includes

an introduction "To the Public," with Villaverde's initials. Some bibliographies and the U.S. Library of Congress cite Villaverde as the author of the "General López" pamphlet; however, the English introduction to the article signed by Villaverde differs in style and syntax from the English of the article, and this raises questions as to whether Villaverde, although fluent in English, worked with O'Sullivan and/or editors at the *Review* to collaborate on the article. My citations are from the pamphlet edition.

[11] The copy of Gonzales' Manifesto in the Library of Congress bears the inscription, "Hon. Caleb Cushing, the compliments of the author."

From Factory to Footlights: Original Spanish-language Cigar Workers' Theatre in Ybor City and West Tampa, Florida

Kenya C. Dworkin y Méndez
Carnegie Mellon University

Introduction

In the introduction to his book *Cuban American Theater*, in a discussion of definition and periodization, Rodolfo Cortina asks: "Cuban literature, Cuban exile literature, Cuban American literature: where does one end and the other one begin?" (7)

Tampa Latin theatre, particularly the Cuban *bufo* variety, actually embodies the elusive answer to the question by simultaneously and severally representing, to some degree, all three of the phases in the literary continuum that Cortina identifies. The dramatic Creole "schizophrenia" to which Cortina and other Cuban theatre scholars ascribe the birth of *teatro bufo* in Cuba, due in part to the antithesis of a Creole desire for independence from Spain and an inability to imagine a national community representative of all of Cuba's people, is played out in Tampa through the antithesis of a Cuban-Spanish-Italian desire to remain faithful to home country and culture, and a need to evolve into Tampa Latins (Americans), in order to be able to participate fully in U. S. society.

In particular, the sociopolitical, economic and cultural situation of Cubans in Ybor City and West Tampa, while not the same as that of their homeland predecesors, was stressful enough, given assimilatory pressures and the restricted environment outside of the Latin ghettoes in Anglo Tampa, to encourage Tampa Cubans to continue in the *bufo* tradition of their island homeland. Whereas Cuban patriots in Cuba had to deal with rising Cuban nationalism and Spanish colonial repression at the time of the birth of *teatro bufo,* during the period between the Ten Years' War (1868–1878) and the Cuban War of Independence of 1895, Cuban *tampeños* had to contend with stresses often associated with post-migratory circumstances, i. e., the negotiation and creation of a new identity, the product of transculturation, a synthesis that resolved the Anglo/Hispanic dialectic.

When Cuban letters, particularly the theatre, sounded the call of *Cuba libre* in Cuba, Spanish censorship and bourgeois disapproval tried to push Cuban popular theatre into virtual oblivion, in the name of national (colonial) integrity and good taste.[1] However, in Tampa, the local version of both imported Cuban popular theatre and the homegrown variety were enthusiastically received by, performed in and even written by an appreciative, predominantly working class society (liberal, progressive and politically astute cigarworkers), who not only identified with the characters and scenes on stage but also consented in the analyses contained in the mostly comic sketches, a clear case of performance and identity construction. However, there are three important characteristics that distinguish the Tampa variety of *bufo* from its Cuban ancestor—the addition of a new stock character, the Italian (or Sicilian), in an effort to accurately represent the demographic reality of the communities of Ybor City and West Tampa, the presence of a more highly-evolved *negrito* character, and the establishment of a careful balance between Cuban identity and an emerging American identity, as will be discussed further on.[2]

A Brief History

In the late 1870s, unhappy with the outcome of the Ten Years' War and the Zanjón treaty with Spain, Spanish-born Cuban cigar factory owners moved much of their industry to Key West, Florida, where cigar making turned the dusty island into a booming economy. By the mid-1880s, after debilitating strikes and a devasting fire, industrialists Vicente Martínez Ybor and Ignacio Haya moved their cigar factory concerns from troubled Key West to newly founded Tampa.[3] With the promise of work and housing, they brought with them urban Cuban cigar makers, who in turn brought with them the culture and tradition of popular theatre. So inherent to their culture was theatre that upon the arrival of the first workers to Tampa, and the inauguration of the first two factories and local boarding houses, the very next public building was to serve as a theatre and meeting house. This building, called the *Liceo Cubano,* was soon after to be baptized *El Círculo Cubano*, its name to the present day, by Cuban freedom apostle José Martí himself.[4] The *Círculo Cubano* became one of many mutual aid societies that cropped up in Ybor City and West Tampa, some of the others being the *Centro Español,* the *Centro Español* of West Tampa, the *Centro Asturiano,* the *Círculo Cubano, Là Unione Italiana,* and the *Unión Martí-Maceo.* There were also numerous other ethnic clubs and lodges, many of which had their own buildings as well, e.g., *La Sicilia* of West Tampa, the Labor Temple and the *Caballeros Leales de América,* in Ybor City. All of the clubs either had their own theatres or made use of neighboring ones.

Building upon an already intact, culturally determined appreciation for music and theatre, a decisive element in the education of cigar workers was the existence of the cigar factory reader, *el lector,* a man who was auditioned, hired and paid by the cigar workers themselves. The reader spent several hours, both in the morning and afternoon, reading newspapers and novels to the cigar workers from a raised pulpit, the *tribuna,* thus becoming a cigar worker's daily source of international, national and local news, in addition, of course, to several multilingual newspapers that were published in both the morning and afternoon. The *lector* also read works of classical literature to the workers. A good *lector* would buy or borrow books that he knew would captivate his audience, and a really good lector, such as Manuel Aparicio, brought the novels of literary giants such as Cervantes, Balzac and Hugo to life, taking care to play out all the parts, inflecting his voice and assuming all the roles in the book.[5] Aparicio was such a *lector,* but he was only one of many. In fact, many a reader-turned-actor polished his craft while reading from the *tribuna* of a cigar factory. From his pulpit, Manuel Aparicio went on to be a theatre great, not only in Tampa, but in cities such as New York. He also directed the Federal Theater Project's Spanish language theatre unit in Ybor City itself, during the late 1930s.[6] This federally funded Spanish-language theatre unit was the only one of its kind in the whole country, a product of progressive New Deal ideology and not a little manuevering on the part of two entrepeneurial *tampeños* who piqued the government's interest by enticing them with information about the highly successful and historically established Spanish-language theatre tradition in Ybor City and West Tampa.[7]

The Plays

Working class theatre, some might think, is not a necessarily unique enterprise. One has only to look to the very origins of Spanish popular theatre, or to more contemporary versions like Nuevo Teatro Popular for evidence. Yet, the Tampa Latin theatre experience *does* distinguish itself from that of other U. S. Latino groups in several ways, i. e., it reached a high level of professionalism while relying primarily on non-professional personnel; performances varied greatly in genre (Cuban *bufo* theatre, drama, opera, operetta, concerts, zarzuela, musical comedy, reviews, and variety shows); it introduced a new stock character, the Italian; it introduced a new, more evolved *negrito* character who was tied to the ideological leitmotif of the plays; most of the people involved in the theatre had full-time jobs and did theatre only as a hobby; Tampa Latins were the only Spanish-speaking group in the United States to have attracted federal funding during the WPA Federal Theater Project, beating out other, perhaps, more obvious choices such as San Antonio or Los Angeles; and, finally, benefit theatre performances and dances helped pay for everything from the 1895 Cuban revolution to supporting the Republican government of Spain during the Spanish Civil War, from building hospitals and clinics, and purchasing operating room supplies, to in-house disability, unemployment and burial insurance, and educational projects. Theatre proceeds were also used to pay for medical travel for society members who needed to leave Tampa and go to Spain, Cuba, North Carolina, Colorado or other places, to recover their health from tuberculosis. In this context, then, one can say that Tampa Latin theatre was a unique marriage of democratic ideals, artistic expression, utilitarianism and social responsibility. Each and every kind of Latin theater that played in Tampa, be it Italian, Cuban or Spanish, reflected the culture of those who both created and enjoyed it. More importantly, though, the Cuban variety often provided a dialogic space in which current preoccupations were problematized, through locally written plays whose themes related directly to the immigrant experience.

Each ethnic mutual aid society had a committee, sometimes called the *sección de declamación*, whose responsibility it was to manage the society's amateur theatrical section and, on occasion, contract professional companies to come on tour from Havana, México and New York to Tampa. More often than not, particularly in the case of the *Centro Asturiano, Centro Español* and *Unione Italiana,* the in-house amateur groups used previously published and copyrighted materials for their performances or, during some periods, showed Spanish-language or American films. Whether much original theatre was performed at the all-black *Unión Martí-Maceo* is not known since little documentary evidence remains, although there is one original manuscript and part of another at the University of South Florida archives and interviews with elderly members reveal that there was a fairly active theatre in their club. However, the *Círculo Cubano,* the all-white Cuban club in Ybor City, in addition to its rich history of visiting *bufo* troupes from Havana, boasted a significant repertoire of locally written and produced plays by Cubans and *tampeños* such as Jaime Fernández, Miguel Govín, "Calvo" López Loyola and Salvador Toledo, the latter of whom is alive and was the subject of an extensive interview that I conducted in summer of 1995. It was during this interview that I discovered, or more appropriately "recovered," from the depths of a hall closet, thirteen original playscripts, most of them written by the above-mentioned playwrights and three others written in the 1920s by Cuban and Tampa authors I have not yet been able to identify. I was also informed that there were many more that were missing. The classification, titles and authors of these plays are:

Zarzuela	"La cortesana" by Mario Sorondo (1927)
Comedy	"Si papá lo manda o la mala hembra" by Teófilo Hernández (1927)
Comedy	"El príncipe coliflor" by Modesto López (1928)
Drama	"La novia del tabaquero o El castigo de su culpa" by Miguel Govín (n.d.)
Comedy	"La familia Tinguillo en Clearwater" by Salvador Toledo (1947; 1952)
Comedy (1943)	"Un blackout en Ybor City" by Salvador Toledo and Jaime Fernández
Comedy (n.d.)	"Tabaqueros a cojer el cheke" by Salvador Toledo and Jaime Fernández
Comedy	"El General Pelusa o Arma Secreta" by Salvador Toledo (1950; 1979)

Comedy	"Casos y cosas o Lío de locos" by Salvador Toledo (n.d.)
Comedy (n.d.)	"Del convento al cabaret o Noche de carnaval" by Antonio López Loyola
Drama	"Sólo Dios lo sabe" by Salvador Toledo (1953)
Comedy (n.d.)	"En busca de placeres o Gallego, cuídame la espalda" by Miguel Govín
Drama	"Amor a gotas" by Jaime Fernández (1947)

In talking to Toledo I discovered that he had not only written plays but also performed in them, many times in *bufo* sketches as the *gallego* or *característico,* one of three or four stock characters who are essential to the genre.[8] In Cuban *bufo* theatre, the Afro-Cuban or mulatto, who often bears the brunt of ridicule, always ends up outsmarting or saving the Spaniard or Cuban (often from the budding merchant class), an aspect of Cuban *choteo* that provided a highly successful vehicle for the criticism and satire of the dominant society.[9] *Choteo,* at its best, can be seen as a verbal discourse strategy, using playful and irreverent language, that permits the exploitation of a topic, for satirical purposes. It is often full of innuendo and double entendre. However, the fact that it may appear to make light of a serious subject is misleading. The more irreverent the farce, the more highly critical the tone, revealing a rebellious, independent view of a strictly hierarchic society. When transposed to the Tampa setting, local *bufo* theatre satirizes the local dominant society, deconstructing the local social hierarchy of Anglos and factory-owning Spaniards on top, white Cuban, Sicilian and Spanish cigar workers in the middle, and Afro-Cubans and African-Americans at the bottom. The ten titles above represent works that range in topic from class struggle, workers rights, the Depression, anti-fascism, and the Korean War, to slavery, orphanhood, lust, the Catholic church and racial anxiety. The plays I have chosen to examine here that are in the *bufo* tradition are "Tabaqueros a cojer el cheke" (Toledo & Fernández) and "El General Pelusa o Arma Secreta" (Toledo). I have also included a brief analysis of "Un blackout en Ybor City" (Toledo & Fernández).

In "Tabaqueros a cojer el cheke," Robusto Peón, a Cuban, is married to an Italian woman, Rosina, signaling the introduction of a new stock character to the traditional three or four. The inclusion of an Italian character married to a Cuban also provides a look at a new kind of marriage that became somewhat acceptable during the lifetime of first-generation Latins in Tampa. Prior to this, marriage between an Italian and a Cuban was deemed totally inappropriate by Tampa Italians, owing, in part, to the perceived racial and cultural impurity of Cubans, and, in fact, the authors have the husband and wife reminisce about the great difficulty they had in getting married during the first scene of the play. Toledo and Fernández, in their effort to make Rosina's character seem more believably Italian to the audience, and to feed the farcical quality of the play, create a constant tension between her Italianized Spanish and what her husband and other characters in the sketch understand her to be saying when she speaks.

This is accomplished by using a kind of bilingual malapropism and codeswitching. While present throughout the work, the most brilliant example occurs toward the end of the play, when Rosina confesses to the terrible mistake she has made in sending her cashed check to her now dead cousin in Italy. There is confusion over the Italian words *cuchino* [cousin] and *mezquino* [unfortunate one], and the Spanish words *cochino* [pig] and *mezquino* [stingy one]:

ROSINA: *Ay Peone, Peone...*
PEÓN: *Peón, Rosina...¿Pero qué rayos es lo que te pasa?*
ROSINA: *Lo cuchino de lo mio cuchino, que se murió.*
MADREÑA (THE GALLEGO): *¿Qué se murió un cochino? Si eso no es para llorar.*
    Que me lo manden que mañana hago un amarillo con puerco que se acabó el mundo.
PEÓN: *Ella quiere decir que el cochino es el primo de ella.*
MADREÑA: *¿Que ella tiene un primo cochino?*
ROSINA: *No. Que es mi primo.*

. . . .

PEÓN: *El pobrecito, aunque no lo conozco lo siento mucho...*
ROSINA: *Mezquino.*
MADREÑA: *Si es mezquino debería haberse muerto antes.*
PEÓN: *No hombre, 'mezquino' en italiano quiere decir pobre.*
MADREÑA: *Entonces el pobrecito.*

. . . .

MARY (THE DAUGHTER): *Bueno, eso es para sentirlo y no para llorar si, total, no lo conocíamos.*
ROSINA: *Yo lloro porque cambié el cheke y le mandé tuto el dinero para allá (7).*

ROSINA: Oh, Peone, Peone...
PEON: It's Peon, Rosina...Well, what the devil is wrong with you?
ROSINA: The *cuchino* of my *cuchino* has died.
MADREÑA: What? A pig has died? That's nothing to cry over. Send it to me and tomorrow I'll make the best pork and yellow rice in the world.
PEON: What she means is that the *cuchino* is a cousin of her's.
MADREÑA: You mean she has a pig for a cousin?
ROSINA: No. I am talking about my cousin.

. . . .

PEON: Poor guy, even though I don't know him I feel bad...
ROSINA: *Mezquino.*
MADREÑA: If he was stingy, he should of died sooner.
PEON: No. *Mezquino* in Italian mean 'poor guy.'
MADREÑA: Well, then. Poor guy.

. . . .

MARY: Well, I guess it's okay to feel bad but not to cry this way. After all, we didn't even know him.
ROSINA: I'm crying because I cashed my check and sent him all the money.[10]

Behind the comic antics of this farce, the action in this play takes place during a time in which the factories are either closed or are experiencing a dramatic work slowdown, due to a change in tobacco tariff laws, making it extremely expensive for the factories in Tampa to get filler and wrapper leaves from Cuba. This meant that many cigar workers were out of work or on limited schedules. In fact, the play opens with Rosina announcing she is about to pick up her last check at the factory, hence the title of the play, "Tabaqueros a cojer el cheke." As a result of this economic difficulty, Robusto and Rosina Peón are trying to marry their daughter Mary off to the pressumed well-to-do Galician, Madreña, who owns a *fonda* (a small restaurant) that caters to cigar workers. What they don't know is that the *fonda* is not doing well at all and Madreña is thinking of closing it. "[L]a fonda, no tiene fondo," he says (7). The very same economic crisis that is putting cigar workers out of work, renders them incapable of patronizing their usual stores, coffee houses and restaurants, thus crippling the economies of Ybor City and West Tampa. Mary, who has acquired more American ideas about courtship and marriage, initially disagrees with her father about marrying Madreña, allowing the authors to interject some of the tension between immigrants and their children, their two languages and their differing values:

MARY: Halló, *dari.*
PEON: *¿Jaló? Aquí nadie jaló nada, mi corazón. Y díme, ¿por qué has tardado tanto?*
MARY: *Es que tenía un* "date," *papa.*
PEON: *Un* "date," *¿no? Y mira, no me digas* "papa" *que eso me sabe a vianda. Díme 'papá.'*
MARY: *Ay, viejo, ¿tú todavía te figuras que estás en Cuba? Despierta que estamos en USA.*
PEON: *Pues, aunque estemos en* "what you say" *yo soy tu padre y usted ha de seguir mis costumbres, para que lo sepa.*

MARY: Hallo, daddy.
PEON: *Hallo**? Nobody has pulled anything, sweetheart. Tell me, why are you so late?
MARY: Oh, I had a date, papa.
PEON: A date, huh? And see here. Don't call me *papa*** because that sounds like the vegetable. Call me *papá.*
MARY: Oh, dad, do you think you're still in Cuba? Wake up. We are in the USA.
PEON: Well, even if were are in "what you said," I am still your father and you have to follow my customs, in case you didn't know.

* Hallo, or *jaló*, as the Spanish version reads, derives from the verb *jalar*, to pull.
** *Papa* means potato in Spanish.

Once Peón has explained to Mary that the *gallego* had twenty thousand dollars (he thinks he does), she is more willing to see things her parents' way, overlooking several negative ideas she has about Madreña that come from

stereotypes about Galicians (they are stupid, unbathed and garlicky-smelling).
However, she is bothered by the idea that Madreña will be, in essence, buying
her, and when she discovers that he actually wants to marry her despite the fact
that he is poor, then she truly wants to marry him, as the following exchange
illustrates:

MADREÑA: Entonces, a mí me querían aquí por mi dinero?
MARY: No. Ahí está usted equivocado. Ahora es cuando lo quiero de verdad, pobre,
porque así los dos aportamos al matrimonio lo mismo, amor....
MADREÑA: Esta es la mujer tampeña, la que se da por amor, no por dinero (8).

MADREÑA: So, you wanted me only for my money?
MARY: No. That's where you're wrong. Now I really love you, poor, because this way
we will both be bringing the same thing to our marriage, love . . .
MADREÑA: That's the Tampa woman, who gives herself for love and not for money.

This celebration of working class values, embodied in a woman, serves to render insignificant any resistance Peón might have to the Americanization of his
daughter since her merits are ascribed to that of a Tampa woman, not an Anglo
one. The same is true for any resistance that Mary might have to marrying a
Galician. The Spaniard, who was first viewed as a good catch for the family
because he was a member of an emerging merchant class, is finally loved by his
bride-to-be because he is now one of them, poor, and they are all in it together.

An Afro-Cuban *bolita* ticket vendor, Pildorita, who tries to sell his friend
Robusto an entry to the daily numbers lottery, takes pity on his friend and picks
a number for him without his knowledge. After Pildorita exits, Peón comments
to himself (and to the audience) on the relative racial tolerance of the Latin
neighborhoods in Tampa:

Este negro es lo más parejero de mi vida. Se mete en casa de los
blancos a vender bolita sin darse cuenta que estamos en la Florida.
Gracias que con nosotros los latinos no existe eso de raza, porque si no
lo linchaban... (4)

This Negro is the boldest guy I know. He goes into white homes to
sell lottery tickets without taking into account that we are in Florida. It's
a good thing that we Latins don't worry about race, because if we did,
he'd be lynched.

This observation on his part serves to ideologically locate Tampa Latins beyond
the binary opposition created by Jim Crow legislation, particularly in Florida,
which led the country in lynchings at one time. Besides, white Latins, and particularly Cubans, were themselves the victims of segregatationist practices such
as being denied access to public parks or swimming holes, or to particular jobs.
While the very different racism of Tampa Latins is not problematized in

"Tabaqueros a cojer el cheke" (it is in one of the other plays I recovered, "La familia Tinguillo en Clearwater"), their treatment of the race issue in the dialectic of Anglo vs. Tampa Latin is resolved through the synthesizing force of workers' solidarity, by a need to form a racial and ethnic alliance against racism, discrimination, exploitation and assimilatory pressures.

Even after Mary has agreed to marry Madreña, despite his poor financial state, and Rosina has discovered that she has sent her last check to a now dead cousin in Italy, it is Pildorita who comes through with a big win and hands over six hundred dollars to Robusto, saving the day. This act of giving on the part of Pildorita, who is now the embodiment of working class ideals (even though he, himself, does not work but rather sell chances to workers), inspires in the final scene an exchange between father and daughter that functions on the level of what I will call an interpellative, hortatory speech, aimed at seeking consensus and consent from the audience on the validity of the representation they have just seen, and at rousing Tampa Latin solidarity. Echoing the historical romance of Dumas and the passionate egalitarianism of Martí, Toledo and Fernández write:

PEÓN: *Esta es la vida. Un pobre salva a otro pobre. Esta es la vida . . .*
MARY: *Sí, papá. Esta es la vida, pero la vida tampeña. Cubanos, italianos, españoles y americanos viviendo todos juntos, pero con un sólo corazón, sintiendo a un mismo tiempo los latigazos de las alegrías o los dolores. Uno para todos y todos para uno.*

PEON: This is what life is all about. One poor man saves another. This is what life is all about . . .
MARY: Yes, father. This is what life is like, but in Tampa. Cuban, Italians, Spaniards and Americans all living together, with one heart, all feeling joys or sorrows at the same time.

This device occurs at the end of several of the locally written plays, which further supports the idea that these plays possessed a sociopolitical and didactic value that far exceeded their worth as "just" working class entertainment. Instead, it becomes quite evident that these works played an important role in the creation of the new Tampa Latin (American) identity, anchored, as it was, in liberal and progressive, working class values.

In "Tabaqueros a cojer el cheke," a ten-page *bufo* sketch, we see a series of alliances being formed, first between an Italian and a Cuban, then between two Cubans, black and white, and finally between a Galician and a first generation Tampa woman. The marriages of Rosina to Peón and Mary to Madreña contribute to the creation and consolidation of the Tampa Latin, respectively. The offspring of the latter marriage will be totally invested in Tampa Latinness and how it represents both old world and new world values and realities. The alliance of Tampa Latins of both races, when pitted against the external pressures of institutionalized racism and segregation, allowed the working class to economically thrive in the relative safety of their ghettoes, while the rest of Tampa, and by extension the South, languished in the paralyzing stupor of ignorance and social decay. While many Anglo southerners devoted their energies to White supremacy and racial hatred, Tampa Latins worked their way into American society, in subsequent generations, through education, politics and economics. Perhaps one of the most important vehicles for Tampa Latin success was the ongoing experiment in identity construction, in which Tampa Latinness was under constant renegotiation in response to sociopolitical and economic realities. This process of experimentation and negotiation was nowhere more evident to or better documented for the public than in their steady diet of Tampa Cuban theatre, which played to capacity crowds for decades, even when other theatrical offerings did not.

Another excellent example of this sort of interpellative hortatory speech appears in the final scene of a play entitled "Un blackout in Ybor City," written by Toledo and Fernández and debuted on May 2, 1943. Set during World War II, the play's title recalls the mandatory blackouts that the U. S. citizenry was asked to endure in their cities, to help prepare for potential bombing raids. A white Cuban rogue and a *negrito*, respectively, plan to simulate an anticipated blackout at the house of a friend who is giving a party, so that they can make off with the food. Once the real air-raid sirens go off, the ensuing darkness that follows the simulated blackout causes all mischief to come to an end, and the citizens of Ybor City turn their attention to the business at hand—the war and national security. It is then that the following exchange takes place between the the rogue Cabecita, another ne'er-do-well, Higuereta, and the Spaniard Regueira:

CABECITA: Pero no teman, quítense de la idea que puedan venir a bombardear a esta tierra, cuna de la democracia...Esos bandoleros...saben perfectamente bien que esta gran nación americana junto con sus aliados, están preparados para en un tiempo no muy lejano borrar por completo del mapa a esos gobiernos facistas...Vivan las democracias del mundo. Abajo para siempre los gobiernos fascistas...Recibamos con los brazos abiertos a los valientes defensores de la libertad del mundo y digámosle adiós y para siempre a los fascistas.
HIGUERETA: (Canta una canción patriótica.)
CABECITA: Bravo, viejo. Usted como siempre; buen obrero, y como tabaquero al fin, siempre al lado de la libertad y Dios quiera que siga imperando en el mundo, como impera en las Américas la buena vecindad.
HIGUERETA: ¿Qué de su opinión, Regueira, que es español?
REGUEIRA: Español, sí; pero Español Republicano. No español de Franco, de ese muñeco de Hitler, de ese que vendió a su madre, a su madre patria por tal de seguir gobernando. Viva España, pero ESPANA REPUBLICANA . . . (4-5)

CABECITA: But don't be afraid. Don't think that they are going to come and bomb this country, the cradle of democracy . . . Those scoundrels . . . know perfectly well that this great nation, and its allies, are ready to erase from the map forever those fascist

governments, in just a short while . . . Long live the democracies of the world. Down
forever with fascist governments . . . Let us receive with open arms the valient defenders of world freedom and say goodbye forever to the fascists.

HIGUERETA: (Sings a patriotic song).

CABECITA: Hurrah, old man! You, as always, a good worker, like a cigar worker
should be, always on the side of freedom and with God's help it will reign around the
world, as good neighborness does in the Americas.

HIGUERETA: What do you think, Regueira, being a Spaniard?

REGUEIRA: Yes, I am a Spaniard but a Republican Spaniard. Not a Franco Spaniard,
that puppet of Hitler who sold his mother, his motherland in order to stay in power.
Long live Spain, but REPUBLICAN SPAIN . . .

Once criticized for being too politically unsophisticated to appreciate
Sinclair Lewis's Spanish-language version of *It Can't Happen Here*, it becomes
clear that Ybor City and West Tampa writers, performers and audiences were
more than aware of the dangers of fascism and the need to support Uncle Sam,
especially after the cruel lesson of the Spanish Civil War.[11] In addition, one can
see that the writers, particularly, knew that this 1940s Tampa Latin audience
was sending its own sons and daughters to fight for the American and Allied
cause. It became their job to fan nationalist sentiments among the Latins and
convince them to buy war bonds.[12] In addition, this hortatory, rhetoric was
aimed at inspiring the Latin immigrants who were not citizens to shift whatever remaining allegiance they had to their old countries and commit it to the
United States. This latter point is emphasized when Cabecita praises Higuereta
for his patriotic song. His praises succinctly define Tampa cigar worker sentiments about themselves and the world around them.

Set in West Tampa, "El General Pelusa o Arma Secreta," by Salvador
Toledo, debuted September 10, 1950, at the *Círculo Cubano*. We have a *gallego*
character named Fungueiro, owner of a bodega, and his neighbor Don Casimiro
(played by Todelo), who owns the bar next door. Immediately, the topic of
Funguiero and his love for the *mulata* Matilde comes up, a common leitmotif
in Cuban *teatro bufo*. This quickly sets up the scene for a quick buck and free
drinks for Don Casimiro, who demonstrates the epitome of *viveza criolla*
(Creole cunning) by convincing Fungueiro to pay him ten dollars for each time
he can get the beautiful girl to smile at him. He accomplishes this by telling
Matilde that Fungueiro thinks her teeth are store bought, thus prompting her to
go over and smile at him several times, each time earning Casimiro ten dollars.

In this play, Toledo introduces a couple of the secondary characters that are
so often seen in Cuban *bufo* sketches. They are incorporated into the plays for
the purpose of reproducing the character of Havana, or in this case, West Tampa
street life. Other characters in this category that appear in "El General Pelusa o
Arma Secreta" are Casilda, a neighborhood busybody who plays the female
característica to the male Casimiro and the *tamalera* (tamale street vendor),
who plays to the *negrito* in this sketch, Pelusita, who is an avocado vendor.

Pelusita, and his counterpart in "Tabaqueros a cojer el cheke," Pildorita, depart from or, perhaps, are evidence of the evolution in this stock character, from its inception in the mid-nineteenth century.

The *negrito* in Spanish and Cuban drama started out by being a *bozal* type, an African who had not yet mastered Spanish.[13] By 1868, a new *negrito* caricature was introduced, one that gave evidence of the Afro-Cuban experience with colonial society, serving as a "neocolonial mimic man." In his attempt to speak the language of the bourgoisie, he distorts it by properly pronouncing but misusing a socially elevated vocabulary.[14] By the post-abolition period in Cuba, this *negrito* became the stock character of the Cuban *bufo* theatre. Yet, in Tampa, by the 1940s and 1950s and, perhaps, earlier, this character had evolved into a still comical but now instrumental figure, who if not a source of nationalist, patriotic or working class sentiments, is at least a catalyst for these interpellative hortatory remarks to occur within a play. In "Tabaqueros a cojer el cheke," Pildorita is the catalyst for Mary's remarks about worker solidarity in Tampa. In "El General Pelusa o Arma Secreta," as we shall soon see, Pelusita inspires his friends to become involved in the Korean War. He accomplishes this by revealing to his potential customers that he has developed a bomb to end the war in Korea.

Claiming genius status, something he has to defend several times, Pelusita explains that his experiment is chemical and that he has invented a bomb that uses three ingredients: avocado, cashew nut, and Spanish olive oil. Pelusita believes that his bomb can end the war in Korea but, of course, he wants to try it out first. His explanation is as follows:

PELUSITA: La semilla la quiero yo para un experimento. Es una química sintética.
CASILDA: ¿Una clínica sin qué?
PELUSITA: Una química sintética, señora. Aquí, donde usted me ve, yo parezco simple aguacatero pero soy un genio. Usted ve, yo he inventado una bomba y pienso que iré a ver al presidente para ver si me facilita los medios y así fabrico dicha bomba y voy a acabar con esa guerrita de Corea.
CASILDA: ¿Qué te parece? ¿Pero están oyendo ustedes? Aquí tenemos a un negro bombero.
CASIMIRO: ¿Un negro bombero? ¿Y dónde está la bomba?
MATILDE: ¿De qué se trata?
PELUSITA: Señores, aunque le parezca increíble, yo, Pelusa, el aguacatero he inventado la bomba más económica que hay" (7).

PELUSITA: I want the seed for an experiment. It's a synthetic chemical.
CASILDA: A sin . . . what clinic?
PELUSITA: A synthetic chemical, madam. I know you see me as a simple avocado seller but I am a genius. See, I've invented a bomb and plan to go to the president and see if he can give me a lab so I can make this bomb and end the war in Korea.
CASILDA: What do you think of that? Are you all listening? We have a Black bomber*
before us.

CASIMIRO: A Black bomber? Where's the bomb?

MATILDE: What's this all about?

PELUSITA: Ladies and gentlemen, although it may seem beyond belief, I, Pelusa, the avocado seller have invented the cheapest bomb ever.

[*There is a play on words here caused by the dual meaning 'un negro bombero' may have. One meaning is the 'Black bomber'; the other is 'Black fireman.']

The positive and negative elements in the explosive are the avocado and cashew nut, but it is a thin layer of Spanish olive oil that separates them. When Fungueiro, the *gallego,* hears the part about the Spanish olive oil, his patriotic sensibilities are so touched that he is inspired to give Pelusita the $5,000 dollars he needs to test his invention. Anxious to oversee his investment, Funguiero, accompanied by the gang, decides to go with Pelusita to Korea. At the end of this first act, it is Pelusita who calls everyone to enthusiastically exit while singing a rhumba: *"Vámonos a Corea a matar chinitos, vamos a demostrarles que somos unos machitos"* [Let's go to Korea and kill little Chinamen, let's show them that we are real tough men], a small preview of the racist overtones that the next scene, when they are in Korea, will have. As for Pelusita, who had just had to repeatedly defend the idea that he, a black man, could invent a bomb, the need to unite forces over the Korean conflict surpasses any measure of resentment he might have felt at the apparent ridicule of his friends and customers.

The next scene opens with the plane having crash landed on some tree tops somewhere in the jungles of Korea. The pilot has been killed but the West Tampa crew is all fine, although Fungueiro has to be brought down out of a tree. No sooner have they assessed their situation than they encounter "natives"— Koreans, one would presume. The language that the natives speak is not understood by them but many of the utterances resemble words in Spanish, which provides for riotous word play in the conversation between the natives Chincha and Mani-Mo, Fungueiro, and Pelusita, who claims to speak the natives' language. Despite the hilarity of the non-stop *malentendus,* the following exchange counterpoises Tampa Latin racism towards Afro-Cubans and American racism towards Asians during the 1950s:

CHINCHA: *Machuca.*

PELUSITA: *Ay, nos partió un rayo.*

CHINCHA: *Machuca allá, machuca allá.*

PELUSITA: *Ay, por tu madre, gallego, si dice que nos machucan allá.*

. . . .

MANI-MO: *(va al negro y riéndose) Cuchi, cuchi, cuchi. Mono lichi.*

FUNGUEIRO: *Dicen algo de mono. Yo creo que hablan de ti, Pelusa.*

PELUSITA: *(Dirigiéndose a Chincha) Oiga, supongo que usted sea aquí el jefe y exijo un poquito de respeto. ¿Cómo me van a llamar mono y usted quién es?*

CHINCHA: *Chincha, yo, Chincha, yo.*
PELUSITA: *Usted será chincha pero yo no soy nada de mono.*
. . . .
PELUSITA: *(A Chincha) Oígame lo que le voy a decir.*
CHINCHA: *Tan chau, tan chau.*
PELUSITA: *(limpiándose los ojos) Compadre, vamos a necesitar un paraguas para hablar con usted.*
. . . .
CHINCHA: *Cuchao, ¿tu va cu cla, cu clu clam?*
FUNGUEIRO: *Por tu madre, va a haber que echar un pie de aquí si nos coge el cu clu clan.*

CHINCHA: Machuca.
PELUSITA: Oh, we're dead.
CHINCHA: Machuca allá, machuca allá.
PELUSITA: Oh my God, *gallego,* he says they're going to squash us over there.
. . . .
MANI-MO: *(walking over to the black guy and laughing)* Cuchi, cuchi, cuchi. Mono lichi.
FUNGUEIRO: They're saying something about monkey. I think they're talking about you, Pelusa.
PELUSITA: *(facing Chincha)* Listen here. I assume you're the boss around here and I demand some respect. How are you going to call me a monkey. Who are you?
CHINCHA: Chincha, yo. Chincha, yo.
PELUSITA: You may be a tick but I am no kind of monkey.
. . . .
PELUSITA: *(to Chincha)* Listen to what I'm going to tell you.
CHINCHA: Tan chau, tan chau.
PELUSITA: *(wiping his eyes)* Man, we're going to need an umbrella to talk to you.
CHINCHA: Cuchao, ¿tu va cu cla, cu clu clam?
FUNGUEIRO: Holy mother, we're going to have to get out of here if the Ku Klux Klan is going to get us.

Misunderstandings prevail and Pelusita is called upon to try out his bomb. Hurling the avocado bomb in the air towards the natives, all that is heard upon its dropping is a sound resembling a Bronx cheer. The West Tampa boys take off running with the natives in hot pursuit. Matilde, Casimiro and Casilda, who are waiting at the airport in Korea, see them all running towards them. By now, Matilde is smitten with Fungueiro's bravery for having gone to Korea and is now truly in love with him. Casilda claims to have possession of a secret weapon, the "real" *arma secreta,* which turns out to be one of Fungueiro's smelly shoes, highlighting one of the negative stereotypes about Galicians. It is soon discovered that the natives speak some Spanish (now they sound like Cuban Chinese) and Chincha tries to pawn off one of his daughters, Mani-Mo, sister of Ini and Mini, to Pelusita, the *negrito.* However, the discussion sours and when the natives once again threaten the Tampa boys, Fungueiro's shoe is brought out. Upon smelling the shoe, the natives run off as quickly as they can. Pelusita takes Mani-Mo home, Fungueiro has won the affection of Matilde, Casilda has caught Casimiro in her amorous web, and all ends with the playing of the National Anthem, to which the whole party rhumbas off stage (!).

In this sketch, Toledo brings to light not only just how real the Korean war was to Tampa Latins but also residual feelings about the bomb that was used to end World War II, in the Pacific, hence Pelusita's desire to create an organic bomb to end the war. By bringing in the Ku Klux Klan, he highlights that although Tampa Latins have their own brand of racism, they have been the victims of discrimination themselves. In introducing a *negrito* who is smart enough to produce a bomb and communicate with the natives, he provides an example of a newly evolved *negrito,* one who participates fully in the ideological scheme of the play.

In addition, while the issue of White racism toward Blacks is not completely resolved by the advent of this more contemporary *negrito,* the alliance formed between Pelusita and Mani-Mo, a Tampa Latin (American) black male and an Asian female, could be perceived as an attempt to mitigate the public's discomfort with once again sending its children to yet another, even more 'foreign' war. It is illustrative of a fairly common reality, particularly in Cuba, but also in Tampa: unions between Afro-Cubans and Chinese. Yet, the offspring of a black man and an Asian woman, in the context of the 1950s, would not be anymore welcome outside of Ybor City or West Tampa than their parents would be, leaving the issue of race unresolved and even more complicated. While the post-war era saw a great deal of Tampa Latin migration to other areas of the city and the suburbs, new Tampa Latins of color would begin where their predecesors did, in the ghettoes.

"El General Pelusa o Arma Secreta" reveals yet another facet in the complex Tampa Latin identity—the profound sense of Americanness and patriotism that had by then developed. Although Pelusita's comical, biochemical invention proved to be ineffective while Fungueiro's shoe was, the true secret weapon in this play is the parody of racial and cultural stereotypes, the *gallego,* the *negrito,* the Koreans, and even the women. Despite all their differences, their feelings of duty to this country, which also became part of their Tampa Latin identity, allowed them to serve both community and country. In this play, we are provided with an excellent example of how Cuban farce in Tampa became American theatre, much in the same way that Cubans (and Spaniards and Sicilians) became Tampa Latins, and thus, Americans.

Conclusion

This paper analyzes, through examples from three original Spanish-language plays by two Tampa Latins, how Spanish, Italian and particularly Cuban immigrants to Tampa maintained their culture, resisted assimilatory pressures and developed a new American identity through the theatre. Tampa Latin theatre, broadly defined, i. e., the cigar factory reader tradition, the variety show, farce, drama, zarzuela and opera, served as the teacher, conscience, and voice of a people who over a period of approximately one hundred years were able to survive exile and immigration, war, racism and discrimination, and bring a new booming industry to Tampa. Tampa Cuban theatre distinguished itself from its predecesor in a variety of ways, the most significant of them being the introduction of a new stock character, the Italian, and the more highly developed persona for the *negrito.* It also provided a means by which the community could experiment with the creation of a new identity—one anchored in old world traditions but incorporating, sometimes critically, U. S. characteristics.

Today, when hardly any Latins still live in Ybor City, the bulk of the Latin population lives in West Tampa and other areas of greater Tampa. As for theatre, there are persistent empresarios like Tony García, who still dreams of one last show, or René González, who some forty years ago took the the Spanish Little Theatre, first from the University of Tampa and the *Centro Asturiano,* and turned it into the now renowned Spanish Lyric Theatre. González, who grew up in the theaters of Latin Tampa, has brought what was originally Tampa Latin theatre to the attention of greater Tampa by striking a balance in his group's repertoire between zarzuela and musical review, on the one hand, and Broadway theatre, on the other. He is also a writer and composer and has written several pieces somewhat reminiscent of the type of plays discussed earlier.[15] Others, like Dennis Calandra at the University of South Florida, have written contemporary theatre pieces for local amateur groups to perform in some of the old theatre houses. For the most part, though, the vibrance of Ybor City and West Tampa theatre is gone, as is the era when the cultural activities of the ethnic mutual aid societies meant physical and cultural survival for their members. Without the theatre, Tampa Latins would have lost their roots long ago, when the big push was for total assimilation into the American melting pot. Had it not been for the availability of this theatre of experimentation and negotiation, especially after the disappearance of the cigar factory reader and the virtual demise of the mutual aid societies, there might be little or no Latin flavor to Tampa at all. Instead, despite the apparent lack of Latin theatre in Tampa, the city retains a highly visible Latin profile, through its many successful city, county and state officials, lawyers, bankers, business people, educators, and artistic enterprises and cuisine. It is also true that the city is experiencing a dramatic increase in Spanish-speaking population, as the result of its more recently arrived Latin American immigrants, who themselves are forming their own societies, and who might well benefit in their adjustment to life in the United States if they follow the Tampa Latin example.

Ybor City and West Tampa writers such as Salvador Toledo and Jaime Fernández, and the others, served as teachers, mediators, and barometers. Through their *bufo* sketches, one can see that they had their collective finger on the pulse of the community. In addition, they were able to purposefully promote ideas that would eventually help Tampa Latins enter Anglo society, through shared causes such as World War II, the Korean War and workers' solidarity. Although not discussed here, the same can be said of their dramatic pieces. The theaters of Ybor City and West Tampa provided the dialogic space where new Americans could discuss their differences and similarities, and practice the culture of their countries of origin while at the same time forging a new identity, that of the Tampa Latin. In a state of constant rejuvenation, the Tampa Latin theatre, and particularly the original *bufo* plays discussed here, evolved with the times, serving the needs of each subsequent generation that supported it.

Notes

[1] For a discussion of the founding of the *Sociedad para el fomento del Teatro,* in 1910, see Bueno, 123-26. This society, and the later *Sociedad del Teatro Cubano* (1913), sought to improve the state of Cuban theatre by imitating European theatre, ignoring any innovations Cuban theatre might have already undergone. Many of the finest writers, professors, and actors of the time became members of these two societies. By 1927, their efforts had evolved enough to produce the *Institución Cubana Pro Arte Dramático,* which cultivated not only Spanish plays but Cuban ones as well.

[2] The *negrito* character in Cuban bufo theatre is often a street-smart rogue who is instrumental in the satirization of the Galician character. There is also a variant called the *negro curro* or *negro catedrático* that is characterized by his incorrect use of educated vocabulary. On occasion, some plays contain female versions of the *negrito* character.

[3] For information on the founding of Ybor City see Mormino and Pozzetta, 63-96; for information on the founding of West Tampa see Méndez, 13-6.

[4] *Liceo* means school or place of learning in Spanish, indicative of the educational value that theatre was thought to have by the Tampa founders of the first theatre in Ybor City.

[5] Manuel Aparicio, Jr., personal interview, 31 July, 1996. Son of reader, actor, and director Manuel Aparicio.

[6] Elisa and Mirella Bermúdez, personal interview, 22 October, 1996. Daughters of one of Tampa's finest Latin actors and prompters, Ramón "El Cabezón" Bermúdez.

[7] For a detailed summary of Tampa Latin theatre see Kanellos, 146-75. According to my interviews with Salvador Toledo and the Bermúdez sisters, and various playbills, Tampa Latin theatre, and in particular the Cuban *bufos,* continued through the 1950s, and to some extent 1960s, with occasional per-

formances being recorded even in the late 1970s and early 1980s.

[8] For a detailed account of the artistic and political origin and development of the Cuban *bufo* genre see Montes Huidobro, 69-79; Tolón, 19-31; Cortina, 7-17; Remos, 195-97.

[9] For a definition of Cuban *choteo,* see Rexach, 51-94.

[10] The translation of this excerpt and all other play excerpts are mine.

[11] For a discussion of this criticism by Federal Theater Project Florida state director Dorothea Lynch, see Dworkin y Méndez, Kenya C., 279-94.

[12] E. J. Salcines, personal interview, 14 August, 1996. In this interview, Mr. Salcines explains how he, as a child, helped sell war bonds with his father, the senior Emiliano Salcines. Furthermore, his father, who was a prominent West Tampa merchant and very respected in both the *Centro Español de* West Tampa and the neighborhood, used to display war bond posters in his store windows, with pictures and clippings attached to the back of the posters about local Tampa Latins who were overseas.

[13] For an explanation and example of *bozal*-type speech in Cuban theatre see Pereira, Joseph R., 13-7.

[14] Ibid.

[15] For a discussion of one such play see Martin Favata, 115-22.

Works Cited

Aparicio, Jr., Manuel. Personal interview. 31 July, 1996.

Bermúdez, Elisa and Mirella. Personal interview. 22 October, 1996.

Bueno, Salvador. *Medio siglo de literatura cubana.* La Habana: Lex, 1953.

Cortina, Rodolfo J. *Cuban American Theater.* Houston: Arte Público, 1991.

Dworkin y Méndez, Kenya C. "The Tradition of Hispanic Theater & the WPA Federal Theatre Project in Tampa-Ybor City, Florida," *Recovering the U. S. Hispanic Literary Heritage Project.* Vol. II. Houston: Arte Público, 1996, 279–94.

Favata, Martin Alfred. "Creativity and Adaptation in the Hispanic Theater of Tampa: Los Claveles de Ybor and Viva Ybor," *Letras Peninsulares.* 5.1. (1992): 115–22.

Kanellos, Nicolás. *A History of Hispanic Theatre in the United States: Origins to 1940.* Austin: University of Texas, 1990.

Méndez, Armando. *Ciudad de Cigars: West Tampa.* Tampa: Florida Historical Society, 1994.

Montes Huidobro, Matías. *Persona, vida y máscara en el teatro cubano.* Miami: Universal, 1973.

Mormino, Gary R. and Pozetta, George E. *The Immigrant World of Ybor City: Italians and Their Latin Neighbors.* Chicago: University of Chicago,

1987.

Remos, Juan J. *Proceso histórico de las letras cubanas*. Madrid: Guadarrama, 1958.

Rexach, Rosario (ed). *Jorge Mañach. La crisis de la alta cultura en cuba. Indagación del choteo*. Miami: Universal, 1991.

Salcines, E. J. Personal interview. 14 August, 1996.

Toledo, Salvador. "El General Pelusa o Arma Secreta." N.p.: n.p., 1950.

Toledo, Salvador and Fernández. "Un blackout in Ybor City." N.p.: n.p., 1943.

————. "Tabaqueros a cojer el cheke." N.p.: n.p., n.d.

Tolón, Edwin T. *Teatro lírico popular de Cuba*. Miami: Universal, 1973.

Looking Backward, Looking Forward: Jesús Colón's Left Literary Legacy and the Adumbration of a Third-World Writing

Tim Libretti
Northeastern Illinois University

Jesús Colón opens his sketch "Something To Read" from *A Puerto Rican in New York* writing, "A piece of working class literature, a leaflet, a pamphlet, a progressive book or newspaper are precious things in colonial and semi-colonial countries under the repressive measures of dictators" (76). Indeed, a prominent theme in many of the skecthes from *A Puerto Rican in New York* is the importance of developing alternative literary institutions to challenge the distortions of the dominant culture and to promote cultural production that comprehends and responds to the issues confronting working-class minority populations in the United States. While I do not mean to argue the extent to which the political structure of U. S. society resembles a repressive dictatorship, I would nonetheless like to suggest that Colón's assessment and valuation of the preciousness of "a piece of working class literature" holds equally true in contemporary U. S. culture and society in which literature of the working classes and of the Left generally has historically been marginalized—even erased—in academic literary study.

As Janet Zandy has noted, working-class literature is "not affirmed or valued in the dominant culture" (Zandy, 1). This critical neglect and devaluation of working-class literature, however, is directly linked to an abiding anticommunist ideology in U. S. literary study and the dominant culture at large. Indeed, as Alan Wald explains,

> as in so many other areas of politico-cultural repression in the United States, the silencing and distortion of the Communist literary tradition has turned out really to be a means of silencing the larger radical and working-class tradition in literature. As has been well-documented by now, the ideology of "anticommunism" in the United States has little to do with genuine opposition to the brutal and authoritarian policies of the Stalin and post-Stalin regimes. It is more often a means of discrediting the entire effort of the Left by tainting all radicals with the crimes of the Soviet ruling group, real or fabricated— although today we must recognize that most of those crimes were real.

One result of this kind of anti-communist ideology in literary studies is the disempowerment of the population of ordinary people who are denied a genuine history of their own cultural activities through access to authors who wrote about strikes, rebellions, mass movements, the work experience, famous political trials, the tribulations of political commitment, as well as about love, sex, the family, nature, and war from a class-conscious, internationalist, socialist-feminist, anti-racist point of view. Instead, the population is often exclusively presented with literary role models that inculcate notions of culture that distort visions of possibilities for social transformation. (Wald, 70)

Jesús Colón is just such a writer as Wald's passage describes: a committed and engaged working-class writer associated with the Communist Party who devoted his life in writing to challenging the distorted historical and social visions of the dominant and colonizing culture, particularly with regard to Third World peoples and cultures, and to developing resistance narratives of class struggle and to rethinking working-class culture and consciousness from a Third World nationalist perspective. But while Colón has certainly been silenced, along with other Left writers in the U. S. literary terrain, Left literary scholars, as I will discuss, have also been complicit in this silencing. In this sense, recovering Colón's writing fills in silences not only in the U. S. Hispanic literary tradition but also in the U. S. Left literary tradition, highlighting the intersection of the two.

It is in this particular context of the dominant U. S. cultural complex, characterized by other attendant cultural developments such as the emergence and critical ascension of post-colonial theory, that the recovery of the writings of the radical Puerto Rican working-class writer Jesús Colón in the recently published collection *The Way It Was and Other Writings* takes on such importance on the various yet related cultural fronts of radical working-class, proletarian, Left, Communist, Hispanic, and Puerto Rican literary traditions. First, Colón provides a model and establishes a tradition for a U. S.-based Puerto Rican anti-imperialist working-class literature of resistance that has been largely erased. Indeed, as Juan Flores argues,

The rebellious young Puerto Rican artists in New York had no way of recognizing their continuity with the working-class traditions of Puerto Rican culture, since it is precisely this component of the national history which imperialist relations are most urgently obliged to suppress. The Puerto Rican cultural outburst of the 1960s could not possibly have been aware of a Puerto Rico as seen by Ramon Romero Rosa, Luisa Capetillo or Edouardo Conde, nor even of the earlier struggle of Puerto Ricans in New York as narrated by Bernardo Vega or Jesús Colón. All of these figures, and above all the political and cultural relations they established between the revolutionary movement in the United States and in Puerto Rico, have been cast into oblivion by the subsequent course of history. (Flores, 135)

But while as Flores also asserts, "Today's Puerto Rican cultural workers, grappling to lend contours to a collective identity that has been battered and twisted by colonialism, have many lessons to learn from their working-class forbears in the United States and in Puerto Rico" (139), so too does the broader cadre of contemporary working-class and radical Left cultural workers. The virtual and complete absence of Jesús Colón from the U. S. Left literary tradition generally and from proletarian and working-class literary traditions specifically represents a significant cultural lacuna in that his writings fomented an awareness of and developed through his representational strategies an analysis of the specific conditions of a nationally oppressed internal Third World working class suffering not only under the conditions of labor exploitation but also of racial oppression experienced as colonization. His writings demonstrate the compatibility and the necessity of a stage of anti-imperialist national liberation struggle with, in, and as part of the class struggle.

Moreover, the Third World perspective generated in his writings provides a global or internationalist dimension to the narrative of class struggle lacking in most U. S. proletarian literature. Indeed, it is the nationalist component of his writing that provides the enabling discursive bridge to an internationalist cultural vision. In this sense, Colón's writings provide models for developing precisely the type of internationalist culture and class consciousness that Marxism theorizes at the most ideal level. His writings highlight, however, that this bridge between nationalism and internationalism is not simply crossed, that crossing requires that the working class of the dominant culture purge itself of its racist and colonialist mentality and recognize the counterproductiveness of and its own complicity with the uneven development of the global economy and the creation and maintenance of a subaltern Third World. Conversely, this crossing also requires that the Third World working class recognize the element of class exploitation underlying the invention of racial difference. Colón's writing attempts to dramatize and enact this dialogue between a First World and Third World working class in exploring the race/nation/class dialectic in the context of the global economy and the persistence of imperialist practice. Colón's conscious and conscientious efforts to inject a Third World anti-colonial perspective into a U. S. working class cultural and political vision are apparent from his sketches in *A Puerto Rican in New York*, most prominently in the sketch entitled "How to Know the Puerto Ricans," in which he writes,

> There is much you can learn by speaking to the Puerto Ricans every time you get a chance at work or in the casual contact of everyday life.
> We must always be ready to learn from the colonial people. They have much to teach. We do not need to elaborate the point to readers of this column. Their gruelling struggle against economic, political and social oppression has steeled the colonial world and taught its people many a way to combat imperialism and war. We colonial people have also much to learn from the working class of the imperialist countries. But if you want to open that door, don't

assume a know-it-all attitude and superior airs just because you were born in the United States. This "superiority" attitude of the imperialist exploiters is unfortunately reflected sometimes in the less developed members of our own working class. (148-9)

This passage neatly reveals the dialogic method of Colón's writing and the narrative bridging mechanism that joins First and Third World working classes, as his narrative position at once representationally holds apart and brings together the dual, or multiple, constituencies of the working class divided by national borders; it at once asserts and negates working class solidarity. Colón identifies himself with both sides of the bridge by counterpointing and moving between narrative subjects in such sentences as "we must always be ready to learn from the colonial people" and "we colonial people have also much to learn from the working class of the imperialist countries." The passage at once orchestrates the virtues and necessity of the both/and of dialectical thinking and the divisive pitfalls of the either/or of non-dialectical thinking. Colón positions himself as part of the "we" who must learn from "the colonial people" as well as part of the "we" who has much to learn from the working class of imperialist countries. Yet these two constituencies are also conflated in the unifying narrative voice of Colón who represents the united embodiment of both sides of the bridge and hence the possibility of a genuine internationalism. Indeed, this heightened international working class consciousness, yielded by adopting a Third World colonial perspective, is in fact assumed as constitutive of Colón's common readership, as he writes that "We do not need to elaborate the point to readers of this column." Indeed, it is in such a passage which implicitly asserts the reality of the common conditions that produce a class-in-itself and the ideologies of racial or national superiority that prevent the class-in-itself from achieving an international solidarity and becoming a class-for-itself, that we see exemplified the solution to the problem of representing the global totality Fredric Jameson seeks a solution to when he calls for "forms that inscribe a new sense of the absent global colonial system on the very syntax of poetic language itself" (Jameson, 349).

Of course, Colón is finally much more critical of the working class of imperialist countries for its racist and self-defeating exclusion of a significant demographic component of the working class, the U. S. internal Third World which represents the strongest link to the Third World abroad and thus to an international working class political vision. Indeed, Colón was one of the few voices on the Left, as a member of the Communist Party, who consistently focussed attention on the U. S. Third World minority working class as a neglected yet potentially vanguard element of class struggle. In 1961, Colón published a piece on Puerto Rican and other Third World migrant labor in *The Worker*, the party organ for which Colón wrote regularly since the mid-1950s. In this piece, which the editors included in *The Way It Was and Other Writings*, Colón asserts, like a lone man in a crowd, "Fifteen thousand Puerto Rican migrant workers, plus other thousands from Jamaica and the other West Indies. Plus thousands from Mexico . . . and white and Negro exploited workers from our own South. This is a problem to which we progressives should be giving more thought and action" (97). And it is in *The Way It Was and Other Writings* that we get Jesús Colón's statement to the Walter Committee on Un-American Activities in which he lambastes the committee for the "inquisitorial invasion of Puerto Rico"; in which he defends Castro and the Cuban people who "have dared to defy American imperialism by refusing to compromise with Wall Street and Washington" and who "have brought new hope and confidence to the anti-imperialist struggle in all the countries of Latin America"; and in which he points out the relationship between imperialist invasions and assaults abroad and racial oppression, or internal colonialism, at home, as he describes the common political commitments of Latin Americans within and outside the U. S. borders. He writes,

> There are millions of Latin Americans living in the United States. Cubans, Mexicans, Puerto Ricans, and many thousands from other republics living here, who support the main progressive leaders and movements in this country. As in New York City with the Puerto Ricans—the followers of the late Vito Marcantonio—the Spanish-speaking people here are becoming a deciding force politically and otherwise. (101)

We see here in these passages from these newly recovered writings Colón's attempt to reconceptualize and develop a deeper and more empirically comprehensive notion of the U. S. working class and to make visible the political existence and emergence of the internal Latin America as a progressive political agent in the making of history and the transformation of U. S. society. Colón's writings make available invaluable documentation of the presence of Puerto Rican and, more generally, Hispanic writing in U. S. Left literary history and, conversely, the presence of the Left literary tradition in U. S. Hispanic literature.

Indeed, the recovery of Colón's stories and articles in *The Way It Was and Other Writings* offers new empirical ground and presents a unique opportunity for theorizing the radical tradition in Puerto Rican and, more broadly, U. S. Hispanic literary history as well as for rethinking U. S. radical Left literary history—particularly that of proletarian literature—more generally from a Third World colonial and internal colonial perspective. This paper will explore the significance of these dual generic or traditional associations of Colón's writing in terms of its potential for leading to the creation of new critical paradigms for organizing and rethinking the contemporary fields of Puerto Rican, Hispanic, and more generally U. S. Third World literatures and for theorizing the intersection of Puerto Rican and Hispanic literatures with other resistance genres, such as that of proletarian literature, with which Colón's writings have not traditionally been associated in major critical studies.

Indeed, major studies of the proletarian literary tradition have generally narrowly periodized the movement or genre, locating its most intense moments of emergence and production in the 1930s and studying its residual persistence and gradual disappearance in the 1940s and 1950s with the onset of the Cold War. Walter Rideout, for example, in his study *The Radical Novel in the United States, 1900-1954* (1956) concludes with a sounding of retreat in Left cultural production. Daniel Aaron's *Writers on the Left: Episodes in American Literary Communism* (1961) writes the obituary for the Left literary tradition with the dwindling of Communism from the political and literary mainstream in the 1950s. Most recently, Barbara Foley has periodized the field even more restrictively in her study *Radical Representations: Politics and Form in U. S. Proletarian Fiction, 1929-1941*. She suggests that one might include later writers such as John Oliver Killens and Thomas McGrath, arguing, however, for their exclusion because they didn't identify themselves as proletarian writers. Chicano, Puerto Rican, and Hispanic writers, such as Américo Paredes, who wrote during the 1930s, do not find a place in these studies.[1] Colón, in fact, because of his direct connection with the Communist Party and literary Communism, would seem to provide the perfect link between pre-Cold War and post-Cold War Left writing, as he wrote well into the 1960s, and to serve as bridge between old and new Left politics and culture in a way that would deepen and extend the Left literary and political tradition from a Third World and Hispanic perspective.

I want particularly to emphasize and focus on the relevance and urgency of Colón's writing, stressing its Third World internal colonial perspective, at this particular juncture in literary and cultural studies given the insidious emergence and ascension of post-colonial theory which, its own denials notwithstanding, prematurely celebrates the pastness of colonialism and hence of the need for national liberation movements as well. It is particularly in *The Way It Was and Other Writings*, even more so than in *A Puerto Rican in New York*, that Colón adumbrates a U. S. Third World writing and anticipates in his writing the advent of the internal colonialism theory. His writing clearly portrays the connection between racial oppression and class exploitation Puerto Ricans endure in the United States as internal colonies and that which Puerto Ricans endured in the "homeland" and demonstrates these connections as linked to the practice of U. S. racial capitalism and imperialism. In *A Puerto Rican in New York* Colón attempts to reconstruct U. S. and international working-class consciousness from a Third World cultural and political perspective. In *The Way It Was and Other Writings*, Colón's writing recognizes the need for a stage of national liberation and consciousness-raising within and by the Third World working-class to eradicate the racism of the First World working class before that internationalism can be achieved. While the individual sketches of each collection might not have been written in different time frames, each collection yields a different rendering of the master narrative of class struggle with respect to national liberation and Third World solidarity.

While in *A Puerto Rican in New York*, Colón looked back, almost nostalgically, to his positive political experiences and to early moments in his development as a writer and as a class conscious citizen in search of resources and models for resistance to class exploitation in the U.S., in *The Way It Was* Colón looks back to life in Puerto Rico and to the early immigrant days to challenge the nostalgia for the homeland and to recall for his readers the colonial conditions and racial oppression and discrimination there as they mirror those Puerto Ricans face in the U. S.

Certainly, *A Puerto Rican in New York* centrally addresses issues of colonialism and represents lives oppressed within and struggling against the colonial experience. The work has a global focus, featuring sketches treating the U. S. government's and Wall Street's involvement in and endorsement of brutal dictatorships in Chile, Nicaragua, the Dominican Republic, and Guatemala. Additionally, Colón also stresses the cultural component of colonization in sketches that explore Hollywood's treatment and historical misrepresentation of Latin American culture as well as a library's distorted exhibits on Puerto Ricans and in sketches that highlight progressive Third World intellectuals and revolutionaries such as Ana Roque and Antonio Maceo. And, of course, in the final sketch titled "A Puerto Rican in New York," Colón provides an analysis of the historical trajectory of Puerto Rican migration, his own included, as motivated by the operations of "this race . . . called imperialism" (199). He presents an understanding "that we Puerto Ricans were part of a great colonialism system. And that not until colonialism was wiped out and full independence given to Puerto Rico would the conditions under which we were living be remedied" (199-200). He asserts that, "Colonialism made me leave Puerto Rico about forty years ago. Colonialism with its concomitants, agricultural slavery, monoculture, absentee ownership and rank human exploitation are making young Puerto Ricans of today come in floods to the United States, if only for a few months to work in the equally exploited agricultural fields" (201). But while *A Puerto Rican in New York* does attempt to construct a global class consciousness based in a comprehension of the colonial operations of world capitalism which at once nationally separate and create the conditions for uniting the international proletariat, the cultural program differs from the cultural vision presented in *The Way It Was and Other Writings* which promotes the necessity of a phase of national liberation as a precondition for a genuine internationalism.

In many ways the differences of cultural representation relate to the means of figuring the relation between "here" and "there," between the U. S. and Puerto Rico, and between past and present—how Colón looks forward and looks back in each work to define the task of day. Juan Flores' description of the relays between "here" and "there" of Puerto Rican cultural production is useful here for setting up this analysis of Colón's writing. Flores writes,

The Puerto Rican presence in the United States does inject a stream of anti-colonial, Latin American, and Caribbean culture into the artery of North American life and, conversely, it has projected the development of Puerto Rican cultural history into a setting of intense multicultural interactions, both events unprecedented . . . within the history of either society. But as long as Puerto Rico remains in direct colonial bondage to the United States, Puerto Rican cultural expression in the United States evokes the relation, above all, between the Puerto Rican people here and there, between the expressive life of the migrant population and the long-standing traditions of struggle and articulation of the Island culture. Whatever else is said about cultural activity of Puerto Ricans in the United States, critical analysis will inevitably hinge on the explanation given to the continuities and interruptions between cultural life in a new setting and its most relevant historical backdrop—Puerto Rican national culture. (14)

In *A Puerto Rican in New York*, the cultural resources inspiring Colón's political vision are drawn from the historical backdrop of a Puerto Rican national culture that is produced out of or called up from the nostalgic memories of his Puerto Rican childhood, which he narrates in multiple sketches as the moment when his artistic and class consciousness emerged and developed hand in hand. In the opening sketch, for example, "A Voice Through the Window," Colón remembers the readers from the cigar factories who would read literature aloud to the workers and who became the collective voice of enlightenment for the people, just as Colón aims to be in his role as a committed writer. The voice also becomes representative of the island working-class culture that serves for Colón as the unifying basis for an international working-class culture of resistance, echoing in the author's ears across generations, manifesting itself in other national idioms across the globe, and drawing together the various national constituencies of the international working class, spanning the globe historically and spatially, as he writes:

I still hear this voice through the window of my childhood. Sometimes I listen to the same themes today. Sometimes in Spanish, most of the time in English, from the halls and squares of this New York of ours. Sometimes this voice comes through the radio, from Europe and Asia, crystallized now in pamphlets and books that have shaken the world to its foundations. But always the theme is the same, the same as the readers from the cigarmaker's factory, coming to my home in my childhood's past. Always the same voice of the reader of my boyhood memories. But now clearer, stronger, surer, devoid of rhetoric, based on facts and history. (13)

In this passage the voice loses its distinct Puerto Rican accent, its distinct national dimension as cultural representation. It becomes the same as any other national voice of the First or Third World, subsuming itself into, as the foundation and model of, for Colón, an international working-class consciousness and cultural expression.[2]

Colón looks to the past to recover a Golden Age of working-class struggle and resistance to direct and fuel the making of history, and the making of the future, in the present. Indeed, the past Colón recovers, albeit grounded in a moment of the history of class struggle, takes on a mythic dimension that divorces it from its historical actuality, just as it becomes divorced from the specific national and historical context of its occurrence and is transformed into a general figuration of an internationally oriented class consciousness and class struggle that glosses over the unevenness of the global economy generated by capitalist and imperialist development.

Colón's use of history and memory in these early sketches work both as a means of recovering a past and also of projecting the past into a utopian future. The act of remembering, constitutive of a figural return to the homeland of the past, works in a way akin to Herbert Marcuse's method of resistance and liberation which emphasizes the anamnesic or psychoanalytic recovery not necessarily of the painful or traumatic events, as with Freudian analysis, but of the pleasurable and promising ones. Within our repressive society, Marcuse sees memory training as functioning in primarily a one-sided way: "The faculty was chiefly directed towards remembering duties rather than pleasure: memory was linked with bad conscience, guilt, and sin. Unhappiness and the threat of punishment, not happiness and the promise of freedom linger in memory" (Marcuse, 232). What we need to remember, Marcuse contends, are those promises and potentialities "which had once been fulfilled in our dim past":

> The liberation of the past does not end in its reconciliation with the present. Against the self-imposed will of the discoverer, the orientation of the past tends toward an orientation on the future. The *recherche du temps perdu* becomes the vehicle of future liberation. (19)

Past gratifications of desire, then, fuel and direct movements toward the future as we seek to restore the conditions of promise and pleasure. Thus, Colón's nostalgic childhood memory of solidarity in struggle is projected as the figure for the possibility of socially transformative working-class political action, even though at times his writing reveals a recognition of the mythic dimensions of the nostalgia for childhood.

Indeed, the return to an idealized past, infected by nostalgia and evacuated of actual historical significance through its projection into a utopian future, begs the question of historical process which Colón's writing attempts narratively not only to unfold but to guide and provoke. Gaston Bachelard, for example, theorizes memory as not so much a recuperation of history and its temporal processes, but rather as a process motivated by changes in spatial relationships. He writes, for example, that "after we are in a new house, when other memories of other places we have lived in come back to us, we travel in a land of Motionless Childhood, motionless the way all immemorial things are" (Harvey, 218). It is in glossing this quote that David Harvey questions the progressiveness of a collective memory that spatializes history and in so doing evacuates any trace of historical time or notion of struggle and transformation, writing:

> Being, suffused with immemorial spatial memory, transcends Becoming. It founds all those nostalgic memories of a lost childhood world. Is this the foundation for collective memory, for all those manifestations of place-bound nostalgias that infect our images of the country and the city, of region, milieu, and locality, of neighborhood and community? And if it is true that time is always memorialized not as flow, but as memories of experienced places and spaces, then history must indeed give way to poetry, time to space, as the fundamental material of social expression. (218)

For Harvey this transformation of history into poetry, from a flowing narrative that marks time to a static lyric that compresses it in space, undergirds a reactionary aestheticization of politics that informs both left and right versions of nationalism.

While Colón can hardly be characterized in any sense of the word as a reactionary, these issues do highlight fundamental quandaries of representing and imagining revolutionary historical process with which Colón's writing struggles. We see Colón almost self-consciously dramatizing and exploring this representational issue in a later sketch entitled "Looking Just a Little Forward." In this comical sketch, Colón tells how he fell asleep reading a copy of Edward Bellamy's *Looking Backward*, a story which features the plot of Julian West, who was mesmerized in a subterranean chamber in 1887, being found and awakened in the year 2000 when a social democratic transformation of society and economy has already taken place. Colón tells us that "the people of the year 2000 were quite informed about the last quarter of the 20th Century, from 1975 on. But for the third quarter of the 20th century, especially the last ten years of this quarter they had only general information. They knew that after the Soviet Union's seventh and eighth Five-Year plans, the superiority of socialism over capitalism was so glaring that most countries were rapidly changing their form of society from capitalist to socialist" (188-9). What those living in the utopian future lack, Colón's story suggests, is a knowledge of the historical process that created their society. By extension, Colón is offering a critique of the inherent problems of utopian visions for a revolutionary aesthetic because of the lack of historical vision, of the how-to of making history. While Colón fills in this quarter century with interesting developments such as an all-inclusive Asian five-year plan, the Soviet Union's supplying the world with food from its surplus, and the tremendous role of the numerically small Communist Party of the United States, the story nonetheless diagnoses the crisis of revolutionary representation and imagination of *A Puerto Rican in New York* as a whole. In retrieving a nostalgic version of the past as means of imagining a utopian future, historical process goes unrepresented. Additionally, while Colón does stress, as mentioned, the reality and effects of colonialism and while he does try to inject a Third World perspective into U. S. working class politics, the writing still makes a qualitative leap to a premature internationalism, skipping the phase of national struggle, assuming the "sameness" of the conditions that will create a class-for-itself and ignoring the reality of combined and uneven development. But in *The Way It Was and Other Writings*, Colón's writing develops a more stridently anti-imperialist nationalist cultural and political vision premised on a different configuration and interpretation of the cultural and historical relays between the "here" and "there" which provide the productive gounding for Puerto Rican literary and cultural production. If in *A Puerto Rican in New York*, Colón attempted to assert a continuity in the U. S. with a Puerto Rican historical and cultural past, albeit a mythic or nostalgic rendering of that history and culture, in *The Way It Was* Colón interrupts this relay and effectively dissociates the grounding of his project in the historical backdrop of a Puerto Rican national culture to develop a Third World cultural vision within the United States, as "the long-standing traditions of struggle and articulation of Island culture" no longer present for Colón a viable or living tradition to comprehend and clarify the particular political exigencies of Third World life in the United States.

In his 1968 piece "The Head of the Statue of Liberty" which Colón had intended for the volume to be titled *The Way It Was*, for example, Colón seems to suggest the need to turn inward and develop a Third World internal colonial perspective to understand the specific conditions of Third World populations in the United States rather than to turn toward Puerto Rico for cultural models to understand the meaning of colonization within the U. S. mainland. He begins the piece reflecting on the lifelessness of the Statue of Liberty, writing,

> Scrutinize those eyes. They have a far off gaze as if the whole head is aiming at solving problems it hardly understands—problems of people far away beyond the seas and the oceans.
>
> If that head could only turn around, just for a minute, and throw its freedom lights on the Harlem slums! If that head could only turn just a few blocks beyond the river and take a look at the Bowery! (41)

While this passage most obviously criticizes the hypocrisy and bankruptcy of U. S. nationalist ideology for asserting itself as a land of salvation and refuge while effectively colonizing the populations in Harlem and the Bowery, this passage also reflects Colón's sense of urgency to direct his political vision to the U. S. internal colonies, not to look abroad for answers to conditions of exploitation and oppression generated in the specific circumstances of U. S. society.[3] Indeed, we see later in this passage Colón's emphasis on developing a Third World solidarity within the United States and a Third World cultural voice and expression, for which Paul Robeson becomes the mouthpiece in this sketch, as Colón imagines the possibility of reinvigorating the Statue of Liberty by having Paul Robeson's voice repeating throughout the statue's head the verses of Emma Lazarus that grace the statue: "If Paul's voice unearths these great verses by Emma Lazarus now on a tablet inside the statue, its ringing words would sound as if they were really coming from the lips of the statue. And then the whole statue would be transformed from an empty lifeless symbol that seems to have joined the credibility gap into something living and meaningful for the black, Puerto Rican, Mexican American, Indian and poor white masses yearning and struggling for peace and freedom in this country today." Indeed, if in *A Puerto Rican in New York* Colón was attempting to inject a Third World perspective into a U. S. working-class consciousness, in *The Way It Was* Colón is as much concerned with injecting a global working-class consciousness into the Puerto Rican community as well as a consciousness of the conditions of internal colonialism that unite people of color in the United States and abroad under capitalism.

In his piece "The Two United States," Colón is effectively urging Puerto Ricans not to turn their backs completely on all elements of U. S. society, that just as there are two Puerto Ricos, that constituted by the ruling class that is complicit with U. S. imperialism and that working-class population which has a long history of resistance to imperialism, so the United States has progressive working class and Third World elements. His concern in this essay is not so much transnational Puerto Rican solidarity as much as it is multi-national solidarity within the United States, as he asks, "Do we Hispanics belong as much as we should to the worker unions that allow us to join with our working brothers and sisters of other nationalities residing in the United States and to know and better protect our livelihood?" (62). Colón is in many ways suggesting and calling for the development a new national culture that can respond to and comprehend the specific ways of life of and problems facing Puerto Ricans in the United States, moving away from "essentialized" or historically fixed notions of national identity in ways that Flores sees as essential in his study of Puerto Rican identity and national culture. He writes,

> There are answers, then, to the question of political alliances, and to the even more vexed issue of national and cultural "identity" so integrally bound up with it. What the emergence and evolution of conscious working-class expression shows is that national culture cannot be understood as an essentially psychological, religious, anthropolgogical, biological or ethnic entity, fixed in time and attached ineradicably to a group of people in some monolithic totality. (140)

While Colón might not be quick to turn back to Puerto Rico for cultural and political direction, however, he does insist that Puerto Ricans in the United States assert themselves as an internally colonized nation and attempt to understand their specific conditions of oppression and resistance from a national perspective, as he states in the piece "A Growing Minority": "One thing is certain and that is that the Puerto Rican national minority is here to stay . . . And so, if we are to think in terms of organizing Puerto Ricans in a way that they will eventually be part of the progressive political currents, we have to study them, their organizations and their leadership from a national point of view" (85).

Additionally, the material in *The Way It Was and Other Writings* also establishes an interruption between the cultural relay of "here" and "there" in its suggestion that the Puerto Rican national cultural tradition no longer provides a usable resource for cultural resistance except perhaps in the nostalgic repository of childhood cultural memory. Indeed, in *The Way It Was*, the Puerto Rican past is not recovered as a Golden Age but rather that idealized past is demystified in the present as underpinning and as historically continuous with the persisting conditions of colonization in the present. In "The *Fanguito* is Still Here," for example, Colón and his spouse visit "the enchanted island" "to see the other side of the tourist model," to find that the sames slums and ghettos still exist and that the conditions of colonialism persist in Puerto Rico as internal colonization presists inside the United States. In this sense, Colón's writing militates against the figuration of Puerto Rico as paradise that would inform later Neo-Rican writing, such that, "When Puerto Rico is evoked, it is not as a society with a history of struggle to build on, but as a fantasized paradise having little to do with contemporary reality" (Flores, 135).

Indeed, the central significance of the title of the collection "The Way It Was," developed in the story "Angels in My Hometown Church," is in its demystification of idealizations of the past as a nostalgic Golden Age and its evocation of a sense of historical process. In this sketch, Colón recalls the racism he endured in Puerto Rico as a child, indicative of the racial/colonialist order as a whole, when he would play with his best friend Pedro, who was "chubby and white." Colón recounts how Pedro's mother would invariably call her son away, chastising him for having "a friend of that color." Seeking solace at these moments, the young Colón found refuge in his hometown church where he "stood for a long time in front of the Virgin Mary's painting on the wall, surrounded with all the white, brown, and black angels around her" (53-4). Colón then writes of his return to this church during a vacation to his hometown in 1965, at which time he finds that the mural has been altered: "The Virgin Mary was still there. She was still surrounded by angels, but all of them were now white. Coats of grey cement covered the space where the brown and black . . ." (54). Curious, Colón asks a white woman praying in the church what happened to the black and brown angels. As she explains that water damaged the wall and that it had to be repainted, Colón asks why only the part of the wall with the brown and black angels had been affected. She summarily cuts him off before he can finish the question, dismissively responding, "Well . . . that's the way it was . . . You know Puerto Rico is becoming a great tourist center. Many, many Americans are visiting our hometown and our church every year" (54). The central phrase here "that's the way it was" registers at once truth and distortion.

While it likely distorts and falsifies the reason for repainting the wall and the history behind the repainting, which we can assume had more to do with racism than with water damage, it also expresses the historical truth that in fact this racism does in fact describe "the way it was" in Colón's youth, lest the older Colón look back with nostalgia to the halcyon days of racial harmony when black, brown, and white angels graced the wall together. Despite the image of angels co-existing in racial harmony, the truth is that racial prejudice, now manifested inside the church, still existed in the community outside the church walls. Thus, the story expresses an historical continuity between racism and colonialism of the past and their persistence in the present in both the U. S. and Puerto Rico. It is this historical perspective that is lacking, that has been nostalgically transmogrified, in *A Puerto Rican in New York.*

It is this sense of historical process that Colón stresses in these pieces which brings to the forefront the necessity of a nationalist phase in the international class struggle. If in *A Puerto Rican in New York* Colón envisions the fertilization of a U. S. working-class perspective with a Third World anti-imperialist working-class politics, in *The Way It Was* Colón, in stories such as "Jesús is Graduating Tonight" and "He Couldn't Guess My Name" despairs over the persisting invisibility of Puerto Ricans, the lack of impact their cultural and political perspective has had on left politics in the U. S., and the stubborn resistance of Anglo-American culture to transformation. In "Jesús is Graduating Tonight," Colón recounts how the principal at his high school graduation earnestly tried to learn the pronunciation of Colón's first name, repeating over and over the sounds "haysoos" as opposed to "geesus." Yet, when Colón takes the stage to accept his diploma, the principal announces his name as "geesus." While the principal expresses despair over the mistake he makes after practicing so long to avoid just that mistake, even greater is Colón's despair for the seeming difficulty if not impossibility of making inroads towards transforming the dominant culture and language so that it can recognize and provide the conditions for minorities of speaking and being heard instead of simply being rendered invisible by prevailing and inflexible cultural and linguistic norms. Indeed, the same theme plays out in "He Couldn't Guess My Name" when the carnival con-artists of Coney Island, who usually "guess" people's names by communicating through some secret code, are confounded by Colón's name which radically differs from the traditional names their code is devised to comprehend. While Colón has the wry pleasure of confounding them, he feels also the bitter fate of again escaping recognition and being rendered invisible by the codes of communication of the dominant culture. In this context, we see the importance of cultural resistance and transformation in Colón's narrative of liberation. Indeed, in the somber sketch "Phrase Heard in a Bus," in which Colón recounts hearing a racist remark from a wealthy woman purportedly involved in "charity" work for Puerto Ricans, we see how the utopian vision of Colón in *A Puerto Rican in New York*, founded in a nostalgic view of history, has been transformed into a steeled and somber recognition of the long view of historical process. He concludes the story, writing of the episode,

> Which should remind us that when, we the people, take full political and economic power, the job will have just begun. It will take years after the people take power to develop a human being without the callousness and insensitivity wrought into millions of men and women by the low morals of capitalism. Even after years when socialism will seem to be well rooted in our land—and there is no doubt that this will come to pass—our grandchildren will still be discovering among themselves some of the tenets of the evil thinking and acting of the so-called civilized society of today. (79)

Here Colón offers a variation on Amilcar Cabral's theme that national liberation is necessarily an act of culture. All of these conditions represented in the stories and essays in *The Way It Was and Other Writings* move Colón to a more insistent working class nationalism as a precondition for a genuine internationalism. His writings implicitly validate Frantz Fanon's political formulations that "national consciousness . . . is the only thing that will give us an international dimension" and that "it is at the heart of national consciousness that international consciousness lives and grows" (Fanon, 247-8). For Colón, as for Fanon, liberation demands the creation of new cultural forms to organize and define social relations and to redefine the human personality generally, but this new culture and this "new humanity," to use Fanon's words, require the invigoration and resurrection of oppressed national cultures in order to ensure that the process of developing that culture is truly democratic and humane. Indeed, Fanon captures the impulse of Colón's creative and political vision when he writes that "it is its national character that will make such a culture open to other cultures which will enable it to influence and permeate other cultures. A nonexistent culture can hardly be expected to have bearing on reality, or to influence reality" (245). Thus, a genuine international culture necessitates overcoming the invisibility imposed on Puerto Ricans and other internally colonized national minorities which Colón describes in such pieces as "He Couldn't Guess My Name" and "Jesús is Graduating Tonight." Becoming visible means asserting one's cultural identity and history against those cultural codes that effectively erase one. This point is especially important given the recent backlash against the politics of nationalism from both the intellectual left and right in contemporary theory in which each tends to equate nationalism with a regressive ethnic absolutism. But as we have seen with Colón's Third World vision, his nationalism is hardly separatist and constrictive but rather is the necessary premise or basis for political coalitions and solidarity. Again, to quote Fanon, "The consciousness of self is not the closing of a door to communication. Philosophic thought teaches us, on the contrary, that it is its guarantee" (247). It needs to be stressed that the resistance to colonialism and internal colonialism through the political subject of the nation is one that for Colón does not simply seek or assert the dominance of another culture over others but rather projects the creation of a new culture and of a new "human being without the callousness and insensitivity wrought into millions of men and women by the low morals of capitalism." Colón's imagination of this cultural process again finds an able glossing in Fanon's assertion that "culture is not put into cold storage during the conflict. The struggle itself in its development and in its internal progression sends culture along different paths and traces out entirely new ones for it. The struggle for freedom does not give back to the national culture its former value and shapes; this struggle which aims at a fundamentally different set of relations between men cannot leave intact either the form or the content of the people's culture. After the conflict there is not only the disappearance of colonialism but also the disappearance of the colonized man. This new humanity cannot do otherwise than define a new humanism both for itself and others" (246). In recognizing the necessity and contemporary efficacy of a nationalist politics, cultural or otherwise, which have been much disparaged in recent theory, we need to move beyond the one-sided approaches of such prominent theorists as Paul Gilroy and Benedict Anderson who tend to focus on official nationalisms of the oppressors and not on the national liberation of the oppressed and who also tend to associate nationalism with nation-states. Rather, we need to take seriously Cherríe Moraga's analysis of the viability of the politics of nationalism when she observes, referring to the struggles of the Cree and Inuit Indians, Palestinians, Kurds, and Chicanos, that "Increasingly, the struggles on this planet are not for 'nation-states,' but for nations of people, bound together by spirit, land, language, history, and blood" (169). Colón's fiction and essays provide fertile ground for rethinking or reimagining the category of nation along these lines.

Colón's writings help us reconceive the relation between race, class, culture, and nation, effectively rewriting the master narrative of class struggle to include the specific conditions of Third World minorities and to highlight the agency of the Third World working class in the class struggle and even as the vanguard of class struggle, as I mentioned earlier. It is particularly in this sense that we can in part measure the importance of Colón's cultural guidance in political practice and consciousness at this particular conjuncture on the Left. Consider, for example, Noam Chomsky's recent study of imperialism and its history. In concluding his 1993 book *Year 501: The Conquest Continues*, a work primarily concentrating on drawing parallels between the genocide of colonial times and the murder and exploitation associated with modern-day imperialism in Haiti, Latin America, Cuba, and Indonesia, Noam Chomsky suddenly shifts his perspective from the Third World abroad to the "Third World at Home" in the United States. He observes that the "internal class war is an inextricable element of global conquest," and, in analyzing "the new imperial age," asserts that "a corollary to the globalization of the economy is the entrenchment of Third

World features at home: the steady drift towards a two-tiered society in which large sectors are superfluous for wealth-enhancement for the privileged." He points to Reagan's replacement of PATCO strikers in 1981 and his destruction of the union as "one of the many devices adopted to undermine labor and bring the Third World model home" (275). What is sudden and surprising in Chomsky's analysis is the unorthodox yet nevertheless enlightening linkage of issues of class and colonial exploitation and oppression suggested by his figuration of the U. S. unionized—or de-unionized—workers as constitutive of a Third World pocket in the United States.

What is lacking in Chomsky's analysis, however, and what is troubling about his identification of the conventionally-defined and predominantly white working class as the U. S. internal Third World is that he neglects to recognize those racialized peoples within the United States who have historically suffered, endured, and resisted internal colonialism and the concomitant enforcement of the racial labor principle which has historically targeted people of color for special exploitation as the cheapest labor concentrated in the least-skilled jobs, the least advanced sectors of the economy, and not infrequently—as we saw mentioned in Colón's article on migrant labor above—the most industrially backwards regions of the nation. That is, his analysis doesn't recognize that the Third World model didn't need to be brought home; it's been at home since the colonization of North America.

Nonetheless, Chomsky's delayed recognition of an internal Third World, and his figuration of that Third World in terms of traditional conceptions of the working class, does yield two interesting insights that can help us understand the importance of Colón to the left cultural tradition. First, it asks us to rethink Robert Blauner's crucial distinction between the colonial and class situation underpinning his pathbreaking internal colonialism theory developed in 1971. Blauner wrote in 1971,

> The colonial situation differs from the class situation of capitalism precisely in the importance of culture as an instrument of domination. Colonialism depends on conquest, control, and the imposition of new institutions and ways of thought. Culture and social organization are important as vessels of a people's autonomy and integrity; when cultures are whole and vigorous, conquest, penetration, and certain modes of control are more readily resisted. (Blauner, 155-6)

If the working class as a whole is defined as an internal Third World, does Blauner's distinction still hold? Pressing Blauner's distinction, we can see that it was never entirely valid. The exploitation and oppression of the U. S. working class as a whole has historically had a central cultural component as well. The imposition and profusion of dominant cultural ideologies of individualism and self-reliance has long served as a means of preserving and validating the U. S. class society. Moments of greatest labor insurgency have been accompanied by the development of a formidable cultural apparatus, such as, in the 1930s, the proletarian literary movement.

The second insight yielded from Chomsky's analysis, then, is that, seeing the working class as a Third World pocket, there is a need for the white working class to begin to look to the Third World constituency of the U. S. working class for leadership in and models of cultural resistance to U. S. racial patriarchal capitalism and imperialism, as Colón mentioned above in the passage from "How to Know the Puerto Ricans." Colón's writings point to ways in which contemporary U. S. Third World literatures can offer new, more comprehensive cultural configurations of class consciousness as well as offer alternative sociocultural models not only for imagining post-capitalist/imperialist socioeconomic organizations but also for theorizing new master narratives of resistance and class struggle that more adequately comprehend the role of culture and nation in that liberation struggle.

At at moment when postcolonial theory is threatening to displace altogether the valuable Third World models of the 1960s and earlier and when the theorizing of U. S. minority literatures and of "race" in general has abandonned the Third World (inter)national, anti-imperialist, anti-colonialist cultural and political vision, the recovery of Colón's writings represents a crucial gesture for the U. S. Hispanic literary tradition and the radical working-class and Left literary traditions more broadly. Colón's nationalism is the dialectical complement of a call for a totalizing global vision that realizes itself in a Third World nationalist political perspective. His Third World vision can stand in the contemporary cultural and political terrain as a corrective to the failure of contemporary postmodernist models of "race" to comprehend the combined and uneven nature of capitalist development that continues to create a Third World and to intensify economic inequality between core and periphery both inside and outside the U. S. Colón's working-class perspective comprehends the unevenness and inequality within the working class itself and provides the context, the conditions of possibility, for Hispanics and people of color generally to speak and be heard in their own words and forms. Barbara Christian has recently pointed out how after the 1960s "ethnic peoples of color were increasingly being lumped together by officials and policymakers under the label 'minority,' a term that implicitly dissociated these groups from the majority of the world who were people of color. The term 'minority' undercut the connotation of that multiuniverse and of the possibility of the strength in numbers that the phrase 'Third World people' had suggested" (247). The recovery of Colón's writings helps us reimagine resistance to racial oppression and class exploitation on a global scale by providing a literary imagination that politically conceptualizes the oppressed nations of people of color as linked by their experiences of colonization and internal colonization.

Notes

[1] For my discussion of Américo Paredes' place in or relationship to the Left literary tradition of the 1930s, particularly the proletarian literary movement, see "'We can starve too': Américo Paredes' *George Washington Gómez* and the Proletarian Corrido" in *Recovering the U. S. Hispanic Literary Heritage,* Vol. II, ed. by Erlinda Gonzales-Berry and Chuck Tatum. Houston: Arte Público Press, 1996.

[2] An apt comparison to Colón's reduction of intra-class differences to sameness is Langston Hughes' early 1930s poem "The Same" in which he also asserts the solidarity of the international working class even in the face of the colonization of Third World working-class peoples across the globe.

[3] Nicholasa Mohr's essay "Puerto Rican Writers in the U. S., Puerto Rican Writers in Puerto Rico: A Separation Beyond Language" provides a helpful gloss to Colón's inward vision as he moves away from Puerto Rico to focus on the specificity of the U. S. context and demystifies the "innocence" or "utopianism" of life in Puerto Rico. She writes, "Except for the attempts of a few writers, I do not see any significant literary movement on the Island of Puerto Rico that speaks for the common folk: the working-class population of the Island. I wonder if the obsession with race, class, Spain, and the use of the baroque Spanish might not be a way for some intellectuals to attempt to safeguard their privilege and power against the strong North American influence that presently permeates Puerto Rico. If this should be the case, then it follows that in safeguarding such a status, a majority who are less fortunate must ultimately be excluded. As I have stated, the separation between myself an the majority of Puerto Rican writers goes far beyond a question of language. The jet age and the acessibility of Puerto Rico brought an end to a time of innocence for the children of former migrants. There is no pretense that going back will solve problems or bring equality and happiness. This is home" (Mohr, 116).

Works Cited

Aaron, Daniel. *Writers on the Left: Episodes in American Literary Communism.* New York: Harcourt, Brace, and World, 1961.

Blauner, Robert. "Colonized and Immigrant Minorities" excerpted from *Racial Oppression in America* in *From Different Shores: Perspectives on Race and Ethnicity in America,* ed. by Ronald Takaki. New York: Oxford, 1994, pp. 149-160.

Chomsky, Noam. *Year 501: The Conquest Continues.* Boston: South End Press, 1993.

Colón, Jesús. *A Puerto Rican in New York and Other Sketches*. New York: Mainstream Publishers, 1961.

————. *The Way It Was and Other Writings*, ed. by Edna Acosta Belen and Virginia Sánchez Korrol. Houston: Arte Público, 1993.

Christian, Barbara. "A Rough Terrain: The Case of Shaping an Anthology of Caribbean Women Writers" in *The Ethnic Canon*, ed. David Palumbo-Liu. Minneapolis: University of Minnesota Press, 1995, pp. 213-240.

Fanon, Frantz. *The Wretched of the Earth*. New York: Grove Press, 1963.

Flores, Juan. *Divided Borders: Essays on Puerto Rican Identity*. Houston: Arte Público, 1993.

Foley, Barbara. *Radical Representations: Politics and Form in U. S. Proletarian Fiction, 1929-1941*. Durham: Duke University Press, 1993.

Harvey, David. *The Condition of Postmodernity: An Enquiry into the Origins of Cultural Change*. Cambridge, Mass.: Blackwell, 1989.

Jameson, Fredric. "Cognitive Mapping" in *Marxism and the Interpretation of Culture*. ed. by Cary Nelson and Lawrence Grossberg. Urbana: University of Illinois Press, 1988, pp. 147-157.

Marcuse, Herbert. *Eros and Civilization: A Philosophical Inquiry into Freud*. Boston: Beacon Press, 1955.

Mohr, Nicholasa. "Puerto Rican Writers in the U. S., Puerto Rican Writers in Puerto Rico: A Separation Beyond Language" in *Breaking Boundaries: Latina Writing and Critical Readings*, ed. by Asunción Horno-Delgado, Eliana Ortega, Nina M. Scott, and Nancy Saporta Steinbach. Amherst: University of Massachusetts Press, 1989.

Moraga, Cherrie. *The Last Generation*. Boston: South End Press, 1993.

Rideout, Walter. *The Radical Novel in the United States, 1900-1954*. New York: Columbia University Press, 1992.

Wald, Alan. "Culture and Commitment: U. S. Communist Writers Reconsidered" in *Writing From the Left: New Essays on Radical Culture and Politics*. New York: Verso, 1994, pp. 67-84.

Zandy, Janet. *Calling Home: Working Class Women's Writings*. New Brunswick: Rutgers University Press, 1990.

Jesús Colón: Relación entre crónica periodística, lenguaje y público

Edwin K. Padilla
University of Houston

Este es el primer trabajo crítico dedicado a las crónicas en español de Jesús Colón. Los escritos de Jesús Colón en español han permanecido desconocidos por más de 50 años y gracias a la intervención del proyecto "Recovering the U. S. Hispanic Literary Heritage" han podido rescatarse de los archivos del periódico Gráfico.[1]

Jesús Colón fue un puertorriqueño que llegó a Nueva York en el año 1917, momento en que se le otorga a los puertorriqueños la ciudadanía norteamericana. Desde sus primeros años en la metrópoli neoyorquina tuvo consciencia de que vino para quedarse y se integra en cuerpo y alma a la lucha social hasta su muerte en el año 1974.

A través de su carrera periodística publicó crónicas y artículos en diferentes periódicos tanto en inglés como en español. En sus publicaciones en inglés presenta una versión de la crónica hispana en los Estados Unidos. Los trabajos más conocidos fueron publicados de los años 1955–57 en Daily Worker[2] en los que denuncia la situación en que viven algunos grupos marginados en los Estados Unidos al igual que opina sobre diversos temas de interés para la comunidad. Muchos de estos trabajos fueron recopilados y publicados nuevamente por el propio Colón en su libro *A Puerto Rican in New York and Other Sketches* en el 1961. Este libro y todos sus artículos periodísticos han sido considerados como precursores de la literatura puertorriqueña en el continente de los Estados Unidos, por el uso del inglés y su interés en los asuntos raciales.[3] En el 1993 Arte Público a través de "Recovering the U. S. Hispanic Literary Heritage Project" sacó el libro titulado *The Way It Was and Other Writings* editado por las doctoras Edna Belén-Acosta y Virginia Sánchez-Korrol en el cual se recopilan otros de sus trabajos periodísticos.

Estas dos publicaciones son los únicos documentos editados que sobreviven a los numerosos escritos de Jesús Colón y ambos fueron publicados en inglés. En éstos se expresa una relación escritor-público diferente a la que se da en la producción en español y de aquí lo interesante o novedoso de estas columnas en español. En otras palabras la relación escritor, lenguaje y público es determinante en el estilo, el tono y los temas de estos artículos periodísticos, sin olvidar factores diacrónicos como los acontecimientos político-sociales y la etapa formativa de un periodista joven.⁴

Las columnas periodísticas de Jesús Colón aludidas en este trabajo pertenecen a la producción en español del periódico Gráfico y serán material de una futura edición por Arte Público. Este periódico tenía entre otras funciones mantener informada a la comunidad latina acerca de lo que acontecía en sus respectivos países, unir a los latinos ante los problemas sociales que existían en la comunidad y mantener viva la configuración cultural latina en los Estados Unidos. En una de las cartas editoriales que abre el periódico, el editor deja ver la ideología del periódico al decir:

> La clase más indefensa de todas las que componen la gran familia hispana e ibero-americana, es la puertorriqueña. Verdad que parece paradoja que siendo los portorriqueños, ciudadanos americanos, sean los más indefensos. Mientras los ciudadanos de los otros países tienen sus cónsules y ministros que los representan, los hijos de Borinquen no tienen a nadie.

Los trabajos de Jesús Colón en el periódico Gráfico son una crónica de lo que les estaba ocurriendo a los hispanos en la ciudad de Nueva York durante los años que siguieron a la Primera Guerra Mundial y los que antecedieron a la gran depresión del 29'. La crónica recoge un juicio pesimista de la condición en que se encontraban aquellos puertorriqueños que llegaron a Estados Unidos con una reciente ciudadanía,⁵ esperando encontrar los empleos que en la isla escaseaban. Al finalizar la guerra, los soldados norteamericanos regresan y se ubican en sus antiguos puestos de trabajo, creándose un caos en donde el sobrevivir económicamente se convierte en combate diario, surgiendo en el barrio una serie de tipos que luchan por ganarse la vida. Al mismo tiempo continúa la inmigración de muchos puertorriqueños, los cuales no tienen especialización ni dominan el inglés. Estos se unen a otros grupos hispanos que llegan al mismo tiempo, creándose así una numerosa comunidad latina.

Es importante señalar que Jesús Colón visualiza una estadía permanente de esta comunidad inmigrante, la cual llegó como toda inmigración económica, con intenciones de regresar a la tierra natal. Esta visión profética hace que su discurso en el periódico Gráfico tenga como uno de sus principales propósitos la de rehabilitar y moldear la imagen del hispano en Nueva York.⁶ No existe, en estos primeros artículos en español la lucha por los derechos civiles, los prejuicios sociales o las preocupaciones económicas que años más tarde Colón caracterizó su producción en inglés. Por el contrario, la voz del escritor tiene una intención anexionista, en el sentido de que busca una aceptación por la comunidad neoyorquina anglosajona.⁷ Con este fin, se propone desterrar todas aquellas costumbres o vicios que reflejan una imagen negativa ante "ese otro". Hay un deseo de "encajar" dentro de una ciudad que tiene ya unos prejuicios preconcebidos, sin que haya un cuestionamiento de la legitimidad de dichos prejuicios. Sin duda, muchas de las observaciones negativas que el cronista hace no son exclusivas de los grupos puertorriqueños, sino que son parte de otros grupos en condiciones económicas similares; sin embargo, nunca se detiene a examinarlas. Esto muestra una etapa joven del periodista en la cual refleja los efectos de toda una ideología prejuiciada en contra de su grupo y la autocrítica se convierte en una reacción impulsiva.

Este trabajo se nutre de veinte columnas periodísticas de las cuales tres han sido firmadas con el nombre propio del cronista, cinco bajo el seudónimo de Pericles Espada y doce bajo el seudónimo de Miquis Tiquis. Estas tres maneras de autorizarse los trabajos tienen estrecha relación con los temas y la problemática que se plantea en los mismos.

En los momentos que utiliza su nombre propio, sus trabajos tienen un parecido con el tono de reflexión político-social de su producción en inglés. Son ensayos cortos en donde expone rápidamente una preocupación de índole social con gran seriedad. Existen otros trabajos en estilo epistolar titulados "Cartas inmorales a mi novia" bajo el seudónimo de Pericles Espada (se aludirán más tarde) en donde se utiliza alegóricamente a la novia como el destinatario del discurso. Y finalmente, bajo el seudónimo de Miquis Tiquis se presenta un Jesús Colón juez crítico de todo el problema que afecta a la comunidad. A través de un mensaje directo y crudo, no toma en cuenta las fronteras que pueda tener su discurso, haciendo unos ataques nunca vistos en su producción en los años posteriores. Por otro lado, como crónica estos trabajos tienen gran valor histórico y el lector puede ver junto al cronista los nacientes personajes del proceso de transculturación latina como los boliteros del barrio, las "flappers" latinas, los vagabundos en busca de trabajo y una nueva versión del hermano explotador-comerciantes latino.

Es imprescindible detenerse por un momento para señalar el significado del seudónimo Miquis Tiquis y qué relación existe entre escritor-lector. La expresión original es "tiquis miquis" y se define como una persona que se siente superior a los que la rodean. Se origina del "tibi et michi", lo cual fue una transmutación del latín de a ti—a mí. Jesús Colón invierte el orden de las palabras y crea el seudónimo: Miquis Tiquis; en donde Miquis—a mí, Jesús Colón viene primero o pasa a un plano superior; y Tiquis—a ti, público, pasa a un plano secundario o inferior. La inversión de las palabras está relacionada con un orden ético, en donde el cronista establece a partir del seudónimo una superioridad sobre el público lector. En este sentido, Miquis se convierte en el acusador de tiquis y esta relación entre escritor y público es la que origina la crónica del barrio en momentos de recesión económica.

Miquis Tiquis no viene a reflexionar o a "vender" ideas políticas sino que presenta: ¿Qué estaba ocurriendo en el barrio? ¿cómo era la gente? ¿qué hacía? ¿Qué valores e intenciones tenían? ¿Cómo se iban formando estos grupos?, etc. A través de un estilo singular logra que un lector contemporáneo pueda palpar el calor de la gente, escuchar el ruido de sus conversaciones, además de reír ante los constantes comentarios del cronista. En una de sus columnas Miquis Tiquis retrata a los puertorriqueños que se reúnen cerca del muelle donde sus paisanos desembarcan diciendo:

Si [por desgracia a][8] una pasajera se le salen un poco las enaguas, eso, para esta ralea social [es motivo de] largo y sucio comentario a toda boca [y] si hay otro pasajero que *tuvo la desgracia de vestirse de acuerdo con la poca adelantada moda de su aldea*, eso [es], para esta brosa acepillada [un] motivo [de] carcajadas infantiles. Y mientras comentan e insultan, y dan a conocer al yanqui su bajo nivel de educación y roce social, no se acuerdan los muy desgraciados, ni por un momento, las condiciones en que ellos mismos vinieron.

Añade:

[Y el] que más vocifera sale a principio de semana, como si fuera a buscar trabajo, y en vez de ir a buscar donde doblar el lomo, que bien grande [que] lo tiene, va derechito para el "35", a criticar los espejos de lo que él mismo era antes de meterse en "spats" y coger fiadas las tres perchas que tiene. (*MT*)[9]

El estilo del cronista hace que el lector se sienta transportado a la calle, haciéndose cómplice por un lado, del comportamiento inmaduro de estos grupos y, por otro, se identifica con la censura que encierra el humor negro de Miquis Tiquis. Su ataque corre en dos direcciones opuestas; por un lado está ridiculizando a este grupo de holgazanes, expresando gran preocupación por la imagen que proyectan hacia afuera; por el otro lado es partícipe de esta burla hacia el grupo recién llegado, añadiendo comentarios personales que levantan una sonrisa compartida con el lector.

Esta inclinación hacia el humor se puede ver en la columna en donde cuenta cómo la "señora X" se cree popular en el barrio por la gran cantidad de personas que asisten a sus fiestas. Sin embargo, Miquis Tiquis pone en duda la calidad de estas amistades porque:

[Como digan] algo acerca de ella es para comentar su "iliteracia", su "antimódico" vestir o su demasiado joven maridito. En fin, si hablan es para "pelarla" de una u otra manera. (*MT*)

Todo lo que ocurre en la comunidad hispana durante estos años viene a servir de semilla para su crónica y esto es lo que se encuentra en el periódico Gráfico. El tono de las meditaciones de sus escritos en inglés de décadas posteriores no está presente en Miquis Tiquis; el cual se expresa "sin pelos en la lengua" censurando fuertemente a su gente. Toma la actitud de un padre que se preocupa y regaña en la privacidad del hogar al hijo indisciplinado; mientras que lo defiende a la luz del público:

Creo que se puede hacer más por la reputación de los nuestros siendo un

poquito más limpios para así ser más
respetados . . . Barran los apartamentos, latinos, por Dios.
No solo pluma y espada,
hacen patria; no señor
Escoba bien manejada
harán patria en Nueva York . . . (*MT*)

La preocupación de Jesús Colón por la imagen, como se indicó anteriormente indica la conciencia de que los hispanos están en los Estados Unidos para largo rato. No es una estadía temporaria, por lo tanto es necesario "restaurar" o exaltar la imagen que se proyecta hacia afuera.

La realidad del barrio está muy presente en Miquis Tiquis el cual aprovecha cualquier observación interesante para usarla como material de su crónica. Por ejemplo, en el momento en que se dirige a las jovencitas que buscan marido, Miquis tiquis señala:

A veces se le oye decir: "El es alemán. Su padre tiene fincas. Casándome con él adelantaré la raza", y así otras cuantas tonterías popularizadas por el vulgo que no razona ni lee—vulgo lleno de prejuicios estúpidos. (*MT*)

Esta idea de pensar que se mejora la raza a través del cruce con la raza "socialmente superior" existe en el caribe y posiblemente en todos los países con una relación binaria de colonizador y colonizados. Jesús Colón no puede ocultar su indignación ante semejantes prejuicios y la exterioriza, convirtiéndose en juez que censura abiertamente todos los prejuicios. Expresa una fijación por lo feo o de mal gusto en las costumbres del hispano en el barrio. Escudado en el seudónimo de Miquis Tiquis, Colón viene a ser el portavoz de la crítica del barrio sin intención de trascender, sino con el único interés de lavar los trapos sucios en casa, impartir disciplina y eliminar los vicios. El propio lector, acostumbrado al tono sarcástico de sus columnas, esperaba leer las novedades que tenía Miquis Tiquis cada domingo por la mañana. Es decir, el seudónimo marcaba el tono esperado por los lectores que seguían su trabajo.

En la siguiente columna Miquis Tiquis narra los cambios que ocurren en los complejos de apartamentos una vez comienzan a llegar los latinos:

Fuí el primer latino
que alquilé donde ahora
Viven más de mil,
Latinos que sobran
Cuando estaba el "building",
Con "gringos" de sobra,
Más he de contarle
Detalladamente
cómo cambió todo,
al llegar "mi gente"

Hay siempre grupitos,
Tapando la entrada
Dando a la que pasa,
Groseras miradas;
Bajan la escalera,
Cual salvajes potros,
Importando nada,
El sueño de otros.
el radio, pianola,
El brinco y el salto . . .
La antigua victrola
Es un sobresalto
Toca que te toca,
Baila que te baila,
¡Y yo que creía,
que iba a estar salvo,
Viviendo contiguo,
A cientos de hispanos!
Y esto es Director,
Lo que yo he sacado:
Dolor de cabeza,
Miles de altercados,
Oír palabras sucias,
Chanchuyos, ¡el diablo!
Si visto muy sucio
Critican, si salgo
vestido de nuevo,
Me miran odiando.
Me roban la leche,
Las cartas, el diario (*MT*)

Con versos simples narra la lucha de gran cantidad de familias latinas que se ven obligadas a vivir asinadas en los barrios pobres de Nueva York. Estas personas hacen todo lo que tienen al alcance por subsistir: se acuestan tarde, interfieren con la tranquilidad del que trabaja al siguiente día y tienen el tiempo para hacer sus fechorías. En esta columna señala una añoranza por el edificio antiguo cuando la población predominante era anglosajona y rechaza todas las perturbaciones que los latinos llevan a cabo. Tal parece que Miquis Tiquis busca identificarse o busca que el latino acepte el modelo anglosajón por ser éste "superior" al que está viendo en su vecindad. En este tipo de columna no existe un análisis socio-económico de los problemas o del por qué estos grupos viven de esta manera, sino que se limita a señalar con el dedo de la misma manera que lo hacía la prensa amarillista de New York. Estas columnas jamás hubiesen tenido lugar en sus producciones posteriores, específicamente en inglés y para un público multi-étnico.

En este ambiente del barrio es que aparecen en su crónica los estereotipos como las "flappers" y los boliteros. En la primera columna, Miquis Tiquis hace una comparación entre la "flapper yanqui" y la naciente flapper del barrio. Usando la segunda persona le dice al lector:

> Si quieres ver lector la caricatura de una flapper no tienes nada más que mirar a una latina que aspira a serlo. La flapper yanqui siempre busca que su conjunto de exageraciones tenga una apariencia *chic,* como se dice en alemán. Además poseen esa divina joya de la frialdad bien imitada. Ese arquear desdeñoso de ojos que al cruzar las piernas casi desde . . . desde . . . parecen no importarle que las miren. *Seeming frigidity, that's the phrase.* La *would be flapper* latina le gusta que la miren y para conseguirlo se pinta como una máscara. Dos chapotas mal puestas en cada buche y cuatro bien pronunciadas montañas de *rouge* en los labios. Critican primero, los nuevos *fads;* después los adaptan, llevándolo hasta la exageración. (*MT*)

Se puede apreciar en la flapper del barrio una manifestación del proceso de transculturación en donde hay un intento por copiar los valores de la época; sin embargo esta copia es un esperpento del cual se burla Miquis Tiquis. La incrementación de esta burla se lleva a cabo a través del contraste o la exaltación de la flapper yanqui.

Con esta misma chispa de ironía trágica con que describe la existencia de las "flappers" latinas; menciona a los boliteros del barrio para decir que los hay buenos y malos; o como dice Miquis Tiquis: "de esos que se desarrollan por esos mundos de Harlem". Según el cronista los boliteros buenos son los que acostumbraban a jugarle los números a sus clientes sin recibir el dinero por adelantado; mientras que al bolitero malo: "se le oyó decir más de una vez que ni a su mamacita que bajara del cielo le [apuntaría] un número fiao". Sin embargo, viendo que perdía su clientela, un día se le apareció a una señora, a la cual nunca dio crédito y se atrevió a exigirle un dinero que nunca fió:

> el [bolitero] bajito como un signo de interrogación, se volvió un artista de película, queriendo imitar un fogón que no sentía, porque sabía que lo que estaba reclamando era un robo, pues no había pensado ni jugar los números. (*MT*)

Este tipo de columna se alimenta directamente de las experiencias del barrio y el cronista se limita a recrearlas dándole su toque personal.

Usando este tipo de ironía festiva, Miquis Tiquis indica las razones por las cuales los hispanos viven en los "top floors" de los edificios. Entre otras razones señala que es:

> para hacerle más ardua, cansada, y miserable la vida a los miles de cobradores que como moscas tras la golosina están persiguiendo eternamente a los hispanos. Hay cobradores que cansados de subir y bajar tantas escaleras dejan de cobrar por un tiempo la Vitrola. Y ¡lo que quería el hispano! ¡Le dió tiempo de mudarse! ¡Y, adiós dinero de la vitrola!

Puede apreciarse a través de todas estas citas grandes rasgos picarescos de estos grupos en búsqueda de sobrevivencia en Nueva York convirtiéndose "el engaño" en una forma de subsistir.

Esta picardía no es exclusiva de los de abajo, sino que también se lleva a cabo por los comerciantes en ascenso económico. Miquis tiquis critica duramente a las compañías de mudanzas latinas las cuales una vez tienen el contrato, "le pelarán todos los muebles, se quejarán a cada paso de las escaleras, le beberán todo el whisky y le cobrarán mucho más caro que el *moving van* americano".*(MT)* De igual forma ataca a las bodegas latinas, las cuales ponen precios exageradamente altos por los productos latinos, aprovechándose de que estos no se encuentran en todas las bodegas:

> ¡Cómo abusaban entonces esos queridos hermanos de la patria y de la raza! En aquellos tiempos, como sabían que si no compraban el plátano al peso de oro que ellos exigían, era que no iba a comer mofongo ese día, se tiraban para atrás pidiendo por sus productos criollos . . .

Finalmente, Tiquis miquis se limita a decir: "Y así en todos los demás oficios y profesiones", lo cual toma características peligrosas debido a que en Gráfico se anunciaban: bodegas, yerberías, restaurantes, reposterías, funerarias, dentistas, abogados y hasta parteras. Esto lo obliga a que al final de la columna aclare:

> Quiero terminar diciendo que hay muchas distinguidas excepciones . . . En las páginas de anuncio de GRÁFICO se encuentran personas "latinas" [de toda confianza], dando servicios en todas las actividades de la vida que son dignas. *(MT)*

Esta aclaración de Tiquis miquis es importante debido a que el periódico Gráfico era patrocinado en gran parte por el comercio latino. Aún así, Miquis tiquis señala que muchos comerciantes se refugian en palabras trilladas dentro del ámbito comunitario como: Unidad, cooperación, fraternidad y ayuda mutua, mientras que: "Lo que necesitamos en la colonia es menos habladuría sobre unidá, fraternidá y hermandá, y más de todas estas cosas en lo práctico." *(MT)*

Esta sátira de Miquis tiquis es llevada a todas las esferas sociales y a pesar del tono severo en que se redacta, levanta sonrisas dentro de sus lectores. Sin embargo, no se puede negar el alto grado de pesimismo de Miquis tiquis, el cual convierte "la burla" en la herramienta para enfrentar la realidad que lo ahoga. En este sentido, podría decirse que ésta va a ser la característica principal de Jesús Colón bajo el seudónimo de Miquis tiquis.

Las cinco columnas bajo el seudónimo de Pericles Espada fueron escritas posteriormente a las de Miquis tiquis y marcan un cambio en el tono del periodista. En estas columnas, escritas como epístolas, tituladas "Cartas Inmorales a mi novia", Pericles Espada se dirige alegóricamente a la patria lejana (Puerto Rico), tratándola como a la novia, y su futura llegada a Nueva York es solamente una justificación para expresar sus preocupaciones y dar consejos. Pericles Espada se dirige a ella en calidad de un novio/maestro que trata de guiar a su novia/patria por los caminos del conocimiento. Al igual que otros cronistas de la época como "Latiguillo", "Samurai" y "Chicote"; el seudónimo de Pericles Espada es usado con el propósito de presentar al público unas ideas liberales en tono "cortante". El nombre Pericles es tomado de la tradición griega, como el político, orador y demócrata ateniense; unido al sustantivo Espada, definido como arma ofensiva que hiere o lastima; da la idea del luchador que utiliza "la palabra" como su arma de combate. A través de las cinco epístolas, Pericles va educando a la novia-patria, de manera que ésta esté preparada para llegada a los Estados Unidos. En un tono íntimo va señalando los conflictos que existen en Nueva York, presintiendo un choque cultural debido a las ideas equivocadas que traen los puertorriqueños de la isla. Presenta la vida en Nueva York como un mundo engañoso que enmascara una cruda y difícil realidad.

> Me he embriagado con el ambiente ilusorio del país de las imágenes; olvidándome de lo rudo y trágico de la vida trepando eternamente por la trenza de Julieta, no sabiendo detenerme a examinar el mundo de las realidades. (*PE*)

A pesar de que Jesús Colón utiliza diferente seudónimo, existe la misma relación de maestro/discípulo en Pericles y la novia/patria que la vista anteriormente en Miquis Tiquis y el barrio. La diferencia se encuentra en que para Miquis Tiquis la realidad del diario vivir se encuentra constantemente en el barrio. Es decir, los compatriotas que llegaron de la isla se han ido transformado ante sus ojos en los tipos aludidos anteriormente y el periodista se siente imposibilitado de cambiarlos. Por el contrario, Pericles Espada percibe con optimismo la próxima llegada de sus hermanos y, por tal razón, no muestra la crudeza de Miquis Tiquis ni su pesimismo agnóstico; sino que sus palabras se proponen preparar a estos hermanos de manera que puedan enfrentar en Nueva York los contratiempos que se avecinan.

Las cinco cartas fueron escritas en el 1928 y Pericles Espada las comienza diciendo: "¡Hoy cumplimos diez años de amores!" lo cual puede referirse a la relación Estados Unidos- Puerto Rico diez años después de la ciudadanía al igual que el tiempo del periodista fuera de la isla. Continúa estableciendo la alegoría novia-patria, marcando la ingenuidad de ambas, a consecuencia de un origen similar.

> Nacida en el ambiente medieval de tu casa empolvada por los años; cerca de la iglesia centenaria y del convento donde residen tus tías monjas . . . (*PE*)

Establecida esta ingenuidad pasa a hablar con "la verdad", sobre religión, guerra, política, y hasta se atreve a exponerle a su novia la teoría filosófica positivista de Comte.

En la primera carta expresa el deseo de romper con los convencionalismos existentes, sustituyendo la idea de "porque mis abuelos así lo hacían" con la de: "Porque la razón y la ciencia así lo dictan . . ."; continúa diciendo:

> Espero que la claridad de mis argumentos triunfe al fin y limpie tu mente de las concepciones hechas por la ignorancia acerca de las cuestiones primordiales de la vida y que empiece para ti la nueva era de luz y del progreso. (*PE*)

A través de las cinco cartas hay un cambio de temas abstractos, como los que se acaban de mencionar, hacia otros relacionados con el barrio. Son los momentos en que su prosa adquiere elementos realistas acercándose más al estilo de Miquis Tiquis. En la última carta se aproxima el encuentro con la novia-patria en Nueva York y Pericles habla abiertamente de la situación existente en el barrio, de manera que no se sorprenda ésta al llegar y señala:

> Me figuro que tú estarás pensando en que vendrás a vivir desde el primer instante en tu propio apartamento, amueblado con juegos profusos de sala, cuarto y comedor . . . (*PE*)

Básicamente Pericles está aludiendo a los mitos que traen los inmigrantes al llegar. Estos vienen con la idea de que el éxito está garantizado una vez se llega a los Estados Unidos. Por eso, enfatiza que en Nueva York se pueden tener todas estas cosas materiales debido a que es la ciudad donde más se compra al fiado; sin embargo le dice: "¿Deseas que te molesten a todas las horas con un continuo tocar de cobradores a la puerta de tu nuevo hogar?" Continúa la advertencia manifestando:

> Después de las primeras dos o tres semanas, cuando ya sepas viajar en el tren subterráneo, es necesario buscar un sitio donde puedas trabajar y ayudarme para la realización de nuestros sueños. Aquí tanto trabaja la mujer como el hombre. A más de ser una costumbre de la mujer americana, es una necesidad . . .

Y cierra la idea con:

> Además, yo no veo la razón que impida a una muchacha joven y saludable, sin niños que atender, a salir y buscarse un dólar de una manera honrada. Así la mujer sabrá mejor lo que cuesta ganarse el pan. (*PE*)

Estas últimas citas muestran la preocupación de Pericles Espada por el choque cultural que va a recibir su novia o la mujer puertorriqueña al llegar a Nueva York para convertirse en fuerza laboral. Le preocupa el cambio de una sociedad en donde la mujer no acostumbraba a trabajar, hacia otra en la que tiene por obligación que hacerlo, presintiendo consecuencias de orden ético.

En la última carta Pericles sugiere un futuro regreso a la isla como la añorada alternativa:

Y si ahora que somos los dos jóvenes sabemos aprovechar nuestro tiempo podremos en el ocaso de nuestras vidas, retirarnos a aquella nuestra tierra donde todo es luz y colorido, paz y tranquilidad. (*PE*)

La idea de un regreso a la isla como el destino final de estos grupos inmigrantes es la misma que más tarde presenta Enrique Laguerre en *La Carreta*. El éxodo continuo es visto como una necesidad económica y el barrio neoyorquino aparece como un gran peligro al que hay que enfrentar y superar. En este sentido el retorno exitoso a la isla vendría a representar el cumplimiento de este objetivo. Por el contrario el estado en que se encuentran los grupos que pinta Miquis Tiquis simbolizan el desastre como consecuencia del choque cultural.

Bibliografía

Acosta-Belén, Edna, and Virginia Sánchez Korrol, eds. *The Way It Was, and Other Writings*. By Jesús Colón. Houston: Arte Público, 1993.

Colón, Jesús. *A Puertorrican in New York and Other Sketches*. New York: Mainstream Publishers, 1961.

Cortina, Rodolfo J., and Alberto Moncada, eds. *Hispanos en los Estados Unidos*. Madrid: Ediciones de Cultura Hispánica, 1988.

Fernández Méndez, Eugenio. *Crónicas de Puerto Rico*. Río Piedras: Editorial de la Universidad de Puerto Rico, 1973.

———. *La identidad y la cultura*. San Juan: Instituto de Cultura Puertorriqueña, 1965.

Forster, Merlín, and Julio Ortega, eds. *De la crónica a la nueva narrativa mexicana*. México, D.F.: Editorial Oasis, 1986.

Flores, Juan. *Divided Borders*. Houston: Arte Público, 1993.

Gutiérrez, Ramón, and Genaro Padilla, eds. *Recovering the U. S. Hispanic Literary Heritage*. Houston: Arte Público, 1993.

Mohr, Eugene V. *The Nuyorican Experience*. Westport, Conn.: Greenwood Press, 1982.

Montalvo, Manuel Alers. *The Puerto Rican Migrants of New York City*. New York: AMS Press, 1985.

Sánchez Korrol, Virginia. *Settlement Patterns and Community Development among Puerto Rican in New York City*. New York: State University of New York at Stony Brook, 1981.

———. *Los puertorriqueños en los Estados Unidos*. New York: Minority Rights Group, 1983.

———. *Puerto Rico, Its History and Culture*. New Jersey: Continental Press, 1989.

Wiener, Markus. *The Puerto Ricans.* New Jersey: Markus Wiener, 1994.

Zavala, Iris M., Rafael Rodríguez. *Libertad y crítica*. Río Piedras: Ediciones puerto, 1973.

Notas

[1] Gráfico fue un periódico que circuló una vez por semana dentro de la comunidad hispana durante el 1927 hasta principios del 1929.

[2] Periódico neoyorkino de orientación socialista-comunista publicado en Nueva York alrededor de los años del 1952–63.

[3] Kanellos, Nicolás, ed., *Biographical Dictionary of Hispanic Literature in the United States* (New York: Greenwood Press, 1989) 63.

[4] Hay que tener en cuenta que este Jesús Colón del 27' es aproximadamente 20 años menor que aquel periodista que escribe en "The Daily Worker".

[5] Puerto Rico recibió la ciudadanía americana en el 1917 a través de la Ley Jones o Acta Jones.

[6] Mohr, Eugene, *The Nuyorican Experience* (Westport, Conn.: Greenwood Press, 1982) 10.

[7] Hay que enfatizar que estos artículos salieron antes de la depresión del 29' y el modelo de vida económico-social que tienen estos nuevos inmigrantes, incluyendo a Jesús Colón, es un mundo anglosajón muy estable en los órdenes político, social y económico. Es claro que, la caída de Wall Street y la influencia ascendente de la revolución rusa vienen a ser factores determinantes en la desmitificación de este modelo de vida. Un futuro trabajo analizará estos cambios ocurridos en las décadas de los 30' y los 40', de manera que los escritos en "The Daily Worker" se aprecien como una continuidad en el pensamiento de Jesús Colón.

[8] Todo lo que aparece bajo corchetes "[ ]" ordena sutilmente la sintaxis sin que se pierda el sentido.

[9] Todas las citas de Miquis Tiquis estarán abreviadas con MT y las de Pericles Espada con PE.

Part V

Using Historical, Archival, and Oral Sources

Social Identity on the Hispanic Texas Frontier

Gerald E. Poyo
St. Mary's University

Introduction

Historians of the United States-Mexico border long ago began to construct the historical narratives of the regions from Texas to California under Spain and later Mexico, but only in the last twenty-five years has socioeconomic and cultural research on this region and time period begun to illuminate the important themes that conceptually integrate the early years to the post-1848 experience of the United States.[1]

United States historiography has generally acknowledged the Spanish and Mexican borderlands historical tradition, but not sufficiently to warrant more than an introductory overview when offering an historical overview of those regions. This is why, for example, we still hear Steven F. Austin referred to as the "Father of Texas."[2] Even the revisionist Chicano interpretations of the 1960s and 1970s, written by Mexican American scholars trained in United States history, viewed the pre-1848 periods as irrelevant for Chicano history.[3] Though this idea continues to be advanced by some Latino historians, for the most part the relevance and importance of the earlier period is now recognized.[4] A solid historiography that demonstrates the continuities across the centuries and sovereignties now exists.[5]

In order to appreciate the processes of integration and change that nineteenth century Hispanic Borderlands communities underwent as they became part of the United States, the societies they came from in the previous century and earlier must be understood. Mexican residents of the Southwest became Mexican Americans. They moved from traditional Hispanic societies into Euro-American dominated societies, giving rise to complex relationships, not only between Hispanics and Anglos, but within Hispanic communities themselves. Much has been written about the nature of relationships between Mexicans and Euro-Americans after 1848, but the processes Hispanic communities themselves underwent in the new political, socioeconomic, and cultural environment are just now being addressed.[6]

In the case of Texas, historians point out that many of the relatively economically well-off leaders of the newly annexed communities tended to make political and economic alliances with Euro-Americans, often by marrying off their daughters to Anglo immigrants, while the *pobres* faced oppression and became a permanent underclass to meet the labor needs of an expanding capitalist frontier.[7] This stratification and indeed definitive splitting of *mexicano* society under United States rule prompted some of the Hispanic landed elites, and others who perceived a need to distance themselves from a Mexican identity, to characterize themselves as Spanish. While the precise process by which this Spanish identity emerged and consolidated in mid-nineteenth century Texas has not been studied, the emergence of a Spanish ethnicity among certain segments of the Hispanic inhabitants of New Mexico is well documented. During 1821-1846, the Hispanic residents of New Mexico generally referred to themselves as Mexicans, but once the region came under United States control *nuevomexicanos* began to refer to themselves as Spanish-Americans. According to Richard L. Nostrand, "In New Mexico, the use of "Mexican" declined while that of "Spanish-American" gained momentum. By the 1920s "Spanish-American" was widely entrenched. By the twenties, moreover, "Spanish-American" or simply "Spanish" had come to be much more than a euphemism for avoiding "Mexican"; it was now a genuine ethnic identity with overtones that were cultural and racial."[8] In the Southwest many members of the Hispanic communities claimed a direct lineage from Spain, and denied any substantive identification with Mexico and Mexican immigrants who arrived in the late nineteenth and twentieth centuries.[9]

While the need by the indigenous Hispanic elites in the Southwest to separate themselves from a Mexican identity was clearly calculated to defend themselves against Euro-American racism and discrimination, it is also true that the concepts chosen by these elites did not emerge from a vacuum or solely from definitions imposed by the arriving Euro-Americans who tended to call the rich "Spanish," and everyone else "Mexican." Spanish/Mexican communities brought with them into the United States already established social attitudes and structures that underwent alterations and transformations as they confronted Euro-American society. To understand why the Mexican indigenous elites in the Southwest appropriated a Spanish identity for their own advantage after 1848, the origins of this identity in the centuries prior to United States occupation must be studied. This paper explores the Texas case.

During the eighteenth century residents of the Spanish American province of Texas developed a regional identity that manifested itself in a variety of ways. The area's relative isolation, and its ranching, agricultural, and commercial economy created a fiercely independent population that jealously defended their autonomous way of life. Scholars have highlighted local politics in defense of autonomy, commercial ties to the east, and a ranching culture as aspects of an emergent Tejano identity during the course of the century.[10] One aspect of Tejano identity that has not received ample analysis relates to social identity.

In 1912, José María Rodríguez, a descendent of San Antonio de Béxar's early settlers wrote in his memoirs that La Villita, a barrio on the east side of the San Antonio river, "was settled by some of the soldiers that came with the Mexican army and those who had intermarried with Indians, and were not supposed to be the very best of people." "In fact," Rodríguez continued, "there was a great distinction between the east and west side of the river." "The west side of the river was supposed to be the residence of the first families here . . . the Canary Islanders . . . [who] took great pride in preventing any intermarriage with mixed races and when one did mix he lost his caste with the rest."[11]

Rodríguez no doubt acquired this uncomplicated understanding of Béxar's late eighteenth century system of social stratification through oral tradition, and it was consistent with the best traditions of the long-standing myth of Hispanic segregation and purity on Mexico's northern frontier provinces. Though racial exclusivity or purity simply did not exist in San Antonio or in any other colonial era communities on the northern frontiers of New Spain, Rodríguez's remembrance does conform with the fact that a Canary Islander or Spanish identity was an important aspect of social organization in the late eighteenth century. While the arrival of Euro-Americans to Béxar in the early nineteenth century clearly changed, deepened and hardened ethnic and racial cleavages within Mexican and Mexican American communities, remnants of the social identity forged during the eighteenth century persisted in the minds of the descendants during the next century. Social stratification existed but how did it evolve and how was it defined?

New Spain's *Sistema de Castas*

Attitudes about social status in late eighteenth century Borderlands communities, as throughout Spain's American empire, derived from the assumptions inherent in the so-called *sistema de castas*, or caste system. The colonial Spanish American social system included a racially inspired hierarchy of status which placed peninsular and American-born Spaniards (*peninsulares* and *criollos*, respectively) at the top and Indians and Africans at the bottom of the social structure. Mixtures of these groups, known as *castas*, fell in-between, each possessing their particular political, economic, and legal place within society.[12]

In attempting to understand New Spain's social system, historians have inquired into the relationship of racial hierarchy inherent in the system to occupational position and social status in general. Some have argued that a person's racial background played a crucial role in defining occupational possibilities and social status. Others suggest that by the middle eighteenth century race had disappeared as the primary determinant of a person's occupational position or social status.[13] Whatever the case, race, class, and social status were intricately intertwined in a complicated hierarchy not easy to sort out that categorized people in census documents according to their *calidad*, "quality," or worth. The difficulty of interpreting the meaning of *calidad* is pointed out by Rodney D. Anderson, for example, when he notes in a study of race and social stratification in Guadalajara that, contrary to expectations, the census of 1821 contained a large number of *españoles* who held low status occupations. In explaining why so many people with Spanish designations held low status jobs, Anderson suggets that "it just might be possible that the low-status Spaniards"...closely resembled Indians and castas because they *were* Indians and castas, generously provided the label of "español" by politically sensitive census takers using more flexible criteria than in the past."[14] This is a crucial observation because it suggests that while the *sistema de castas*, with its clearcut *español, criollo, casta, indio* and *negro* designations, created the fundamental frame-of-reference for categorizing people socially in the census throughout the empire, in reality, the practical workings of the system was subject to highly complex manipulations of the census according to the political, economic, and social crosscurrents of particular communities. Anderson's observation is useful for our analysis of the Texas frontier.

The categories of *calidad* recorded in census documents theoretically attempted to conform to the ideal system of racial hierarchy required by law, but in fact, a person's *calidad* designation also included other considerations such as wealth, military rank, or other characteristics that might lend individual prestige. Spanish censuses often did not register an individual's race at all, but rather his "quality" or status in the community beyond race. The problem with making generalizations about what *calidad* meant in eighteenth century New Spain, of course, was that its definition varied from community to community. In some places *calidad* might relate closely to race while in other locations economic position or some other indicator of status might be more important than racial background. Thus any analysis of social status in a particular colonial Latin American historical setting confronts the fundamental problem of discerning something about the history of how the local community defined *español, mestizo*, or any other designation, which takes us back to Anderson's observation about Guadalajara in 1821. If, in fact, the low status *españoles* Anderson alludes to were actually Indians or *mestizos* it seems evident that in Guadalajara the meaning and usage of categories of *calidad* had moved away from a racial definition. In the case of Texas, the exact meaning of a category of *calidad* and its implications for local social relations may only be understood and evaluated through research into the specific dynamics the province's individual communities.[15]

Bexar's Demographic Development

An analysis of San Antonio de Béxar's census of 1793 seems to confirm José María Rodríguez's remembrance that his ancestors were Spanish. The census reveals that 63 percent of Béxar's household heads were *españoles*, while only 24 percent were *castas* and another 13 percent were *indios*. But at the same time, Rodríguez's historical memory does not incorporate Anderson's insight that what you see in the census documents may not be what was. In fact, the historical literature suggests that social development in eighteenth century Texas was indeed fluid and flexible. Alicia Tjarks observed some years ago that "as a consequence of the mixture of race and classes, Texan society [of the late eighteenth century] experienced an increasing upward mobility." "It is remarkable," she continued, "that, along with the continuing concept of a caste society, differences due to skin color and other related circumstances were reduced to such a point that a society definitely heterogeneous, both in its origin and its composition, emerged in Texas." The socioeconomic dynamics in the late eighteenth century, she concluded, "encouraged a strong social and ethnic mobility, tending toward a free and heterogeneous society."[16]

Tjark's article supported the generally held assumption that racial distinctions on the frontier were less sharp than in more settled areas, but the article is less successful in providing an understanding of the interplay between *calidad* and social status in Spanish Texas. Texas frontier communities were socially fluid but how did this fluidity also contribute to the emergence of a Spanish or Canary Islander social identity that endured in oral tradition for over a century?

We may begin by looking at Béxar's demographic development during the century. In 1718 Indians and soldier-settlers from communities in northern New Spain such as Saltillo, Monclova, and Monterrey founded the mission and presidio communities that eventually became San Antonio de Béxar.[17] Béxar's military rosters did not include information on racial background, but frequent testimonials by missionaries and Spanish officials indicates that most residents were *castas*. Fray Antonio de Olivares of Mission San Antonio de Valero complained that almost half of Alarcón's recruits were "mulattoes, lobos, coyotes, and mestizos." He expressed prevailing *criollo* attitudes toward people of color when he noted that the inhabitants were "people of the lowest order, whose customs are worse than those of the Indians."[18] Of the fifty-four families living in the presidio in 1726, most were of mixed racial backgrounds according to the military commander. Demographic growth during most of the century came as a result of immigration. Béxar received a one-time influx of 56 Canary Islander immigrants in 1731 and a larger number of immigrants (reflected in the censuses of 1790s) of mixed-blood heritage who arrived from Los Adaes [close to Natchitoches, La.] and New Spain especially during 1760s-1780s.[19] By the late 1770s, Fray Agustín Morfi estimated that the town, presidio, and missions that composed the community of Béxar included 514 families. Of the 2,060 persons, "324 are Spanish or as they commonly say 'de razón,' 268 Indians, 16 mestizos, and 151 'de color quebrado.' According to Morfi, over half the residents of the settlement were identified as non-Spanish.[20]

For the most part people who travelled to Texas came from the lowest rungs of northern New Spain's economic strata and, as the testimonials and data suggest, they were heavily of mixed-blood social backgrounds.[21] At the same time, as we have seen, by the 1790s most residents in Béxar appeared as *españoles* in the official census returns. The *calidad* designation of *español* was clearly preferred, but, given the demographic history of the region, it cannot be understood as an accurate racial indicator. What then did *español* mean? Clues to this may be gleaned by tracing Béxar's social development.

Defining *Español* in Bexar

To begin with, it is helpful to recognize that the founders of Béxar recognized the importance of being español in colonial New Spain. Recruited primarily in Coahuila and Nuevo León where they participated in the *sistema de castas*, the soldier-settlers who resided in the presidio associated status with being *español*. As leaders of this new and isolated community, the prominent *vecinos* (residents) took the opportunity to define social categories, which they did to their own benefit.

Despite their mixed-blood heritage, almost from the beginning the most prominent military settlers in Béxar, with the cooperation of the friars, recorded themselves as Spanish in offical marriage, baptismal, and death records.[22] They became the community's *españoles* and, very often, the children of these Spaniards by Indian wives also received an *español* designation. Already during the 1720s the emergent community conformed to the prejudices inherent in a *caste system* that gave preferences to people of Spanish or white backgrounds. Despite the fact that few in the community were actually ethnically Spanish, even on this isolated frontier inhabitants understood that to be declared Spanish in official documents carried a certain distinction. The most prominent residents took on the Spanish designation and established the rules for gaining access to it.

While a concern with being known as Spanish already existed among Béxar's early settlers in the 1720s, this concern seems to have become even more exaggerated with the arrival in 1731 of a contingent of Spanish immigrants from the Canary Islands. They established the formal villa or town of San Fernando next to the presidio and missions along the river. These *isleño* immigrants did not occupy high socioeconomic rank in their place of origin, but on immigrating to their new home the Crown empowered them economically, socially, and politically. On arriving to Béxar, they received titles as *hidalgos* and obtained the best lands in the area. They also gained exclusive control of the *cabildo*, or city council, which they used to try to maintain a monopoly over farm lands and water rights in the region. They emerged as the region's recognized, though bitterly contested, elites and, as a result, the importance of being known as an *español* grew even more dramatically.[23]

The value of having an *isleño* or Spanish identity is evident in many documents of the era. Those with the appropriate genealogical credentials often prefaced their requests for land grants with allusions to their Canary Islands origins or parentage, hoping that their cousins on the city council would reward this distinction with the best grants. Others without such backgrounds often had to be content with smaller, less strategically located lands without water rights. When the mixed-blood Mexican soldier-settlers complained to authorities in Mexico City about their displacement and obtained decrees ordering distribution of farm lands and water to them, the cabildo ignored the directive for most of the century. The cabildo provided the Canary Islanders with the political authority to maintain their advantages and status to redefine social relations in Béxar.

While the Canary Islanders attempted to maintain an exclusive position within the community, their small number resulted in frequent interactions with the Mexican families of the presidio community. Intermarriage and economic cooperation led to an overall integration that blurred distinctions between the two groups. By the end of the century, the children and grandchildren of these two groups composed the local elite and it is evident that they established the standard for being Spanish in the local version of the caste system. Since the offspring of the two groups were in the majority of mixed-heritage, presumably representing many shades of color, actual race receded as an important determinant for attaining the Spanish designation in Béxar's census and other documents. In fact, since most people were actually mestizos or some other race mixture, Spanish simply became the term used for most people in Béxar, including 63 percent of the town's household heads in 1793.

The Workings of *Calidad* and Status in Bexar

Clearly, by the end of the eighteenth century Bexar's system of social stratification in principle adhered to the caste system which by its very nature discriminated against non-whites. Indeed, residents of Béxar aspired to be *españoles* because it was a prerequisite for obtaining respectability, and for being a member of the elite. *Españoles* held most of the land, were eligible for the honorific title of *don*, and held political office. The 1793 census reveals that a strong relationship existed between *calidad* and occupation. Take, for example, the relationship between being *español* and being a *labrador*, or an individual with access to land. In Béxar, only 23 percent of household heads were *labradores*, a rather restricted percentage. Of these *labradores*, 73 percent were Spanish. This relationship suggests that residents of Béxar perceived advantages in being recognized as *españoles*.

Nevertheless, despite the ideal of stratification in the *sistema de castas*, fluid local practice allowed the great majority of the town's inhabitants to define themselves, or be defined, as *españoles*. Béxar's society incorporated the ideological framework of the caste system but circumvented its exclusionary aspects in local practice by allowing "worthy" people of any racial background "to pass" as Spaniards. In effect, the designation of *calidad* in Béxar's census records and other documents did not reflect an individual's race but rather the level of acceptance or status in the town. People born in the town or individuals who gained a certain recognition had a greater possibility of being *español* than a person without status, who remained a *casta* or Indian in official documents for a longer time, particularly if his skin was dark. This is reflected in the census documents when comparing *calidad* and nativity. It is also reflected in the case histories of individuals.

The relationship in the 1793 census between *calidad* and nativity suggests that immigrants to Béxar could not expect to be recognized as *español* immediately. In 1793, 74 percent of the native born enjoyed the designation *español*, but only 49 percent of immigrants achieved this desired status. The dynamics of *calidad* designations in Béxar seem to have made distinctions between long-time community residents who descended from the *primeros pobladores* (founding settlers), and new arrivals.

It seems, then, that a desire to be recognized as Spanish existed and that, in general, native born people had a birth right to that status while immigrants usually achieved it by proving their "worth" to the community. But how did this passing of people into *español* status actually happen? While this is extremely difficult to know for sure, one interpretation may be that their status changed as they achieved reputation. Land acquisition provided one avenue. By the time of the 1793 census lands around Béxar were at a premium. The threat of Indian raids meant that only lands within the vicinity of the presidio could be effectively used, limiting the lands available for official distribution by the Governor and Cabildo. People competed for land and distribution criteria had to be established. The statistics suggest that land was technically only for people who fit the local definition of Spanish, but the reality of the local practice, which allowed for "passing," provided opportunities for *castas* to recieve land. They merely became Spanish, it seems, once they acquired land based on their individual merit and reputation in the community.

But the process was even more complex than just land acquisition. Two individual case examples illustrate more effectively how newcomers in Béxar managed to establish themselves as respected Spanish residents of the community. In the 1770s, José Manuel Berbán arrived to live in Béxar from the east Texas community of Los Adaes. A former member of the Adaes presidio, Berbán and his neighbors relocated to Béxar in compliance with the governor's orders to abandon the village. Béxar's first census taken in 1779 described Berbán as a *mulatto* (of black and white heritage) of 38 years who worked as a *campista* or farm/ranch hand. Between that time and 1792, Berbán married Teresa de Armas, daughter of a prominent Canary Islander family. In the 1792 census he appeared as a *mestizo* (of indian and white heritage). In 1796 Berbán gained election as a member of Béxar's city council and five years later he became the cabildo's city legal officer. He also gained sufficient position in the community to file a complaint against an important citizen, Santiago Seguín, for assault. In Béxar's 1803 census, our subject is registered as Don Manuel Berbán, *español, labrador*. During his thirty years or so in Béxar, Berbán had risen from obscurity to prominence and respectability. Bérban, however, was not unique.[24]

Also consider the case of Pedro Huízar, a *mulatto* from Aguascalientes, who probably arrived in Béxar in the 1770s. The census of 1779 lists his occupation as sculptor, and he worked at Mission San José. He and his wife, Trinidad Enriques, a *coyota* (of Indian and black heritage), had several children beginning in 1779. During the early 1780s, Huízar purchased several lots of land in the town from prominent Bexareños, suggesting a financially rewarding employment at San José. Huízar also became a surveyor. In 1791 he conducted a survey in La Bahía to determine the feasibility of digging an irrigation system and in 1794 he became the official surveyor for the mission lands secularized the previous year. Huízar then became the alcalde of the former mission community of San José. In the census of 1793, Huízar appeared as an *español*, thus like Berbán he too gained sufficient prominence and respectability to achieve the most desired ethnic status in Béxar.[25]

While most Bexareños achieved classification as *españoles*, that designation did not necessarily translate into elite status. Apparently, once a family became part of the community, members retained the designation of *español* even if they did not distinguish themselves economically. The 1793 census includes many cases of *españoles* who were servants and day laboreres. They did not lose their status as *españoles* simply because they failed to reach elite status, and, presumably, they retained Spanish identity for themselves and their children even if they married people darker than themselves providing they enjoyed a good name and reputation.

The data seems to suggest that race played a role in defining social categories for non-whites just entering the community, but race could be disposed of as a concern once a settler proved his individual "worth" (or *calidad*) to the broader community. Strategic marriages, acquisition of land, personal friendships, or leadership capabilities all operated to establish a person's worth and reputation. Immigrants had to gain the community's respect before becoming an accepted "Spanish" member of Béxar's society.[26] In general, Béxar's *españoles* were those who achieved full-blown acceptance as legitimate members of the community, regardless of economic or racial background. But their identity as *españoles* also depended on the existence of a group not accepted as full members of the community.

As revealed earlier, according to José María Rodríguez's historical memory, the established Spanish/Canary Islanders of Béxar's society lived in the town, San Fernando, on the west bank of the San Antonio River, while the non-established (and thus non-Spanish) group lived east of the San Antonio River on lands of the former Mission San Antonio de Valero. Once again nativity played an important role in defining status and belonging in Béxar. In 1792, local authorities finally implemented an order, originally issued in 1779, to secularize Mission Valero. The next year Texas Governor Manuel Muñoz distributed irrigable farmlands to fourteen mission Indian families, forty-two heads of household from the abandoned east Texas presidio of Los Adaes, and fourteen others.[27] Valero also became the home for hundreds of soliders and their families who arrived from Mexico during the next decade and a half. Few Indians remained in the mission at the time of secularization, but those that did maintained an Indian or at least a *casta* identity. The immigrants from the presidio of Los Adaes received the largest number of land grants. Forced by the Crown to leave Los Adaes for Béxar in 1772, after Louisiana became Spanish, many of these refugees rented lands from the missionaries, worked as day laborers and tenant farmers, or served in Bexareño households.[28] Only after twenty years, with the secularization of Valero did they succeed in obtaining lands. By the time of the census of 1804, seventeen of the thirty-three household heads (51%) of the pueblo de Valero were designated *españoles*, while the rest were *mestizos*, *coyotes*, and *indios*.[29] Seeminly, the residents of the pueblo slowly attained *español* designations, but a new development redefined the barrio de Valero once again. In 1803, La Segunda Companía Volante de San Carlos de Parras arrived in Texas and took up residence at Valero mission and its environs. While some soldiers lived in the mission itself, many lived with their families along the river south of the mission complex in a neighborhood that became known as La Villita.[30] By 1810, the 69 soldiers from the Parras del Alamo Company, were joined by 50 soldiers from the Punta de Lampazos garrison, and 508 militiamen from Nuevo León and Nuevo Santander.[31] It is likely that many of these also took up residence in La Villita. While the military roster of the Parras Company of 1807 does not include the *calidad* of the soldiers, the list does reveal that most of their wives were *castas*. This demographic history explain's Rodríguez's description of the residents of the Alamo as not among "the very best people."

The Case of Nacogdoches

Béxar's complex social process reflected an adaptation of the *sistema de castas* to local conditions, but it is also useful to compare Béxar's experience with another community in the province to demonstrate the uniqueness of these processes of local identity formation. In the east Texas community of Nacogdoches different conditions resulted in different attitudes about social status despite a similar demographic history.

In 1720 the Marqués de Aguayo, newly appointed governor of Coahuila and Texas, departed Monclova with some five hundred soldiers for east Texas. He established a presidio garrisoned by twenty-five men.[32] During the next fifty years the community of Los Adaes emerged. Initially the presidio provided the primary means of economic livelihood, but in time residents farmed, raised cattle, and traded with the nearby French garrison of Nachitoches. Many of the twenty-five Mexican soldier-settlers from Coahuila, which later grew to sixty-one, brought wives and families with them and their community grew to some 500 by mid-century. Like in Béxar, most were of mixed racial heritage. Among the members of the presidio in 1731, twenty-nine were classified as *españoles* (probably American-born Spaniards), while the remaining thirty-two were *mestizos* (Spanish-Indian mix), *mulattos* (Spanish-black), *lobos* (Indian-black mix), *coyotes* (Indian-mulatto mix), and *indios* (Indian).[33] In 1770, a frontier reorganization resulted in Los Adaes' abandonment and most of its residents subsequently founded Nacogdoches. The continuity in population from the first settlement to the second is clearly revealed in the family names found in the census data of the 1790s.[34]

It is evident that Nacogoches's demographic experience was not dramatically different from that of Béxar. Each was founded by a contingent of people of color and in general reflected a population of mixed background, but by the end of the century the census reveals that a significant divergence in social identity had emerged. As we have seen Béxar's household heads were 63 percent Spanish in 1793, but an analysis of Nacogdoches' census reveals that only 28 percent of household heads were *españoles*. Forty-seven percent were *castas*, 12 percent were *indios*, and 13 percent were of some other designation.[35] The differences in the number of *españoles* in the two communities is striking and cannot seem to be explained through divergent demographic experiences.

Nacogdoches' social system operated so differently, in fact, that the underlying assumptions used in the Béxar census do not apply in interpreting the Nacogdoches census of 1793. The analysis of the 1793 Nacogdoches census data departs from the assumption that *calidad* in the Nacogdoches case is probably more realistic indicator of the community's racial composition than was the case for Béxar. For a number of reasons people in Nacogdoches were not as concerned as people in Béxar with attaining the status-laden designation of *español*.

An interesting difference in the census statistics relates to the relationship between *calidad* and nativity. Nacogdoches reveals an opposite pattern from Béxar. In the east Texas community, 77.5 percent of residents born in Nacogdoches/Adaes were *castas*, mostly *mestizos*, while only 55.3 percent of immigrants to Nacogdoches from the Spanish empire were *castas*. In addition, at Nacogdoches a considerable number of European and American French contributed to diluting the traditional caste designations. While immigrants to Béxar were mostly defined as *castas*, and natives were mostly *españoles*, in Nacogdoches *españoles* were immigrants in higher proportion. This suggests that the isolated residents of east Texas simply cared little for New Spain's social attitudes and accepted whatever designation they were given. On the other hand, new arrivals in Nacogdoches were more conscious of the *sistema de castas* and considered an *español* designation important.

Similarly, the relationship between *calidad* and occupation in Nacogdoches reveals a different pattern from Béxar. In Nacogdoches, 47 percent of household heads were *labradores*, and, of these, only 33.3 percent were Spanish. In Béxar a smaller percentage of residents were *labradores* and they were to a greater extent Spanish. Clearly, in Nacogdoches a much weaker relationship existed between *labrador* status and Spanish *calidad* than in Béxar. To some extent this probably reflected the fact that land was simply more plentiful in the Nacogdoches areas due to the generally cordial relations with the Indians. Since pressures on land were not great, no system of stratification evolved to define its distribution. In fact, it seems that since land was readily available few residents in the area bothered to acquire official title.

Another difference to consider relates to what must have been dramatically different attitudes about race as a result of the divergent relations each community maintained with their surrounding Indian populations. While the census indicates that the actual number of Indians who were heads of households living within Béxar and Nacogdoches were about the same, we might speculate that the attitudes about them were different. While settlers in central Texas had to contend with the warlike Apaches and Comanches and did not often mix with them socially, Adaesanos coexisted with the more settled and sedentary Caddoes of east Texas for a half century or more.[36] Adaes' general population characteristics differed from Béxar only in that perhaps the Native American influence was more recent and culturally alive. From the perspective of *mestizo* Bexareños who called themselves Spanish (most already culturally removed from Indian ways) the residents of Nacogdoches were viewed as highly influenced by Indian culture. The psychological, political, and socioeconomic need to reject Indian and mixed-blood designations of *calidad* among people in Nacogdoches was simply not as intense as in Béxar.[37]

Furthermore, in Nacogdoches no institutional basis for stratification existed as in Béxar. The local elite in Nacodoches did not have at its disposal a cabildo that it could use to manipulate class relations. This is reflected in the weak relationship that existed in Nacogdoches between the Spanish designation and the occupation of *labrador*. While a local Spanish elite did exist, whose leader Antonio Gil Y'Barbo was himself evidently a *mulatto* or *mestizo*, this elite did not enjoy the benefit of a cabildo through which to link certain social standards to acquisition of resources as was obviously the case in Béxar.[38]

If this analysis is correct, when Manuel Berbán lived in Los Adaes he probably did not have to worry excessively about becoming *español* to advance his economic interest and obtain community respectability. Nacogdoches's political and social dynamics made for a society relatively lacking in distinctions, consistent with generally accepted notions of frontier communities. The case of Nacogdoches highlights Béxar's more stratified society. For reasons peculiar to

San Antonio's political, social, and economic development, prominent early settlers fervently sought Spanish status in order to more effectively manipulate the social system to their advantage. The flexibilities inherent in the system resulted in a significant majority claiming Spanish ethnic designations, which, in turn, contributed to creating a local identity based on that ethnic designation.

When José María Rodríguez wrote about his eighteenth-century ancestors in Béxar, he revealed their clear sense of social identity apart from the Mexican soldiers who had settled in La Villita in the early nineteenth century. But when they spoke of being Spanish or Canary Islanders, they did not refer specifically to nationality or race, but rather to a definition born of the old *sistema de castas* and transformed by local reality, culture and custom. Perhaps the residents of Béxar did attempt to maintain themselves separate from the soldiers in La Villita, but this stemmed not exclusively from racial motivations. Their desire for separateness was a more generalized need to defend their community definitions of social status and identity from immigrants unfamiliar with local traditions. To be Spanish meant to be an accepted member of Béxar's community to which all could aspire in one way or another but only after meeting certain conditions. People of light complexion would be accepted more easily than people of darker skin tones, but people of color could also be *españoles* by being born in Béxar, establishing a good "reputation," or attaining some level of economic or political "respectability." In Nacogdoches, on the other hand, social identity operated in a different way. To be known as Spanish was not so necessary. Despite similar demographic profiles each community created its own standards of social status and thus community identity.

Conclusion

Shortly after the arrival of the Parras military company in Béxar, the community entered a period of considerable crisis as insurgents in Mexico led by Father Miguel Hidalgo y Costilla initiated the Mexican war of independence against Spain. Texas became embroiled in the insurgencies and on two occasions during 1811-1813 Tejanos in Béxar displaced Spanish authority. Nevertheless, Spain reasserted its power in Mexico and San Antonio, and independence came peacefully in 1821. Béxar's residents became Mexican citizens of the State of Coahuila y Texas. In an 1832 petition of the *ayuntamiento* of Béxar to the state legislature in Saltillo, the local councilmen made clear their allegiance to a Mexican identity at the same time that they complained of the inadequate attention the Mexican republic gave their region. "Being persuaded, your honors, of the importance and need of this manifesto, you will surely appreciate the language of sincerity and frankness with which this body has explained its cause. In so doing, it represents the emotions that inspire its inhabitants. It does so openly, without remote thought of calling into question the sweet and valued glory of being Mexican."[39] In Nacogdoches, the Mexican population also expressed its firm allegiance to Mexico in the face of Euro-American immigration into their region.

Nevertheless, in 1836 political confrontations between Euro American settlers and Mexican authorities resulted in an insurrection that led to Texas independence from Spain and incorporation into the United States in 1846.[40] This was followed by the United States war against Mexico which resulted in the conquering by the United States of the entire Southwest. Texas' Mexican inhabitants became Mexican Americans who had to contend with entirely new circumstances and a new national identity. San Antonio's Mexican residents attempted to conform to the imposed system while those in Nacodoches actually rebelled against the new order.[41] Regardless of these distinct survival strategies, in both regions Mexicans found themselves confronted with the threat of political, economic, and social subjugation.[42]

As Euro-Americans flooded into Texas after 1836, the Spanish or Canary Islander social identity took on a new importance for Mexican residents in both San Antonio and Nacogdoches. Mexican independence from Spain had brought to an end the official designations of calidad in the census as the new nation set out to implement republican ideals. An *español* or Canary Islander identity had diminished as the region became more integrated into the Mexican nation, but the racist social attitudes toward Indians, Blacks, and Mexicans brought to Texas by Euro-Americans produced incentives for Tejanos to revive a Spanish identity as a way of separating themselves from their brethren to the south.[43] As United States racism penetrated Texas, Tejanos reinvented the social definitions from their own tradition of social identity in the eighteenth century. José María Rodríguez's reassertion of his own Spanish or Canary Islander heritage, and emphasizing its distinction from the Mexican identity "across the river," was consistent with a need to maintain a social identity acceptable within the borders of the nation to which he belonged. While the centrality of race had diminished as a feature of Tejano social identity during the eighteenth century, racial concerns clearly regained force and hardened with Texas' incorporation into the United Sates. Indeed, even into the late twentieth century, many Mexican American descendants of eighteenth century settlers in San Antonio and Nacogdoches continue to identify with their Spanish—not Mexican—heritage.

Notes

[1] For a discussion of this idea see Gerald E. Poyo and Gilberto M. Hinojosa, "Spanish Texas and Borderlands Historiography in Transition: Implications for United States History," *Journal of American History* 75

(September 1988), pp. 393-416.

² Stephen F. Austin's designation as the "father of Texas," has been universally utilized in Texas history texts since their inception.

³ The classic expression of this view is Juan Gómez-Quiñones, "Toward a Perspective on Chicano History," *Aztlán*, 2 (Fall 1971).

⁴ A more recent restatement, arguing from an economic rather than sociocultural point of view, is Gilbert González and Raul Fernández, "Chicano History: Transcending Cultural Modes," *Pacific Historical Review*, 63:4 (November 1994), 469-497.

⁵ For examples of studies that deal with the Spanish/Mexican communities across time, cultures, and sovereignties see John Chávez, *The Lost Land: The Chicano Image of the Southwest* (Albuquerque: University of New Mexico Press, 1984); Juan Gómez-Quiñones, *Roots of Chicano Politics 1600-1984* (Albuquerque: University of New Mexico Press, 1990); Thomas Hall, *Social Change in the Southwest, 1350-1880* (Lawrence: University Press of Kansas, 1989); Gilberto M. Hinojosa, *Laredo: Borderlands Town in Transition* (College Station: Texas A & M University Press, 1983); Antonio Ríos-Bustamante, "Los Angeles, Pueblo and Region, 1781-1850: Continuity and Adaptation on the North Mexican Periphery" (Ph.D. diss., University of California, 1985); Ramón Gutiérrez, *When Jesus Came, the Corn Mothers Went Away: Marriage, Sexuality, and Power in New Mexico, 1500-1846* (Stanford: Stanford University Press, 1991); Douglas Monroy, *Thrown Among Strangers: The Making of Mexican Culture in Frontier California* (Berkeley: University of California Press, 1990).

⁶ See Arnoldo de León, *They Called them Greasers: Attitudes Toward Mexicans in Texas, 1821-1900* (Austin: University of Texas Press, 1983) and *The Tejano Community, 1836-1900* (Albuquerque: University of New Mexico Press, 1982); Timothy A. Matovina, *Tejano Religion and Ethnicity in San Antonio, 1821-1860* (Austin: University of Texas Press, 1995); Gerald E. Poyo, *Tejano Journey,1770-1850* (Austin: University of Texas Press, 1986).

⁷ For a sophisticated study of the nature of relations between Euro-Americans and Mexicans in Texas, and the implications of these relations for Mexican American social structures see David M. Montejano, *Anglos and Mexicans in the Making of Texas* (Austin: University of Texas Press, 1986).

⁸ Richard L. Nostrand, *The Hispano Homeland* (Norman: University of Oklahoma Press, 1992), p.16. See also Nancie L. González, *The Spanish-Americans of New Mexico: A Heritage of Pride* (Albuquerque: University of New Mexico Press, 1967).

⁹ For an excellent overview discussion of this issue see the final chapter of David J. Weber, *Spain's Northern Frontier in North America* (New Haven: Yale University Press, 1992), pp. 335-360.

¹⁰ See Gerald E. Poyo and Gilberto M. Hinojosa, *Eighteenth Century Origins of the Tejano Community of San Antonio* (Austin: University of Texas

Press for the University of Texas Institute of Texan Cultures at San Antonio, 1991).

[11] José María Rodríguez, *Rodríguez Memoirs of Early Texas* (San Antonio: Passing Show Printing, 1913; reprint, San Antonio: Standard, 1961).

[12] For a useful introduction to social relations in colonial Latin America see Magnus Morner, *Race Mixture in the History of Latin America* (Boston 1967).

[13] For an overview of this literature see Benjamin Keen, "Main Currents in United States Writings on Colonial Spanish America, 1884-1984," *Hispanic American Historical Review*, 65:4 (November 1985) and John E. Kicza, "The Social and Ethnic Historiography of Colonial Latin America: The Last Twenty Years," *William & Mary Quarterly* 45 (July 1988), 468-470.

[14] Rodney D. Anderson, "Race and Social Stratification: A Comparison of working-Class Spaniards, Indians, and Castas in Guadalajara, Mexico in 1821." *Hispanic American Historical Review* 68:2 (May 1988), 339-240.

[15] For an interesting discussion of the *sistema de castas,* including visual depictions created by eighteenth century artists, see María Concepción García Sáiz, comp. *La Castas Mexicanas: Un género pictórico americano* (Italia: Olivetti, 1989).

[16] Alicia Tjarks, "Comparative Analysis of Texas, 1777-1793," *Southwestern Historical Quarterly* 77, no.3 (January 1974).

[17] For information on the Alarcón expedition see Fritz Leo Hoffman, ed. and trans. *Diary of the Alarcón Expedition into Texas, 1718-1719, by Francisco de Céliz* Los Angeles: Quivira Society, 1935 and "The Mezquía Diary of the Alarcón Expedition into Texas, 1718," *Southwestern Historical Quarterly* 41, no. 4 (April 1938). For the most thorough discussion of San Antonio's demographic development during the eighteenth century see Jesús F. de la Teja, *San Antonio de Béxar: A Community on New Spain's Northern Frontier* (Albuquerque: University of New Mexico Press, 1995).

[18] quoted in Jesús F. de la Teja, "Forgotten Founders: The Military Settlers of Eighteenth Century San Antonio de Béxar," in Gerald E. Poyo and Gilberto M. Hinojosa, *Tejano Origins in Eighteenth Century San Antonio de Béxar* (Austin: University of Texas for The Institute of Texan Cultures at San Antonio, 1991), 33.

[19] See Gerald E. Poyo, "Immigrants and Integration in Late Eighteenth Century Béxar," in Gerald E. Poyo and Gilberto M. Hinojosa, eds. *Tejano Origins in Eighteenth Century San Antonio*, 85-104.

[20] Fray Juan Agustín Morfi, *History of Texas, 1673-1779*, trans. and annotated by Carlos Eduardo Castañeda (Albuquerque: The Quivira Society, 1935; Arno Press Reprint, 1967), 99.

[21] See de la Teja, *San Antonio de Béxar*, 17-29.

[22] See baptismal, marriage and death records of mission San Antonio de Valero. Photocopies available at University of Texas Institute of Texan

Cultures, San Antonio.

[23] See Gerald E. Poyo, "The Canary Islands Immigrants of San Antonio: From Ethnic Exclusivity to Community in Eighteenth-Century Béxar," in Gerald E. Poyo and Gilberto M. Hinojosa, *Tejano Origins in Eighteenth Century San Antonio* (Austin: University of Texas Press for The University of Texas Institute of Texan Cultures at San Antonio, 1991).

[24] For information on Berbán see "Estracto General de la tropa de dicho [San Antonio de Béxar] Presidio y Vezindario de la Villa de San Fernando en que se Comprende el Padron de sus Familias, Armamentos, y Bienes Raizes que cada uno tiene. 1, 2 y 3 del mes de Julio de 1779," Archivo General de Indias (AGI), Audiencia de Guadalajara (AG), legajo 283; "Padron de las almas que ay en esta villa de San Fernando de Austria (*sic*). Año de 1793," Bexar Archives Microfilm (BAM), reel 2; "Padron de las familias que hay en esta Villa de San Fernando, y Presidio de Béxar . . . Año de 1803," BAM; and Frederick C. Chabot *With the Makers of San Antonio* (San Antonio: Artes Gráficas, 1937).

[25] For information on Huízar see "Padron de las almas . . . Año de 1793," household entry no. 325; Land sales Pedro Huízar, Béxar County Archives, Land Grant Series (LGS)-322 (1783); LGS-323 (1784); LGS-278 (1784). Carlos E. Castañeda, *Our Catholic Heritage in Texas, 1519-1936*, 7 vols. (Austin: Von Boeckmann-Jones, 1936-1958) v. 5, pp. 40, 42, 51-58, 177, 197.

[26] Poyo, "Immigrants and Integration."

[27] See "Distribution of Land of Mission San Antonio de Valero, January 11, 1793," Bexar County Archives, Mission Records.

[28] See Herbert Eugene Bolton, "The Spanish Abandonment and Re-Occupation of East Texas, 1773-1779," *Quarterly of the Texas State Historical Association*, 9:2 (October 1905) and "Expediente promovido por los vecinos del extinguido presidio de los Adaes para que se les conceda algun establecimiento donde pueden subsistir con sus familias," AGI, AG, legajo 103. Copy of transcript in Barker Texas History Center.

[29] "Census Report of the Town of San Antonio Valero, December 31, 1804," BA, in Carmela Leal, comp. *Residents of Texas, 1782-1836* 3 vols (San Antonio: University of Texas Institute of Texan Cultures, 1984), 3: 378-380.

[30] Randell G. Tarín, "The Second Flying Company of San Carlos de Parra," *The New Handbook of Texas* 6 vols. (Austin: The Texas State Historical Association, 1996), V: 960-961.

[31] Statistics found in Jesus F. de la Teja, "Rebellion on the Frontier," p.17, in Gerald E. Poyo, ed. *Tejano Journey, 1770-1850* (Austin: University of Texas Press, 1996).

[32] On the Aguayo expedition see Charles Wilson Hackett, "The Marquis de San Miguel de Aguayo and His Recovery of Texas from the French, 1719-1723," *Southwestern Historical Quarterly*, 49, no.2 (October 1945); Peter P.

Forrestal, "Peña's Diary of the Aguayo Expedition," *Preliminary Studies of the Texas Catholic Historical Association* 2, no.7 (January 1935).

[33] "Lista, y relazion jurada . . . de los ofiziales, y soladados de este presidio de Nuestra Señora del Pilar de los Adais, 27 de Maio de 1731," Archivo General de la Nacion (AGN), Provincias Internas, vol. 163.

[34] Castañeda, *Our Catholic Heritage,* v.4, pp. 273-302.

[35] "Census of the Town of Nacogdoches. 1793," *BA,* in Leal, *Residents of Texas,* v.1.

[36] For information on the Caddo tribes and their ongoing relationships with the Spanish and French see Timothy K. Perttula, *"The Caddo Nation": Archaeological and Ethnohistoric Perspectives* (Austin: University of Texas Press, 1992); Timothy K. Perttula, ed. "Commemorating the Columbian Quincentenary," *Bulletin of the Texas Archeological Society,* v. 63 (1992), special issue; H.F. Gregory, ed. *The Southern Caddo: An Anthology* (New York: Garland Publishing Co., 1986); F. Todd Smith, "The Red River Caddos: A Historical Overview to 1835," *Bulletin of the Texas Archeological Survey,* v. 65 (1994), 115-127. For information on the combative Spanish-Indian relations in the San Antonio area see Elizabeth A. H. John, *Storms Brewed in Other Men's Worlds: The Confrontation of Indians, Spanish, French in the Southwest, 1540-1795* (College Station: Texas A & M University Press, 1975).

[37] Castañeda, *Our Catholic Heritage,* v.4, pp.273-302,

[38] Herbert Eugene Bolton, *Texas in the Middle of the Eighteenth Century* (Austin: University of Texas at Austin, 1970), 388-389.

[39] David J. Weber, ed. *Troubles in Texas. 1832: A Tejano Viewpoint from San Antonio with a Translation and Facsimile* (Dallas: Southern Methodist University, 1983), 29.

[40] See Paul Lack, *The Texas Revolutionary Experience: A Political and Social History, 1835-1836* (College Station: Texas A&M University Press, 1992)

[41] See Gerald E. Poyo, ed. *Tejano Journey, 1770-1850* (Austin: University of Texas Press, 1996)

[42] See David Montejano, *Anglos and Mexicans in the Making of Texas, 1836-1986,* (Austin: University of Texas Press, 1986)

[43] On Euro-American racism in Texas in the nineteenth century see Arnoldo De León, *They Called Them Greasers* (Austin: University of Texas Press, 1983) and James Ernest Crisp, "Anglo-Texan Attitudes toward the Mexican, 1821-1845." Ph.D. dissertation, Yale University, 1976. For a profile of nineteenth century Tejanos after Texas independence from Mexico see Arnoldo de León, *The Tejano Community, 1836-1900* (Albuquerque: University of New Mexico Press, 1982).

Reading Early Neomexicano Newspapers: Yesterday and Today

Doris Meyer
Connecticut College

If there is one kind of writing for which time is crucial, it is the newspaper. Since old news doesn't sell, journalists race the clock to beat their competitors with the day's latest headlines. Timeliness is critical to both the publisher and the reader whose demand for news increases as the outside world becomes more familiar. Newspapers bring the local and the global into focus on the printed page, wielding an ephemeral power to draw attention and stir debate. In the public forum of the press, multiple voices mingle to define and contest a reality that's constantly changing.

The passage of time also affects the reader's take on the news. We read differently today because we know more than yesterday. And, like it or not, our attitudes toward what we read are shaped by the media just as the media is influenced by public demand for its product.

This market-driven interdependence may be obvious today and understandably objectionable to those who blame the media for society's current ills. But what about a century ago in the Southwest? Was the press equally powerful in shaping public opinion when type was laboriously set by hand and when only a small segment of the population was able to read? What about Hispanic communities on the so-called frontier? Was the Spanish-language press able to compete with its English-language counterpart as Anglo immigrants arrived in droves with a culture that glorified the printed text and disparaged the oral traditions of Hispanics and Native Americans? These are questions to be pondered as we study the history of Hispanic culture in the United States and the role played by the press in its expression and diffusion.

A century ago in the Southwest the fundamental dynamics of journalism wasn't so different. In New Mexico, where the Hispanic population was numerically dominant and newspapers in Spanish flourished despite a small reading public, the press played a powerful role in articulating neomexicano cultural identity during the era of transition to statehood. This process took longer in New Mexico than in any other western territory due to the reluctance in Congress to grant statehood to a population that was predominantly Catholic, Spanish-speaking and non-Anglo. From the late 1870s, when the railroad facilitated massive Western migration, to the granting of statehood in 1912, the Spanish-language press was instrumental in opening up a new discursive space in which neomexicanos defended their own interests and voiced their concerns about statehood and its implications. Even after statehood, the Hispanic press served as a watchdog to protect the constitutional rights of Spanish-speaking New Mexicans and to make sure their voices continued to be heard.

My own fascination with the dynamics of Hispanic journalism in the Southwest began in the mid 1970s. Back then, I spent several summers in New Mexico reading neomexicano newspapers and looking for evidence of literary expression. Out of this came a half-dozen articles on subjects ranging from the nature of anonymous poetry to responses to negative stereotyping in the press. Later, I turned my attention to other research, and almost twenty years passed before I looked at this material again with renewed interest. In the interim my way of reading texts had changed by exposure to critical approaches like discourse analysis, cultural studies and feminist theory. This time I read the newspapers differently, seeing them more holistically, more as cultural than literary texts. As a result, it became clear that these newspapers were replete with evidence of a cultural identity crisis in the late 19th and early 20th centuries—a crisis in which neomexicanos struggled to retain interpretive power in a highly charged socio-economic environment that threatened their values on multiple fronts. So I decided to write a book incorporating past insights and new material into a comprehensive study, and I called it *Speaking for Themselves: Neomexicano Cultural Identity and the Spanish Language Press, 1880-1920* (University of New Mexico Press, 1996). In New Mexico, which produced more Spanish-language newspapers in the nineteenth century than any other region of the Southwest, it is essential to understand the climate that promoted newspapering, the role the Hispanic press played in the social and intellectual history in this era of transition, and particularly the impact newspapers had on the evolution of neomexicano cultural identity. I hope that my research sheds light on the unique history of New Mexico as well as the struggle to be American on Hispanic terms.

In his seminal work published in 1969 on the territorial press of New Mexico, Porter A. Stratton documents and describes the history of New Mexican journalism concentrating almost entirely on the Anglo-American experience. When discussing the Spanish-language press, his observations are useful but they suffer from an Anglocentric bias. Nonetheless, Stratton makes some general obervations that apply to both Anglo and Hispanic newspapers in territorial New Mexico: for example, many lasted only a short time due to the economic difficulties of sustaining a newspaper with low readership, recalcitrant subscribers, high advertising rates, and the lack of outside printing contracts. Newspapers were often propaganda vehicles for political campaigns and thus tended to disappear after elections, but the relative ease with which an owner-editor could start one up with a characeristic blend of optimism and opportunism meant that when one ceased publication, another would grind into operation. The Washington hand press that was commonly used on the western frontier was a time consuming and labor intensive device that was not replaced until the end of the century with the more costly steam-driven press because the number of subscribers—usually no more than a few hundred for the average paper—could not justify the expense. News reporting in a typical four-page layout was allocated differently then, with items of territorial and local interest given much more attention than national and international news. Provincial mores also tolerated an unpolished and lusty use of language that could lapse into mud-slinging and rowdy editorial battles. On the whole, however, newspaper editors had an above-average education and a wide range of business and cultural experiences. As public figures with a high profile in the community, they were conscious of their power to shape public opinion. Since their trade depended on reader response, however, they took pride in knowing their constituencies and cultivating their support. As Stratton points out for both English and Spanish-language papers, "the core of these papers became the editorials, which were made interesting by the prestige and insight of the editors and their strongly partisan support of political allies. . . ."[1]

Politics and the press had been mutually dependent but distrustful of one another ever since newspapers first came into existence and joined the power structure as the fourth estate. In a freewheeling frontier society, the press could take the moral high road and influence public policy or follow the low road and sell out to vested interests. In New Mexico between 1880 and 1920, there were ample reasons for Hispano and Anglo journalists to be tempted by one course or the other and only minimal ethical standards to rein them in.[2] Although some papers professed an independent stance, objectivity was not the norm and editors usually declared their allegiances on the front page and without ambivalence. At stake during these early years of uneasy bicultural coexistence were issues of crucial importance which would determine when and how the territory would join the union of states, who would wield economic and political power, and how the major ethnic groups would adjust to one another within this jockeying for power. According to historian Marc Simmons:

> The entire history of New Mexico from 1850 to the present is interwoven with attempts by the Indian and Hispano populations to come to terms with an alien Anglo society. Through principles supplied by the Declaration of Independence, they have tried to win equality while remaining different and have sought liberty to pursue a time-honored way of life. That history also includes a long story of the Anglo-American's adjustment to things that are uniquely and engagingly New Mexican.[3]

For this reason, New Mexico remained different, unlike other emerging Western states where Hispanic and Native American cultures were relegated to isolated and marginated communities. The evolution of cultural identities from

1880 to 1920 would determine the shape of the future of the state of New Mexico.

One scholar has suggested that two New Mexicos—Anglo and Pueblo-Hispanic—existed between 1885 and 1925:

> One of "what is," that of the pragmatist-realist, concerned with material things, reflecting the economic and political order; the other, that of the mind and spirit, of "what might be," concerned with non-material realities, reflecting human yearning for truth, brotherhood and eternal meaning in the universe.[4]

Although such broad characterizations can be misleading, there is abundant historical evidence of a clash of cultures and value systems that reached its culmination in the bicultural negotiation and accomodation that produced the New Mexican Constitution of 1910 which brought both New Mexicos together to achieve the goal of statehood in 1912. This bipartisan document pledged to protect the rights of neomexicanos that had been guaranteed by the Treaty of Guadalupe Hidalgo and to recognize the equal status of their culture by making New Mexico an officially bilingual state—the only one in the nation. Such an agreement would not have been possible had not the Hispanic population in New Mexico been almost ten times larger than that in Texas or California at the time. Nor would it have occurred without the Spanish-language press which kept the concerns and demands of neomexicanos in the public eye, constantly reinforcing neomexicano cultural identity in the struggle for interpretive power in New Mexico.

Joshua Fishman pointed out back in 1966 that the "naturalization" process for immigrants to America since the end of the nineteenth century has carried with it an expectation of de-ethnization and yet, in spite of this, "ethnicity is one of the strongest unrecognized facets of American life—in politics, in religion, in consumer behavior, in life-styles and in self-concepts."[5] He spoke of "the anomalous half-life of ethnicity in present-day America" and warned that Americans needed to face the contradictions this implied. Fishman noted a further irony: for most ethnic groups in America, their ethnicity only assumed conscious importance (awareness of their "groupness") *after* immigration, thereby suggesting that anti-foreign sentiments in the social core might in fact precipitate a defensive reaction.[6] When we look at the historical case of New Mexico in the territorial period the tables were turned in one sense but not in another: it was the Anglos who immigrated to a new, albeit American soil, but it was the Hispanic majority that responded with a new awareness of its communal identity and the need to resist a de-ethnicizing, culturally rootless Americanization.

The early Spanish-language press was the primary vehicle for articulating and galvanizing this cultural imperative. Because the press bridged the gap between local tradition and imported modernity, it was able to articulate an intellectual connection between the remembrance of the past and the anticipation of the future.[7] In so doing, it energized and motivated its readership, consciously assuming the role of cultural interpreter and interlocutor with the larger Anglo majority beyond New Mexico's borders. A typical editorial in *La Voz del Pueblo* of November 14, 1891, shows this self-conscious stance:

> En fin esperamos que el sufrido pueblo Neo-Mexicano colecte sus mentes y obre con deliberación en materias públicas; que despierte del letargo en que ha dormido por tantos años, y que aprecie el valor intrínseco de una sana y verdadera educación, y que reconosca que el periódico y la literatura generalmente es el camino más seguro para la ciencia y la prosperidad . . . .

Ordinary neomexicanos experienced the jolt of massive Anglo immigration on a personal and non-ideological basis: they saw communal property threatened by land-grabbing tactics, their families affected by intermarriage, their produce devalued in a highly competitive market, and their way of life disdained by foreign intruders. The historical record and a few surviving texts, such as the autobiography of Rafael Chacón,[8] show that Anglo intrusion was met with vocal native resistance. Many popular poems reflecting the neomexicano spirit of defiance can be found in the newspapers, confirming that the press was not a tool of the Anglo-affiliated Hispanic *ricos* to indoctrinate the masses but rather a vehicle for autocthonous expression on many levels.[9] In a pre-capitalist society such as New Mexico's at the end of the century, however, traditional Hispanic ways of life did not prepare neomexicanos to resist en masse the incursions of an aggressive foreign culture. Thus, it is doubly significant that the neomexicano press assumed, among other functions, the unofficial role of a public forum and community bulletin board where aggrieved citizens could speak out.

Defending Hispanic ethnicity and its rightful claim to interpret American citizenship on equal terms with Anglos became a recurrent topic of Spanish-language journalism at the turn of the century. A handful of aggressively outspoken editors and local writers refused to relinquish this claim or lower their guard despite decades of bicultural coexistence and volumes of newsprint that had revisited the topic many times. This included men like Luis Tafoya—descendant of an early neomexicano family—whose traditional poetry and satiric prose brought attention to the political infighting that was tearing neomexicanos apart. Or José Escobar and Pedro García de la Lama—emigrés from Mexico—who adopted New Mexico's identity crisis as if it were their own, helping to resist the threat of cultural oppression that had stifled Mexican culture under Porfirio Diaz. Or Benjamin Read—a bilingual, bicultural historian and local attorney—who amassed a valuable archive of old documents in order to rewrite New Mexico's past and correct the errors of Anglo historiography. These men sustained a crusade in print that was both externally and internally directed: to Anglos, they repeatedly contested unjust, negative stereotypes of neomexicano culture, while to Hispanic readers, they called for unity, self-determination, and the preservation of their native language and culture. This dialectic of affirmation and resistance anticipated the aggressive stance of Chicano writers many years later and is clear proof that the discourse of identity politics began a century before in the Southwest.

Educational opportunities for Hispanics improved after the passage of a comprehensive school bill in 1891, but the growing readership in the neomexicano community could not offset the effects of a national economic recession in the 1890s that increased the financial hurdles all papers faced; additional problems for neomexicano newspapers included the higher proportion of literate Anglos and their deeply ingrained habit of reading newspapers; the political patronage Anglo papers obtained in the form of govenment printing contracts that rarely went to neomexicano newspapers; the higher advertising revenues Anglo papers were able to demand; and the unknown number of readers who were literate in Spanish, or both languages, but chose to read bilingual newspapers. Considering these obstacles, a neomexicano newspaper editor needed a degree of conviction and determination even greater than his Anglo counterpart.

There is no doubt that a cultural gap of varying dimensions existed between editors and the average neomexicano farmer, miner, laundress or storekeeper. Newspaper editors were generally well educated, middle-class, male city dwellers who had probably read and traveled more than 95 percent of neomexicano men and women. These differences notwithstanding, an editor had to communicate with, speak on behalf of, and represent the people of his community or he would not succeed. His own voice, and the news he and his co-workers printed, had to find appropriate rhetorical strategies to speak to the interests and needs of his constituency; if his advocacy of one political stance or another became too strident, he ran the risk of reducing readership or shortening the paper's already precarious lifespan. In essence, the Spanish-language papers—especially those that became well-known and were widely read, such as *La Voz del Pueblo*, *El Independiente*, *El Nuevo Mexicano*, and *La Opinión Pública*—were metatexts of the Hispanic community with a polyphonic resonance that incorporated directly or indirectly the voices of the common people as well as those of the educated elite who formed the power structure of community politics, business, and society.[10] As one might expect in a traditionally Hispanic patriarchal society further reinforced by Victorian attitudes in vogue at the time, females were not expected to participate actively in journalistic enterprises. Despite this, their presence is felt in subtle ways and their subdued voices are heard in the background.

Neomexicano newspapers were the de facto literature of their time. The contemporary reader who hopes to understand their significance must take into consideration the discursive strategies of the medium and the context of its message. Like any literary text, newspaper writing is a form of discourse that reflects the institutions of power in society and it has both a conscious and unconscious effect on its target audience. As part of a social dialogue in New Mexico, the Spanish-language press participated in an intricate semiotic system, or what Clifford Geertz has called the "webs of significance" that make up a culture.[11] Embedded in the newspapers are references to other texts that figure in the neomexicano cultural heritage, both popular and learned in their origins. In order to interpret the role neomexicano newspapers played and the impact they had we must try to understand them as multi-layered constructs that served different objectives in different ways, reflecting a plurality of voices and subject positions. Rather like archaelogical terrain, the newspapers must be explored and studied in their problematical "otherness," as complex communicative sites where we look for clues to the *ongoing narrative of identity* rather than definitive answers or essential truths. Out of the dialogic discourse of their pages—to borrow a familiar Bakhtinian term—emerge the contours of a changing neomexicano cultural identity which, as Stuart Hall reminds us, is "subject to the continuous 'play' of history, culture and power."[12]

True, the Spanish-language press enabled those who enjoyed the advantages of literacy to sustain an intellectual exchange both within the Hispanic community (north and south of the border) and across cultural borders (with the Anglo power structure in the U.S.). But it also gave representation and voice to those who were ex-centric to the traditional power structure within Hispanic society. Enjoyed by many and financially supported by only a few, neomexicano newspapers were a far cry from the established cultural industries of the mass media today. They were products of their turbulent era, appearing and disappearing with the regularity of the political seasons. Timeliness was their main objective and obsolescence their eternal threat. Despite this vulnerability, some neomexicano papers endured long enough to command respect and influence. As the bulletin boards of public opinion they served the powerful and the weak, those in authority and at least some of those who protested against it. Bringing neomexicanos into this typically American public dialogue, the Spanish-language newspapers became, as Francisco Lomelí has noted, a middle ground for oral and literary traditions which mingled there without dichotomizing and formed a chronicle of living history in the making.[13]

The Spanish-language press survived in the New Mexico borderlands long enough and with sufficient strength to affirm the political clout of an indigenous Hispanic community that was undergoing a transformation more dramatic than it had known since the beginning of its long history in the Southwest. As an organic element of its time and place, the press shaped and was shaped by the multicultural context in which it evolved over the better part of a century. Its pages form our only broad picture of the cultural matrix of a long-standing Hispanic and American community affirming its right to define itself and be heard. This affirmation, and the challenge it entailed, brought with it an inevitable process of change for the Spanish-speaking community. The press gave voice to the people but it also transformed their consciousness and thus transcended the realm of the spoken word by which they had lived. By the time its influence waned in the 1920s, the Spanish-language press had left its mark in many ways, not the least being the enhanced value of literacy in a society steeped in orality. The growing image of authority associated with the press underscored the power of the printed word and diminished the importance, if not the ubiquity of oral culture in New Mexico. As a tool of modernity, the emerging industrial society, and the globalization of knowledge, the neomexicano press may have actually undermined the traditions of the neomexicano past. Yet without their own newspapers and the subversive power they could wield, Hispanic New Mexicans would never have had the same leverage in the struggle against Anglo domination. Nor would we now have the detailed record of Hispanic cultural identity that can be found in microfilmed archives throughout the Southwest.

Notes

¹ Porter Stratton, *The Territorial Press in New Mexico*, 21-22.

² A libel law enacted in New Mexico in 1889 stimulated an increased consciousness of press responsibility. When the libel law was repealed in 1893, under criticism that it was stifling free expression, press association activity decreased. Porter Stratton, *The Territorial Press*, 37-38. On press standards in the late nineteenth century, see also Hazel Dicken-García, *Journalistic Standards in Nineteenth-Century America*: "Critics after 1850 struggled to define appropriate journalistic conduct and were more specific than their predecessors in citing abuses and corrections. But by 1890 they were still groping with what had become an immense social institution of overwhelming capabilities," 221.

³ Marc Simmons, *New Mexico: An Interpretive History*, 12. My focus is on the Hispanic and Anglo ethnic groups in New Mexico as the main interlocutors of a cultural dialogue during this period but it would be a grave omission not to recognize the importance of Native Americans in the shaping of New Mexico's collective identity as a state. Although the Pueblo Indian tribes after 1692 lived peacefully at some remove, with minimal interaction with the majority populations, the Comanche and Apache tribes resisted pacification and were not subdued by federal troops until approximately 1890. The Navajos surrendered earlier, in 1864, at which time the U. S. government abolished the common practice of peonage and Indian slavery in New Mexico. For the most part, Anglo and Hispano editors in these years showed little concern for the welfare of the exploited and mistreated Native Americans, although occasional editorials called for improvement of living conditions on the reservations and backed the establishment of Indian schools. See also Porter Stratton, *The Territorial Press*, 117-126.

[4] Joseph Franklin Sexton, "New Mexico: Intellectual and Cultural Developments, 1885-1925: Conflicts Among Ideas and Institutions," 181. A recent essay by Rudolfo Anaya, the well-known Chicano author who writes about his New Mexico roots, echoes the concept of two New Mexicos by contrasting the traditional harmonious ways of life of the Indo-Hispanic Southwest with the destructive development of a materialistic urban environment. Anaya sees the battle for New Mexico's future as one of epic proportions: "The first step in answering these questions is to realize that we have turned away from our inner nature and from our connection to the earth and old historical relationships. We have allowed a political and economic consciousness from without to take control. How we engage this consciousness not only describes us but also will inform future generations of our values." Anaya, "Mythical Dimensions/Political Reality," 30.

[5] Joshua A. Fishman, *Language Loyalty in the United States: The Maintenance and Perpetuation of Non-English Mother Tongues by Amerian Ethnic and Religious Groups*, 31.

[6] Fishman, *Language Loyalty*, 27.

[7] On the role of the communications media in mediating betweeen tradition and modernity in Latin America, see William Rowe and Vivian Schelling, *Memory and Modernity: Popular Culture in Latin America*.

[8] See Jacqueline Dorgan Meketa, *Legacy of Honor: The Life of Rafael Chacón, a Nineteenth-Century New Mexican* and Genaro Padilla, *My History, Not Yours: The Formation of Mexican-American Autobiography*.

[9] The complex nature of New Mexico's political history in the territorial period has been the subject of many studies. Two by Robert W. Larson are recommended to give the interested reader some background in this subject: his article,"Territorial Politics and Cultural Impact," and his book, *New Mexico's Quest for Statehood, 1846-1912*.

[10] Bruce-Novoa, in a recent article entitled "Dialogical Strategies, Monological Goals: Chicano Literature," has pointed out that the "tribal orientation" of the Chicano movement could not produce a cohesive nationalistic group because a we/they dichotomy does not reflect the dialogical reality of cultural production. "Heteroglossia is the undeniable state of contemporary culture. Dialogized language makes the return to the monological a nostalgic illusion," 241. I would add that even in the late nineteenth century, intercultural dialogism made the idealized theory of monologic anti-Anglo resistance impossible.

[11] Clifford Geertz, *The Interpretation of Cultures*, 5.

[12] Stuart Hall, "Cultural Identity and Diaspora," 222.

[13] From a taped lecture on neomexicano literary and cultural history given at the University of New Mexico in 1990. I am grateful to the UNM Southwest Research Collection for furnishing me a copy of the tape and to Francisco Lomelí for his insights in an area of research where we have many parallel interests.

Works Cited

Anaya, Rudolfo A. "Mythical Dimensions/ Political Reality." *Open Spaces, City Places: Contemporary Writers on the Changing Southwest.* Ed. Judy Nolte Temple. Tucson and London: University of Arizona Press, 1994: 25-30.

Bruce-Novoa, Juan. "Dialogical Strategies, Monological Goals: Chicano Literature." *An Other Tongue: Nation and Ethnicity in the Linguistic Borderlands.* Ed. Alfred Arteaga. Durham and London: Duke University Press, 1994: 225-245.

Dicken-García, Hazel. *Journalistic Standards in Nineteenth-Century America.* Madison: University of Wisconsin Press, 1989.

Fishman, Joshua A. *Language Loyalty in the United States: The Maintenance and Perpetuation of Non-English Mother Tongues by American Ethnic and Religious Groups.* The Hague: Mouton & Co., 1966.

Geertz, Clifford. *The Interpretation of Cultures.* New York: Basic Books, 1973.

Hall, Stuart. "Cultural Identity and Diaspora." *Identity, Community, Culture, Difference.* Ed. Jonathan Rutherford. London: Lawrence and Wishart, 1990:222–237.

Larson, Robert W. *New Mexico's Quest for Statehood, 1846-1912.* Albuquerque: University of New Mexico Press, 1968.

———. "Territorial Politics and Cultural Impact." *New Mexico Historical Review* 60:3 (1985): 249-269.

Meketa, Jacqueline Dorgan, ed. *Legacy of Honor: The Life of Rafael Chacón, a Nineteenth-Century New Mexican.* Albuquerque: University of New Mexico Press, 1986.

Padilla, Genaro M. *My History, Not Yours: The Formation of Mexican American Autobiography.* Madison: University of Wisconsin Press, 1993.

Rowe, William and Vivian Schelling. *Memory and Modernity: Popular Culture in Latin America.* London and New York: Verso, 1991.

Saxton, Russell Steele. "Ethnocentrism in the Historical Literature of Territorial New Mexico." Diss. U. of New Mexico, 1980.

Sexton, Joseph Franklin. "New Mexico: Intellectual and Cultural Developments 1885-1925. Conflict Among Ideas and Institutions." Diss. University of Oklahoma, 1982.

Simmons, Marc. *New Mexico: An Interpretive History.* 1993 rpt. Albuquerque: University of New Mexico Press, 1977.

Stratton, Porter A. *The Territorial Press of New Mexico, 1834-1912.* Albuquerque: University of New Mexico Press, 1969.

Recovering Neo Mexicano Biographical Narrative: *Cuarenta años de legislador,* the Biography of Casimiro Barela

A. Gabriel Meléndez
University of New Mexico

There is properly no history; only biography.   —Ralph Waldo Emerson

La historia, cual relicario santo, guarda en su seno las acciones buenas y malas de los hombres: las primeras para que las imitemos y las segundas para que evitemos su repetición. [History, like a holy reliquary, holds in its bosom the good and evil acts of men: the first that we might imitate them and the latter so we might avoid their repetition.]   —José E. Fernández, 1911

Biography, by definition, is a finite narrative form in the sense that it most often follows the chronology of the life of a biographical subject from cradle to grave. When it is produced as a posthumous tribute, biography labors to resurrect the life of its subject for a ready audience of readers who share the biographer's wish to attach collective significance to the individual's agency and experience. Complicit in such aims, biography (today we would include film biography as well) cannot help but disclose the subjective nature of its intent.

For traditionally excluded populations, biography that opens onto a politics of identity can be invalueable for mapping notions of self in relationship to the social standing of a group or community. For often such narratives are a means to assess the social or historical circumstances of a group, nation or community. In spite of their chronic erasure from dominant historical discourse, *Mexicanos* in the Southwest have consciously worked across generations to represent themselves positively in social and historical terms. In this paper I wish to open a space to consider how biography has been a particularly salient means of self-representation for Mexican Americans, and to consider how even the panegyric text, rendered as a postumous tribute to a fallen member of the group, encodes ethnic and gender-identified constructions of self which in turn assist in the development of social communitas.

Nineteenth-Century Mexicano Life-Narratives
As Symbolic Biography

In October, 1878, Josefa Ortiz de Barela, a resident of Trinidad, Colorado, sat down to pen a five-page profile of her father-in-law, José María Barela, who had died a day or two earlier. Her thumbnail sketch became the basis of a number of obituaries that appeared in Spanish-language newspapers in northern New Mexico and southern Colorado and by which the passing of a citizen of note in the Mexicano community was collectively acknowledged and lamented.

In titling the work "Biografía de Don José María Barela escrita por Josefa Ortiz de Barela, su hija política" [Biography of Don José María Barela written by Josefa Ortiz de Barela, his daughter-in-law], Josefa Ortiz claims her agency as the author of the text, raises her work a notch above the funeral oration that was commonplace in her day, and draws attention to her own participation in a narrative of settlement of southern Colorado by Mexican pioneering families.

Josefa's work is not unique as Mexicano cultural mores go. Rather, it is part of an older practice of verse-memorializing and extemporaneous funeral oration that was common practice in Hispano oral traditions. Such practices intesified with the advent of Spanish-language newspaper publication in the Southwest after 1880. This is not an unimportant development for it is in Mexicano newspapers, and, precisely through the collective act of reading fostered by publication whereby eulogy and funeral oratory become transformed into "symbolic biography," a form whose function, Michael T. Gilmore suggests is "to compose the collective biography of an entire people." (1978, 131)

Along with the *boceto* (biographical sketches), these self-reflexive texts celebrate as praiseworthy the lives of individuals deemed worthy of emulation by virtue of their achievements. Whether written to memorialize the loss of a community leader or to get out the vote, these micro-narratives encode positive self-representation in the face of the hegemonic effacement and historical erasure to the Mexican American community was subject to after 1848. Political *bocetos* had the effect of supplying models of behavior to the community-at-large, but they also validated the historicity of actions undertaken by members of the group in the name of community. The *boceto* as it appears in newspaper publication is but one example of the way print had come to shape communitarian expression among the Spanish-speaking, (a subject I have documented in my work on Spanish-language newspapers) for unlike the *corrido* and other oral narratives, such texts produce expository narration and move away from the figurative embellishment associated with oral narratives.

For Hispanos in New Mexico and Colorado during this period, every social act and every inscription of action in print is complicated by a politics of conquest and by the subaltern status they occupy after 1848. Like funeral oration, the *boceto* is a micro-text that discloses as much about personal character as it does about the ethical norms of the community. These are textual "snap-shots" taken from a subaltern vantage point that suggests a will to historical and cultural presence. Thus, their value as socio-biographical narrative, credentials the preferred forms of individual agency within Mexicano communities after 1848.

From *Boceto* to Biographical Communitas

Through the early twentieth century biography remained a fertile field for Neo-Mexicano self-representation and self-objectification. Life-writing permitted a kind of factual conflation of the past and present through which the deeds of Neo-Mexicanos long dead might be compared to the lives of contemporary men and women. Moreover, biography also filled the desire to authenticate experiences compounded by the circumstances of the present society. Using biography to authorize the ethos of the group is an idea consistent with creating a code of ethics and a morality of community around the aestheticized, that is, the biographed life. Neo-Mexicano bio-historical discourse had the effect of strengthening a reciprocal system of meaning connecting the biographical subject to community. It is biography's capacity to encode self-representation and to sustain self-objectification as a narrative strategy which Bakhtin sees as "proceed[ing] in indissoluble unity with the collective of others, it is interpreted, constructed and organized (with respect to all the constituents it shares with the world of others) on the plane of another's possible consciousness of my own life; my life is perceived and constructed as a possible story that might be told about it by the other to still others (to descendants)" (1990, 153).

A particularly attractive means to document achievement over time, Neo-Mexicano bio-texts familiarized history for a community of readers in a way other writing could not. Newspaper editors were aware that through the eyelet of an individual life and agency, could be threaded socio-historical events that impinged on present circumstances. Several editors in the 1890s had in fact launched what today we might label "recovery projects." Their aim was to produce works of history through the compilation of biographies of notable figures in the history of the Southwest.

Among the first such historiographic projects to be touted in the Neo-Mexicano press is José Escobar's "Nuevo México y sus hombres ilustres. 1530-1894." [Illustrious Men of New Mexico, 1530-1894]. In October of 1893 *El Boletín Popular* of Santa Fe ran the item, "De interés para los Neo-mexicanos." ["Of Interest to New Mexicans."] This work, reported *El Boletín*, was to be a collaboration between Trinidad editor José Escobar and Trinidad attorney Eusebio Chacón, and was to be published by *El Progreso,* a newspaper owned by Casimiro Barela in the same city. Mindful of questions of self-representation, Escobar promoted the book as one that would register the history of Nuevomexicanos in a dignified way. Escobar writes:

Con la confianza que acompañan siempre las acciones que tienden al bien y al la proseperidad de una raza esperamos que los amantes á las letras, lean el libro de que venimos hablando en el folletin de "El Progreso," para que cuando el mismo esté elegantemente encuadernado, y adornado con finas y bellas ilustraciones que representarán los monumentos antiguos y modernos del suelo de Nuevo México, asi como los retratos de los hijos ilustres del mismo Territorio procuren hacerse de un ejemplar. ("De interés para Neo-Mexicanos" *El Boletín Popular,* Santa Fe, New Mexico, 12, Oct. 1893)

[Confident in those actions that tend to accompany the betterment and prosperity of a race of people, we hope that those who are fond of literature will read the book, which we have talked about in *El Progreso* [we hope this is the case] so that when it has been elegantly bound and adorned with fine and beautiful illustrations that represent the ancient and modern monuments upon our New Mexican soil, as well as with the portraits of the illustrious sons of the territory, [its readers] will be sure to obtain a personal copy].²

Mikhail Bakhtin has commented on the capacity of biography to form axiomatic relationships that graft the actions of the biographical subject to the world he or she shares with a group or nation (1990, 154). Such observations provide a particularly useful theoretical frame for viewing the narratives of the type fostered by Escobar and which were meant to counter social subordination.

Keeping to the idea that biography illuminated historical *communitas* and a sense of shared experience, part IV of Benjamín Read's *Historia Ilustrada de Nuevo México* [Illustrated History of New Mexico], published in Santa Fe by *la Compañía Publicista del Nuevo Mexicano* [Publishing Company of the New Mexican] in 1911, includes one hundred and forty-six biographical sketches of contemporary men and women along with those of notable personages from Neo-Mexicano history. Read's biographical appendix provided readers with the rare opportunity to learn about the accomplishments of their contemporaries, and thus, added popular appeal to the book.² The inclusion of this material in a book of history was a strategy meant to reverse the intense negativism of the eastern press toward New Mexico and Neo-Mexicanos.

The weight of proving the merit, worth, loyalty, and accomplishments of Nuevomexicanos within Anglo society had been cast upon them since the American conquest. The sting of discrimination determined to a large degree the social station Nuevomexicanos occupied during the period. Nuevomexicano aptitudes and qualifications as citizens were continually judged by a small, but powerful Anglo elite. Read and other members of his generation could not escape the urgency to "put one's best foot forward," hence this public biographical tally of the accomplishments of Neo-Mexicanos in diverse walks of life. The appending of *bocetos* also was a way to make history, or so Read intimates in his prologue to *Historia Ilustrada* ". . . this last book carries some appendices and the biographical sketches of many of the sons and prominent citizens of the Territory along with the photos of many and other illustrations of extreme historical importance . . ." (Read 1911, 8).

Bringing the lives of contemporary Nuevomexicanos into the public record intensified in anticipation of statehood in 1912. Read's inclusion of profiles on prominent New Mexicans in *Historia Ilustrada* parallels the writing of more complete biographies, the most important of these being, *Cuarenta años de legislador, o la biografía del Senador Casimiro Barela,* [*Forty Years as a Legislator, Or the Biography of Senator Casimiro Barela* (1911),[3] a work written by José E. Fernández[4] and published just across the New Mexico border at Trinidad, Colorado[5] by Barela's own *El Progreso* Publishing Company of Trinidad. For Nuevomexicanos struggling for statehood, the publication of Barela's biography could not have come at a better time, for it told the story of one of their own who, not only had succeeded in the political arena, but had superseded Anglos in achievement and this, in a state where Mexicanos were a decided minority. Benjamín Read, who had included a *boceto* of Barela in *Historia Ilustrada,* consented to write the introduction for the book.

"*Biografiar es historiar*" [To write biography is to write history], declares José E. Fernández as a preface to his biography of the southern Colorado legislator Casimiro Barela. Contemporary theorists of historical narrative might readily agree with Fernández, when considering the discursive strategies that constitute bio-narrative disclosure. New historicists, on the other hand, would be much less concerned as to whether the subject of the narrative deals with real or imagined events, with truth or invented truth. The stance of such theoreticians gives Hayden White cause to state, "In point of fact, history—the real world as it evolves in time—is made sense of in the way the poet or the novelist tries to make sense of it . . ." (White 98). José E. Fernández, on the other hand, a nineteenth century Nuevomexicano biographer, was not thinking of the philosophy surrounding historical narrative, rather his intent was to convince his readers that his praise of Barela rested squarely upon the factual record. In equating *Cuarenta años de legislador* with history, Fernández speaks to the dialectic of representation faced by nineteenth century Mexican Americans in view of their virtual exclusion from other means of self-representation. Fernández conceived of the book as documentation, as a means to leave to posterity some record of Mexicano collective (historical) and individual (biographical) experience.

In introducing the biography, Benjamín Read underscores the point that its reading will improve Neo-Mexicano self-esteem and identity since it holds up to public scrutiny an example of success and attainment. He writes,

> Por eso yo, que desde años he tenido la honra de contarme entre sus amigos particulares, he sentido un verdadero regocijo en lo de obsequiar los deseos del dicho autor escribiendo, con toda sinceridad de mi corazón, estos apuntamientos en forma de introducción á la obra que ha de perpetuar en los corazones de los hispano-americanos de Colorado, y Nuevo México, los grandes servicios é incontables beneficios que han recibido de uno de los más fieles y más desinteresados de sus compaisanos y consanguíneos —Nosotros

los Neo-Mexicanos lo reconocemos y lo apreciamos, como hijo de este suelo, pues que en efecto lo es; y de ello tenemos orgullo (Fernández 1911, xviii).

As a result, I who for many years have had the honor to include myself among his [Barela's] close friends, find it a sincere joy to grant the wish of the author, and write these notes in the form of an introduction to a work that is destined to bring to life in the hearts of the Hispanos of Colorado and New Mexico, the great service and innumerable benefits that has come to them from one of the most loyal and selfless of its countrymen, [he is] blood of our blood —We *New* Mexicans recognize and appreciate him as a son of this earth, which in effect he is, and of this we are proud.

Barela's origins in the Embudo-Mora area gave his biographer cause to remark, *"Aquí hallarán como un joven de humilde cuna, de limitada educación y pobre de recursos ha llegado a distinguirse no solamente entre sus paisanos sino ante el mundo entero."* [Here [readers] will find how a young man of humble birth, with limited education and financially impoverished, has come to distinguish himself not only among his countrymen, but before all the world . . .] (Fernández 1911, xii).

Fernández records that Barela's genealogy included forebears who in the Colonial Period settled in San Francisco, San José and Los Angeles, California. He writes that some family members left California, traveled east and settled south of Albuquerque at the ranching community of Tomé early in the nineteenth century. Once in New Mexico the family relocated to Taos, New Mexico in 1839. A few years later Barela was born amid the chaos of the American invasion and the Taos revolt. Fernández writes:

En los años 1846 y 1847, durante la invasión de los norteamericanos á Nuevo México, se despertaron los odios entre estos y los nativos colonos como también con los indios; y como las persecuciones eran terribles como se recordarán con pavor los sucesos del 19 de enero de 1847 en Fernández de Taos, así fue que la familia de don José María Barela, domiciliada en Mora, tuvo que salir, regufiandose en El Embudo, Condado de Río Arriba, Nuevo México, donde ya estaba destinado por el Arquiteco Supremo que la Señora María de Jesús Abeyta de Barela, presentara á su esposo, el día 4 de Marzo, de 1847, con el niño que hoy llamamos el Senador Casimiro Barela (1911, 4).

In 1846 and 1847, during the invasion of the North Americans of New Mexico, hatred built between them and the native colonists as well as among the Indians, and, as there were terrible persecutions, like those that are recalled with horror at Fernández de Taos, so it was that the family of *Don* José María Barela, which made its home in Mora, had to leave and take refuge at El Embudo in Río Arriba, County, New Mexico, where it was destined by the Supreme Architect that *Señora* María de Jesús Abeyta de Barela would present her husband on March 4, 1847 the child who we today call Senator Casimiro Barela.

Having registered the matter of a family origin, Fernández in turn takes up other elements of biographical credentialing. He recounts the details of Barela's formation as a student of the Christian Brothers in Mora, New Mexico, his apprenticeship under the Rev. Juan B. Salpointe, his rags-to-riches ascent from a humble freighter of goods to a wealthy landowner in southern Colorado, and his election to the territorial legislature of Colorado at age 25 in 1871. Laced throughout the narrative are numerous references to Barela's moral character and, as if this were not enough to convince any reader that here are *"actos dignos de imitarse"* [acts worthy of emulation], Fernández adds a twenty-one page conclusion, a gushing tribute really, in which the author delves into the virtues of his biographical subject as family man, entrepreneur, politician, civil libertarian, community and church leader, and so forth. Throughout, Fernández does not pretend to offer an impartial and objective account of the public and private life of his biographical subject. As biographer his impulse is to be commendatory and to promote a sharing of his subject's virtues in the imagination of his readers. The work reflects a perspective in keeping with panegyric biographical narrative of the type in which Bakhtin observes a conflation of values between biographer and subject, "What the hero believes in, the author as hero believes in as well; what the hero regards as good, the author regards as good . . ." (1990, 163).

Fernández's enthusiasm in the re-telling of his subject's life is cause to look for the meaning of the work within and outside the text. While Fernández's high praise of Casimiro Barela may ring hollow to contemporary readers, it is axiomatic to Nuevomexicano socio-historical disposition and its intense desire for a re-integration of communitas, even as that sense of communitarianism is compromised in U.S. society after 1848.

Yet, biography, however exuberant, must be buoyed by factual information. In the Barela narrative the factual reference remains the struggle for the civil and cultural rights of the Spanish-speaking of southern Colorado. The narrative painstakingly records the names of dozens of Barela's fellow Nuevomexicanos and reproduces important documents from Barela's personal papers to substantiate the collective nature of the struggle for political and electoral representation. The biography all the while points—in the way the *boceto* points to shared aspirations—to Barela as the foremost spokesman and political leader of the Mexicano community of southern Colorado.

Barela's record as lawmaker and his active participation in the development of Colorado suffice to make his story worth telling. The Barela biography is the record of a legislative and political career filled with firsts for Mexicanos, a fact Fernández underscores repeatedly when showering his subject with the epithets: "Perpetual Senator," "Father of the Colorado Senate," and "Forty Years a Legislator." Among Barela's accomplishments is his election as President Pro Tempore of the Colorado Senate in 1893, his appointment in the same year by the Mexican government as Consul in Denver and his appoint-

ment to a similar post by the government of Costa Rica in 1897. Above all,
Barela is shown to be a steadfast advocate for the Spanish-speaking community of southern Colorado, a noteworthy accomplishment considering that
Colorado was a place where anti-Mexican sentiments ran high and often resulted in intimidation and open violence against the Spanish-speaking. Barela often
asserted that, *"Al tratarse de mi raza, especialmente si se trata de discriminar,
abdico mis ideas en política y me dedico á su defensa en todo tiempo y lugar."*
[If it concerns my race, especially if it is a matter of discrimination, I abdicated
my political ideologies and dedicate myself to its defense at all times and at all
places.] (1911, *xvi*).

Barela's five hundred and four page biography revolves around the same
kind of bio-discursive credentialing that informs the *bocetos* of local
Nuevomexicano political figures. Even Barela's vanity in having commissioned
the biography is masked by the work's emphasis on community building.
Barela's biography is, after all, about a life aestheticized in the name of communitas. Or so biographer, Fernández, would have the reader believe when he
writes, *"Esta obra no está escrita por el sentimiento de la adulación, está escrita para que el pueblo conozca actos dignos de imitarse . . ."* [This work is not
written out of a sentiment of adulation, it is written so that the people might
come to know actions worthy of imitation . . .] (Fernández 1911, xii). As with
political *bocetos,* the elements selected for re-telling reflect the prevailing sense
of communitas for Mexicanos in the Southwest at the end of the nineteenth century, a time when aspects of character constituted the dominant themes in the
emplotment of life narratives.[5]

Resurrected Meaning(s)

Since both testament and testimony are present in the Barela narrative it is
fair to ask how modern readers might arrive at critically discerning the meaning inscribed in it by Fernández, a commissioned writer, and the veracity of
Barela's achievements. Moreover, what are we to make of Barela himself?

Chicano historian Juan Gómez Quiñones regards Barela as "a centrist and
a pragmatist" (1994, 266) and includes him among a handful of Mexican elite
politicians that wielded influence in electoral politics in Colorado and Arizona
after the American takeover of those areas. Gómez Quiñones holds that
Mexicanos exercising any social agency after 1848 had varying motives, the
result of a complex weave of class and social membership in a subaltern community. Moreover, he notes that these attributions of motive often masked the
links that tied elites to a common origin in community. Gómez Quiñones identifies the following points as operating after 1848:

... the Mexican elite shared at least two commitments: one the devotion to
Catholicism, which grew more pronounced perhaps than in other periods; and
the other, the determination not only to survive but to insist on recognition of
both their political and social credentials. They also shared a consciousness of
local tradition and identity. Apart from these commitments, and as in the period before the conquest, they came to be characterized both as individuals and
as groups, by varying political factions, regional and personal divisions, and
motivations and loyalties; but now outsider elements, primarily influential
Anglos, were ultimately their audience, and a varying community and regional awareness of general and particular Mexican interests prevailed. (ibid., 196)

Gómez Quiñones's description is extremely useful for understaning the status
of subalterns, but it does not go to the particular motivations that drive the
actions of someone like Casimiro Barela. In the political arena, the legislative
record and the tallies of votes give some indication of the sympathies of these
Mexican politicos, but the intimate side of their personalities remains half-hid-
den beneath the protective layers of nineteenth century conventions and social
mores. In Barela's case it is at those points where the narrative facade might
breach and give way to intimate disclosure as in the discussion of family,
women and employees, and that Fernández, the biographer-confidante, glides
over the contentiousness of patriarchal privilege, private ambitions and class
allegiance. A rare instance that departs from the image of Barela as a self-made
man comes in Barela's tribute to his first wife Josefa Ortiz de Barela. Fernández
notes, *"Hablando de su primera esposa el Senador Barela ha dicho: 'Mi
primera esposa me hizo hombre; era una muchacha de mucho sentido y estaba
mejor educada que yo. Ella me enseñó el inglés, y veía por mis negocios en mi
ausencia. A ella le debo todo."* [Speaking of his first wife the Senator has said:
'My first wife made me a man; she was a woman of great judgement and she
was better educated than I. She taught me English, and she looked after my
businesses in my absence. I owe her everything.] (1911, 409)

It is perhaps the absence of corroborating evidence regarding Barela as *"un
ser humano,"* a human being, that has fueled conjecture from other Barela biographers. Such concern inhabits the work of Inez Hunt, a curriculum developer
for the Colorado Springs Public Schools who produced a children's reader in
1971 based on Barela's life. As with other resurrections of the Barela life story
the motivation is more symbolic than factual, one of the unavoidable deriva-
tives of a biographical method whenever the biographer inflects collective
significance to the individual agency and experience of the biographical subject. That Hunt's reader was begun in the wake of the Chicano Movement and
the mobilization of the Mexican American community by Corky Gonzales and
the Denver-based, Crusade for Justice, is also cause to look for the meaning of
the re-telling of the Barela story within and outside of this text.

The Barela Brand

> Senator Barela really did all these things. We have only added the conversa-
> tions as we imagined he would have spoken. —*The Barela Brand* (1971)

Attempts to resurrect meaning from Barela's public record are found in commemorative newspaper articles that celebrate the virtues of the early pioneers of Colorado. With rare exception, the roster of southern Colorado settlers adjoined to these local interest stories is headed by Casimiro Barela. Examples include: "Early Trinidad Legislator Called Perpetual Senator," *Pueblo Chieftain*, April 3, 1966; "Conquistadores Influenced State," *Pueblo Chieftain*, Pueblo, Colorado, June 6, 1971 and "Barela Helped Life Blossom in the Trinidad Area," *Trinidad Plus*, February 28, 1990.

Two works outside the commemorative vein need to be mentioned: first, Hunt's *The Barela Brand*, and second, a chapter-length sketch of Barela in *Colorado Profiles* published by Monnet and Michael McCarthy in 1987. Unlike the commemorative articles meant to turn the reader's attention to deeds of local interest, these life-narratives are set on the goal of resurrecting the Barela story for contemporary, Hispanic and non-Hispanic audiences. Both projects assist multicultural educational objectives that arise as a response to the Mexican American civil rights movement of the last three decades.

Hunt's reader, *The Barela Brand*, produces the most altered palimpsest of "our subject" by recasting Barela as a Franklinian hero in the tradition of American biography, the obvious result of the author's desire to make the reading meaningful to youth. *The Barela Brand* published in 1971 was the second in a series of children's books written by Hunt as part of a curriculum development project for the Division of Instructional Services of the Colorado Springs Public Schools. A local reporter hearing Hunt lecture before the Rho Chapter of Delta Kappa Gamma, an international sorority for teachers, described the genesis of Hunt's multicultural children's books,

> Her interest began, she said, when she took large groups of children on ghost
> town tours. She said she then became aware of minority groups among the
> children. Later a teacher asked Mrs. Hunt if she knew of any history books in
> the region that told about minority figures. Mrs. Hunt discovered they were
> few and far between. Mrs. Hunt met with Dr. William Liddle, director of ele-
> mentary education in School District 11, to discuss writing books for children
> on minority figures. At the time Mrs. Hunt had written an adult book on a
> black run-away slave named Barney Ford.[6]

Inez Hunt's *bios* is not included here to digress, rather to readjust the frame around the process of bio-narrative credentialing that informs her treatment of the Barela biography, and by which is produced a retro-fitting of the Casimiro Barela biography in the name of diversity and multiculturalism.

The Casimiro Barela revived by Hunt in 1971, like the Hale-Bopp comet streaking across the skies in 1997, drags in its wake the debris of Hunt's own biographical inflections. How best to describe Hunt then? Local news stories on the author (and there are many) reiterate her passion for Colorado lore. Described as "a busy writer, poetess, lecturer and teacher," newspaper stories report that she "taught hundreds something of the lore of Colorado's 'ghost' trails."[7] The title "ghost hunter," seems a most apt description for Mrs. Hunt's penchant for researching Colorado lore. In one account we find her leading the uninitiated—even the most reluctant among them, a convention of Colorado assessors no less—through the minutiae of pioneering days in Colorado. The news story begins by saying: "A wispy, piquant, Inez Hunt, dressed like the ghost she pursues, Tuesday guided Colorado assessors through the 19th century pioneer towns from which Colorado grew and introduced them to the legendary figures which peopled their streets and log cabins."[8] The spectral in Colorado's restless past also increased public reception of Hunt's books. Judging from tributes in the local press Hunt worked diligently to cast herself in the role of "biographer of the state's ghosts and ghost towns." A local reporter noted, "Mrs. Hunt notes that sometimes she feels haunted once she gets started. 'You think the ghosts are looking over your shoulder and pushing you on,' she says."[9]

Inez Hunt prided herself on being a good storyteller, yet there is much to suggest that other aims beyond spinning a good yarn drove her work, particularly her series on "minority subjects." The Barela story is a case in point. Regardless of the spectral trappings with which Hunt may have thought to bedeck the story, the need for multicultural curriculum in Colorado's public schools seems ultimately to have convinced her that stories of "minority ghosts" might make good reading. Hunt explained how she came to do the Barela book, "School District 11 was pleased with the first book [*The Adventures of Barney Ford—A Runaway Slave*]. The children were delighted and Dr. William Liddle, School District 11 director of elementary education, asked Mrs. Hunt to do more."[10]

With *The Barela Brand,* Hunt turned her attention to Mexican Americans, Colorado's largest ethnic minority group. In Barela she met up not with a ghost, but with a political legacy: "Mrs. Hunt said she met Barela the very first time by picture. He was one of 16 pioneers who had been chosen for stained glass portrait immortality in the capitol building in Denver because of his outstanding contributions to the state." Hunt is quoted as saying, "The authoress said she looked at the portrait and at the name and said, "I don't know you, but sometime I will."[11] Hunt was correct. There of course, was a story behind the portrait in the rotunda, one which she would easily telescope into her children's reader from the original biography in Spanish.

Highly selective in her use of documented sources Hunt draws heavily on the Fernández biography even to the point of paraphrasing its powerful admonition on the "good and evil deeds of men" in her forward. Hunt puts her own spin on it:

> All of us leave a brand or a mark on the world by the kinds of things we do, whether they are good or bad. It like putting our hands in wet cement which will harden in time and tell what we did. Its like the dinosaur which leaves a footprint in the mud which becomes rock and tells us what he was like millions of years later. The man whose story I want to tell you was named Casimiro Barela. He left his mark on Colorado history to last forever, so I call his story, The Barela Brand. (1971)

Employing the basic outline of the Barela story Hunt illustrates her work with historical photographs, most of which were previously published in the Fernández biography. In the move to make the narrative more palatable to the requirements of the local school board, Hunt's version conflates information and de-traumatizes the socio-historical elements of Barela's life story, (an idea I shall return to later) especially as concerns racial and class contentions.

Hunt's reconstruction of the Barela narrative is reminiscent of the "inter-polative narrative" built around the memoirs of yet another nineteenth century Neo-Mexicano, Rafaél Chacón (coincidentally Barela's compadre).[12] *Legacy of Honor,* Jacqueline Dorgan Meketa's restoration of the Chacón memoirs is a case where Genaro Padilla believes that, "In supplementing Chacón's memoirs, Maketa gives us a version of Rafaél Chacón that in the process of thickening the biographical subject, eventually so disperses Chacón's own narrative that the autobiographer himself is displaced" (1993, 158). In an opposite narrative shift Hunt cuts away the details of Barela's life so that the biographical subject is winnowed down to little more than an outline. By far the greatest alteration results from Hunt's imaginative re-invention of dramatic dialogue which the protagonists (Barela and others) are made to voice. Hunt then stages the action of Barela's life story in a few, highly stylized, narrative blocks or scenes.

Hunt opens the narrative with a romanticized southwestern scene which has José María Barela (Casimiro's father and the subject of Josefa's *boceto*) standing at the doorway of his adobe house in Embudo. Hunt's description turns on heavily canned tourist images of the Southwest, the house at Embudo that Hunt describes is typically adorned by "red chili peppers" that "looked like copper in the moonlight." (1971, 1). We are told that "troubles with the Indians" (ibid., 1) have forced the recent move of the family to Embudo. The narrator follows José María as he gathers wood to keep the house warm for the new baby, and then going to María, his wife, we see the couple discussing the name they will give their "unusually fine child." José María urges that the child be named in honor of his distant ancestor, Casimiro Varelas, (note the spelling) who settled in California. Hunt's, José María, relates the following bit of family history: "Casimiro was the name of this great ancestor. He brought a colony of eighty people with him from Spain to Mexico. Casimiro joined General Anza and went to California in 1777. On a beautiful spot, they built a mission, a fort and a city for Saint Francis." (ibid., 1) The scene ends with José María inscribing the propitious name into the family record book.

Hunt's novelized biography transforms Barela from a defender of human and civil rights—the central view of the Fernández book—to Barela as a minority entrepreneur whose "success" in securing a livelihood becomes the measure of his life. Dramatic reconstruction aside, Hunt's reader alters some basic facts of the story and de-emphasizes others. Hunt writes, for example, that the Barelas's relocation in 1847 to Embudo from their residence at Mora was due to "Indian" not "American troubles." In reality, the "terrible persecutions" recalled by José E. Fernández were the result of the American Invasion. These events are corroborated by Rafaél Chacón who tells us that the American arrival produced havoc across the whole on northern New Mexico:

> When the American troops advanced toward Taos in two divisions, one by way of El Embudo and the other by way of El Chamizal, the people, with their families and animals fled and found refuge in the Cañon del Rio between Picuris, Las Trampas, and El Embudo. There they lived, suffering many mishaps among the shady groves of pines. I remember that there was such terror instilled by the Americans that when a dog barked the people killed it, the burros were muzzled so that they could not bray, and if the roosters crowed at daylight they killed them. Only at night were fires permitted in order that the enemy not discover the smoke from the huts. After the assault on the pueblo of Taos, where the Indians fought with much vigor, the Americans seized some Indians and Mexicans and executed them after which all was peaceful once more. As soon as they considered the countryside conquered, they sent some companies of soldiers to Mora. The people fled in terror and the soldiers burned the public markets, the granaries, and everything the people were not able to carry away. (Meketa, 1986, 67)

Fear of reprisal from American soldiers, not fear of Indian depredations held grip over northern New Mexico throughout the spring and summer of 1847. Quite a different social reality to be born into, especially when one considers that Mexicans and Indians at Taos had found common cause in resisting a foreign invasion. By altering this part of the story and attributing the relocation of the Barelas to "Indian troubles" Hunt manages to avoid scripting the unpleasant and upsetting facts of the American conquest of the Southwest.

What is altered more substantially is the groundwork that explains Barela's advocacy for the Spanish-speaking in his adult life. Hunt, in essence, de-traumatizes history for her young readers, and in doing so narrates against the expectations set for the historian as set forth by Hayden White:

> Moreover, the greatest historians have always dealt with those events in histories of their cultures which are "traumatic" in nature and meaning of which is either problematic or overdetermined in the significance they still have for

current life, events such as revolutions, civil wars, large-scale processes such as industrialization and urbanization, or in situations which have lost their original function in society but continue to play on important role on the current social scene. (1978, 87)

The Fernández text, in contrast, never loses sight, just as Barela never loses sight, of the massive change that is wrought on Mexican Americans by the signing of the Treaty of Guadalupe Hidalgo at the close of the Mexican American War. Whereas Fernández's narrative is about Barela, his people and his race and its *raison d'etre* is to bolster an Hispano sense of self-worth, Hunt proclaims detachment as her preferred method for writing books on ethnic difference: "Its not necessary to repeat the outrages of these people. They should be respected for what they did, not their color."[13]

While school administrators in the early 1970s were apt to crow about the multicultural bent Hunt's series of children's books provided the school district,[14] Hunt's narrative focus does little to encourage the interest of Hispanic students, a prime reason, one suspects for creating the curriculum project in the first place. By flattening out the socio-historical events that frame Barela's life, the Hunt narrative dulls the motivation of such acts.

Absent from the Hunt emplotment of the Barela life-narrative is the axiology between the author and the biographical subject. In contrast to Fernández's estimation that the biography is intended to be "un estímulo para la juventud que no debe desmayarse porque su origin sea humilde y sus ventajas limitadas." [a stimulus for young people that should not be faint of heart because they are of humble origin and of limited means.] we have only District 11 school administrators attesting to the reader's value to minority and non-minority students.

It is curious, nonetheless, that Hunt opens her biography with Barela's admonition on racial discrimination, the same words Fernández cites in the epigraph that opens his biography: "If it concerns my race, especially if it is a matter of discrimination, I abdicated my political ideologies and dedicate myself to its defense at all times and at all places." (Fernández 1915, xvi). It must be noted that Hunt does not substantiate by example the premise upon which Barela's assertion rests. In fact, the greater part of the Hunt reader dwells on Casimiro Barela in his leisure activities. The image Hunt forges of Barela is of a successful landowner whose prowess in politics allows him to enjoy the fruits of his achievements. Hunt for example recreates an idyllic picture of life at Barela's *quinta* at Rivera, Colorado, the town he built for his second wife, Damiana. These descriptions are reminiscent of California pastoral narratives as found in Hubert Howe Bancroft's *California Pastoral* (1888), Henry Dana's *Two Years Before the Mast* (1840) and Helen Hunt Jackson's *Ramona* (1884). Not surprising is Inez Hunt's devotion to her writer-namesake, Helen Hunt Jackson. Once asked if she was related to the author, Inez Hunt answered that she was not. A reported added, "But she is a close personal friend of Helen Hunt

Jackson's relatives and memorializes her in "[To Colorado's] Restless Ghosts" for Helen's "Ramona." The reporter added, "Miss Hunt feels the novel "Ramona" is the "Uncle Tom's Cabin" of Indian sufferings.[15] In *To Colorado's Restless Ghosts* Inez Hunt offers her own panegyric of her name-sake. Hunt's inflection of romantic descriptions of California hacienda society onto Barela are clear. Hunt's Casimiro Barela is a gentleman farmer with a decided preoccupation for pastoral refinement that outweighs his concern for his "raza." Hunt's narrative is thickened with descriptions of the Barela's country home at Rivera, Colorado:

> Four acres of lilacs and roses made a colorful garden in front of Rivera. Great clumps of peonies blossomed in June. Daisies and lilies bloomed all summer. It was so spectacular that travelers on the train would ask the conductor, "Is that a public park or just a private garden?" When the Senator had built all the buildings, sidewalks, and ditches to water the flowers, he thought of something else he needed for the house. He wanted lights both inside and outside the house. (ibid., 27)

Hunt's twelve short chapters present the image of the aging Senator in a godfatheresque adipose sitting at the veranda of his *quinta* at Rivera, Colorado advising his fellow citizens or musing over the questions of destiny and fate. What is clearly absent is the story of a man in struggle with his society.

Like the Hunt project, the Monnet and Michael McCarthy profile of Barela in *Colorado Profiles* shares in the project of creating "diversity" and "multiculturalism" in Colorado. That both projects follow in the wake of the Chicano Movement is telling, for each in its own way responds to the indictment by Corky Gonzales and others who had made the charge of racism a mantra in Colorado. Brief and schematic, the McCarthy profile details only the most important aspects of Barela's political career. The authors note his entrance into the Colorado legislature, his introduction of legislation to translate the law of Colorado into Spanish and German for the benefit of excluded populations. In speaking of his role as Denver consul to Mexico and Costa Rica, the authors add that these were crucial "to aid Hispanic immigrants in transition to American culture." (1987, 155) The authors also see as important Barela's advocacy on the behalf of Hispanic ranchers to protect their grazing rights against the powerful interests of the Colorado Fuel and Iron Company.

The McCarthy tract, a straightforward summation of Barela's public life does occasionally lapse to the panegyric tone of the Fernández biography. This is especially true in passages that describe Barela's oratory and eloquence in public speaking: "Barela used eloquence as a speaker to advance his many causes. Not with a sharp temper, he had the ability to out shout the best of them on the floor of the Senate. He always seemed to get his point of view across in boisterous fashion. Within a very short time, many people believed that Casimiro Barela would become a major force in the Colorado Senate. And they

were right." (1987, 154)
   The McCarthy profile does not avoid addressing the socio-historical context of Barela's life. The authors note the origins of racial and cultural antagonism between Anglos and Mexicans in Colorado and speaking of conditions at the end of the previous century they note:

> As long as the Mexicans remained confined to the southern portion of the territory, they posed no threat to the glorious pageant of Manifest Destiny being played up north. The politicians in Washington had made them an instant minority group within the boundaries of the new territory, and the Anglo-Saxon population wholeheartedly approved. (1987, 152)

   Having acknowledged racial, class and ethnic conflict, the authors assign a civil and human rights coefficient to Casimiro Barela's presence in the hallowed chambers of the Colorado assembly. One which they affirm provides the earliest challenge by any minority population in Colorado to Anglo absolutism in matters of political power and electoral representation.
   Sharing the view held by Juan Gómez Quiñones, Monnet and Michael McCarthy label Barela as the political pragmatist par excellence, saying, "More notable than his financial accomplishments, however is his record of achievement in helping the Hispanic people of Colorado while concurrently displaying pragmatic political sense to keep himself in a position of power during an age of severe racial prejudice." (1987, 154) Barela's pragmatism they conclude was only possible in the measure that Barela managed "to bridge the gap between the interests of the two ethnic groups [Anglo and Hispano] in his constituency and in the state at large." (ibid., 158) They extrapolated significance from the Barela example for their own time affirming that "old militancy of the 1960s and 1970s" in Colorado had given way to a "modern sense of pragmatism" embodied in the person of Denver's Federico Peña, the only minority mayor of an American city "not dominated by minorities." For Monnet and Michael McCarthy the parallels to present day Colorado are clear, "Federico Peña was able to bridge the gap between ethnic communities once again." (ibid.,158) The authors further conjecture that Casimiro Barela "would heartily approve of that position."
   The fascination of biography, indeed, may be the changing palimpsest produced by the reiteration of the life-narrative in subsequent generations of readers. Commendatory news articles that compare Barela to the Spanish Conquistadores (i.e. "Conquistadores Influenced State," *Pueblo Chieftain,* Pueblo, Colorado, June 6, 1971) reflect the enduring fascination with the epic of Spanish exploration in the Southwest. One might however rightly ask why Barela, "the son of a poor farmer and freighter," would have any more connection to a Spanish Conquistador than a yeoman farmer would have to King George of England.
   Several degrees of complexity shade the significance of the Barela life-nar-

rative, each governed by succeeding attempts to resurrect meaning from the story of an Hispano immigrated to Colorado from New Mexico and whose tenure in the Colorado legislature in 1876 that would last until 1916, one of the longest of any state senator in the nation.

The Metaphor of the Empty Filing Cabinet: Recovering the Casimiro Barela Biography

A small mahogany filing cabinet which once belonged to the esteemed long-time state senator, Casimiro Barela who served in the state legislature from 1876 to 1916 from Las Animas County, has been presented to the Colorado State Historical Society by J. M. Romero of Denver.
—"Romero Makes Donation to State Historical Society," *Trinidad Chronicle-News,* January 20, 1970.

Recovering and restoring a narrative that has been dormant for three quarters of a century is a remarkable undertaking.
—Genaro Padilla, *My History, Not Yours* (1993)

After undertaking exhaustive searches at my request, the archivist at the Baca House / Trinidad Historical Society informs me that precious few documents from the Barela household are in the collection of the Colorado Historical Society in Denver. The Baca House has only two original receipts from "Casimiro Barela y Cía," [Casimiro Barela and Company]. It also owns a Bible, a rifle and a filing cabinet, items reputed to have belonged to Barela.

Senator Barela's filing cabinet, empty of its original papers, was donated to the Colorado Historical Society by a Mr. J. M. Romero of Denver. An item in the *Trinidad Chronicle News* in January of 1970 relates how Mr. Romero came to own the cabinet. Mr. Romero bought the item from some of the last members of the Rivera family who were still living at El Moro, Colorado in the late 1950s. Interestingly, Mr. Romero, a caseworker for the welfare department, had read José E. Fernández's *Cuarenta Años de Legislador.* His interest was piqued when family members announced that they were selling some of Barela's personal items. Romero notes, "I was interested in having a momento of the famous Las Animas pioneer." Most of the furniture has been sold but the filing cabinet was still there. Romero bought it and kept it for some twenty years before donating it to the Historical Society.

The cabinet, long emptied of documents and correspondence, is a sobering metaphor of historical loss for Hispanos in the West. For as Fernández notes, Barela was meticulous in his record keeping, *"Jamás desperdicia una sola carta de su correspondencia, guardándolas en filas* (sic) *dedicadas á ese fin y arregladas alfabéticamente y puede referirse á cualquier correspondencia y hallarlas cuando las necesita porque tiene su lugar separado para cada cosa."* [He never throws away a single letter from his correspondence, keeping them in files that are arranged alphabetically for this purpose, and he can refer to any correspondence and find it when he has to because he has a place reserved for each thing.] (1911, 410) Certainly the filing cabinet must have contained a rich and detailed cache of missives, files, correspondence, texts of speeches, legislation, etc. So, it is indeed fortunate that Barela did in fact open his personal archives to his biographer since it is only by way of Fernández's narrative that any such record survived to the present.

Though altered in many ways, José E. Fernández's first telling of the Casimiro Barela story remains the authority for the re-tellings by Hunt and the McCarthys. Throughout these latter reinventions traces of the original text remain in place. That such is the case is testimony to the power of the originating inscription of the Fernández biography.

The significance, for those of us who re-encounter these biographical lections from Hispanics as they create a sense of community in the face of hegemonic erasure at the end of the nineteenth century is manifold. The question to be answered in a re-encounter with this text is not, "Who was Barela?" but what did/does Barela represent and how is our understanding of what his story represents framed by ideological discourses that seek to dissolve, mute or ignore his role as an advocate of Hispano civil rights?

Barela's life, like that of most real people straddles class, ideological and humanitarian boundaries. This being so, one must ask to what extent is the work worthy of reconsideration by a contemporary readership?

One is drawn to those instances where Barela fulfills a collective mission to improve the lot of his *gente,* thus making him worthy of the praise José E. Fernández heaps on his person. In this light his story is clearly of interest to contemporary readers who are drawn to those who have championed social justice issues. But in the record are also instances where class interests, political power, patriarchal privilege and social hierarchy add to his personal advantage. Because Barela occupies a position of power both tendencies surface over the course of his life. Gómez Quiñones sees a case where, "Barela practiced a politics that exhibited an ambition for wealth and power that was concurrent with an interest in protecting the rights of his people." (1994, 265).

When one returns to Fernández "originating inscription," one finds instances of the twin nature of Barela's motives, though, clearly, Fernández elects to tell only of those things favorable to constructing the image of Barela as intelligent, hard-working, honest and so forth. We see Barela operating in the name of his community and defending his race from insult and racial attack, but we are just as likely to see him exercise his political privilege and personal power to enhance his social stature. That Fernández found no inconsistency in registering the latter is of course consistent with a politics of the exploitative and extractive capitalism that reigned in Colorado and the West at the turn-of-the-century. My point is that the complex Barela is not reducible to a paragon of virtue, and neither is his story material for hierography. No Saint Casimiro shadows our subject and no amount of high praise in the Fernández account can camouflage Barela's ambition, nor his shrewd political and business instincts. The detail in Fernández's biography results from Barela's insistence that his biographer build the narrative upon the factual record. Barela instructed his biographer at the outset of the writing, *"Escriba mi biografía, tal cual es, para que aquellos que deseen leerla, hallan allí solamente hechos que se puedan substanciar con los registros, y que no dé cabida á un pensamiento de querer exagerar mis acciones."* [Write my biography just as it is, so that those who wish to read it will find there only those facts that can be substantiated by the record and which will not give way to the thought of wanting to exaggerate my actions.] (1911, x) More to the point, is the importance Fernández accords to the archival record from which he fashioned Barela's life story:

Esta advertencia, que no he podido menos que respetar, me ha limitado á tratar de su biografía con la mayor precaución para preparar esta obra, teniendo en mi posesion un verdadero archivo de documentos coleccionados de diferentes personas y lugares, en los cuales hay infinidad de datos relativos á su persona, á los cuales, si me he atrevido á comentar brevemente es porque en ellos campea la verdad absoluta: cuyos comentarios van dictados por la buena fé y no por incienso (sic) que pretenda quemar á su alrededor, pues soy de la opinión que su biografía por sí sola es aún más interesante.

[I have been able to do no less than respect this warning and in preparing this work I have limited myself to treat his biography with the utmost caution. I have in my possession a virtual archive of documents collected from different persons and different places and in these there are an infinite number of facts concerning his person and of which, when I have dared to comment on them, I have done so only because that commentary is driven by good faith and not in the form of incense to burn around him, for I am of the opinion that his biography is of its own merit interesting.] (ibid., x–xi)

In a very real sense, the Fernández narrative is inextricably linked to Barela's mahogany filing cabinet for it stands in place of it, replicating in large measure the contents of Barela's papers. One supposes that the mahogany filing cabinet also contained Barela's private *calaveras*, his personal skeletons in the form of unpaid debts, legal shenanigans, documents registering the malcontent of Barela's business and political enemies, the correspondence of illicit love affairs (perhaps), and other dark secrets? In short, all those things we suspect round out the life story of a nineteenth century patriarch. But as we do not have direct notice of such activity we must weight the significance of Barela's life against that part of the record that does survive.[16]

The table of contents for *Cuarenta Años de Legislador* lists 136 discreet entries. Each entry, arranged chronologically follows Barela from "humble origins" to his last term in public office, but also the list exhibits a superimposition that results from Barela's filing habits. Fernández's chapter titles could well have come from those files he had at hand. Consider the following partial list: "The Colorado Constitutional Convention," "Judge Caldwell Yeaman's Arbitrary Action," "His Trip to Mexico," "Comments by the Press," "Correspondence with the Honorable Antonio Joseph," "The 1895 Legislative Session," etc. Evidence that Fernández inventoried Barela's files is his verbatim inclusion of names, correspondence, lists, certificates, etc. found in the master files. For example Fernández includes 16 letters from well-wishers on the occasion of Barela's sixtieth birthday; a detailed list of 73 endorsements supporting Barela nomination to be foreign minister to Guatemala in 1893; a list of 87 Hispanic and Anglo, male and female voters who changed over to the Democratic party with Barela in 1904; and, 71 "Cartas de apreciación" [Letters of Appreciation] from friends, supporters and business associates written in support of Barela's nomination to be General Consul to Costa Rica. From a stylistic point of view such minutia interrupts the narrative flow of the Barela story. Yet as the empty filing cabinet shows they are extremely valuable to the historian and researcher. For his part, Fernández justifies his decision to include such items with comments to the effect that, *"sólo para sustanciar mis aserciones"* [simply to substantiate my assertions] (ibid., 146).

Insignificant as it may seem on the surface, it is important to learn that Casimiro Barela was a meticulous and detailed record keeper for in a real sense this makes him the shadow narrator, a fact that blurs absolute distinctions between autobiography and biography in the telling of the story of his life. Fernández gives us a succinct description of Barela's personal record keeping: *"Conserva también un diario de todo lo que hace ó de que se ocupa cada un día del año. Es tan estricto en sus negocios que sabe cuantos tones de alfalfa le producen cada corte de cada rancho, lo cual lleva por medio de su diarios. Por escrito consta lo que le cuesta cada cosa y lo que se consume en su casa ó en sus empresas."* [He also keeps a diary of everything he does and of everything he undertakes each day of the year. He is so strict in his businesses that he knows how many tons of alfalfa that each cut on each of his ranches produces, something he records in his diary. His written records provides him an accounting of the cost of everything and of what is consumed by his household and his businesses.] (ibid., 410] What stories might his records have revealed had they survived the ravages of time?

In re-reading the Fernández biography the heteroglossia of Barela's actions must be considered not to tally virtue against vice (as Fernández himself thought) but as a means to understand from whence proceeds the complex social, economic and inter-ethnic position occupied by the subaltern subject in the socio-historic moment he or she occupies.

In Barela's instance this heteroglossia of activity reflects the habits of one studied in the art of compromise, a skill that must be developed by the subaltern if only to survive. Barela's accomplishments and to an extent those of his fellow Spanish-speaking citizens are out of the ordinary as the history of ethnic minorities in this country is concerned, since not only do they survive but for a short time they prosper under highly competitive, even antagonistic social expectations.

Barela's life story mirrors those conditions. Fernández's narrative inbricates Barela in the socio-historical milieu that prevail for his community and provides an account, in Bakhtinian terms of the "co-experiencing" of the social moment.

High on the list of accomplishments is Barela's defense of language-rights for the Spanish-speaking. Fernández notes that Barela's advocacy on the issue came from his first days as a legislator,

> Ya hemos dicho que en el primero período que desempeñó el Senador Barela como representante, se prentendía que las leyes fueran publicadas en el idioma inglés solamente, y hemos dicho también que por mociones del Sr. Barela y por sus reñidas defensas en favor de la raza nativa del Territorio, se dispuso que fueran publicadas también en el idioma español. Cada término legislativo tenía que suscitarse esta cuestión en la Cámara de Representantes y el día que allí faltara quien saliera a su defensa, los habitantes de la parte Sur de Colorado tendrían que quedarse sin que las leyes se publicaran en su idioma.

> [We have already said that in Senator Barela's first term as a representative moves were afoot to have the laws published only in the English language, and we have also said that it was by Senator Barela's motions and through his energetic defense of the native race of the Territory, that provisions were made to have the laws published in Spanish as well. At each legislative session the matter had to be brought up again and the day that no one was there to come its defense was the day the inhabitants of southern Colorado would be left without the laws being published in their language.] (ibid., 57)

Barela's handling of the language question is strategic. Unable to outright defeat the linguistic xenophobia of his fellow members of the legislature, Barela's tact is to hold off the attacks of his political (read cultural) enemies until more favorable conditions prevail. The breach in the hegemony of political power in Colorado that Barela sought came with the 1875 Constitutional Convention. Barela was convinced that provisions written into the constitution of the state to protect the language-rights for the Spanish-speaking would bring to an end the legislative battles that he had to wage each year in the territorial legislature to have the laws published in languages other than English. Seizing political opportunity, not acquiescence, is a strategic factor in Barela's art of compromise. Barela explains:

> En aquel tiempo uno tenía la oportunidad de que si no admitían los provistos que les sugería con respecto a mejorar ó cuidar por mis paisanos, les amenazaba con que estos votarían en contra de la admisión del estado, y como estaban ansiosos por la adminisión tenía que acceder, y como yo, consideré que tan

pronto como se volviera a reunir la legislatura tratarían de enmendar aquella parte por lo tanto hice que el provisto de que no pudiera enmendar hasta cumplidos los 25 años.

[At that time one had the opportunity to say that not working to improve and protect my fellow countrymen would mean that they [the Spanish-speaking] would vote against the admission of the state, and since they [the lawmakers] were anxious for admission they had to acquiesce, and as I considered that as soon as the legislature met again, they would try to amend that section, and therefore I made a provision that it could not be amended until 25 years had past.] (ibid., 58)

The point never lost to Fernández is that he is writing the story of a representative and defender of the Mexicano minority. In his mind Barela's political agenda is the agenda of southern Colorado's Spanish-speaking community. Barela, for example, presses for legislation to support elementary education in Spanish in 1884. His reasons for supporting instruction in Spanish at the elementary level include what bilingual educators today label the "two way immersion" method. Barela argues before the Senate, *"siendo que los habitantes de la parte sur de Colorado eran casi todos de raza mexicana, y desconciendo el idioma inglés, podía dárseles la instrucción elemental en español, y así les sería fácil adquirirla en breve tiempo, estudiando á la vez el idioma inglés, lo que daría por resultado que cuando aprendieran el inglés, estarían ya instruidos elementalmente* [being that the inhabitants of southern Colorado were nearly all of the Mexican race and not knowing the English language, they could be given elementary instruction in Spanish and it would be easy for them to acquire English in a short time, while studying English at the same time, the result would be that when they learned English they would already have obtained elementary instruction.] (ibid., 92)

Not surprisingly, it is politics and, in particular, moves to disenfranchise the Spanish-speaking from their constitutional right to vote that is by far Barela's greatest concern. Moves to limit access to the vote by the use of language requirements was a constant threat to Barela and his community. In 1883, for example, District Judge Caldwell Yeaman, ruled that jurors in Colorado's Third Judicial District could serve on juries only if they could read and write the English language. The Judge's ruling further stipulated that such a requirement superseded other criteria for eligibility.

At the head of a protest meeting organized in Trinidad in March 1884, Barela called the ruling arbitrary and discriminatory. A coalition of Hispanos and concerned Anglos at that meeting drafted a set of six resolutions demanding that the Judge recant his decision. Calling into question the faulty logic of Judge Yeaman, the committee challenged officials of the court to review the record of service that Mexican jurors had established over the years, moreover, they appealed to the Constitution and to the rights of citizenship guaranteed to them by the Treaty of Guadalupe Hidalgo. Points five and six speak most clearly to their concerns:

> 5to. *Que demandaremos en todo tiempo nuestros justos derechos, los privilegios é inmunidades comunes á todos los ciudadanos de esta república, la cual fué fundada sobre la idea sublime de justicia é igualdad. Tampoco olvidaremos ni dejaremos de exigir aquellos otros derechos garantizaos á nosotros como un pueblo por el solemne compacto y tratado entre el Gobierno de los Estados Unidos y el de la República de México conocido como el Tratado de Guadalupe Hidalgo.*

[Fifth, that we demand our just rights at all times along with the privileges and immunities that are common to all citizens of this Republic founded on the exalted idea of justice and equality. We also do not forget to demand those additional rights guaranteed to us by the solemn compact and treaty known as the Treaty of Guadalupe Hidalgo between the government of the United States and the Republic of Mexico].

> 6to. *Que los Mejicanos somos nativos del suelo en que vivimos, y no extranjeros; que en todo tiempo los principios del derecho universal han sido reconocidos por nuestro pueblo, y hemos tratado con hospitalidad y deferencia á los pobladores de habla inglesa que vinieron á compartir con nosotros las vicisitudes de la primera población de este suelo; que nos adherimos firmemente á la creencia de una justicia universal, que es el complemento de la ley natural; y la cual demanda que nadie sea excluido del goce de todos aquellos derechos y privilegios acordados á los más favorecidos ciudadanos de un gobierno.*

[Sixth, we Mexicans are natives to the land where we live and not foreigners, that at all times the principles of universal rights have been recognized in our community and that we have treated with hospitality and distinction those English-speaking settlers that have come to share the hardships endured by the first settlers of this land, that we adhere firmly to the belief in universal justice that is a compliment to natural law and which demands that no one be excluded from the enjoyment of those rights and privileges accorded to the most favored citizens of the government.] (ibid, 81–82)

Barela's intervention in the matter did not end with the speechmaking at the Trinidad protest rally. Fernández reports that among his first acts as a newly elected Senator at the next session of the Colorado legislature was to introduce a measure to nullify Judge Yeaman's decision. Fernández savors the victory of the bill's passage for his readers by noting, "La oposición al proyecto fué grande, pero los razonamientos expuestos por el Senador Barela fueron tan poderosos, sus esfuerzos tan persistentes y sus razones tan convincentes que su proyecto pasó y la disposición del Juez Yeaman quedó sin efecto y el Juez en ridículo. [Opposition to the bill was great but the reasons put forth by Senator Barela were so powerful, his efforts so persistent and his reasons so convincing that the bill was passed and the disposition of Judge Yeaman was without effect and the Judge was made to look ridiculous.] (ibid., 87) Beyond Barela's censure of the good judge is Barela's longevity as a public official. His tenure and his contravention of racist and elitist social engineering in Colorado is not easily dismissed. Fernández repeatedly calls his readers' attention the significance of that tenure:

> Los cuarenta años que el Senador Barela ha estado en la legislatura han sido para él una continua lucha en pro de sus constituyentes y especialmente en pro de proteger á su raza, cuyo sólo hecho debía de merecer más común y absoluto reconocimiento de parte de cada hispano americano que le conoce y que no puede negar los beneficios del Senador Barela hacia su pueblo.

> [The forty years that Senator Barela has been in the legislature have, for him, been a continuous struggle in favor of his constituents and especially in favor of the protection of his race, a single fact that should be more commonly and more decisively recognized by each Hispano who knowing him cannot deny Senator Barela's benefits to his community.] (ibid., 215)

The complexity of Fernández's description is matched by the diversity of Barela's interventions in his society. Fernández writes of Barela's disinterested altruism (51), but also of the inclusion of his portrait among those of 15 other prominent Coloradans in the rotunda of the state capitol building (167); of his defense of Mexicano land grants (127) and of his membership in Anglo-dominated civic associations (257); his defense of New Mexico (his birth place) in its bid for statehood (242) and of his penchant for raising fine racing horses (400); of his work in creating Baca county in recognition of Hispanic pioneering efforts in southern Colorado (93) and his work in establishing the Columbus Day holiday in Colorado (190); of his call for the return of war trophies taken from Mexico during the 1846-1848 war (152) and his collaboration with the Díaz dynasty (122); of his commutation of the death sentence for Librado Mora, an Hispano found guilty of murder (190) and of his passage of legislation that would force prisoners in Colorado to labor in the construction of the state's roads (258); his support of women's suffrage (160) and his preoccupation over not having a male heir (Dedication).

Much of the above suggests that Barela openly courted fame and basked in the public recognition it brought him, albeit, that the such self-aggrandizement was highly disapproved of in Barela's cultural group. Fernández's mission as a biographer-confidante is clear. His role is to democratize aggrandizement and pretentiousness and to refract Barela's achievement across the whole of the Spanish-speaking community in southern Colorado, New Mexico and the greater Southwest. This axiology of purpose constitutes a chief characteristic of this formative moment in Mexican American biographical inscription and it is one that must remain in any re-reading of the Barela biography.

Works Consulted—Primary Sources

"Barela Helped Life Blossom in the Trinidad Area," *Trinidad Plus,* Trinidad, Colorado, February 28, 1990.

Biografía de D. Jesús María Barela escrita por Josefa Ortiz esposa de Casimiro Barela, printed monograph, Colorado Historical Society, Denver, Colorado.

"Casimiro Barela: "The Perpetual Senator," *Trinidad Chronicle-News,* Trinidad, Colorado (no date).

"Conquistadores Influenced State," *Pueblo Chieftan,* Pueblo, Colorado, June 6, 1971.

"Cuarenta años de legislador ó la vida del Senador Casimiro Barela," El Progreso Publishing Company Circular, August, 1911, Trinidad Public Library.

Encyclopedia of Biography of Colorado: History of Colorado by William N. Byers, Volume I, Chicago: Century Publishing and Engraving Co., 1901: 330-331.

"En Memoria del Finado Senador de Colorado, Don Casimiro Barela," *El Nuevo Mexicano,* Santa Fe, New Mexico, December 30, 1920.

"Early Trinidad Legislator Called Perpetual Senator," *Pueblo Chieftan,* Pueblo, Colorado, April 3, 1966.

Fernández, Emilio, E. *Cuarenta Años de Legislador: La vida de don Casimiro Barela.* Trinidad: Compañía Publicista de El Progreso, 1911.

Hunt, Inez. *The Barela Brand,* Colorado Springs: Instructional Services Colorado Springs Public Schools, 1971.

History of Colorado, Volume II, by Frank Hall for the Rocky Mountain Historical Company, Chicago: Blakely Printing Co., 1890: 312, 535, 536, 546, 547.

History of Colorado, Volume III, Chicago: S. J. Clark Publishing Co., 1918: 666-670.

History of Colorado: Biographical, Five Volumes, Volume V, Denver: Linderman Co., 1927: 439-440.

Representative Men of Colorado in the Nineteenth Century, Denver: Rowell Art Publishing Co., 1902: 16.

"Senator Casimiro Barela Draft (*sic*) First Colorado Constitution," *Nuestras Raíces,* 2, 4, (October, 1990): 154-155.

"Senator Barela Shot," *Trinidad Chronicle-News* (no date).

Sketches and Portraitures of the State Officers and Members of the Ninth General Assembly of Colorado, Denver: Carson, Hurst & Harper, 1893.

Secondary Sources

Bakhtin, M. M. *Art and Answerability: Early Philosophical Essays by M. M. Bakhtin.* Translation and notes by Vadim Liapunov. Austin: University of Texas Press, 1990.

Clifford, James, "Hanging Up Looking Glasses at Odd Corners: Ethnobiographic Prospects," in *Studies in Biography,* Daniel Aaron, editor. Cambridge: Harvard University Press, 1978 : 41-56.

Denzin, Norman, K. *Interpretive Biography.* Newbury Park: Sage Publications, 1989.

Deutsch, Sarah. *No Separate Refuge: Culture, Class and Gender on an Anglo-Hispanic Frontier in the American Southwest, 1880-1940.* Oxford: Oxford University Press, 1987.

Gilmore, Michael T. "Eulogy as Symbolic Biography: The Iconography of Revolutionary Leadership, 1776-1826," in *Studies in Biography*, Daniel Aaron, editor. Cambridge: Harvard University Press, 1978 : 131-157.

Gómez Quiñones, Juan. *Roots of Chicano Politics: 1640-1940.* Albuquerque: University of New Mexico, 1994.

Gonzales, Rodolfo "Corky." *I Am Joaquín.* New York: Bantam Books, 1967.

Meketa, Jacqueline. *Legacy of Honor.* Albuquerque: University of New Mexico Press, 1986.

Meléndez, A. Gabriel. *So All Is Not Lost: The Poetics of Print in Nuevomexicano Communities, 1834-1958.* Albuquerque: University of New Mexico Press, 1997.

Rewa, Michael P. *Reborn as Meaning: Panegyrical Biography From Isocrates to Walton.*

White, Hayden. *Tropics of Discourse: Essays in Cultural Criticism.* Baltimore: Johns Hopkins, 1979.

Notes

[1] The translations to English from newspapers and other primary sources are my own except in the case of Rafaél Chacón's memoirs; in this case I have used Jacqueline Dorgan Meketa's 1986 edition. In citing these sources I have elected to quote them in their original form noting only on rare occasion instances where anglicisms, common useage or grammatical form obstructs the meaning or intent of the writer.

[2] Of the one hundred and forty-six *bocetos* or profiles included in the book, six are of prominent women in the *Nuevomexicano* community. Read also included group profiles representing the participation of women in development of New Mexico. Included in these descriptions is the work of the

Sisters of Charity and the Sisters of Loretto.

[3] An original copy of this work formed part of the small library kept by my own family. For years I spied the small volume wedged between our set of encyclopedias and the family Bible, not knowing nor suspecting its significance. I am grateful to my mother and father for guarding and keeping this very valuable cultural heirloom through the many years of their marriage. It is one I have turned to often in doing this study.

[4] A biographical profile in Read's *Historia Ilustrada* provides the whole of what is known about Fernández. It reads, "José Emilio Fernández was born at Trinidad, Colorado, April 10, 1882, the son of Jesús María Fernández, a prominent figure in the 70s in Taos County and Mrs. Rosita Martínez. Mr. Fernández was educated in the country schools of Colorado. At the age of 15 he taught at a private school at Catskill, New Mexico and started his first public school at Gulnore, Colorado, December 12, 1898. He taught in the public schools until 1907 when he took charge of *El Progreso* of Trinidad, Colorado. At 14 Mr. Fernández was assistant postmaster at Madrid, Colorado. Since 1907 he has been writing several Spanish works and in May, 1911, he wrote in Spanish *Forty Years as a Legislator,* or *Biography of Senator Casimiro Barela.* At present Mr. Fernández is writing Senator Barela's Biography in English. Mr. Fernández has also been prominent in politics in Las Animas County for the last five years" (Read 1911, 750).

[5] Writing in a circular promoting the publication of the biography, poet and attorney, Eusebio Chacón, could not help but appeal to this same shared valuation when he remarks, "Mr. Fernández paints all with good result, placing here and there a light commentary of his own, adding at another point a deep felt apostrophe, and ending with some sentence of admiration." Book circular, *Cuarenta años de legislador,* Trinidad, Colorado, August, 1911.

[6] "She Collects the Past," by Cyd Shewchuk, *Colorado Springs Sun,* Colorado Springs, Colorado, November 10, 1972.

[7] "Mrs. Inez Hunt Receives Award," *Colorado Springs Sun,* May 21, 1970.

[8] "Inez Hunt Takes Assesors On 'Ghost-Hunting' Tour," *Colorado Springs Gazette-Tribune,* Colorado Springs, Colorado, September 6, 1967.

[9] "Desire—It's What Makes An Author," by Donnie Smith, *Colorado Springs Sun,* October 10, 1971.

[10] "Author Uses Pen to Nail Colorado's Ghosts," by Donnie Smith, *Colorado Springs Sun,* no date.

[11] ibid.

[12] Sofía Barela the fifth daughter born to Casimiro and Josefita Ortiz de Barela on January 29, 1874 married Eusebio Chacón. According to Meketa the Chacón-Barela union was the source of great celebration for Casimiro Barela: "He [Casimiro] had three daughters and, being a wealthy, gregarious, important public figure intent on preserving his culture, when his daughter Sofía

married Eusebio Chacón the senator put on a wedding of great proportion at his ranch named El Porvenir. It was reported that on the occasion of the November 8, 1891, wedding almost the entire population of Trinidad and Las Animas county was present." (1986, 406 n 37).

[13] "She Collects the Past," by Cyd Shewchuk, *Colorado Springs Sun,* November 12, 1972.

[14] A *Colorado Springs Sun* reporter informed the public that the response from the District 11 administrators to Hunt's first book, *The Adventures of Barney Ford —A Runaway Slave,* was extremely positive. Another local news story in April, 1974 notes the enthusiam, "Dr. William Liddle, District 11 director of elementary education, said pupils responded very well to the Barney Ford story in [*sic*] they will find the "Barela Brand" equally interesting. "Not only children from minority groups but all children should be inspired by these two men. They overcame extreme hardship to become prosperous businessmen but more importantly they also contributed to the welfare of others." "District 11 Classes Use Biography by Inez Hunt," *Colorado Springs Tribune-Gazette,* April 4, 1974.

[15] "Inez Hunt, Wanetta Draper Combine to Write About Colorado's Ghosts," *Colorado Springs Gazette-Tribune,* May 18, 1969.

[16] It is not difficult to imagine that a man in Barela's position would have been disliked, perhaps even despised by political enemies, litigants, dismissed employees, even estranged family members. Fernández records the attempt on Barela's life in Hoehne, Colorado on the evening of October 31, 1896. In this incident Barela was shot in the face but rather miraculously was wounded only superficially. The motive for the attack was never fully known, although newspaper accounts suggest that Barela's political enemies had hired his assailants. Less violent enmities also surfaced. One involved a falling out between Casimiro Barela and the New Mexican editor, Felipe Maximiliano Chacón. While at *El Independiente* in Las Vegas, New Mexico, Chacón kept a running attack on Barela for several years beginning in 1915. Chacón, who formerly had been a good friend of Barela's apparently parted ways with Barela after a business deal between the two men soured. Chacón published a number of very venomous editorials accusing Barela of being a dishonest and corrupt politico. The bilious sentiment of Chacón's newspaper pieces is expressed even by their use of headlines which by contemporary standards would be considered libelous: "Al viejo babas," *El Anunciador,* Trinidad, Colorado, April 20, 1915, "El viejo babas Barela," *El Anunciador,* Trinidad, Colorado, April 20, 1918, "Ex-Senador, idolo roto y fracasado del C. F. & I.," *El Anunciador,* Trinidad, Colorado, May 11, 1918.

En torno a Joaquín Murrieta: Historia y literatura

Luis Leal
University of California at Santa Barbara

I

Antes de entrar en materia es necesario que me detenga con el propósito de hacer algunos comentrios sobre el método histórico. El término, como todo concepto crítico, requiere un deslinde, ya que se presta a diversas interpretaciones. Por ejemplo, se puede referir a la historia de la literatura, ya sea de la literatura en general, de aquélla de una nación o un grupo étnico, o la de una modalidad literaria, como la poesía, la ficción, el drama; o la de un género, ya sea la poesía lírica, la novela histórica, etc.; o a las formas, como el soneto, el romance o el corrido, para mencionar sólamente tres de ellas. Al mismo tiempo, el historiador que aplique el método histórico puede cubrir cronológicamente todos los tiempos, o limitarse a una época, un período, o una década.

Una variante del método histórico es aquella que se detiene a examinar las relaciones entre la historia propiamente dicha y la literatura, dedicando espacio sobre todo al examen de las fuerzas históricas que determinan la naturaleza de la obra literaria. Este enfoque, durante el siglo pasado y parte del presente, abusó del método, aplicando conceptos de la crítica histórica positivista, como el de causa y efecto, el del progreso, el de la objetividad y otros. La obra era interpretada a través de hechos históricos concretos, supuestamente objetivos, resultado de la investigación científica. No menos importante era la idea de interpretar la obra literaria atribuyéndole las características culturales de un pueblo durante cierta época, lo que dio lugar a la crítica nacionalista, esto es, el deseo de interpretar la obra literaria con el propósito de descubrir sus características nacionales. A la literatura de hispanoamérica, por ejemplo, se le aplicó el concepto del tropicalismo, sin hacer distinciones entre regiones tropicales y otras áreas no tropicales como el altiplano, la pampa, los desiertos, etcétera. También importante fue la separación que se hizo de la historia y la literatura, atribuyendo objetividad a la primera y subjetividad a la segunda. Por lo tanto, se consideraba que era imposible que la literatura trascendiera la historia. No es hasta las primeras décadas del siglo veinte cuando los formalists rusos establecen la crítica literaria como una disciplina independiente de la historia. La obra literaria deja de ser un objeto cultural para convertirse en un objeto de arte, independiente de la historia. Por lo tanto, fue necesario establecer una ciencia de la literatura, independiente de las otras ciencias. Es curioso que se use el concepto "ciencia," que implica objetividad, para estudiar lo que se considera subjetivo. Sea como sea, los formalistas, para interpretar la literatura, aplican un enfoque literario, no histórico, sociológico, psicológico, político o propio de otra ciencia positiva. Además, eran los críticos literarios los que debían estudiar la literatura y no los especialistas en otras ramas del saber humano, para quienes la literatura sólo tiene un valor utilitario, ya sea como fuente de información o para apoyar teorías científicas.

Para los formalistas, en cambio, lo importante en el texto literario es la forma, el lenguaje, la estructura. El mundo lingüístico en la obra es lo que hay que estudiar, no su contexto, esto es, el mundo histórico que la produce. La literatua deja de ser referencial, deja de tener un valor documental, deja de representar valores históricos; lo cual indica que no puede ser explicada por medio de los métodos históricos, que tienen como base lo referencial. Si existe una historia literaria, debe de ser la historia de las formas. Eso es precisamente lo que en 1957 propuso Northrop Frye en su ensayo "The Historical Method," el primero de los cuatro que componen su libro *Anatomy of Cirticism*. Según Frye, la historia literaria debe de incluir no solamente un estudio diacrónico de las formas, que va de lo mítico a lo irónico, sino también el aspecto sincrónico, esto es, el estudio de las estructuras literarias. A pesar de las nuevas tendencias críticas, lo mismo que del llamado nuevo historicismo, el método histórico tradicional no ha desaparecido, si bien modificado y ejercido principalmente por críticos de la literatura y no por historiadores o especialistas en otras materias, como ocurría en el pasado. Para ilustrar los problemas a los cuales tiene que enfrentarse el crítico que enfoca el texto literario a través del método histórico paso a discutir el problema de las relaciones entre la historia y la ficción según se presenta en las obras dedicadas a la vida y las aventuras de Joaquín Murrieta.

II

Los dos más famoso historiadores norteamericanos que se ocuparon de Murrieta como ser histórico fueron Hubert Howe Bancroft y Theodore Hittell, el primero en su *California Pastoral* (1888) y su *History of California* (1890), y el segundo en su *History of California* (1898). Bancroft, en *California Pastoral*, incluyó un capítulo sobre los bandidos californianos, en el cual dice: "Permítanme que les presente algunos de los más famosos salteadores, quienes tienen, sin duda alguna, tanto derecho de figurar en las páginas de la historia como los que se hacen famosos robando sin salirse de las reglas aceptadas por la sociedad" (1888: 644-45; mi trad.). Murrieta aparece allí como persona histórica, sin cuestionar su existencia. Ese capítulo se convierte, en su historia de

California, en una larga nota sobre los *banditti* californianos, entre quienes predominan los mexicanos (1890: 203-205). Para reconstruir la vida de Joaquín en ambos libros Bancroft se vale de obras consideradas como literarias, esto es, ficticias, cuya información acepta sin cuestionar su historicidad. Hittell es un poco más riguroso en su método, pues dice: "Joaquin, according to the best but still to a great extent unreliable reports about him, was born in Sonora and came to California soon after the discovery of gold" (1898: 713). También: "It would be impossible, on account of the numerous contradictions as well as the apocryphal accounts of the doings of Joaquin, and his band, to affirm with certainty as to many of the murders and robberies attributed to him. It is certain, however, that he was for several years at the head of a desperate band of villains" (1898: 721-722). Ambos historiadores se valen de la información contenida en el libro de *Yellow Bird* (pseudónimo de John Rollin Ridge), *The Life and Adventures of Joaquin Murieta*, publicado en 1854, un año después de la supuesta muerte de Murrieta. Para caracterizarlo utilizan la segunda edición de esa obra de Ridge, publicada en 1871, aunque sin mencionarla.

Un historidor más reciente, Joseph Henry Jackson, cree que fueron precisamente Bancroft y Hittell quienes dieron autenticidad histórica a Murrieta. Dice Jackson: "By this time [1880], the Murieta legend was doing very well indeed. Joaquin had grown far beyond his original, purely local stature. All that that was necessary to give this Murieta the final stamp of authenticity was acceptance by a recognized historian. Two men stepped forward to perform this office, Hubert Howe Bancroft and Theodore Hittell, whose histories of California have been standard reference works ever since they were published in the 1880s" (1955: xxxviii). Hoy, entre los histiadores, sin embargo, predomina la tendencia a considerar a Murrieta como un ser histórico; así lo presentan en sus historias, entre otros, Remi Nadeau, Frank F. Latta y Manuel Rojas.

III

A pesar de su corta vida y su corta actuación, Joaquín Murrieta dio materia a historiadores y fabuladores para un buen número de composiciones. Numerosos son los poetas que lo cantan y los novelistas que lo han convertido en un héroe mítico Si bien la información histórica concreta sobre Murrieta es escasa, las novelas en las cuales aparece como protagonista son numerosas; y lo mismo puede decirse de otras formas artísticas como el drama y la poesía.

Desde la perspectiva de la crítica histórica, los problemas que se presentan al estudiar la literatura sobre Murrieta son numerosos. En este corto estudio sólo podremos mencionar los principales, que nos parecen ser las relaciones entre la historia y la ficción, los plagios de la obra de John Rollin Ridge y la nacionalidad de Joaquín, ya que México y Chile se lo disputan. Si bien ya en 1850 los periódicos de California hablan de un tal Joaquín, a quien se le atribuyen innumerables muertes, robo de caballos y otras atrocidades, el nombre completo del héroe no aparece hasta el 17 de mayo de 1853, al lado de otros cuatro Joaquines: Joaquín Muriati (¿Joaquín Murrieta?), Joaquín Ocomorenia (o sea Joaquín Ochoa Moreno) Joaquín Valenzuela, Joaquín Botellier (o sea Joaquín Batelas) y Joaquín Carillo (o sea Joaquín Carrillo), escasos dos meses y siete días antes de su supuesta muerte el 24 de julio de 1853.

En la historia, Joaquín, como nombre genérico para designar a un bandido mexicano a quien se le atribuyen toda clase de crímenes, aparece primero en los periódicos, a partir de 1850. En la ficción el primer relato, "Joaquin the Mountain Robber, or the Bandits of the Sierra Nevada," no aparece hasta el año siguiente de su muerte, publicado en el *Pacific Police Gazette* en mayo de 1854. En julio del mismo año la *California Police Gazette*, en sus dos primeros números, incluyó las primeras cuatro partes de la historia, "Joaquín, the Mountain Robber! Or the Guerilla of California". Este título sugiere que se trata del mismo texto de la *Pacific Police Gazette,* lo que no podrá ser esclarecido hasta que no se encuentren ejemplares de esas gacetas. Lo que sí sabemos es que en estas tempranas historias sobre Joaquín no se identifica todavía al héroe con el apellido Murrieta. Pero si el nombre completo de Joaquín no se encuentra en esos tempranos relatos, ya lo hallamos un mes más tarde, escrito con una *ere,* en la obra de Ridge), publicada, como ya dijimos, en 1854.

Muy discutido ha sido el problema de la veracidad histórica del libro de este autor. Para algunos es una simple novela, una ficción inventada por Ridge. El historiador Jackson, por ejemplo, acepta la idea de que Murrieta, como hombre de carne y hueso, existió, pero que la biografía de Ridge, aunque basada en su vida, es pura ficción: "It is true that in the early years of the gold rush there was a Murieta. But it was Ridge's *Life* of that outlaw, as preposterous a fiction as any the Dime Libraries ever invented, that sent this vague bandit on his way to be written into the California histories" (1955: xi-xii). Para crear su obra, dice, Ridge se vale de una estratagema muy común, el pretender que se escribe una historia verdadera, cuando lo que se hace es usar elementos folklóricos e imitar los episodios melodramáticos de las novelas baratas ["dime novel variety"], lo mismo que el uso de elegantes discursos en boca del héroe y la presencia de actos y provocaciones vívidamente imaginados. Estos y otros historiadores consideran a Ridge como el creador de la leyenda de Murrieta, no como su biógrafo, y citan posibles fuentes ficticias.

En cambio, ya el editor de la primera edición del libro de Ridge, en su corto Prefacio, había dicho que *Yellow Bird*, "no ha lanzado su libro al mundo descuidadamente, sin autoridad para sus asertos. En general, se verá que [lo que dice] es estrictamente verdadero" (1955: 4; mi trad.). Pero tal vez fue criticado por haber dicho lo anterior, ya que en la edición de 1871 se hace referencia de cuando en cuando a fuentes de información que no aparecen en la primera edición, sin duda para contestar a los que dudaban de la veracidad de los hechos narrados. A pesar de ello, la edición de 1871 se acerca más a la ficción que la de 1854.

IV

Pronto las obras de ficción sobre la vida de Murrieta, con elementos históricos revisionistas, se multiplican. En varias novelas y en el drama de Charles
E. B. Howe, *Joaquín Murieta de Castillo, the Celebrated California Bandit*,
publicado en 1858, el conflicto no es entre Murrieta y sus hombres y los anglo-
americanos, como en Ridge, sino entre Joaquín y pérfidos intrigantes
mexicanos o californios. La ficción ha logrado cambiar la historia, como pode-
mos ver en las novelas *Joaquin, the Claude Duval of California, or the
Marauder of the Mines* (1865), de Henry Llewellyn Williams; *Joaquin, the
Saddle King* (1881), de Joseph E. Badger; *A Plaything of the Gods* (1912), de
Charles Caldwell Park; *The Crimson Trail of Joaquin Murieta* (1928), de Ernest
Klette; *The Robin Hood of El Dorado* (1932), de Walter Noble Burns; *Gringo
Gold, A Story of Joaquin Maurieta the Bandit* (193), de Dane Coolidge, y *The
Dream Ends in Fury* (1949), de Samuel Anthony Peeples.

En la novela de Williams—calificada por Jackson como "a fearfully bad
novel" (1955: xl)— Joaquín no muere asesinado por el capitán Harry Love y su
acordada, sino ahogado en un lago cuando el barco en que se encuentra se
hunde. La obra es de interés, sin embargo, porque en ella se mitifica a Joaquín
comparándolo con Claude Duval, el bandolero inglés del siglo diecisiete. El crítico Kent L. Steckmesser, en cambio, humaniza a Murrieta comparándolo con
Billy the Kid (1859-81), el famoso bandolero que vivió la mayor parte de su
vida en Nuevo México, donde murió a manos del Sheriff Pat F. Garrett, su biógrafo.

Otra transformación de Joaquín la encontramos en la novela de Joseph E.
Badger, *Joaquin, the Saddle King* (1881), en la cual Murrieta es un joven
español rubio que apoya a los revolucionarios texanos y después pelea al lado
de los norteamericanos en la guerra del 47. Alguien le pregunta por qué adora
a los americanos y Joaquín dice: "¡Ah! porque son muy hombres; he vivido con
ellos, he comido, peleado y cabalgado con ellos. Estoy orgulloso de que sean
mis amigos. Cómo deseo que fueran mis compatriotas" (citado por Paredes
1973: 182). Así, al rechazar su cultura, Murrieta se convierte también, en la
novela de Badger, en un héroe de todos los norteamericanos.

V

El crítico que trate de esclarecer la historia de un texto literario a veces se
tiene que convertir en verdadero detective. Eso ocurre en el caso de la novela
*Vida y aventuras del más célebre bandido sonorense, Joaquín Murrieta; sus
grandes proezas en California*, de la cual existen varias ediciones —algunas
publicadas en Los Angeles antes de los 20— todas ellas atribuidas al novelista
mexicano Ireneo Paz. Sin embargo, al consultar la *Bibliografía de novelistas
mexicanos* del cuidadoso bibliógrafo Juan B. Iguínez, descubrimos que en la

lista de novelas de Ireneo Paz no se encuentra la dedicada a Murrieta. Esto despertó nuestras sospechas y decidimos investigar la omisión en tan prestigiosa bibliografía. Al revisar las varias ediciones que existen de la obra, descubrimos que en ninguna de ellas se dice que Paz es el autor; solamente que fue publicada en México, en la la Tipografía y Encuadernación de Ireneo Paz, 2a.de Relox número 4. ¿A qué se debe, pues, que se le atribuya? Sin duda a que en 1925 apareció en Chicago un libro titulado *Life and Adventures of the Celebrated Bandit Joaquin Murrieta; His Exploits in the State of California.* Translated from the Spanish of Ireneo Paz by Frances P. Bell. La traductora, no conociendo el historial del libro, pensó que era obra del editor, Ireneo Paz. Y se podría creer que lo es, como lo ha afirmado el mismo Octavio Paz, nieto de don Ireneo. En las bibliotecas, esta edición atribuida a don Ireneo aparece bajo su numbre; la más antigua es de 1904.

La historia de este texto es más que complicada. He aquí lo que hemos podido deslindar. En 1939 el historiador Jackson ya había notado las semejanzas entre la traducción de Bell y la obra de Ridge. Lo que no explica es la complicada historia de la trayectoria del texto, desde Ridge hasta Bell. He aquí lo que hemos investigado aplicando el método histórico. En 1859 aparece una edición pirata, anónima, de la obra de Ridge en la revista *Police Gazette* de San Francisco, en la cual se introducen algunas variantes que nos ayudan a trazar el origen de ediciones posteriores. Uno de esos cambios es el del nombre de la amiga de Joaquín, que en la obra de Ridge se llama Rosita, y en la edición pirata "Carmela"; además, cuando ésta muere la reemplaza un nuevo personaje, "Clarina," que no aparece en la obra original de Ridge. Murrieta sigue siendo considerado como sonorense. Esta edición pirata, llamada "Carmela-Clarina," es la que fue traducida, primero al francés y después al castellano, y la que dio a conocer a Murrieta en Europa y el mundo hispano, pero sobre todo en México y Chile, donde se convirtió, como en California, en héroe popular y literario. El francés Robert Hyenne, que había estado en California, tradujo la versión *Police Gazette* y la publicó en París en la imprenta de Lécrivan et Toubon en 1862 bajo el título *Un bandit californien (Joaquin Murieta).* Esta edición, de la cual existe un ejemplar en la Biblioteca Nacional de París, es conocida solamente a través de las traducciones españolas, la primera de las cuales es la que hizo el dramaturgo chileno Carlos Morla Vicuña y que publicó en Santiago de Chile en 1867 bajo el título *El bandido chileno Joaquín Murieta*, y firmó con las iniciales C.M. Existen numerosas ediciones de esta traducción, algunas atribuidas a un tal Profesor Acigar. Otras aparecen con el nombre de Hyenne y otras anónimas, como la que se publicó en Santa Bárbara en 1881 en el periódico *La Gaceta,* que quedó incompleta. Murrieta aparece como chileno solamente en la traducción de Morla y las reediciones de esa traducción. Que Murrieta fue chileno lo creyó nada menos que el poeta Pablo Neruda. En la "Antecedencia" de la cantata que le dedicó en 1966, *Fulgor y muerte de Joaquín Murieta,* nos dice: "Pero Joaquín Murieta fue chileno. Yo conozco las pruebas. Pero estas páginas no tienen por objeto probar hechos o sombras" (10). Existe una edición de la traducción de Hyenne al español, sin año de publicación, que lleva el pie de imprenta "Barcelona: V. Acha, Editor | México: Maucci Hermanos", y el título *El bandido chileno Joaquín Murieta en California.* Según parece, no tenemos información concreta, la edición Acha/ Maucci Hermanos, publicada bajo el nombre de Roberto Hyenne, pero con diferente ilustración en la cubierta y, como todas estas ediciones, sin año de publicación, es la edición que en 1904 Ireneo Paz publicó en su tipografía en México, con el título, *Vida y aventuras del más célebre bandido sonorense Joaquín Murrieta: sus grandes proezas en California.* El título es casi idéntico al de Ridge, al cual se le agregó la palabra "sonorense." Como el libro no se publicó bajo el nombre de Hyenne, o Morla, se ha creído que es obra original de don Ireneo, lo cual no se afirma en ninguna de las ediciones conocidas. Lo que hizo Ireneo Paz fue solamente retocar el texto con el objeto de recobrar la nacionalidad mexicana de Murrieta, para lo cual le agregó al título la palabra "sonorense," que no aparece en ninguna de las otras ediciones españolas traducidas del francés. Comparando algunos párrafos, como los siguientes, nos es fácil verificar que el texto de Ireneo Paz es una refundición de la traducción al español que se hizo de la traducción francesa de Hyenne, quien la tomó de la versión *Police Gazette* , así como ésta es una refundición de la obra de Ridge. Ejemplo:

RIDGE: "Joaquin Murieta was a Mexican, born in the province of Sonora of respectable parents and educated in the schools of Mexico" (1955: 8).
PG: "Joaquin was born of respectable parents in Sonora, Mexico, where he received a good education"(1969: 2).
MORLA: "Joaquín vio la luz en Santiago. Su familia originaria de la misma ciudad y muy honorable bajo todos sus aspectos, le hizo educar convenientemente y tuvo excelentes maestros" (p. 5).
PAZ: "Joaquín Murrieta nació en la República de los Estados Unidos Mexicanos. Su familia, originaria de Sonora, y respetable bajo todos conceptos, le hizo criar en su pueblo natal, en donde recibió una buena educación" (1953: 5).

El siguiente ejemplo es importante porque confirma que Murrieta era mexicano y no chileno. Ridge no menciona esta aventura, que aparece primero en el texto del *Police Gazette,* lo que indica que los traductores al español usaron esa edición.

PG: "Shortly after his arrival at the City of Mexico, he called upon one of his father's old friends, señor Estudillo, and presented a letter of recommendation. El Señor received him warmly and soon obtained for him a situation as groom in the magnificent stables of President Lopez de Santa Anna" (1969: 2).
MORLA: "Habiendo muerto su padre en esta fecha [1845], se trasladó a casa de un antiguo amigo de su familia, el señor Estudillo, y este buen hombre le hizo objeto de una cogida excelente. Muy pronto su protector obtuvo para él una plaza de oficial en una

de las compañias del regimiento que servía de escolta al Presidente Bulnes" (p. 5).
PAZ: "En 1845 Joaquín abandonó su pueblo en Sonora para ir a buscar fortuna en la
Capital. [...] Llegado a México , se dirigió a la casa de un antiguo amigo de su padre,
el Sr. Estudillo, entrególe una carta de recomendación, la cual fue muy bien acogido
por ese señor. "Muy pronto su protector obtuvo para él un destino como palafrenero
en las caballerizas del Presidente López de Santa Anna" (1953, 5).

Es obvio que Joaquín Murrieta no pudo ser chileno y mexicano al mismo
tiempo. No queremos insinuar que el método histórico sea superior a ningún otro.
Sólo hacer ver que para resolver ciertos problemas que presentan algunos textos literarios su uso es indispensable. Si nos propusiéramos hacer un estudio del
discurso narrativo de Ireneo Paz basándonos en su edición de la vida de
Murrieta, sin saber que no es de él, cometeríamos un imperdonable error.

Obras Citadas

Acigar, El Profesor. *El caballero chileno bandido de California: única y ver-
dadera historia de Joaquín Murieta.* Barcelona: Biblioteca Hércules, sin
fecha.
Badger, Joseph E. *Joaquin, the Saddle King.* New York: Beadle & Adams,
1881. "The Bell Dime Library."
———. *Joaquin, The Terrible.* New York: Beadle & Adams, 1881; Reimpr.
Brookling, NY: Dime Novel Club, 1947.
Bancroft, Herbert Howe. *California Pastoral 1760-1848.* San Francisco, CA,
1888.
———. *History of California.* vol. 24 of *The Works of Herbert Howe
Bancroft.* San Francisco, CA, 1890.
Bell, Frances P. *ver* Paz, Ireneo.
Burns, Walter Noble. *The Robin Hood of El Dorado: The Saga of Joaquin
Murrieta, Famous Outlaw of California's Age of Gold.* New York:
Coward-McCann, 1932.
California Police Gazette. "Joaquín, the Mountain Robber! Or the Guerilla of
California". 1-2, July 1854 (cuatro capítulos).
———. "Life of Joaquin Murieta, the Brigand Chief of California." San
Francisco, 1859.
———. *Idem.* San Francisco, CA: Buttler and Co., 1861.
———. *Joaquin Murieta, the Brigand Chief of California.* Ed. Francis P.
Farquhar. San Francisco, CA: Grabhorn Press, 1932.
———. *Idem.* Fresno, CA: Fresno Valley Publishers, 1969. Supplement of
Notes by Raymund F. Wood and Charles W. Clough. C.M. *ver* Morla
Vicuña.

Coolidge, Dane. *Gringo Gold. A Story of Joaquin Murieta the Bandit.* New York: E. P. Dutton & Co., 1939; reimpr. Boston: Gregg Press, 1980, 1981.

Corcoran, May S. "Robber Joaquin, As Seen in Statutes of California Legislature Journals and by One Living Ranger." *Grizzly Bear* (June, 1921): 4.

Frye, Northrop. *Anatomy of Criticism: Four Essays.* Princeton, NJ: Princeton University Press, 1957.

Gaceta, La. "Vida y aventuras de Joaquín Murrieta." Capts. I-IV. Santa Bárbara, CA, Año 2, números 98-106 (Junio 1—Julio 30, 1881).

Hittell, Theodore H. *History of California.* 4 vols. San Francisco, CA: W. T. Stone, 1898.

Howe, Charles E.B. *A Dramatic Play Entitled Joaquín Murieta de Castillo, the Celebrated California Bandit.* San Francisco, CA: Commercial Book and Job Steam Printing Establishment, 1858.

Hyenne, Robert. *Un bandit californien (Joaquin Murieta).* Paris: Le'crivan et Toubon, 1862.

———. *El bandido chileno Joaquín Murieta en California.* Ed. Ilustrada. Barcelona: V. Acha, editor / México: Maucci Hnos, sin año de publiación.

———. *Idem.* Trad. del francés por C.M. [Carlos Morla]. Santiago [de Chile]: Centro Editorial "La Prensa", 1906.

———. *Idem.*15a. ed. Valparaiso, Chile: Sociedad Impresora y Litografía Universo, 1910.

———. *Joaquín Murrieta, el bandido chileno en California.* San Antonio, TX: Editorial Martínez, 1926. 2a. ed., 1929.

———. *Vida y aventuras de Joaquín Murieta.* Prólogo de Ricardo Donoso. *Excelsior.* Santiago de Chile, año I (1936), Suplemento No. 1, pp. 31-90.

Iguínez, Juan B. *Bibliografía de novelistas mexicanos.* México: Secretaría de Relaciones Exteriores, 1927, 1926.

Jackson, Joseph Henry. *ver* Ridge, 1955.

Klette, Ernest. *The Crimson Trail of Joaquin Murieta.* Los Angeles, CA: Wetzel Publishing Co., 1928.

Latta, Frank F. *Joaquin Murieta and His Horse Gangs.* Santa Cruz, CA: Bear State Books, 1980.

Life of Joaquin Murieta, Brigand Chief of California. San Francisco, CA: California *Police Gazette*, 1859); 2a. ed. (San Francisco, CA: Buttler and Co., 1861); reimpr. por Francis P. Farquhar. San Francisco, CA: Grabhorn Press, 1932; reedit. Fresno, CA: Valley Publishers, 1969 (ed. facsimilar).

Klette, Ernest. *The Crimson Trail of Joaquin Murieta.* Los Angeles, CA: Wetzel Publishing Co., 1928.

[Morla Viçuña, Carlos]. C.M. *El bandido chileno Joaquín Murrieta en California* [Santiago de Chile: Imprenta de la República, de Jacinto Núñez, 1867].(traducción del francés de Hyenne) [2a. ed., 1874]. 3a. ed. 1879. 15a. ed., *ver* Hyenne, Robert.

Nadeau, Remi. "Joaquin, Hero, Villain, or Myth?" *Westways*, Jan. 1963.

————.*The Real Joaquin Murieta. Calfornia's Gold Rush Bandit: Truth v. Myth.* Santa Barbara, CA: Crest Publications, 1974.

Neruda, Pablo. *Fulgor y muerte de Joaquín Murieta, bandido chileno ajusticiado en Caifornia el 23 de julio de 1853.* Santiago de Chile: Empresa Editorial Zig Zag, 1966; reimpr. 1967. (drama)

Pacific Police Gazette. "Joaquin the Mountain Robber or the Bandits of the Sierra Nevada." May 1954. "No copy of this 'biography' has ever come to light" (Nadeau 1974: 115).

Paredes, Raymund A. "The Image of the Mexican in American Literature." Diss. U of Texas at Austin, 1973.

Park, Charles Caldwell ("Carl Gray"). *A Plaything of the Gods.* Boston: Sherman, French, 1912. [novela]

Paz, Ireneo ed. *Vida y aventuras del más célebre bandido sonorense Joaquín Murrieta; sus grandes proezas en California.* México: Tipografía y Encuadernación de Ireneo Paz, 1904. (ejemplar en la Biblioteca Bancroft de la U de California en Berkeley). 4a. ed. 1908. 5a. ed. Los Angeles, CA: Oscar? Paz y Cía, 1919. 5a. ed. [*sic*] México: Ediciones Don Quijote, 1953.

————. *Life and Adventures of the Celebrated Bandit Joaquín Murrieta. His Exploits in the State of California.* Translated from the Spanish of Ireneo Paz by Frances P. Belle. Chicago: Regan Public Corp., 1925; reimpr. Chicago: Charles T. Powner, 1937.

Ridge, John Rollin ("Yellow Bird"). *The Life and Adventures of Joaquin Murieta, the Celebrated California Bandit.* San Francisco, CA, 1854.

————. *The History of Joaquin Murieta, the King of California Outlaws, Whose Band Ravaged the State in the Early Fifties.* 3rd.[*sic*] ed., "with much and hereto unpublished material." San Francisco, California: Fred MacCrelish, 1871; revised ed. Hollister, CA: Evening Press, 1927.

————. *The Life and Adventures of Joaquin Murieta, the Celebrated California Bandit.*ꞏ New edition with Introduction by Joseph Henry Jackson. Norman: University of Oklahoma Press, 1955.

Rojas, Manuel. "*Joaquín Murrieta, el patrio*". *El "Far West" del México cercenad M*exicali, B.C.: Gobierno del Estado de Baja California, 1986. 2a. ed. corregida. Mexicali, B.C.: Instituto de Cultura de Baja California, 1990.3a. ed. corregida, 1992.

Steckmesser, Kent L. "Joaquin Murieta and Billy the Kid." *Western Folklore* 21.2 (April 1962): 77-82.

Williams, Henry Llewellyn. *Joaquin, the Claude Duval of California, or the Marauder of the Mines.* New York: Pollard & Moss, 1888.

Varela's *Jicoténcal* and the Historical Novel

Rodolfo J. Cortina
University of Houston

Introduction

The novel *Jicoténcal* is the work of Félix Varela, a Cuban priest living in the United States after his death sentence was pronounced *in absentia* by Fernando VII of Spain in 1823. The novel deals with the conquest of Mexico by Hernán Cortés with the help of the Tlaxcalans, bitter rivals of the Aztecs, focusing on the relationship between Xicontencatl, the Youth, who served as chief of the Tlaxcalan army, his forced ally, Cortés, and the maiden, Teutila, whose love for Xicotencatl is part of the non-historical portion of the story. The novel has been called the first historical novel in Spanish, or, at least, in the New World, the first indigenist novel, the first Cuban novel, and one of the first novels of U.S. Hispanic literature.

The purpose of this paper is to examine the contexts in which this text can be read within the tradition of the historical novel. The tradition, as discussed by Gyorgy Lukács in his *Theory of the Novel* and in his *The Historical Novel*, places the novelistic discourse within the philosophical current of historicism as conceived by the Romantics, that is taking into account the idea of a collective subject moving over time and conscious of the act. But in addition to this, it might be interesting to briefly explore the notion of autobiography as personal history, especially since at some level the chain of historical signifiers relate to contemporary signifieds. Further, it might prove instructive to expose those hidden possiblities of reference to a natural history, viewed in anthropological terms, as these reveal philosophical notions on the founding of a civil society. It would probably be better to begin the examination with the more intimate context of autobiography, move to the public historical discourse, and then to the more apparently vague and diffuse level of anthropological—read human archeology—reconstruction.

The Novel as Autobiography

The usual approach for the study of an autobiographical text is to begin by exploring its motives, examining its methods, and divining its meanings. At

450

another level, autobiography has been the subject of its connection to the world of fiction, much like history has been by Hayden White and others. For some, it is not only fictive, but patently not possibly true. But the world of theory has often leaped itself into its own oblivion, so we will keep to the text for now.

When looking at motives, one has to question why would Varela write *Jicoténcal*, and then, having gone to all the trouble, leave off his name? It is in this regard that the speculation on his motives has to be tied to his novelistic methods. By using Greek allegory, he is interested in establishing a link between his world and that of the conquest of Mexico. But it is a connection that may appear difficult to accept given the contemporary reduction of nineteenth-century Cuban writing to those texts that treat the African presence in the island. Naturally, this is so because abolitionism was a code word for independence and it was a way of writing about the political independence based on the emancipation of the slave population. Indeed, Gertrudis Gómez de Avellaneda wrote *Sab* to explore the possibilities of uniting a black male slave to a white female owner. For her the possibility of Cuba was in that union. Yet she also wrote a novel about *Guatemozín* which also deals with the Indian question in the Mexican context.

The question for us remains, why Indians? At one level the answer could be historical—that the Arawaks were victims of Spanish genocide in the Caribbean—but troublesome because Varela's choice is not Hatuey, the Arawak from Hispaniola who goes to Cuba to warn the Indians that the Spaniards were not good gods, but cruel tyrants. Rather, he chooses Xicotencatl, whose grandeur was more evident both within the conquest of Mexico and within the awareness he held about the consequences of not fighting Cortés. Indeed, Varela's identification with his character Jicoténcal, the historical Xicoténcatl, the Youth, is indisputable, since the latter never ceased in his call for his country's freedom from any outside domination, be it Aztec or Spanish, though it was to defend Tlaxcala, from Spain and his desire to confront Cortés that moved the historical figure. Senator Maxiscatzín is his Arango y Parreño, the traitor to the independence of the fatherland. Cortés is his Fernando VII: cruel, astute and deceiving. Tlaxcala is Cuba, Fray Bartolomé the Catholic Church. Perhaps that is the main reason for hiding his authorship of the novel: the speeches which he attrributes to the indigenous populace reveal a dichotomy in his thought about the Church which is very dangerous flowing from a priest's pen, though Varela always kept his personal faith. Diego de Ordaz is his Alacalá Galiano, and Teutila his great love for his country's freedom.

While Varela establishes the allegory, he also works with diptychs. For him, the characters appear in philosophical pairs some in opposition, some in conjunction: for example, Magiscatzin, the treacherous Tlaxcalan senator, is opposed to Xicotencatl the Elder, whose wisdom may diminish with age, but not his loyalty to Tlaxcala; or Cortés and Ordaz, the first being the cruel Spaniard and the second the noble one, or even the analogy between Teutila and

Marina which suggests that example is more powerful than persuasive words. And this may be done with all the characters. But the priest Olmedo appears contraposed to no one except the author, who for his part identifies himself as "el filósofo," not as a priest himself. One may relate his singular identification as the philosopher to the fact that he had been a teacher and a writer of philosophical concepts that revolutionized the Hispanic world. Yet Olmedo is an instrument of Cortés: dull-witted, obedient, blind to all the foibles of the conqueror, and loyal to the Spanish crown without question or doubt. It is small wonder that Varela, who had been maligned by that crown as worn by Fernando VII, would spare the figure of such a servile tool of Spanish imperial policy. It is in the negation of himself as such an instrument, that Varela projects his public persona as that of a philosopher rather than as a priest. In his own life he continued serving the Irish immigrants in New York where as founder of schools and parishes and ultimately as Vicar General, he also found the Spanish ambassador to the Vatican successfully pleading that he not be made Bishop of New York. With his life bedeviled by the long arms of Spanish revenge, including the hiring of an assassin to come to New York from Havana to send him to an early grave, Varela was left with little choice about his feelings for the mother country.

The Novel as History

The most effective critical approach for the study of a historical novel is to begin by learning what is the relationship between narrative and discourse, which may be seen from another angle as to what is the link between telling and showing. In *Jicoténcal* Varela poses the question of legitimate government, of motives and ultimate meanings of the governors and their actions.

The most important lesson of historicism for Varela had been that he, as a public figure, and Cuba, as a Spanish overseas province and potential republic, were elements travelling through historical time. He perceived his existence and that of his home as historically conditioned. The transformations all around him of republics emerging from former Spanish colonies were too large and too real to evade the gaze of even the most oblique observer. He likens all of it to those transformations which took place with the nations of the Mexican main as Cortés moved in with his small army.

Varela portrays the life of Tlaxcala as that of a republic in which civil discourse takes the place of discord. The novel opens with the speeches being presented by those envoys which represent Cortés and Spanish interests. These are followed by reasonable commentaries and allocutions which reveal the practice at the Spanish Cortes under the Spanish liberal regime. Varela's interests in parliamentary discourse and practice included his translation into Spanish of Jefferson's *Handbook of Parliamentary Practice for the Use of the U.S. Senate* which appeared the same year as the novel.

In his description of the events that took place he follows Antonio de Solís whose *Historia de la conquista de México* [History of the Conquest of Mexico] presents the wrenching event as a reasonable enterprise. He does so some twelve times where his mimetic impulse takes him to follow the historian textually, (though one must add that since Solís only takes two pages in his history to tell the story of Xicotencatl, the author could hardly have copied everything that appears in the novel). There is only one exception. In recounting the betrayal by the Spaniards against Moctezuma, Varela follows the more damning account of Las Casas, something that Solís himself anticipates in his history, but which leaves Varela undeterred. The strategic intertextuality reveals the calculus of the novelist in using the historian's words to promote his own views within the walls of fiction. For Lukács this strategy is fundamental to understand two things: the present as seen through the past, and the past as seen from the present. This makes the historical novel a window to the past, but a window with a mirror beyond it looking back through it.

The Novel as Anthropology

From the standpoint of anthropology, the novel opens by positing some implicit questions about the nature of civil society, and like all good questions, suggesting some possible answers. From the start of humankind, one may well wonder which of the possible stories is the story through which we enter civil society; that is, how do we abandon those behaviors that we consider primitive and engage those that we consider civil. Going back to the transition of ape to human we may find very instructive where the story takes a turn from one species to the other, and the answer is not biological, as may be seen immediately. Most ape groups or bands from chimpanzees to gorillas tend to be ruled by an alpha male. This male is the strongest, the most intelligent and the one who gets to eat first, to choose his female for the night first, and so forth. The killing of the alpha male by the rest of the male apes, born of the resentment and envy that each feels makes it possible for a number of things to happen:

1) the first revolution within society in which blood is shed to advance the cause of the rebels,
2) the encounter with guilt which, in turn, will lead to other encounters, among them
   a) exogamy, or marrying away from the group, inherent in which is the organization of the population in clans, families or other divisions to facilitate recognition of available mates and of legal unions, and implicitly accepting incest as a taboo;
   b) the totem or the selection of an animal which, when slaughtered at the feast celebrated on the anniversary of the killing of the alpha male, will represent it;
   c) the divine, or the symbolic anthropofagy devolving from eating the

totemic animal and acknowledging and sharing the sin of having killed
the father of the tribe, and then finding the image of fire in the circle of
dancing around it.

The novel opens with the description of Tlaxcala [Land of Bread] in which,
besides the social commentaries about the absence of castles and palaces that in
European societies have always served to contrast with the hovels of the poor,
the population is divided into four towns or neighborhoods. The people are
described as being belicose, as having suffered, as being frank, not taken with
ostentation, and enemies of effeminacy. Its government is defined as a confederate republic where soverign power rested on a congress or a senate composed
of elected officials from each of the four parts. The executive and the judicial
power resting on the local officials, yet all subordinated to the senate. Each of
the four parts was to be considered as an independent district. There was a
remote memory still remembered that once Tlaxcala had been ruled by one
powerful ruler, but that the people had arisen against his abuse of authority and
having recovered the popular soverignty, established a republic. Their pride and
self-sufficiency prevented them from trading for salt with Moctezuma's vassals
because they were enemies of the Aztecs with whom they were always at war.
Their army was led by a general who was also part of the senate. In short, they
had established a civil society. Reading this account reveals the concerns of the
philosopher in creating a utopia in which all the conditions were to be met. But
like all Edens, there was to be discord which would lead to a Fall. Together with
the Greek allegory stands the figural allegory in which the prophecy of the Fall
is enunciated at the very opening of the text: "The Fall of the great empire of
Moctezuma, under whose ruins would be buried the republic of Tlaxcala and
other governments of a beautiful part of America, was written in the fatal book
of destiny." Cortés here is the alpha male, who already foreshadows all those
who would follow him in the New World: dictators, despots, and tyrants.
Tlaxcala the edenic utopia that will be destroyed, and the possibility of a civil
society buried under the Spanish boot.

In anthropological terms, considered within the parameters of natural law
in philosophy, it is fundamental to understand the results of contrasting those
findings obtained from probing the depths of group memory in the collective
unconscious and of the quasi-official social memory in the historical record. All
Varela has done is to compare the findings, and they are very revealing.

Meaning of the Novel

This brief allegorical reading relies on Georg Lukács's idea that historical
novels contain a rewriting of the present utilizing designs from the past that
speak to today's problems. The author, according to Lukács, is never interested
in his historical subject, rather in its use for his contemporary purposes. The

reading also shows the parallels between Varela's intimate biography and those feelings of the character Jicoténcal in the novel that bears his name. The reading confirms the authorship, but also reveals the bitterness felt by Varela when his reasonable behavior was defeated by Fernando VII's exercise of royal power.

In his public life Varela always tried to adhere to proposals about the Island of Cuba thinking about his compatriots, including the landed aristocracy, even when Varela himself lived in penury and was able to join the priesthood and obtain a teaching post for his sustenance only with Bishop Espada's assistance. In contrast to Arango y Parreño, the aristocrat, on whose proposals one could always find evidence of his selfishness, Varela followed his conscience as well as his practical sense of finding solutions to those problems that would make sense for everyone involved. That is why we find projects of autonomy and not of independence; of recognizing the independence of the other liberated American republics; of freeing the slaves, while compensating the owners; of proposing reform projects for the clergy, or for the improvement of education. In sum, useful proposals full of common sense.

However, after his reasonable involvement in the Spanish Cortes as a Cuban delegate and his confrontation with Fernando VII's intransigent idiosincracy which demanded blind obedience from the legislators—and which many offered—Varela had to leave for the United States with the profound conviction that only Cuban independence from Spain would allow the Island to prosper materially and spiritually. As a former Spanish legislator the Mexican president sent a ship to New York harbor to invite him to Mexico to discuss diplomatic strategy in the recognition of Mexico by Spain and by other republics, an offer he declined, though he negotiated for the Mexican and Colombian invasions of the Island of Cuba to begin the liberation of it from Spain's grasp. The United States, however, did get the plans cancelled in exchange for diplomatic recognition from Russia for the two emerging republics.

Alone and in search for Cuban independence, Varela wrote *Jicoténcal*, a novel in which allies are not loyal either. Thereafter he castigated his disciples who subsequently would visit him in Philadelphia or in New York or even in St. Augustine, a few days before his death, to offer proposals of autonomy within the Spanish realm or of annexation to the United States . . . with his own call to arms.

Select Bibliography

Alonso, Amado. *Ensayo sobre la novela histórica.* Buenos Aires, 1951.
Goldmann, Lucien. *Towards a Sociology of the Novel.* Translated by Alan Sheridan. London: Tavistock Publications Ltd., 1975, 1977.
Lukács, Georg. *The Historical Novel.* London: Merlin, 1962.
———. *The Theory of the Novel.* Translated by Anna Bostock. Cambridge, Mass.: MIT Press, 1971, 1994.
Varela, Félix. *Jicoténcal.* Edited by Luis Leal and Rodolfo J. Cortina. Recovering the U. S. Hispanic Literary Heritage. Houston: Arte Público, 1995.